American Foreign Policy Making and the Democratic Dilemmas

JOHN W. SPANIER
UNIVERSITY OF FLORIDA

ERIC M. USLANER
UNIVERSITY OF MARYLAND

American Foreign Policy Making and the Democratic Dilemmas

SIXTH EDITION

MACMILLAN PUBLISHING COMPANY
NEW YORK

MAXWELL MACMILLAN CANADA
TORONTO

Editor: Robert Miller
Production Supervisor: Betsy Keefer
Production Manager: Francesca Drago
Cover Designer: Proof Positive
Cover Illustration: Tom Post

This book was set in 10/12 Baskerville by American–Stratford Graphic
Services, Inc. and was printed and bound by R. R. Donnelley & Sons.
The cover was printed by Phoenix Color Corp.

Macmillan Publishing Company
866 Third Avenue, New York, New York 10022

Macmillan Publishing Company is part of
the Maxwell Communication Group of Companies.

Maxwell Macmillan Canada, Inc.
1200 Eglinton Avenue East
Suite 200
Don Mills, Ontario M3C 3N1

Library of Congress Cataloging-in-Publication Data

Spanier, John W.
   American foreign policy making and the democratic dilemmas / John W.
Spanier, Eric M. Uslaner.—6th ed.
      p.   cm.
   Includes bibliographic references and index.
   ISBN 0-02-414201-8
   1. United States—Foreign relations administration.   I. Uslaner, Eric M.
   II. Title.
JX1706.A4   1994
   353.0089—dc20   93-914
                                                                       CIP

Printing: 1 2 3 4 5 6 7   Year: 4 5 6 7 8 9 0

Preface

This sixth edition of *American Foreign Policy Making and the Democratic Dilemmas* appears in a vastly changed world. Communism has collapsed throughout most of the world and the United States is the only remaining superpower, yet there remain many danger spots throughout the world. Foreign policy still deals with security issues, but economic and environmental concerns now occupy larger roles than ever before. Many would even say that economic policy is now the preeminent factor in international politics. For many citizens these changes in the international arena are an occasion to look inward, perhaps now more than ever before.

Our original purpose in writing this book was to explain the ways in which foreign policy (further subdivided into crisis and noncrisis security policies) is made differently than is domestic policy. At that time, most texts on the policy process focused on *domestic* policy making. *American Foreign Policy Making and the Democratic Dilemmas* was written to fill the need for an introduction to the actors and elements in the foreign policy decision process and to the analytic approaches most useful in understanding and criticizing it. In the second edition, we added intermestic policy as a further category to our two types of foreign policies because of the increasing erosion of the distinction between foreign and domestic policy in this area. This threefold distinction is examined in greater detail by additional case studies.

Contemporary conflict over foreign policy demands, too, that we not only deal with the processes of foreign policy making, but also confront the question of whether the outcome of these processes can be both effective and democratic. We felt this issue critical enough that we have explained it at greater length in what we call the *three dilemmas* of democratic policy making. For this purpose, we examine the variations in the constitutional and political power of the president and Congress in both domestic and foreign policy formation. We also examine the actual access to foreign policy decision roles and various possible participants; the parts that may be played by members of Congress, political parties, and interest groups; and the impact of the media and expressions of public opinion.

The rational-actor and bureaucratic models of decision making are suggested as aids to a clearer understanding of the interaction of all these forces. The utility of the rational-actor model is demonstrated in case studies of the Cuban missile crisis and the Gulf War. The bureaucratic model elucidates policy making on the antiballistic missile system and Ronald Reagan's Strategic Defense Initiative and such intermestic issues as energy, trade, agriculture, and the environment.

Among the changes in this edition are our focus on the Gulf War, an entire new chapter on public opinion (Chapter 5), and a discussion of the environment as an international issue (Chapter 9). We focus extensively on how the world has changed, but believe that our original framework stands up to the "New World Order." If anything, we may have been ahead of our time in stressing the importance of intermestic issues and domestic constraints. We rely heavily on surveys of citizens' attitudes in our chapter on public opinion. The proliferation of such surveys not only gives us more information than ever; it also forces public officials to become more attentive, some would say reactive, to the public mood.

Conflict between the president and the Congress has become endemic in foreign policy making. These conflicts arise under both divided government and single-party control of the legislative and executive branches. The Congress is now a major player in foreign policy, much to the consternation of presidents. Can a foreign policy with such a great degree of congressional and public participation be effective? Are democracy and effective policy making compatible?

These are complex issues and we do not claim to have resolved them. Our goal is more modest: to outline for the introductory student of American foreign policy how the decision-making process works and to highlight the problems we believe are most important. In any such endeavor, particularly a joint one, some arguments are bound to remain incomplete in the eyes of the specialist. Our problem was somewhat compounded by differing views on what would constitute a "good" foreign policy and on how much of a say Congress should have. Over the almost two decades since the first edition, our views have become closer. Yet, the disagreements we had—and sometimes still have—led us to produce what we hope are balanced arguments on different sides of critical issues and to examine the feasibility of proposed reforms regardless of our personal biases.

We are grateful to Frank Kessler, University of Wisconsin at Milwaukee; Kevin Mulcahy, Louisiana State University; Martin Sampson, University of Minnesota; and Paul Watanabe, University of Massachusetts at Boston for comments on a previous edition and to Philip R. Baumann, Moorhead State University; Larry Elowitz, Georgia College; B. David Meyers, University of North Carolina at Greensboro; Dennis Pirages, University of Maryland; and Blake Strack, University of Southern Maine for their help on this one. Bruce Nichols did such a good job in shepherding this book through that he got a promotion—from which perch he can deny responsibility for anything we have written.

J. S.
E. M. U.

Contents

CHAPTER 1

Foreign Policy in a Democracy

The Cold War is over. But, as after World Wars I and II, the defeat of an enemy does not mean the end of international conflict. The U.S. victory over the Soviet Union after four decades of global conflict and competition, the subsequent disintegration and disappearance of the Soviet Union, and the spread of democracy raised hopes for a more peaceful world in the post-Cold War era. Democracies were unlikely to commit aggression against other states, especially other democracies. But Iraq's seizure and annexation of Kuwait and the subsequent U.S.-led United Nations coalition war against Iraq was one early sign that the post-Cold War era might not be as peaceful as expected.

As the Cold War was ending, euphoria was widespread. The countries of Eastern Europe threw off their Soviet-imposed regimes, the Soviet army withdrew from Hungary, Czechoslovakia, and Poland and was scheduled to withdraw from what used to be called East Germany by 1994; the Berlin Wall, which had divided the city and become a symbol of the Cold War's struggle between freedom and totalitarianism, came down, and shortly thereafter the reunification of Germany followed, four decades after the American-Soviet conflict had started. The two former rivals signed two major arms-control agreements, one sharply reducing strategic nuclear weapons, the other conventional forces in Europe. And they settled various regional conflicts in Africa, Asia, and Latin America that had only recently bitterly divided their various countries.

But the removal of the Soviet Union's power and control over Eastern Europe unleashed the nationalist and ethnic passions that had plagued the area both prior to World War I and between the two world wars. Yugoslavia disintegrated into civil war. Czechoslovakia was divided into two states peacefully. Nor was the Soviet Union immune. Moscow's central command structure weakened as Mikhail Gorbachev sought to reform the Soviet Communist system, and each of the fifteen republics that composed the Soviet Union claimed that it was sovereign. For a while, they sought to negotiate a new, looser union in which most of the power would rest with the republics. The failure of the attempted coup in August 1991, by the old guard, to overthrow Gorbachev and prevent the flow of power from the center, however, led to a stampede, as republic after republic, distrusting Moscow and fearing a reestablishment of its authoritarian power, refused to remain part of the Soviet Union. The three Baltic republics, incorporated into the Soviet Union against their will in 1940, regained their independence as nations. The other republics, with the exception of Georgia, organized the Commonwealth of Independent States (CIS); its members committed themselves to cooperating on foreign affairs, defense, and, most important, economic affairs. Whether the Commonwealth will endure or fall to its own quarrels, however, remains unclear. Russia, the largest republic in size, population, and wealth of resources, however, is clearly the successor state to the former Soviet Union.

While the nations of Eastern Europe were breaking apart, the countries of Western Europe were moving, although haltingly, toward greater unity. Originally founded to create a United States of Europe in the age of continental-size superpowers, the European Community (EC) in 1992 took its last step toward full integration; originally incorporating six states, it now was composed of twelve. Eventually, it would grow even larger; for the EC, with a population of 380 million people, attracted a long line of applicants. But the critical change in Europe, besides the collapse of the Soviet Union, was the reunification of Germany. Unified initially in 1870, Germany was too strong for its neighbors. In both world wars, which she began, it took a combination of almost all the other great European states plus the United States to defeat her. Even divided among the victors after the second war, West Germany, upon recovery from defeat, was the strongest member of the North Atlantic Alliance, one of whose purposes was to restrain the former enemy and reassure her new allies and former victims. Containing West German power was also a prime motive for European integration. West Germany was no longer to control the industrial basis for its power and aggression; it was to be integrated into a European framework. Germany's reunification in 1990, creating the largest nation west of Russia, 80,000,000 in population and economically the strongest in all of Europe, therefore, made her neighbors nervous. Europeans have long historical memories. Should the EC speed up the integration process to ensure Europe's continued ability to restrain this new Germany's power? Or would Germany be able to dominate the EC? Or would the fear of Germany break up the EC and lead to a new and unstable balance of power, as in interwar Europe?

The end of the Cold War also had effects in the underdeveloped world to which the Soviet Union and the United States had extended their competition. Moscow and Washington tended to support opposing sides in the civil wars that wracked many developing countries, as well as rival states competing for regional influence, if not hegemony. Thus the superpowers' conflict was often imposed upon domestic and regional quarrels as they sought to expand their influence at one another's cost, and those competing for power internally or externally looked to them for political support, economic assistance, and weapons. This interaction intensified what might otherwise have been only local disturbances and made them potentially quite dangerous. But the drawing in of the two superpowers also placed a lid on these conflicts, because neither wanted their confrontations to escalate into a direct clash.

The end of the American–Soviet rivalry, therefore, threatened to result in more regional rivalries that would follow their own dynamics. The reasons were several: the retrenchment of American and Soviet power, creating power vacuums that were likely to attract regional rivals no longer restrained by their patron superpowers; the rise of small, radical, potentially reckless states that sought not only to play a major regional, if not hegemonic, role but, in some instances, a larger international role; and these states' efforts to acquire, if they did not already possess, weapons of mass destruction (nuclear, chemical, and biological) which, when placed on top of missiles, are capable of hitting targets far beyond their immediate neighbors. Thus, as Iraq's invasion of Kuwait—widely referred to as the first post-Cold War crisis—suggested, the end of the Cold War did not necessarily mean a more stable world.

The emergence of the United States as the sole superpower in the wake of the Soviet Union's disappearance, which eliminated the military threat to American security, also meant that military power would no longer play its former preeminent role. Rather, economic power and practices would occupy a more prominent place. The developing countries were still trying to develop. The eleven republics composing the new Commonwealth of Independent States sought to replace the failed centralized Communist economy with market economies, as did the former Soviet-controlled states in Eastern Europe, not only to reverse their economic decline but also to preserve their new and fragile democracies. Western Europe was moving toward a huge common market as the twelve EC members joined with the seven members of the European Free Trade Association, composed largely of states that had remained neutral during the Cold War, to form the largest trading bloc in the world. On the one hand, the EC was making what it claimed to be its "final push" toward a united Europe. Its members had committed themselves to eliminating the remaining economic barriers to a single European-wide market, a single European currency, and common social as well as foreign policies by the end of the decade. At the same time, the EC was also attracting new members in Western Europe (such as Sweden, Norway, and Austria) and being beseeched for associate status and eventual membership by countries ranging from Poland and Hungary to Turkey. And two U.S. allies, Germany and Japan, the losers in World War II, had become economic superpowers while the United States, whose economy had been the basis of its World War II and Cold War victories, was declining economically in an increasingly interdependent and competitive global market.

One U.S. industry after another—steel, textiles, shipbuilding, automobiles—was ravaged by foreign competition; other industries, to stay competitive, went overseas where workers' wages were cheaper. The result was a partial "deindustrialization" of the United States. Even high-tech industries—supercomputers, semiconducters, machine tools, robotics, telecommunications—which were supposed to be the basis of the postindustrial U.S. economy, were experiencing difficulties in competing. The symptoms were all too evident in 1992. Pan American Airways, the first and for many years the world's number one airline, went bankrupt. IBM, for long the world's premier computer company, announced that despite having already slimmed down the number of its employees, it needed to reorganize to reenergize the company and make it more profitable in the highly competitive computer market. And General Motors, not just the world's largest motor company but the world's largest corporation, which had already lost a sizable share of the U.S. car market and had closed plants and laid off workers, announced an even more drastic set of closings and lay-offs of over 70,000 more workers. Three once-great companies, symbols of American technology, workmanship, and service, had either died or were fighting for their survival as major players.

As if this were not bad enough, it might be remembered that the color television set, the microwave oven, the VCR, and the fax machine were all invented in the United States. Not a single one of these American inventions is produced anymore in the United States. The reasons for this situation include poor business management, with short-term outlook focused on the quarterly dividend return for stockholders rather than long-term investment to ensure survival, growth, and profitability in the new *global* marketplace; insufficient nonmilitary research and development and slowness in getting those new products that were developed from the design stage to production and retail; low savings rate, as distinct from a high consumption rate, and lack of investment in technological innovation; adversarial management–labor relations and low labor-productivity growth; and an increasingly unskilled labor force (educational tests in math and science—and in geography and history—repeatedly showed American students to be last or next to last among all industrial countries, one result being the insufficient production of engineers and scientists). Indeed, during the 1980s foreign investments had bought up ever-increasing numbers of U.S. corporations, commercial real estate, and farmland, which raised questions about who would control the economy in the future.

Thus, as the security issue was declining in importance, the critical concern facing the United States—once the world's leading creditor nation, now the world's largest debtor—was economic growth. The revival of the U.S. economy became priority number one, as in the recession of the early 1990s not only blue-collar workers lost their jobs, but white-collar workers and even executive personnel were laid off. U.S. corporations, long used to having the American market largely for themselves, now had to fight for sales, if not survival, against foreign competition even in the domestic market. But the issue, to underline the point, was not just economic recovery, as in past recessions, but economic revival. And this had to be done when the country's debt was approaching $4 trillion and the interest on the debt had become the federal government's most expensive program, ahead of Social Security and defense, let alone health, transportation, crime, drugs, etc.

On the international scene, where power had long been associated with military might, economic robustness and strength were becoming the leading indicators. No issue could have symbolized the changing and ambiguous nature of power on the international scene more than the war against Iraq in 1991. On the one hand, the United States demonstrated its military superiority with a dazzling display of high-tech weaponry; on the other hand, this country had to beg its allies, especially Japan and Germany, to pay for the war. The United States, in short, could not afford to wage the war it felt necessary to fight; in the future, it might need the permission of its more affluent friends before deciding to use force. In the post-Cold War world, reversing America's economic decline had become the primary issue. Because the consequences of economic growth for employment and rising wages—or economic decline for lower wages and unemployment—were so blatantly obvious, the clear-cut distinction between foreign and domestic policies was fading. A vital economy was not only the basis of the nation's military strength and influence in the world, it was also the basis for the nation's ability to compete economically internationally and maintain its welfare and prosperity. Thus the number one issue in foreign policy had also become the number one issue in domestic policy.

As economic issues came to the fore and the threat of nuclear war receded, Americans began to look inward. The victory over Iraq in the Gulf War was soon followed by the breakup and eventual dissolution of the Soviet Union. Yet the postwar euphoria gave way to gloom over the domestic economy. As the new republics of the Soviet Union and the formerly Communist countries of Eastern and Central Europe struggled with crumbling economies, Americans found themselves unwilling to share their decreasing bounty with citizens of the new democracies. When Yugoslavia fell apart into civil war that threatened its neighbors in 1992, even President George Bush—who had proclaimed himself defender of the free world—said that America could not become the "world's policeman." Buffeted by a stagnant economy and a neoisolationist challenge in the Republican primaries from Pat Buchanan, Bush followed the lead of public opinion. As Thomas Friedman wrote in the *New York Times,* "Many Americans . . . are beginning to see foreign policy as a luxury they can no longer afford, even though America's economic involvement with the rest of the world has never been greater, and dangerous security issues remain."[1] Would there be one superpower or none in the last decade of the twentieth century?

The Different Types of Policies

Security Policies

All states need a foreign policy because they all exist in an essentially anarchical world in which each state lives in fear and must seek its own security. There is no world government to protect individual states. Each must guard itself in a system in which states tend to view each other as potential adversaries rather than friends. The analogy is the proverbial town of the "old West" where there was no "law and order" and where men lived in fear of one another and wore guns to protect themselves against those who might want to rob them, take away their land, or who were just plain ornery and mean. State A might look at its neighbor B and see it is arming itself. Is B strengthening itself to deter a possible attack (a defensive action), or is it preparing to attack (an offensive action)? State B might declare that its intentions are peaceful and that it is increasing its military power only to ensure that A or other states will not attack it. But why should A believe that statement? Once B's capabilities have grown, it may attack; the declaration of peaceful intent may have been deceitful. Or, even if B had been sincere about its defensive intentions earlier, it can, after all, change its mind once it realizes its improved power position.

The point of this simple analogy is that, in general, states distrust one another. Even when one state extends the hand of friendship, the other wonders why. Is one state trying to deceive the other to strike later? Where their security is concerned, if not their survival, states are cautious and careful. No one guarantees them either; each is its own guardian. States, therefore, rarely take chances; the stakes are too high. The basic rule is "protect yourself." This is fundamental since security is regarded as the prerequisite for a nation to preserve its way of life. Forgetting this basic rule is to risk endangering one's territorial integrity and political independence.

The principal mechanism to ensure state security is in fact the balance of power. If one state matches another in strength, neither is likely to attack the other; but an imbalance may entice the stronger one to attack. Consequently, in the state system, in which each state sees an increase in power and security of another state as a loss of power and security for itself—a loss it regards as unacceptable—preserving the balance of power constitutes the heart of foreign policy. American Cold War foreign policy after World War II was largely concerned with the central balance with its principal adversary, the Soviet Union, and a series of regional balances in Europe, Asia, the Middle East, and, after the 1970s, sub-Sahara Africa. Thus the United States was involved in virtually every area of the world, with many different nations as adversaries, allies, and developing countries. Military power—the threat and the actual use of force—played a major deterrent and coercive role in this foreign policy, although other instruments, such as economic aid to strengthen an ally, were also used widely.

American foreign policy was primarily concerned with assuring the nation's security, but there were also more *specific* policies that sought to preserve the nation's security. These included (but were not limited to) such policy areas as the defense budget (procurement and deployment of arms and personnel), arms control, limited war, alliances, arms transfers to allies and other countries, economic and technical aid, and intelligence operations against other states. Most of these policies were continuing ones because they involved long-term interests. The United States, as one of the world's two nuclear superpowers, had an additional interest not only in balancing Soviet military strength but in seeking to reduce the intensity of the arms competition and stabilizing the balance in an environment of rapid technological innovation in weaponry. Foreign aid programs and arms transfers went on from year to year, although the recipients and the amounts they received changed. Limited wars obviously—and fortunately—were not an everyday concern, but when they occurred, as in Korea and Vietnam, the fighting went on for periods of three to eight years and they consequently required major commitments of troops, arms, and money. And the use of force in other contingencies remained a constant possibility.

The need for security policies did not end with the disappearance of the Soviet military threat and the collapse of the Soviet Union and its replacement by the Commonwealth of Independent States, which may yet disintegrate as Russia, the Soviet Union's successor state, and Ukraine continue to squabble. The war with Iraq testifies to the different—diminished but continuing—security threats that exist. Regional shuffles and the likelihood of accelerated diffusion of nuclear, chemical, and biological weapons of mass destruction, accompanied by the pervasion of missile technology, are but two of the more potent threats. The rapidly changing post-Cold War environment, while perhaps posing less of an immediate security threat to U.S. interests, does not promise to be more stable. The fragmentation of the Soviet Union with its huge nuclear establishment; the violent collapse of Yugoslavia and the potential disintegration of other Eastern European states, such as Czechoslovakia, testifying to the power of ethnicity and nationalism to break up formerly stable nation-states; and the potential failure of Russia, Ukraine, and other republics of the CIS, as well as Eastern European states, to make the transition to democratic and free market states—all suggest that the world remains a dangerous and unstable place.

Crisis Policies

Crisis policies are distinguished from security policies by their relative infrequency and their short duration, but they make up for the lack of numbers by their utter seriousness and atmosphere of great danger. Frequently characterized by surprise, crisis policies are even more prominently featured by the perceived threat to a nation's vital interests and the lack of time the policy makers feel they have to deal with it. If they do not act quickly, the crisis situation, which in all probability took them by surprise and is in any case seen by them as endangering the country's fundamental security, will go against them. In these circumstances, the most critical element of a crisis is that the possibility of the threat or actual use of force—which underlies much of traditional international politics—is very high. In short, the likelihood of war erupting suddenly becomes a real danger. While during Soviet–American crises the initial clash was at the level of threats or low levels of force, the possibility of escalation to a nuclear confrontation was always present. Whether in Berlin, Cuba, the Middle East, or elsewhere, the repeated confrontations between the superpowers always posed the frightening possibility of an escalation to nuclear war and national suicide. As a result, the emphasis during the Cold War was understandably on crisis management—defending vital interests when threatened by an adversary and simultaneously avoiding nuclear war—and, even more important, crisis prevention. While crises in the post-Cold War era are less likely to threaten the United States, or much of the rest of the world, with the possibility of a nuclear conflagration and destruction, threats to important interests, such as Iraqi to Saudi Arabia and its oil fields, on which the Western industrial powers depend, may recur.

Intermestic Policies

If these two security policies comprise what is sometimes today called the "old" international politics, the increasingly important "new" foreign policy revolves around economics, specifically the issue of prosperity. Major domestic cause for governmental growth, and especially the power of the presidency and executive branch, has been the increasing demand by citizens for more and more services. Governments all over the world, especially in democratic states where the electorate can hold its representatives accountable, are held responsible for the welfare of their peoples and for satisfying their ever higher expectations. This "welfare state" must, therefore, concern itself with economic growth, creation of jobs, higher incomes, and social programs for the disadvantaged. If political leaders do not want to lose office, their concern with social services must be at least as great as the military services. Security issues, except in moments of crisis, rarely touch the mass of the electorate personally, even if they are aware of important foreign policy events from watching television news or reading newspapers. But employment, salaries, and prices affect their pocketbooks. Bread-and-butter issues arouse them quickly, certainly in time for the next election.

Most nations do not have the natural resources or industrial/agricultural capacity to ensure their own prosperity. They must import raw materials, manufactured goods, and food items. Nations, and especially their economies, are thus increasingly a part of an interdependent world. Even a government like that of the United States, a country possessing many of the resources it needs, an enormous industry, and productive agriculture, no longer completely controls its economic destiny. Ever since 1973 and the dramatic increase in oil prices, it has become clear that the economic prosperity of the United States is both sensitive to events overseas and increasingly vulnerable in a more and more interdependent world.[2] America's welfare can be undermined if, for example, a less developed country possessing a vital resource such as oil withholds that resource or dramatically raises the price. OPEC's (Organization of Petroleum Exporting Countries) 1973 price increase and the 1979 jump after the Shah of Iran was deposed lowered America's living standards at the time, increased inflation, precipitated the worst recession since the 1930s, and made it more difficult to resume a rapid rate of economic growth.

Only after oil prices had shot to close to $35 a barrel did this country begin a serious policy of conservation, switching to non-OPEC oil and greater use of coal; in addition, the closing of factories and production cutbacks helped lower oil imports. Lower American, as well as European, demand suddenly produced an oil surplus and a price reduction to $29 a barrel. Later, oil prices plummeted briefly to below the 1973 level of $12 per barrel before they once more rose to $18 per barrel.

By 1991, however, Iraq's dictator, Saddam Hussein, had seized Kuwait's oil fields. America went to war for the purpose, among others, of preventing Iraq from either invading Saudi Arabia, as well as the other tiny oil kingdoms, or threatening those fearful states so as to dictate OPEC's oil supply and price policies. Saddam Hussein's voracious appetite for money to rebuild Iraq after its eight-year-long war with Iran and to make Iraq the premier Arab power and himself its leader by creating large, modern armed forces equipped with the newest and most powerful weapons, including nuclear and chemical weapons, demanded a sharp upward rise of oil prices. The United States and its principal allies, however, did not want to experience a repetition of the 1970s economic catastrophe.

The oil issue in the 1970s erased once and for all the distinction between international and domestic policies. Caught up in both, it could best be characterized as "intermestic." In an increasingly interdependent world, no nation any longer fully controlled its own economic destiny; what Washington decided to do about inflation or recession might be less important than what Saudi Arabia or Iran decided. Because jobs and income were involved, these intermestic issues became critical to the electorate, which was profoundly affected by more than the oil policy. The United States, for example, used to be the world's breadbasket; American farmers were the most productive in the world. During the 1970s agricultural exports were a main source of earning dollars, paying for some of the imported oil, and keeping the resulting trade imbalances—the difference between what is spent on imports and earned on exports—from widening further. But by the 1980s, other countries had also become productive food producers and were exporting as well. Some of these countries, such as China, Australia, France, and other members of the European economic community (Common Market), were friends and allies. As they undercut one another's prices, tensions between these nations grew, affecting their political-military relationships. A collective solution to the problem was widely promoted since no national one was possible: to cut the subsidies farmers received to produce their staples. But that was a difficult solution, given the political power of farmers in all countries.

U.S. and other farmers were not the only group that was upset; so too were U.S. workers. American industry, as noted earlier, once the world's most powerful and prosperous, had never depended on exports or been threatened by imports. U.S. goods were well made—items labeled "Made in the U.S.A." were sought after throughout the world—and because they were mass produced, they were more affordable than equivalent foreign-made goods. But during the 1970s this changed drastically as foreign—especially Japanese—cars poured in during the oil crisis while American-made cars were in the main poorly assembled, unreliable gas guzzlers. Never having had to be competitive in the world economy, the U.S. industries, not just autos, suddenly found themselves exposed to the global economy and unable to compete effectively. Foreign labor was less expensive and often more educated and skillful; foreign products were desirable, well made and finished, and competitively priced. America, confronted not only by an economically revived Europe but, more competitively, by Japan and other export-oriented economically developing Asian states such as Taiwan and South Korea, suffered in the international marketplace. The Reagan administration's decision in the early 1980s to cut taxes drastically while financing a large increase in military spending resulted in an enormous budget deficit of over $200 billion, and a jump in the value of the dollar. These factors made American products too expensive for foreigners while rendering imports more affordable. The result was a great influx of imports, a further weakening of industries that could not compete in price abroad, and a piling up of a huge trade deficit. While the value of the dollar has since been forced down—with the cooperation of our principal allies and competitors—reducing the trade deficit as U.S. products became less expensive and more competitive, there have been two major results: increasing pressure for protectionism and growing tensions with Japan, with whom the trade deficit remains very sizable. While "Japan bashing" has become very popular in the United States, the basic problem remains the uncompetitiveness of the U.S. economy in the global economy.

Policies and Stakes

A key element in any situation in which any of these governmental policies may be invoked is how the various actors involved in decision making perceive the consequences of their actions. The differences between foreign and domestic policy making are due, at least in part, to the different stakes involved and how the actors perceive them. In domestic policy making, participants can often differentiate between the "winners" and the "losers." In foreign policy making, on the other hand, the entire nation is usually seen as either "winning" or "losing." Most foreign policy decisions do not result with one group in the population gaining at the expense of others.* In domestic policy, the most clear-cut example of the winners-losers dichotomy may be antipoverty programs, which are specifically designed to provide aid to an identifiable group in the

---

* Not everybody sees foreign policy in this way. Notably, radical critics (on both the left and the right) do see foreign policy decisions as involving domestic winners and losers. Critics on the left, for example, may view foreign policy decision making as a conflict between capitalists and the workers (just as they do in domestic politics).

population (the poor), who are classified as losers by such standards as income or housing. The poor are viewed as a "have-not" group, and the debate surrounding antipoverty programs is marked by arguments about what the government should do to aid disadvantaged groups at the expense (in taxes or prerogatives) of the "haves" in society—those people who have more or less "made it." The goal, then, is to turn some of the losers into winners.

On the traditional issues of foreign policy, however, decisions are not generally viewed in terms of winners against losers. Foreign policy decisions are more frequently viewed based on the entire country (rather than any particular group in the population) winning or losing. This is most noticeable when a country goes to war or is involved in a crisis. The winners and losers are the nations (or alliances) involved, not specific groups like the oil companies, the farmers, or the poor. Tensions within the country on domestic legislation are put aside as the population "rallies around the flag" in support of the president's actions as commander in chief.[3] Simply stated, the stakes are very different in foreign and domestic politics.

In domestic politics, there are a multitude of interest groups concerned with the decisions of government and attempting to influence them. Each group wants to be a winner rather than a loser. Even though the president initiates more domestic legislation than does Congress, the chief executive's hands are tied to a much greater extent in domestic politics than in foreign politics. Groups and individuals looking out for their own interests attempt to influence Congress on how money should be spent, which tax loopholes should be closed or left untouched, and how business and labor should be regulated. The process of raising revenue and spending it for domestic programs is marked by a relatively high degree of conflict among the groups contending for special benefits. The mediating actors in domestic politics are Congress and the executive departments that draw up the federal budget. To some extent, the very large scope of the demands made can also serve to moderate these demands made by interest groups. The president simply cannot spend his time listening to all of these demands. He must in many cases give up a large part of his power to Congress.

All of these conflicts and more are found on intermestic issues. In addition to the aforementioned actors on domestic policy, we find the president trying to balance a whole series of conflicting interests: the vitality of the American economy, the coherence of American policy, and the various pressures from multinational companies who often have divided loyalties. The president will have to balance the American demand for oil against the traditional policy of providing strong support for Israel. Oil companies, as well as other businesses operating abroad, find themselves active participants in the intermestic policy process. To meet their goals of making as large a profit as possible, they might pursue policies (such as advocating a tilt in Middle Eastern policy toward the Arabs) that might be at odds with that of official U.S. policy.

There are, then, so many different actors, foreign and domestic, and the issues involved may be vital to the nation's security and certainly to its economic well-being. International politics and economics, as well as intermestic policies, clearly involve very high stakes. There are "winners," "losers," and sometimes "non-winners" as well—groups that might not be affected by a particular change in policy through careful strategic planning or simple happenstance. Indeed, we find not only winners and losers but also many "high rollers"—actors willing to take major risks, such as the oil-producing nations, which steadily raised their prices during the 1970s in the belief that their strategic position was superior. What makes intermestic politics so complicated is that it encompasses not only the divisions we find on domestic policies, but also the "we-they" conflicts of foreign policy.

The situation is quite different with crisis and, to a large extent, security policies. Since foreign policy decisions are not perceived either by the public or by the decision makers as involving methods of "dividing up the spoils," the conflict over decisions made will involve a much smaller circle of actors. Interest groups become mobilized only when they see the potential to "win" something for themselves, but on most foreign policy issues either the entire country wins or the country loses. This is not to deny that some citizens or groups may differ vastly on foreign policy questions from other citizens or groups. But, significantly, each group views its own position as the one that is in the "national" (or even "international") interest.

The basic distinction then, between conflicts over domestic and foreign affairs concerns the way participants view the stakes of the policy process. On most domestic policies, including intermestic policies, there are more likely to be winners and nonwinners than winners and losers. These policies, also called "distributive" policies, are "perceived to confer direct benefits upon one or more groups [but are] determined with little or no conflict over the passage of the legislation but only over the size and specific distribution of the shares."[4] On crisis decisions, however, the whole nation either wins or loses, and the nature of the conflict on such policies will be quite different. Conflict on these crisis decisions is most likely to resemble the less fequent but loudly argued cases of domestic policies that propose to redistribute income from the haves in society to the have-nots, where again we see a clash between inevitable winners and losers. Security policies involve many actors who may have diverse goals and different perceptions of the stakes involved. Crisis decisions, on the other hand, involve only a small number of actors, and the stakes involved are generally quite clear. Indeed, the high stakes involved in crisis decisions are a key reason why the president is the dominant actor in this area. The president is the only actor in the American political system capable of the swift and decisive action required in crises.

The Growth of Presidential Primacy

In an effort to give the president the authority he needs to conduct foreign policy, yet not accumulate dictatorial power to threaten the democratic needs of the domestic order, the framers of the U.S. Constitution vested exclusive responsibility for the conduct of foreign policy in the federal government and then divided its authority in this field, as in the domestic, between the president and Congress. The president could receive and send ambassadors—that is, deal with representatives of foreign powers—but the Senate had to give its consent to treaties by a two-thirds vote as well as confirm top diplomatic, military, and political appointments. The president was appointed commander in chief of the armed forces, but only Congress was empowered to declare war, appropriate funds for the maintenance of military forces, and regulate commerce with other nations. It could also investigate the operations of the various executive departments, including those that participated in the formulation and implementation of the foreign policy of the United States.

Thus, while this sharing of the foreign policy power by separate branches was intended to ensure a check on presidential power, the president clearly was constitutionally the nation's chief diplomat and commander in chief. But a number of changes in the social and economic environment increasingly have upset the balance between the executive and legislative branches and shifted power toward the president. Most of these new conditions have affected the conduct of both foreign and domestic affairs in all nations, but particularly in those of the West. First, and perhaps most fundamental, is the general growth of "big government"—which has usually meant *executive* government. Running a highly urbanized, complex, industrial society has required big government and large bureaucracies to serve its manifold needs. The mass vote and the mobilization of new groups and classes into the political process have multiplied demands on government for services ranging from unending economic growth, high employment, subsidies of all types, stabilization of the economy, and the redistribution of power, status, and money to create a more equitable society. The list is endless.

Indeed, it was the growth of the role of the government in the domestic economy, as much as any international event, that, in the United States, marked the sharp shift in the balance between the president and the Congress. The Great Depression of the 1930s focused people's attention on Washington. The traditional forces of the marketplace had failed to readjust themselves to an era of great economic crisis, and the administration of Franklin D. Roosevelt, which began in 1933, committed the national government to direct intervention in the economy. Even during the pre-World War I administration of Woodrow Wilson, known for his liberal economic policies (which he called the "New Freedom"), total federal expenditures constituted less than 2 percent of the gross national product—(GNP), the value of all goods and services produced in the country. Half of those expenditures went for defense. By the 1930s, the figure for total spending rose to 7.7 percent, most of which (4.9 percent) was domestically oriented. The federal share of the GNP has continued to rise so that it was approaching 25 percent by the early '80s. This great increase in federal spending gave broad new responsibilities to the national government—and to the president who proposes and (at least indirectly) administers the programs.

Presidents and prime ministers in the relatively open societies of the West, as leaders of political parties from whom the electorate expects the satisfaction of certain demands, have become the central figures; as heads of their party and government, they draw up the social and economic programs, as well as foreign policies, and it becomes their responsibility to submit and shepherd bills through their respective legislatures. For the most part, legislatures do not act on their own. They wait for the executive to submit a program. And it is on this record of achievement that the parties and their leaders run in the next election and seek to renew their mandate to govern. The fact is that presidents have become the authors of and spokesmen for national legislative programs and, by the 1980s, trillion-dollar budgets.

Even nations that are neither democratic nor economically developed share this global trend toward executive government. States that do not possess a constitutional tradition (as, for example, the former Soviet Union) may have a legislature, but such a body has no independent status and power. The executive has complete authority and governs unchallenged. In the new, former colonial, economically developing countries power has also tended to be centralized in the executive. One-party governments and military regimes were until recently common throughout the Third World; parliamentary bodies, with few exceptions, were in decay. Only lately has a new trend toward democracy emerged. But by and large, executive dominance, whether justified by efficiency, ideology, or impatience, has been widely justified as the way to ensure results or for an individual to retain power.

In the case of the United States, another obvious fact needs to be noted in this regard. The president is nationally elected, and he, more than any other figure, represents the national mood and is the spokesman for the nation's interests, domestic and foreign. Congress, on the other hand, represents local interests; its representatives in the House and "ambassadors from the states" in the Senate respond mainly to their constitutents' interests. By contrast, in Great Britain, elections are organized around the parties and their national platforms. One votes for a member of Parliament because he or she represents one of the parties whose leader, if the party wins, becomes prime minister. But, unlike in Britain, the U.S. chief executive is also chief of state. He is more than a partisan leader and chief of government. In short, when he occupies the office of the presidency, he becomes the symbol of national unity and can thus draw on most citizens' patriotism and loyalty. In a nation increasingly diverse and fragmented, that symbolic role is very important. In Britain, the monarch is chief of state and stands above politics and differences over public policy, while the prime minister is chief of government. Therefore, a United States citizen may often feel politically schizophrenic, hating and loving the president at one and the same time (as a partisan and an American). In Britain, the citizen can hate the prime minister and still love, respect, and feel patriotic about the king or queen.

Only the president can instantly communicate with the people. Television, especially, has done much to expand the president's powers, but even in the days before the widespread use of radio, Theodore Roosevelt referred to the White

House as a "bully pulpit." This is all the more true today when the people look toward the president for everything from national defense to social justice. Harry Truman once said that the president is the lobbyist for all the people. As chief of state, whether receiving a distinguished foreign dignitary or visiting other nations, he is covered by the press and television cameras and therefore can remain first in his nation's eyes, if not always in its heart. In either capacity, whether he attends a summit conference with other Western leaders or Soviet leaders, or wishes to make a statement to the public via a press conference, television is present and is his to command; he has no problem getting on the nightly news.

Presidents play many roles: chief of state, chief executive, chief legislator, chief of party, chief diplomat, and commander in chief. But President Reagan added a new role: chief pastor. On several occasions when servicemen or civilians were killed (as in the Challenger space shuttle explosion in 1986), the president attended the services, eloquently eulogized those who had died serving their country, and afterward spent a few minutes, together with Mrs. Reagan, embracing and consoling each of the bereaved families. These moving ceremonies were clearly "a byproduct of television and the constant airing of foreign policy, which effectively makes the president personally responsible for its outcome, including casualties."[5]

Since World War II and the advent of the nuclear era, the president's foreign policy role has reinforced his central role in government to the point where he is no longer merely the "first among equals"; during the Cold War he became, as one writer has said of the English prime minister, the "sun around which planets revolve."[6] The Constitution gave the presidency specific grants of authority with a great potential for expansion. These grants, such as that of commander in chief, were written in such a way that they were open to future interpretations as circumstances changed. In a real sense, what was not said in the Constitution "proved ultimately more important than what was."[7] Often called the Constitution's "great silences," they gave presidents—especially strong presidents such as Lincoln, the two Roosevelts, Truman, Kennedy, Johnson, and Nixon—freedom to do what they thought needed to be done in unprecedented circumstances on behalf of the nation's interests as they defined these and to test the powers and limits of the office.

They were, to put it simply, "missing powers" in the Constitution. For example, the Constitution did not say where the powers to recognize other states or to proclaim neutrality were located. If the president and Senate must cooperate in the negotiation and ratification of a treaty, do they both have to agree also on when to terminate a treaty or can the president do so on his own? If Congress must declare war, does it also make peace? Who proclaims neutrality, the president because he is commander in chief or Congress because of its authority to declare war and regulate commerce? Does a president have the authority to send U.S. troops into Korea, Lebanon, or Grenada, or launch air attacks on Libya, or conclude military base agreements with foreign nations? Could a president, some ultimate day, believing Moscow was about to attack the United States, launch a preemptive strike on his own authority? One frequent manner of determining who exercises these powers has been to assume that the foreign affairs powers explicitly granted imply other powers: The president's power to appoint and receive ambassadors, for example, implies the power to recognize or withhold recognition from other states. The "implied powers" doctrine, however, leaves much room for struggles between the executive and legislative branches for control of the conduct of foreign affairs—as the former enhanced its powers, especially during this century. As Louis Henkin has noted, the powers specifically allocated to the president are so few that "a stranger reading the Constitution would get little inkling of such large presidential authority, for the powers explicitly vested in him are few and seem modest, far fewer and more modest, than those bestowed upon Congress."[8] It seems incredible that these few meager grants support the most powerful office in the world and the mul-tivaried, wide-flung webwork of foreign activity of the most powerful nation in the world."[9] One obvious reason for this is that the Founding Fathers did not foresee the United States soon playing an active and major role in international politics. In his farewell address, President Washington counseled his countrymen to take advantage of America's "detached and distant situation" from Europe and stay isolated from the "toils of European ambition, Rivalship, Interest, Humor or Caprice."[10] Today, even in the post-Cold War period, the president is leader not only of the United States but, in a sense, of the West. And whether he provides firm or fumbling leadership, his actions will have global consequences. Television coverage of foreign policy crises, dramas, and glamor magnifies the public's awareness of the president's leading role and its need for his leadership.

In short, whether the cause was domestic or international, presidential power has grown and presidential leadership has become a necessity. Initially, during the Great Depression, President Franklin Roosevelt laid the foundations of the *welfare state*. The system was later broadened and strengthened by Harry Truman, John F. Kennedy, and, especially, Lyndon Johnson in order to provide a minimum standard of living for all citizens. The emergence of the Cold War following World War II led President Truman and his successors to organize the *national security state*, establishing new organizations, such as the National Security Council in the White House, the Defense Department, and Central Intelligence Agency, to contain the perceived threat of the Soviet Union and Communism in general. In the present post-Cold War phase, the United States government will have to become a *competitive state* whose aim will be to revive American economic competitiveness and strength, the basis of both the United States' influence in the world and its military strength.[11]

The big question is: How can a democratic American domestic order be reconciled with an executive powerful enough to safeguard the nation's security and advance its prosperity so that it can continue to enjoy its way of life? Former Senator Fulbright during the Cold War admitted he was a pessimist. "I for one am fairly well convinced that neither constitutional government nor democratic freedoms can survive indefinitely in a country chronically at war (presumably the Cold War), as America has been for the last three decades. Sooner or later, war will lead to dictatorship."[12] Fulbright's prediction was wrong; nevertheless, in a democracy, the tension between a strong president powerful enough to conduct relations with other nations and the preservation of a democratic society is a constant problem.

The Three Dilemmas of Democratic Foreign Policy Making

The United States officially has one president, but he occupies two presidencies.[13] One deals with the domestic political system, the other with the international one. Inherent in that division lies one of the three major dilemmas the United States, as a democracy and as a superpower, faces as it conducts its foreign policy. This fundamental dilemma might be summed up as *governmental checks and balances versus concentration of presidential power*. In domestic matters, it has always been considered vital to limit presidential power to preserve the constitutional design of American democracy. The nation's historical tradition has been one of fear and suspicion of concentrated power, whether it existed in the governmental or economic area. The possession of power has been equated with its potential abuse, and power was therefore domestically distributed vertically between the federal government and the states; within the federal government it was separated horizontally among the executive, legislative, and judicial branches.

By contrast, the conduct of foreign policy—whose principal aim is safeguarding the nation's security so that life may be preserved and enjoyed—requires a concentration of executive power. In the international, or state, system, in which each state is its own protector and must rely primarily on its own resources and strength, the chief executive is usually considered the defender of the "national interests." This was as true in America in the days before democracy, under the rule of the British Crown, and it is true in contemporary democracies, and in authoritarian and totalitarian states. Survival in an essentially anarchical international system whose principal rule is self-help requires a single source of authority so that a state can, if necessary, act speedily, secretly, with continuity of purpose or, when demanded, with flexibility. From the beginning of the modern state system it was taken for granted that legislatures, especially as the democratic representatives of the people, were incapable of conducting foreign affairs; public opinion was felt to be too ignorant, too impassioned, and too unstable. Parliaments as legislative institutions were by their very nature thought to be incapable of rapid decisions; to pass wise legislation, they were expected to debate at some length and reconcile conflicting interests and viewpoints. In short, the primacy of the executive in foreign policy was essentially a response to the nature of the state system.

Because of the domestic system's requirements to restrain executive power and the state system's need for ample executive power, tension between these two aspects of the presidency in the United States is inevitable.[14] On the one hand, if the president is limited sufficiently to protect American democracy, the danger is that he might also become so enfeebled that he will not be able to defend effectively the nation's interests. On the other hand, if the president accumulates enough power to act with the necessary authority, dispatch, and secrecy to protect the nation, he might become so powerful that he will erode the restraints on his power that were intended to preserve the constitutional nature of the American political system. Thus, what is a virtue domestically might become a vice internationally, as the nation falls victim to its democratic organization; and what is a virtue externally might become a vice internally, as the nation loses its democratic soul in seeking to protect its democratic order from foreign threats.

Interestingly, this fundamental dilemma—how to preserve a democratic order at home while investing the government and especially the presidency with enough authority to effectively guard the nation's security and welfare—was first noted by the English political philosopher John Locke, who is usually regarded as the theorist whose political philosophy underlies the Declaration of Independence and the Constitution. Locke asserted that man possessed certain natural or inalienable rights that in society would be protected by the election of representatives who, through the legislature, would restrain the executive from abusing these rights and undermining the democratic nature of society. Externally, however, nations continued to live in a "state of nature" with one another. Therefore, the executive—which in the conduct of foreign affairs Locke called the federative power—could not be similarly contained.

> These two powers, executive and federative, though they be really distinct in themselves, yet one comprehending the executive of the municipal laws of the society within itself . . . ; the other the management of the security and interests of the public without. . . . And though this federative power in the well or ill management of it be of great moment to the commonwealth, yet it is much less capable to be directed by antecedent, standing, positive laws than the executive; and so must necessarily be left to the prudence and wisdom of those whose hands it is in, to be managed for the public good.[15]

It was Locke, then, who first distinguishsed between the two presidencies—the executive and the federative—both embodied in one person, the president, situated at the crossroads where the domestic and international systems meet and overlap.

The second, and closely related, dilemma might be summed up as *process versus output*. The American government is supposed to represent the "will of the people." This will is expressed in many different ways. A nationwide election is held every four years for president, the only nationally elected figure in the United States; elections are held every two years for one third of the Senate and the entire House. And those who hold grievances are able to organize themselves, express their legitimate interests, and, as interest groups, can strive to achieve their goals by supporting candidates for office during elections and, in between elections, by bringing their influence to bear at the legislative, executive, and judicial levels of government (both state and federal). Clearly, in domestic policy, the emphasis is on widespread participation of many different groups and interests in society and government and the reconciliation of their diverse and conflicting interests as they are reflected in the bureaucracy, Congress, and competing interest groups. The preferences of the majority emerge through this political process.

In foreign policy, as in domestic policy, the executive and legislative branches share responsibility and power. This does not, however, necessarily produce the "right" policies. The concern for producing "correct" foreign policies—or at least not the wrong ones—is certainly understandable, especially in this highly volatile era. President John F. Kennedy once said that foreign policy can kill us, while domestic policies can set us back. This description may be overdrawn. Not all foreign policies are likely to result in nuclear war nor are all domestic policies necessarily salvageable and correctible if mistakes are made. But Kennedy did state a simple truth underscoring the difference between foreign and domestic policies: the first, unlike the last, may be irreversible and result in the destruction of American society, indeed, much of the world. Kennedy's own estimate in the early 1960s was that 100 million Americans, 100 million Europeans, and 100 million Russians would become casualties in the opening hours of an all-out American–Soviet nuclear war. A Carter administration study placed U.S. casualties at 140 million and Soviet casualties at about 110 million.

From the beginning of the Cold War in the late 1940s there was agreement that foreign policy should therefore be decided differently than domestic policy. Indeed, there was some precedence. During World War II (1941–1945), the balance between the president and Congress was virtually suspended, and the president was given emergency powers for the duration of the conflict. After hostilities had ceased, the Congress reasserted itself. Not surprisingly, the concentration of power in the presidency was therefore considered the most effective way to deal with the Soviet Union. Partisan rivalry and executive-legislative conflict—the norms in domestic policy—would play havoc with foreign policy. Presidential primacy and congressional and bipartisan support would provide a more effective pattern.

The Cold War, being neither war nor peace (as usually understood), meant that the president had to wield a kind of emergency power on a continuing basis. This was a novel situation. The United States had overnight become the leader of the "free world," with extensive and long-term commitments. Many of the situations it confronted, and could expect to confront, needed speedy decision and action, for delay could be costly, and the issues that had to be dealt with were varied and complex. American foreign policy required that the president be given the authority he needed. Only he had the capacity to act quickly and, thanks to the large bureaucracy whose responsibility it was to deal with the world beyond America, he also possessed the expertise. He did, however, need legislative support, for "correct" policies were not always popular. Conflicts between the president and Congress on the one hand, and between the Democrats and Republicans on the other, would undermine such support and were, therefore, intolerable. "A nation which excuses its own failures by the sacred untouchableness of its own habits can excuse itself into complete disaster."[16] The domestic ways of making policy were unfit for making foreign policy.

Successive presidents—with the general support of Congress—expanded the powers of the office to avoid such disaster. After the United States became deeply involved in the Vietnam War in the 1960s, however, it was precisely this growth of presidential power that was called into question. The "imperial presidency" was said to be responsible for a policy that had overcommitted the United States and led to "global policemandship" beyond the capacity of America's "limited power." Vietnam was considered the logical conclusion of the unchecked growth of presidential power. In turn, the imperial presidency was said to be the offspring of the disregard for prescribed procedure. Senator J. William Fulbright (D-Ark.), chairman of the Senate Foreign Relations Committee during the 1960s, said:

> Out of a well-intended but misconceived notion of what patriotism and responsibility require in a time of world crisis, Congress has permitted the president to take over the two vital foreign policy powers which the Constitution vested in Congress: the power to initiate war and the Senate's power to consent or withhold consent from significant commitments. . . . So completely have these two powers been taken over by the president that it is no exaggeration to say that . . . the United States has . . . become . . . a presidential dictatorship.[17]

Recent presidents, Fulbright said, had claimed the unlimited right to use the armed forces as they saw fit under an inflated interpretation of their powers as commander in chief and had ignored Congress' authority to declare war.[18] Similarly, the Senate's treaty power had been weakened by the president's contracting obligations with other nations by executive agreements or declarations; the interpretation of existing treaties in "extravagant and unwarranted ways"; and the revision of treaties by executive agreements after Senate approval of the treaties.[19] Fulbright's charges were widely accepted at the time.

By the late 1970s, however, as disillusionment with U.S.–Soviet détente grew, demands arose for the weakening or removal of at least some of the restraints placed on presidential power in the wake of Vietnam. These restraints seemed to be obstacles to the conduct of a more vigorous assertive foreign policy seemingly required by the continued expansion of Soviet influence, the demands of developing nations for a new international economic order, and the growing importance of and tensions in the Persian Gulf–Indian Ocean area for American and Western security and economic viability. The fear now was that the imperial presidency had become the "imperiled presidency," and that if the shift of power from the presidency to the Congress that occurred after Vietnam was not partially reversed, the United States' ability to define and defend its vital security and economic interests might be jeopardized. In short, greater congressional participation in foreign policy was compatible with a more limited American role in the world, but this larger legislative involvement, or what the critics called congressional "interference" and "restraint," was not deemed compatible with the enlarged global role that seemed to be the lot of the United States in the 1980s.

The third dilemma follows from the other two: *broad democratic participation versus foreign policy making by a small elite.* The ethos of the American political system points to the widespread involvement of the many actors involved on a particular issue. Certainly domestic policies follow this practice. The emphasis is on representativeness. In foreign policy, however, it is on expertise. Too many cooks spoil the broth seems to be the adage. Most cooks are assumed to be amateurs. The small number who are professionally skilled in foreign affairs should be in charge and be the president's advisers. By contrast, the foreign policies of a president who feels he must reflect public opinion, as represented by the polls and Congress, will be short term and erratic, for the public's mood tends to change rapidly. We are then condemned to "diplomacy by dilettantism," as one expert has called it.[20]

The degree of participation is critical in the two principal models of decision making presented in this book (Chapters 8 and 9); bureaucratic/governmental politics and rational. The first part of the former is so named because the most important domestic policies and virtually all foreign policies are initiated in the executive branch; whether the ideas for the policies are the president's own brainchildren or not, it is the bureaucracy that spells out the details of proposed policies (and later administers them). Governmental refers to the wider participation in the policy process of other actors such as Congress, interest groups, and affected segments of public opinion. And the word *politics* is included because with so many actors with different views and interests at stake, the only way of arriving at a decision is by negotiations and compromise—that is, politics. If the necessary accommodations are attained, most of the participants will gain something, although most likely not all they wanted. Such an accommodation, then, is considered a satisfactory solution even though the policy output may not be the best one in terms of solving a particular problem. There clearly is no such thing as a "correct" policy. The issue is how to reconcile conflicting interpretations of what the correct policy ought to be. The result of the compromises made is bound to be a watered-down version of what rationally would be the best (although not necessarily the correct) policy solution. In short, bureaucratic politics involves multiple actors. The decision-making environment is decentralized and the focus is on both the conflictual nature of and the necessity for accommodation if decisions are to be made.

The rational model refers to the *best* solution to a particular problem. The focus, instead of being on the internal dynamics of the decision-making process, which democratically allows all major actors to participate in formulating policy, is on the specific issue at hand and the most appropriate way of enhancing the chief value or goal that the policy makers select and seek. Which way, for example, can they best attain a goal such as the nation's security or welfare? Of the several possible alternatives usually available, which option is the most likely to achieve this end? The search is for a successful policy, not necessarily a popular one; the emphasis is on the solution to the problem, not the attempt to satisfy the many actors involved, which all too often results in a policy that no participant fully favors. The assumption is that the government is a unitary actor and rationality refers only to choosing the best among several ways of attaining a specific aim. In fact, decision making is highly centralized, made by those policy makers occupying the "command post positions." In real life, of course, the assumption underlying rational decision making—that these policy makers have the time and information to consider all aspects of a problem before deciding on the best possible solution—falls short.

In our scheme, the bureaucratic/governmental politics model best explains the domestic policy process, while the rational actor model is most useful in explaining foreign policy crisis situations. Our other two policies, noncrisis security policies and intermestic policies, the last a mixture of *inter*(national) and (do)*mestic* policies,[21] are also best understood in terms of the bureaucratic/governmental politics model. While rational policy stands largely by itself, the other policies are part of a continuum.

Crisis policy is made by the few deciding rationally (see Table 1.1); other policies by the many arriving at a decision politically. The more a policy resembles domestic policy, the larger the number of actors and the more intense the bargaining is likely to be. At the cost of some repetition, let us be clear about the distinction. Crisis policy focuses on the external situation confronting the nation

TABLE 1.1   Presidential Freedom and Policy Making

Rational Decision Making	Bureaucratic/Governmental Politics		
Crisis Policies	Noncrisis Security Policies	Intermestic Policies	Domestic Policies

⟶

Increasing number of actors and bargaining involved in the policy-making process; less presidential leadership

⟵

Fewer participating actors; increasing presidential freedom and leadership and on finding a correct response in that after a full examination of the alternative ways in which the national security or welfare can be protected in the situation at hand, the most effective means of achieving that goal at the least possible cost is chosen. Noncrisis security and other policies, by contrast, focus on the preferences of the many participating actors in the bureaucracy and legislature, their varying and differing policy preferences, purposes and power, the negotiations among them, and the policy "outcomes" that occur as a result of the compromises struck. In short, the last emphasizes the dynamics of the decision-making process and its central feature, the constant bargaining and trade-offs arranged among the players. It ought to be added that crisis policy, decided quickly by a few at the pinnacle of the executive branch, resembles policies made by authoritarian regimes, while noncrisis policy, characterized by the widespread participation of the bureaucracy and Congress over a fairly lengthy time period, tends to be highly democratic.

Our third dilemma for most security policies has been summed up as follows.

> A democratic government must accomplish two tasks: On the one hand, it must pursue policies which maximize the chances for success; on the other hand, it must secure the approval of its people for these foreign policies.... The necessity to perform these tasks simultaneously faces a democratic government with a dilemma; for the conditions under which popular support can be obtained for a foreign policy are not necessarily identical with the conditions under which such a policy can be successfully pursued. A popular foreign policy is not necessarily a good one.[22]

Yet is there an alternative in a democracy?

Characteristics of Foreign Policy Decision Making

The principal characteristics of decision making in the foreign policy sphere may be summed up as follows.

1. The actors and processes of foreign policy decision making differ for each of the three types of foreign policy decisions: crisis decisions, security decisions, and intermestic policy decisions.

    Crisis decisions, as noted, usually involve an element of surprise. The leaders have not been anticipating a threat from a foreign power; when the threat does occur, they perceive the need for a quick response lest the situation deteriorate to the detriment of the nation's security and violence ensues. For this reason, crisis decisions are made by the small number of actors at the very top of the executive "policy making machine."

    Security decisions, on the other hand, involve long-term policies. Most security policies, although formulated by the president and the various foreign policy bureaucracies, involve money and thus require congressional approval. Because many actors must participate, these policies may require lengthy deliberation. Furthermore, because security policies express continuing goals and commitments, they tend to involve stable sets of actors.

Intermestic decisions may involve both short-term and long-term considerations. Energy, for example, is an issue of enduring importance but it may also be subject to short-term factors such as an oil embargo or temporary loss of supplies. These issues affect both relations among nations and politics within nations. Intermestic issues, therefore, mobilize all the actors that domestic policies usually do: the executive agencies whose jurisdiction is basically domestic, Congress, interest groups, and public opinion. Consequently, the State Department, articulating the "national interest," will hardly be heard above the din of voices of the Departments of Treasury, Agriculture, Labor, and Commerce, their respective congressional committees, and interest groups in each of these and other policy areas. All these actors feel expert in these areas, possess major stakes and can articulate their viewpoints, and usually have a good deal of clout, since they represent specific, well-organized, and well-financed groups who normally represent millions of voters.

2. The foreign policy elite is a relatively small group located in the executive branch, primarily the political leadership and the professional officers of the principal foreign policy bureaucracies. More specifically, this includes the president (who is elected), special assistants on national security affairs, secretaries, under secretaries and assistant secretaries (political appointees), as well as senior professional officers of both the Departments of State and Defense and the Central Intelligence Agency. On a secondary level, there are the upper ranks of the Arms Control and Disarmament Agency, the U.S. Information Agency, and the Agency for International Development, as well as other departments and agencies that have an intermittent interest in specific foreign policy issues, for example, the Department of the Treasury's interest in monetary policy or the Department of Agriculture's desire to export food products.

3. Most noncrisis foreign policy decisions are arrived at through bureaucratic politics. Different bureaucracies have different perspectives and training for their professional staffs, a need to enhance their prestige, budgets, and influence—the more so if they are convinced of the importance of their contribution to the nation's security and well-being. The different departments and agencies, in short, have their own biases and tend to see the same problem and therefore come up with varying and conflicting policy recommendations. The result, on the one hand, is bureaucratic conflict; on the other hand, the need to make a decision produces a "strain toward agreement or consensus."[23] Policy, therefore, results from a process of bargaining and compromising. This is particularly the case on intermestic issues, where even more diverse interests are involved than we find for security policy or most domestic issues. This multi-

plicity of actors, many of them outside of the executive branch, makes bargaining particularly difficult—and there is no guarantee that a satisfactory compromise will be reached. Stalemate remains a strong possibility.

4. The central and key figure in the foreign policy process is the president. Although noncrisis policy is largely the product of bureaucratic conflict, this does not mean—as models of bureaucratic struggle often imply—that the president is merely one player among many, one chief among many departmental chiefs. He is more than merely a first among equals; he is by far the most important player.[24] He, after all, appoints the chiefs; presumably to a large degree they reflect his values and owe him, as well as their departments, a degree of loyalty. They can be fired if they no longer serve the president's purposes. He can also "stack the deck" by assigning a policy to a particular chief and department or set of people. If he selects "hawks" to investigate whether to intervene militarily in Vietnam, as Kennedy did, he is likely to receive a report favoring intervention; had he chosen "doves" he would in all probability have gotten back quite a different answer.

Moreover, many problems require the consideration of so many political, economic, social, and psychological elements that nowhere short of the presidential level can these factors really be balanced off against one another and integrated into an overall policy. But perhaps the most important factor—in an era in which presidents have grown increasingly fond of being their own secretaries of state—is that presidents will seize for themselves specific areas of policy (for instance, arms control) or policies (for instance, negotiating an end to the war in Vietnam). "The ability of bureaucracies to independently establish policies is a function of presidential attention. Presidential attention is a function of presidential values. The chief executive involves himself in those areas which he determines to be important."[25] Bureaucratic power is thus to a large degree a function of presidential—and, even further, congressional and public—inattention. In practice this means bureaucracy plays its largest role in routine day-to-day matters, its smallest during crisis periods.

The comparative presidential ability to gain legislative support for his foreign as distinct from his domestic policy has been summed up by one leading scholar of American politics as follows.

> The president's normal problem with domestic policy is to get congressional support for the programs he prefers. In foreign affairs, in contrast, he can almost always get support for policies that he believes will protect the nation—but his problem is to find a viable policy. . . .
>
> In the realm of foreign policy there has not been a single major issue on which presidents, when they were serious and determined, have failed. The list of their victories is impressive: entry into the United Nations, the Marshall Plan, NATO, the Truman Doctrine, the decisions to stay out of Indochina in 1954 and to intervene in Vietnam in the 1960s, aid to Poland and Yugoslavia, the test-ban treaty, and many more. Serious setbacks to the president in controlling foreign policy are extraordinary and unusual.[26]

On intermestic policies, not surprisingly, the president's ability to initiate, lead, and maneuver will, as in domestic policies in general, be more constrained than on security issues. As one writer, referring to the growth of intermestic issues, which he calls nondefense issues, has said:

> There is likely to be an increasing emphasis on *nondefense* foreign policy issues, most of which will have a great impact on *domestic* politics and great attraction for domestic interest groups. Problems with the monetary system, trade deficits and surpluses, energy policy, and the import or export of things such as inflation, unemployment, technology, and pollution will consume more and more of the foreign policy effort. This will occur . . . because these nondefense issues will have a larger absolute impact on American society. . . . As post-Vietnam foreign policy becomes more constrained, on the one hand, by independent foreign actors he will not be able to outmaneuver, such as economic institutions and foreign governments' economic policies, and on the other hand, by the fact that his decisions will have real domestic impact. . . . Indeed, the seamlessness of the distinction between foreign economic and domestic economic policy may simply extend the president's weakness in domestic policy to foreign policy as well.[27]

Whereas in foreign policy, presidents can usually take the initiative and gain great satisfaction from the role they play on the world stage—an opportunity few can resist—in policies that affect the domestic arena, presidents find themselves more constrained by the Congress, interest groups, media, and, on some issues, public opinion.

5. The role of parties in foreign policy has been defined in terms quite different from those applied to domestic policy by politicians themselves as well as by journalists and scholars. Largely stirred by the memory of the defeat of the Versailles treaty following World War I in the conflict between a Democratic president and a Republican Senate, the post-World War II partisanship mood was one of the usual type of political considerations that, it was held, had no place in the conduct of foreign affairs. The national interest was to be placed ahead of party interest. In protecting the nation against external threats, the president deserved the support of both parties. "Bipartisanship" became the new slogan and the patriotic policy to follow; partisanship was to be confined strictly to domestic affairs. Executive–legislative hostility and party controversy over foreign policy might undermine the stability and continuity of U.S. policy, make it impossible to speak with one national voice in world affairs, and erode the nation's credibility in its dealing with friends and foes.

Since Vietnam, bipartisanship has been on the decline. As the Democrats swung more to the left and Republicans to the right, the gap between the parties grew. One pursued "world order politics," focusing on the interdependence between the industrial Western democracies and the less-developed countries of Asia, the Middle East, Africa, and Latin America. The other continued to concentrate on the U.S.–Soviet rivalry; the Cold War, far from being over, had entered a new and more competitive phase. While security issues were increasingly subject to partisan conflict, intermestic issues like trade remained partisan. For instance, the Democrats have traditionally supported lower tariffs while Republicans have sought to protect industry; today, the Democrats are more disposed to support protectionism while the Republicans oppose protective tariffs. Still, on these types of issues, regional and economic interests may cut across party lines. But on security issues, party differences have become clear, especially during the four Carter and eight Reagan years.

6. The Congress has been traditionally supportive of the president in foreign policy. Legislators to a large extent felt a lack of familiarity and sense of incompetence on foreign affairs. Viewing them as esoteric matters beyond their personal experience, in contrast to farm or labor problems, confronted with expert civilian and military witnesses at committee hearings, they usually have tended to subordinate their own presumed expertise—political judgment of the feasibility and acceptability of administration policies—to that of the president and his phalanx of bureaucratic help.

But since Vietnam, Congress has become more assertive and less willing to accept presidential dominance on foreign policy. There has been a renewed concern for the establishment of a balance of power between the president and Congress in policy making, although this reassertion of congressional power does not mean that the legislature has become an equal partner with the president. While more members of the Congress are more interested in foreign policy today than at any time in recent history, they are still a substantial minority within the Congress. Most legislators remain primarily concerned with domestic policies—and with their reelection campaigns. Most foreign policy questions are not salient to voters, so members of Congress tend to downplay their importance and devote their time to issues and services that are more rewarding. Thus, only a minority of the legislators are strongly concerned about foreign policy and even they tend to be supportive of the president in crisis situations.

There are more challenges than before on security decisions, but the greatest congressional involvement is found on intermestic policies. These issues (energy, trade) have great impacts on the day-to-day lives of the people in members' districts and the stakes are perceived as very high. Members see themselves as the only protectors of their districts' interests. The key intermestic policy battles are fought in the legislature, where presidential programs are often held hostage and do not always escape alive. Regional and economic controversies surrounding intermestic politics are clearly reflected in the localism of Congress and its decentralized (many say parochial) system of committees and subcommittees.

7. Interest group representation, articulation, and influence, while pervasive in domestic politics, are not nearly as extensive or intense in the traditional area of foreign policy concerned with security issues. In this area interest groups tend to lack the interest, experience, and, above all, the knowledge they possess on domestic issues. Nonetheless, ethnic groups in a nation of immi-

grants have often pressed for policies favorable to the former mother country. In contrast, as already suggested, on intermestic issues so many groups have interests in the outcome of policies and see the stakes as so high that these groups may control much of the policy process. Businesses, banks, agricultural and shipping interests, and labor organizations have a natural interest in trade, foreign investment, and tariff issues. Virtually nobody fails to perceive a critical interest in energy policy (Chapter 7).

8. The public has, like the Congress, largely been supportive of the president's conduct of foreign policy, particularly before Vietnam. One reason is that most Americans simply are poorly informed and uninterested in foreign policy issues. Their knowledge and experience, like that of most senators and representatives, relate to affairs nearer home, such as family and professional life; the political opinions they do hold are more likely to be about national politics. At best, policy makers may sense a general mood, which may set broad limits on what they regard as feasible and permissible, but they do not receive specific operational cues. In general, it would be more accurate to say that public opinion on foreign policy is a response to the policy makers' decisions and to public presentation of the issues. On intermestic issues, however, much of the public does not make a clear-cut distinction between domestic and foreign policy considerations. Thus, these issues can easily become a source of great controversy, since citizens may expect that domestic political considerations will determine how to resolve questions involving the state of the economy. The public is less supportive of the president during times of domestic hardship, for they expect him to provide immediate relief for these sorts of pocketbook problems and display little patience when he cannot do so.

We can sum up these characteristics with the following diagram of concentric circles. In these circles (see Figure 1–1), the central decision-making locus on foreign policy is the president and his key advisers. In the second circle are the major foreign policy agencies and the armed services, the second-rank and less-influential foreign policy departments, presidential and other executive departmental advisers, and cabinet members whose primary responsibility is in the domestic sphere but who may be consulted on foreign policy questions. The innermost circle is composed of a select few members of the administration; the other circles have successively more members of the administration; the outer circles have successively more members and correspondingly less impact on foreign policy decisions. Congress is in the third circle, while political parties, interest groups, "personal diplomacy," public opinion, and the mass media are in the fourth circle. But the issue is not solely one of numbers and how close the various actors are to the inner circle; it is also a matter of time. The longer a policy is debated and the more prolonged the process of making policy, the more likely that it will spill from the inner circles to the outer circles and become part of the public debate. On intermestic policies, of course, the outer circles

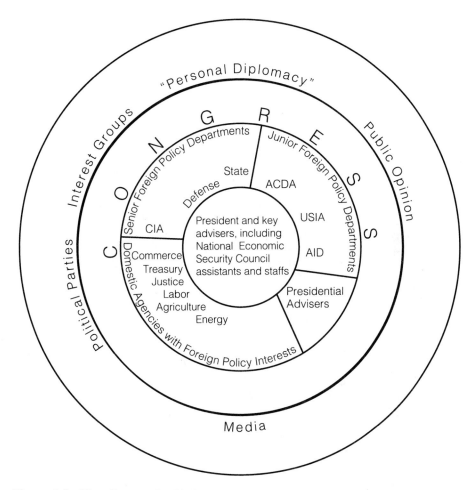

Figure 1.1 The Concentric Circles of Power in Foreign Policy Decision Making. (*Source:* Adapted from Roger Hilsman, *To Move A Nation*, New York: Doubleday Publishing, 1967, pp. 541–44.)

tend to be involved early and may be more influential than the inner circle, circumscribing presidential leadership.

All three types of policies revolve around the central question of democratic decision making on foreign policy. How much participation, and by which actors, do we want or can we tolerate? The larger the number of participants involved in making decisions, the more difficult it will be to reach a consensus on what ought to be done. That is why in a crisis, participation is kept narrowly confined. More broadly, the question is whether American democracy, with its checks and balances and its goal of preserving individual freedom and preventing political tyranny, can also effectively protect and enhance the nation's security and well-being in a dangerous and more interdependent world.

Notes

1. Thomas L. Friedman, "Rethinking Foreign Affairs: Are They Still a U.S. Affair?" *New York Times* (February 7, 1992), A10.
2. Robert O. Keehane and Joseph S. Nye, *Power and Interdependence* (Boston: Little, Brown, 1977), pp. 11–15.
3. See Kenneth N. Waltz, *Foreign Policy and Democratic Politics* (Boston: Little, Brown, 1967), pp. 274–75, and John E. Mueller, *War, Presidents, and Public Opinion* (New York: John Wiley & Sons, 1973), p. 211.
4. Robert H. Salisbury, "The Analysis of Public Policy: A Search for Theories and Roles," in *Political Science and Public Policy*, ed., Austin Ranney (Chicago: Markham, 1968), p. 158. See also Salisbury and John Heinz, "A Theory of Policy Analysis and Some Preliminary Applications," in *Policy Analysis and Political Science*, ed., Ira Sharkansky (Chicago: Markham, 1970), pp. 39–60.

   On the original distinction between distributive and redistributive policies in the literature of political science, see the pioneering article by Theodore J. Lowi, "American Business, Public Policy, Case Studies, and Political Theory," *World Politics*, July 1964, pp. 677–715. On the applicability of distributive and redistributive policies to the study of foreign policy, see James N. Rosenau, "Foreign Policy as an Issue Area," in *Domestic Sources of Foreign Policy*, ed., Rosenau (New York: Free Press, 1967), pp. 11–50; and Lowi, "Making Democracy Safe for the World: National Politics and Foreign Policy," in ibid., pp. 295–331.
5. Henry G. Graff, "Presidents Are Not Pastors," *New York Times*, May 27, 1987.
6. Ivor W. Jennings, *Cabinet Government* (Cambridge: Cambridge University Press, 1951), p. 183.
7. Paul Seabury, in *Power, Freedom and Diplomacy* (New York: Vintage, 1967), p. 196.
8. Louis Henkin, *Foreign Affairs and Constitution* (Mineola, N.Y.: The Foundation Press), p. 37.
9. Ibid., p. 41. See also his "Foreign Affairs and the Constitution," *Foreign Affairs*, Winter 1987/88, pp. 284–310.
10. Quoted by Felix Gilbert, *To the Farewell Address* (Princeton, N.J.: Princeton University Press, 1961), p. 145.
11. Samuel P. Huntington, "Advice for a Democratic President," *The National Interest*, Spring (1992), pp. 16–17.
12. J. William Fulbright, *The Crippled Giant* (New York: Vintage, 1972), p. 241.
13. Aaron Wildavsky, "The Two Presidencies," *Trans-Action* (December 1966), p. 7.
14. Seabury, *Power, Freedom and Diplomacy*, p. 189.
15. John Locke, *Two Treatises of Government* (Cambridge: Cambridge University Press, 1960), pp. 383–84 (italics and capitalization of nouns omitted).

16. George F. Kennan, *American Diplomacy 1900–1950* (Chicago: University of Chicago Press, 1951), p. 73.
17. Fulbright, *The Crippled Giant*, p. 193.
18. Ibid., p. 198.
19. Ibid., p. 218.
20. Kennan, *American Diplomacy*, pp. 93–94.
21. Bayless Manning, "The Congress, the Executive and Intermestic Affairs: Three Proposals," *Foreign Affairs*, January 1977, pp. 306–24.
22. Hans J. Morgenthau, *A New Foreign Policy for the United States* (New York: Praeger Publishers, 1969), pp. 150–51.
23. Roger Hilsman, *To Move a Nation* (New York: Doubleday Publishing, 1967), p. 541.
24. See Stephen D. Krasner, "Are Bureaucracies Important?" *Foreign Policy*, Summer 1972, pp. 159–79, for an incisive critique of the bureaucratic model.
25. Ibid., p. 168.
26. Wildavsky, "Two Presidencies," pp. 7–8.
27. Donald A. Peppers, "The Two Presidencies: Eight Years Later," in *Perspectives on the Presidency*, ed., Aaron Wildavsky (Boston: Little, Brown, 1975), pp. 463–64, 469.

CHAPTER 2

Presidential Preeminence in the Making of Foreign Policy

Presidential Primacy in Foreign Affairs

The preeminence of presidents in the domain of foreign policy is visible in the names attached to specific policies: Washington's Farewell Address, Jefferson's Embargo, the Monroe Doctrine, Theodore Roosevelt's Big Stick, Wilson's Fourteen Points, Franklin Roosevelt's Good Neighbor Policy, the Truman Doctrine, the Eisenhower Doctrine, the Nixon Doctrine, and the Reagan Doctrine. During his years in office, President Nixon even issued an annual State of the World message to supplement the yearly State of the Union message. (The last formerly included a president's assessments and general recommendations on foreign and domestic policies; Nixon separated the two.) President Carter, after the Soviet invasion of Afghanistan in 1979, declared the Carter Doctrine, which committed the United States to preserving the independence of the oil-producing states bordering the Persian Gulf. The Reagan Doctrine embodied U.S. support for guerrillas trying to overthrow Marxist regimes in some Third World countries.

Indeed, between the end of World War II and Vietnam, most of our presidents have been primarily interested in and concerned with foreign policy issues. Truman had little choice; circumstances made it necessary for him to give most of his time to foreign policy. President Eisenhower, the general who had led Allied armies to victory in Europe, was elected during the protracted Korean War, which he promised to end. John Kennedy left no doubt that he sought his fame and reputation by his handling of foreign policy; in his inaugural address he confidently asserted that the United States ''shall pay any price, bear any burden, meet any hardship, support any friend, oppose any foe to assure the survival and the success of liberty."[1] President Nixon, too, clearly considered foreign policy his particular area of expertise and showed far less interest in domestic affairs. Before his inauguration, he was quoted as saying that the country needed a president for the conduct of foreign policy; the cabinet could take care of domestic policies. His reorientation of American policy toward Communist China and his negotiations with the Soviets on a broad front from arms control to trade preoccupied the president in his attempt to lay the foundation of a "generation of peace."

By contrast, President Lyndon Johnson's fate tragically symbolized the plight of a president whose principal experience was domestic and whose fundamental wish was to enact a social reform program to rival that of his mentor, Franklin Roosevelt. Unfortunately the world would not go away. Thus Johnson, on succeeding President Kennedy after the latter's assassination, pushed more liberal social legislation through Congress than any president in the twentieth century, including Franklin Roosevelt. But foreign policy proved his undoing. Feeling inexperienced in this area, he kept Kennedy's advisers, all of whom had been counseling the escalating intervention in Vietnam and therefore had a vested interest in the success of the Vietnam policy; he thereby almost unthinkingly committed himself to a larger intervention. Johnson refused to do what he should have done—appoint men he knew and whose judgments he trusted. Thus, when it was too late he appointed one such man, Clark Clifford, as secretary of defense. Clifford, after reevaluating the war effort, recommended de-escalating the war and beginning peace negotiations. But feeling cowed by what he called Kennedy's "Hahvuhd" types, Johnson kept them around, believing they had the knowledge and experience he lacked; he was mistaken. Johnson paid for his mistaken judgment; he decided not to run for reelection in 1968.

Gerald Ford, Nixon's successor had little experience in foreign policy. After long service in the House, he became president only by the rarest of circumstances. First, the vice president was forced to resign because of kickbacks he had taken while governor of Maryland and, second, the president left office because of a pending impeachment proceeding in the Congress. Ford, however, had a very experienced and forceful secretary of state in Henry Kissinger. Carter was the first governor in the postwar period to become president. Even though he had served on the Trilateral Commission, the purpose of which was to bring about closer relations between the United States and its democratic and industrial allies in Western Europe and Japan, he had no foreign policy experience and relied heavily on a number of advisers. The point, however, is clear: whatever the president's background and however much or little he is interested in foreign policy, he soon becomes immersed in foreign policy issues. One of the ironies of the Carter presidency in this respect was that the president was widely perceived as having failed as a manager of the economy and that his achievements really were in the foreign policy area: the Panama Canal treaties, Camp David and the Israeli-Egyptian peace treaty, the official recognition of the People's Republic of China, and the SALT II treaty (even though the Senate never ratified it). President Reagan, another former governor, also focused on domestic policy during most of his administration. More than any of his predecessors, Reagan was uninterested in foreign policy matters; at press conferences he frequently displayed his ignorance by making gross factual errors when asked about international events—errors that later had to be "corrected" or explained by White House statements. A strong anti-Soviet, Reagan would issue broad directives such as a military buildup, while avoiding the specifics of policies (except in the cases of his involvement in the covert war against the Nicaraguan government and his proposal for Strategic Defense Initiative). He believed in delegating authority to the responsible cabinet officers. Yet it was Reagan the "great communicator" who, with his patriotic speeches and generally tough rhetoric, stirred the nation. He made Americans feel good about themselves again, and gave them pride that the United States was once more "standing up" to the Soviet Union and terrorists. It was also Reagan who was to lead the country away from the Cold War as he responded to changes in the Soviet Union after 1987.

And it was President Bush, Reagan's vice president for eight years, who ended the Cold War and forged a cooperative relationship with the Soviet Union during his first three years in office—until the revolutionary events of those years ended in the disintegration of the former Soviet superpower. Presidential leadership reached its apex during the months following Iraq's seizure of Kuwait as Bush organized an international coalition to oppose Iraq and finally to compel its withdrawal from Kuwait by going to war. Without his leadership, there would have been no opposition to Saddam Hussein. In the post-Cold War period, the United States remained the premier power and the U.S. president the leader of the world. Indeed, he seemed so preoccupied with foreign affairs that during the 1992 campaign for presidential nomination his Democratic contenders and his Republican opponent charged that his preoccupation had led to a neglect of domestic affairs.

The Selection and Campaign for the Presidency

The Recruitment of Presidential Candidates

The central role of the president in foreign affairs has been reflected during the post-World War II period—from the eruption of the Cold War to the end of the war in Vietnam—by the pattern of recruitment of presidential candidates. Until World War II, the governorship had supplied a long list of presidential candidates. Since the end of the Civil War, the list included, among others, Wilson, Theodore Roosevelt, Coolidge, and Franklin D. Roosevelt. While the United States was largely an isolationist country, this training ground for presidents was incomparable. It was at the state level that they gained experience in dealing with the problems of pre-Depression domestic America; four of the presidents since 1945 have served in the Senate. At a time when the United States was one of the two leading powers in the world, when nuclear weapons would mean the deaths of tens of millions of Americans if war erupted, this is not really surprising. The expertise for dealing with these key issues of war and peace was in Washington, not state capitals. And in Washington, the Senate is the senior legislative body and is more involved in foreign policy making than the House. Thus the emergence of the Senate as a launching platform for presidential candidates is natural. Truman was a senator, although he was not selected by Roosevelt as vice president in 1944 because of his knowledge of foreign affairs. But what is striking about post-Truman presidential and most vice presidential candidates until 1976—especially the winners of each nomination in both parties—is (1) the predominance of U.S. senators and (2) membership of those senators on either the Foreign Relations Committee or the Armed Services Committee, with a slight edge for the first. The standout exception was Eisenhower, a military officer and public servant with much experience in foreign policy and diplomacy.

Two senators who were unsuccessful in their first tries for a place on their parties' national tickets and were successful the second time had in the interim become members of the key Senate committees. John Kennedy (D-Mass.) in 1956 was a member of the Senate Government Operations Committee when he sought the Democratic vice presidency; four years later, when he became his party's presidential nominee, he was on the Foreign Relations Committee. Barry Goldwater (R-Ariz.), unsuccessful in 1960, was successful in 1964 and had in the meantime become a Senate Armed Services Committee member. Edmund Muskie (D-Maine), the Democratic vice presidential candidate in 1968, joined Foreign Relations before the next election, when in the early going he was considered the front-runner for the Democratic presidential nomination.

In contrast George McGovern did not become a member of the Senate Foreign Relations Committee until after he had lost his race for the presidency in 1972. McGovern's concern for foreign policy was said by his opponents in Senate races in 1974 and 1980 to lead to a neglect for his constituents' concern with domestic issues (see Chapter 3 for a more general discussion of this theme). In 1980 he lost his Senate seat but remained an active voice in Washington, particularly on foreign policy; indeed, his 1984 quest for the Democratic nomination stressed international issues. Almost all of the Democratic aspirants in 1984 had foreign policy experience, ranging from service on Senate committees to former Florida Governor Reuben Askew's position as Carter's special trade representative. Only the Reverend Jesse Jackson, who had not held public office, lacked an active foreign policy background. To compensate for this, he, as Carter did in 1976 and Reagan did before the 1980 election, toured Western Europe before announcing his candidacy. He later gained the release of first an American navy flier shot down in an engagement with the Syrians in Lebanon and then some Americans (mainly alleged drug runners) and a number of Cuban political prisoners while visiting Castro in Cuba.

Governors were generally unsuccessful presidential aspirants from 1945 to 1976—until after Vietnam and the resulting disillusionment with foreign policy and increasing domestic economic concerns. Two governors were nominated during the Cold War: Thomas Dewey (R-N.Y.) in 1948 and Adlai Stevenson (D-Ill.) in 1952 and 1956; the last had some foreign policy experience. State executives who made bids for the presidential nomination and failed—Nelson Rockefeller, William Scranton, and W. Averell Harriman—had considerable foreign policy experience. But most governors did not; because their experience was primarily domestic, they were not even nominated. A state's chief executive who demonstrated an interest in foreign policy but also an inability to handle international problems was even worse off than a governor who stressed domestic concerns almost to the exclusion of foreign policy. A case in point is former Michigan Governor George Romney. Romney was considered the front-runner for the Republican nomination in 1968 until he stated that the Johnson administration had succeeded in "brainwashing" him on the proper course of action in Vietnam. The charge backfired on Romney, who appeared to many to be too gullible on any policy. The first governor actually elected on a national ticket in the postwar years was Spiro T. Agnew in 1968 and 1972, who had not aspired to the post and was surprised at being selected by candidate Nixon in 1968 to balance the GOP ticket geographically and ideologically. Both Nixon and Agnew, of course, left office involuntarily; Agnew was then replaced by Nelson Rockefeller who, as noted, had considerable foreign policy experience (indeed, he introduced Henry Kissinger to national political life). At the time of his nomination, Rockefeller was serving as the head of a self-financed research organization analyzing both foreign and domestic policy alternatives.

As surveys indicated a declining trust in government, Washington experience became less critical for candidates seeking the presidency. Former Georgia Governor Jimmy Carter gained the Democratic nomination in 1976 by running against the "Washington establishment." Four years later former Governor Ronald Reagan of California was the Republican nominee. Both were elected to the White House despite—or, perhaps, because of—their lack of Washington experience. Walter Mondale, with impeccable insider credentials, was crushed by Reagan in 1984. He had served on the Select Intelligence Committee in the Senate and as vice president. There was a modest increase in trust in government in the mid-to-late 1980s. The insider candidacy of George Bush—Reagan's vice president, former director of the Central Intelligence Agency, and representative to the People's Republic of China—met less resistance. The Democrats reverted back to a Washington outsider, picking Massachusetts Governor Michael Dukakis, but balancing the ticket with Senator Lloyd Bentsen (Texas) of the Intelligence and Commerce Committees for vice president. Dukakis's main challenger for the Democratic nomination was civil rights leader Jesse Jackson, even more of an antiestablishment candidate than the Massachusetts governor.

With trust in government at an all-time low in 1992, Washington experience became a burden. A strong anti-incumbent mood led both the chair and the ranking minority member of the House Foreign Affairs Committee to join the ranks of the congressional retirees. The 1992 elections set a record for congressional retirements. Washington insiders with foreign policy experience—Bentsen, Senator Bill Bradley (N.J.), Senator Albert Gore (Tenn.), and Congressman Richard Gephardt (Mo.)—decided early in 1991 that the swift victory in the Gulf War made Bush invincible. They declined to seek the Democratic nomination. All three major candidates—Arkansas Governor Bill Clinton, former Senator Paul Tsongas (Mass.), and former California Governor Jerry Brown—portrayed themselves as anti-Washington. Even Bush claimed to be an outsider: The "permanent government" was the Democratic-controlled Congress. Even though he grew up in Washington as the son of a senator and had worked there for most of the past two decades, Bush portrayed himself as the new kid on the block trying to change a corrupt system. Even as the electorate was preoccupied with domestic issues, Democratic nominee Clinton decided it was essential to balance his outsider strategy with a vice presidential nominee (Gore) who served on the Senate Armed Services Committee and had established a reputation as an expert on arms control.

From Truman to Reagan, presidents had been so involved with foreign policy problems, including crises when the threat of nuclear war became especially acute, that domestic problems were bound to suffer neglect. The fact that there are only so many hours in a day and that the president can pay attention to only some of the many problems that he should deal with (had he unlimited time) means that he has to make a choice, and when the external danger is perceived as high by the president and his advisers, foreign policy will preoccupy them. Since throughout most of the post-1945 period the threat from the Soviet Union and China (from 1950 to 1972) was seen as global in scope, it is not surprising that before Reagan domestic affairs were delegated to a secondary status. One analyst even asserted that "foreign policy concerns tended to drive out domestic policy."[2] Indeed, in a situation where even potential foreign crises like Vietnam did not receive sufficient attention, and therefore tended to blow up into full-fledged crises, domestic affairs often seemed to gain consideration only when they too became critical. Sometimes, in fact, it appeared that only domestic violence would attract sufficient attention and bring results, as, for example, when rioting during the 1960s dramatically demonstrated the frustration and anger of American blacks at their status and treatment 100 years after the Emancipation Proclamation.

This subordination of domestic to foreign policy has occurred with increasing frequency during this century, as America has more and more become involved in world affairs. Every president who has come into office bent on reform at home has sooner or later found himself confronted by external threats that came to preoccupy his attention and led to the subordination of domestic problems. Wilson's New Freedom program was overtaken by the German menace and

World War I; Franklin Roosevelt, or "Dr. New Deal," as he called himself, became "Dr. Win-the-War" early in his third term, as Hitler, Mussolini, and Tojo made it impossible to complete domestic reforms; after 1945 Truman's Fair Deal quickly became subordinated to the policy of containment; Kennedy's New Frontier became a victim of one foreign crisis after another; and Johnson's Great Society was devoured by Vietnam.

This does not mean that, without the appearance and perception of external threats, presidents supported by Congress would have spent the resources used up by recurrent military preparations on domestic problems and reforms of various kinds. Roosevelt's New Deal was stalled in Congress by 1938. Truman's Fair Deal made modest progress in 1949 and 1950, but was overshadowed by congressional criticism of the Korean War in the last two years of his administration. Eisenhower had no social program to speak of, and Kennedy's New Frontier remained largely rhetoric since Congress wanted no part of it. Johnson's Great Society was the exception. It was made possible by the exceptional circumstances of his immense persuasive skills, a landslide presidential victory that also elected a sizable number of Democratic congressmen, and the president's concentration on the enactment of his social legislation. Simultaneously, he conducted the escalating Vietnam War in a business as usual atmosphere that demanded no sacrifices from the American people. This strategy worked until the 1966 midterm election and the recapture by the Republicans of many of their former House seats. Nixon, in his turn, had few domestic interests except to dismantle some of his predecessor's social programs.

It was the widespread disenchantment with foreign policy and increasing concern with domestic affairs in the late 1970s that resulted in senators no longer having the inside track on being nominated for the presidency. The first challenge came, as already noted, from the ranks of governors. Carter, of course, was renominated in 1980 despite a strong challenge from Senator Edward Kennedy. Reagan in the Republican party had the field virtually to himself; he was an old campaigner, the darling of the conservatives, and had almost taken the nomination away from President Ford in 1976. After his nomination in 1980, presidential candidate Reagan, inexperienced as he was in the area, stressed foreign policy heavily.

Like Carter, it was predictable that Reagan would have to give much of his attention to foreign policy. He would, like his predecessor, have to learn on the job. There is an irony to Carter's record as president: if he had any successes they were in foreign policy, not domestic affairs. He was the father of the Israeli–Egyptian peace treaty of 1979; he negotiated a strategic arms limitation with the Soviets; he formally recognized the People's Republic of China; he negotiated a new status for the Panama Canal; and he was active in seeking a peaceful solution to the Rhodesian problem. He also energetically promoted human rights and responded strongly to the Soviet invasion of Afghanistan. By contrast, the energy problem, unemployment, and inflation grew worse under Carter—not because Carter did not devise programs to manage these problems, but because Congress and the president were unable to agree on approaches to these complex issues. Carter was widely perceived as an incompetent president and, most ironic of all, it was his handling of the Iranian hostage issue and Afghanistan that rallied the country around him, helped stifle Kennedy's campaign on domestic issues, and helped the president survive the late presidential primaries.

Carter, with a limited background in foreign policy, chose a running mate in 1976 with a Washington background and foreign policy experience and capitalized on Ford's blunder in a foreign policy debate. He campaigned as an outsider against the "Washington establishment" candidate. Four years later, he found himself the "insider" candidate against Reagan, who also chose a running mate with Washington experience and an extensive foreign policy background. Reagan's campaign against Carter very much resembled Carter's against Ford in 1976. Reagan attempted to make up for his lack of foreign policy background by attracting knowledgeable assistants and issuing policy statements. Experience itself would be gained on the job. Even as incumbent in 1984, Reagan continued to campaign as an "outsider," and stressed Mondale's role as Carter's vice president in attacks that most analysts felt were important to his reelection. President George Bush is a departure from this pattern. In his campaign, he stressed his experience in foreign policy as vice president (see Chapter 5). Immediately after the election, he met with German Chancellor Helmut Kohl and British Prime Minister Margaret Thatcher; prior to his inauguration he met with Soviet leader Mikhail Gorbachev. Bush's first cabinet appointment was Secretary of State James A. Baker, his best friend and former campaign director.

Few presidents have devoted themselves so heavily to international relations as George Bush. He became known as the "foreign policy president." In his first year in office—1989—he sent American troops to invade Panama to topple General Manuel Noriega and bring him to trial in the United States on charges of trafficking in drugs. (Noriega was convicted in 1992.) The Soviet Union unraveled while Bush was in the White House, and the president claimed credit for its demise. The crowning achievement was the victory in the Gulf War in early 1991 and the apparent renaissance of the United States as a world power. Yet critics charged that Bush was preoccupied with foreign policy because he had no domestic agenda. When the American public began to doubt whether the war against Iraq really was a victory and began to focus more on domestic policy, the Bush administration seemed to have lost its way.

Candidates who lack foreign policy background have sought to overcome this handicap by making trips abroad, hiring foreign policy experts as consultants, and making political advertisements suggesting their toughness on foreign policy issues. Gary Hart visited the Soviet Union to hold talks with Soviet party leader Mikhail Gorbachev in 1986. Jesse Jackson made a trip to Damascus where he arranged the freedom of American pilot Robert Goodman, who had been shot down in Lebanon, and later paid a surprise visit to the Geneva summit between Reagan and Gorbachev; he engaged in a brief televised dialogue with the Soviet leader. While contemplating running, Mario Cuomo hired many foreign policy experts and used his position as governor of New York to meet with visiting heads of state such as Italian Prime Minister Bettino Craxi and Garrett Fitzgerald of Ireland; he also made a trip to Moscow. Even if candidates have no direct foreign policy experience, it is important that they try to establish some background so that they appear equipped to handle crisis decision making. And Michael Dukakis, the 1988 Democratic nominee, made a famous television advertisement that seemed totally out of character and became the subject of considerable hilarity. It featured the Massachusetts governor, complete with helmet, riding around standing in the turret of a tank. Bill Clinton strove to overcome Bush's charges that he had little foreign policy experience. During his tenure as Governor of Arkansas, he travelled out of the country less than most other state chief executives. In his 12 years, he visited Asia three times, Western Europe twice, and the Soviet Union once. Clinton made a series of speeches on foreign policy in 1992 and portrayed himself as more ready to give foreign aid to the former Soviet Union than was Bush. When Russian President Boris Yeltsin came to the United States for a summit with President Bush three weeks before the Democratic convention, Clinton held a widely publicized meeting with him to demonstrate foreign policy credentials. He met with CIA Director Robert Gates for a security briefing two months before he was elected President and stressed his agreement with much of Bush's foreign policy.

Presidential Campaigns and Foreign Policy

Obviously, who gets elected president matters in foreign policy. It is hard to believe that President Walter Mondale, Ronald Reagan's opponent in 1984, would have bombed Libya to persuade it not to engage in further terrorist acts. Equally, it is not credible that President Michael Dukakis would have drawn a line in the sands of Kuwait in 1990, sent more than a half million troops to Saudi Arabia, and attacked Iraq after the United Nations deadline for its withdrawal had passed. Moreover, no one would have expected an anti-Communist hawk like Richard Nixon to make détente with the Soviet Union and reconciliation with Communist China the foundation of his foreign policy after he became president. Nor would anyone have expected Reagan, the most conservative and anti-Communist president in postwar America, to have become the architect of the deepest U.S.-Soviet arms control cuts and the chief promoter of the end of the Cold War. Ironically, conventional wisdom contends that the outcome of a presidential race turns primarily on domestic or "pocketbook" issues. Foreign policy issues are not similarly relevant to most voters. Others argue for the salience of foreign policy and point to the elections of 1952 and 1968, when the Korean and Vietnam wars exerted a major influence on voting behavior by defeating the Democratic presidents who had intervened in these wars; or to 1980 when the electorate reacted to Iran's holding of U.S. hostages and President Carter's inability to gain their release. What seems beyond dispute is the fact that the voters are very much concerned over the relative capacity of rival presidential candidates to deal effectively with foreign policy issues, even though they may have little knowledge of, or concern with, the substance of these issues. Clearly, presidential candidates themselves believe this to be the case. One of the chief ways in which presidential hopefuls demonstrate their qualifications for the high office they seek is by exhibiting knowledge and competence in matters affecting the national security of the United States. When a candidate fails to radiate a reassuring image in foreign affairs, his campaign is gravely damaged.[3]

Republican candidates have, by and large, benefited from this more than Democrats since Vietnam and the election of Nixon. Republicans have pounded the theme that it was under Democratic leadership that the country had become involved in the two world wars, Korea, and Vietnam. Just as the Democrats had, after the Great Depression, tagged the Republicans as the party that mismanaged the domestic economy, so the Republicans called the Democrats the "war party." Whether the electorate believed these myths, the fact remains that Democratic candidates have not provided the country with the image of strong defenders of American interests in the world who would, if necessary, be willing to use force.

What is not debatable is that presidential campaigns can have critical impacts on foreign policy.[4] One negative impact, as we have already stressed, is that the election campaign may bring to the fore inexperienced leaders. Another negative is the use of a particular issue to beat the opponent; a "loss of China," a "missile gap," and other specious issues that divert attention from the real issues, yet afterward may have profound—largely negative—effects on the conduct of foreign policy (see Chapter 3). Additionally, the campaign can lead to promises that simply cannot be or are not kept, such as Eisenhower's pledge to liberate the then Soviet satellites in Eastern Europe, or Lyndon Johnson's statement that American boys would not be sent to Vietnam to do the job Asian boys should do. In domestic policy Congress is the principal obstacle, but in foreign policy it is Congress *and* 160 other nations. Promises rashly made may lead to cynicism and disillusionment when they remain unfulfilled. Each presidential candidate is increasingly tempted to criticize his opponent and promise that he can do better—much better; the gap between promises and achievements is almost inevitable, as is later public disillusionment and cynicism.

This temptation to promise easy and painless solutions is exaggerated by two aspects of the campaign: the increasing number of primaries and the use of television appearances and radio/television advertisements. Complex issues are boiled down to simple solutions and catch phrases that can be presented in a minute and a half on the evening news; in a long campaign, there tend to be lots of such phrases and broad promising generalities. These changes in presidential campaigns have led increasingly to an emphasis on personality rather than on policies (see Chapter 5). While personality is not unimportant, it must be stressed that this emphasis denies voters ways of assessing the various candidates' knowledge of foreign affairs and their sense of judgment on foreign policy issues. Personality is often just "image making"; a candidate seeking votes does not state his views but rather takes polls to find out what he should say or not say. As Robert Strauss, Democratic National Committee chairman from 1972–77, has said:

> There can be no laboratory test in foreign policy. . . . U.S. history is full of surprises about the men who have become presidents. Most often these have been pleasant surprises, as was the case with Harry Truman. Yet trusting to luck is not enough. However imperfect a basis it is for judgment, the amount and quality of information available to the American people about prospective presidents and their foreign policy capabilities and intentions must be increased.[5]

One more negative aspect of the campaign needs to be discussed, namely, the temptation to avoid controversial topics that might cost votes. For example, no candidate for the presidency during the Cold War had advocated a peace process between Israel and some of her Arab neighbors that would have required the United States to pressure Israel to be more accommodating on territorial issues and perhaps the Palestinian situation in exchange for peace. Despite the enormous difference in power, and Israel's dependence on U.S. military and economic assistance and diplomatic support, U.S. presidents—who have usually taken an evenhanded position between the Israeli and "moderate" Arab points of view—had little leverage, except possibly in the second and third years in office. A president running for reelection was unlikely to be so bold as to take a tougher position with Israel as reelection time neared (or election time for his successor); if he had done so, the opposing candidate would have criticized him for endangering Israel's security. It became almost a ritual for presidential candidates to visit Israel and express their commitment to her security and welfare. Israel was obviously not the only controversial issue.

In fact, former Secretary of State Cyrus Vance so despaired of the heavy intrusion of domestic politics into foreign policy issues that he has advocated one six-year presidential term. Since it takes a president from six to nine months to learn his job and feel comfortable in it, Vance said, he can operate with assurance only for the next eighteen months.

> But during the last year or so, he is running for reelection and is forced to divert much of his attention to campaigning. As a result, many issues are ignored and important decisions are deferred. Sometimes bad decisions are made under the pressures of months of primary elections. And at home and overseas, we are frequently seen as inconsistent and unstable.[6]

Whether the end of the Cold War will reduce this impact of domestic politics on foreign policy—or accentuate it—remains to be seen.

Presidential campaigns can, however, have positive effects. Despite the greater salience of domestic issues, the campaigns every four years can bring to the public's attention some of the key issues facing the nation, such as Soviet–American relations, arms control, and nuclear proliferation, the military budget and U.S.

military strength, trade (and jobs), and American policy toward South Africa or Latin America. Some of these issues do raise differences between candidates in the primaries, as well as between the two final contenders in the presidential debates that have become part of the campaign ritual every four years, and may thus educate the electorate about some of the foreign policy alternatives.

Instead of putting off critical issues, campaigns may advance them because some presidents see these issues as helping them get reelected. President Nixon's overture to China and summit conference in Moscow, which concluded the SALT I agreement and antiballistic missile treaty, were all-important foreign policy achievements that created the public perception of a creative statesman deserving reelection. They counteracted much of the criticism for Nixon's continued conduct of the Vietnam War. (Nixon, too, countered that criticism by advancing the diplomatic process enough to enable Henry Kissinger, his national security adviser, to say that "peace is at hand" just before the election.) President Ford might have been reelected in 1976 had he signed SALT II and not been frightened off by right-wing criticism of détente and arms control from Ronald Reagan, who was vying with Ford for the Republican nomination. And President Carter might have benefited from his extraordinary risk taking in personally brokering Israeli–Egyptian differences and moving these countries toward peace, had it not been for the adverse consequences for him of Iran's seizure of U.S. hostages in Teheran and the administration's subsequent floundering and inability to gain their release in time for the president to benefit.

A critical advantage of the election is that it compels presidents and candidates to move toward the center of American politics. This has become especially important because since Vietnam, as we shall see below, the two parties have taken more divergent approaches to foreign policy. President Reagan is particularly instructive in this respect. The darling of the conservatives, strongly anti-Communist and antiarms control, the president had, by the time of his reelection campaigns, shifted to accepting the necessity for a strategic relationship with Communist China against the Soviet Union, despite earlier statements suggesting closer U.S. relations with the Nationalist Chinese regime on Taiwan. Then he began to talk of the importance of arms control and of his commitment to a summit conference with the new Soviet leader, Mikhail Gorbachev, in 1985. In this way, fears that Reagan's recklessness and cowboy approach to foreign policy might get the United States into war were allayed. He did not send the marines into Nicaragua or El Salvador, only into Grenada (which was very popular with the American public); and in Lebanon, Reagan pulled the marines out before battle casualties rose, thereby maintaining a high performance rating in the public opinion polls.

More fundamentally, election campaigns can sometimes educate the American public to the necessity for change. Franklin Roosevelt took the lead in 1940 by slowly shifting public opinion from isolationism to the need for supporting Britain after France's defeat by Germany that year; and that effort continued after the election. The president took risks in adopting this position, but he was an effective leader of a public shocked by the defeat of France. The 1948 and 1952 campaigns contributed to the death of isolationism and the mobilization of public opinion in favor of the United States playing a leading role in the world. Conversely, campaigns allow candidates to gain a better sense of the issues that are on the electorate's mind. Reagan's shift toward arms control was undoubtedly in large part a response to widespread concerns that were conveyed to the president by, among other things, his travels around the nation and the popularity of the nuclear freeze movement. In the 1984 primaries, all of the Democratic contenders but one (Senator John Glenn) favored the nuclear freeze; the president needed to defuse the peace issue and identify himself with it, as he had begun to do by 1983.

An interesting phenomenon is that other countries increasingly seek to exploit the open nature of the U.S. political system, especially the presidential campaigns, for their own purposes. North Vietnam was particularly shrewd in this respect, launching major offensives in 1968 and 1972 to affect the course of the war and American opinion. The Tet offensive in 1968 was especially successful because it undermined public support for the war with the result that the subsequent presidential campaign focused not on winning the war, but on de-escalating and getting out. While it was clearly North Vietnam's purpose to strengthen pressure in the United States to withdraw, South Vietnam's was the opposite. In the peace negotiations that had just started, they resisted any concessions in the hope that the Republicans would win and that they would get a better deal from Nixon. In 1972, with mounting criticism of Nixon and unrest in the country at the continuing U.S. involvement in the war, the Democrats nominated Senator George McGovern as the peace candidate. But Nixon's moves toward China and Russia, and the fact that the war appeared close to being over favored Nixon. North Vietnam played the election cleverly. It made some key concessions in the now four-year-long peace negotiations; then, before they were concluded, the North Vietnamese announced diplomatic breakthroughs and the imminent end of hostilities. Once it became apparent that McGovern, who might offer them better terms, would not win the election, they were clearly keen on getting the administration committed to end the war before the election. They feared that Nixon's reelection for a second and final term would allow him first to continue the heavy and damaging use of U.S. airpower against North Vietnam (U.S. ground troops had largely been withdrawn from the fighting by then); and second to offer less favorable terms than before the election. After the United States withdrew from Vietnam in 1973, the big North Vietnamese offensive to finish off South Vietnam was reportedly scheduled for 1976. The election campaign would presumably ensure against reintervention by the United States. In fact, however, South Vietnam had collapsed in 1975 under its own incompetence in dealing with the daily fighting.

In 1980, the Iranians played the same game. Having seized the U.S. embassy and its occupants in Teheran in early November 1979, the Ayatollah Ruhollah Khomeini's Islamic regime held these hostages month in and month out. Nothing seemed to gain their release. Only after Iraq attacked Iran in September 1980 did Iran's attitude begin to change. The U.S. presidential election campaign also played a role in finally gaining freedom for the hostages, for Ronald Reagan had strongly denounced the Iranians, calling them "barbarians," and the general sense was that Reagan, unlike Carter, might take strong military action. Just as the North Vietnamese had wanted to commit Nixon before the election in the expectation of getting better terms, so now the Iranian leaders calculated that a president fighting for his political life would be more accommodating than one assured of four years in office—if Carter were reelected. The Iranians proposed ending the crisis by November 4, but internal quarrels and the war with Iraq delayed them several weeks and Carter was unwilling to accept a number of the conditions submitted on November 2.[7] Had a settlement been reached at a dramatic last moment, would Carter have been reelected? Once Reagan was elected, the Iranians were determined to end the crisis before he took office, in fact, the hostages were released on the day of his inauguration.

The Soviets took the opposite tack in 1986–87. In part to slow down the Strategic Defense Initiative (SDI), President Reagan's plan for a defense of the United States against nuclear missiles, and in part to slow down the arms race so that he could divert funds into the stagnating Soviet economy, Soviet leader Mikhail Gorbachev was eager for arms control agreements, both on intermediate-range missiles based in Europe and on strategic arms (intercontinental missiles and bombers). He appeared particularly anxious because he correctly assumed that if he and Reagan signed an agreement, the president would be able to mobilize the two-thirds vote necessary for a treaty in the Senate. In 1979–80, Carter had been unable to muster the necessary sixty-seven votes, partly because of the unhelpful Soviet invasion of Afghanistan. Gorbachev clearly believed that if the strongly anti-Soviet and previously antiarms control Reagan signed a treaty, most conservative Republican senators would be in no position to oppose the treaty, as they might have been with a more liberal Democratic president. Reagan's anti-Communist credentials would ensure the necessary votes. Gorbachev's calculations proved to be correct: the arms control agreement on intermediate nuclear forces (INF), signed in December 1987, was passed by the Senate by a vote of 93–4, despite the fierce opposition of a few die-hard Republican conservatives.

Presidential Stakes in Foreign Policy

Foreign policy and presidential authority are organically and intimately tied together. The welfare state is one reason for the enormous growth of presidential power, but foreign policy is the primary one. Presidential power has clearly grown with America's global role; during the Cold War, presidents achieved a clear-cut primacy, while Congress subordinated itself to a secondary, if not peripheral, role. In the post-Vietnam, Watergate period, congressional attempts to restrain the president were linked to attacks on America's Cold War role as "global policeman." A more limited presidential role was tied to a policy more consistent with America's "limited power" as an institutionally greater congressional role. In short, the executive-legislative conflict revolved around America's world role. A strong presidency had a vested interest in not retreating from its overseas commitments; a strong Congress—reasserting itself at the cost of the presidency—had a vested interest in precisely such a retreat to what was called a more responsible, discriminating foreign policy.

It may also be true that while Democratic presidents have been in the forefront of expanding executive authority, it has been Republican presidents before Reagan who have had an even greater vested interest in making foreign policy their strong suit. Democrats were in power when the United States became involved in World Wars I and II, the Korean War, and the Vietnam War. Democrats could, however, also run on their domestic record—the New Deal, the Fair Deal, the New Frontier, and the Great Society. By contrast, the Republicans, the party of Herbert Hoover and the Depression, had no domestic record on which to run; they had to run on foreign policy and demonstrate to the nation that they could more effectively manage the country's foreign affairs. Thus Eisenhower was urged to run in 1952 by the eastern, moderate, internationalist wing of the Republican party. Senator Taft (R-Ohio), the leader of the dominant conservative, nationalist-isolationist, Midwestern wing of the party, was favored in 1952 as the Republican presidential candidate. Eisenhower, elected after three years of the Korean War, was followed eight years later by Nixon, elected after three years of the Vietnam War. Nixon's only interest was foreign policy. Détente with the Soviet Union, with SALT I as its centerpiece, rapprochement with Communist China, a gradual disengagement from Vietnam which left the anti-Communist Thieu regime in power in Saigon, was the foreign policy record that Nixon successfully ran on in 1972. And Reagan sounded the alarm once more about Moscow after the years of détente, Vietnam, and the humiliation the United States suffered in Iran in Carter's last year; he summoned the country to "stand tall" once more and successfully appealed to its pride and patriotism.

A president's interest in foreign policy is a matter of personal and political self-interest. A president's foreign policy record allows him to establish a reputation for leadership and effective stewardship of the nation's affairs which, in turn, also helps his party's reputation and fortunes. Until the Vietnam era, foreign policy was the one area in which the president was able to exercise a degree of initiative and autonomy that did not exist in domestic affairs. By and large, the president could count on public support and congressional deference on foreign policy issues. The temptation to be an activist president in foreign policy is thus very great. After Vietnam this temptation remained great, even if congressional support was no longer always a certainty. For one thing, a president's historical reputation remained tied to his foreign policy accomplishments. Not only did President Nixon's reputation as a foreign policy leader restore some of his luster after he was forced to resign the presidency in disgrace, but President Reagan's eagerness for arms control agreements with the Soviets, after years of opposing such agreements, testified to his desire (and reportedly, even more Mrs. Reagan's) to leave a record of important accomplishments in the key area of war and peace. Indeed, ironically, the most anti-Communist president since World War II was the first to recognize that Mikhail Gorbachev might represent a change in the Soviet Union and was willing to explore how genuine and fundamental this change might be. By the time Reagan left the presidency, he and Gorbachev had defused the Cold War, laying the foundation for the end of that four-decade-long conflict, which came during the first year of the Bush administration.

But the end of the Cold War is likely to have two consequences, one of which may be bad news for Republicans. First, the Cold War presidential primacy, already eroding since Vietnam, is likely to erode further. With domestic policy achieving greater prominence, Congress will likely be even more assertive, especially on trade issues. Second, the Republican party had been the prime beneficiary of the Cold War since Vietnam. Although most presidential contenders generally took a tough anti-Communist line during the presidential campaign—including Jimmy Carter, who attacked President Ford's détente policy as being too soft—the Democrats after Vietnam were widely perceived by the public to be "soft" on defense. This perception was reinforced by the congressional Democrats' overwhelming stance against permitting President Bush to use force to expel the Iraqis from Kuwait (see Chapter 8). But victory in both the Cold War and in the subsequent hostilities with Iraq deprived the Republicans of their main claim to power; it also gave the Democrats their first opportunity to reclaim the White House on the basis of better management of the economy, an issue that had also favored the Republicans during the Reagan years.

Conducting Foreign Policy

The Inner Circle: The National Security Council

At the center of the inner circle, helping the president conduct foreign policy, is the National Security Council (NSC). In addition to the president, its members are the vice president and the secretaries of state and defense, plus three advisers: the director of Central Intelligence, the chairman of the Joint Chiefs of Staff, and the director of the Arms Control and Disarmament Agency. All are statutory members whose appointments were designated by Congress when it organized the National Security Council. Two additional categories of officials have been appointed from time to time. One consists of those officially designated by the president—for example, the National Security Adviser (NSA), the director of the Office of Management and Budget, the secretary of the Treasury, the chairman of the Council of Economic Advisers, the permanent U.S. representative to the United Nations, the director of the United States Information Agency, and the secretary of energy. A second category of officials includes those whom the president informally asks to attend occasional meetings, such as the White House chief (or deputy) of staff, the president's press secretary, and the president's counsel. For example, during his second term, Reagan chose to include Attorney General Edwin Meese, Secretary of the Treasury James Baker, Budget Director James Miller, and U.N. representative Vernon Walters.

The National Security Council was founded in 1947 by the same act that established an independent air force, the Defense Department, and the Central Intelligence Agency. The rationale behind its establishment was to centralize decision making on national security issues, to ensure that the political, military, and intelligence strands of foreign policy issues would be more related to one another than previously, and to make certain that the major foreign policy advisers would be included in the decision-making process. Under Franklin D. Roosevelt, the decision regarding which high officials or agencies to include or exclude in a specific decision was entirely in the president's hands. As a result, political and strategic issues had often not been coordinated. The NSC was supposed to be a check against such presidential discretion and lack of coordination. The fact that the NSC was placed in the White House reflected the president's roles as chief diplomat and commander in chief, and the recognition that the president must lead the country and formulate a comprehensive and integrated foreign policy.

Nevertheless, presidents have not used the council as either the formal or actual locus of foreign policy making. Truman, Eisenhower, Johnson, and Ford relied heavily on their secretaries of state. Both the Truman–Dean Acheson and Eisenhower–John Foster Dulles relationships were close, and both secretaries jealously guarded the relationships against interlopers. Johnson relied heavily on Secretary Rusk and Ford was very dependent on Kissinger. Kennedy relied on his secretary of defense, Robert McNamara, as well as his brother, Attorney General Robert Kennedy, and close staff aides like Theodore Sorensen, less than on his secretary of state. It was during this period that the NSA first gained a degree of influence and prominence, largely because he was McGeorge Bundy, a well-known academic from Harvard who took an active role. His predecessors, especially during the Eisenhower years, had not only been prominent public figures but had confined their role to managing the council and ensuring that policy decisions were left for the president. Bundy, however, became a major player in the policy process because Kennedy encouraged him to state his own views on foreign policy. President Johnson retained most of the Kennedy people and also consulted from time to time with a group of "wise men," individuals with extensive foreign-defense policy background who no longer held formal positions in the government (the best known of these was Dean Acheson). President Nixon restricted his circle of advisers largely to Henry Kissinger, the NSA from 1969 to 1975 and secretary of state from 1973 to 1977. During the years he was not secretary, Kissinger was clearly the most important foreign policy official, far more influential than the secretaries of state and defense; as secretary of state, Kissinger continued to dominate, especially during President Ford's administration. Nixon transformed the NSA's role from that of being one of several key policy figures to that of the president's chief adviser on foreign policy. Both Presidents Carter and Reagan, however, vowed that their primary foreign policy adviser and spokesman would be the secretary of state, but their efforts were not always successful. Secretary Cyrus Vance and NSA Zbigniew Brzezinski—like Kissinger a well-known academician, and an articulate man of strongly held views—were often in conflict. Even the initial reduction of the NSA's authority and prominence, including the appointment of a number of undistinguished NSAs and two prominent secretaries of state during the Reagan years, did not fully restore the secretary of state's position as the president's primary policymaker and spokesman. Bush was more successful than his predecessors in this respect. James Baker, his secretary of state, was clearly the principal administration spokesman on foreign policy; Brent Scowcroft, the NSA, a former Air Force general who had previously served President Ford in the same position, deliberately eschewed public positions and statements.

This brief review of whom the president relied on for foreign policy advice suggests two conclusions. One is that the president consults pretty much whomever he wants; his informal circle of advisers is likely to include both key NSC officials and others with whom he has a close relationship. In short, membership on the NSC does not guarantee any official a place in the inner circle. Among President Carter's closest non-NSC advisers were his wife Rosalynn, Chief of Staff Hamilton Jordan, Attorney General Griffin Bell, press secretary Jody Powell, and Robert Strauss (who held a variety of positions from chairman of the Democratic National Committee to chairman of the 1980 reelection campaign). Just as Carter relied heavily on the people he had come to know and trust in Georgia politics, so Reagan relied heavily on longtime friends and officials from his California days, especially during his first administration: White House Chief of Staff Edwin Meese; his deputy Michael Deaver; William Clark, his second NSA and later secretary of the interior; Secretary of Defense Caspar Weinberger; and, although he shied from publicity, William Casey, director of the CIA. The only non-Californian who gained access to this group was James Baker, a Texan who in 1980 had been George Bush's key aide, and who became chief of staff after Meese left that position. President Bush continued this trend, naming Baker as secretary of state, Dick Cheney as secretary of defense, and Scowcroft as NSA. The four men had all served the Ford administration and gotten to know each other well. Indeed, they had become good friends and basically viewed themselves as team players.[8]

A second conclusion is the increasing visibility of the NSA and his emergence as a rival to the secretary of state. This perhaps is not as surprising as it sounds. As presidents in this century have become more and more preoccupied with foreign policy issues, they have also increasingly wanted—or felt compelled—to

become their own secretaries of state. Wilson set the precedent; he clearly overshadowed William Jennings Bryan, the former Democratic presidential candidate and great orator, as well as Bryan's successor, Robert Lansing. Franklin
Roosevelt paid very little attention to his secretary of state, Cordell Hull. During
World War II, in his meetings with Churchill and Stalin, he usually left Hull at
home and uninformed. Kennedy deliberately selected a relatively weak secretary
of state, Dean Rusk, a former assistant secretary of state during the Truman
years, and from 1969 to 1973 Nixon chose a friend, William Rogers, precisely
because he had no experience in foreign affairs. Nixon replaced Rogers with
Henry Kissinger, a strong figure, at the beginning of his second administration
and Kissinger remained as President Ford's secretary after Nixon resigned in
1974.

As presidents have increasingly exercised their authority as the nation's chief
diplomat, they have also come to rely more and more on a personal adviser who,
starting with Eisenhower, came to be called a special assistant on national security affairs. Wilson had his Colonel House, and Franklin Roosevelt his Harry
Hopkins. Kennedy appointed Bundy, Johnson appointed Walt Rostow from MIT
after Bundy resigned, and Nixon chose Kissinger, who, like Bundy, came from
Harvard. Under Nixon the position became institutionalized, and a sizable foreign policy staff of about fifty was assembled in the White House (Bundy had
twelve). This growth marks perhaps better than anything else the pre-Reagan
shift of the locus of foreign policy decision making from the State Department
to the White House. Even when appointed secretary of state, Kissinger kept his
White House position until 1976 when he gave up the national security post
because of political pressure on Ford. Yet, the new security adviser was General
Brent Scowcroft, Kissinger's deputy. Carter followed the past pattern of employing an academic adviser on foreign policy, Brzezinski of Columbia University,
whose staff was about forty. Ironically, the staff grew to its largest, about seventy,
when the NSC and NSA were at their most ineffective. By 1986, the NSC's main
function almost appeared to be giving everyone a title: one NSA, one deputy
assistant, one assistant to the president who doubled as special counselor, three
additional deputy assistants, one special assistant, fourteen senior directors, forty
directors, and nine deputy directors! There were five committees dealing with
U.S.–Soviet affairs, and the staff had become involved with bureaucratic minu-
tiae "at the cost of providing strategic direction and imposing policy coordination."[9]

Secretary of State versus National Security Adviser

In a real sense, the national security adviser had become a second secretary of
state. This was not the original intention; the NSA was merely to arrange meetings of the National Security Council (NSC) and manage the paperwork. Cre-

ated in 1947 to coordinate the political and military strands of foreign policy, the NSC did not initially play a prominent role. Truman's and Eisenhower's assistants remain unknown figures; these two presidents relied on strong secretaries of state. But Kennedy, wishing to play a more direct foreign policy role than his two predecessors—especially wanting to be his own secretary of state—made the NSA's position more prominent by appointing Bundy. The latter, however, largely remained out of the limelight. The NSA's job was to ensure that the president would receive all the necessary information and the full range of options he needed to make decisions, coordinate the work of all departments involved, and ensure that presidential decisions would be carried out. He was to be a largely anonymous manager. It was Kissinger, serving a president whose principal interest was foreign policy, and Brzezinski (with a somewhat smaller staff of about thirty to thirty-five), who gave the position public prominence. Kissinger was in charge of the Vietnamese peace negotiations, SALT, China and, after the 1973 Yom Kippur War, the first Israel–Egyptian steps toward peace in the Middle East. Brzezinski was not quite as dominant, although he was active, especially on policies toward the Soviet Union and China. A hard liner concerned about the Soviet's rapidly growing military power and expansion of influence, his advice became more prominent after the Soviet invasion of Afghanistan disillusioned Carter with U.S.S.R. behavior and Secretary of State Cyrus Vance's more accommodating stance. His position was reinforced by Vance's resignation in 1980; had Carter been reelected, Brzezinski would undoubtedly have been his primary foreign policy adviser.

Thus, one result of appointing a prominent national security adviser has—with two exceptions*—been friction with the secretary of state, officially the president's chief foreign policy adviser. Conflicting policy statements from the president's adviser and the secretary of state also raise questions among friends and foes about what U.S. foreign policy is and who is in charge. Another result is tension with Congress, which does not confirm the assistant's appointment; as the president's assistant he cannot be called on to testify before congressional committees, even though he may give television or newspaper interviews. A cabinet officer is confirmed and must testify (at best, the assistant meets informally with the Senate Foreign Relations Committee, for instance, or individual members of Congress). Perhaps the greatest danger is that the NSA, if he is someone with strong policy preferences, will not ensure that all points of view on issues reach the president. It has been said that Rostow, who was considered a hawk, shielded Johnson from critical views on the Vietnam War. The NSA cannot be both policy advocate and neutral policy manager. Institutionally, it is impossible; it is not primarily a matter of personality.

---

* One was the period when Henry Kissinger occupied both positions during the second Nixon administration; and then when President Ford (who succeeded Nixon after his resignation in 1974), during his last months, replaced Kissinger with retired Air Force General Brent Scowcroft, Kissinger's former deputy at the NSC.

Not surprisingly, it has been suggested that the NSA's position should be either abolished or downgraded to that of a basically neutral manager and that the secretary of state should be restored to the position as the president's chief adviser on foreign policy. Interestingly, after he left office Kissinger himself came out against a strong NSA and recommended a strong secretary of state. An active adviser, he said, is bound to reduce the secretary of state's prestige and influence. If the president does not have confidence in his secretary of state, Kissinger claims, he should replace him. Secretary Vance too, after resigning from office in 1980, urged that there be only two spokesmen for the government on foreign policy issues: the president and the secretary of state. Reagan, who reflected on the frequent Vance (and later Muskie)–Brzezinski tugs of war during his predecessor's tenure, chose as his first secretary of state General Alexander Haig, Kissinger's former assistant and later NATO commander in chief. Haig, a strong personality, was to be Reagan's chief foreign policy maker and spokesman and prevent the rise of a rival like a Kissinger in the White House. The appointment of Richard Allen, not previously well known as a foreign policy activist—he had been an economic consultant, largely in matters of trade, after a brief stint as a political science professor at Georgia Technological University—was to emphasize the secretary of state's primacy in foreign policy. The fact that the NSA would no longer report directly to the president as did his predecessors, and that the president's counselor, Edwin Meese, would serve with cabinet rank and would be in charge of both the national security and domestic policy staffs, underlined the determination to avoid having what amounted to two secretaries of state.

This arrangement did not, however, work out well in practice, as might have been foreseen. A strong secretary of state may not be able to avoid conflict with the national security assistant.[10] First, departments deal with policy only from their own perspectives; this is as true of the State Department as of other departments. Brzezinski, in his memoirs of the Carter administration, has said that the State Department tends to confuse foreign policy with diplomacy, but diplomacy is only a tool, as is the use of force or covert operations. Political considerations must be integrated with military, intelligence, and economic/commercial/financial factors. But this cannot be accomplished from a departmental perspective; each will fiercely resist giving another department the lead in formulating policy. Given the fierceness of bureaucratic politics, the institutional fragmentation of policy in Washington, and the weakness of political parties, the NSA can provide a degree of balance by centralizing policy direction.

Second, the State Department is reputed as cautious, often timid, unimaginative, and slow. This reputation for lack of risk taking and avoidance of controversial issues has been strengthened by the history of those foreign service officers who, in the 1940s, went out on the proverbial limb by predicting Nationalist China's collapse and suggesting that the United States make overtures to the Chinese Communists, who would shortly control mainland China. The careers of most of these officers were destroyed as they were charged with wanting that outcome and abetting it in the anti-Communist hysteria of the 1950s. Other officers who favored a specific policy in other areas have found their careers set back when a new administration favoring a different policy has come into power. In short, prudence dictates caution, "going along," and "getting along" rather than "getting out in front."

In addition, the State Department lacks the capability for long-range planning. Its Policy Planning staff has neither the power nor the prestige to do so and gain the cooperation of other responsible departments. This raises a question about the desirability of State acting as the president's chief adviser on foreign policy; indeed, Presidents Kennedy and Nixon questioned whether State had the ability to act in any advisory capacity. One reason for the growth of the NSA's authority is precisely that presidents have felt they could not depend on State for quick or sound advice. Recent presidents have felt the need for someone other than the secretary of state to ask for judgments and independent opinions not influenced by departmental biases and perspectives; the NSA has been that individual.

Third, the State Department is surprisingly weak in the very areas that ought to be its strengths. Perhaps because foreign service officers are supposed to be generalists, they often lack area expertise despite frequent rotation in a particular region, as well as knowledge of foreign languages, especially Russian, Chinese, Japanese, and Arabic dialects. In an era of increasing specialization, the State Department also misses other skills that it needs to hold its own against other departments: science and technology, international economics and, to a lesser extent, political-military expertise. The last illustrates the point: the State Department has had to bring in outside experts because foreign service officers still lack sufficient knowledge of defense and arms control policies.

Fourth, even if the department should be the primary spokesman, it would not be the only one—or the most powerful. Defense, Central Intelligence Agency (CIA), and—now that economic issues have become as prominent as political-strategic ones—Agriculture, Treasury, Commerce, and Labor are all more powerful spokesmen for their viewpoints than is State. These agencies all represent major sectors of the society and economy such as the defense industries, farming, labor, and the banking or business community, all of which have political clout and can mobilize support for their views in Congress and among the public in general. State, even though it may claim to represent the "national interest," has no constituency. Its chances of determining policy through coordinating the varying views of the different departments is, therefore, likely to be contested. By contrast, the NSA, as the president's alter ego, is in a better position to coordinate the many strands of policy and the conflicting views on what policy should be, and to impose on foreign policy the direction the president wishes. As Richard Allen perceptively noted later about Secretary Haig's difficulties:

> Haig, an experienced and exceptionally skilled operator within the bureaucracy, clearly believed that the conduct of United States diplomacy was actually synony-

mous with the broader, presidential concept of "national security." In the 1980s, "national security" is in itself an all-encompassing term too often narrowly construed as having to do only with foreign policy and defense matters. In reality, it must include virtually every facet of international activity, including (but not limited to) foreign affairs, defense, intelligence, research and development policy, outer space, international economic and trade policy, monetary policy and reaching deeply even into the domains of the Departments of Commerce and Agriculture. In a word, *"national security" must reflect the presidential perspective, of which diplomacy is but a single component* [italics added].[11]

The NSA cannot only represent that perspective, but if it is known that he has the president's personal confidence and can speak authoritatively on his behalf, he can resolve the bureaucratic conflicts and impose some order and direction on U.S. foreign policy consistent with the president's wishes.

Fifth, the very fact that foreign and domestic policy have become intertwined on so many issues means that the president is, by definition, paying constant attention to foreign policy. Not only do traditional security policies have an impact on domestic policy because of the demand for money and personnel, but such issues as energy or farm or environmental policies have both foreign *and* domestic policy implications. The NSA, sitting next to the president, can keep the president far better abreast of what is happening so that he can calculate the domestic feasibility and costs of a particular policy as, for example, on trade matters in which a president has to calculate which domestic constituencies are benefitted or hurt. The secretary of state does not sit at the crossroads between the "two presidencies." Only the occupant of the White House does.

Last, the very qualities that constitute the "essence" of its work do not help the State Department in its struggles for influence on policy among other departments in Washington. Diplomacy requires that foreign service officers be sensitive to the interests of the countries to which they are posted. After all, the State Department represents America's desire to get along with other nations. In Washington, however, the department has acquired the perhaps unfair reputation of representing foreign interests at home rather than U.S. interests abroad. More to the point, however, the department's skills are supposed to lie in compromising differences and accommodating conflicting perspectives and interests. But being influential in Washington requires an aggressive, pushy style. Bureaucratic politics is a rough game.

And hardly least—perhaps it should be first—presidents want action and results in order to demonstrate their leadership capacity. Given State's slow work habits, its tendency to produce fudge, and its reacting to White House proposals with an emphasis on professional caution and experience, advising one step at a time (clearly suggesting that the president's men should leave the conduct of foreign policy in their expert hands), presidents soon look elsewhere and are tempted to go around the department. Foreign policy is also a glamorous field. Its innate importance, especially at critical moments, the crucial contribution of foreign policy to a president's historical reputation, the ability to act on security issues with less opposition from Congress and interest groups than in domestic policy (although that is declining), draws almost immediate presidential attention. And when it comes to political judgments, no president is going to take a second place to "a bunch of bureaucrats." So presidents do not hesitate to make bold and innovative suggestions and take the initiative in the conduct of foreign policy.

Thus the NSA is likely to remain in a powerful position, helping the president achieve an overall view and giving the president counsel when he seeks it. It is the president, at whose pleasure the assistant serves, who defines the job and the balance he wants between his assistant and his secretary of state. He may dislike conflict and appoint a figurehead to the State Department, as Nixon did during his first administration; or he may, like Carter, welcome diverse advice and conflict, which leaves him greater freedom to choose. (Franklin Roosevelt regularly encouraged conflict among *all* his advisers.) Or he may not give him direct access, as Reagan did initially with his first NSA. But it is unlikely the president can do without the NSA, for in the words of the Senate Subcommittee on National Security Organization:

> The president at all times should have the help and protection of a small staff whose members work outside the system, who are sensitive to the president's information needs, and who can assist him in asking relevant questions of his departmental chief, in making suggestions for policy initiatives not emerging from the operating departments, and in spotting gaps in policy execution.[12]

These reasons may be reinforced by differences of opinion among the president's cabinet members and White House staff. In the absence of a consensus, the NSA may well be the person asked by the president to present the options and his own preferences. Thus, conflict between the NSC adviser and the secretary of state may be unavoidable, not because of the personalities involved but because of the structure of decision making. Perhaps it would be more appropriate to say that the increasing impingement of the world on the United States makes such conflict almost inevitable; this century has forced American presidents to become ever more involved with the conduct of foreign policy. As chief diplomats, commanders in chief, and chiefs of state, they have had no choice but to become activists in foreign policies. In doing so, they have looked for assistance from within the White House. The rise of the powerful national security adviser reflects the leading role the United States plays in the world and that increasingly, presidents want—or feel compelled—to be their own secretaries of state, qualified or not.

The Reagan Administration Melee

Conflict between secretary of state and national security assistant was evident very early in the Reagan administration. This was so despite President Reagan's determination to make his secretary of state his number one foreign policy man and to demote the NSC. One reason for the conflict was that Alexander Haig was suspect by the Reaganauts, the ideological conservatives who had come with Reagan from California and who ran the White House. Haig had served Kissinger, who was associated in their minds with détente and arms control, policies the Reaganauts condemned even though they had been in effect during a previous Republican administration. Haig was therefore denied frequent access to the president; he saw him only once a week and then always with a White House staffer present. In these circumstances, Haig was unable to achieve the type of relationship that Dean Acheson had stated was necessary for the effective conduct of foreign policy: a close relationship in which the secretary of state has the president's confidence and meets alone with him regularly so that the two can and do speak frankly to one another about the state of the world. Acheson had that kind of relationship with Truman and so, Haig observed, did Kissinger with Nixon. But Haig claimed to be "mortally handicapped" by his lack of access to Reagan, meaning he had to formulate policy without knowing the president's thoughts and methods, or having the opportunity to discuss policy details with him.[13]

What made the Reagan–Haig relationship even more difficult was that Haig took the president literally when Reagan said that his aim was to restore the secretary of state as his "vicar"—as Haig called his role—of foreign policy. And, as already noted, the secretary was not modest about defining the scope of his jurisdiction. Virtually all matters beyond the nation's borders were included; this encompassed not only traditional policy areas such as defense but also economic policy. Clashes with the secretary of defense, a close personal friend of the president, soon erupted; so did other conflicts, such as with the secretary of commerce when it came to negotiating limits on Japanese automobile imports. But most of all, tension occurred with the White House, where the staff felt that Haig was attempting to overshadow the president, perhaps to establish his own reputation in preparation for a run for the presidency. (He was a weak candidate in 1988.)

The result of this infighting was the worst of all systems for conducting foreign policy, one that fell somewhere between the secretarial system of a Truman and Eisenhower and the presidential system of a Kennedy and Nixon (see Table 2–1). Not only did the NSA report to the principal domestic adviser (who had no foreign policy competence) instead of directly to the president, as had become custom, but the White House, while asserting that crisis management was, as in the past, within its jurisdiction, placed Vice President Bush in charge. Since the vice president is not involved in daily foreign policy making, how could he take charge at critical and dangerous moments when he had not participated in decisions that preceded the crisis? Moreover, since the vice president has virtually no staff of his own, would he not have to depend on the president's NSC staff during a crisis? Clearly, the early Reagan system was a confusing and disorganized one in which the secretary of state frequently found himself at odds with—and checked by—the White House.[14]

TABLE 2.1   Organization for Foreign Policy—President and National Security Assistant

Presidential System	Falling in between	Secretarial System
Kennedy (Bundy) Nixon (Kissinger)	Carter (Vance–Brzezinski) Reagan (Allen–Haig–Clark/ McFarlane/Poindexter/Carlucci/ Powell–Shultz)	Truman (Acheson) Eisenhower (Dulles) Johnson (Rusk) Ford (Kissinger) Bush (Baker)

Of course, the fundamental problem was Ronald Reagan himself. He was completely inexperienced in foreign policy; his prime area of concern—the one in which he had both experience and a sense of competence—was domestic policy. The president, to be sure, had strong feelings. For example, he was militantly anti-Communist and committed to a large military buildup. However, some specific policies ran headlong into his inexperience, unfamiliarity, and lack of interest on most issues. His press conferences revealed a startling lack of knowledge of the details of policies; and what was later politely to be called his *management style* was one of "hands off."[15] In late 1986, when a foreign policy scandal, referred to by such names as Irangate, Iranamok, Contragate, and Contra(de)ception (see Chapter 3 for case study), broke out the president repeatedly defended his ignorance of events by claiming that his aides had not told him! His predecessors would all have demanded to know what was going on. Thus while the secretary of state was not in fact given the authority to be Reagan's spokesman and number one policy maker, the president's lack of interest and competence in foreign policy meant that the conflicts that naturally erupt in any administration were usually not resolved. The result was that the secretary of state, secretary of defense, CIA director (the last two being Reaganauts), and others were continuously feuding. Instead of a battle between the secretary of state and NSA, the Reagan administration ended up with a confused melee.

Efforts to resolve this matter were only partially successful. The initial step taken was to replace Richard Allen with William Clark after one year. Clark, a California rancher, close Reagan friend, and executive assistant to the president when governor of California, had later been appointed to the California Supreme Court. He too had no foreign policy knowledge or competence but had gained some familiarity and experience when he was appointed the number two man in the State Department. But his service there was short and he had none of the intellectual background and expertise Bundy, Kissinger, and Brzezinski had brought to the NSC position. He was expected to be essentially a good manager and mediator and to reduce the amount of conflict among the president's principal foreign policy advisers, especially between the White House and the secretary of state, his former boss. Clark was given access to the president, and the NSC position was upgraded so that Clark's authority was equal to that of the other principal White House officials. Second, Haig was replaced in the second year after the White House made several decisions he had opposed. His replacement, George Shultz, a former professor of economics at the University of Chicago and secretary of Labor and the Treasury under Nixon, had a calm personality and was more sensitive to the presidential need to show who was in charge. This new arrangement with Clark and Shultz appeared initially to provide the president with a system more comfortable to him for the conduct of foreign policy.

As Clark gained a degree of foreign policy knowledge and experience, however, he became more assertive, especially on Central America, Middle Eastern, defense, and arms control issues; and, at the end of eighteen months as the NSA, he had become the Reagan administration's most influential foreign policy figure and the Clark–Shultz relationship had become more strained. At this point, Clark, not totally comfortable in his foreign policy post, opted to become secretary of the interior. He was replaced by ex-marine Robert McFarlane, a loyal staff officer who had gained some experience and knowledge in foreign policy. But McFarlane was not a member of the Reagan inner circle and soon found himself in trouble with the president's chief of staff, Donald Regan, who was determined to run the White House as he had run Merrill Lynch—as a corporation, hierarchially organized, with the president as chief executive officer, the chief of staff as chief operating officer, and all others in a subordinate role. Any staffer who sought to play an independent role or have his own power base was not tolerated. In short, all access to the president went through Regan.[16]

As if this were not bad enough, McFarlane was also confronted with the ongoing rivalry between the secretary of state and secretary of defense, a rivalry that was more than institutional or ideological. The NSA was never given the authority to resolve this bitter personal conflict and to make decisions; the result, in McFarlane's opinion, was paralysis and drift in policy. Moreover, as McFarlane reported, "I had countless times with the president when I felt he wasn't absorbing what I was telling him. He did not have a good deal of interest in foreign affairs." He quit in frustration after two years, convinced that while he knew more about these affairs than anyone else in the cabinet, "I wasn't being listened to because I didn't qualify to be in the inner circle." In McFarlane's words:

> The president is a man who admires men who have accumulated means and become wealthy and demonstrated considerable accomplishments in a chosen endeavor . . . I haven't done that. I had a career in the bureaucracy. I didn't really quite qualify. It didn't do any good to know a lot about arms control if nobody listened.[17]

The problem was that the president would not resolve the Shultz–Weinberger disputes; it was not Reagan's style to knock heads to resolve differences. The absence of a strong-minded NSA placed a premium on cabinet offices being combative to win the president's personal support. This style of decision making did not change with McFarlane's replacement, Vice Admiral John Poindexter, who, like his predecessor, lacked clout. He also lacked foreign policy experience. While a nuclear physicist by training, he had picked up the military's post-Vietnam distrust of the press and Congress. A man without political experience as well, highly secretive in the conduct of his job, he was soon caught up in the Iran–Contra scandal and resigned. Reagan's fifth NSA in six years, Frank Carlucci, a veteran of government service in the CIA and Defense Department, was the first genuinely competent person to occupy that key position during the Reagan presidency. But by the time of his appointment in late 1986, Reagan was not only entering his last two years in office, but he was gravely weakened by the Iran–Contra affair. When Carlucci succeeded Weinberger as secretary of defense, he was followed by General Colin Powell, the third military man out of six NSAs in seven years.

The succession of weak NSAs did not, however, solidify the secretary of state's position as the president's "vicar" on foreign policy. Secretary Shultz's position was always a somewhat tenuous one. He did not have Haig's aggressive personality to prevail in the bureaucratic struggle, and he was not, like Kissinger, a conceptualizer. His principal skill was that of a negotiator; he had been a labor relations expert concerned with collective bargaining. A good secretary of state has to have a broader vision and be an architect; negotiating skills by themselves are not enough. Although a man of undoubted personal integrity, Shultz's accomplishments have been basically negative.[18] After watching his first efforts at diplomacy—arranging for Israel, Syria, and the Palestinian Liberation Organization to leave Lebanon—end in disaster with the killing of 241 marines in 1983, he did not try any new initiative in the Middle East until very late in the second term. Four visits to the area did not advance the peace negotiations one iota. The Contra war in Nicaragua and the Strategic Defense Initiative (SDI), the proposed shield for protecting America's population in a nuclear war, were managed by the NSC and the Defense Department. While Shultz basically washed his hands of Central America (although his Assistant Secretary of State for Latin-American Affairs, Elliott Abrams, largely managed the covert war together with the director of the CIA and the NSC staff) he loyally supported the president's policy, despite his own apparent preference for a negotiated solution.

Shultz sought to make arms control his issue and, given his lack of expertise, he took the unprecedented step of hiring a veteran, Paul Nitze, as his own adviser. Nevertheless, Shultz's success was rather mixed. He fought a rear-guard action on SDI, opposing the Defense Department's effort to reinterpret the 1972 antiballistic missile treaty to allow testing of SDI components in space; but he lost that one eventually to Secretary of Defense Caspar Weinberger. Shultz also opposed the Defense Department's efforts to abandon the SALT II limits on strategic weapons, arguing that this would publicize the president's lack of interest in arms control; Weinberger won that one too in November 1986. Moreover, at the 1986 Iceland summit meeting between Soviet leader Gorbachev and

President Reagan, Shultz was unable to persuade the president to use SDI as a bargaining chip and compromise on SDI research and development so that the United States could accept the Soviet proposal of a 50 percent reduction in Soviet and U.S. missiles (see the case study in Chapter 9). Nor was he able to follow up on this potential "grand compromise" because Weinberger's freedom to negotiate on strategic arms was severely restricted.

Ironically, Shultz's effort to separate himself from the Iran–Contra scandal, which damaged his standing in the White House, strengthened Weinberger's influence even though he too had distanced himself on this issue. Shultz's major preoccupation, largely a result of the marine deaths in Lebanon, was terrorism. He repeatedly urged the need to use force and exact a price for terrorism against Americans. Weinberger opposed such a use of force, even reportedly aborting a planned U.S.–French air strike against the terrorist camp following the killing of 241 American marines and 59 French paratroopers. Shultz, the leading advocate of attacking Libya's Colonel Qaddafi, was successful on this issue after Qaddafi provided the provocation. But on the whole, the secretary of state was eclipsed by the secretary of defense, especially on arms control issues, so he largely confined himself to damage limitation. Although he was successful in persuading the president to moderate his strong anti-Soviet language, Shultz's overall record was a negative one.

Until his last two years in office, the Reagan foreign policy record contains no diplomatic achievements like his predecessor's Panama Canal treaties, the SALT II agreement, the Camp David accords, or the official recognition of Communist China. It consists largely of the invasion of a tiny Caribbean island, an attack on Libya, and support of a number of anti-Marxist guerrillas against Marxist governments (mainly in Nicaragua, Angola, and Afghanistan). It is notable too that the secretary of state, despite his professional interests and background, including having been President Nixon's secretary of the treasury, did not exert himself on issues such as the protection of U.S. industries, the huge debt problem of Latin-American and other less-developed countries, and other economic issues. Neither did he challenge the Treasury's primacy in international economic policy. Even in his own area, as noted, he distanced himself from the Iran hostage crisis when it became clear that Reagan was determined to try to swap the hostages for arms. He apparently did not see it as his responsibility to continue to object and, if he could not dissuade the president, he did not feel he should resign. Yet, as one observer has noted:

> The case of . . . George Shultz is probably illustrative of the maximum influence future secretaries can expect to have. . . . Shultz's prominence is due to an unusual combination of factors. Reagan has had no desire to act as his own secretary of state, no deep personal interest in international affairs and little knowledge of the subject. Fortuitously, the secretary of state's frequent competitor, the NSA, has been strapped by presidential preference. Reagan's NSAs, except William Clark, have had their policy advisory roles restricted, and some NSAs were weak and ineffectual

or unschooled and inexperienced in foreign policy. Despite this, by January 1982, the NSC, not State, had the primary interagency coordinative function.

Moreover, Shultz is a skilled, experienced, bureaucratic operator regarded highly by Congress and by many within the administration. His effectiveness was further enhanced ... by his self-effacing, team-playing style. ... Above all, Shultz has developed an unusually cordial personal rapport with the president ... always a crucial factor.[19]

It was only in the Reagan administration's final phase, after 1986, that it became productive in foreign policy. This was the period when Reagan was served by three men whose outlook was similar and who sought solutions— Shultz, NSA Carlucci, and, after he became secretary of defense, NSA Colin Powell, later to become Bush's chairman of the Joint Chiefs of Staff. It was in 1987 that Gorbachev decided to call off the Cold War, in order to focus on the Soviet Union's domestic affairs, and began to take a more accommodating position. The president responded, in part because he sensed that Gorbachev was a different type of Soviet leader than his predecessors, and in part because— after Weinberger's resignation—principal advisers too favored changing the past course of confrontation. Reagan was never interested in specifics; his three advisers translated Reagan's general positions into negotiating positions and then worked out the compromises with the Soviets and within the U.S. government. This applied particularly to the elimination of middle-range nuclear weapons, which was a key arms control agreement, less because of its substance than because the Soviets, after years of refusing to even negotiate, suddenly accepted virtually the entire American proposal, thereby signaling their capitulation in the Cold War.

There are, of course, problems with the NSA's domination of foreign policy as well.[20] Any system run out of the White House risks not availing itself fully of the bureaucracy's expertise; a staff of 30 to 50 people is not a substitute for the larger body of experts throughout the executive branch. Moreover, to the degree that the White House runs policy and bypasses interested bureaucracies, the danger is that the president and the NSA may not gain support for their policies in the executive, let alone the Congress and the public. Third, the president and the NSA can only manage a certain number of policies. These are likely to be the ones that they judge as key issues and/or that need handled immediately; other important and long-term issues are postponed and neglected. Finally, if the NSC is abused by the use of covert operations, as in Irangate, the operation, narrowly held and not subjected to sufficient criticism from the experts, is likely to turn into a disaster (see Chapter 3).

The NSC's original functions need therefore to be reemphasized: preparing options for the president, acting as a neutral arbitrator in finding compromises between departments, ensuring that presidential decisions are implemented, selecting issues for the president's attention, and providing the president with independent judgment on what policy the administration should adopt.

> The degree to which the NSA should also be a policy adviser to the president also must be resolved. A major concern is that the NSA cannot be both an influential policy adviser and a neutral arbiter. Moreover, an assumption of the former role would invite friction with the secretary of state. On the other hand, to be an effective manager and institution the NSA must have an advisory role. This gives the NSA the stature and political clout to deal with powerful members of the cabinet. . . . Many presidents will naturally solicit advice from NSAs with whom they are in daily contact. Yet the NSA must not usurp the rightful role of the secretary of state.[21]

This clearly will not be an easy task. But since in the next century the United States will be even more deeply involved in world affairs, and both its national security and economic well-being will be intimately related to events and decisions made beyond the nation's borders, pressure for the NSA to play the central role in foreign policy making is likely to grow as well. Presidents will continue to take the leading foreign policy role because of their constitutional responsibility, the benefits such a role brings them politically, and the necessity to do so in the nuclear age. It is also only at the White House that a view transcending the various foreign policy bureaucracies can emerge and be imposed on policy. Thus the NSA can no longer be only or mainly a "manager"; he cannot avoid being a policy advocate also.

Obviously, whether this occurs or not, it would not mean the end of the rivalry between the NSA and the secretary of state, as well as others. That is normal. Such a system, given capable men, can serve the president well. The battles royal and guerrilla warfare Secretary Shultz talked of during the Iran–Contra hearings, are almost commonplace and not necessarily unhealthy, for they expose the president to a range of options and the cost, risk, and opportunities of each option. But if the system is abused, as in the Iran–Contra affair, when the NSA with little foreign policy experience seeks to make policy by cutting out the secretaries of state and defense who had opposing views, and transforms the NSC into an operating agency, it will fail the president and U.S. interests. But in the final analysis, if the system is to work well, it needs a president who does more than give general guidance; he must show continued interest in policy, including the details of some key issues, ask critical questions, demand policy reviews if policies do not work, and not exclude the foreign policy experts in the bureaucracies. Bush, of course, was heavily involved in foreign policy decision making. He clearly felt at ease in this area, as opposed to that of domestic policy where he had little knowledge and few real ideas of what he wanted to do. Bush was preoccupied with foreign policy concerns. In part, this was simply in response to the revolutionary events of 1989–91 and to the fact that the domestic economy was in reasonable shape; even when recession hit, the economy was expected to revive by the summer of 1991. Basically, Bush enjoyed conducting foreign policy; among other things, he was constantly calling foreign leaders on the telephone and consulting with them. In addition, as noted earlier, Bush's principal foreign policy advisers were personal friends who believed in being team players. The administration was not plagued by the fierce rivalry between the NSA and the secretary of state as in the Nixon and Carter administrations, or the intense rivalry between the secretary of defense and the secretary of state, as in the Reagan administration. Prior to the Bush administration, interestingly enough, only two NSA–secretary of state relationships had worked quietly and smoothly: Scowcroft and Kissinger during the Ford years and Powell and Shultz in the closing days of the Reagan administration. In both cases, the NSA was a military officer, trained to subordinate his ego to superior officers.

But the post-Cold War era poses a new issue, namely, whether the NSC system for foreign policy can be responsive to the new world in which bipolar confrontation has ended and military power, although hardly irrelevant, as demonstrated by the war in the Persian Gulf in 1991, is likely to be less salient. The new emphasis will be on economics; on issues of competitiveness and fierce trade rivalries; on environmental issues like global warming; on diplomacy in a new world of disintegrating empires, such as the former Soviet Union, and collapsing nations, such as Yugoslavia as ethnic hatred and quarrels lead to new conflicts and instabilities; on containing such anti-Western and antisecular forces such as Islamic fundamentalism; and on the increasing threat of the diffusion of weapons of mass destruction—nuclear, chemical, and biological—plus the missiles to deliver them—to Third World nations. Many of these issues impinge on domestic policy, and most can be managed only on a multilateral basis. The NSC system is not equipped for this new world; for example, there has been no place to bring together the conflicting views within the government on trade issues—for example, with Japan—and arrive at a common position. The absence of such an arena allows foreign countries, including Japan, to play one department against another, weakening the U.S. position on trade while strengthening that of its rivals and souring relationships with our allies, our principal economic competitors. Nor was there any way to balance foreign policy against domestic considerations. The NSC was not designed to deal with intermestic policy; not only are none of the relevant domestic departments statutory members, but the question is whether such a collective group could overcome the traditional departmental turf battles, subordinating their natural rivalry for transdepartmental, multiagency solutions.

The Clinton administration is moving to correct these shortcomings. It has organized an economic counterpart of the NSC. Yet the foreign policy team, ironically, reflects an absence of economic expertise. Warren Christopher is a lawyer, a cautious man and very patient and persistent negotiator, identified mainly with the cumbersome and procrastinated negotiations leading to the freeing of the American hostages seized by Iran during the revolution. He was the number two man to Cyrus Vance at the State Department during the Carter years. Zbigniew Brzezinski, Carter's NSA, was constantly critical of the Vance–Christopher State Department for its belief that foreign policy was a matter of endless negotiation and excessive faith that all problems could be resolved by compromise, and how they shied away from a willingness to use the threat of force or force as an incentive to adversaries to be more compromising. (There is no record that Christopher favored the use of force against Iraq, or rejected it as did Peter Tarnoff, Christopher's Under Secretary for Political Affairs.)[22] Anthony Lake, Clinton's NSA, was a former foreign service officer who worked for Henry Kissinger on the NSC until he resigned over the Vietnam War and directed the State Department's policy planning during the Carter years. If Secretary Christopher has been primarily a tactician—unlike Kissinger or Brzezinski, who had broad strategic visions and political agendas when they were appointed—he shares with Lake the lack of any strong intellectual or political influence that either brings with them to their respective positions. Neither has a commanding stature or movie-star type personality and each "will have to prove he's tough and worthy."[23] This may, of course, result in what President Clinton may want: a White House–centered foreign policy. Only Secretary of Defense Les Aspin, who had served previously in the Defense Department, and has been in the House for two decades, eight years of which he was chairman of the House Armed Services Committee, could be called a defense intellectual who has thought long and hard about the post-Cold War and the changing requirements of the U.S. military. None of these three has the economic expertise which is so necessary in this post-Cold War era; and it remains unclear how they, the NSC, and the new Economic Security Council will relate to one another and devise a coherent and consistent economic strategy.

The Second Circle: The Bureaucrats

While the secretaries of state and defense—and often their under secretaries and assistant secretaries—and the CIA director are attending meetings of the president's inner circle, one may wonder, Who's minding the store? Each department has a set of second-rank officials including assistant secretaries and other officials. There are also the ambassadors who report back to the State Department, the ambassador to the United Nations, and the military and civilian officials in the army, navy, and air force in the Pentagon. In addition, there are junior foreign policy agencies. These cannot match the political influence of State, Defense, and the CIA. These less influential foreign policy bureaucracies include the Arms Control and Disarmament Agency (ACDA), the United States Information Agency (USIA), the Agency for International Development (AID), and the major foreign policy bureaucracies (the foreign service and the military services), and the scientific and academic advisers to the executive branch. These advisers include the Rand Corporation, a "think tank" for scientists—and social scientists—in California; the Harvard Center for International Affairs and centers at other major universities; and the largely Washington-based professionals (see below).

Another set of actors in this second circle are cabinet members whose departments are only partially concerned with foreign policy issues. The Department of

Commerce plays a major role in all aspects of international trade as well as in matters of immigration. The Department of the Treasury is a key actor in such decisions as the valuation of the dollar in the international money market and, of course, has an abiding interest in the cost of U.S. foreign policy. The Agriculture Department is consulted on such issues as wheat sales to the Soviet Union and China and the use of surplus commodities in the foreign aid program. Indeed, food exports have become a major issue. In the 1970s the United States was the "food basket" of the world; in the 1980s, after the European Common Market countries, India, China, and others, had stepped up their production of everything from grain to butter, U.S. exports declined sharply. Washington found itself under great pressure to help agricultural exports, resulting in strained relations with allies ranging from France to Australia. Other departments with an interest in foreign policy are Labor and Energy (see Figure 2–1).

Compared with the inner circle, there is greater continuity among the lower-level officials. A new administration does not result in massive changes in the executive departments. In particular, the military service personnel are quite durable. The country desks at State, the scientists at the Pentagon, the small staff at ACDA, and many career diplomats who have obtained their posts by rising through the Foreign Service remain in place as the people at the top change. The second circle thus provides a continuing organizational basis for foreign policy decision making at lower levels. However, the bureaucrats at the various country desks (for instance, the African desk, the Western Europe desk, and so forth) at State and in the three services at Defense also develop vested interests to protect. They served in their departments before their respective secretaries, under secretaries, and assistant secretaries were appointed and have established their own standard operating procedures.

A change in those at the top may mean at least a minor shakeup of bureaucratic procedures. The lower-level officials may attempt to resist such changes, as the services did under Secretary of Defense McNamara. In addition, if a member of the inner circle is occupied with settling problems and conflicts in his own department, he faces the problem of presenting a unified departmental position to the White House. The problem is particularly acute for secretaries of state. The State Department is divided into various "desks," each dealing with a different geographical or functional area: African Affairs, Inter-American Affairs, East Asian and Pacific Affairs, Near Eastern and South Asian Affairs, and International Organization Affairs, as well as Economic and Russian Affairs, Oceans and International Environmental and Scientific Affairs, International Narcotic Matters, Humanitarian Affairs, and Politico-Military Affairs. The various desks not only have their own operating procedures, but also their own policy positions, and these are often in conflict with each other, as well as with the views of the secretaries. The Middle East desk, for instance, has long been charged with displaying a pro-Arab and anti-Israel bias, while most secretaries of state have been disposed the other way.

Figure 2-1 Administration of U.S. Foreign Affairs

Foreign Affairs Branch

Political Affairs (general foreign policy and conduct of relations with foreign countries)	Politico-Military Affairs (mutual defense, strategic policy, arms control)	International Commercial and Economic Affairs (trade, investment, monetary affairs, foreign aid)	Information and Educational and Cultural Exchange (contact with foreign audiences through government media; promotion of people-to-people relations)	Intelligence (collection and analysis of information bearing on the conduct of foreign relations)

Departments and Agencies Involved

	Department of Defense, Arms Control and Disarmament Agency	Departments of Agriculture, Commerce, Energy, Labor, Treasury; Export-Import Bank; International Trade Commission; Overseas Private Investment Corporation; U.S. Trade Representative; International Development and Cooperation Agency; Agency for International Development	United States Information Agency	Intelligence Community

Department of State
Responsibilities in all foreign affairs branches

Interagency Policy Coordination

National Security Council
Economic Security Council
Flexible system of interagency committees at various levels and of varying composition depending on subject matter

Constitutional Responsibility

President
Head of government/Head of state

SOURCE: United States Department of State, Bureau of Public Affairs, *Atlas of United States Foreign Relations*, 2d ed., (Washington, D.C.: U.S. Government Printing Office, 1985), p. 5.

The function of the second circle is to provide ideas, information on policy alternatives, and to make policy recommendations that the members of the inner circle can then debate. The second circle also carries out the daily operations of the nation's foreign and military policies. It does not play a direct role in crisis decision making or even in most foreign policy decisions, but it serves the members of the inner circle by providing background information and analyses for decision makers.

How well the members of this second circle perform their information functions may affect how influential their spokesmen in the inner circle are. Presidents normally want accurate information and sound analysis from their principal advisers (although on rare occasions a president is determined to do something to which some of these advisers object, as in the case of President Reagan's determination in 1986 to exchange arms with Iran for the release of U.S. hostages seized by pro-Iranian terrorists in Lebanon). These men, in turn, depend on the professional people, such as the Foreign Service or Officer Corps. The State Department has fared less well than Defense in the role of providing key information to its top-level bureaucrats. The large bureaucracy at State leads activist presidents to circumvent the department in making foreign policy innovations. Because the department is compartmentalized, there is the insurmountable problem of coming up with a unified position on foreign policy. There are simply too many vested interests in the department to achieve a consensus on what ought to be done and to arrive at one set of recommendations on how to do it (see Figure 2–2). The policy statements that the secretary of state receives from his subordinates therefore often take a long time to write and tend to be ambiguous. On the other hand, the policy recommendations of Defense tend to be produced relatively quickly and are quite specific, reflecting the military's characteristic "can-do" attitude.

The Pentagon is not without its own vested interests: there are *inter*service rivalries and vigorous *intra*service rivalries (such as that between the Strategic and Tactical Air Commands in the air force or between the carrier navy, the rest of the service navy, and the nuclear submarine navy). But the Defense Department's policy recommendations to the president are usually more specific than those of State, because, despite the rivalry among the services, the military's analysis emphasizes the "threat" and potential danger, and preparations to counter it. The focus, in short, is on capability, specifically the enemy's hardware and on the American forces that would be needed should a confrontation and possibly a war occur.

The State Department, by contrast, begins its analysis with another country's intentions and the general context of a particular problem or dispute. Its professional bias is the opposite of the military's, namely, to have the best relations with other countries, which tends to make it minimize problems and discount threats. To the foreign service officer, the military's stress on capability, action, and quick solutions may seem simplistic, but to the military, the former's concern with the intentions is too general, vague, and unlikely to bring about a

Figure 2–2 Responsibilities in the Department of State

			Duties				
Leadership and overall direction	Policy development and coordination	Development of policy toward and conduct of relations with foreign countries and international organizations	Policy development and conduct of relations in special fields	Policy development in and conduct of consular affairs (passports, visas, citizens' services overseas)	Specialized support	Congressional, media, and public liaison	Management of the department
			Responsible Officers				
Secretary of State / Deputy Secretary of State	Under Secretaries for Political Affairs, Economic Affairs, and Security Assistance, Science and Technology / Counselor of Department / Director of Policy Planning Staff	Assistant Secretaries for (heads of bureaus of) African Affairs, Inter-American Affairs, East Asian and Pacific Affairs, European and Canadian Affairs, Near Eastern and South Asian Affairs, and International Organization Affairs	Assistant Secretaries for (heads of bureaus of) Economic and Business Affairs, Oceans and International Environmental and Scientific Affairs, International Narcotics Matters, Human Rights and Humanitarian Affairs, and Politico-Military Affairs / Directors of Bureau of International Communications and Information Policy and Bureau for Refugee Programs	Assistant Secretary for Consular Affairs	Legal Adviser / Assistant Secretary for Intelligence and Research / Chief of Protocol	Assistant Secretary for Legislative and Intergovernmental Affairs / Assistant Secretary for Public Affairs and Spokesman of the Department	Under Secretary for Management / Inspector General / Assistant Secretary for Administration / Assistant Secretary for Diplomatic Security / Director General of the Foreign Service and Director of Personnel / Comptroller of the Department / Director of Management Operations / Director of Foreign Service Institute

resolution. In addition, if one of the services sharply disagrees with the recommendations of the secretary of defense, its chief of staff can state his objections directly to the president, for the Joint Chiefs of Staff are almost always in the inner circle. In contrast, the secretary of state *may* be the only representative of that department in the inner circle. Even if the under secretary and assistant secretaries are on occasion in the inner circle, they do not ordinarily have the same influence as the Joint Chiefs.

Interestingly enough, though, Defense is not necessarily the most influential when it comes to the use of force. The military advisers have usually been divided, as were their civilian counterparts. "Military leaders were less anxious than the majority of involved civilians to initiate United States commitments about as often as they were aggressive. Joint Chiefs of Staff (JCS) members' views were virtually the same as the dominant civilian attitude more than half the time. . . . In no case did a fully united set of military advisers oppose united civilians." The real difference was that once a commitment was made, the military wanted to employ force massively and quickly to win. Ironically, the "only cases in which military recommendations on use of force were considered irresistible were the instances in which they opposed intervention."[24] In the post-Vietnam years, the military was united in resisting further intervention. During the eight years of the Reagan administration, there was a consistent pattern, whether in Grenada, Lebanon, Nicaragua, or elsewhere: the secretary of state took the lead in advocating the use of force, with the secretary of defense usually resisting.

The difficulties the State Department has in developing clear-cut policy proposals further weaken the stature of its department in the inner circle by leading activist presidents to assume the political functions of the department. After all, diplomacy is something presidents think they know something about. Bargaining and accommodation between conflicting interests are the essence of the political process, and its summit is reached in the White House. This preemption further lowers departmental morale. As Henry Nash has stated: "To the extent that crises in Asia and the Middle East have been 'managed' by the president's White House staff, the skills of state have eroded through disuse."[25] Kissinger himself argued the following before becoming NSA and, later secretary of state in the Nixon administration:

> Because management of the bureaucracy takes so much energy and precisely because changing course is so difficult, many of the most important decisions are taken by extrabureaucratic means. Some of the most important decisions are kept to a very small circle while the bureaucracy happily continues working away in ignorance of the fact that decisions are being made, or the fact that a decision is being made in a particular area. One reason for keeping the decisions to small groups is that when bureaucracies are so unwieldy and when their internal morale becomes a serious problem, an unpopular decision may be fought by brutal means, such as leaks to the press or to congressional committees.[26]

We thus have a kind of vicious circle in which the frequently ambiguous policy recommendations of State are often rejected and in which this rejection leads to a further weakening of the influence of State in the inner circle. The public's image of State is a function of the department's performance, of what people believe it stands for, and of how the department is viewed in comparison with Defense. The public, including Congress, sees State as representing foreign interests rather than American labor, business, agriculture. State brings a troubled world in which there are no quick and easy solutions to the door of American citizens. But instead of facing the world as it is, the public and especially Congress make State a scapegoat. The department is frequently called *Foggy Bottom*. Originally this term referred to the haze surrounding the department's building in a valley in the District of Columbia; in more recent years, the term has been used to characterize the type of thinking in the department. If State thought "correctly" and represented American interests abroad more vigorously, it seems to be suggested, there would be no foreign policy problem. State represented foreign headaches because it brought world problems to the United States, and the department was supposed to find the aspirin to make them disappear. The public's view of State is not one of admiration. Francis E. Rourke has noted that

> The nonmilitary sector of the foreign affairs bureaucracy has been on the defensive before the bar of public opinion, confronted with a deficit of public support rather than the surplus which the military ordinarily enjoys. Over virtually the entire period of the cold war the State Department had been in a precarious position with respect to its public image.[27]
>
> On the other hand, "the military role exerts a symbolic appeal that is as rare among bureaucratic organizations in the United States as it is in other societies. The identification of the military with national pride and achievement—in a word, with patriotism—is a quite extraordinary bureaucratic resource—setting the Defense Department apart from all other executive agencies in the country.[28]

This does not mean that the Defense Department does not have its own severe problems; it does, largely in the operational area. Since Korea, the military has been criticized for its consistently poor performance, whether in Vietnam, the rescue of the merchant ship *Mayaguez* seized by the Cambodians in 1975, the humiliating and botched-up rescue of U.S. hostages in Iran in 1980, the avoidable 1983 tragedy in Beirut, Lebanon, in which 241 marines were killed, the successful but poorly planned Grenada invasion, also in 1983, or the shooting down of an Iranian airliner with 290 people aboard by the USS *Vincennes* in the Persian Gulf in 1988. The problem has been essentially "grossly overelaborate planning . . . supervision by vastly overstaffed headquarters very remote from the scene of combat . . . with no real center of higher decision." The Joint Chiefs of Staff were basically only a committee of service chiefs, resulting in clumsy planning for combat because "the interests of each service must be accommodated, . . . because everything must be done by committee, bureaucratic compromises displace tactical ingenuity, operational art, and sharp choices that strategy always demands.''[29] To try to dampen interservice rivalry and plan and execute military operations more effectively, in 1986 Congress passed a defense reorganization bill. Its purpose was to make the chairman of the Joint Chiefs the principal military adviser to the secretary of defense and the president rather than, as in the past, being merely a first among equals; to improve the quality and timeliness of military advice that had too frequently represented a bland consensus; to strengthen the authority of theater commanders, whose forces would include troops from all the services to reduce interservice disagreements; to make these commanders responsible only to the chairman of the Joint Chiefs and the secretary of defense, thereby shortening the chain of command and clarifying who was responsible for actions taken; to pay more attention to strategy, roles, and missions of the various services and for the more efficient use of resources, especially money; and to reward rather than punish officers who place the national interest above service interests by promoting officers to generals and admirals only if they have previously served in a position on a joint staff.

While State is usually less influential in the inner circle than Defense, there are even weaker agencies in the second circle. The functions of ACDA, concerned with arms control, overlap with those of State because it is concerned with the overall diplomatic position of the United States, and Defense, which is charged with devising military strategy and evaluating the level and kind of armaments needed to defend the country. Therefore, ACDA, small by comparison with State and a midget compared to the giant-sized Defense Department, must walk a very thin line between these agencies and at the same time serve the president. ACDA's fortunes have gone up and down. In the 1960s, as arms control became a prominent issue, its influence rose; in the SALT I negotiations, its influence reached its highest levels (although much of the negotiating on key issues was done not by ACDA's director but by Kissinger negotiating in the back channels with the Soviet ambassador in Washington). After SALT I, its influence declined as Kissinger completely took over the arms control negotiations. Under Carter, ACDA's director conducted most of the negotiations. But with the growing disillusionment with détente, the renewed emphasis by the president and Congress on rebuilding military strength, and the death of SALT II in the Senate, the stature of ACDA declined sharply. The question was even raised of whether it was needed at all; the agency could be integrated into the State Department or abolished altogether. Influence varies, among other things, with time and circumstances. During the Reagan administration its influence was small, symbolized by the initial appointment of a hard-liner who had opposed SALT II; when he was fired he was replaced by Kenneth Adelman, a young, inexperienced, and politically uninfluential figure who shared the administration's generally negative attitude toward arms control.

The second circle thus provides decision makers with information on policy questions. It also runs the bureaucracies, which in turn gather the information for the mid-level officials. This circle has its own sphere of decision making as well, but its decisions concern more routine types of foreign policy questions, which the president and his inner circle have neither the time nor the inclination to answer. Will the administration agree to a particular request for foreign aid? Will it send a trade mission to a newly emerging country? These are the questions usually reserved for the bureaucracies.

The distinction between the actors in the first or inner and second circles is not clear-cut over all decisions on foreign policy issues. Because the first and last circles may at times overlap, a sudden crisis in a remote area in the world can elevate a bureaucrat—for example, a Soviet specialist—to the inner circle. Or, if one president pays more attention to the recommendations of his secretary of state and another to his secretary of defense, different policy areas or issues may find the same actors in different circles.

In this connection, it is worth emphasizing a function of the NSC that is normally overlooked. A lower-level official may write a policy paper on either a current policy or a future issue. As it slowly makes its way up the vertical channels to the top of the department or across the horizontal channels between departments sharing responsibilities for a problem, it is likely increasingly to be watered down or, at some point, buried. It is NSC staff members, dealing with specific areas, who usually know other members throughout the executive branch also working in these areas. They can cut across bureaucratic lines (in our concentric circles), establish informal links with those they believe able (given these links, the last will also take the initiative and send their papers or talk to the NSC staff), thereby enlisting the "best and brightest" in the process of policy formation. A good NSA encourages this process to make sure that good ideas do not get lost somewhere in the bureaucratic maze. Establishing such links should not be regarded as an act of insubordination; it is intended to ensure that senior officials gain access to the best information and ideas.

Presidential Powers and Primacy

The Ability to Act: Information as a Political Resource

One reason why the president is looked to for leadership on foreign policy and why Congress has generally played a subordinate role is his advantage over Congress in foreign policy in the vast amounts of information he has at his fingertips. "Power is knowledge," and the foreign policy bureaucracy possesses such knowledge. The president can call on the State and Defense Departments, the Central Intelligence Agency, the Arms Control and Disarmament Agency, the U.S. Information Agency (propaganda), the Agency for International Development (economic aid), and the foreign staffs in such other departments as

Commerce, Treasury, and Agriculture. All these agencies are represented in the embassies abroad and participate in the making of foreign policy in Washington; abroad, they are also amply represented outside the embassies, often by delegations of at least equal size to that of the State Department's foreign service. Indeed, the State Department, of the senior agencies, is the smallest one. In the White House alone the president has the help of special bureaus on a whole range of topics—including the National Security Council, Office of the U.S. Trade Representative, Office of Science and Technology, Council of Economic Advisers, Council on Environmental Quality and, not least, the Office of Management and Budget.

It is not surprising that in these circumstances Congress should be dependent on the executive for its information. This is particularly true when compared to domestic affairs. Here, as already noted, a representative or senator can call on the appropriate executive departments dealing with the problem as well as on numerous interest groups, or can rely on his or her own familiarity with the problems being considered by the committee (for instance, congressmen from agricultural areas may serve on the agriculture committee). A member of Congress has, in brief, means not only to check out what the facts really are, but also experience from which to gain a sense of perspective on executive policy recommendations. But on foreign policy issues Congress has relied—and largely still does—primarily on information supplied by the president and the foreign policy bureaucracy. And given the facts of life for most congressmen—that they must devote a lot of time to their constituents' affairs, that they are members of one or more committees in which most of Congress' work is accomplished, and they feel that they usually have less competence and knowledge of external than of internal problems—this reliance is understandable.

This dependency is, in fact, twofold. First, it applies to the "facts" that most congressmen do not even have the time to digest. The year 1987 was the fortieth anniversary of the Marshall Plan for the reconstruction of postwar Europe, a highly imaginative policy that signaled a revolutionary shift of American policy from its prewar isolationism to a postwar commitment to Europe (a course Congress had rejected in 1919). During the hearings on it, this exchange occurred between the staff director of the Republican Policy Committee and Republican Senator Homer Ferguson (Mich.):

> *Mr. Smith:*   Now, Senators, for your amusement as well as to bear out my point on the impossible work load put upon members of Congress, I have gathered here a group of the books and reports, limited solely to an official character, which you should be reading now on the Marshall Plan.
>
> [Mr. Smith here presented a stack of material 18-inches high.]
>
> You are going to take the momentous step in the history of this country when you pass upon the Marshall Plan. . . . That

is what you ought to be studying. It contains the Krug report, the Harriman report, the State Department report, the reports of the Herter committee, the Foreign Relations Committee digest; it includes part of the hearings just completed of the Foreign Relations Committee. It does not include hearings yet to be held by the Appropriations Committees. This is one work load you have now on a single problem out of the many problems you have to decide.

Senator Ferguson: How long would it take in your opinion . . . for a person to read it?

Mr. Smith: Well, Senator, I have been reading for the last 35 years, nearly all my life, in the field of research; and if I could do an intelligent job on that in two months of solid reading excluding myself from everything else. . . . I would credit myself with great efficiency.

Senator Ferguson: A normal person would probably take four to five months.[30]

How in these circumstances can a legislator become familiar with such intricate problems as the strategic arms control negotiations, the nature of nationalism in a Third World region, the intentions of the Soviets toward the major non-Communist states, or the strategic doctrine and force structures of the U.S. military? These and the multiple other issues confronting Congress are issues on which even the experts may not have all the facts and on which, even with sufficient facts, they would disagree about meaning, consequences, and policies.

Of course, all of this assumes that Congress gets the information. After it was disclosed in 1973 that the United States had been secretly bombing Cambodia during 1969–70, a number of senators were critical of Secretary of State Rogers for not discussing this issue with them fully at the time. A State Department spokesman said in reply that Rogers had mentioned the raids on two occasions while testifying before the Foreign Relations Committee, although he admitted the secretary had not volunteered information on the magnitude of the raids. He added that if Rogers had been asked for details of the bombing, the secretary would have provided any requested information. But how were senators to ask questions about a military operation of which they were unaware and about which they had learned only a few details from the *New York Times*? This utter dependence of senators on executive information was also vividly demonstrated when in 1983–84 it became public that the United States was involved in mining Nicaraguan harbors, a warlike act but a matter mentioned so briefly before the Senate's supervisory committee on intelligence activities that the senators felt deceived. If the executive withholds information, Congress is likely to remain ignorant. This was starkly revealed when the administration's efforts to privatize foreign policy after the Congress cut off military assistance for the Nicaraguan resistance fighters, or Contras, in 1984 became public. Clearly, information was withheld to maximize the administration's freedom of action and minimize congressional interference (see Chapter 3).

But Congress is dependent on the executive not only for the facts but for their interpretation as well. For example, in 1947 the Truman administration had to reach a decision about intervening in the eastern Mediterranean, where the Soviet Union was putting great pressure on Turkey for control of the Dardanelles and on Greece, where a civil war involving the Greek Communists was raging. There was little precedent for American involvement in that area of the world. While Congress had become increasingly anti-Soviet during spats with Moscow in 1946, it was also in a fierce budget-cutting mood and averse to vast expensive external commitments in January 1947. Thus when in February the British informed the State Department that they could no longer support both endangered countries, the Truman administration decided that American power had to contain what it perceived to be Soviet expansion. Western Europe was drained by war, and Britain's role as a major world power was ending; in its place, the postwar bipolar balanced emerged.

On the Eurasian continent, the Soviet Union was emerging as the dominant state; only the United States, separated from Eurasia by the Atlantic and Pacific oceans, could supply the countervailing power. President Truman called together a congressional delegation to declare his intentions, but it initially reacted skeptically and interpreted Truman's proposed action as one of pulling British chestnuts out of the fire. Secretary of State George C. Marshall and Under Secretary Dean Acheson contested this interpretation, and Acheson particularly stressed American security considerations. Convinced, the congressmen insisted Truman explain his dramatic reversal of traditional American policy before Congress and the nation. In an address to a joint session of both houses, Truman informed Congress of the situations in Turkey and Greece and then outlined the basis of the new containment policy. He disguised the basic power realities motivating U.S. actions, however, and justified them on ideological grounds.[31] The Truman Doctrine was, for the United States, the beginning of the Cold War.

Another pertinent example is the American involvement in Vietnam. Johnson inherited a situation in which only ad hoc decisions had been made in response to immediate problems. The Kennedy administration, Arthur Schlesinger, Jr., has suggested, was occupied with other, more urgent issues, such as the abortive Cuban invasion, the Berlin Wall, crises in Laos and the Congo, the Alliance for Progress, and the limited nuclear test ban.[32] Only piecemeal economic and military commitments had been made; each constituted the minimal step necessary to prevent a Communist victory. At no point were the fundamental questions and long-range implications of an increasing Vietnam involvement analyzed: Was South Vietnam vital to American security? Would its fall represent the consolidation of one country under a nationalist leader or constitute a "falling domino" in the communization of all Southeast Asia? Did the political situation in South Vietnam warrant or preclude American intervention? Were political conditions both in the United States and in South Vietnam conducive to effective military action? How large a commitment would the United States be required to make, and what costs should be expected? What role should Saigon and its forces play?

If these questions were even asked by President Kennedy and his advisers, the answers did not provide guidelines for the policies that were ultimately followed. The assumption was that South Vietnam was vital, a test of the credibility of America's commitments and power. Policy was built on that assumption. The approach was incremental and, as the overall situation deteriorated badly, Johnson, like Kennedy, continued to react to the symptoms of the problem and applied short-range solutions: first covert operations, then increasingly frequent air strikes against North Vietnam, followed by around-the-clock bombing and, finally, the use of U.S. ground forces in South Vietnam.

What is noticeable, in retrospect, is not only the administration's lack of questions, but also Congress'.[33] Congressmen may not always know the facts or be sufficiently expert in foreign policy, but their expertise is supposed to be something more fundamental, a political judgment about the viability of policy, an ability to question the experts' views based on specialized knowledge. But neither the Senate nor any of its committees, including Foreign Relations and Armed Services, raised any of the fundamental questions that should have been answered before the 1965 intervention. As before, the Senate and House followed the executive's lead; their criticism came after the intervention, and then only after the intervention went sour.

It is unlikely that the information and interpretation "gap" between the executive and legislative branches will disappear. It has, to be sure, been narrowed as congressional committees have obtained larger and more expert staffs to develop their own sources of information and policy advice, taken more investigative trips abroad, and have been critical in cross-examining administration witnesses. The Vietnam War has led the Congress to concern itself more with the assumptions underlying specific policies and the likely consequences of their adoption. Still, the resources of the executive remain overwhelming by comparison. An administration that insists its policies are of vital importance to the national interest and can make a convincing case for its position still usually prevails, as Carter did in extending U.S. commitments to the Persian Gulf and Reagan did despite a great deal of justified skepticism in Congress about his policies toward El Salvador, Lebanon, and reflagging Kuwaiti oil tankers in 1987.

The Willingness to Act

THE CHIEF DIPLOMAT AND THE CONSTITUTION.   Besides the advantage of knowledge, the president possesses the further advantage of being able to act. It is, of course, this capacity to initiate action—especially the commitment of U.S. forces when the president deems it necessary—that has been greatly responsible for the expansion of presidential power in foreign policy since the Nazi and Japanese threats of the late 1930s; and it is this capacity that is at the heart of the contemporary controversy over the extent of presidential powers. Not that this expansion started in the 1930s. For example, the Constitution states that the president can receive and send ambassadors. President Washington, for example, interpreted this as conferring on the presidency the power of diplomatic recognition when he received Citizen Genêt of the French Republic. Congress, of course, has on occasion exerted its influence in this area, as it did after 1949, when it consistently warned successive presidents not to extend recognition to Communist China. Still, a determined President Nixon visited China in 1972 and in effect established all but formal relations with the People's Republic.

President Carter extended full diplomatic recognition in 1979. The decision did not go unchallenged. Opponents of the recognition of China, which involved withdrawing our embassy from the Nationalists on Taiwan, took the issue to the courts. Senator Barry Goldwater, who brought the lawsuit, argued that since the Senate had given its consent to the 1955 mutual security treaty with Taiwan (the treaty would be null and void one year after the transfer of recognition), the Senate had to consent to ending the treaty and, by implication, the recognition of the People's Republic of China.[34] A federal judge ruled that the Senate had to approve the president's decision by a two-thirds vote or a majority of both houses of Congress, even though the treaty contained the standard clause allowing either party to withdraw from the treaty at any time after proper notification of the other party (a clause approved by the Senate with the rest of the treaty). But on appeal, the judge was overruled, and the president's right to recognize a nation by accrediting diplomats was upheld. This is a legal right that a president will exercise when political circumstances are favorable or, at least, not hostile to a recognition.* On China, Congress had for thirty years opposed recognition and made it very clear that the president would recognize Peking as the legal government of China at his risk. The resulting Asian policy bordered on the irrational, reflecting emotions, even hysteria, not hard calculations of what American national interests required. But presidents refused to exercise their power for fear of Congress. Only after a costly and divisive war and the election of a conservative president who could never be accused of appeasement was U.S. policy once more set on a path of rational calculation—and then only gradually.

Presidents not only exploited the "great silences" of the Constitution to "make foreign policy" and enhance the powers of their office, but also used their position as the nation's chief diplomat to strengthen their position against Congress. In this connection, presidents have long resorted to setting policy through declarations or by means of a variety of individual initiatives. A Monroe announces his famous doctrine or a Truman declares, as he did in early 1947,

---

* The Supreme court has never ruled on the question of the president's right to extend recognition. The judges have always hesitated to interfere in foreign policy and left such issues to be settled politically.

that it must be U.S. policy to support free peoples who are resisting attempted subjugation by armed minorities or outside pressure, and more recently, the Carter Doctrine committed the United States in the Persian Gulf–Indian Ocean area. Or a president may visit West Berlin, as Kennedy did, thus reinforcing in the minds of his NATO allies and Soviet adversary the American commitment to that city and Western Europe; he may visit the capital of a nation not previously recognized, as Nixon did on his trip to Peking, signaling a radical shift of policy; or go to the Middle East to indicate U.S. interest in the area and a more "evenhanded" policy between Israel and the Arab states. Or he may, as Carter did after the Soviet invasion of Afghanistan, decide that the United States should boycott the 1980 summer Olympic games in Moscow.

President Reagan, early in his administration, announced that the United States would not permit Saudi Arabia to fall into the hands of any internal or external forces threatening to cut off oil supplies to the West. The president, clearly trying to suggest to the world that his administration had more resolve than his predecessor's in defending America's friends, said that "we will not permit [Saudi Arabia] to be an Iran."[35] Reagan's words were immediately seen as a broadening of the Carter Doctrine, which had seemingly committed the United States to Saudi Arabia's defense against external threat. Now the United States also appeared to be committing itself to the defense of the ruling royal family against domestic revolution or insurrection. The president's words were followed by the stationing of four AWACS (Airborne Warning and Command System) planes on Saudi soil to protect that country from potential air strikes from Iran, which was then at war with Iraq and hostile toward Saudi Arabia. Later, against great opposition in Congress, the administration sold the Saudis five of these planes. Both moves were cited by the administration as evidence of a deepening American commitment.

President Reagan, like earlier presidents, also expressed his support for Israel. Thus, although no formal treaty of security existed between Israel and the United States at the time, repeated presidential pronouncements over several decades have constituted a de facto defense treaty despite the absence of Senate approval. Indeed, congressional figures often protest such presidential "commitments." One congressman complained that Reagan's statements had "spelled out a dangerous strategic doctrine. . . . They have asserted, in effect, a right to commit United States prestige, power, and military might to the defense of remote areas of the world without the advice, much less the consent, of the Congress." Many in Congress, if not most, were skeptical of Reagan's commitment in 1987 to protecting Kuwaiti oil tankers in the Persian Gulf, but they were reluctant to oppose him outright after the president had already announced U.S. policy (see "War Powers Resolution" section).[36] Presidential words, as well as acts, create obligations.

The point of these examples is threefold. One, the president, by what he says and does—and, on occasion, by not saying or not doing—sets the direction and tone of U.S. foreign policy. Two, by exercising his initiative, the president usually leaves Congress with little option but to follow him, unless it wishes publicly to humiliate him and undermine his position as the nation's spokesman in international affairs. He may also keep the Congress ignorant. This was starkly revealed when the administration's efforts to "privatize" foreign policy after the Congress cut off military assistance for the Nicaraguan resistance fighters, or Contras, in 1984 became public. Clearly, information was withheld to maximize the administration's freedom of action and minimize congressional interference (see Chapter 3). And three, the president has an array of tools—informal, such as discussed above, as well as more formal ones—at his disposal, which enable him to use his advantages.

One of the more formal tools the president can use to draw public attention to certain issues and his suggested solutions is the draft treaty. Although the Senate may be consulted during the drafting and negotiating of a treaty and may give its consent when it is submitted, the end of the negotiating process really commits the United States, unless the Senate wants to erode other nations' confidence in the president's ability to represent and articulate America's international interests. Ever since defeat of the Versailles Treaty concluding World War I, the Senate has been reluctant to deny ratification. For example, when a president negotiates a limitation on strategic arms, the publicity alone by the time the treaty reaches the Senate floor may make the draft difficult to defeat. Arms control measures are probably unique in this respect. If an administration has initialed a draft treaty that has the support—or at least the acquiescence—of the various interested executive agencies involved, such as the Joint Chiefs of Staff, it is likely to be able to "sell" such measures to Congress and the public. (Arms control often takes on the appearance of a combination of motherhood and salvation and can be easily identified with that most cherished of values, peace.) When such a measure is signed in Moscow by the president himself, as Nixon did in 1972 with the Strategic Arms Limitations Treaty (SALT I) and the event is fully covered by television (as were the president's return to the United States and his immediate journey to Capitol Hill to report the success of his negotiations in building a more stable "structure of peace"), who can really do more than raise some objections and then approve such a clearly worthy enterprise, especially when, in effect, the president has already gone over Congress' head to the country?

SALT II, however, reaped considerable opposition even though the Carter administration consulted Congress, especially the Senate, far more than had Nixon or Ford for the earlier arms control negotiations. Despite that opposition, which ranged from liberals who thought the number of strategic weapons allowed each side were too high to conservatives who felt that the treaty ratified Soviet strategic superiority and endangered U.S. deterrence capability, to moderates who found the treaty acceptable if the administration would simultaneously increase defense spending 5 percent per year, Carter was short of the votes needed for ratification when other events overtook him and jeopardized passage of the treaty. Carter used these other events—the Shah's fall in Iran, the

Soviet invasion of Afghanistan, among others—to toughen his policy toward the Soviet Union, invoking a number of diplomatic and economic sanctions, and withdrawing SALT II before the Senate—in its anti-Soviet mood—defeated it (see Chapter 6). By contrast, Reagan's public signing of the INF agreement in December 1987, in Washington, D.C., where the summit was covered by the television networks, gained overwhelming public support for the treaty, even among most conservatives.

Although some of the most fundamental U.S. policies since 1945 have been submitted to the Senate to let the American people know what commitments their government has undertaken on their behalf and to signal to the adversary the nature of American interests, treaties are few and far between. Presidents often bypass the Senate, where a two-thirds majority is required for approval of treaties. In a Senate representing fifty states, it takes only 34 votes out of 100 to defeat a treaty. That means a majority of senators may in fact favor a treaty, which was certainly true of SALT II. Indeed, given the fact that a highly urbanized state with a large population has the same representation as a rural state with a smaller population, the thirty-four senators opposing the treaty may in fact represent less than 5 percent of the population. The two-thirds majority required for treaties in fact places a premium on opposition so that the president, to mobilize those sixteen votes he needs over a fifty-one majority, has to literally ''buy'' these votes by acquiescing or supporting policy decisions such as increasing the defense budget or a pet project that a senator wants for his state. These may add millions, if not billions, to the nation's federal budget.

Given the uncertainty of Senate treaty approval, it is understandable why presidents prefer to use executive agreements that do not need legislative approval. (Executive agreements may, of course, also be negotiated and signed in pursuance of a particular objective authorized by Congress—for instance, specific tariff agreements with individual countries after Congress has approved a general tariff bill.) Indeed, executive agreements outnumber treaties by 17 to 1 (see Table 4–2, Chapter 4). The vast majority of these were executive agreements to implement congressional legislation or congressional–executive agreements; and only a small minority were executive agreements based on the executive branch's constitutional authority. But these agreements may be the most significant of all the executive agreements and indeed more important than most of the treaties, for they may commit the United States to the defense of other countries or involve the use of force. Thus, for example, a series of executive agreements with Spain for American military bases since 1953 are tantamount to a military commitment to Spain, even though the Senate in 1970 adopted a nonbinding resolution expressing the view that the 1970 executive agreement signed by Spain and the Nixon administration should not be construed as a U.S. commitment to the defense of Spain. In 1976, an agreement for the continued use of American bases in Spain was finally put in treaty form giving the United States the opportunity to deny the existence of a defense commitment to Spain. The issue of a bilateral U.S. defense is now moot. Spain, finally a democratic state, is now a full-fledged member of NATO.

The trend toward executive agreements on important issues is demonstrated by two other Nixon agreements: The Paris peace agreement of 1973 ending the Vietnam War (at least, officially) and the five-year freeze on offensive arms negotiated as part of the SALT I package; both of them were executive agreements. But no executive agreement is ever likely to be more dramatic than the destroyer deal arranged by President Roosevelt in 1940. One more example, perhaps more of presidential ability to commit the United States than of executive agreement, was a letter President Nixon sent President Thieu of South Vietnam to soften his opposition to the Vietnam peace agreement. While such letters do not usually constitute executive agreements, Nixon assured Thieu that if North Vietnam did not abide by the terms of the agreement, he would "take swift and severe retaliatory action."[37] Nixon repeated this assurance at a later date. Confronted by these reassurances and faced with U.S. determination to go ahead and sign the cease-fire agreement on its own and disengage from the war, Thieu signed too. Nixon had just been reelected by a very large majority; he had won all states except Massachusetts. With Nixon at the zenith of his power, Thieu obviously believed his promise was credible. Watergate and the congressional war powers resolution were to undermine that promise.

Nixon had also embodied the SALT I five-year freeze on offensive nuclear arms in an executive agreement, while the antiballistic missile agreement was incorporated in a treaty. When President Carter later began to note mounting opposition to SALT II as the negotiations proceeded, he stated that he might make the document an executive agreement. But after vociferous objections from the Senate, he backed down and submitted it to the upper chamber as a treaty, only to find he had to withdraw it when it became clear he could not mobilize the two-thirds approval required for treaties.

THE COMMANDER IN CHIEF WIELDS THE SWORD.   The president's authority as commander in chief has become the greatest source of his expanded power in this century. In 1900 President McKinley sent troops to China to join an international army to crush the Boxer Uprising, which had besieged foreign embassies in Peking. Theodore Roosevelt, Wilson, and Coolidge used the marines at will throughout the Caribbean. Woodrow Wilson sent troops into Mexico to pursue Pancho Villa and had Vera Cruz bombarded before the outbreak of World War I. In early 1917, when the Germans declared unrestricted submarine warfare on all shipping, belligerent and neutral, to starve Britain into submission, Woodrow Wilson armed American merchant marines taking supplies to the British. Wilson acted after the Senate refused to sanction his request to authorize armaments for the self-defense of the ships. When, during the Russian Civil War of 1918–1920, the Japanese sought to exploit that conflict and establish themselves in Siberia by landing troops, Wilson sent American troops to counter the Japanese and to protect allied interests in western Russia against the Germans. After the eruption of World War II and the fall of France, President Roosevelt, as we already know, used American warships to escort the English and Canadian merchant ships as far as Iceland, where the

British Royal Navy took over, and ordered American ships to "shoot on sight" at German raiders or submarines.

Since World War II, recurrent crises—many with the potential of exploding into nuclear war—as well as two limited wars, have built on these precedents and further expanded the president's authority as commander in chief. When the Soviets blockaded Berlin in 1948, President Truman responded with an airlift to supply the population of the western half of the city. When the North Koreans attacked South Korea in 1950, the president ordered first air support for the South Korean army and then the landing of American ground forces in Korea when the air support seemed unable to stem the invaders. Congressional leaders were informed of these decisions by the president, but he did not ask for their approval. Truman felt that as commander in chief he already possessed the authority to commit U.S. forces when he believed American security was endangered. After Communist China's intervention in Korea, he sent several divisions to Western Europe to enhance Western strength and deter a possible Soviet move in Moscow's "front yard" while America was becoming more deeply involved in Asia; again Congress was not asked for approval.

Both Eisenhower and Kennedy, as we know, made commitments to South Vietnam. The first initiated a large-scale program of economic and military assistance to support the non-Communist government there. "The United States had gradually developed a special commitment in South Vietnam. It was certainly not absolutely binding—but the commitment was there."[38] Kennedy would enlarge this into what the Pentagon Papers refer to as a "broad commitment"[39] and would leave his successor feeling that the commitment was virtually binding. Kennedy also launched the Eisenhower-planned invasion of Cuba in 1961 and blockaded the island a year later to compel the Soviets to withdraw their missiles. After his assassination, his successor intervened in the Dominican Republic in 1965 with troops to forestall "another Cuba" (Eisenhower had earlier, in 1954, covertly used the CIA, rather than the marines, to overthrow the government of Guatemala when it was feared to be moving in Moscow's direction). And in 1983, President Reagan sent the marines and Rangers into Grenada.

It was, however, the increasing unpopularity of America's first modern limited war, the Korean War, that led President Eisenhower, after the Democrats had been defeated in 1952, to ask for congressional resolutions granting him legislative support to use the armed forces when he felt this was necessary in the national interest. The administration's idea was that "the resolution process, by involving Congress in the takeoff, would incriminate it in a crash landing."[40] In other words, a principal purpose was to ward off the type of later congressional criticism and retribution that had hurt the Truman administration. These resolutions did not, however, indicate that Eisenhower, any more than his predecessors or successors, felt that in the absence of congressional support he lacked the legal authority to use the armed forces as he saw fit—as, for example, in Lebanon or the Formosa Straits. In any event, Congress gave him virtually a blank check; in fact, it was more an expression of approval than a grant of authority.

In 1964, Johnson received a similar broad grant known as the Tonkin Gulf Resolution, after the gulf where North Vietnamese torpedo boats allegedly attacked two American destroyers. It reads, in part:

> [Be it] Resolved by the Senate and House of Representatives of the United States of America in Congress assembled, that the Congress approves and supports the determination of the President, as Commander in Chief, to take all necessary measures to repel any armed attack against the forces of the United States and to prevent further aggression.
>
>   The United States regards as vital to its national interest and to world peace the maintenance of international peace and security in Southeast Asia. Consonant with the Constitution and the Charter of the United Nations and in accordance with its obligations under the Southeast Asia Collective Defense Treaty, the United States is, therefore, prepared, as the President determines, to take all necessary steps, including the use of armed force, to assist any member or protocol state of the Southeast Asia Collective Defense Treaty requesting assistance in defense of its freedom.[41]

Johnson, unfortunately for the nation as well as himself, was neither lucky nor shrewd and wound up using force.[42] Both he and Eisenhower requested congressional resolutions for the areas in which action was contemplated when tensions there appeared to be quite high. In each case Congress, once the president had publicly requested its support, had acceded. Eisenhower, however, was either lucky or shrewd. In neither crisis was he required to use force overtly. In the Middle East, troops landed in Lebanon but were not involved in any fighting, and in the Formosa Straits the Seventh Fleet "showed the flag" but did not need to shoot. Johnson, however, was drawn deeper and deeper into war.

Johnson had hoped that the Tonkin Gulf Resolution, passed by the Senate with only two dissenting votes and by the House unanimously, would be read by Hanoi as an indication of American determination to prevent a Communist takeover of South Vietnam. But nothing, including escalating military force, led Hanoi to "leave its neighbor alone," as Secretary of State Dean Rusk phrased the American objective. More punitive moves, it was felt, were needed to attain this aim. Sustained air attacks that avoided bombing cities were launched in the spring of 1965; when those also did not frighten off Hanoi, Johnson felt he had no choice but to send American troops into South Vietnam as the military situation there deteriorated rapidly and the Vietcong appeared to be within reach of victory. But as the increasingly Americanized war dragged on and victory seemed more and more distant, congressional and public support for the war declined, as it had earlier for the war in Korea. As the criticism mounted, the Tonkin Gulf Resolution offered no protection to Johnson. The conclusion would, therefore, seem to be that congressional support in the form of a resolution for presidential use of force is politically largely immaterial, especially if the conflict turns against the United States. If a president is successful, he will receive little or no criticism—indeed much praise—even without a congressional resolution; if he is unsuccessful, he will reap large amounts of criticism and abuse, even if he has hundreds of congressional resolutions.

In any event, once the country is involved in a war, whether it is legally declared by the Congress or not, presidents make the basic political decisions and choose the appropriate military strategy to achieve the chosen political objectives. Thus, Roosevelt during World War II decided that Germany should be defeated before Japan since Germany was the stronger power and the United States, as a belligerent, had allies whose existence was threatened primarily by Germany, not Japan. Later, Roosevelt chose to invade continental Europe through France rather than, as Churchill wanted, to drive into the Balkans from northern Italy and Yugoslavia, thereby trying to limit the Soviet army's advance and the establishment of Soviet influence to Eastern Europe. A cross-channel invasion, which would come to grips with the German army on the plains of Europe, where it could be defeated, seemed to Roosevelt a more feasible way to end the war quickly; it undoubtedly was, but it did mean that the Soviet army had reached the heart of Europe by the time of Germany's collapse.

During the Korean War, President Truman, who had already made the key decisions to drop two atomic bombs to force Japan's surrender and to intervene in Korea, made two further significant decisions: one, to cross the 38th parallel dividing North and South Korea after the North Korean army had been pushed back; and two, not to extend the war even farther by bombing and blockading China after the Chinese had responded to the U.S. invasion of North Korea by intervening, just as the North Korean invasion of the South had precipitated American intervention. This brought Truman into a fierce confrontation with the commanding general, Douglas MacArthur, a great war hero who was supported by the conservative and dominant wing of the Republican party in Congress. When MacArthur refused to stop publicly criticizing the administration's policy and strategy in Korea with the assertion that there was "no substitute for victory," Truman fired him amid a public furor.[43]

For Johnson, of course, all the decisions in Vietnam proved fateful: the decision in 1965 to escalate the American intervention with air power and troops until U.S. forces in Vietnam stood at over 500,000; further decisions to escalate to appease congressional hawks and deescalate to satisfy the doves; and the decision to fight a "painless war" until 1967 by deferring many students from the draft and postponing a war tax to counter the rising inflation, among other measures. But as the intervention turned sour, it precipitated an executive-legislative struggle, badly divided the nation, deeply divided the Democratic party, and helped the Republicans win the presidency that year.

After President Nixon came into office, the Senate repealed the Tonkin Gulf Resolution not once but twice! Nixon even supported this move, claiming that he did not need it, and thereby added insult to the injury the Senate already felt at what it claimed was Johnson's deception at the time he requested the resolution. Although it had given him a broad grant of authority, senatorial critics now asserted, it had done so on the assumption that Johnson would use it only for retaliatory strikes, *not* to justify the widening of the war with large-scale American intervention.[44] But Nixon, whose policy was to withdraw U.S. ground forces gradually while letting the South Vietnamese army increasingly take over the fighting, claimed that as commander in chief he had the authority to use the armed forces in any way he wished to protect the remaining American forces in Vietnam.

As more and more U.S. troops were pulled out and Hanoi's temptation to attack in South Vietnam increased, Nixon undertook a number of actions—vigorously criticized in the Senate—under the authority he claimed as commander in chief. He ordered American forces into Cambodia to search for and destroy North Vietnam supplies and Vietcong headquarters. (Before this action in 1970, as noted earlier, U.S. bombers had carried on bombing attacks in Cambodia, which were hidden from congressional and public scrutiny.) Nixon also sent American planes from time to time for "protective reaction" raids on the North; authorized the mining of North Vietnamese ports and the heavy bombing of Hanoi and Haiphong after Hanoi launched a large conventional attack on South Vietnam; and, when the Paris peace negotiations stalled, launched B-52s during the Christmas season to compel a settlement (in January 1973, a settlement was signed). After the Paris peace agreement, when the understanding that a cease-fire and withdrawal of U.S. forces from South Vietnam would be followed shortly by cease-fires in Laos and Cambodia failed to materialize in Cambodia, B-52s were used to stem the successful Communist forces. Since the president could no longer invoke his need to protect American troops after they had departed, he claimed that the failure of the Communists to abide by the Paris agreement meant that he could wage the war in Cambodia until a cease-fire had been agreed on. He had possessed the authority to wage the war in Vietnam; this authority continued until the war in Cambodia ended as it had in South Vietnam. The Congress disagreed and cut off funds for further bombing in 1973.

In an attempt to terminate the bombing even before the cutoff date, a suit was brought in federal court on the basis that Congress had not declared a war in Cambodia and that consequently the president's action was unconstitutional. A similar suit was brought to the courts by over 100 congressmen trying to compel President Reagan to invoke the War Powers for his commitment of the U.S. Navy in the Persian Gulf. Both suits were unsuccessful, but at some point it is likely that the Supreme Court will have to rule on the whole issue of the president's war power. In the past, the Court has generally been reluctant to challenge the president's exercise of his power, even when he has exercised it in unprecedented ways. Whether it can or will continue this general absention on the crucial central issue of the use of force remains to be seen.

The War Powers Resolution

In the wake of the Vietnam War, the Congress took a number of actions to hold the executive more accountable. Collectively, they constituted a congressional assertion to play a larger and more active foreign policy role than before and, simultaneously, to restrain the president from presumably getting the country into "another Vietnam." "No more Vietnams" was the slogan and the mood of the country throughout the 1970s. Closer congressional supervision of presidents was viewed as the best means of keeping the country out of new and costly overseas adventures. America was no longer to be the world's policeman; it was to play a more limited role only. To ensure this was Congress' responsibility.

Congress' determination to play a more energetic part in this process was reflected in the following actions.

1. The War Powers Resolution, which was passed by the Senate and the House over President Nixon's veto in 1973, was to restore Congress' role in decisions involving the use of force.
2. Executive agreements had to be reported to Congress, and the Congress has tended to insist that important agreements be submitted as treaties.
3. An increasing number of restrictions have been imposed on security or military assistance, including a congressional veto of specific arms transfers over a few million dollars.
4. Intelligence operations—that is, CIA covert interventions or subversions—must now be reported to a number of Senate and House committees.

We shall focus on the War Powers Act because it is as commander in chief that presidents have enormously expanded the powers of their office, and because it was the Vietnam War that led the Congress to assert its responsibilities on the use of force. The resolution states that in the absence of a declaration of war the president shall consult the Congress before introducing U.S. armed forces "into hostilities or into situations where imminent involvement in hostilities is clearly indicated by the circumstances." The resolution also provides for three emergency situations in which the president can commit American forces without prior congressional declaration of war: to repel or forestall an attack on the United States; to repel or forestall an attack on American forces located outside the country; and to rescue endangered American citizens in carefully defined circumstances. Beyond these emergency categories, the president would need "specific statutory authorization."[45] This requirement aims to replace the blank-check resolution with precisely worded authority, jointly devised by Congress and the president. Even when the president uses his emergency powers, the War Powers Act requires that he immediately make a full report to Congress and obtain congressional authority to continue the action after sixty days, with an extension of thirty additional days if troops are in danger. If he fails to receive legislative concurrence, he must terminate the action at that time. Even before his sixty-day deadline Congress can terminate the action through a concurrent resolution, which would not be subject to a presidential veto. As one of the bill's sponsors said, "The real danger is that presidents can—and do—shoot from the hip. If the collective judgment of the president and Congress is required to go to war, it will call for responsible action by the Congress for which each member must answer individually and for restraint by both the Congress and the presidents."[46] The War Powers Act, in short, grants the Congress the potential to play a greater role in decisions involving the use of force through the use of the legislative veto. Indeed, to be more precise, the resolution no longer permits Congress to avoid its political responsibility.

The Ford–Carter Years

The act, in one sense, recognized "reality," for it changed the Constitution from reading that war cannot be waged without the consent of Congress to the president can wage war until Congress stops him. When the U.S. merchant ship *Mayaguez* was seized in what the American government claimed to be the high seas by the Cambodians shortly after the final collapse of South Vietnam in 1975, President Ford used American military forces to recover the ship and its crew on the island where they were and, to prevent any retaliation, ordered some bombing of certain airfields and port targets on the mainland. The president did inform the Congress, as the War Powers Act required, of what had occurred and what he intended to do. But he no more consulted Congress than had his predecessors. The ship and crew were recovered, although at the time the rescue operations began, unknown to the United States, the crew was being released. Despite loss of life and equipment, the action was generally applauded as successful and as saving a tattered American prestige that had been badly deflated by the fall of South Vietnam to the Communists.

The lesson from this incident appeared clear and was probably of no comfort to the proponents of the War Powers Act. If a president is unsuccessful when he uses force, he will be damned even if he has legislative support; if successful, he will be acclaimed even if he does not possess congressional support. Subsequently, there were a number of more ambiguous tests of the War Powers Act. One incident that, ironically, failed to become a test was the abortive 1980 rescue mission of the American hostages held by the Iranians in Teheran. While there were some mutterings in Congress about President Carter using military forces, which Carter termed a "humane mission" rather than a military one, no one was really willing to bring the issue to a head. The mission's failure, the loss of life among the rescuers, and the humiliation of the whole affair were apparently considered tragic enough. Yet this rescue mission had anticipated the possibility of escalation. The marine-piloted navy helicopters, with their armed men aboard, were backed up by a powerful carrier-based group of naval ships; careful preparation had been made so that the mission would be undiscovered not only by the Iranians but the Soviets. There was some concern about Soviet intervention.

Reagan and Lebanon

During Reagan's eight years in office, force was used on several occasions but the president, like his predecessors, refused to invoke the War Powers Resolution. One incident was the U.S. involvement in Lebanon from 1982 to 1984. Since 1975, Lebanon had been a nation in turmoil deeply divided within by ethnic and religious quarrels among Christian and Muslim factions, then occupied by Syria, and finally, in 1982, invaded by Israel to destroy the Palestine Liberation Organization (PLO). In the hope of ending the fighting by protecting the withdrawal of the PLO fighters, the United States together with France, Italy, and Britain sent an "international peacekeeping force," as it was called, to the capital city, Beirut, in 1982. Later, in 1983, the United States tried to assist the new Lebanese government to establish and extend its authority to the city and, it was hoped, beyond. The marines then ended up in the middle of the civil war. When in 1983 several marines died in the shelling of their position, the president refused to invoke the War Powers Resolution. Lebanon was a peace-keeping operation, he said, not a war. The Congress, however, insisted that he had to do so since the marines were involved in a combat situation and naval gun fire was used to support Lebanese government forces. The issue was resolved by compromise.

The president, on the one hand, did not recognize the authority of the War Powers Resolution. *Congress,* however, determined it was in effect. This meant that the president did not have to send Congress formal notification, and Reagan thereby avoided directly acknowledging the validity of the act as it applied to Lebanon. Indeed, in signing the legislation authorizing the marines to stay in Lebanon, he specifically said that he could not cede any of the authority he already held as commander in chief, in fact suggesting he really did not need congressional approval to keep the marines there. On the other hand, the Congress was willing to authorize the continued deployment of the marines in Lebanon for eighteen months rather than sixty or ninety days, after which the president would have to go back to the Congress for authority to keep them there another two or three months. This longer term would, it was expected, give the president the time to both secure his objectives in Lebanon and avoid injecting Lebanon as an issue into the 1984 presidential election campaign. But in early 1984, after a terrorist drove his truck filled with explosives into the marine barrack in late 1983, killing more than 241 men, the president pulled the marines out; so did the other "peacekeepers," leaving most of Lebanon under Syrian influence and a southern strip on Israel's borders under Syrian control. Despite the eighteen months' mandate, congressional and public pressure to withdraw from Lebanon was too intense to resist in an election year.

Reagan and Central America

Concurrent with the crisis in Lebanon, President Reagan undertook another action as commander in chief: he sent the Marines into the tiny Caribbean island-nation of Grenada (110,000 inhabitants). Here a pro-Cuban regime was deposed and the prime minister murdered by an even more radical faction. The United States acted, the president said, to protect the 1,000 Americans on the island—most of them medical students—and to forestall a possible Iranian-style hostage seizure. He also responded to the concerns of several eastern Caribbean states about instability in the region resulting from a Cuban military buildup in Grenada. A third, and real reason, was U.S. concern about Cuban control of Grenada, which lies in the southern part of the Windward Islands in the Caribbean, just north of oil-rich Venezuela. Additionally, the use of U.S. troops was intended to send a message to the Sandinista regime in Nicaragua that the United States might some day use force against it as well.

The president sent Congress a letter informing its leaders of the invasion, as he is required to do by the War Powers Resolution, but he did not invoke the resolution. Again, Reagan insisted that the law could not tie his hands as commander in chief. Democrats, particularly in the Senate, were especially critical of the president's action. Both houses of Congress insisted on invoking the War Powers Act, forcing the president to remove the troops within sixty days unless Congress approved an extension. But a showdown was avoided when Congress—especially the Democratically controlled House whose leader, Speaker Thomas O'Neill, denounced the invasion as "gunboat diplomacy"—seeing how popular the invasion was with the public and viewing the returning students fall on their knees to kiss American soil, decided not to push the issue. In any event, U.S. troops had been withdrawn before the sixty-day limit. When United States planes attacked Libya in 1986 to retaliate for its reported involvement in terrorist attacks in which Americans were injured and killed, the Congress did not even bother to insist on the War Powers. The president's action was greeted with great enthusiasm.

The Central American situations in which the United States supported the government of El Salvador against left-wing guerrillas and the Contra guerrillas in their war to overthrow the Sandinista government in Nicaragua, also ironically failed to become tests of the War Powers Act. Neither involvement ever gained much public support and Congress throughout remained anxious lest the United States become involved in another Vietnam. Congressional concerns certainly made it impossible to use United States forces, especially in Nicaragua. Thus the War Powers Act may have had an indirect effect but, probably even in its absence, the Reagan administration would not have intervened directly. There would have been considerable domestic opposition and, if United States forces had not quickly succeeded in toppling the Sandinistas, the resulting turmoil might have been reminiscent of the Vietnam days. Hence in Nicaragua, the administration became involved in a covert war that ended in a major scandal. (See Chapter 3 for a more detailed discussion.)

In brief, the Central American situation arose from the administration's perception that events there were part of the broader Soviet–American rivalry. Therefore, it sent fifty-five military advisers to El Salvador to assist government forces. Because of congressional concerns about increasing the size of this group—a buildup of advisers had preceded the United States military intervention in Vietnam—the administration sent the additional advisers to neighboring Honduras. But legislative concerns remained high about the possibility of the conflict escalating and about intervening in a country whose civil war seemed the result mainly of decades of governmental political repression and social injustice. While it reluctantly went along with the president's requests for military and economic aid, the administration stilled some of the criticisms by finding and supporting centrist and democratically inclined political leader Napoléon Duarte. It also made clear its opposition to the powerful political right wing, which had long dominated El Salvadore with its death squads that were indiscriminantly killing "Communists," including centrist political and religious figures. Congress played an important role in this respect: by making its aid conditional on a greater respect for human rights, it compelled the administration to pay more attention to these matters and made the Salvadoran army restrain its own forces' often unnecessary killing of civilians and, perhaps even more important, restrain the death squads with which the army was often involved. With training by the United States, the Salvadoran army became more of a professional fighting force and achieved greater success in its war, although the civil war continued.

The situation in Nicaragua, however, increasingly became the focus of the Reagan administration's efforts. Nicaragua was controlled by the Sandinista government which, after the ouster of the American-supported Somoza regime in 1979, increasingly suppressed criticism, ousted its moderate partners, and turned toward Cuba and the Soviet Union. The Reagan administration accused the Sandinistas of permitting arms from the Soviet bloc to flow through their country to the Salvadoran rebels. The administration, through the CIA, organized the opponents of the Sandinista regime, and provided them with arms and other assistance in their camps in Honduras and Costa Rica in an effort to pressure the Nicaraguans to cut off arms shipments. The CIA was thus involved in an undeclared war against the Sandinistas that, despite administration denials, seemed aimed mainly at overthrowing the Nicaraguan government. This kind of covert operation, in brief, fell between the cracks of resolving an issue either by diplomatic negotiation or the direct use of American military forces.

Therefore, the congressional restriction on actions aimed at overthrowing the Nicaraguan government became hard to enforce. Where exactly was the line to be drawn between actions that blocked the supply of arms from Nicaragua to the Salvadoran guerrillas and those that destabilized the Nicaraguan regime? The first presumably was legal, but the last was not. Moreover, while the president officially maintained that the United States only wanted to stop the flow of arms, he called the anti-Sandinista rebels "freedom fighters" opposing a government that had betrayed its original democratic commitments, including the promise to hold genuinely free elections. Reagan also said it would be difficult to bring stability to Central America if the Sandinistas remained in power. One result of these and similar statements was a stalemate: the Democratically controlled House voting repeatedly to cut off funds for the CIA's covert activities in Nicaragua, and the Republican-controlled Senate going along with the administration. But even the Senate rebelled when it was revealed that the CIA had been active in organizing and directing the mining of Nicaraguan harbors. Opposition to the covert war thus mounted in both Houses.

The congressional cutoff of funds for the Contras in 1984 and 1985 (except for $27 million for "humanitarian" assistance, which by definition was not to include the buying of arms) did not, however, discourage the administration. Convinced of the correctness of its actions, it did an end run around Congress, shifting the direction of the conduct of the Contra war from the Central Intelligence Agency to the National Security Council to avoid congressional oversight while replacing congressional funding of arms with private and foreign government funding. In essence, it privatized the conduct of the war. To say the least, this was a novel idea but since, according to the Constitution, U.S. foreign policy was supposed to be made by the president and Congress, the discovery in November 1986 of what was going on, after years of suspicion and rumors, led to a major crisis for the Reagan administration (see Chapter 3).

Reagan and the Persian Gulf

The administration also refused to invoke the War Powers Resolution in the Persian Gulf where Iraq and Iran were waging their war. In this war, which had started in 1979 with an Iraqi attack to exploit Iran's instability in the early days of the Islamic revolution after the fall of the Shah, the odds were with Iran as the war dragged on year in and year out after the Iraqis failed to win a quick victory. Iran's population was three times larger than Iraq's and while Iraq had better and more arms, Iran could and did sacrifice more of its men in battle than Iraq. Iraq even used poison gas, but that too did not bring an end to the war. (Had Israel not taken out its atomic reactor in 1981, would Iraq have used nuclear bombs?) In desperation, the Iraqis in 1984 began attacking ships going to and from Iran where they loaded oil; the aim was to strangle Iran financially so that it would have to call off the war rather than continue the fighting until it had achieved its declared aim of deposing the Iraqi regime. Iran retaliated, starting in late 1986, by attacking ships to and from Kuwait, not just Kuwaiti-owned shipping, thus setting off a tanker war. It also intermittently threatened to close the Persian Gulf to all shipping, which would have shut down oil exports from the various Arab countries on the Gulf, who were pro-Iraqi in sentiment and supported it with financial aid. The Iranian acquisition of Chinese-made short-range missiles and their emplacement at the mouth of the Gulf was therefore considered an ominous sign.

The United States repeatedly reaffirmed its commitment to keeping the Gulf open: the navy, which had been in the Gulf since 1949, would ensure this goal. But freedom of the seas was never threatened, for Iran depended on the Gulf for its oil exports; it was in fact Iraq, which used pipelines, that threatened this freedom with its attacks on ships carrying Iranian oil. A more obvious reason was U.S. support of the pro-Western oil sheikdoms, all of whom feared an Iranian victory and the spread of Islamic fundamentalism. In the war itself, while declaring neutrality, the United States in fact favored Iraq because an Iranian victory was not in America's interest. However, since Iraq could not win, the U.S. preference was for a stalemate.

It is in this context that the president's thoughtless, if not reckless, sale of arms to gain the release of a few U.S. hostages in Lebanon became pertinent. Among other consequences, it shocked the Arab Gulf kingdoms and other Arab states who feared that the United States was tilting toward Iran. One result was that Kuwait, lying to the south of Iraq and an ally of Iraq, turned to the Soviet Union for help. Moscow agreed and chartered three of its tankers to Kuwait. Kuwait was basically a city-state with oilwells and a port through which Iraq's trade and arms flowed. Kuwait was in all but name an ally of Iraq. The United States, which had also been asked for its protective services in December 1986 but had not given any answer to Kuwait, quickly assented in March 1987 to forestall a larger Soviet role and presence in the Gulf. The United States could not afford to lose even more of its prestige and influence than it had already as a result of the shipment of arms to Iran. The aim was clearly to eliminate the Arab perception that the United States had become pro-Iranian, or had become irresolute and was therefore a less desirable guardian of the sheikdoms' security than Moscow. A refusal to protect Kuwaiti tankers would, in Washington's eyes, have had that result, with a corresponding increase in Moscow's prestige and influence.

A Soviet presence in the Gulf, located near two thirds of the world's oil reserves—probably the greatest geopolitical prize of the late twentieth century—had therefore to be opposed. The plain fact is that the United States cannot permit the oil kingdoms to fall under the influence of any hostile power, regardless of whether it is the Soviet Union or Iran. Thus the fallout of Irangate had a profound impact on U.S. foreign policy. To prove U.S. reliability to the Arabs, the administration rather quickly agreed to a major step, assuming that its escort service could be carried out with ships then present in the Gulf and that Iran would not dare provoke the American Navy.

If Washington's decision, therefore, was largely a response to a Soviet move in an area where Russia has historically sought control since tsarist days, it soon became clear that the Reagan administration had not thought this move through any more than it had its earlier intervention in Lebanon, where a small force of marines was sent in as part of an international peace-keeping force. As Lebanon's bitter civil war resumed, the United States took sides and supported the Christian-dominated government, which did not even control the capital city, against the Muslim opposition. The marines now became targets. The result was a tragedy and a timely but humiliating withdrawal by a humbled superpower. Would that sequence be repeated now, for reflagging Kuwaiti tankers and escorting them with U.S. warships would be taking sides in the Iran–Iraqi war? The issue of the Reagan administration's policy-making processes—already prominent because of Irangate—came to be questioned even more closely as the U.S. frigate *Stark* was inadvertently attacked in May 1987 by an Iraqi jet with a French-made missile. Not expecting an attack by "friendlies," the ship took no defensive measures and suffered a loss of thirty-seven lives.

Now the Congress, which had previously not voiced any objections, became worried, for the new rules of engagement—shoot first, ask questions later—plus the U.S. intention to reregister eleven Kuwaiti oil tankers as U.S. vessels to be commanded by a U.S. captain and escorted by U.S. warships meant that the risks of conflict with Iran and more casualties had grown. What would happen if the Iranians would not be deterred by the likelihood of U.S. retaliation, as the administration contended they would? What kind of retaliation and risks did it have in mind? What if a Kuwaiti ship with a U.S. flag were attacked, or the escorting U.S. ships or planes? Would the United States then strike back at Iranian missile or air bases? If attacks became more frequent, would the United States continue to retaliate or strike preventively? Could U.S. warships defend themselves properly? Did they need air protection and, if so, how was that to be assured if none of the Gulf states would give the United States landing rights? And should the United States not insist on help from its allies to whom most of the Gulf oil was shipped? Obviously, while making its commitment to Kuwait, the administration had not thought through the consequences and prepared for them. For instance, on March 7, 1987, the secretary of defense announced the policy but only on May 24, after the Iraqi attack on the U.S. frigate on May 19, did Weinberger assert that air cover for U.S. ships was essential. Yet no agreement for land air bases for U.S. planes had been negotiated before the policy was announced; nor was such an agreement concluded afterward. Administration officials stated that they would examine the above questions and others *now*. This lack of preparation was dramatically illustrated when the Pentagon, having underestimated Iran's shrewdness and the danger of mines, was immediately confronted by the first tanker being hit by an Iranian-planted World War II mine, leading the U.S. naval ships to line up behind the damaged tanker to avoid hitting other mines. Having spent its money on high-technology weapons, the navy now found itself without the lowly minesweepers it needed, leaving the United States to plead with its European allies for help—which it got.

Despite the obvious risks of its policy, the administration refused to invoke the War Powers Resolution; the president contended that conditions at the time did not meet the resolution's description of a "situation where imminent involvement in hostilities is clearly indicated by circumstances." Yet the navy was giving sailors dangerous duty pay because they were "subject to hostile fire or imminent danger"! Indeed, there were a number of incidents in which American forces opened fire, sinking Iranian oil rigs and more than half of its navy. The Congress therefore repeatedly objected to the president's failure to invoke War Powers; indeed, over 100 congressmen took the issue to the courts to compel the president to invoke the resolution, although their suit was rejected. While Congress remained nervous about the entire Persian Gulf commitment, leading members stated that they realized that once committed, the United States could hardly withdraw without disastrous consequences in the area because such an action would reinforce the Persian Gulf countries' perceptions that the United States was an unreliable protector who could not be counted on, exactly the impression the administration wished to counter. That is why the administration remained suspicious of Congress' intention and tended not to believe the reassurances of support. It continued to believe that if there were a major Iranian attack on a U.S. naval ship with high casualties, Congress would seek a U.S. withdrawal. Indeed, the passage of the War Powers Resolution might provide precisely the incentive the Iranians needed for an attack.

A Reassessment: The Role of the Congress and the Military

The continuing debate about the War Powers Act touches on a number of issues: the wisdom or stupidity of the policies that involve the use of overt or covert force; the institutional struggle between the executive and the legislature; and not unexpectedly, partisan politics. The War Powers Act, then, requires the Congress to stand up and be counted—"Put blood on our hands, too," as Senator Jacob Javits (R-N.Y.) reportedly said—instead of hiding behind the president and letting him take sole responsibility.[47] But, of course, the Congress has always possessed the power to intervene in that it must approve of a president's actions by appropriating funds for the conduct of any hostilities. Events in Central America, Lebanon, and Grenada had made it clear that Congress no longer intended to be passive on matters of war and peace, and uncritically accept presidential explanations. Nonetheless, the limits of presidential discretion in the use of force remained cloudy. Perhaps only a major large-scale intervention abroad by U.S. forces will resolve the issue.[48]

What happens if the president and Congress differ in their respective definitions of what constitutes "imminent involvement in hostilities," that is, whether a crisis exists? Would the Congress have accepted Roosevelt's definition of the German threat after the fall of France as a menace to U.S. security and supported the transfer of destroyers to Britain, the convoying of British merchant ships by U.S. warships as far as Iceland, or the "shoot on sight" order against German raiders? The War Powers Act simply assumed the unassumable: that imminent involvement in hostilities is clear to any beholder and therefore does not need a definition. This may not always be true, as Lebanon, Grenada, and the Persian Gulf suggest. The president may simply refuse to recognize imminent involvement in hostilities is at hand to keep Congress from interfering and perhaps insisting on U.S. withdrawal.

Even if they agree on what an emergency is, how, from a practical point of view, can the president be given sufficient authority and flexibility to act without evading congressional involvement and responsibility to participate in key decisions affecting war and peace? In short, how can one find the spot halfway between authority that is too broad and that which is too narrow, between giving the president the flexibility he needs to protect American interests and handcuffing him so that he does not involve the country in needless conflict? In the weeks before the abortive rescue attempt of the American hostages in Iran in 1980, the Senate Foreign Relations Committee chairman and ranking minority members insisted that the Carter administration consult with the committee before any potential use of force. Rumors were rife that Iran's ports were about to be mined in an effort to increase economic pressure on Iran. But how can any administration consult the Congress in advance on plans for the use of force without placing the world on notice, giving its adversary time to mobilize international opinion (including American opinion) against such an effort, and placing its military forces on alert to foil the American effort? Is this any way for a great power to conduct its foreign policy and protect its interests?

A third problem remains equally vexing: How can Congress really participate in crisis decision making? President Ford after the *Mayaguez* said that it could not and cited several reasons, some of which President Kennedy before him and Carter after him also cited.[49]

1. Key legislators were out of town and communicating with them was difficult, slow, and in some instances impossible. (Kennedy had the air force pick up the important congressional figures and return them to Washington during the Cuban missile crisis.)
2. Congressmen have a multitude of concerns that prevent them from focusing over a period of time only, or primarily, on one issue.
3. Time is of the essence and this requirement is incompatible with developing a consensus among congressional leaders in case of disagreement, especially if they are not in town.
4. Even if a consensus were reached, many congressmen among today's independent-minded legislators might not accept it.
5. The likelihood of information leaking out from some members of Congress about a forthcoming military operation inhibits any executive consultation with the Congress or with more than just a very few members.

One might add to these reasons cited by President Ford that in the contemporary Congress it is doubtful that many members would consider presidential consultation with key congressional leaders sufficient. The days when a few men could speak for the Congress appear to be over. Paradoxically, however, one might question how many congressmen really want to know what the president is planning. It is one thing to blame him for failure afterward and suggest that had he consulted Congress this failure could have been avoided; it is another matter to also be held accountable for disaster. Perhaps it is for this reason that not too many voices were raised in protest about the lack of consultation after the failure of the hostage rescue mission in Iran.

The War Powers Act and the increasing concern of the Congress to limit presidential discretion on foreign policy ran into a major Supreme Court decision on June 23, 1983. The Court that day swept away the fifty-year-old congressional practice of blocking executive action with a "legislative veto" after it had delegated authority to the president. A legislative veto occurs when Congress gives provisional authority to the executive to make a decision, subject to ultimate legislative approval. In the case of foreign policy, the War Powers Act gives the president the power to dispatch troops as he deems necessary, but Congress reserves the right to reverse such decisions. Depending on how Congress has written the original legislation, a veto may be made either by one house or by both.

The Court ruled that once Congress delegated a decision to the executive branch, either the president or the bureaucracy, it could not simply decide to overrule that branch. Such an action would constitute a breach of the separation of powers between the two branches. The veto itself had come about because Congress has been willing to grant the president broad powers to set policy, whereas legislative initiatives require narrow and specific legislation. The idea behind the veto, then, was to permit the president or the bureaucracy to determine the specifics of policies, subject to congressional disapproval. The Supreme Court ruled, however, that Congress must make its specific decisions *before* the executive branch acts. The War Powers Act, the Arms Export Control Act of 1976, which gave Congress a veto over arms sales, and the Jackson–Vanik amendment of 1974 denying preferential trading status to Communist nations that restrict Jewish emigration were the key foreign policy tools threatened by the decision. Since the Court ruled only on an obscure emigration case, it was not clear that these acts were immediately invalidated. Earlier, the House Foreign Affairs Committee attempted to evade the Court's decision by including a provision that permits Congress to vote on a joint resolution to suspend aid to El Salvador. A joint resolution of the two houses can be vetoed by the president, whereas a concurrent resolution, which has been used previously, was not subject to presidential approval.[50] Joint resolutions are virtually identical to ordinary bills, while concurrent resolutions merely express the "sense of Congress" that something ought to be done.

The Court decision does not affect the portions of the War Powers Act that require the president to report to Congress when American troops are sent overseas and face either combat or imminent hostilities that prohibit the president from keeping troops in such situations for more than ninety days unless

Congress declares war or approves an extension. What Congress cannot do, at least according to the president's interpretation of the Court decision, is to force withdrawal of troops engaged in hostilities. The Congress has not admitted defeat on the War Powers issue, claiming that the Supreme Court decision on the immigration bill may not cover all aspects of the legislative veto. Yet there is little evidence that Congress has developed any alternatives to the current procedure that might work effectively.

Despite the ruling, however, the executive branch is not likely to regain more freedom to use force. A lawyer for the Reagan administration dealing with foreign policy commented: "From our point of view, nothing has changed. We never conceded the constitutionality of the legislative veto in the first place. But as a practical matter, we would be fools to thumb our noses at Congress now."[51] A president will still have to live with Congress, which clearly remains determined to participate in decisions involving the use of force, especially ones that unlike Grenada may lead to lengthier military interventions against more formidable opponents. It would be very impolitic for a president not to be sensitive to congressional opinion about issues of war and peace; the political cost would be too high. Presumably, this is the reason the executive has not challenged the War Powers Resolution in the courts and presidents have consulted with Congress if time permitted and have reported to Congress "consistent with the War Powers Resolution" while asserting that the president as commander in chief has the authority to use the armed forces.

Overall, the Reagan administration was in its way sensitive to congressional and public opinion when it contemplated the larger scale use of U.S. forces. Its resort to covert operations in Nicaragua reflected its awareness that it could not use U.S. troops; short, successful, and relatively cost-free operations in terms of situations like Grenada and the air strikes on Libya created their own public support and did not therefore pose a War Powers issue, as the Democrats discovered. Even with initial War Powers support in the Congress, Reagan was quick to cut losses in Lebanon after the deaths of 241 marines rather than escalate the relatively limited intervention of 1,200 marines, suffer a greater number of casualties, and risk public disaffection. In the post-Vietnam period, lengthy and costly interventions in losses of lives were to be avoided; whenever the possibility of the use of force was even discussed, concerns were expressed about another Vietnam.

At no time was this more true than in August 1990, after Iraq invaded and annexed the tiny oil kingdom of Kuwait. President Bush decided almost immediately to reverse this aggression by Iraq's dictator, Saddam Hussein. The reasons were several. One, the post–Cold War era could not be allowed to start with such flagrant aggression against a member state of the United Nations; if met with inaction, it would send the wrong signal to other regional bullies who wanted to prey on their neighbors. The result would be an unstable international system. Two, Kuwait was a neighbor of Saudi Arabia, the non-Communist world's largest oil producer. The seizure and removal of the royal family was an ominous warning to the Saudi royal household. Iraq wanted to raise oil prices both to wipe out huge debts outstanding from its recently concluded eight-year war with Iran and to earn more money to spend on the vast armaments program intended to turn Iraq into the region's most powerful state. Saudi Arabia, the most influential member of the Organization of Petroleum Exporting Countries (OPEC) on oil prices, was thus faced with a painful dilemma: to obey Iraq's wishes or to be invaded. The Saudis would be no match for the Iraqis. In either case, Saddam Hussein would have his hands on about half of the industrial world's oil supplies. Three, ever since the Islamic revolution in Iran in 1979–80, Iraq had sought to replace Iran, the most populous state in the Persian Gulf area, as its preeminent state. That was why Iraq had invaded Iran in 1980, but its expectation of a quick victory ended in a long war of attrition in which Iraq, using poison gas, among other means, outlasted Iran. Believing itself to have won that war, it now sought to turn its victory into regional hegemony by menacing Saudi Arabia and the other Persian Gulf oil kingdoms, overthrowing moderate pro-Western Arab governments throughout the Middle East, and, as the Arab world's radical leader, unite all Arabs against Israel and the West.

Thus President Bush felt it necessary to act. The implications of Iraq's action were multiple and serious, affecting the interests of the United States and the other industrial nations, indeed, the entire post-Cold War world. In initially sending U.S. forces to Saudi Arabia to defend that country in case of invasion and to demand that Iraq withdraw from Kuwait, the president had the support of the Democratically controlled Congress. But although Saddam Hussein did not invade Saudi Arabia, he did not pull out of Kuwait either. To make the U.S. demand more credible, the president in November began a buildup that was to increase American forces in the Gulf to over 500,000 troops, larger than the forces that had invaded France in 1944 and about the size of those sent to Vietnam in the 1960s. If Saddam Hussein did not withdraw voluntarily, the United States would have sufficient troops in place to compel the withdrawal of an Iraqi army of approximately the same size.

At this point, the Democrats protested. They considered the deployment of this many troops to be a buildup for offensive action. They preferred the president's course of defending Saudi Arabia and placing an economic embargo on Iraq. Since Iraq was dependent for 90 percent of its revenues on oil exports, the assumption was that it was only a matter of time until its economy would collapse; force was therefore unnecessary to accomplish the goal the United States sought. When that did not happen within the first few months, it was suggested to wait for nine months, or eighteen months, or two years, if that is what it took. The Democrats' counsel, in short, was patience; the president should not "rush into war." Traumatized by Vietnam, a war in which they had intervened without success, the Democrats were reluctant to repeat that trauma.

President Bush thus faced a constitutional dilemma. If the Congress supported the president, it would make his threat to use force against Saddam Hussein more credible and enhance the Iraqi leader's incentives to withdraw from Kuwait and restore its legitimate government without war. But if the president went to the Congress seeking its backing and it refused to support him, voting instead to give the embargo more time to work, in effect postponing indefinitely any use of force, American diplomacy would be weakened. This would be true even if Congress' advice were sound. By advertising to the world that it disagreed with the president, even if it disguised that disagreement by declaring that it supported the president but simply wanted to wait a bit longer before using force—to make sure that American lives would not be spent—until it was clear that economic sanctions would not work, Congress would undercut the president's efforts to make the threat of war believable to Saddam Hussein and thus weaken U.S. policy.

It was frequently said during the Gulf crisis that Saddam Hussein, while ruthless, was not suicidal; that if he really believed that war was imminent, he would withdraw rather than face defeat. But the American political system, with its checks and balances, and Republicans in charge of the White House and a Democratic majority in the Congress, made it difficult to use the threat of force credibly in an attempt to avoid having to fight a war. Saddam Hussein tried to manipulate this situation by, among other things, releasing the several thousand foreign hostages, including Americans, he had held. Confessing that holding these hostages had been against "established norms," he specifically thanked Senate Democrats who had held hearings of the Armed Services and Foreign Relations Committees, which had concluded that economic sanctions needed to be given more time to work.

President Bush was, therefore, reluctant to go to the Congress. Yet he could not really avoid doing so. Moreover, since he had made such a huge commitment of troops, and a war with Iraq might involve major casualties—the military's own estimate ranged up to 20,000—he could not really rely on his authority as commander in chief or even on the War Powers Resolution. The president therefore turned to the United Nations. He had already mobilized an unprecedented coalition in the United Nations, consisting of the America's principal Western allies, Japan, Arab countries (who had never before joined the West against another Arab state), the Soviet Union (Iraq's former patron), and Communist China. With such support, the United Nations had condemned Iraq, demanded its withdrawal from Kuwait, imposed economic sanctions, voted for the enforcement of the embargo on the sea and in the air, and condemned Iraq's cruel treatment of Kuwait. Bush now sought—and got—a U.N. Security Council resolution declaring that if Saddam Hussein had not obeyed the earlier resolutions demanding withdrawal from Kuwait by January 15, 1991, force could be used to eject the Iraqis. Bush argued that the Security Council's resolution granted him all the authority he needed to commit U.S. forces. The vote in the Security Council also conveyed to Saddam Hussein that the coalition against him was holding fast.

Bush's critics, however, argued that even with the U.N. resolution the president needed congressional approval. Some of the president's advisers, including the vice president, also urged him to seek legislative support. Otherwise, he might take the country into war in a divided state. Thus, after receiving the

United Nations' authorization to use force after mid-January, Bush focused on mobilizing the support of Congress for the United Nations' decision. He did so by first offering to "go the extra mile" diplomatically. He proposed receiving Iraq's foreign minister in Washington and sending the secretary of state to Baghdad. If these talks did not result in Iraq's withdrawal from Kuwait, Bush expected to isolate his critics and to be able to muster the country's and Congress' backing for the use of force. But all the diplomatic maneuvering produced only a barren meeting in Geneva between the secretary of state and the Iraqi foreign minister.

It was only after the failure of the Geneva meeting that President Bush asked Congress for authority to use force after January 15, that is, a functional equivalent of a declaration of war. Congress voted its support, although by only a slim 52 to 47 majority in the Senate—three votes could have turned the whole thing around—and by a 250 to 183 majority in the House. Four-fifths of the Democratic senators and two-thirds of Democratic representatives voted against the authority to use force, preferring to rely on economic sanctions. The Democrats had placed themselves in a precarious position. If there was no war, their votes would not matter much. But if there was a war and it resulted in a quick victory, the Democrats risked reviving the electorate's memory that they were "soft on national security" just as the 1992 presidential campaign was beginning. (At this time the recession was not expected to be the main issue, since the economy was supposed to recuperate in the summer of 1991.) Yet, on the other hand, if the war dragged on and the number of casualties mounted, the Democrats could say that they had warned the country against going to war and had wanted to rely instead on peaceful means to compel Saddam Hussein to withdraw from Kuwait. Bush, of course, was aware of these calculations. A long, drawn-out war with heavy casualties would ensure that he would be a one-term president; politically, he needed a short war and a quick victory with relatively light casualties.

What is striking is the contrast between the U.S. effort to mobilize international support and domestic support and the very narrow margin of victory in the congressional vote for the use of force. Indeed, this is all the more striking because the president had boxed Congress in by first gaining United Nations' support. Would Congress really be the only party to oppose the war and undermine the world's opposition to Iraq? The close votes in the Congress reflected a divided public opinion (see Chapter 5). Especially after Vietnam, the American public has been reluctant to use force.* As Vietnam had demonstrated, public

---

*A contrary view holds that Congress' acquiescent role demonstrated the meaningless of the War Powers Resolution. Bush had committed the United States to the defense of Saudi Arabia; then he declared that the Iraqi invasion of Kuwait "would not stand"; and finally, he doubled the forces in Saudi Arabia so that they could compel the Iraqis to withdraw. On none of these occasions had the administration sought congressional authorization; nor had the Congress sought to force the administration to involve the Congress. Thus, essentially, the administration had placed the nation on a path to war by facing it with a number of *faits accompli* and the Congress had just acquiesced.[52]

support for such interventions is lacking because of the fear that hostilities would be costly and long and casualties heavy.

Thus, as in the situation with Iraq, a president risks his political career and his reputation when he decides to resort to war and seeks congressional support for what is essentially a declaration of war, especially until Clinton's election to the presidency in 1992 when partisan and ideological differences have accentuated normal executive-legislative tensions.

Notes

1. *New York Times,* January 21, 1961.
2. Aaron Wildavsky, "The Two Presidencies," *Trans-Action,* December 1966, p. 3.
3. Francis E. Rourke, Robert E. Osgood, Robert W. Turner, et al., "The Domestic Scene: The President Ascendant," in *Retreat From Empire?* (Baltimore: The Johns Hopkins University Press, 1973), p. 106. See also Leslie H. Gelb and Richard K. Betts, *The Irony of Vietnam* (Washington, D.C.: The Brookings Institution, 1979), pp. 223–24.
4. Robert S. Strauss, "What's Right with U.S. Campaigns," *Foreign Policy,* Summer 1984, pp. 3–22; and Stephen Hess, "Foreign Policy and Presidential Campaigns," *Foreign Policy,* Fall 1972, pp. 3–22.
5. Ibid., p. 19.
6. Cyrus Vance, *Hard Choices* (New York: Simon & Schuster, 1983), p. 13.
7. Gary Sick, *All Fall Down* (New York: Random House, 1985), pp. 363–77, especially 376–77.
8. David Jerge, "Bush's Very Own Ford Foundation," *The Washington Post,* April 2, 1989; Dan Oberderfer, "Baker's Evolution of State," ibid., November 16, 1989; Andrew Rosenthal, "Scowcroft and Gates Team Rivals Baker," *New York Times,* February 21, 1989; and R. W. Apple, "A Mover and a Shaker Behind Bush Foreign Policy," ibid., February 6, 1989.
9. Zbigniew Brzezinski, "NSC's Midlife Crisis," *Foreign Policy,* Winter 1987–88, pp. 91–92.
10. Duncan L. Clarke, "Why State Can't Lead," *Foreign Policy,* Spring 1987, pp. 108–42.
11. *New York Times,* January 25, 1983. See also Zbigniew Brzezinski, *Power and Principle* (New York: Farrar, Straus, Giroux, 1983), pp. 53–55.
12. Quoted in *New York Times,* May 21, 1980. Also see I. M. Destler, "A Job That Doesn't Work," *Foreign Policy,* Spring 1980, pp. 80–88; and Flora Lewis, "The Parts and the Whole," *New York Times,* September 30, 1980.
13. Alexander Haig, *Caveat* (New York: Macmillan, 1984), pp. 352 ff.
14. Interview with Zbigniew Brzezinski, *New York Times,* January 6, 1982.
15. See the Tower Commission Report on the Iran arms for hostages deal, *New York Times,* February 27, 1987.
16. Norman J. Ornstein, "Reagan's Mismanagement Style," *New York Times,* February 5, 1987. Also, Donald T. Regan, *For the Record* (San Diego, Calif.: Harcourt Brace Jovanovich, 1988).
17. *New York Times,* March 2, 1987.

18. Ronald Steel, "Shultz's Way," *New York Times Magazine,* January 11, 1987, pp. 17 ff; Also see George W. Ball, "A Report Card on Secretary Shultz," *New York Times,* July 3, 1988.

19. Clarke, "Why State Can't Lead," pp. 141–42.

20. I. M. Destler, *Presidents, Bureaucrats, and Foreign Policy,* rev. ed. (Princeton, N.J.: Princeton University Press, 1974), pp. 298–319; and "Can One Man Do?" *Foreign Policy,* Winter 1971–72, pp. 28–40.

21. Clarke, "Why State Can't Lead," pp. 140–41.

22. Zbigniew Brzezinski, *Power and Principle* (New York: Farrar, Strauss & Giroux, 1983), pp. 42–44.

23. Leslie H. Gelb, "Clinton's Security Trio," *New York Times,* December 20, 1992.

24. Richard K. Betts, *Soldiers, Statemen, and Cold War Crises* (Cambridge, Mass.: Harvard University Press, 1977), pp. 4, 6.

25. Henry T. Nash, *American Foreign Policy: Response to a Sense of Threat,* 3d ed. (Homewood, Ill.: Dorsey Press, 1985), p. 151.

26. Henry A. Kissinger, "Bureaucracy and Policy-Making: The Effects of Insiders and Outsiders on the Policy Process," in *Readings in American Foreign Policy,* Halperin and Kanter, eds., p. 89.

27. Francis E. Rourke, *Bureaucracy and Foreign Policy* (Baltimore: Johns Hopkins University Press, 1973), p. 32.

28. Ibid.

29. Edward N. Luttwak, *The Pentagon and the Art of War* (New York: Simon & Schuster, 1984), pp. 19–20. On the new military reforms, see Arthur T. Hadley, "Military Coup," *The New Republic,* January 18, 1988, pp. 17–20. For this author's critique of the U.S. military, see *The Straw Giant* (New York: Avon Books, 1987).

30. Quoted by Robert A. Dahl, *Congress and Foreign Policy* (New York: Harcourt Brace Jovanovich, 1950), pp. 129–30.

31. Joseph Jones, *The Fifteen Weeks* (New York: Viking Press, 1955) pp. 138–41.

32. Arthur M. Schlesinger, Jr., *The Bitter Heritage* (Greenwich, Conn.: A Fawcett Crest Book, 1967), p. 47. See also, Larry Berman, *Planning a Tragedy* (New York: W. W. Norton, 1982).

33. William Conrad Gibbons, *The U.S. Government and the Vietnam War,* Part II: 1961–1964 (Princeton, N.J.: Princeton University Press, 1986).

34. *New York Times,* October 18, 1979.

35. *New York Times,* October 2, 1981.

36. *New York Times,* October 27, 1981.

37. Guenter Lewy, *America in Vietnam* (New York: Oxford University Press, 1978), pp. 202–5.

38. J. William Fulbright, *The Crippled Giant* (New York: Vintage Books, 1972), pp. 218–20; and *The Pentagon Papers* (New York: Bantam Books, 1971), p. 25.

39. Fulbright, *Pentagon Papers,* p. 79.

40. Arthur M. Schlesinger, Jr., "Congress and the Making of American Foreign Policy," *Foreign Affairs,* October 1972, p. 98.

41. Quoted by Joseph C. Goulden, *Truth Is the First Casualty* (Skokie, Ill.: Rand McNally, 1969), pp. 50–55. See also Eugene C. Windchy, *Tonkin Gulf* (New York: Doubleday Publishing, 1971).

42. See, for example, David Halberstam, *The Best and the Brightest* (New York: Random House, 1972); Stanley Karrow, *Vietnam* (New York: Viking Press, 1983).

43. Spanier, *The Truman-MacArthur Controversy and the Korean War,* rev. ed. (New York: W. W. Norton, 1965).

44. Fulbright, *The Crippled Giant,* pp. 188–91. On the intervention, see Berman, *Planning a Tragedy.*

45. Thomas F. Eagelton, "Whose Power Is War Power?" *Foreign Policy,* Fall 1972, pp. 29–31. John H. Sullivan, *The War Powers Resolution: A Special Study of the Committee on Foreign Affairs* (Washington, D.C.: U.S. Government Printing Office, 1982).

46. Ibid.

47. Jacob Javits in the *New York Times,* February 14, 1972. See also Javits, *Who Makes War* (New York: William Morrow, 1973).

48. Pat M. Holt, *The War Powers Resolution* (Washington, D.C.: American Enterprise Institute, 1978); and Robert F. Turner, *The War Powers Resolution* (Philadelphia: Foreign Policy Research Institute, 1983).

49. Cited by Richard G. Head, Frisco W. Short, and Robert C. McFarlane, *Crisis Resolution* (Boulder, Colo.: Westview Press, 1978), p. 254.

50. "Panel Skirts Legislative Veto Ban," *Congressional Quarterly Weekly Report* 41 (July 30, 1983), p. 1576.

51. John Felton, "Hill Weighs Foreign Policy Impact on Ruling," *Congressional Quarterly Weekly Report* 41 (July 2, 1983), p. 1324.

52. Michael J. Glennon, "The Gulf War and the Constitution," *Foreign Affairs,* Spring 1991, pp. 84–101. Also see Jean Edward Smith, *George Bush's War* (New York: Henry Holt, 1992).

The Presidency and Executive–Legislative Relations

The Background: 1940–41

It must be clear by now that no issue is of greater importance than the relationship between the executive branch and Congress in the conduct of foreign policy. Even before the United States became a world power, one observer noted:

> America has never yet devised a sound or efficient technique of diplomacy.... Nearly every important treaty the country has been called upon to make has become a bone of contention between the executive and the Senate. It is certain that in years to come if we are to go forward in the new paths and stand for a clear-cut world policy, we must devise some method of speaking to the world promptly and with an undivided voice. Our present system leads to utter weakness, muddle, and delay; it forces both sides to play politics, and instead of meeting the issue squarely, to indulge in a vast controversy over the prerogatives of two coordinate branches of the government. The deadlock between the executive and the senate every time we face a really critical foreign problem is intolerable. It not only disgraces us before the nations, but in some future world crisis may ruin us.[1]

Since the United States did become a superpower, executive–legislative relations have grown more important. In a Cold War situation, where presidents have come to wield virtually emergency powers that in the past they would have exercised only temporarily—mainly in wartime—they need the support of the Congress. Treaties require a two-thirds Senate vote, diplomatic appointments must be confirmed, control over the military is shared with the president as commander in chief and, most important, appropriations must be authorized for all sorts of foreign and defense policies. Nevertheless, all recent presidents have consistently and repeatedly complained about congressional restrictions and interference with their efforts to carry out U.S. policy. These criticisms have often been summed up by the comment that Congress is composed of 535 secretaries of state.

Actually executive–legislative conflict is as old as the Republic and institutional rivalry and partisanship are its principal causes. If mounting U.S. involvement in world affairs is the main reason for the growth of presidential power, another important cause has been congressional obstructionism. Three phases of U.S. policy in this century need to be mentioned if one is to understand not only why the presidency has established preeminence in the conduct of foreign policy, but, equally important, why until Vietnam, this trend received popular approval and academic blessings.

The starting point is the Versailles Treaty of 1919, which concluded World War I and established the League of Nations. The intensity of the conflict between President Wilson, a Democrat, and the Senate, controlled by the Republicans and directed by Senator Henry Cabot Lodge (Mass.), resulted in the treaty's defeat. Executive–legislative rivalry, partisan considerations, and personal hatred of the two men toward each other thus contributed to the U.S. withdrawal from an active world role after the war. This return to isolationism, many Americans later felt, was partly responsible for the outbreak of World War II. The defeat of the Versailles Treaty thus dramatically raised the question of America's ability, with its institutions, to conduct a foreign policy to protect its interest.

The second period, from the German defeat of France in the spring of 1940 to Pearl Harbor in late 1941, reinforced this concern.[2] This was a period in which the president had to confront the threat of an increasingly powerful Germany while Congress remained in the grip of isolationism. Indeed, during the 1930s the Congress had passed a series of neutrality laws that were supposed to keep the United States out of any future European war. On the eve of that war in 1939, when the administration asked for changes that would allow the government to sell arms to the allies who seemed less well prepared than the Nazis, Senator William Borah (R–Idaho), chairman of the Foreign Relations Committee and himself an ardent isolationist, not only rejected the request, but asserted that *his* sources of information were superior to those of the State Department, and that they had told him there would be no war!

After hostilities erupted, the problem for President Roosevelt was how to do the "right thing" and be able to do it despite the continued isolationist sentiment in the Congress. For Roosevelt, the right thing meant supporting Britain after the fall of France, the low countries (the Netherlands, Belgium, and Luxembourg), and Denmark and Norway. American policy makers have historically considered the domination of Western Europe by a single power as a potential threat to American security. Even Thomas Jefferson, a Francophile, voiced the possibility of aligning with England as Napoleon proceeded to conquer Europe.

In Roosevelt's words, the defense of American democracy would be difficult and would certainly result in the sacrifice of the democratic ingredient if the United States were to become a lone island of peace surrounded by a world of brute force (German, Italian, and Japanese). America would have to turn itself into a garrison state; the Atlantic Ocean was no longer a barrier to attack but a highway to the Western Hemisphere.

The president therefore wanted to help Britain, first of all, to defend itself against a possible German invasion. But despite entreaties by Prime Minister Churchill for some old World War I–vintage destroyers, Roosevelt, at a time of great emergency, procrastinated. The Congress, anticipating him, had imposed a legal barrier by decreeing that the president could not transfer the destroyers unless the chief of naval operations certified that such ships were not needed for U.S. defense. The distrust of the president was abundantly clear. Roosevelt finally outflanked the Congress with an executive agreement but only after four months of hesitation. The president had to secure a pledge from the Republican presidential nominee that he would not make the transaction a political issue; at the same time, the Committee to Defend America by Aiding the Allies had mobilized domestic support through intensive propaganda, and Churchill had agreed that in return for the destroyers the United States could lease bases on British islands in the Atlantic and Caribbean. This deal allowed Roosevelt to present the destroyer transfer basically as an American acquisition of bases and thus a means of enhancing American security; nonetheless, the destroyers were hardly mentioned in Roosevelt's speech to the country. What would have happened had the Germans invaded, as expected, during these months?

After his reelection in 1940, Roosevelt was successful in obtaining congressional support for the Lend-Lease Act by which Britain, soon unable to pay for American arms and ammunition, could acquire these on a lease basis. The United States was to become "the great arsenal of democracy." The Congress went along with the president because of the view—probably shared by Roosevelt too—that the best chance of staying out of the war was by helping the British to strengthen themselves and win the war. "Give us the tools and we will finish the job" was Churchill's cry. But the key problem was getting the supplies to Britain. In the battle of the Atlantic, the Germans were sinking British and Canadian merchant ships faster than they could be built. But Britain's survival remained the critical issue. Yet, what was the point of giving the arms to the British if their ships were sunk? Roosevelt felt inhibited, however, from doing anything. He had, in the summer of 1941, sent the marines to Iceland to prevent the Germans from stationing air reconnaissance and submarines there to cut Britain's lifeline to America. But he continued to hesitate in authorizing American warships, which were taking supplies and mail to the marines, from also convoying British and Canadian merchant ships to Iceland, even though that would relieve the already thinly stretched British navy (which would then have to convoy ships only the last half of their journey across the Atlantic). One senator had introduced a resolution specifically forbidding the president from authorizing convoys. Again, not until after several months of hesitation did Roosevelt as commander in chief of the armed forces authorize such protection.

He did so only after a German submarine had attacked the U.S. destroyer *Greer*. In publicly explaining that the navy would from then escort all merchant ships and "shoot-on-sight" at German submarines and raiders, the president was in effect involving the United States in a limited naval war in the western Atlantic. But he did not explain in his "undeclared war" speech that the destroyers had for several hours pursued the German submarine, that in desperation to escape the submarine had turned on the destroyer and fired its torpedoes, after which the destroyer had dropped depth charges on the submarine. Thus a German act, which could not have been anticipated, finally permitted the United States to do what was needed to ensure that the arms required by Britain—America's first line of defense—would get there. Had the submarine been able to slip away and had other German submarines not sunk several other American ships, what could the president have done? For congressional sentiment on the eve of World War II was clearly shown in two separate votes—one on extending the Selective Service Act, which passed the House by only one vote, and the other, finally repealing the last major neutrality-law constraint blocking American ships from carrying supplies directly to British ports, squeezed through a very narrow House majority of 212 to 194 and Senate majority of 50 to 37. These last two votes came right after a German submarine had torpedoed a U.S. destroyer near Iceland.

Franklin Roosevelt thus set a precedent for his successors. He felt compelled to resort to executive agreements to expand the powers of the commander in chief. His problem, as he saw it, was that if he did not undertake the various measures he used to help Britain, Hitler might win in Europe and then threaten the United States. If he had sought to gain congressional approval for such steps as the destroyer deal or the convoying of allied merchant ships by U.S. warships as far as Iceland, he might have failed, eroding his own authority and effectiveness as president and encouraging Hitler. Indeed, had he come out more openly for intervention, he might have lost his unprecedented third-term bid for the presidency.

It is interesting that even the critics of the president's war powers do not question Roosevelt's judgment of the peril to national security. But they do question the constitutional propriety of his actions. Thus, quite typically, Merlo Pusey, after admitting that had the president gone to Congress he would have been turned down even though "human freedom was gravely endangered on a global scale," says: "On grounds of expediency and of international power politics, the argument [for the actions Roosevelt took] is very impressive. But where does it leave us in terms of democratic principles and the maintenance of constitutional government?"[3] By the juxtaposition of such loaded terms as *expediency* and *power politics* with *principles* and *democracy*, Pusey stacks the odds and avoids the issue of (1) what Roosevelt should have done, and (2) how to reconcile American democratic government, with its separation of powers, with the protection of national security. Pusey dismisses this concern as "one of the inescapable risks in democratic government."[4] The worst, he says, that would have happened had Roosevelt gone to Congress for support and been rejected, would have been more aggressive behavior by the Nazis on the assumption that the United States would do nothing to stop them; they might even have struck the first blow, as Japan finally did.

In short, what Pusey argues is that U.S. institutions could not cope with the critical situation in 1940 and 1941; they could not take the initiative to protect U.S. security, but could only react to the enemy's initiatives. But no matter. America's paralysis would have provoked its enemies so that after they had attacked this country Congress could legally have declared war.[5] The integrity of the Constitution in these circumstances could have been preserved. In other words, American democracy—separation of powers style—unable to act wisely would be saved by its enemies' stupidity.

But Pusey's argument avoids the central issue of the effectiveness of American institutions in meeting critical foreign policy situations and of the ability of the political process to produce the best policy outcome. What would have happened had the Japanese bypassed Hawaii and had Hitler not declared war on America? Could Roosevelt have mobilized sufficient congressional and public support to declare war on the Axis powers? It is doubtful, even though by late 1941 Germany had conquered all of Western Europe except Britain, stood at the gates of Moscow and Leningrad, had captured much of North Africa, and was soon to move within sight of the Suez Canal, while Japan was poised for the conquest of British, French, and Dutch colonies in the Far East with a possible linkup via India with the Germans in the Middle East. But for German *and* Japanese mistakes, these two powers might have finished off their opponents and then confronted a psychologically and militarily unprepared America at the peak of their power and self-confidence. The ultimate decision—to make war on the United States—was made by Japan and Germany. The United States did not make this decision for itself despite the fact that the balances of power in Asia and Europe were at stake. As Robert Divine has aptly said:

> From the first signs of aggression in the 1930s to the attack on Pearl Harbor, the United States refused to attack until there was no other choice. . . . Although it was the single most powerful nation on the globe, the United States abdicated its responsibilities and became a creature of history rather than its molder. By surrendering the initiative to Germany and Japan, the nation imperiled its security and very nearly permitted the Axis powers to win the war. In the last analysis the United States was saved only by the Japanese miscalculation in attacking Pearl Harbor.[6]

Given the experience of 1940–41, it is not surprising that students of American foreign policy have often seen the executive–legislative relationship as a chief obstacle to the formation of a sound American foreign policy in the postwar era.

Presidential Primacy, Bipartisan Support, and the Cold War

The triumphant victories over Germany, Italy, and Japan under Franklin Roosevelt's majestic leadership only reinforced the trend toward strong presidential leadership. This strong leadership would allow the United States to act with authority, speed, steadiness, and, when necessary, flexibility. An active congressional role raised the possibility that U.S. foreign policy would be characterized by divided counsel, frequent policy changes, if not occasional paralysis, slow reactions, and inability to exploit rapidly changing situations—all of which would raise questions as the Cold War began about U.S. leadership and reliability. Under the new circumstances of American–Soviet conflict, the country could not afford constant executive–legislative quarrels; indeed, as noted earlier, it was in recognition that such conflict would be harmful that the policy of bipartisanship or "nonpartisanship" was born. The aim of a bipartisan foreign policy, is, in the words of a former State Department official, "to make it virtually impossible for 'momentous divisions' to occur in our foreign affairs" and to provide a "continuity and consistency" in decision making from one administration to another.[7]

The bipartisan formula, which accepted presidential primacy and congressional acquiescence, was probably unavoidable during the Cold War, even had the memories of Versailles faded and those of 1940–1941 been less vivid. For the Cold War was attended by an almost universal American perception that the country's security was under threat. It was not called *Cold War* for nothing. The United States was engaged in a war, even if it was not a hot one. But the adversary was as much, if not more, of a threat than Germany had been. The Soviet Union was the other superpower, the only nation in the world that could threaten our security—indeed, our survival. It was a threat not only because the Soviets were a great power but because they were also a totalitarian state, representing beliefs and values completely antithetical to those of American and Western democracy. The Soviet challenge, like the German one that preceded it, constituted a menace to America's physical and political survival.

This perception of threat was reinforced by frequent high tensions. Each superpower watched the other carefully to preserve the precarious balance of power. Frequent confrontation and crises were the result: Greece and Turkey (1946–1947), Berlin (1948–1949), the Korean War (1950–1953), Quemoy–Matsu (1954–1955), the Suez War and Hungarian uprising (1956), Quemoy–Matsu (1958), Berlin (1958–1962), Cuba (1961–1962), and the deepening Vietnam involvement after 1961 and, finally, war after 1965. Lack of time and the need to make rapid decisions often meant that presidents spent most of their time consulting their advisers; they then usually informed Congress of their decisions. When there was more time for consultation between the two branches of government, policy might be modified. Congress frequently put its imprint on the president's policy, but the essence of executive policy remained intact. In any event, the recurrence of crisis brought home the perceived danger to America and reinforced the popular and congressional rallying-around-the-flag phenomenon that external danger always encourages.

During this period, Congress also recognized the executive's expertise in foreign policy. The president has at hand a large bureaucracy to help him. Senators and congressmen, therefore, rely on executive officials for information and interpretation of events. In foreign affairs, members of Congress lack the confidence they have on domestic matters. As citizens and representatives, they hold views on many of the problems their constituents experience, whether inflation, unemployment, busing, education, subsidies, or health care. Whatever their own professions, they presumably have wide acquaintanceship, via their constituencies, with individuals in other walks of life and their specific problems as doctors, farmers, or workers. Moreover, they can call on a whole range of interest groups for other views of the facts and alternative policy views. But foreign problems—the question of Sino–Soviet relations, Soviet intentions, Third World nationalism, military strategy, force levels, and weapons systems— are for most congressmen just that—"foreign." This is also true for most interest groups; their expertise is essentially domestic. Deference to executive judgments followed logically. Congress tends to be not only supportive, therefore, but permissive in giving the executive a good deal of leeway.

Congressional subordination, the result of a consensus on foreign policy, was also very important. For over two decades after World War II, the president and Congress shared a common set of beliefs about the role and objectives of the United States in the world. The central conflict in international politics was the conflict between the Communist world led by the Soviet Union and the free world led by the United States; that any expansion of Communist influence and power was a loss of influence and power for the free world; that the fundamental role for American and Western policy, therefore, was to oppose such expansion; that the United States, by far the strongest Western power, had the primary responsibility for containing communism; that military power was a principal tool for preserving the strategic balance between the superpowers and deterring a Soviet first strike against the United States and its European allies as well as for opposing any limited Communist aggression around the Sino–Soviet periphery; that firmness in negotiations was essential because concessions only whetted the unlimited ambitions of the totalitarian rulers of the Soviet Union and China and would not therefore resolve key issues but lead to further demands; that other means for waging the struggle against communism—ranging from economic aid and arms sales to subversion—were legitimate in what was essentially a global competition between two giants whose rivalry would determine which of the two antithetical ways of life would dominate the world—freedom or despotism. Permeating this consensus was the feeling that this conflict between despotism and democracy was a struggle between the forces of good and evil. This set of "shared images" between the two branches of government meant that conflict between them largely revolved around the problem of means. The ends or objectives of American policy were agreed on; controversy was focused on implementation.

One other critical reason for the success of bipartisanship—a reason not present after the Vietnam War—was the advice and support that the Truman, Eisenhower, and Kennedy administrations enjoyed from a relatively small group of individuals, collectively referred to as the Eastern Establishment.[8] Its members were white, Anglo-Saxon, Protestant, and by profession, largely Wall Street lawyers and investment bankers, with a few international corporation executives and academics, especially from M.I.T. and Harvard. They were generally well off, though not necessarily rich, for wealth was not a membership requirement; Dean Acheson and John Foster Dulles, secretaries of state to Presidents Truman and Eisenhower, respectively, and men who had served the government in important positions before that, were both sons of clergy. All, however, were members of "good" families that had received an elite education at private preparatory schools, most notably Groton (where the ethic of public service was strongly emphasized), and at elite private universities such as Harvard, Yale, and Princeton. Few of them were New Dealers or liberal Democrats; indeed, the most prominent were Republican. In addition to Acheson and Dulles, there were distinguished figures such as Robert A. Lovett, John J. McCloy, Paul Nitze, Thomas K. Finletter, and Averell Harriman (one of the few members who ran for public office and won—the governorship of New York state). Around them were a small number of soldiers, such as Generals Marshall (the architect of the military victory in World War II), Eisenhower (victor in Europe, the first NATO commander, and later president), Bradley (Eisenhower's deputy in Europe during the war and later chairman of the Joint Chiefs of Staff), and diplomats such as George Kennan, Charles Bohlen (the government's chief experts on the Soviet Union), and Allen Dulles (first deputy director and later, director of the CIA), all of whom were nonpartisan.[9]

The core group of lawyers and bankers was essentially New York based. The members were generally from the prestigious Council of Foreign Relations. Also included was the publisher of *Foreign Affairs*, the distinguished quarterly journal.[10] Indeed, the Establishment and the council became synonymous. Council members were distinguished by their internationalist outlook and their rejection of prewar isolationism. They had become active in the period after France's defeat in 1940. At that time the key issue confronting the United States was whether to help Britain, who was fighting Hitler all alone and in jeopardy of invasion, or cling to the traditional policy of isolationism from Europe. These council members took the lead in arranging the famous Destroyer Deal and helped to mobilize public opinion in favor of aid to Britain. Once the United States was in the war, many of the younger members served in the Office of Strategic Services, the CIA's predecessor. After the war, they were united in opposing a return to isolationism. They also opposed any appeasement of Stalin, as the Soviet threat appeared to be growing. They remembered the British–French appeasement of Hitler which, together with American isolationism, they held to be the chief cause of World War II. They were committed to containing the Soviet threat, by force if necessary. Having served Roosevelt, they now remained to help Truman, or to be available if called on. They became "ins" and "outers." Individual members would join an administration, later leave, and then if requested, rejoin the same or another administration in a different capacity, each time occupying a higher position. These individuals were among the postwar presidents' most reliable and capable advisers.

It should be noted that isolationism was still strong on the far left and right after the war. Henry Wallace, vice president during World War II, who abandoned the Democratic party to run for president on his own ticket, was the most prominent of the leftists. He charged that there was no Soviet threat, that Stalin's actions in Eastern Europe were limited to that area and basically defensive, and that U.S. meddling in that area was provoking Moscow. Wallace believed that the United States should stop interfering abroad and concentrate on its domestic and hemispheric affairs. At the other extreme, the conservative wing of the Republican party, dominant in Congress, remained strongly committed to its historic opposition to European involvement. Senator Arthur Vandenberg, an isolationist before Pearl Harbor, an internationalist afterward belonged to a minority in the party. Largely composed of easterners, this group, often referred to as Republican liberals or moderates, supported the Truman foreign policy toward Europe.

Bipartisanship thus served several important functions. First, it ensured that U.S. foreign policy would be centrist, containing both extremes. Second, it ensured a high degree of continuity in policy, despite changes of administrations every four years and possible shifts in the public mood. In 1948, when Truman was expected to lose his bid for the presidency, Vandenberg made it clear to Moscow that a Republican president would be as committed as was Truman to the United States staying in Berlin and that the airlift to the western half of the city, under blockade by the Soviets, would be continued. Third—and most important—in 1952, when conservative Republican Senator Robert Taft was the leading presidential candidate, prominent members of the internationalist wing recruited General Dwight Eisenhower, who became the Republican nominee. Eisenhower was brought in to maintain continuity in foreign policy and to convert the party, out of power since 1933, to a responsible internationalist position. Finally, the cooperation that bipartisanship produced between the executive and legislative branches provided for stability and avoided the kinds of separation of powers conflicts that typically had accompanied domestic policy making.

All of the above reasons favored presidential leadership and Congress' willingness to accept, or at least acquiesce in a secondary—if not at times peripheral—role in foreign policy making. Ironically, therefore, the problem of executive–legislative relations, which many observers in the mid to late 1940s expected would obstruct the formation of a policy responsive to America's international needs, was largely—although not completely—avoided.[11] Bipartisanship, it should be noted, involved the use of various techniques. President Franklin D. Roosevelt had, as early as 1940, named Republicans Henry Stimson and Frank Knox as secretaries of war and of the navy, respectively. By appointing members of the opposition party to high-level government positions, Roosevelt sought to dramatize the idea that foreign policy decision making involved the welfare of the entire nation and transcended any partisan lines. Truman continued the bipartisan foreign policy after World War II. James Forrestal and Robert A. Lovett, both Republicans, served as secretary of defense under Truman; Lovett also served as under secretary of state. Among Republicans appointed by Kennedy were McNamara as secretary of defense, William C. Foster as head of ACDA, John A. McCone as head of the CIA, and Henry Cabot Lodge as ambassador to Saigon. Democrats have followed this pattern of bipartisanship more than Republicans, probably because Democratic presidents have been more concerned with warding off charges of being too "soft" on communist regimes than have Republicans (the charges having come mainly from Republicans). A Democratic administration with Republicans playing a major role in the formation of foreign policy, Democrats believed, would be less susceptible to such attacks.

The appointment of opposition party members was just one method presidents used to gain bipartisan support for their foreign policy. Truman, as well as Acheson, as we know, worked closely with Vandenberg, particularly during 1947–1948, when the Republicans controlled Congress. The White House openly brought Congress into the decision-making process on foreign policy. The Marshall Plan and the establishment of NATO probably marked the high points of congressional involvement in foreign policy making. Truman pursued a bipartisan foreign policy not only because he believed that the international stakes were extremely high and that they transcended partisan grounds, but also because his party simply did not have the strength in Congress to adopt his proposals without Republican support. In 1947–1948 particularly, cooperation with the Republicans was a necessity.

In this respect, Republican chief executives also resemble their Democratic counterparts. Eisenhower had to deal with a Democratic Congress during six of his eight years in the White House, and he found Senate Majority Leader Lyndon B. Johnson's support of his foreign policy more dependable than that of his own party leaders. Democrats have generally been more cohesive on foreign policy votes in Congress than have Republicans. Furthermore, Eisenhower's dealings with his own party majority in 1953–1954 were rather strained. Senator Robert Taft (R-Ohio) was Eisenhower's first majority leader; Taft had been Eisenhower's main competitor for the 1952 Republican nomination, and the two men sharply disagreed on certain foreign policy questions. Following Taft's death in 1953, the president received only slightly more support from Majority Leader William Knowland (R-Calif.), who had presidential ambitions of his own.

In 1953, the bipartisan foreign policy of more than a decade was almost upset by the efforts of Republican Senator John W. Bricker (Ohio). Bricker wanted to limit severely the president's authority to conduct foreign policy by amending the Constitution to prohibit the executive from entering into any agreement that committed American troops to any foreign conflict without specific congressional approval. Knowland, in a rare spirit of cooperation with Eisenhower, agreed to be the floor leader for an administration-sponsored substitute to the Bricker amendment. All three of these Republicans belonged to the right wing of the party. In general, bipartisan foreign policy is accentuated when control of the White House and Congress is split between the two parties.

Indeed, bipartisanship during the Cold War seemed a necessity if the nation were to have any type of coherent foreign policy in a situation of divided control. When one party controls both the executive and legislative branches, as occurred in 1949–1955 and 1961–1969, arguments over foreign policy may increase because bipartisan support is no longer strictly necessary. Conversely, when the opposition controls Congress, it may well be reluctant to oppose the president outright, for he can then accuse it of subordinating the nation's interests to partisan politics and advantage. Yet a president cannot be sure in advance from which direction criticism will come. Eisenhower received the bulk of his criticism from fellow Republicans, Johnson from other Democrats. Kennedy and Truman, on the other hand, found their own parties more united in their support and the opposition split.

Partisanship and Domestic Politics in Foreign Policy: The Example of U.S.–Asian Policy

One exception to this largely bipartisan Cold War consensus ultimately developed: American policy in Asia. Its occurrence was a constant reminder of what could happen to U.S. foreign policy in a situation of congressional assertiveness and partisan rivalry, for its effects on policy was twofold: (1) to transform U.S. policy in Asia into a rigid anti-Communist Chinese mold, deepen Sino–American enmity and delay until 1972 a reconciliation between the two countries. From the early 1960s on, they had shared a common interest in containing the Soviet Union; and (2) to help precipitate the tragic American intervention in Vietnam. Whether Vietnam was avoidable is debatable; what is not debatable is that congressional pressures, and the anticipation of such pressures by Presidents Kennedy and Johnson, made Vietnam inevitable.

Since presidents run for office, wish to be reelected, or want successors elected who will keep control of the White House in their party, foreign policy cannot be divorced from domestic politics. This is not to say that foreign policy positions are adopted only, or primarily for, domestic political reasons, but it does say that the last may, to varying degrees, depending on the president and international and domestic circumstances, influence the conduct of the nation's international behavior.

Nowhere was this more clearly demonstrated than in America's post-World War II Asian policy.[12] After three defeats of Republican presidential nominees in 1940, 1944, and 1948—elections in which the Republicans were led by candidates from the moderate-liberal eastern wing of their party—Republican conservatives felt that only a presidential candidate from their wing of the party could regain control of the White House. A conservative candidate would give the country (to quote the 1964 Republican nominee) "a choice, not an echo." Since the party of Herbert Hoover and the Depression was hardly likely to attract a popular majority on domestic issues, foreign policy became their target. The collapse of Nationalist China in 1949 presented one such opportunity. Until then the Republicans had supported containment in Europe and had not been very critical of U.S. policy toward China. But when Nationalist China disintegrated because of its war weariness, corruption, inefficiency, and brutality and the country "fell" to the Communists, the loss was exploited by Republican conservatives and led to vicious attacks on Democrats. China, it was charged, had been sold out; the administration had "coddled communism" and "appeased" the Kremlin; Communists and "Communist dupes" in the State Department and other high places in government—whether they had infiltrated or been appointed by Roosevelt or Truman—had betrayed an ally and friend as well as their own country. China, in brief, had not fallen because the Nationalists had been incompetent or because Communist morale, organization, and fighting ability had been superior; it was "lost" because of a deliberate conspiracy within the Democratic administration to lose Nationalist China. These charges of a deliberate betrayal and conspiracy within the U.S. government are still associated with its principal proponent, Senator Joseph R. McCarthy (R-Wisc.), even though other leading Republican figures like then Senator Nixon were also involved.

The results of these vicious and continuing attacks had profound consequences for U.S. policy. They particularly affected the Democrats whenever they controlled the White House. To avoid further charges of betrayal or of selling out allies, they were disposed to preempt such a charge with policies that tended toward strong anticommunism, military intervention, and (until Jimmy Carter) no diplomatic recognition of Communist China. Thus, during the Korean War, once the North Koreans had been driven back to the 38th parallel where they had begun their attack on South Korea, an end to the war based on the prewar status quo was attacked as appeasement by Republicans. Undoubtedly, such attacks on a solution short of total victory influenced the Truman administration's decision to advance into North Korea. Its neighbor, Communist China, seeing American armies march toward its frontier, then intervened and enlarged the war. When the Korean War began in 1950, the Republicans exacted a price from the Democrats for political support and domestic unity: the protection of the island of Formosa (Taiwan), to which the Nationalist leader Chiang Kai-shek had fled. Thus, the United States, which had finally washed its hands of Chiang and his losing cause in January 1950, had, in effect, reintervened in that civil war by June. No wonder the new China, seeing the United States protect the rival claimant to legitimate authority over all of China, and American armies advancing toward its borders, defined the United States as its enemy and intervened to protect itself. This intervention embittered U.S.–Chinese relations for two decades and played into the hands of those opposing any reconciliation.

One can only speculate about whether the Chinese intervention in the Korean War, the escalation of the hostilities, and the subsequent rancorous Sino–American relationship could have been avoided had the United States had its own diplomatic representatives in China. Chinese warnings of intervention if the United States advanced toward the Korea–China frontier were dismissed in Washington as a bluff. Would American personnel in China not have told Washington that these warnings had to be taken seriously? If one cannot argue with certainty that two costs of American nonrecognition of the People's Republic were the intense fighting in Korea and the political alienation of the two countries, there is much less uncertainty that two *real* costs were the Vietnam War and the failure to recognize and exploit the Sino–Soviet dispute by the late 1950s. Instead, even as late as the early to middle 1960s, any moves toward the diplomatic recognition of the People's Republic of China were politically dangerous—indeed, for the Democrats, suicidal. Not surprisingly, without U.S. personnel in China, the differences between the Soviet Union and China were often dismissed as tactical rather than fundamental, and North Vietnam viewed as essentially a tool of an expansionist oppressive China. Hanoi was not understood to have any degree of independence or nationalism outside the orbits of both Moscow and Peking. Surely, American observers in Peking would have known better and so advised the U.S. government. The Vietnam War may thus have been one of the highest prices the United States paid for the congressional hard-line attitude toward recognition of Peking.

The decision to intervene with U.S. military forces in Vietnam was made by President Johnson. He did so because by early 1965 U.S. options regarding the fate of South Vietnam had run out. His predecessors had stalled and done only what each had judged necessary to prevent the fall of South Vietnam to the Communists. For each postwar president, increasing involvement in Indochina was calculated as *less* costly domestically than doing nothing and writing it off as an unwinnable situation in the long run. In the context of American domestic politics and a government characterized by a separation of powers, the acceptance of defeat was believed to be unacceptable. The costs of nonintervention in the loss of congressional and public support were measured as exceeding the cost of intervention. The basic rule was "Don't lose Indochina." As Daniel Ellsberg summed up this imperative for each White House incumbent: "This is a bad year for me to lose Vietnam to communism."[13] Thus, each time the possibility of disaster stared an administration in the face, it escalated the involvement and its commitment to *not* losing Vietnam.

Note the negative nature of the goal: to prevent a disaster. It was hoped that if they could not win, the North Vietnamese would eventually desist. Even before the French defeat in 1954, the Truman administration, by the time of the Korean War, was sending aid to help the French and prevent a Communist victory. The Eisenhower administration, while not intervening militarily, talked a great deal in public about the strategic importance of Vietnam, raised the U.S. financial contribution to the French conduct of the war, and organized and supported the new anti-Communist Diem government in Saigon politically, economically, and militarily. The Kennedy administration fortified this commitment with U.S. military "advisers" and tacitly consented to the South Vietnamese military's overthrow of the increasingly despotic and ineffective Diem regime. Hence the link was provided between the United States and the U.S.-encouraged military government in Saigon, which Washington hoped could conduct the war more effectively than its predecessor. But it was Johnson who sent in the military to prevent the collapse of South Vietnam. The intervention was the logical culmination of the acts of his predecessors; with the exception of Eisenhower, none of them had had to make a decision about the use of force in Vietnam to prevent Communist domination. Johnson did; he could not avoid it. Each of Johnson's predecessors was responsible for an increasing commitment and escalation in Vietnam; but if each one was an architect of intervention, each was also a "part, and prisoner of the larger political system that fed on itself, trapping all its participants in a war they could not afford to lose and were unable to win quickly."[14]

Why was it that charges of appeasement from the opposition party made it impossible to recognize the People's Republic after its birth, negotiate with it on a continuing basis on outstanding issues, and later exploit China's quarrel with the Soviet Union? Why was American diplomacy frozen into a rigid anti-Communist posture that finally led the nation into the quagmire of Vietnam? Because if nation X collapses, a president lays himself open to political attack by the opposition party. One of the resulting casualties may be his prestige and reputation. For a man who has sought the presidency, worked and sacrificed for it, and perhaps long dreamed about it, a major failure is a blow to the strong ego that drove him to the top and made him believe that he could be a successful president. Even after they leave office, presidents are not forgotten; they become immortals because their heads appear on postage stamps, and their records go into the history books. So major political criticisms of alleged failure that might endanger their reputations, so to speak, are not desirable. To paraphrase Johnson, he was not going to be the first president in American history to lose a war.

But more than personal prestige is at stake for any president. He has to be concerned with his own reelection or, if he does not run again, his successor's election. In a democracy, the president's focus on his own political fortunes and those of his party cannot be neglected; to suggest that there is something immoral about such considerations is to ignore how U.S. politics works. Even if the public does not "punish" the president at the polls for the "loss" of country X, the president's calculations about the possible electoral impact of such a setback are understandable. Of crucial importance is what presidents believe might happen. Laurence Radway has said that "American incumbents tend to overinsure against even a remote possibility of defeat. They can be sobered to the point of paranoia by the realization that quite a few congressional elections and fully 50 percent of all presidential elections since World War II have been decided by only a handful of votes."[15]

Closely related is another cost: the president's domestic program. The fall of China, followed by the Korean War, helped slow Truman's Fair Deal, which was followed by a Democratic defeat in 1952. Kennedy's perceived setbacks in Laos, Cuba (Bay of Pigs), and Berlin at the time the Berlin Wall was built hurt his chances of achieving his New Frontier. Johnson did not want to jeopardize his Great Society program but also did not want to be tagged as the president who "lost Indochina" as Truman had "lost China." Until 1966, he was able to convince Congress to give him both social spending and military escalation in Vietnam.

Despite frequent invocations of "bipartisanship" in the postwar era, an administration's foreign policies have been fair game for attack. Thus a loss of a China or Vietnam or other countries was portrayed as a serious blow to U.S. interests in other areas. No wonder, confronted by such electoral pressures and partisan attacks, the president calculates that tough foreign policy postures, including intervention or nonrecognition of an "evil" government, are preferable to more accommodating and noninterventionist postures, and frequently will cost *less* politically at home. Even before congressional or partisan pressures are exercised, the mere anticipation of such pressures will have a prenatal effect on the president's conduct of foreign policy, leading to rigid policies ranging from the pretense that Nationalist China's government on the island of Taiwan was still the government of all of China to the escalation of U.S. involvement in South Vietnam. During both of the limited wars the United States has fought in Asia—Korea and Vietnam—Truman and Johnson felt that they were pressured from the right to escalate even further. It has been said with great perceptiveness that Congress, like the Strategic Air Command, possesses both the power of deterrence to prevent the president from doing what Congress feels he should not do (such as recognizing the new regime in Communist China) and the threat of "massive retaliation" if he does what Congress wants him not to do (such as lose South Vietnam, which Congress in the early-middle 1960s was as much opposed to as the president).*

By contrast, conservative presidents were able to withstand domestic pressures

---

* Even in areas other than Asia, presidents are susceptible to doing whatever is necessary to avoid such political attacks. Thus, after becoming president, John Kennedy discovered the CIA plans for the Bay of Pigs operation. He felt uneasy about the feasibility of the operation but proceeded anyway lest he subsequently be accused of weakness and cowardice when compared to his predecessor, Eisenhower, who had conceived of the operation and presumably would have carried it out (or left that to his heir apparent, Richard Nixon). Similarly, when, in 1965, "pro-Castro communists" were allegedly involved with the opposition in an attempted overthrow of the Dominican Republic's right-wing military-supported government, Lyndon Johnson intervened. The Democrats had to avoid the accusation of having allowed "another Cuba" in the hemisphere.

for intervention and escalation (although they might also do so for international reasons) and could meet and negotiate with Communists. Thus Eisenhower could sign a Korean peace treaty based on the *status quo ante bellum,* which Truman had been unable to do. Confronted by the possible collapse of the French position in Indochina in 1954, Eisenhower threatened intervention but then decided against it, and no one accused him of a sellout. In 1955, he became the first Cold War president to meet the Soviet leaders and was not labeled "pro-Communist" for so doing. Nixon, while escalating the air war in Vietnam, could bring U.S. ground forces out and eventually disengage the United States from that war. Above all, he initiated a détente with Moscow to negotiate seriously over a whole range of issues, including strategic arms limitation, and he began the American rapprochement with Peking. The last, particularly, would have been impossible under a more liberal president. More conservative presidents, immune to attacks from the right of appeasement and coddling communism, have far greater flexibility in the conduct of foreign policy.

Not that they are immune to such attacks. To protect himself from the right wing of his own party, Eisenhower resorted to tough talk of "liberation," "unleashing Chiang," and "massive retaliation." Initially, he permitted Senator Joseph McCarthy (R-Wis.) a free hand in his general witch hunt for alleged security risks in the State Department, the U.S. Information Agency, and the army, among other institutions of government. Eisenhower also allowed congressional Republican leaders in the Senate occasionally to constrain his foreign policy options. Even in Indochina, although Eisenhower did not intervene there in 1954, neither did he disengage the United States. Rather, he substituted an American presence for that of France; American dollars, military equipment, and men to train South Vietnamese forces flowed to the new country, and the SEATO alliance was formed to permit unilateral U.S. intervention if it failed to deter future "communist aggression." Eisenhower, in Gelb and Betts' neat summation, "kept America out of war, and he kept America in Vietnam."[16]

Similarly, when Eisenhower's former vice president, Nixon, came to office in 1969 at a time of growing disillusionment with anticommunism as a rigid foreign policy, he made the initial moves toward opening relations with China secretly and presented his trip as a fait accompli so that any opposition would not have time to organize itself. And the reality of the final withdrawal from Vietnam and the peace negotiations were well disguised by the heavy bombing of North Vietnam, including a pounding of Hanoi by B-52s during the 1972 Christmas season. Even Nixon and Kissinger were haunted by the fear of another right-wing, appeasement-type of attack at home if they "sold out" in Vietnam. It is surely a devastating comment on executive–legislative relations and American political institutions that the overture to China, the prerequisite for the détente of the 1970s, could probably not have been accomplished through normal diplomatic channels. From the time he entered government, Kissinger's secretive, closely held style of making policy was often condemned for creating confusion and low morale—if not bad policy—in the bureaucracy. However, who can doubt that without it, the new and strategic American–Chinese relationship could not have been achieved when it was? Another critical commentary is that a conservative administration was fearful of attacks from its own party's right, in and out of Congress. Thus, one reason for the Christmas bombing was to pre-empt such attacks. The United States had to disguise its leaving of Vietnam with an act of toughness.

What Has Happened to Executive–Legislative Relations Since Vietnam?

Before Vietnam, Congress, public opinion, and the press had all looked to the president for leadership in foreign policy. He and his leading foreign policy advisers defined the situation facing the United States, the key issues, and what the nation should do about them. Bipartisanship, with the one significant exception of Asian policy, ensured the president's ability to mobilize legislative support. Public opinion was also supportive. All in all, presidents until Vietnam took and held initiative and leadership while public opinion not only supported their decisions and actions, but gave them a high degree of freedom and maneuverability. Rarely, as noted earlier (Chapter 1), was a president defeated because of foreign policy issues, unlike the situation surrounding domestic policies.

After Vietnam the bipartisan consensus disintegrated. The fact that the two presidents who came to power following the collapse of South Vietnam in 1975 were "outsiders," governors who ran against Washington and were inexperienced in foreign policy, is itself revealing. The collapse of bipartisan foreign policy making was strikingly embodied in Carter's and Reagan's personal visions of what U.S. policy should be.[17] Not only did Carter denounce past policy as an over-reaction to an exaggerated Soviet threat, but he specifically condemned it for its lack of morality. In the name of anticommunism, Carter believed, the United States had linked itself with too many right-wing dictatorial regimes. Carter's vision of morality led him to reject the SALT II ceilings on weapons which Kissinger had almost finished negotiating, but Ford had put off a decision about until after his expected reelection. As the newly elected president, Carter thought these ceilings were too high, that they sanctioned the arms race. He was going to seek "real" arms control, that is, very deep arms reductions. The result was a Soviet rejection of the Carter proposals, three more years of negotiations, and a postponement of SALT II until a time when détente was in decline and the president could not mobilize two thirds of the Senate in support of the treaty.

Morality also demanded a concern for human rights. But since Carter could do little to ensure against the violation of human rights in the Soviet Union (his one attempt to denounce Soviet violations delayed the arms control negotiations, whose successful conclusion was also demanded by morality), the president enforced the human rights policy on the weaker U.S. allies who were dependent on this country, thus causing turmoil within the nation's various alliances.

Reagan's morality, by contrast, was so intensely anti-Communist that during his initial years in office, he repeatedly and undiplomatically denounced the Soviet leadership. More importantly, he strongly opposed negotiations, especially arms control, with the Soviet Union, seemingly preferring (at least in his rhetoric) confrontation with an enemy he condemned in religious terms as evil and the source of all sin in the world. Carter viewed his predecessor as not having vigorously enough pursued radical arms reduction. Reagan believed his predecessor had not been tough enough on Moscow. The Reagan diplomatic legacy was thus rather bare. Its one outstanding exception—on medium- and short-range missiles in Europe—was the result of a U.S. plan deliberately conceived in such a way that Moscow would reject it, which initially was the case. When, to Washington's surprise, Moscow later turned around and announced its readiness to accept Reagan's offer, the president could hardly say "no." Even more illustrative of Reagan's morality was his personal vision of a strategic defense shield to protect America's population. This shield was to replace the deterrent policy that had given the United States and its allies security and peace for four decades. That policy was now denounced as immoral and bound to break down some day, causing nuclear war. These were the same arguments the antinuclear movement was making at the time.

Apart from these breaks with preceding policies—and, of course, the widespread criticism in Congress and society about superior presidential wisdom and expertise in foreign affairs—an additional critical change in the post-Vietnam period was the decline of the Establishment's influence and the usurpation of its role by think tanks and their staffs, which have been called the *professional elites.* Many of these think tanks, often also referred to as *beltway bandits,* provide basically technical services, especially for the Pentagon. Living on government money, they are concerned with everything from personnel policies to management and logistical problems to seeking ways of joining high technology to weapons systems. Our focus will remain with those whose preoccupation is strategy and foreign policy, and the shift of power from the former Establishment to these "professional service industries."

This shift was perhaps most aptly symbolized by the attacks on the Council of Foreign Relations. The Establishment, which had supported the containment policy, including the intervention in Vietnam, became divided by the war and lost much of its prestige.[18] Former Secretary of State Henry Kissinger, who had first achieved prominence in his famous book *Nuclear Weapons and Foreign Policy,* sponsored by the council, was rejected in 1981 when he was renominated for the board of directors. During his 1980 campaign for the presidential nomination,

George Bush, a moderate Republican, had resigned his council membership so as not to further alienate his party's conservatives; the resignation no doubt made it easier for Ronald Reagan to choose Bush as his vice presidential running mate. After the Reagan–Bush victory, Republican Senator Jesse Helms' standard question for foreign policy appointees was whether they were council members; not being a member became a test of the ideological purity of a true conservative. (The council was allegedly too liberal.) This type of reaction to the council was not limited to the right wing. In Jimmy Carter's campaign for the presidency, his close adviser and future White House chief of staff, Hamilton Jordan, stated that he would not serve in an administration that appointed council members to leading positions. Later, when Cyrus Vance became the secretary of state and Zbigniew Brzezinski the NSA, Jordan suppressed his concerns and stayed on, but the council's elitism and reputed conservatism from the left side of the political spectrum clearly made it a target from this direction too. The later Vance–Brzezinski disputes over policy were symptomatic of the council's inner divisions. Its pre-Vietnam reputation was one of being tough-minded and hard-nosed, but the war transformed many members from hawks on foreign policy issues to doves; those who remained hawks like Brzezinski became a minority. *Foreign Affairs* articles reflected this shift in the middle to late 1970s.

The Establishment's prestige and prominence as a centrist organization were now taken over by the professional elites on the left and right.[19] Foreign policy had become increasingly complex and specialized, requiring expertise in topics ranging from arms control to currency exchange, from trade issues to population control. Full-time experts were needed; as the new "ins" and "outs," they tended to identify more with either the Democrats or Republicans. While Establishment figures usually were Republicans, they served both Democratic and Republican administrations; in fact, since the Democrats were more vulnerable to attacks for being "soft" on foreign policy, they were more visible when Democrats controlled the executive. The new elites were not only full-time professionals as political, military, or economic experts, but they were more ideologically inclined and loyal. They gained their prominence—as council members Kissinger and Brzezinski had done—by being university professors at the right schools (mainly Ivy League, but no longer as exclusively as before). They wrote articles and books, gaining their fame this way and thereby becoming consultants to government agencies and making contacts, largely in the Boston–New York–Washington area.

Both Kissinger and Brzezinski were immigrants. Kissinger became close to Nelson Rockefeller, governor of New York and a liberal presidential aspirant in the Republican party; it was Rockefeller who recommended Kissinger for the NSA's position to President-Elect Nixon. Brzezinski latched onto David Rockefeller, Nelson's brother, and became a member of the Trilateral Commission, which was organized to promote closer U.S.–European–Japanese ties; while serving on the commission, Brzezinski, who also wrote a column for *Newsweek,* met Governor Carter of Georgia, another member. Less-famous figures followed basically the same path. The Establishment shunned publicity; they had access in Washington and used their influence quietly. The new professional elites had to gain public visibility first, then promote themselves to find their political connections and acquire influence. This required time, patience, push, a large ego, party identification—and often picking the winning candidate even before the primaries.[20] In short, expertise was not enough; being a good combatant was at least as important.

When they were not in an administration, the new professional elites usually returned to a think tank, if they did not (re)join a university faculty, or, on occasion, a Wall Street firm. Rarely did they go into business or law. If they did so to make money, they kept themselves in the limelight with articles and frequent television appearances. They hoped they were "outs" only temporarily. Perhaps the best known think tank, often referred to as the Democrats-in-exile, was the Brookings Institution. "Its principal purposes are to aid in the development of sound public policies and to promote public understanding of issues of national importance."[21] A moderately liberal, slightly left-of-center organization, Brookings is staffed by experts who publish actively. One of its strong suits is the defense-arms control field, in which it offers considerable and alternative expertise outside of the Pentagon. The Republican equivalent, slightly right of center, is the American Enterprise Institute, although it publishes less than Brookings and focuses more on helping Republican legislators bolster their arguments against their usually more numerous Democratic colleagues. A more actively liberal institution is the Carnegie Endowment for International Peace, which publishes the quarterly *Foreign Policy* journal. Many of its editors and contributors became members of the Carter administration, devotees of interdependence and "world order" politics, and critical of the power politics outlook. A very ideologically conservative and Republican organization is the Heritage Foundation, which was to sponsor General Daniel Graham's High Frontier advocacy of strategic defense, one of the early, although not the most influential, forces in what was to become President Reagan's Strategic Defense Initiative (SDI) or Star Wars. A prestigious conservative center for foreign-defense policy expertise is Georgetown University's Center for Strategic and International Studies, among whose members are such luminaries as Kissinger, Brzezinski, former CIA Director and Secretary of Defense James Schlesinger and other distinguished "outs," mainly Republicans.

Almost all these institutions hold regular conferences and take a generally scholarly approach to issues. Interestingly, many Democrats—often officials in past administrations—who remained faithful to the containment policy and continued to place priority on the U.S.–Soviet rivalry (instead of favoring an interdependence policy) now found new outlets for their growing criticisms, especially of the Carter administration. Calling themselves *neoconservatives,* these people, often former liberals, finding themselves without a voice in the Democratic party, formed a lobby, the Committee on the Present Danger, and regularly published their critiques in *Commentary,* a monthly magazine historically devoted to Jewish affairs. Many of the committee's members and *Commentary*'s authors were later to join the Reagan administration.

These think tanks are all Washington based. While there are some think tanks outside of Washington, such as the conservative Institute for Foreign Policy Analysis in Cambridge, Massachusetts, and the Hoover War and Peace Institute in Stanford, California, most are in the nation's capital because this is where most of their consumers are and where they can gain influence and hopefully power by staffing an administration. These and other less well-known think tanks illustrate the fragmentation of the pre-Vietnam consensus while simultaneously ensuring that a variety of views about the role and purposes of U.S. foreign policy will continue to be aired. Administrations may at election time move toward the proverbial center of American politics, but the experts who increasingly identify ideologically with one party or the other often take sharply contrasting views of, for instance, the desirability and character of an arms control agreement, how much emphasis should be placed on human rights in American policy, or the importance of Nicaragua to U.S. security interests.

The greater "ideologicalization" of foreign policy issues is more basically a reflection of the shift from bipartisan agreement to a more partisan stance on foreign policy between the two parties, as well as within each party[22] in the post-Vietnam period. When President Nixon resigned and Gerald Ford assumed the office and ran for the presidency in 1976, Ronald Reagan challenged and nearly beat an incumbent president in the primaries, an almost unheard of occurrence when a party controls the highest office in the land. Reagan attacked his own party's president for his pursuit of the Nixon–Kissinger détente with the Soviet Union. Ford dropped the word *détente* entirely from his vocabulary during the primary season and told his secretary of state (Kissinger, whom he had already removed as NSA) to maintain a low profile until the nomination was his. Ford, in fact, ran on a platform that included a plank inserted by the Reagan conservatives repudiating his détente policy! After Ford's defeat at the polls, the conservatives captured the party and the moderate or liberal Republicans, who had played such a key role in the 1940s and 1950s, now became a shrinking minority as the party swung to the right. It had been the conservatives who, in the days of bipartisanship, had dominated the congressional Republican party. From 1946 to 1952 they had tolerated the liberal wing's support for Truman's containment policy. Only after their fifth consecutive loss of the presidency in 1948 did they reject what was now called *me-tooism* and try to capture the presidential nomination for one of their own kind, Senator Taft. Defeated again as the moderates continued to control the Republican presidential party with the nomination of General Dwight Eisenhower, a popular hero, the conservatives finally achieved their first success in 1964 with the nomination of Senator Barry Goldwater. After his defeat, former Vice President and 1960 Republican standard-bearer Richard Nixon was renominated in 1968. Conservatives were not to forgive him in the late 1970s and early 1980s for what they considered his naiveté at best, and betrayal at worst, in adopting a policy of détente with the Soviet Union.

Indeed, the conservatives who during the Truman years had largely clung to their historic nationalist/isolationist stance and opposed the Democrats' alliance with the states of Western Europe and intervention across the Atlantic to contain Soviet power, now ironically adopted the liberal Democrats' Cold War policies. Labeled Cold War internationalism or conservative interventionism, the Republicans gave priority to the East–West struggle. In their perception the central conflict remained the one with the Soviet Union; national security was still the key consideration; the chief threat to the United States was Soviet expansionism and growing military might; and the motivating drives behind this expansionism were Communist ideology and Soviet totalitarianism. In short, the Republican party in the post-Nixon/Ford period shifted to an antidétente and promilitary orientation until the late Reagan years. Kissinger's prodétente and proarms control perspective was anathema to the conservatives. This explained not only why Kissinger could not get an appointment in the Reagan administration, but it was one reason why his former deputy in the NSC, Alexander Haig, was probably doomed from the start when Reagan appointed him secretary of state.

The Democrats too had flip-flopped from Cold War liberalism to post-Cold War internationalism or liberal internationalism. Presidents Truman and Kennedy/Johnson had pursued vigorous anti-Communist and interventionist policies. These policies reflected the liberal Democrats' basic commitments to individual dignity and freedom, racial equality, and social justice. These were not only considered good values for America at home, they were to be promoted overseas as well. Communism and totalitarianism were the antitheses of these values; therefore, Soviet expansion had to be resisted. It was precisely because the Democratic party—certainly the presidential party—was liberal that it initiated the containment policy and became strongly interventionist. After Vietnam, this stance was condemned and Cold War liberalism became a term of condemnation because of its anti-Communist and militarist character. As the Cold Warriors became a small minority that now found their voice largely outside of the Democratic party, as in the Committee on the Present Danger (Chapter 5) and *Commentary* magazine, post-Cold War liberal Democrats now divorced themselves from the party's earlier hard-line stance.

The new liberal internationalism viewed the nations of the world as increasingly interdependent. The key issues were social/economic/humanitarian: overpopulation, hunger, poverty, ill health, ignorance, lack of resources, and environmental issues. The Democrats' chief concern was not the East–West axis, but the North–South axis (which was also consistent with the party's commitment to the New and Fair Deals, that is, welfare issues at home). National security issues were regarded as subordinate to the transnational problems confronting all of humanity. The Democrats especially identified themselves with the less-developed countries' (LDCs) demands in the 1970s for economic justice: they called for a new international economic order between the West and the LDCs. The Democrats were also opposed to the status quo within the LDCs because it was often associated with American-supported, politically repressive regimes. Wanting to be on "the right side" of history, the party favored social change, called *national liberation*. Liberal internationalism did not ignore the Soviet Union, which was considered merely a traditional great power, not a militant revolutionary state. Russian expansion was seen mainly as defensive, the product of a deep sense of insecurity produced by frequent past invasions (and defeats). American–Soviet arms control, plus nuclear nonproliferation, was therefore desirable to help defuse the American–Soviet conflict and to take a first step toward a new world order.

The Democrats' main thrust was antimilitary, anti-interventionist, and pro-human rights. Vietnam had seared the party's conscience. "No more Vietnams" became the party's motto whether the issue was Angola or Nicaragua. While the party recognized that in principle military power remained an instrument of policy, in practice it abhorred the use of violence and opposed its use in any actual situation anywhere, just as fervently as the Founding Fathers had counseled against "entangling alliances." When Reagan invaded the tiny Caribbean island of Grenada in 1983 to overthrow a pro-Cuban and pro-Soviet regime, leading Democrats both in and out of Congress immediately voiced their concern and opposition until this operation gained widespread popular approval, leaving them little choice but to join in praise of Reagan's action. In 1988, Dukakis, who had been critical of Grenada, was weakened by what was widely seen as his inexperience and softness on defense; Bush had experience and claimed to be tough on defense.

These different post-Vietnam Republican–Democratic views of the world, with one party swinging more to the right and one more to the left, emerged fully after the Nixon administration. Characterizing belief systems by outlining the differences between them may somewhat exaggerate actual partisan differences; nevertheless, these characterizations do represent genuine differences. (In fact, there was a third position, called *semiisolationism*. It emphasized that the main threats to the United States were internal ones, such as inflation, unemployment, racial conflict, and so on, and that genuine superpower conflicts of interests were few and could be resolved. According to this view, the Soviet Union represented no genuine threat to the United States, and Soviet fears and insecurities could be assuaged by a friendly United States policy. This position was largely identified with the Reverend Jesse Jackson in the Democratic party.) Interestingly, congressional Republicans had supported the Nixon administration despite its prodétente, although also promilitary (as well as proarms control) outlook. This was due in part, of course, to the fact that the administration was Republican. It can also be explained by noting that while the administration pursued détente it pursued the Vietnam War, refusing to "bug out" despite a great deal of political pressure to do so. By Ford's time, however, the hearts of these congressional Republicans were with Reagan, even if their heads warned them against dumping an incumbent president. Thus, when Carter won and later signed the Strategic Arms Limitation Treaty (SALT II), Republicans in large numbers opposed it despite Ford's and Kissinger's endorsements and the fact that negotiations for it had started with Nixon, who had fathered SALT I. SALT II was now the Democrats' treaty. The same held true for the Panama Canal treaties, concluded during the Carter years.

By contrast, the Democrats favored détente but they opposed Vietnam. Once they were out of office, it became "Nixon's war," although it was Kennedy and Johnson who had militarily intervened in Vietnam. When the war was over, they became more vocal about the Republicans' alleged lack of concern for human rights, as well as their effort to modernize U.S. strategic forces, which was often criticized for provoking a new arms race and being antiarms control. Partisanship now became the order of the day and foreign and defense policies tended to become enmeshed in controversy. Because partisans in both parties were convinced of their rightness, indeed the morality of their particular perspective, these controversies often became tinged by ideological convictions that embittered foreign policy debates in and out of Congress. Policy issues became matters of "right" and "wrong," of "morality" and "immorality."

Public opinion also changed (see Chapter 5).[23] Once rather passive and willing to allow the president to lead while it was quite content to follow, the public had grown increasingly distrustful and suspicious of political leadership. It thus tended to swing from left to right to the other end in response to current concerns and anxieties and could no longer be discounted as in the Cold War days. Whereas bipartisanship had once protected presidents against the extremes on the left and right and volatile changes in the public mood, its decline meant that there was little to prevent wild swings in foreign policy.[24] These changes in party outlooks and public opinion are nowhere more visible than in the Congress, which no longer was willing to play "president knows best."

The President and Congress in the Post-Cold War Era

In short, the relationship between the president and Congress is an ever-changing one. In the 1930s, the Congress was clearly the dominant partner. During World War II and the Cold War the president was supreme. Since Vietnam, the Congress has reasserted itself and sought to restrain the president's conduct of foreign policy lest he get the country involved in another war. This has created the situation many feared in the early postwar years of a president and Congress pulling in different directions, either paralyzing U.S. policy or undermining the possibility of the wise, long-range, and steady course required of a leader of a coalition of nations. This worry was well taken; executive–legislative conflict and partisan differences between Republicans and Democrats were the norm.[25] The peace treaty with Spain at the turn of the century after the United States had emerged on the international stage—for a brief performance, as it turned out—squeaked through by two votes with a majority of Republicans supporting it and the Democrats opposed. The 1919 Versailles peace treaty, which involved U.S. entry into the newly organized League of Nations, went down to defeat in the bitter rivalry between Democratic President Woodrow Wilson and Republican Senate Majority Leader and Chairman of the Senate Foreign Relations Committee Henry Cabot Lodge. Both men, besides disliking each other personally, were also strong partisans. The interwar period was one of isolationism but executive–legislative differences surfaced again even before President Roosevelt began moving to help Britain in 1940. In 1935, Roosevelt barely mobilized enough votes—helped by telephone calls from the postmaster general threatening a cutoff of patronage from recalcitrant Democrats—to defeat the Ludlow amendment 209 to 198, requiring a popular referendum before Congress could declare war.[26] After France's defeat, the president, with the major exception of the Lend-Lease Act, preferred using executive agreements for his policies rather than going to Congress. The reason is obvious. On August 10, 1941, the Congress passed by only one vote the renewal of the Selective Service Act. "In favor were 203 House members (182 Democrats, 21 Republicans); opposed were 202 members (65 Democrats, 133 Republicans). But for a single vote the nation might have been left with an army in dissolution, only a few months before Pearl Harbor."[27] Another historian noted that "fundamentally the close ballot indicated that the American people were not convinced that Germany and Japan truly endangered the security of the United States."[28]

Given this historical pattern, it appears that the twenty years of bipartisanship after 1945 were an exceptional period rather than a norm that must be restored. Only a "clear and present danger" appears to unite the nation and the two branches of government. Otherwise there is conflict. That was, of course, the intention of the Founding Fathers in establishing the separation of powers, a rather ill-termed phrase because the reality is a separation of institutions sharing powers. It is this sharing that produces the sparks.

The Founding Fathers' design was deliberate. They expected institutional conflict. Their aim was to prevent domestic tyranny and ensure individual freedom. The question today is whether an institutional arrangement of checks and balances designed for that purpose is capable of making policy to deal with external threats to American security and prosperity at a time when there is no agreement on what the U.S. role and aims should be in the world, how those goals should be achieved, and at what risk and cost. In any event, the current executive–legislative relationship is probably nearer the norm than the now largely defunct bipartisanship.

The split in the post-Vietnam consensus is also a major cause of today's institutional conflict. Liberal Democrats had earlier been the strongest advocates of presidential preeminence and leadership. First the New Deal and then the vigorous prosecution of the Cold War had led the party to champion executive power. It was conservative Republicans, who had opposed the New Deal and later the European orientation of U.S. foreign policy, who became the spokespersons for a more vigorous Congress that would limit presidential power. The liberal Democratic/conservative Republican reversal on policy after Vietnam also led to a flip-flop on executive–legislative relations. The Republicans, who controlled the White House from 1972 to 88 (with the exception of 1976–80), were now the Cold War party, focusing their attention on the continuing Soviet threat and need for U.S. containment. Thus, they became the champions of presidential leadership. In fact, the Republicans have controlled the presidency for twenty-four of the thirty-six years since Eisenhower. The Democrats, badly hurt by Vietnam and unable to forget it, did not share this perspective and became especially wary of new commitments and any use of force. Since they tended to control at least one of the Houses, if not both, they pressed for a strong congressional role to restrain the conduct of U.S. foreign policy vis-à-vis the Soviet Union. The Democrats have controlled both Houses of Congress for twenty-eight of the thirty-six years since 1952, and at least one House for six more years. Executive–legislative conflict thus reflected more than the institutional prerogatives and sensitivities of the two branches; it also reflected the growing partisanship and ideological gap between the two parties, with each occupying the opposite end of Pennsylvania Avenue.

If post-Vietnam circumstances can be projected backward, it is legitimate to ask whether President Roosevelt would have been able to lead the country to Britain's support in 1940–41. Or would his resort to executive agreements to circumvent restraints imposed by the Congress' strong isolationist sentiment have led to extensive Senate and House hearings and the passage of an amendment constraining the president's leadership? Indeed, had the War Powers Resolution been in place, what could Roosevelt have done? In retrospect, no one quarrels with the fact that Nazi Germany constituted a threat to U.S. security, but in 1939–41 that was not as clear; it was not even taken for granted after France's defeat in 1940 when Britain stood alone.

In Roosevelt's time, one might add, the president could still expand his powers as commander in chief, but by Reagan's time, the Congress had reined the president in. Fearful of what a president might do, Congress had written into law a number of restraints and, as presidents saw it, sought to micromanage his conduct of foreign policy. As the restraints mounted, was the attempted privatization of foreign policy not perhaps inevitable, even if illegal? It might be well to remember that before Reagan, presidents did not hesitate to intervene—especially in this hemisphere—when they deemed U.S. interests to be at stake. Eisenhower acted covertly in Guatemala in 1954; Kennedy acted covertly in Cuba in 1961; and Johnson used the marines in the Dominican Republic in 1965. Reagan could not use overt or covert intervention; the news was soon all over the front pages and the television screen.

The Privatization of Foreign Policy: The Iran–Contra Affair

The scandal that enveloped the Reagan administration in late 1986 was initially likened by many to President Nixon's Watergate debacle. Although the nation clearly was unwilling to go through such a wrenching experience again so soon, President Reagan remained personally popular, even though most Americans thought he was lying about his involvement.[29] Nixon had sought to deal with certain domestic problems, including his 1972 reelection, in extralegal ways by misusing the CIA and other agencies, deceiving Congress, and engaging in efforts to cover up crimes. Collectively, these matters led to the drawing up of the articles of impeachment. At the heart of the resulting impeachment proceedings was the finding that President Nixon had violated the duty of his office that, according to the Constitution, the president "take care that the laws be faithfully executed."

The abuses of power by the Reagan administration were considered more serious and fundamental because of their effects on U.S. foreign policy. Through the National Security Council the White House had organized a "shadow government" that secretly sold arms to Iran to gain the release of six U.S. hostages held in Lebanon in violation of the Arms Export Control Act banning arms shipments to states that sponsor terrorism (which had been applied to Iran by a Reagan executive order). The Reagan administration also violated a requirement to notify Congress' intelligence committees if the president authorized covert arms sales (done only retroactively). It further established a network of private individuals, mostly former government officials, some of rather unsavory reputation (because of their earlier association with Edmund Wilson, who had supplied Libya's Colonel Muammar Qaddafi with terrorist capabilities, including arms and training by former Special Forces personnel),[30] as well as foreign personnel, including Iranian, Saudi, and Israeli arms dealers. It employed these men as agents of the U.S. government to carry out an arms-for-hostages exchange with Iran. It then used some of the profits from this deal to supply arms to the U.S.-organized and supported Contras against the Nicaraguan government. This was done in clear violation of a congressional cutoff of military aid for the Contras from mid-1984 to late 1986. (Indeed, after it became clear that the hostages still held would not be released, the arms sales continued to fund the Contras.) Money for the Contras was solicited from wealthy private individuals in the United States and from foreign governments, thus violating the constitutionally approved method requiring a president to seek approval and funding from the Congress for his policies. As revelations of these activities surfaced in November 1986, the White House and NSA, together with the director of the CIA and the attorney general, attempted a cover-up by constructing a false chronology of events to protect the president by minimizing his role. Incriminating documents were altered and shredded to conceal extralegal covert activities—enough "to fill up half a box car"—as well as smuggled out of their files.

The president himself changed his story about when he first learned of the initial secret shipment of U.S. arms to Iran via Israel in September 1985 and about whether he had authorized it to gain the release of the U.S. hostages. He claimed a loss of memory on this radical shift of policy from his own earlier and repeated insistence that the United States would never deal with terrorists. Reagan denied ever having been told of the Contra diversion. The president's stated unawareness of important details and the factual errors in his public accounts of the Iran affair led the Tower Commission, established by the president to investigate the matter, to be highly critical of his hands-off "management style."* One of its members, former Senator and Secretary of State Edmund Muskie, said that he and his two colleagues on the commission "were all appalled by the absence of the kind of alertness and vigilance to his job and to these policies that one expects of a president."[31] On circumventing the Congress' restrictions on aid to the Contras, the president first asserted that he had obeyed the law and had not solicited funds. As the evidence piled up during the congressional investigation of this matter that Reagan and several members of the NSC staff had done precisely that, he changed his defense and asserted that helping the Contras with private and foreign funds was his idea, that he had been kept fully informed (undoubtedly true for the Contras were his favorite cause), and that the legislative restraints did not apply to him and the NSC staff. In fact, Reagan claimed that the restraints were an unconstitutional encroachment on the president's right to conduct foreign policy.

Yet, throughout the period of Congress' cutoff of military aid, the administration had repeatedly deceived Congress when questions were raised about what it was doing to help the Contras. It never challenged the congressional restrictions in the courts. Reagan had, in fact, signed the law he now claimed he was above! Consistent with that claim, the NSA and others involved with both policies systematically and deliberately lied and deceived not only Congress, but the secretaries of state and defense and other NSC members, in order to keep secret what they were doing to implement what they had every reason to believe were President Reagan's policies.

Reagan became president the day the U.S. hostages, held by Iran for 444 days, were released. From the beginning of his administration he vowed to deal firmly with terrorists, whether sponsored by states like Iran or not. His administration would not bargain with terrorists since that would only encourage further acts of terrorism. But as terrorist actions multiplied throughout the Middle East and

---

* President Reagan appeared to feel relieved by this critical assessment, for it seemed to support his contention that he had been unaware of what was being done in his name. That a president would feel pleased by being publicly told that he was not doing the job expected of a chief executive is a commentary in itself.

Europe—especially in Lebanon, a state disintegrating in civil war—the administration remained passive. These actions included the 1983 blowing up of the U.S. embassy with over 50 lives lost and some months later the blowing up of 241 marines who were in Lebanon as part of an international peacekeeping force. Similar attacks on Israeli and French troops led to quick retaliation on the terrorist camps. But after several more terrorist attacks in which Americans were killed, the United States attacked Libya in response to what was said to be a Libyan-planned attack on a West Berlin discotheque frequented by U.S. service personnel. The president's actions were finally forging a Western consensus on how to deal with the terrorists. Up to this time Western Europe had been reluctant to act against Libya because it was economically profitable to maintain good relations with Libya and because of the fear that Qaddafi would retaliate on their territory, not in the United States. Following a wave of bomb explosions in Paris and a reported Syrian-sponsored attempt to plant a bomb on an Israeli airliner in London, Europeans, who had already begun to watch Libyan personnel at their people's bureaus or embassies more closely, adopted a British plan for an arms embargo and diplomatic sanctions against Syria.

Apparently because the president was deeply moved by the plight of the U.S. hostages taken by Iranian-sponsored terrorist groups in Lebanon, the administration approached Iran to gain their release (the midterm election in 1986 may have increased the incentive for an early release). Iran, at war with Iraq since 1979, needed spare parts for its largely American military equipment purchased by the Shah's pro-American regime (which had preceded the Ayatollah Khomeini's militantly anti-American government). While the president was later to explain the U.S. shipment of arms in geopolitical terms—as an approach to so-called *moderates* with whom the United States could, after Khomeini's death, establish better U.S.–Iranian relations—a memorandum written by CIA Director William Casey showed that this was a rationalization to be used as a cover story if the hostage swap were discovered. The United States was concerned not with strategic goals, but with the hostages' release.* In fact, NSA Robert McFarlane and NSC staffer Lt. Col. Oliver North accompanied one shipment of arms, bringing their Iranian hosts not only antitank missiles, but a Bible signed by Ronald Reagan and a cake in the shape of a key (to unlock the door of U.S.–Iranian friendship). When his hosts did not release all the hostages, McFarlane recommended ending the exchange. (The secretary of defense, when first informed, contemptuously remarked that the whole idea was too absurd even to comment on.) Shortly thereafter McFarlane resigned as NSA, but the White House went ahead with additional shipments of arms.

---

* The original "finding" authorizing shipment, signed by the president only after the arms shipment had started, stated this purpose only. But this original copy has disappeared and in at least two subsequent findings, the broader reasons to disguise the arms for hostage trade were stated: the geopolitical "strategic initiative," to establish relations with "moderate elements" and so on. The initial cover-up got lost in the later congressional hearing, which focused more on the diversion of funds for the Contras and on whether the president knew about it.

U.S. interest in continuing to deal with the Iranians was triggered by the fact that the more cash that was brought in by the arms transaction, the more could be diverted to the Contras. In any case, only one hostage was released after each of three shipments. But three more U.S. hostages were seized in Lebanon! It was clear that the administration's decision to trade arms for hostages gave the terrorists an incentive to replace the ones released. Depressed by the failure to gain the hostages' release and feeling in general that he had let the president down, former NSA McFarlane attempted suicide.

Quite apart from not gaining all the hostages' freedom and violating U.S. laws, the Reagan administration exposed itself as hypocritical and undermined its own tough antiterrorist public posture of never surrendering to terrorist blackmail. It sanctioned the usual European approach of bartering for hostages and undermined the British effort to lead Europe to adopt Reagan's publicly stated position of not dealing with terrorists. Arms for Iran violated not only the administration's prior proclamation of neutrality in the war but, if it helped the Iranians to defeat the Iraqis, would endanger all the Persian Gulf oil sheikdoms, which controlled two thirds of the non-Communist world's oil reserves (a key reason why in 1987 the United States committed itself to naval protection of some Kuwaiti oil tankers). An Iranian victory might also spread Islamic extremism to Egypt and Jordan, as well as to the Shiite Muslims in southern Lebanon on Israel's northern frontier, thereby endangering moderate pro-American Arab regimes and placing Israel in greater jeopardy (which is why questions might at least have been raised in the NSC about Israel's policy of helping the Ayatollah's Iran against Iraq). In return for the arms, the administration had not even gained concessions on terrorism or the war.

It was hard to understand how the president could place the lives of a few individuals over America's broader and longer-run national interests. At the very least it jeopardized the nation's and his own authority, reputation, and credibility at home and abroad. To trade arms in a war in which it is against America's national interest for Iran to win, and to do so in a way that would encourage further hostage taking—all this with a regime that had only recently humiliated and mocked the United States and blown up over 200 American marines and diplomats in Lebanon—raised serious questions about the president's judgment and competence and the whole manner in which the Reagan administration made policy. The Iran decisions appear to have been made by the president and the director of the CIA, with the support of the NSA, first McFarlane and then Poindexter, over the protests of the secretaries of state and defense, who were then cut out of the decision-making process. The government's experts on Iran in the State Department, Defense Department, and the CIA were never brought into the process to evaluate whether the arms deal would gain the release of the hostages and strengthen the so-called *moderates* in the Iranian government—if they existed. Nor were any outside experts consulted about whether the shipment of arms was indeed a sound way to move toward the laudable objective of improving U.S.–Iranian relations and helping to bring about an Iranian–Iraqi peace, an additional justification stated by the president for his move when it was embarrassingly revealed. Iran's leaders—radicals, not moderates—still virulently denounced the United States, continued to sponsor and finance the groups carrying out terrorist actions against the United States in Lebanon, and were in fact using the hostages to manipulate the U.S. approach for their own purpose of acquiring arms. In the secretary of state's words "we got taken to the cleaners." The Reagan administration's behavior in these circumstances could only enhance their contempt for the "Great Satan," as they called America, and incite them further to undermine U.S. interests throughout the Middle East–Persian Gulf area rather than moderate or change their behavior. The White House officials running the Iran operation clearly knew little about Iranian politics and personalities. Good intentions thoughtlessly pursued, subject to no checks and balances, could only end in disaster—and did.

For the administration, the revelation of its dealing with Iran was bad enough since there probably was no country—not even the Soviet Union—more despised by American public opinion. Even worse, however, was the additional revelation that some of the profits from the arms sales to Iran had been diverted illegally to fund the Contras in Nicaragua. From its first days in office, the Reagan administration had focused on what it perceived and defined as the Communist threat in this hemisphere. In El Salvador, the government was fighting against left-wing guerrillas and the administration contended that Nicaragua was transmitting Soviet and other Eastern bloc weapons shipped via Cuba to the rebels. It therefore organized the rag-tag remnants of former American-supported dictator Anatasio Somoza's National Guard into a Contra guerrilla force, ostensibly to pressure Nicaragua's Sandinista government to halt these arms deliveries. In reality, the aim was to overthrow the Marxist Sandinista regime. Having come into power in a genuinely popular revolution against Somoza, the Sandinistas, once in control of the government, squeezed its former partners (the Roman Catholic Church, the business community, trade unions, intellectuals, student groups and others) out of the coalition. It became increasingly authoritarian in its rule at home and shifted toward the Soviet Union in foreign policy, betraying its previous promises of political democracy, a mixed economy, and nonalignment in world politics. The Reagan administration, admittedly, stated that its goal for Nicaragua was free elections. But once in power the Sandinistas, already convinced that they represented the popular will, were hardly likely to allow such "bourgeois" practices, especially as they began to alienate segments of the population with their policies of economic austerity, political suppression, Miskito Indian resettlement, and military conscription. The administration, determined to prevent a "second Cuba" in this hemisphere and the "first Cuba" on the mainland, and convinced that the Sandinistas, committed to a "revolution without frontiers," would seek to undermine not only El Salvador but other Central American countries, therefore committed itself to the support of the Contras. The president rather generously called their leaders the "moral equals of our Founding Fathers."

Central America was seen as part of the East–West struggle, a new front in the Cold War opened up by Somoza's overthrow and the resulting Soviet–Cuban–Nicaraguan decision to exploit this opportunity to weaken the United States in its own backyard. In a sense, the administration viewed the area and the possibility of spreading the Sandinista revolution to Nicaragua's neighbors as creating an "Eastern Europe" for America on its southern border, a result it sought to avoid. American foreign policy, in extending U.S. power across the Atlantic and Pacific Oceans, had always taken its security in this hemisphere for granted; it could extend American power precisely because it did not have to worry about enemies close to home. Thus, despite Nicaragua's small size and population, and the overwhelming military power the United States exercises in this hemisphere, the administration was convinced that U.S. security was at stake in Nicaragua. Besides SDI, there was no issue about which President Reagan felt more strongly.

The administration was, however, constrained in how to deal with the Sandinistas. The memory of Vietnam was still vivid and the use of U.S. forces to topple the Nicaraguan regime was therefore not a genuine option, even though the administration kept this possibility alive by building airstrips in Honduras, transporting U.S. troops for "exercises" on Nicaragua's borders, deploying warships on Nicaragua's east and west coasts, and invading Grenada. Another option it rejected was the diplomatic solution. While, on occasion it pretended to support the Contadora process (the effort by Mexico, Venezuela, Colombia, and Panama to arrange a peaceful settlement), the United States remained opposed because such a settlement would have left the Sandinistas in power. The issue was not defusing the situation by having the Sandinistas send the Soviet bloc and Cuban military personnel home, reducing the size of the Sandinista army so that it could not be a threat to its neighbors, having the regime promise not to support revolutionary groups in neighboring countries or permitting the establishment of a Soviet base in Nicaragua. The issue was eliminating the Sandinistas. Thus the Contras were the administration's principal alternative. CIA Director Casey and United Nations Representative Jeane Kirkpatrick, both influential in the Reagan inner circle, believed that the support of the Contras would lead to the Sandinistas' collapse.

Thus the United States escalated the covert war. The CIA organized the Contras into more of a fighting force, which eventually grew to approximately 15,000 men; and CIA personnel became involved in the mining of Nicaraguan harbors, the blowing up of oil storage depots, and other operations. The Congress was outraged. Its intelligence oversight committees, which are supposed to supervise covert actions, had not been informed of these American-run operations. Apart from the sense of being deceived, the principal congressional concern was that the growing U.S. sponsorship of the war would eventually draw the country into another Vietnam. Even if no Americans were involved, once U.S. prestige was committed, could it avoid not "finishing the job" itself if the Contras failed to overthrow the Sandinista regime? Congress—led by the Democratically controlled House—therefore cut off military aid to the Contras in the spring of 1984 for that year and for 1985, although it restored $27 million in "humanitarian aid" (allegedly, food, bandages, and the like) when the Sandinista leader traveled to Moscow. Not until 1986 did the Congress—nervous about administration charges that if Nicaragua were "lost" it would be their fault—vote $100 million once again for military assistance to the Contras. In the meantime, Congress' intent was clear. It was not a question of whether President Reagan approved. He did sign the law, no doubt with misgivings, but Congress had enacted it. Undoubtedly, the president would try to get Congress to change its mind. Until that happened, however, he did not have the right to subvert the law by implementing the rejected course of action in secret. Specifically, the Boland amendment prohibited the CIA, Pentagon, or any other entity of the U.S. government involved in intelligence from "directly or indirectly" aiding the Contras militarily. At the time, neither the president nor anyone close to him in the administration claimed that the amendment did not apply to the president or the NSC staff; and no one denied that it prevented administration officials from encouraging other nations to finance and arm the Contras. In 1985 Robert McFarlane, as he did in 1987 during the Iran–Contra congressional hearings, stated that it was always his belief that Congress' intent was that the Contras were not to receive U.S. assistance and that therefore the NSC was not exempt from the Boland amendment. Even more specifically, Robert Motley, the assistant secretary of state in charge of Central American affairs, said the amendment prohibited the entire administration from giving any help, direct or indirect for the Contras, and that this implied soliciting or encouraging foreign money. The fact that the administration did raise funds and organize military help so furtively suggests that it was well aware that it was circumventing the will of Congress, whatever its rationalizations once the whole matter had been exposed. It is hardly surprising that the Boland amendment did not include the NSC, for the NSC had not been established to be an intelligence, let alone a paramilitary organization, but an advisory body to the president.

That is, however, what it became as Reagan, frustrated with the results of democracy at home, decided to work for democracy in Nicaragua by transforming the NSC into a secret government. The president's commitment to the Contras—whom he called *freedom fighters*—was firm. But the CIA, which normally runs covert operations, could no longer do so; top officials expressing their skepticism of the arms deal, had opposed the agency's involvement. Thus its director, a close confidante of the president, shifted the operation to the NSC, which had not been listed in the Boland amendment;* and Casey's zealous point man in the NSC, a "can-do" officer par excellence, later to be called the only five-star lieutenant colonel in the U.S. military, was a marine

---

* North's testimony about Casey's role, while very persuasive, was offered to exculpate North and could not be contradicted by Casey, who had recently died. Yet a book by *Washington Post* reporter Bob Woodward of Watergate fame on Casey's directorship of the CIA makes North's testimony plausible. See Robert Woodward, *Veil* (New York: Simon & Schuster, 1987).

officer, Oliver North. The NSA, certainly McFarlane, appeared almost irrelevant, outflanked by the Casey–North alliance (although Admiral Poindexter supported the policy and was thus included in the small circle of men who ran the Iran and Contra operations). North, a relatively junior officer whose authority came from Casey, could command help from officials in the CIA, State Department, and Pentagon. The NSC thus became the shadow government to ensure the Contras' survival until Congress would hopefully change its mind and fund the Contras again.

Perhaps it would be more appropriate to call the NSC a shadow CIA. North organized a network of operatives led by retired Major General Richard Secord. Most were veterans of the failed 1961 Bay of Pigs operation to overthrow Castro in Cuba and the disastrous 1980 Desert One rescue operations of U.S. hostages in Iran (hardly a good omen for success this time). It was this "private aid" group that took over the purchasing of weapons, their shipment to the Contras, and the training and direction of the Contra war. Secord and his men organized, among other things, an air service to supply the rebels; the main air base was in El Salvador, but airstrips were laid in other countries as well. Ships were also acquired to help this supply operation. U.S. government help, usually through Lt. Col. North in the form of CIA maps, intelligence information, tactical advice about military strikes and—causing quite a stir at the time—a CIA-prepared manual on assassination, was, however, never far away. Administration officials were always at the other end of a telephone line: calls were placed from El Salvador to Lt. Col. North's private line at the NSC. The U.S. ambassador in Costa Rica was ordered to help this clandestine operation, reportedly run by North with the help of Assistant Secretary of State for Inter-American Affairs Elliott Abrams and the CIA official heading the Central American Task Force; calls were also made to Stanford Technology Trading Inc., an arms firm half owned by General Secord.

This shift of field operations from the CIA to the NSC to General Secord's warriors—this privatization of covert action—left the NSC mainly in the role of fund-raiser. North and his cohorts were not only a shadow CIA, but became a shadow Treasury, raising millions to buy arms for the Contras. Secord and another retired major general, John Singlaub, played key roles. Secord opened a Swiss bank account and deposited $30 million earned from selling arms to Iran in it. As chairman of the World Anti-Communist League, Singlaub had many overseas contacts and he collected large funds from, for instance, South Korea and Nationalist China. Both men were in frequent contact with North and occasionally even met with CIA Director Casey. When in 1986 funds reportedly began to dry up after potential donors realized that the United States would resume funding after Congress had appropriated $100 million, Abrams successfully solicited $10 million from the ruler of Brunei. (These funds disappeared until May 1987 when it was discovered that Abrams had deposited the money in the wrong account!)

North also contacted private fund-raisers in the United States. Conservative anti-Communist organizations like the tax-free National Endowment for the Preservation of Liberty (later indicted for tax fraud) raised more millions for arms. North himself often addressed Endowment meetings, talking about the Contras. While he did not himself solicit funds, others did so after his speeches. In addition, North arranged for large contributors ($300,000 minimum) to be taken to the White House to meet the president, who thanked them for their donations (which he later claimed he thought would be used for television spots supporting the Contras, although the private donors knew their contributions went to buy arms). The president, too, addressed some conservative groups, stopping just short of asking for funds. While administration officials pressured or enticed the Central American democracies with economic and military aid to assist the Contras, the president himself reportedly talked to Saudi King Fahd when the king visited the White House. The Saudis, who had paid $1 million per month after the congressional cutoff in mid-1984, raised that sum to $2 million a month after the king had talked to the president in early 1985 for a total of $32 million. While Reagan denied soliciting these funds or doing anything illegal, Saudi generosity is hard to explain except as a contribution to Reagan's favorite "charity" in return for the president's past help in obtaining AWAC surveillance planes—never before sold to non-NATO countries—and other advanced weapons despite strong congressional resistance and favorable consideration in the future. Still, someone at some point must have suggested a contribution to the Contras; and someone must have proposed doubling the contribution.[32]

In fact, the line between public and private assistance for the Contras is difficult to draw; the two were inextricably merged. For operators like Secord, the 50 percent markup of weapons sold provided a sufficient profit to make his participation more than just the matter of patriotism he presented in his defense. Secord did not consider himself financially accountable to the government, although the cash raised by his company was from the sale of U.S. arms bought with taxpayers' money. He and his partner made $4 million from the arms sale; the Contras received only $3 million. On the other hand, Secord could enlist the cooperation of the NSC, CIA, or State Department, or show Iranian visitors through the White House's private quarters and the Situation Room, where the most secret military planning is done, when the president was away. Thus he was also an agent of the U.S. government. Where was the line between private citizen and U.S. representative, when North, virtually assuming the powers of the president, Secord, and his Iranian-born business partner tried to sweeten the pot for the Iranians by promising that the United States would go to war against the Soviet Union if it invaded Iran, help depose President Hussein of Iraq, and pressure Kuwait to release seventeen pro-Iranian terrorists who, among their deeds, had attacked the U.S. embassy? As Senator Daniel Inouye (D-Hawaii) commented, it was a "sad state of affairs" when a lieutenant colonel and two private citizens without security clearances could conduct such sensitive negotiations.

We find an American general who should know better, an American lieutenant colonel who everyone suggests is second only to the president of the United States, committing this country, its power and majesty to defend Iran is just unbelievable.

And then to come out that we will participate in deposing a chief of state of a country, and we're supposed to be neutral in that area.[33]

North and other government officials also pressured officials among Nicaragua's neighbors to permit "private operations."

But the U.S. Constitution intended that the basic foreign policy of the country be decided by the president and Congress after consultation and debate; foreign policy, like domestic policy, needed public support and confidence, and these could not exist if policy were made secretly. Nowhere does it say that private groups can conduct the nation's foreign policy in secret. If this were permissible, a president could at any time propose a controversial policy to Congress and if Congress turned him down, he could then ask wealthy individuals or foreign countries to finance his policy. The State Department would hardly be needed anymore. And who, for that matter, would need Congress? The president could franchise his diplomacy and raise money privately. However, it is a fundamental principle of the American political system that Congress decides whether to support a policy by appropriating funds.

Placing the NSC in charge of carrying out what everyone knew was the "old man's" favorite cause, then, was intended to do an end run around Congress. The NSA and NSC staff appointments are not subject to Senate confirmation. Therefore, an administration zealously committed to a cause, distrustful of Congress, and filled with a passion for secrecy and covert operations turned to the NSC, thumbing its collective nose at the Constitution. The White House communications director articulated this mood when in praising Lt. Col. North he said that North's "distracted and indifferent" countrymen could not be counted on to recognize what U.S. interests were in Nicaragua. North's loyal secretary put it more succinctly: "Sometimes you have to go above the written law."

Indeed, as a kind of logical culmination to this effort, CIA Director Casey reportedly had planned to use the profits from the arms sales to Iran not just for the Contras, but to establish a privately funded "off-the-shelf, self-sustaining, standalone" fund (to use Lieutenant Colonel North's description) to pay for covert operations beyond *all* governmental controls. Thus, the resumption, at inflated prices, of arms shipments had its own incentive, despite McFarlane's recommendation to call the hostage deal off and the opposition from cabinet members. The CIA director wanted money to support a super-secret, self-financing intelligence operation outside the CIA to fund programs that were either not known or not authorized by Congress and had they been known, might have been rejected by Congress.[34] Neither the president nor the vice president was told about the fund; the Congress too was not informed. Casey, who was not even in the NSC chain of command, would direct operations of this private spy agency with NSC staffers like North and perhaps even CIA personnel—all away from the watchful eyes of the Congress.

President Reagan had for six years, despite his enormous budget deficits, the bungled 1983 intervention in Lebanon, and frequent policy misstatements at press conferences, survived with his reputation and popularity high. Mistakes just bounced off him, and he became known as the "Teflon president." But the Iran–Contra affair scratched that Teflon and left him badly damaged as he faced his last two years in office. To be sure, as the president had said, "There ain't no smoking gun," but that was hardly the point. He was the president, he should have known what was going on. Even if he did not, he is responsible for his administration's actions. Reagan had wanted to avoid being a lame duck president, as most presidents are when they do not run for reelection; and he had already lost the Senate to the Democrats in the 1986 midterm election. His judgment, sense of competence, and credibility with the Congress, the press, and public were now badly hurt. A large majority of Americans believed that he was lying about what he knew of the diversion of funds. His approval ratings dropped sharply, reportedly affecting his sense of self-confidence, placing him on the defensive, and affecting his ability to lead the nation for the rest of his term.[35]

NSA Admiral Poindexter later testified that he had not informed the president of the diversion of funds. However, he did say that had he asked for the president's approval, he was certain he would have had it. The president, of course, denied that he would have approved, but Poindexter's point was that the policy had been established: to support the Contras. Therefore, using profits from the arms sale was only an "implementation" of this basic policy. Poindexter did admit that he also did not ask the president for his approval because, if this use of funds ever became public knowledge, it would be politically damaging. He wished to protect the president and provide him with "future deniability." Indeed, Poindexter emphasized that in no other decision of equal importance had he failed to bring a matter to the president's attention and get his approval or disapproval. Only on this decision had he decided that "the buck" stopped with him, rather than with the president. This was a rather incredible decision for a subordinate official, a quintessential staff officer, to make, given its significance and political importance and the fact that, if discovered, the president would have had to take the responsibility for it. Equally as obvious, the president was the kind of man who did not ask the questions his predecessors would have asked. Thus, given his general lack of interest in policy details, he let his NSAs make decisions that he should have made. A staff officer does not usually make such critical decisions; elected and accountable officials do. The picture that emerged from the congressional investigation into these matters certainly raised questions about whether the president was capable of managing the foreign policy of a world power. Ironically, however, more Americans were upset by Reagan's dealings with the Iranians than the Contras. As Senator Dole, Republican minority leader said, the only way the American people wanted arms delivered to the Ayatollah is from a B-1 bomber. But most ironically, the president had by his actions probably jeopardized future support for the Contras in Congress.

In the longer run, apart from having stained his historical reputation and leaving the question open of whether Poindexter offered himself as the "fall guy,"* the president's modus operandi in this matter may also have created a new issue about which to fight with Congress:

> The strange two-year episode of the private covert war may have uncovered a power of the presidency that has never before been fully illuminated: the power to persuade private citizens and friendly governments, each eager to cultivate Washington, to do what Congress will not. It is a blunt and unwieldy instrument, but it is not easily susceptible to legislative restriction—and that alone may recommend it to future presidents and open a new field of conflict between the executive and legislative branches.[36]

This prediction may well be correct because one of the results of the Iran–Contra affair was to confirm the importance of the checks and balances system, the necessity of both branches being involved in policy making. The tendency toward abuses of power and mistakes in policy requires that each branch keep watch on the other while simultaneously insuring that any U.S. policy will first be properly debated and have the support of the American people. No important foreign policy moves can be sustained without it. The problem is that as the executive has sought to evade congressional restrictions, Congress has increased the restrictions and sought more and more to micromanage policy, leading the president to seek new ways of evading legislative supervision.

The War Against Iraq

At the opposite extreme was the executive–legislative cooperation on Iraq. Yet the fragility of even this cooperation needs further underlining to demonstrate the difficulties the country will confront in the post-Cold War era in attaining some kind of consensus about the role of the United States in the world. We have already noted that Iraq's invasion and annexation of Kuwait had vital security and economic consequences for the nation, and that the Congress supported

---

* Lt. Col. North had offered himself, but CIA Director Casey had told North that the administration might need a figure with higher rank. He specifically named Admiral Poindexter. His testimony, therefore, raised a serious credibility question and almost as many Americans believed he had told the president despite his denial, as believed he had not told him.

  Poindexter said he withheld the information to protect the President.

  One key reason many congressmen on the investigating committees did not believe the admiral was that he testified that on the day he resigned, neither the president, vice president, chief of staff, nor attorney general, all present when he submitted his resignation, asked him any questions about the diversion. Had they not known anything about the diversion, which was one of the principal reasons for the scandal, they surely would have asked the admiral to explain what happened. The fact that they did not suggests that they already knew, either from Poindexter or Casey, or both.

the president's initial strong stand against Saddam Hussein, including the sending of U.S. forces to Saudi Arabia. But this consensus broke down over the issue of economic sanctions. Would they be sufficient by themselves to compel the Iraqi strongman to reverse himself? The Democratic party's answer was to give the sanctions time to work; only if after a year or eighteen months or two years they had failed to compel Saddam Hussein's withdrawal from Kuwait would it approve the use of force. But until then American lives were not to be sacrificed.

The problems were several. Saddam Hussein was quite willing to tolerate a high level of pain suffered by his people if he could achieve his goals; he and his entourage would not feel any discomfort. In addition, there was a serious question as to whether the U.N. coalition would hold. The U.S.–European–Arab–Soviet coalition was very vulnerable to disruption and breakdown. A Palestinian–Israeli clash, or a turn of events in the Soviet Union that might topple Gorbachev, or Israeli military intervention provoked by Saddam Hussein's threat to attack the Jewish state with missiles (as he was to do later) might destroy the coalition. Time was not necessarily on the coalition's side, as the advocates of continuing the embargo assumed.

In retrospect, we know this to be true. Only after six weeks of intense aerial bombardment on Iraq and Iraqi troops in Kuwait, only after the coalition's invasion of Kuwait had begun and Saddam Hussein faced imminent defeat, did he reverse his annexation of Kuwait. What chances, therefore, were there that economic sanctions would, after a year or two, have compelled Iraq's withdrawal from Iraq and giving up its claim of annexation? Moreover, we know now that Saddam Hussein's efforts to acquire weapons of mass destruction—nuclear, chemical, and biological—were far more advanced, extensive, and sophisticated than had been believed before the hostilities erupted. Indeed, the U.N. inspectors, whose task after Iraq's defeat was to find the facilities involved in these efforts and destroy them, estimated that Saddam Hussein was twelve to eighteen months away from getting an atom bomb or two while he was also working on a hydrogen bomb. Therefore, allowing sanctions up to two years of time might in all likelihood not only have failed but radically changed the political and military context of the conflict.

Thus President Bush's decision to use force if persuasion failed to convince Saddam Hussein to withdraw from Kuwait appears in hindsight to have been the correct course. But congressional opposition made both courses difficult. How could he persuade the Iraqi leader to pull out voluntarily when the latter knew that the opposition party, which controlled both the Senate and the House, was opposed to using force and, as a result, that President Bush might not be able to take such action—especially if he sought support from the Congress in the form of a resolution that was the functional equivalent of a declaration of war? From the Iraqi leader's perspective, why not wait to see what would happen, hoping that in the meantime the coalition against him would fall apart? Saddam Hussein was very much aware of the fact that the crux of the opposition to using force against him was fear of another Vietnam. Since that conflict the United States had been unwilling to fight a long war and suffer substantial casualties. He knew that the United States had withdrawn from Vietnam after suffering the deaths of 58,000 troops and had withdrawn more recently from Lebanon after 241 marines had been killed by a terrorist attack. He had specifically and derisively told the U.S. ambassador to Iraq, just before the seizure of Kuwait, that the United States was unwilling to accept 10,000 casualties in a battle; he intimated that he thought nothing of such a sacrifice. During the eight-year war with Iran, he had suffered up to a million casualties and not blinked an eye at the cost.

Saddam Hussein sought to reinforce this fear of war by arguing that any war would be a protracted one. He declared that his goal would be to hold out and survive the American onslaught for several months. He would absorb the initial blows inflicted upon Iraq by allied air power—he was really in no position to challenge the coalition in the sky—and wait for the ground battle. Then with his sizable and well-equipped forces, with the experience they had gained in the long war with Iran in defensive warfare, and possibly using poison gas among other means, he expected to inflict heavy casualties on American forces in a war of attrition. This would, he assumed, encourage a growing peace movement in the United States.

Thus when President Bush in January 1991, eighteen years after the U.S. withdrawal from Vietnam, asked the Congress to give him the authority to use force if the U.N.-set deadline of January 15 for an Iraqi withdrawal from Kuwait had not been met, he could not be certain of mobilizing sufficient support. He won by a slim majority in the Senate; only ten Democrats (and of these, only one from north of the Mason-Dixon line) were part of the slim majority of 52 to 47 that voted for the resolution supporting Bush's request; in the House, a greater number of Democrats helped the president gain a comfortable majority of 250 to 183. But overall, the vast majority of Democrats in the upper and lower chambers, including the entire senior leadership in both Houses, voted against what was in effect the functional equivalent of a declaration of war. This was the smallest vote for the use of force in the history of the United States since 1812. In the words of one of the small minority of Democrats in the House who voted for the war resolution:

> The Democrats must ponder the political consequences of a reflexive refusal to even consider the use of force. The party has suffered in too many elections from the popular perception that it is categorically and emotionally unwilling to use force under almost any circumstances other than a direct attack on the United States itself. If Democrats are not prepared to support the use of force in a situation like this, when the aggression is so unambiguous, the international community is so cohesive, and the stakes so great, how can anyone expect the Democratic party to support the use of force in defense of vital American interests in the far more common circumstances of confusion, ambiguity, and uncertainty?[37]

The president was well aware that a war against Iraq could not be allowed to become another Vietnam—if he wanted to remain president. He also knew that if the conflict did turn into a bloody war, despite his repeated assurances to the contrary, the Democrats would point out in the next election campaign that they had tried to warn the country against the danger of using force and giving up so quickly on economic sanctions. But the defensive nature of Iraqi strategy, which had worked so well against Iran, and the absence of any air power to protect Iraqi positions or attack allied forces, in fact left the Iraqi army in Kuwait and southern Iraq a sitting duck against modern, hi-tech forces. In the memorable words of Colin Powell, chairman of the Joint Chiefs of Staff, the coalition would isolate Iraqi forces and then "kill them." Communications and logistics were heavily bombed, and when that objective was successfully achieved and the Iraqi forces in Kuwait isolated and without supplies, the weight of an air war was turned against them. By the time the ground war was launched, the Iraqis were only too happy to surrender; those who could not surrender retreated or would not fight. The war lasted forty-three days. The Iraqis suffered an estimated 100,000 deaths and at least 60,000 were taken as prisoners of war during the 100-hour land offensive—twice the numbers the United States suffered during eight years of the Vietnamese war. Bush's decision to fight turned out to be a popular one. But it remains a fact that the executive–legislative conflict and the partisan–ideological disputes had made it difficult to persuade Saddam Hussein that President Bush's threat to go to war was a credible one; in turn, that had helped to make war unavoidable. It was not a good start for the new post-Cold War international order.

The Dilemmas Revisited: The Price of Power

The purpose of the separation of powers has been to guard against executive concentration of power. Such a concentration, it was feared, might constitute a threat to the liberties of American citizens. Yet the conduct of foreign policy requires just such a concentration; a powerful president is a fundamental prerequisite. But as even Alexander Hamilton, an advocate of a strong executive, said in *Federalist 75*, history did not warrant such an "exalted opinion of human virtue" that it would be wise for the United States to leave its relations with other nations to "the sole disposal of the magistrate created and circumstanced as would be the President of the United States."[38] The first dilemma might therefore be rephrased as "What does foreign policy do to American democracy?"[39] Former Senator Fulbright and chairman of the Senate Foreign Relations Committee was pessimistic on this question. "The American Constitution was never meant to operate in a condition of permanent warfare and crisis." The effect would be to transform the United States into a "presidential dictatorship" for it would gradually erode established constitutional procedures. Foreign policy "has become subversive of the very ends it is meant to serve."[40] Writing in 1972, Fulbright said that in protecting democracy, presidents had seized the authority to initiate war from the Congress, as well as the Senate's treaty power by the extensive use of executive agreements and by interpreting existing treaties in unwarranted ways.

One reason isolationists resisted international involvement was precisely this: the domestic effects. Becoming a major player in world politics meant big government and a shift of power from Congress to the presidency; it meant vast appropriations for a large military establishment. The resulting tax increases, isolationists feared, would stifle private enterprise. In brief, the cost of foreign policy would be freedom; the American promise would be betrayed. "An extreme sensitivity to, and consequently an obsessive fear of, the domestic effects of foreign policy has been one of the hallmarks—perhaps the hallmark—of the isolationist outlook."[41] A war, hot or cold, to preserve democracy elsewhere would result in the destruction of democracy in the United States.

Obviously, America's global involvement over four decades has yielded some of the results about which isolationists were concerned: the centralization of power in Washington, the enormous expansion of the executive branch, the growth of presidential power, the rise of a large military establishment and military-industrial complex, the violations of civil liberties during the infamous McCarthy period of the 1950s, the distortions of priorities as domestic needs gave way to defense concerns, and the widespread use of secrecy in the conduct of many government activities such as covert operations by the CIA. The isolationists were correct in this respect: there is a price to be paid for being a world power. The privatization of foreign policy to help the Contras is a recent, very disturbing, and blatant example. It does demonstrate the danger that in fighting an undemocratic adversary a democracy may become like its enemy. In Nicaragua, the Reagan administration stated that its aim was to bring about democracy—apparently by ignoring democratic processes at home. This potential cost of the attrition of the prescribed constitutional methods for making policy, even covert operations, is the inherent possibility that worried Senator Fulbright.

The isolationists were wrong, however, on one fundamental point, namely, that the United States could survive as a democratic state in a world of hostile antidemocratic states. Nazi Germany and the Soviet Union were both totalitarian states that represented a threat to the balance of power and democratic values. The survival of democratic values in the United States depends on their survival in other nations as well, especially in Western Europe. That is why when France and Britain were threatened twice by Germany, the United States came to their assistance and made a commitment to Western Europe's defense after World War II. Moreover, the fact remains that despite occasional associations with authoritarian regimes, the basic thrust of U.S. foreign policy since World War II has been the support and promotion of democratic values.

Similarly, the expansion of presidential-bureaucratic power has not seriously jeopardized America's democratic liberties or the executive–legislative balance.

The institutional balance seems very much alive and well and it cannot seriously be argued that the United States is a less free society today than it was before its deep involvement in world affairs. Whatever infringements there have been from time to time on civil liberties during wartime or during the Cold War, the American people have obviously accepted the trade-off between tolerating some violations of American democratic norms at home and the defense of the United States against antidemocratic threats from abroad. In wartime, democracies usually abandon democracy temporarily. Power is basically concentrated in the executive and everything is subordinated to the conduct of the war and the achievement of victory. Freedom of speech or assembly, the right to strike, and other normally accepted rights may be constrained or set aside temporarily. Such "democratic Caesarism" ends when the last shot has been fired. What is, therefore, remarkable about the lengthy Cold War is that despite the growth of executive power and the need for a strong presidency to conduct U.S. policy, Americans enjoy more freedoms today than ever before. As an increasing number of citizens have involved themselves on various foreign policy issues, including such issues as nuclear weapons, which had previously been left to the experts, the United States has indeed become more of a "participatory democracy" than before. The insistence that this country support human rights abroad as one of its objectives has also grown stronger. All in all, the United States has been able to flourish as a democratic society while simultaneously concentrating power in the executive, despite the historical fear of such power; power has been held accountable. The very fact that in the 200th year of the Constitution, congressional hearings were publicly exposing Irangate suggests that however embarrassing all this was, U.S. democracy remained alert and vital.

The issue of presidential power is directly related to the third dilemma, the character of the policy process: elite policy making versus broad democratic participation. At the beginning of the Cold War, George Kennan, a respected foreign service officer and a specialist in Soviet affairs who provided the rationale for America's postwar containment policy, reviewed the first fifty years of U.S. foreign policy in this century and concluded:

> A good deal of our trouble seems to have stemmed from the extent to which the executive has felt itself beholden to short-term trends of public opinion in the country and from what we might call the erratic and subjective nature of public reaction to foreign policy questions. . . .
>
> . . . I firmly believe that we could make much more effective use of the principle of professionalism in the conduct of foreign policy. . . . However, I am quite prepared to recognize that this runs counter to strong prejudices and preconceptions in sections of our public mind, particularly in Congress and the press, and that for this reason we are probably condemned to continue relying almost exclusively on what we might call "diplomacy by dilettantism."[42]

This plea for leaving foreign policy to an elite small group of officials and experts because public opinion and the Congress could not be trusted was not novel.

The conduct of foreign policy has traditionally been the province of the executive, absolute kings and their ministers before the rise of democracy, and prime ministers and presidents responsible to elected legislatures after. But even in Britain, a democracy, the House of Commons did not become continuously and closely involved in foreign affairs until after the enormous casualties suffered by that island-nation during World War I. After that disaster, foreign and military policy experts were no longer trusted to be always wise enough or to care enough to avoid war. Representative legislative bodies claimed that foreign, like domestic, policies must be publicly debated and approved. The public was to be informed and participate in making policy. Persons professionally engaged in the conduct of international politics were no longer to do so by themselves.

Consistent with the tradition of executive primacy in foreign policy making, presidents have long claimed to be the spokesmen for the national interest. They are the only nationally elected officials and therefore feel they have a popular mandate. The Constitution grants them the authority as the nation's leading foreign policy official; they are the country's chief diplomat and commander in chief. And as the single figure in the U.S. government to whom the public in an increasingly dangerous and changeable world looks for leadership and solutions—indeed, public expectations are probably too great to be fulfilled—presidents not unnaturally believe that they should be given wide latitude to conduct foreign policy as they, advised by experts, see fit.

On the whole, even Congress has recognized the need for presidential leadership, but it does insist on being informed and consulted on foreign policy issues. Given institutional differences, which are strengthened by conflicting partisan views, executive–legislative cooperation has been difficult and frequently frustrating. Yet, obviously, democratic norms give the Congress that right to participate. The Contra issue vividly demonstrates, however, what may happen if the two branches of government disagree and the executive is willing to live with the resulting stalemate.

The conservative Reagan administration, with its strong Cold War outlook, was obviously absolutely convinced that Nicaragua was part of the superpower rivalry and that the Sandinistas represented a "Soviet beachhead" on the mainland of the Western Hemisphere. Therefore, the Congress, under the leadership of a liberal Democratic House, was totally wrong when it banned military assistance to the Contras. Whether that mistake was due to incompetence, shortsightedness, Democratic control, or any combination of these, the conclusion the administration drew was that Congress had to be cut out of the decision-making process because it was a nuisance and an impediment. Those in the executive branch who were competent to judge what U.S. interests were and how to advance them had therefore to continue the policy, regardless of what Congress wanted. Congress did not seem to know what it wanted, they argued. It changed its mind six times in five years, first favoring aid, then opposing it, and finally favoring it again. Only in one year did Congress absolutely ban assistance to the Contras, for even in 1985 it voted for humanitarian aid. That appropriation came as the Sandinista leader slapped Congress in the face after it had banned assistance for the Contras by immediately flying to Moscow to consolidate Nicaragua's links with the Soviet bloc. Thus, Congress half changed its mind, voted funds for the Contras, but insisted that they could not be used to buy arms. In short, this vote represented not a clear act of legislative conviction, but indecision and embarrassment.

In these circumstances, the president considered it his duty to hold the Contras' "body and soul together" until the Congress changed its mind once more. The long-term security interests of the United States demanded no less. In the meantime, as Lt. Col. North repeatedly insisted during his testimony from July 6 to 14, 1987, the president and the NSC had the *right* to withhold information from the Congress, deceive it and lie to it repeatedly, and to destroy records and alter documents as the whole covert operation started to unravel. In fighting the "good fight," North represented the attitude of the NSC well when he characterized the Contra affair as a conflict between good and evil, between a small band of patriots and hostile forces in Washington as well as Moscow.[43] Without remorse or any sense of guilt, he defiantly stated that he and his colleagues had acted as they had only because Congress seemed blind to the threat; although they felt beleaguered, they had carried on against what should have been a readily visible security threat to everybody. North indicted Congress. Doubting that Congress would conclude it had been wrong in restricting the executive or that it would commend the executive for sustaining the Contras, he said

> Plain and simple, the Congress is to blame because of the fickle, vacillating, unpredictable, on-again-off-again policy toward the Nicaraguan democratic resistance. . . . The Congress of the United States allowed the executive to encourage them to do battle and then abandoned them. . . . When the executive branch did everything possible, within the law, to prevent them from being wiped out by Moscow's surrogates in Havana, in Managua, you then had this investigation to blame the problem on the executive branch.[44]

Even if this affair was a rather extreme case, the product of a group of men who believed that the ends justified the means, who did not for a moment entertain the thought that they might be wrong, that the conflict with Congress over the Contras represented a legitimate expression of differences of opinions, the fact remains that since 1940 presidents have repeatedly sought to bypass Congress with executive agreements. They have acted by not informing it at all, telling it only part of the story, or mobilizing the Congress by exaggerating the threat the United States faced and/or going over Congress' head directly to the people. If Congress is part of the solution—indeed, must be part of the solution—it has also been a major part of the problem from the Versailles peace treaty to SALT II.

As we saw earlier, one major reason for the presidential growth of power has been the obstructionist character of Congress on foreign policy issues. It was in recognition of this that Congress until Vietnam was willing to accept a subordinate role in foreign affairs. But Vietnam's destruction of the Cold War consensus, conflicts over what the U.S. role in the world should be, a continued public cautiousness, if not unpredictability, about foreign commitments have led Congress to once more reassert itself. On the whole, Congress represents caution and skepticism about commitments, especially ones that involve risks and costs, while the presidency, because of its responsibility, tends to be more activist and willing to define U.S. security interests broadly. Congress has therefore tried to restrict the president's freedom of maneuver, from the War Powers Act to specific issues such as the Boland amendment or attempts to block funds for arms exceeding SALT II limits. On occasions, it even seeks to upstage the president and make policy, as in 1987, when House Speaker Jim Wright intervened between the administration and the Sandinistas and, acting as secretary of state, sought to mediate between them. Indeed, he and the secretary later made their own peace pact after the furor died down. Congress is also concerned with executive evasion, and when it catches the executive doing so, it tries to micromanage, in turn leading the presidency to try all the harder to evade legislative restraints. The result is conflict and, on occasion, paralysis—unless the president decides to ignore congressional opinion, as President Reagan decided to do, go ahead with his policy, and lie to the Congress. But deception hardly provides a sound basis for policy; nor does lack of public support.

Thus, finally, we return to the second dilemma, process versus output, which as should be clear by now, is intimately linked to the third dilemma. More specifically, the issue is whether democratic policy making yields the "right" decisions on crucial issues. Another way of phrasing this is by reversing our initial question—What does foreign policy do to democracy?—to What does democracy do to foreign policy? It is the lack of confidence that broad popular participation will produce the correct policies required to deal with particularly troublesome issues that provides the rationale for elite decision making. Since the public remains largely uninformed on most foreign policy issues despite television and newspaper coverage, and since most of these issues are not really of major concern to most citizens, the impact of democratic participation in foreign policy making has generally been regarded negatively. The public has been criticized for relaxing its vigilance, ignoring rising threats, and being unwilling to spend the funds necessary to ensure the nation's defense. Therefore, while the public may be rational in its response to foreign policy events retrospectively and over the long run, it is not a good guide for action in the shorter run. While in wartime public fervor tends to be aroused and engages in ideological-military crusades, this jeopardizes the emergence of a stable postwar balance. Furthermore, once peace has been reestablished, the public prefers to focus its energy and resources on domestic issues, thereby endangering the preservation of the balance of power against its adversaries.

In a classic formulation of the resulting democratic dilemma, Walter Lippmann, journalist, philosopher, and man of affairs, said many years ago that "The rule to which there are few exceptions . . . is that at the critical junctures, when the stakes are high, the prevailing mass opinion will impose what amounts to a veto upon changing the course on which the government is at the time proceeding. Prepare for war in time of peace? No. It is bad to raise taxes, to unbalance the budget, to take men away from their schools or their jobs, to provoke the enemy." The people, Lippmann continued "have compelled the governments, which usually knew what would have been wiser, or was necessary, or was more expedient, to be too late with too little, or too long with too much."[45]

One does not have to believe that this statement is necessarily true or at least always true to recognize that tensions may arise between democracy and its international role. Britain and France were two of the great powers in Europe in the interwar period (1919–39). After 1933, when Adolf Hitler assumed power in Germany, and the Nazi leader began to undermine the status quo as he built up his military machine, it was in Britain's and France's self-interest to preserve the balance of power. But the two Western democracies failed in this task and war resulted because public opinion in the 1930s preferred to appease Germany in the hope of avoiding war rather than rearm and take a firm stand against it. British leaders were particularly reluctant to tell the public what needed to be done. A conservative party prime minister refused to make rearmament an issue in the mid-1930s because he thought he would lose the election; he won the election but Britain remained unprepared. The policy of appeasement was clearly popular. A later conservative prime minister was wildly cheered in the House of Commons when he announced that he would meet Adolf Hitler, Germany's leader, to settle differences over Czechoslovakia; he achieved this by giving in completely to Hitler's demands. Peace was preserved and the nation felt relieved. Not until Hitler attacked Poland in 1939 did the two Western democracies make a stand; but from 1933, when Hitler gained power, to 1939, they did not, making war unavoidable. Both failed. Worse, France was defeated in 1940 and Britain was saved from defeat by the English Channel, the bravery of its own people, and especially its ability to fall back on the United States to save it from defeat and help it achieve victory. That makes the issue of American democracy's performance all the more critical. Democracy can, as in the 1930s, fail to make the "right" decisions, and it can be fatal.

During the Cold War, we noted the collapse of bipartisanship on the China issue. Had the United States recognized the People's Republic when it was established and had American diplomats been present in China when the Korean War broke out in 1950, would not U.S. intelligence on Chinese concerns about the U.S. advance to China's border have been received with more credibility in Washington? And might diplomatic arrangements not have been worked out or the advance halted short of China's frontier, thus avoiding China's intervention with the bitter consequences it had on Sino–American relations for twenty years? Even more pertinently, had the United States been represented in Beijing, China's capital, would the United States not have been dissuaded from its belief that North Vietnam was a Chinese puppet and that a North Vietnamese victory would therefore be damaging to U.S. interests since it meant an increase in the power of China, then still seen as an enemy and a member of the Sino–Soviet bloc? It was these beliefs that led to the intervention in Vietnam's civil war, a war that ended in the damaging collapse of the consensus underlying the nation's postwar foreign policy.

The rational or right policy toward Communist China after Nationalist China's collapse was never in doubt. What was in doubt was the rationality of public opinion and the Congress on the issue of recognition. After the Democrats' accusations of being "soft on communism" and "appeasement" following Nationalist China's demise, it is not surprising that President Johnson did not want to be accused of "having lost" Indochina. Johnson did not want to jeopardize his domestic program and his ability to conduct foreign policy, as Truman's had been after the vicious attacks on him for "having lost" China. No president, not even a conservative Republican like Eisenhower, wanted to be attacked by the anti-Communist right. None therefore disengaged from Vietnam. Each did just enough by sending economic aid, military assistance, and finally, military advisers to prevent South Vietnam's collapse and avoid domestic attacks. President Johnson, faced with an imminent South Vietnamese defeat, was not so lucky. He could not procrastinate as had his predecessor, deferring any final decision on what to do if the crunch came. He had to make a decision and he followed his predecessors by escalating U.S. commitment and involvement. He paid dearly for that intervention.

This Asian pattern of grievous errors in policy, admittedly, must be set against the European pattern of correct decisions. The Truman Doctrine, the Marshall Plan, the Berlin Airlift, and the North Atlantic Treaty Organization were among a series of imaginative and daring policies adopted by the United States, a novice in international politics, to resurrect Western Europe after World War II. These created a framework of security for all the Western democracies that still stands over forty years after the end of that conflict. Still, the undeclared war with China, after its intervention in Korea, remains a serious and avoidable blunder. After the late 1950s, the growing Sino–Soviet schism was becoming quite clear, but until 1972 the United States failed to exploit this schism for its own security benefits. A rational great power confronts only its primary enemy. It does not get bogged down fighting secondary enemies in areas of secondary importance, wasting its resources. It husbands these to defend areas of vital importance against its principal adversary. The United States was unable to follow these simple but cardinal rules in its conduct of foreign policy. It is worth repeating for the sake of emphasis that when he decided to play "divide and rule" and attract China into strategic cooperation against the Soviet Union, President Nixon did not first consult his vice president or cabinet, let alone Congress. He kept his decision secret to prevent leaks to the news media, sent his NSA to China to open relations with it and prepare for a presidential visit, and confronted the nation with a fait accompli.

But, more recently, Iraq is a vivid reminder of the consequences in a breakdown of bipartisanship. Iraq's naked aggression threatened the Western economic lifeline, as well as U.S. allies and friends in the region; moreover, if unpunished, it would set a precedent for other regional bullies. These perceptions, which were almost universally shared by member states in the United Nations, permitted the president to mobilize an unprecedented U.N. coalition against Saddam Hussein. Despite this, and the support of 82 percent of the American public, only ten Democratic senators voted for the president to use force; even those votes were the result of intense White House lobbying. This margin was much too close for comfort. It is surely not surprising that until the moment of the U.S. attack Saddam Hussein did not believe that a government so divided on an issue so vital to U.S. interests would use force, nor that this lack of unity was one reason that Saddam Hussein did not take the twelve U.N. resolutions seriously, thus making war unavoidable. The virtual global support for the U.S.-led coalition was no substitute for a president who could not count on the support of a Congress controlled by the opposition. The executive–legislative sharing of powers may have the laudable goal of preventing the exercise of arbitrary power. Nevertheless, the institutional conflict between the two branches of government has become embittered by the huge ideological gap between the two parties on national security issues, by the long control of the presidency by one party and the opposition's long control of the Congress, and by the Democrats' determination before 1992 that if they could not capture the White House they would try to control policy from the Congress. The "problem is not one of congressional participation, oversight, or comment," said one observer in 1991. "Rather, it is that the scales have tipped too far. More than any time in recent memory, Congress is entrenched in an institutional, partisan, and ideological approach to national security that is at odds with the executive, and there is little indication that this downward-spiraling trend will be reversed."[46]

Thus the question raised by Merlo Pusey earlier in our discussion of President Roosevelt's policy during 1940–41, remains: Can a democracy, if it is a great power, deal responsibly with the threats and problems it confronts? Above all, can it mobilize the will to carry on over a long period of time when it is at peace? There is really only one answer in a democracy: if a particular course of action, like helping the Contras, is unacceptable to the Congress, a president has no choice but to take his case directly to the public. If he cannot persuade the Congress or the public, the policy cannot be pursued. Thus if Congress forbids military aid to the Contras, that is the law. It is not a license to substitute the president's will for the popular will, however strong the temptation to act covertly and illegally. If the result turns out to be an error, that remains one of the inescapable risks of democratic government. Although in some instances it is very clear what should be done, as in the case of helping Britain in 1940–41 or dealing with China after 1949, in most cases the correct policy is not clear at all. We tend to know only afterward. Public opinion certainly judges afterward, rewarding or punishing its political leaders. In a democracy, in any case, established and legitimate democratic policy making procedures cannot be ignored in the search for the "right" policy. Totalitarian states do that; self-appointed leaders, claiming to know what the correct policies are, arrogate to themselves the right to rule. But the difference between democracy and totalitarianism lies precisely in the method of decision making. Just as economic systems, seeking to provide certain goods and services to satisfy human wants and needs, are distinguishable from one another by *how* economic decisions are made, political systems are distinguishable by how public policies are made and justified. Democratic theory rejects the concept of the right answer or that a few know what is best for the country. It suggests instead that in a free society there may be many versions of the right answers on any issue. Confrontation and debate before the public ought to decide which is the best solution to a specific problem.

Democracy is a method of seeking the best solution. Failure, as France and Britain demonstrated, is always an inherent possibility. The basic test of any political system is surely its ability to protect itself. The Western democracies' failure was precisely their unwillingness to pay sufficient attention and invest the necessary resources to protect themselves. Thus Congress may have been in error on the Contras, but as democracy can fail, it can, however, also correct its mistakes and change policy. Senator Warren Rudman (R-N.H.) said at the Iran–Contra hearings, "The American people have the constitutional right to be wrong." Public opinion did not favor the Contras. This was the reason, he said, Congress had vacillated on Contra support.[47] Therefore, we return to the beginning. U.S. foreign policy aims to protect the security of a democratic United States.

The problem of executive–legislative tension may, however, ease during the Clinton years. The partisan differences between the Democrats and Republicans are vanishing as Democrats for the first time in twelve years occupy both ends of Pennsylvania Avenue. In addition, the ideological differences on the issue of military intervention have changed. The Democrats, who have overwhelmingly opposed the assertion of American power and the use of force since the Vietnam entanglement, for which they were largely responsible, have since the post-Iraqi war collapse of the Soviet Union lost their fear that any regional intervention would escalate into protracted conflict. Indeed, the very Democrats who were so intensely opposed to the war against Iraq were subsequently the enthusiastic supporters of military intervention for more idealistic and humanitarian goals, such as preventing the starvation of hundreds of thousands of Somalis as the collapse of the Somali government in that East African country spawned violence and anarchy, or curbing Serbian "ethnic cleansing"—that is, genocide—of Croatians and, especially, Muslims in Bosnia–Herzegovina, as this former state of Yugoslavia disintegrated after the retreat of Soviet power from Eastern Europe.

By contrast, Republicans lost much of their former enthusiasm for the use of force after the end of the Cold War and the conflict with Iraq. Military power, they contended, should be used where vital U.S. strategic or economic interests were at stake, not for open-ended humanitarian and idealistic goals. For if the prevention of starvation in the midst of civil chaos or massive killing of one ethnic group by another is the goal of U.S. policy, why not intervene in other countries where people were enduring the same terrible conditions? An intervention in Somali, moreover, where the only military opposition consists of groups of young armed gangs headed by opposing warlords might be relatively costless in lives. But in Yugoslavia there was not only what was left of the former Serbian-dominated Yugoslav army, but thousands of well-armed Serbs, as well as rival Croats who were cleansing their territories—and the memory that during World War II more than thirty German divisions had been unable to quell guerrilla resistance and pacify the country. Would military intervention, initially with air power, suffice to end the slaughter of innocent non-Serbian civilians; or would it fail, leading step by step to further intervention, eventually requiring a large-scale commitment of ground troops and risking extensive casualties? And, in the final analysis, why should not African or European regional organizations take the lead in what are essentially problems in their own areas? Bush's interventions in Somalia and steps toward increasing intervention in Bosnia were clearly belated and reluctant, taken largely in response to the awful heartrending barrage of daily television pictures from both countries. But for the media—and perhaps Bush's desire after his electoral defeat to bolster his place in history—these interventions did not occur.

Whatever some Republican objections and hesitations in becoming involved militarily in such ventures, one thing was clear: that if President Clinton wanted to pursue a more interventionist, internationalist foreign policy, he would be less likely to be opposed by those members of his party who for twenty years were as opposed to the use of force as the Founding Fathers were to entangling alliances; indeed, they seemed to welcome interventions to help the helpless and persecuted or to promote democracy.

Notes

1. Ray Stannard Baker, quoted by Cecil V. Cabb, Jr., *Bipartisan Foreign Policy* (New York: Row, Peterson and Company, 1957), p. 9.
2. Robert A. Divine, *The Reluctant Belligerent* (New York: John Wiley & Sons, 1965): and Diriner, *Roosevelt and World War II* (Baltimore: Penguin Books, 1969).
3. Merlo J. Pusey, *The Way We Go to War* (Boston: Houghton Mifflin, 1971), p. 74.
4. Ibid., p. 75.
5. Ibid.
6. Robert A. Divine, *The Illusion of Neutrality* (Chicago: University of Chicago Press, 1962), pp. 280–81.
7. Ernest A. Gross, "What Is a Bipartisan Foreign Policy?" *Department of State Bulletin* (October 3, 1949), pp. 504–5.
8. Godfrey Hodgson, "The Establishment," *Foreign Policy,* Spring 1973, pp. 3–40; and I. M. Destler, Leslie Gells, and Anthony Lake, *Our Own Worst Enemy* (New York: Simon

& Schuster, 1984), pp. 102–6; also see Kai Bird, *The Chairman: John J. McCloy* (New York: Simon & Schuster, 1992).

9. Walter Isaacson and Gran Thomas, *The Wise Men* (New York: Simon & Schuster, 1986) tells the story of six of these men: Harriman, Lovett, Acheson, McCloy, Kennan, and Bohlen.

10. Hodgson, "The Establishment," p. 13.

11. For example, Daniel S. Cheever and Field H. Haviland, Jr., *American Foreign Policy and the Separation of Powers* (Cambridge, Mass.: Harvard University Press, 1952); and James M. Burns, *Congress on Trial* (New York: Harper & Row, 1949).

12. See Foster Rhea Dulles, *American Foreign Policy Toward Communist China* (New York: Thomas Y. Crowell, 1972); John W. Spanier, *The Truman–MacArthur Controversy and the Korean War*, rev. ed. (New York: W. W. Norton, 1967); and Leslie H. Gelb and Richard K. Betts, *The Irony of Vietnam* (Washington, D.C.: The Brookings Institution, 1979).

13. Daniel Ellsberg, *Papers on the War* (New York: Simon & Schuster, 1972), pp. 101–2.

14. Gelb and Betts, *The Irony of Vietnam*, p. 25.

15. Laurence I. Radway, "Electoral Pressures on American Foreign Policy," prepared for delivery to the International Studies Association convention, Los Angeles, March 21, 1980, p. 6.

16. Gelb and Betts, *The Irony of Vietnam*, p. 68.

17. James R. Schlesinger, "The Eagle and the Bear," *Foreign Affairs*, Summer 1985, p. 957.

18. Hodgson, "The Establishment," p. 15.

19. Destler et al., *Worst Enemy*, pp. 110–26. For a parallel fragmentation of foreign policy magazines, see Ousa Sananikone, "The World of Journals," *The Washington Quarterly*, Spring 1988, pp. 209–14.

20. See, for example, "Democrats in Exile Count the Days," *New York Times*, June 4, 1987.

21. Statement printed in Brookings Institution books describing its purposes.

22. Ole R. Holsti and James N. Rosenau, *American Leadership in World Affairs* (Boston: Allen & Unwin, 1984), especially pp. 130–32, for a table summarizing the three foreign policy belief systems: Cold War internationalism, Post-Cold War internationalism, and semiisolationism. Also see update of Holsti and Rosenau, "Consensus Lost. Consensus Regained?: Foreign Policy Belief of American Leaders, 1976–1980," in *International Studies Quarterly*, December 1986, pp. 375–409.

23. See Michael Mandelbaum and William Schneider, "The New Internationalisms"; and Schneider, "Conservatism, Not Interventionism: Trends in Foreign Policy Opinion, 1974–1982"; and " 'Rambo' and Reality: Having It Both Ways" in *Eagle Entangled* (New York: Longman, 1979), *Eagle Defiant, and Eagle Resurgent?* (Boston: Little, Brown, 1983 and 1987), eds. Kenneth A. Oye, Robert J. Lieber and Donald Rothchild, pp. 34–88, 33–64 and 41–72, respectively.

24. Destler et al., *Worst Enemy*, p. 126.

25. Daniel S. Cheever and H. Field Haviland, *American Foreign Policy and the Separation of Powers* (Cambridge, Mass.: Harvard University Press, 1952), pp. 56–96.

26. Divine, *The Reluctant Belligerent*, p. 49.

27. William L. Langerand and S. Everett Gleason, *The Undeclared War* (New York: Harper & Row, 1953), p. 574.

28. Divine, *The Reluctant Belligerent*, p. 131.

29. Based on the Tower Commission Report, *New York Times*, February 27, 1987; Doyle McManus, "Dateline Washington: Gipperdämmerung," *Foreign Policy*, Spring 1987,

pp. 156–72; Robert Parry and Brian Barger, "Reagan's Shadow CIA," *The New Republic*, November 24, 1986, pp. 23–27; the daily *New York Times* throughout the congressional hearings of Irangate, the final congressional committee's report, *The Iran–Contra Affair* (Washington, D.C.: U.S. Government Printing Office, 1987); Robert Woodward, *Veil* (New York: Simon & Schuster, 1987); and Jane Mayer and Doyle McManus, *Landslide* (Boston: Houghton Mifflin, 1988). Also on Iran–Contra, see Theodore Draper, *A Very Thin Line* (New York: Hill & Wang, 1991) and William S. Cohen and George J. Mitchell, *Men of Zeal* (New York: Viking, 1992).

30. Peter Maas, "Oliver North's Strange Recruits," *New York Times Magazine*, January 18, 1987, pp. 20 ff.

31. *New York Times*, March 2, 1987.

32. It was later revealed that the Saudis had contributed billions of dollars since the early 1970s to governments and movements to further anti-Marxist, Western interests, often at the suggestion of the United States, although this was also clearly in the Saudi interest. *New York Times*, June 21, 1987. The newspaper's report, titled "Prop for U.S. Policy: Secret Saudi Funds," however, omitted Saudi policies contrary to U.S. interests such as support for the Palestinian Liberation Organization, isolating Egypt in the Arab world after its peace agreement with Israel, and the 1973 oil embargo against the United States.

33. *New York Times*, June 6, 1987.

34. *New York Times*, July 7, 1987; Woodward, *Veil*, p. 467.

35. Ibid., June 28, 1987.

36. McManus, "Dateline Washington," p. 172.

37. Stephen J. Sularz, "The Stakes in the Gulf," *New Republic*, January 7 and 14, 1991, p. 25.

38. Quoted in J. William Fulbright, *The Crippled Giant* (New York: Vintage Books, 1972), p. 216.

39. Charles Krauthammer, "The Price of Power," *The New Republic*, pp. 83–85.

40. Fulbright, *Crippled Giant*, pp. 178, 193, 208.

41. Robert W. Tucker, *A New Isolationism* (New York: Universe Books, 1972), p. 35.

42. George Kennan, *American Diplomacy 1900–1950* (Chicago: University of Chicago Press, 1951), pp. 93–94.

43. *New York Times*, July 9, 1987.

44. Ibid., July 10, 1987.

45. Walter Lippmann, *The Public Philosophy* (Boston: Little, Brown, 1955), pp. 19–20.

46. Jay Winik, "The Quest for Bipartisanship: A New Beginning for a New World Order," *The Washington Quarterly*, Autumn 1991, p. 123.

CHAPTER 4

Congress: How Silent a Partner?

The First Branch of Government

The president is the major actor not only in foreign policy but in domestic policy as well. But the intentions of the Founders of the American republic had not envisaged this. The legislative branch is the first one discussed in the Constitution, and this was not accidental.[1] The type of government planned by the Founders was one of legislative dominance. The Constitution gives the Congress a large number of specifically enumerated powers and a wide-ranging grant of "implied powers." In contrast, as noted earlier, the president has constitutionally been given only three specific powers: (1) the position as commander in chief of the armed forces and as the principal officer in each of the executive departments; (2) the power to negotiate treaties and to appoint ambassadors, in each case with the advice and consent of the Senate; and (3) the power to make executive appointments during periods when the Senate is in recess.

Two of the three powers specifically granted to the president deal with questions of foreign policy, but this hardly is evidence that the Founders expected the executive branch to dominate policy making in this arena. George Washington's farewell address to the nation warned against the country becoming involved in *entangling alliances*, and the Founders generally expected the president to execute the laws of the country as passed by the Congress in domestic policy. The scope of foreign policy making was viewed as quite limited—and not terribly important to a new nation thousands of miles away from the European powers. Foreign policy was simply too inconsequential to take up much of the time of the Congress, the first branch of government. In the unlikely event of armed conflict, however, the legislature retained the sole power to declare war on foreign countries.

Two centuries later, however, presidential preeminence in foreign policy was an established fact. The impetus of decision making had shifted dramatically, and many members of the Congress after Vietnam sought to reclaim their historical role as at least a coequal policy maker on foreign questions. The arguments raised in this debate over which branch should be most powerful have been reminiscent of those which marked the original debate over the Constitution. The Founders selected a president rather than a king because they did not want one individual to hold excessive and unchecked power. The powerful president, so highly regarded when people respected the men occupying the office, became in the 1960s and 1970s the "imperial presidency,"[2] an American king. Congress, in contrast, was the "voice of the people," the men and women directly elected by the mass public. As such, a representative government should place great emphasis on reflecting public opinion in policy making.[3]

A president, sitting in Washington, might become too isolated from public opinion and carry out policies which do not have widespread support. The Congress, on the other hand, might prove to be too parochial: members of the House of Representatives are elected from legislative districts and thus have little incentive to consider the great issues of international politics. There are two senators representing each state and, initially, senators were chosen by state legislatures rather than by popular vote. The Senate possesses more formal foreign policy powers than the House because the Founders feared what a political body so closely linked to mass opinions might do. The House, with its smaller districts and elections held every two years, would tailor its policies to the popular sentiment of the moment. The Senate, chosen for six-year terms and supposedly the more elite body, would be more concerned with the long-term consequences of its decisions. For it is, or at least calls itself, the "world's greatest deliberative body."

How, then, should policy be made? Should it follow the will of the public, or are the masses too uninformed and unconcerned to be trusted? What differences are there between foreign and domestic policy formation? These are the large issues which concern us in this and succeeding chapters. Furthermore, since the Congress has taken many steps to reassert its power in foreign policy, what is the actual balance between legislative and executive initiatives on foreign policy? Can a bicameral legislature with 535 members formulate any sort of policy? If not, what is the most appropriate role for the legislature to play?

The constitutional theories of legislative supremacy, or at least equal sharing of decision making by the two branches, are discussed more these days in the literature on Congress than on foreign policy making. Indeed, the dominant model of foreign policy decision making is that of the concentric circles.[4] In these circles (see Figure 1–1), the central decision-making locus on foreign policy is the president and his key advisers. In the second circle are the bureaucracies in the major foreign policy agencies and the armed services, the second-rank and less influential foreign policy departments, presidential advisers, and cabinet members whose primary responsibility is in the domestic sphere but who may be consulted on foreign policy questions, and scientists. The innermost circle is composed of a select few members of the administration; the outer circles have successively more members and correspondingly less impact on foreign policy decisions. We have placed Congress in the third circle. The fourth, outer circle comprises public opinion, and the media, political parties, local activists, and interest groups.

Foreign policy decision making has been viewed, as represented in the concentric circles, as basically hierarchical. There is one president and then there is everyone else. Occasionally, as the situation warrants, an adviser might move into the first circle from the second. But the norm is that the president, as the only nationally elected politician, chooses whomever he wishes to occupy the innermost circle with him. The outer circles are expected to be at the beck and call of those in the inner circle, thus establishing the hierarchy. The difference is highlighted by a story involving President Johnson and Senator Frank Church, a ranking Democrat and future chairman of the Senate Foreign Relations Committee, at a White House reception. Johnson queried the senator, an early opponent of the Vietnam War, about where he was getting his information on the war effort. Church replied that his information came from the columns of the noted journalist Walter Lippmann. The president reportedly replied, "Well, the next time you want a dam in Idaho, ask Walter Lippmann for it."

The concentric circles analogy stands in sharp contrast to the decision-making process in domestic policies. Here lines of authority cut across the national, state, and local levels and across the executive, legislative, and judicial branches as well. The stakes are generally perceived as less critical and policies are, at least in principle, more easily reversible. The actions taken are viewed as the results of bargaining and coalition building by actors who are intensely interested in their own priorities and often could not care less about other issues. Thus a legislator from the Midwest will fight long and hard for agriculture subsidies to wheat farmers and work with representatives of farmers' groups and the Department of Agriculture to ensure that their programs are protected. These well-structured relationships among legislators, bureaucrats, and interest groups have been called *policy subsystems*[5] and, somewhat less admiringly, *cozy triangles.*[6] The dilemma that the agriculture subsystem has to face is that the farm bloc in the legislature is not large enough to provide a voting majority on the floor of either the House or the Senate to get its programs enacted. Thus, it is forced into seeking out votes from "uninterested" members[7]—such as legislators from New York City or Cleveland, who may want public housing projects or government-backed loans to their cities to prevent imminent bankruptcy. Intermestic policies are much like domestic policies, at least with respect to decision-making patterns. Indeed, the number of actors may be greater on some intermestic policies because the decisions involved affect more than a single nation. This is particularly true on energy politics as well as on most trade issues.

Legislators thus trade votes and, ideally, interests are not in direct conflict, so that most major groups can get what they want from the Congress. When interests do conflict, a group that feels very intensely about its position can often block the passage of a bill adverse to its position. The political processes of domestic politics hardly guarantee good policies. Instead, they are designed to ensure that each important group gets heard before a decision is reached.[8] The power of an interest lies in how often it can get its way and how strong its ties are to legislators and bureaucrats who formulate and administer the policies which affect the routines of the interest. Bargaining takes place among equals, although as George Orwell has reminded us, some are more equal than others. But every member of Congress, no matter how much power or seniority he or she might have, still has to face the electorate every two or six years. Once elected, or reelected, each has the same mandate as every other.

The concentric circles, then, indicate the amount of centralization or hierarchy in decision making on foreign policy. Restriction of foreign policy initiatives to the innermost circle, the president and his closest advisers, fits the hierarchical model nicely and best describes crisis decision making (Chapter 8). On the other hand, congressional action on foreign policy necessarily includes more actors, and since the legislature is itself not hierarchically structured, the potential for widespread participation by legislators and their supporting and opposing constituents (interest groups, political parties, public opinion, and the media) is enhanced. But what does this do to the quality of decisions made on foreign policy?

We note that in contrast to the executive branch, congressional decision making is parochial rather than national or global in focus, with members rarely putting their districts' concerns out of mind; indeed, because members rely so heavily on constituency contacts rather than strong national parties for reelection, this local focus may be inevitable in the Congress. Second, the executive branch can respond quickly to changing events; the legislature is a "deliberative" body (or, as critics might have it, an obstructionist one which succeeds by employing delaying tactics). Third, the Congress is only intermittently interested in foreign policy, does not have the staff expertise on international questions that the administration does, has had weak foreign policy committees in the House of Representatives, and has not developed the resource base in information that the executive branch has on foreign policy issues. We shall examine each of these issues. But we first turn to a discussion of perhaps the most important occurrence of recent years: the increased activism of Congress on international issues.

Congress and Foreign Policy: Revival Fires

The Congress has become more involved in foreign policy in recent years. The most celebrated action it has taken, as noted earlier, is the War Powers Act. Other actions have also been largely directed toward amending, or restraining, executive initiatives. Congress has not taken upon itself the problem of formulating alternative policies. That is, as we shall see shortly, simply impractical. But the legislature can be an effective check on the executive branch. In 1974, for example, it passed what has been called the Hughes–Ryan amendment, after Senator Harold Hughes (D-Iowa) and Representative Leo Ryan (D-Calif.), which significantly restrained the president's leeway to use the Central Intelligence Agency as he wished.[9] The bill forbade the CIA to use public funds for foreign operations, excluding the gathering of intelligence, unless the president decides that the activity is important to the national security. Even in that event, the chief executive was required at one time to report such actions to as many as *eight* committees in the House and the Senate. This was finally limited to two (House and Senate Intelligence) in 1980. Furthermore, the Case–Zablocki Act of 1972, named after Senator Clifford Case (R-N.J.) and Representative Clement Zablocki (D-Wis.), established new requirements for the reporting of executive agreements to the Congress. A 1974 amendment sponsored by Senator Gaylord Nelson (D-Wis.) and Representative Jonathan Bingham (D-N.Y.) established procedures for reporting arms sales to the Congress and provided for a legislative veto over some sales. Although this legislation had a large loophole (only sales of over $5,000 had to be reported, so that multiple sales of $4,999.99 could go undetected) and there were relatively few instances of administration proposals actually being defeated, the impact of the amendment should not be underestimated. Despite an unsuccessful effort to prevent the sale of jet fighters in 1978 to Egypt and Saudi Arabia by leading Jewish groups and many members of Congress, arms sales to Turkey, Chile, Argentina, Libya, Iraq, and other nations were either defeated or stalled in committee and not pressed further by the administration. In some cases, such as Libya and Iraq, the issue was not strictly over military sales but about the purchase of aircraft that had potential military applications. In several cases, including Turkish aid, the increased congressional role threatened to disrupt the NATO alliance, while in others, such as the cutback of aid to Nicaragua in 1980 following the revolution in that country, the legislative actions ran directly contrary to the Carter administration's announced foreign policy toward developing nations.

Other legislative initiatives include an amendment, sponsored by Representative Thomas Harkin (D-Iowa) in 1975, which established criteria for determining aid eligibility based on a nation's human rights record. Except in a few cases (mostly in Latin America), the Congress did not exercise the veto power it granted itself over executive decisions that could waive this provision. In 1973, Senator Henry Jackson (D-Wash.) and Representative Charles Vanik (D-Ohio) shepherded through the Congress an amendment that linked favorable trade relations with the Soviet Union to more liberal emigration procedures by that country, particularly for Jewish dissidents. Many of these actions occurred during the Nixon administration and constituted a congressional assault on the president's refusal to be forthcoming on both foreign and domestic questions with the Democrats who controlled the Congress. Nixon strongly believed in the command style of decision making and was also much more interested in foreign policy than domestic issues. The foreign policy clashes thus were part of a pattern of poor legislative–executive relations that marked his administration. But the roots of the congressional resurgence and assertiveness go deeper—to Vietnam and a reluctance to have the United States too widely committed throughout the world and especially to become involved in wars that might not be winnable (Angola in 1976) or in countries where the leadership may have been only marginally more popular than that in Vietnam. The cry was "No more Vietnams."

While the examples point to attempts by Congress to regain control over foreign policy and indicate that the president may well face strong constraints (as demonstrated especially by the two very close Senate votes on the Panama Canal treaties in April 1978), the greatest challenge to presidential preeminence on foreign policy occurred in 1979 on the second Strategic Arms Limitation Treaty or SALT II (see Chapter 9 for a detailed analysis). The second SALT treaty was favorably viewed by the Senate Foreign Relations Committee, but faced considerable opposition from the Senate Armed Services Committee, a much more hawkish group of legislators. Jackson, a senior member of Armed Services who had been offered the position of secretary of defense in the Nixon administration, joined several conservative senators from both parties in opposing the treaty. Some moderate Republicans, including ranking minority member of Foreign Relations, Jacob Javits, supported the treaty, and press reports variously indicated that the treaty would either pass with several votes to spare or be soundly defeated. The administration's political problems were compounded by the decision of then-Minority Leader Howard Baker to oppose SALT II. Baker had been a key, if not decisive, backer of the Panama Canal treaties, maintaining the tradition of bipartisanship in foreign policy that dated back to at least the administration of Franklin D. Roosevelt. But in 1979 Baker specifically argued that it was time to reassess the wisdom of restraining partisan criticism of presidential foreign policy decisions. After Baker announced his position, press estimates of vote counts in the Senate tilted heavily toward defeat of SALT II. The minority leader may not have made his decision based on the desirability of bipartisanship in foreign policy; Baker was on the verge of announcing his own bid for the Republican nomination for president and had been roundly criticized by GOP conservatives for supporting the Panama Canal treaties. Following the Soviet Union's invasion of Afghanistan in December 1979, President Carter asked the Senate to defer further consideration of SALT II. While it was a presidential initiative that took the treaty off the Senate calendar, there was little doubt that Carter's action was taken as much to prevent his own political embarrassment as to punish the Soviets.

The bipartisan consensus on foreign policy, which had crumbled during the Johnson administration as political conflict over Vietnam crossed party lines and deeply divided the Democrats, has not been restored. When Nixon had assumed office in 1969, the Asian war had become a "Republican war," which was widely criticized by Democrats of various political persuasions. Splits within both parties developed over Reagan's Central American policy as well. The administration sent fifty-five "advisers" to El Salvador to train government troops battling Cuban-backed insurgents. Members of Congress, as well as the public, feared "another Vietnam," however, and were worried that the United States might be supporting militarily a government it could not justify supporting politically. Many members of Congress believed that the cause of the rebellion in El Salvador was not just Cuban or Soviet provocation, but poverty and a long history of political repression. Terrorism had been widespread in that country on both the left and the right and critics charged that the government cared little about stopping the rightist "death squads" that carried out political assassinations throughout the country. In late 1980, four American churchwomen, three of them Catholic nuns, were murdered, and in 1981 two other Americans serving as labor advisers were killed. It took some time for the government to begin an investigation, and the trial of the El Salvador national guard members charged in the former murders was delayed several times until 1984. An election held in 1982 replaced a right-center government with an interim government dominated in the constituent assembly by a far-right coalition. Until the election of 1984, a negotiated solution was thus impossible.

By then, however, Congress had already acted to restrict the scope of American involvement, albeit weakly. In 1981 it enacted legislation that forced the president to report every six months on the progress of land reform, the movement toward democracy, the capacity of the El Salvadoran government to control the "death squads," and compliance with "internationally recognized human rights." The press reported 5,331 civilian "death squad" casualties in 1981 and 2,630 in 1982.[10] Future U.S. aid would depend on reports of satisfactory progress.

The early opponents in Congress to Reagan's El Salvador policy were Democrats, particularly those from the party's liberal wing. In 1983, however, the president began to lose support among moderates in both parties. In May of that year the House Foreign Affairs Committee adopted a proposal to withhold half of the foreign aid granted to El Salvador until after the government prepared a plan for unconditional negotiations, created an effective judicial system, brought the accused murderers of Americans to trial, and completed land reforms. Furthermore, within ninety days of enactment of the legislation, all military aid would be suspended unless the government had begun negotiations with the opposition over participation in new elections. However, the proposed legislation provided no *automatic* cutoff in aid; Congress would have to vote anew any such restriction. The Senate Foreign Relations Committee proposed much milder restrictions on administration policy limiting the amount of aid El Salvador could receive and demanding that the United States push the government toward negotiations.

The Congress was even more assertive on the other aspects of Reagan's Latin American policy. As far back as 1977, during the Carter administration, it had suspended military assistance to Guatemala because of human rights violations. In 1983 the House Select Committee on Intelligence voted strictly along party lines to cut off covert CIA assistance to American-backed insurgents attempting to overthrow the left-wing government in Nicaragua. Overt aid had already been cut off in December 1982 by the Boland amendment, named after House Intelligence Committee chairman Edward P. Boland (D-Mass.). An Intelligence Committee report in 1983 concluded that American assistance to the insurgents was actually strengthening internal support for the Nicaraguan regime.[11] Thus, the entire House, in July, followed the Foreign Affairs Committee and voted to bar covert aid. The vote was largely on party lines, although House Democrats were more split than their Republican colleagues. To a considerable extent, the vote was viewed as a rebuke to then-National Security Adviser William P. Clark, who had not revealed details of American military maneuvers in the Caribbean to Congress.[12]

Many Democrats strongly opposed the president's policy of attempting to overthrow a government and were also anxious to rein in the Central Intelligence Agency. The Congress had last paid close attention to the CIA in the late 1970s and was fearful that the agency might become a mechanism for an administration to evade legislative scrutiny of foreign policy. However, Democrats were also concerned that the president might charge them with being "soft on communism" and demand to know "who lost El Salvador or Nicaragua?"[13] Thus, the Congress went along with Reagan's decision to appoint a bipartisan commission on Central America, headed by former Secretary of State Henry Kissinger, to recommend a new course of action for that troubled area.

Reagan regained much of the initiative in foreign policy making compared to many recent presidents. Much of his success can be attributed to his large margins of victory in the 1980 and 1984 presidential elections and his high approval ratings in public opinion polls. Carter appeared to be a weak president following the Soviet invasion of Afghanistan and the taking of hostages by the Iranian government. There was considerable public support for increased defense spending and a more aggressive foreign policy, especially toward the Soviet Union. Defense spending sharply increased in 1981–82 even as many domestic programs were drastically curtailed. In 1984 Congress agreed to provide assistance to anti-Soviet rebels in Afghanistan and Cambodia. It also repealed the Clark amendment prohibiting aid to the South Africa-backed guerrillas fighting the Angolan regime, despite strong opposition from American oil companies that were still operating in Angola. The legislative branch further approved "nonmilitary" assistance to the Contras in Nicaragua and, following the 1984 reelection of moderate President Jose Napoleon Duarte against right-wing opposition, the Congress once again approved assistance to El Salvador. The invasion of Grenada in 1983 and the bombing of Libya three years later were both popular moves that confirmed to the public the president's assertion that the United States was once again "standing tall" in the eyes of the world.

However, Reagan's foreign policy proved contentious even before the Iran–

Contra affair (see Chapter 3), which in late 1986 demonstrated to Congress that its worst fears about secret foreign policy making within the administration were well grounded. In contrast to previous administrations that tried to maintain some form of bipartisan spirit, if not consensus, on domestic as well as foreign policy, the Reagan team proposed a radical program of budget and tax cuts, deregulation, and an aggressive foreign policy that it hoped would create a new Republican majority in the country. Reagan's strategy, then, was less to seek congressional support for his programs than to pursue what he believed was right and what he thought the public might approve (in hindsight if not immediately). Gaining control of the nation's policy agenda from the Democratic party and from the House of Representatives in particular was paramount to this strategy of long-term political gain. The Republican victory in 1980, based much more on foreign policy concerns than most previous contests (see Chapter 6), led many in the administration to believe that they had a mandate for a new direction in policy.[14]

The sale of arms to Iran and the diversion of funds to the Contras is the prime example of administration officials pursuing policies that they believed to be correct, even when Congress had dictated otherwise. When Congress recessed for a week without acting on the president's aid for El Salvador Proposal in 1984, the administration announced that it would bypass the legislature and use a special emergency defense fund to send the aid.[15] The administration also attempted to politicize the historically nonpartisan Foreign Service, which staffs American embassies and consulates overseas. Traditionally, 75 percent of American ambassadors have been career Foreign Service officers; this figure fell to 60 percent under the Reagan administration. Some Foreign Service officers charged that there had been a "wholesale purge" of career diplomats in the Bureau of Inter-American Affairs, which handles Central American policy.[16] The administration also charged the House and Senate Intelligence committees with jeopardizing the nation's intelligence through their investigations of covert actions in the Third World.[17] It and its friends in the Congress clearly viewed foreign policy formation as a presidential preserve. Representative Dick Cheney (R-Wyo.), a key ally of the president, argued that the president has "to put up with every member of Congress with a Xerox machine and a credit card running around the world cutting deals with heads of state."[18]

The Congress has not stood still in the face of these administration initiatives toward reasserting executive prerogatives. The legislature's responses to the Reagan administration predated the Iran–Contra affair. As the economy slipped into a severe recession in 1982, public support for increased defense spending fell sharply (see Chapter 5) and Congress reacted accordingly. The unpopularity of aid to the Contras (see Chapter 5) meant that every year the president had to struggle to get his requests through the legislature, usually by the narrowest of margins. In 1986 the Congress passed a strongly protectionist trade bill that did not become law only because of a presidential veto.

The administration had actually lost much of its initiative before the revelations of the Iran–Contra affair. The Democrats recaptured control of the Senate in November 1986, shortly before the initial revelations of the secret arms deals. These events, however, weakened support for the president within the Republican party as well, as many legislators charged that the president had not told them the entire truth. Emboldened Republican members of Congress, including their Senate leader Robert Dole (who had announced his intention to seek the presidency), were much more ready to criticize the president on other foreign policy initiatives such as protecting Kuwaiti ships from Iranian fire in the Persian Gulf. The congressional mood was said to be "bold and bitter."[19]

The Bush administration was more willing than its predecessor to compromise with congressional Democrats. When the Sandinista government of Nicaragua agreed to hold elections in 1989, tensions over Central American policy abated. Congressional Democrats and the administration agreed on an aid package for the Contras that would end upon the transition to an elected government. The opposition was caught off guard when the Bush administration sent troops to topple Panamanian dictator Manuel Noriega. Some in Congress charged that the administration acted unconstitutionally in sending troops without congressional approval. However, the charges that Noriega was conspiring with Cuba to send narcotics into the United States blunted the criticism. The president and Congress reached agreement on an aid package for the new government, with each side trying to outbid the other.

The president and Congress compromised only when Bush had the upper hand with the public. On domestic issues, where congressional Democrats more clearly reflected public preferences compared with Republican presidents,[20] the president and Congress fought continuously. At the beginning of Bush's administration, the Senate had the upper hand in the nomination for secretary of defense. Bush selected former Senator John Tower (R-Texas), who had to face charges of marital infidelity, alcohol abuse, and potential conflict of interest. Tower had earned almost $800,000 in 1988 serving as a political consultant to defense firms. The Senate defeated Tower's nomination 47 to 53 on an almost strict party-line vote. When Communist governments fell in Poland and Hungary in 1989, the Congress (both Democrats and Republicans) pressed Bush for more generous foreign aid. Congressional Democrats offered a plan in late 1991 to allow the president to shift $1 billion from the defense budget to aid the Soviet Union, but Bush would not agree. The president and Congress were most strongly split on China. Conservative Republicans joined with Democrats of all stripes to strip China of its favored trading status with the United States after the Tiananmen Square massacre in Beijing in 1989. Bush argued that the United States would have more leverage with China if it continued normal relations. In 1990 the House overrode Bush's veto of Chinese sanctions legislation, but the Senate fell four votes short of an override. The Senate vote in 1991 was twelve votes shy of a veto-proof majority; seven farm-state Democrats defected, fearing the loss of a $500 million annual market for American wheat.[21]

The president and Congress battled over the proper American role in freeing Kuwait from Iraqi occupation. As early as October 1990, congressional leaders from both parties complained that the administration was not consulting them. Secretary of Defense Dick Cheney showed little inclination to bring the leaders into the decision-making process: "It was an advantage that Congress was out of town" when the United States sent forces to the Gulf. "We could spend August doing what needed to be done rather than explaining it."[22] In December fifty-four Democrats filed suit, contending that the United States could not begin hostilities without a declaration of war. As the president's self-declared deadline (January 16) for the initiation of hostilities grew closer, tensions between the president and Congress increased. Bush gained the backing of House Foreign Affairs Committee chair Dante Fascell, but failed to sway the most powerful Democratic leaders: House Speaker Tom Foley (D-Wash.), Senate Majority Leader George Mitchell (D-Me.), and Senate Armed Services Committee chair Sam Nunn (D-Ga.). As one of the most conservative Democrats, Nunn might have been expected to support Bush. When he did not, other Southern Democrats joined him so that the Senate could muster only a 52 to 47 majority in favor of the resolution approving military action passed in January 1991. The House provided stronger support for the president. The vote in that chamber was 250 to 183. Republicans in both chambers were virtually unanimous in backing the president. House Democrats cast votes 2 to 1 against the president, while Senate Democrats were almost 5 to 1 against Bush.

Congressional Democrats backed the president when the war started and became very popular. When the war was over and Saddam Hussein remained in power in Iraq, Democrats took the offensive again. In the summer of 1992, the Democratic-dominated House Judiciary Committee appointed a special prosecutor to investigate the administration's support for Iraq before its 1990 invasion of Kuwait. Democrats charged that administration officials wanted to expand American agricultural markets that they ignored the illegal sale of defense-related materials to Iraq. Congressional Democrats continued to raise the Iran–Contra scandal, establishing a task force to examine charges that Reagan-Bush campaign officials convinced Iranian leaders to delay the release of American hostages until after the 1980 presidential elections.

These challenges not only reflect a willingness of Congress to assert itself more vigorously on foreign policy (during the entire eight years of the Nixon and Ford presidencies the Congress was controlled by Democrats), but also indicate that some of the traditional differences in congressional determination to participate in policy making between domestic and foreign policy are weakening. Domestic policy has traditionally involved multiple groups and interests. All of these forces are represented in the Congress, where their spokespersons argue forcefully for their positions. There is no presumption of greater administration experience and expertise on domestic policy as on foreign policy. A member of the House Education and Labor Committee, interviewed by Richard F. Fenno, Jr., in the 1960s, made a dramatic (and still valid) point:

Hell, everyone thinks he's an expert on the questions before our committee. On education, the problem is everyone went to school. They all think that makes them experts on that. And labor matters are so polarized that everyone is committed. You take sides first and then you acquire expertise. So no one accepts anyone as impartial.[23]

In contrast, there is still the "we–they" attitude on foreign policy issues, with the United States pitted against other nations. A president's popularity increases whenever he is involved in a major foreign policy achievement or a crisis. There were virtually no critics of Carter following the Camp David accord between Israel and Egypt; a confrontation with the president over the handling of the Iranian hostage issue was viewed as unpatriotic. Indeed, Vice President Mondale charged Senator Edward Kennedy with a lack of sufficient patriotism when the Massachusetts senator told a San Francisco television station that the president should not have let the Shah back into the United States for cancer treatment when there were indications that such a decision might lead to problems at the American embassy in Teheran. As the Congress moves toward greater activism in foreign policy, we must consider its institutional capacity to take concerted action in this arena.

The Reelection Imperative: "Afghanistan's Not in My District"

As foreign policy making moves beyond the innermost circle to include participation by the Congress, more actors and perspectives become involved in making decisions. While Congress has become more active on foreign policy to check any potential "imperial president," greater participation has its costs as well. In particular, members of the House and Senate tend to see policy alternatives in the districts and states they represent. Representatives and senators see the stakes based on the people they represent; the views of a Midwest farmer are not necessarily similar to those of a New Yorker or a Floridian.

Unlike most parliamentary systems, the American Congress is elected by congressional districts in the House and by states in the Senate. Representatives face constant reelection battles, while senators, because of their six-year terms, are more insulated from the mass public. House members always face the electorate at the same time as the president, but they also must run in even-numbered years when the president is not on the ballot. Only one third of the Senate is elected at the same time as the president. This type of electoral system puts even stronger pressures on legislators to pay more attention to local issues than to national concerns and to define national issues in local terms. Furthermore, the United States does not have strong political parties at the national level (Chapter 6).

There is no country in the world where individual legislators are as free of pressures from national political parties and where the ties to local constituencies are as strong as the United States. The electoral system and weak parties reinforce localism in American politics. And it is difficult, if not impossible, to conduct a coherent national foreign policy if decision makers do not see the stakes in the same way.

In international crises, support for the president by the public and the Congress is generally strong and lasts for a considerable amount of time. On more routine foreign policy issues, legislators from different regions with different types of constituencies will, as on domestic policy questions, see questions in terms of alternative stakes. Consumers want lower prices at the grocery stores, farmers want protection from meat and vegetables which sell at lower prices in other nations. Steel and automobile workers also fear foreign competition and clamor for protection against cheaper imported materials and products from Europe and Japan. Automobile manufacturers—who might favor higher tariffs on foreign cars—might fight any move to restrict imports or less expensive steel. Legislators from the steel-mining area of Pittsburgh and the automotive center of Detroit, although representing the same political party and both espousing the "national interest," will see the stakes in foreign policy decision making quite differently. It is unlikely that they will perceive the issues as involving primarily foreign policy, since the economic well-being of their constituents is at stake.

The electoral cycle and the weak party system explain much of the parochialism of members of the Congress, but so do the attitudes of members toward their jobs and their constituencies. Former Representative Frank Smith (D-Miss.) stated: "All members have a primary interest in being reelected. Some members have no other interest."[24] For representatives, the reelection drive begins the day after the previous contest ends. The overwhelming majority of members of Congress, and particularly the House, not only seek reelection but attain it. And, as we shall see below, they realize what former Speaker Thomas P. O'Neill said: "In all my years, I have yet to meet a politician who was elected to anything on the basis of his foreign policy."[25] In 1986 almost 99 percent of House members seeking reelection won. Fewer than one in eight won by less than 55 percent of the vote, compared to one in five in 1956. In 1988 once again almost 99 percent of incumbents on the ballot won, and this time fewer than one in eight received less than 60 percent of the vote. However, incumbent safety is not a completely new phenomenon. The *lowest* percentage of incumbents reelected since 1950 was 87.1 in 1974 when many Republicans were ousted in the Democratic landslide that followed the Watergate scandal.

How do members get reelected? In the past, congressional elections were referenda on the standings of the political parties. Within Congress, the parties and their leaders dominated the Congress in the late nineteenth and early twentieth centuries. In the House, the speaker appointed members of all standing committees and controlled the flow of legislation; members voted the party line in the vast majority of instances. But in 1910–1911, a revolt against the strong speakership by the progressive wing of the Republican majority and the minority Democrats stripped the leader of the House of much of his power and transferred it to committees. Since then, committee and party leaders have struggled for dominance in the Congress, with the former being victorious much of the time. The growth of subcommittee government has further weakened the congressional parties, as members are free to pursue their own policy interests without much concern for formal positions of power. When a member cannot obtain some jurisdiction over a bill in subcommittee, he or she is likely to propose an amendment to it on the House or Senate floor. This is a role that was proscribed for junior members in the past. But today independence is valued more highly than party or committee discipline. As the congressional parties have weakened, so have the parties in the mass electorate. There are more ticket splitters and fewer strong attachments among voters to political parties today than at any time in our recent history; to many, political parties are anachronisms.[26]

Taking the place of parties are single-interest groups representing a wide spectrum of issues: proabortion and antiabortion forces, antigun control activists, environmentalists, antinuclear groups, and so forth. While it is unclear what impact such forces have on actual election returns, the proliferation of these political action committees (PACS) has changed the political landscape. Although candidates for office no longer can depend on strong party organizations to turn out loyal supporters, many do not lament the passing of the parties. The increased incumbency advantage for members seeking reelection can be traced to some of the perquisites of office that members have provided for themselves: in 1954, the Congress had a staff of about 5,000 people; by 1978, the figure had risen to over 17,000, where it has stabilized. Thirty years ago, House members were limited to five members on their personal staffs; senators were allowed six. These figures are very generous by comparison to almost any other legislative body in the world. In Britain, for example, all but the most senior members of the majority party have their correspondence handled by a typing pool. The contemporary House, however, allows members to hire up to twenty-two personal staff members. Senators' staffs are based on the population of the states the members represent. The salary, staff, travel, and other perquisites of office for House members are worth at least $1.5 million for each representative over a two-year term.[27] In addition to personal staffs, members of both chambers who chair committees or subcommittees have access to several more staff assistants through their committee positions.

These staff assistants do work on legislation, but many concentrate on "casework," providing such services as finding lost Social Security checks, writing letters of congratulation or condolence, or sending out copies of government publications. Many staffers do little more than answer mail for constituents. The cost of official mail from Washington to constituents has risen more than sevenfold from 1971 to 1989: from $11.2 million to $85.2 million, while the average cost of each item mailed has almost doubled (from 8 to 15 cents). This massive postal bill is not paid for by the members. Correspondence dealing with the "official business" of Congress can be mailed without postage under the member's signature (called the *frank*); other mail, much of it oriented toward reelection, does require stamps, but the members have virtually unlimited postage.

In the quest for reelection, there is no place like home. Even while in Washington, legislators maintain a considerable presence back in the district. Over 40 percent of House employees worked in district offices in 1990, compared with just over one-fifth in 1973. Thirty-five percent of Senate employees toiled back home in 1990, almost three times the 1972 level.[28] Not only has the percentage of staff assigned to the district increased, but so has the total number of staff members. This at least doubles the impact of the increase. But going home is also important.

Members of the House are now authorized unlimited trips back home, subject only to the amount of money in their total office budget. Most members go home at least three weekends every month. Senators go home somewhat less frequently. Many believe that they do not have to pay such close attention to their constituents because they face the electorate only once every six years. Furthermore, most senators would clearly prefer to be interviewed on "Face the Nation" or "Meet the Press" than discuss some constituent's personal problem at a garden club meeting back home. Yet, senators who neglect this advice are becoming increasingly vulnerable to challengers who promise better constituency service.[29]

Such close attention to the constituency no doubt helps the members gain reelection, but it also reinforces parochialism in congressional decision making. To members of the Senate and particularly the House, the national interest is usually defined in terms of local priorities. The reelection imperative as well as the success that members have in exploiting these advantages work against the development of a national or international perspective. In a rare burst of introspection, a survey of representatives conducted by the House in 1977 found that 57 percent of the legislators believed that constituent demands interfere with other aspects of the job, especially the legislative role.[30] By contrast, the president is the only nationally elected political leader and thus has greater leeway to balance competing interests in both domestic and foreign policy. The chief executive can thus take a more detached view of policy alternatives and can— indeed must—consider the reactions of our allies and enemies to foreign policy decisions as well as the long-term consequences of decisions.[31] The vast foreign policy bureaucracy serves the president and his secretary of state—who, in turn, can be dismissed at any time the president chooses.

Reelection is not the only goal of members of Congress, however. Fenno examined three other major goals which characterized legislators to varying degrees: (1) seeking influence within the House or Senate; (2) making good public policy; and (3) a career in politics beyond the House or Senate.[32] (For House members, this career generally means the Senate or a governorship, for senators the goal is the White House.) Indeed, some members, a minority to be sure, try to strive for the making of sound national and international policy without excessive concern for the parochial interests of their own districts or even the political consequences of their decisions. A somewhat jaundiced member of the House commented to Fenno:

> All some House members are interested in is "the folks." They think "the folks" are the second coming. They would no longer do anything to displease "the folks" than they would fly. They spend all their time trying to find out what "the folks" want. I imagine if they get five letters on one side and five letters on the other side, they die.[33]

The goal of making good public policy is held in varying degrees by all members. But what is good policy? For many, it is meeting the needs of the district. It is hardly surprising to find that a member from the Midwest or South would be primarily concerned with agriculture policy or that a black representative from New York or Chicago would be most interested in civil rights and labor policy. For most members, what is good for the district is good for the country—and, to a certain extent, each is correct. But the balance between district demands and the nation's priorities is difficult to determine. The policy-oriented member must not neglect his or her district, but he or she is also compelled to consider the claims of other members. Domestic policy making is generally not discussed in these terms. Legislators, who must face constituencies back home as well as among their fellow members, prefer policies which produce only "winners" and "nonwinners," the politics of the pork barrel and the agriculture and housing subsidies. Probably only a small minority of elected officials are concerned with resolving the issues involving "winners" and "losers," the sorts of questions that arose when over 100,000 Cuban refugees entered the United States during the 1980 recession. When unemployment is rising, how do you distribute jobs to the new Americans? An even smaller number direct their attention to foreign affairs. Those who do often have studied international relations in college and traveled extensively.[34] In the House, they tend to come from urban areas and have relatively safe seats, and they are also more likely to be members of ethnic groups particularly concerned with foreign policy (Jews regarding Israel and blacks on Africa). In addition, as noted earlier (Chapter 2), many members of the foreign policy committees have ambitions beyond the Congress.

Most members of Congress do little more than cast roll-call votes on foreign policy. Legislators who spoke on the floor or tried to shape foreign policy legislation came from constituencies that favored a more active role, according to a study of participation in four key decisions in 1984. Supportive constituents were the key to the initial decision to participate actively. The degree of involvement reflected a member's personal policy interests, committee or leadership positions, and the desire for personal influence in the House. Yet members see foreign policy as risky; they must see some electoral payoff to venture into these waters.[35]

These diverse goals may often come into conflict. Particularly on questions of foreign policy, legislators recognize that concern for foreign policy is often not appreciated back home.

A member of the Senate Foreign Relations commented:

> It's a political liability, . . . You have no constituency. In my reelection campaign last fall, the main thing they used against me was that because of my interest in foreign relations, I was more interested in what happened to the people of Abyssinia and Afghanistan than in what happened to the good people of my state.[36]

Foreign policy is often not very salient to many candidates either. In 1950 the Democratic challenger to Senator Robert A. Taft (R-Ohio) was asked his position on two controversial islands off the coast of China, Quemoy and Matsu. He reportedly replied: "I'll carry 'em both."[37] More recently, only one of four candidates in the 1986 Maryland Senate election could answer correctly more than half the questions on foreign affairs posed to them by reporters. Among the answers missed by most was the name of the prime minister of Israel. Among those who fared poorly in the "pop quiz" were the state's governor and two sitting members of the House, one of whom chaired the Foreign Affairs Committee's Subcommittee on the Western Hemisphere.

Issues can be hazardous in congressional elections, and foreign policy concerns have proven particularly deadly. When voters cast ballots for Congress, they ask themselves: How much do I like the incumbent and the challenger? Nonpartisan activities such as casework and direct contact with voters increase incumbents' favorability ratings. Issues more often help than hurt, but few other factors—scandals excepted—damage incumbents' ratings at all.[38] Voting records matter more in Senate elections than in House contests. Challengers are far less well known than incumbents in House elections; they are thus in a poor position to exploit incumbents' voting records since few people are listening. Voters are more likely to identify the names of Senate challengers and to know where both they and the incumbents stand on issues.[39] Challengers are thus in stronger positions to use issues to defeat incumbents in Senate contests.

Legislators are vulnerable to defeat on issues, and Senators have found foreign policy concerns particularly troublesome. Thomas McIntyre (D-N.H.) and Richard Stone (D-Fla.) attributed their defeats in 1978 and 1980 to their votes in favor of the Panama Canal treaty. In 1980 four of five members of the Senate Foreign Relations Committee lost their reelection bids. Three of the last five chairs of the Senate Foreign Relations Committee—J. William Fulbright (D-Ark.), Frank Church (D-Idaho), and Charles Percy (R-Ill.)—were turned out of office on foreign policy issues. The current chair, Claiborne Pell (D-R.I.), won reelection in 1990 by 62 percent—a nine-point drop from 1984—before he assumed the top position. Senators who have run for president and addressed foreign policy issues—Church, George McGovern (D-S.D.), Alan Cranston (D-Calif.), and Paul Simon (D-Ill.)—either lost reelection bids or saw their previous victory margins slashed. Representative Richard Gephardt (D-Mo.), who ran for president in 1988 and stressed the trade issue, fell from 80 percent of the vote in his congressional district in 1988 to 57 percent in 1990.

House members have not fared so poorly on foreign policy issues, largely because the role of that chamber on international affairs has not been so important or visible. The House Foreign Affairs Committee is classified as a "minor" committee by the congressional party organizations that assign members to committee positions. A member on a minor committee can also serve on another committee. The additional committee assignment of House Foreign Affairs members is usually more politically beneficial to them. House members have traditionally sheltered themselves from contentious issues, including foreign policy concerns, by paying more attention to constituents' personal problems than Senators do.[40]

For senators, the goal of making good foreign policy may often conflict with that for reelection. This is not quite the case in the House, but probably because those members attracted to the House Foreign Affairs Committee are among the most electorally secure. The Senate Foreign Relations Committee is a high-profile committee; Foreign Affairs in the House is almost invisible. Indeed, in an attempt to call greater attention to its role, the committee changed its name in 1971 to International Relations. A senior committee member commented: "We were sick of that old (former senator and vice president) Alben Barkley joke, the House committee only had affairs, not relations. Basically, we were considered a throwaway committee—our only bill was foreign aid. So we changed our name to fit our image."[41] But, despite the increasing activism of the body, the House did not stand up and take notice, so the name was changed back to Foreign Affairs in 1979 because members found the new title confusing and "difficult to remember."

Perhaps because so many senators seek (or wish to seek) the presidency, the Senate Foreign Relations Committee has served to help members attain institutional power. The House Foreign Affairs Committee is not the road to power in the House. Once the role of the committee as a critic of administration foreign policy had been institutionalized, its attractiveness declined. Very few members were willing to leave more desirable assignments to serve on Foreign Affairs. Freshman members comprised two thirds of all new appointments to the committee from 1973 to 1981, almost twice the percentage of a decade earlier. No other committee had such a large increase in junior membership.[42] In contrast to previous years when a large percentage of the committee's membership had considerable seniority and was generally reluctant to challenge the administration, the new junior-dominated committee is composed of members anxious to make their mark. They do not have "institutional memory"; since few legislators served in the pre-Vietnam War days, there are not many who recall the era of bipartisan foreign policy.

The Senate, long the bastion of both reasoned and unprincipled opposition to—and support for—administration foreign policy, is becoming more and more like the House. Senators are finding foreign policy concerns to be politically costly. The goals of members of Congress may often be conflicting, and legislators may be called on to decide whether to cast a vote in favor of a controversial foreign policy issue supported by the president or to ensure their reelection or quest for higher office. In a parliamentary system, Howard Baker, who was to become the Senate Majority Leader, would have been the odds-on choice to gain the Republican nomination for president (or party leader) in 1980. Instead, an outsider to the legislative party, Ronald Reagan, captured his party's nomination with ease, and Baker took considerable criticism within his own party for supporting the Canal treaties. In 1988, an informal poll of House Democrats indicated that their clear first choice was House Majority Leader Thomas Foley (D-Wash.), but Michael Dukakis, also an outsider to national politics, prevailed in the primaries.

The ideological attacks by conservative groups on senators who supported the foreign policy of the recent Democratic *and* Republican administrations have increased Senate parochialism on foreign policy. Foreign policy is less important in House contests because representatives have paid more attention to their constituents than have senators and because House members have not expressed a very strong concern for foreign policy issues. The prevailing attitude has been: Let sleeping dogs lie. When the House has taken initiatives on foreign policy, it has generally done so in response to some sort of a constituency pressure—from the demands of ethnic lobbies to economic interests in the district. One of the ultimate ironies of recent Congresses has been the tremendous increase in size of House and Senate staffs, but the lack of new efforts to challenge the executive branch in staff expertise on foreign policy. Congressional staffs concentrate on public relations activities designed to aid reelection efforts but, when they are concerned with policy, it is with domestic issues. The reason is straightforward: most members of Congress do not have a primary or even a strong interest in foreign policy. The issues raised stand in the way of reelection and often institutional power. Since each member can allocate staff resources, time and interests as he or she wishes, the Congress is capable of producing 535 separate foreign policies, each based on a different conception of national and local interests with no strong organizing force such as political parties to produce more coherent choices.

House members have won reelection in recent years by playing down issues. It seemed like a magic formula for ever-increasing success. Yet, something happened in 1990: While only 15 incumbents were defeated, the average vote share for incumbents fell by almost 5 percent—to 63.5 percent—the lowest level since 1974. The share of incumbents winning less than the magical 60-percent level separating "safe" from "competitive" seats doubled from 1988.[43] The 1990 results set the stage for 1992, when House retirements set a record and 43 incumbents were defeated in either primary or general elections for the House and 5 for the Senate.

The rebellion against congressional incumbents stemmed from the same anti-

Washington sentiment that fed the independent presidential candidacy of H. Ross Perot. Shortly before the 1990 elections, the president and Congress launched a civil war against each other. Their battle over budgetary priorities was so ferocious in 1990 that the entire federal government shut down for a brief period. The public lost confidence in both the Congress and President Bush—and, more broadly, in government generally. People felt that the president and the Congress did little more than bicker with each other while pressing national problems were unmet. The 1990 elections were a warning shot that incumbents were in trouble. The heady days of the Gulf War restored public confidence in the government; President Bush's popularity rose to record levels (see Chapter 5). Public office holders rested easy. The afterglow of the Gulf War faded quickly as public attention turned toward the recession and away from foreign affairs. Americans' confidence in their leaders at all levels plummeted. Bush and the Congress resumed their quarreling, and the people expressed their disapproval with both.

The sour public mood toward the government in Washington corresponded with a turning away from foreign involvement by the American people. This turning inward, combined with a hostility toward Washington officials, made Congress even more timid on foreign policy. If people trust their legislators, they are not only likely to reelect them, but also to give them some leeway in their Washington behavior.[44] Yet, even under these supportive circumstances, few legislators have any incentives to become active on foreign policy. When citizens are wary of their legislators, there is less room for policy innovation. Senators and especially Representatives, always cognizant of public opinion, become hypersensitive when the threat of defeat looms large. When the policy message is that Americans don't care much about foreign policy, a frightened Congress will turn away from international issues.

The handful of activists who are concerned with foreign policy have become increasingly isolated. Virtually no one now claims constituency benefits as a reason for seeking positions on either the House Foreign Affairs Committee or Senate Foreign Relations Committee. These were never core "constituency" committees, but in the past some members cited electoral reasons for serving on these panels.[45] Is a chastened Congress good news for a president with an activist foreign policy? Hardly. The legislature will not simply lie low. It is likely to obstruct executive initiatives, arguing that the public has no tolerance for them.

Committees: Centers of Congressional Power

A camel, it is said, is a horse designed by a committee. Congressional government is committee government—and, in recent years, government by subcommittees, the littlest legislatures of them all. The camel analogy is quite appropriate, for committee government does not move much faster than that desert animal. Whereas foreign policy, or at least crisis decision making, is marked by the need for action that is both *unified* and *quick*, responsiveness to public opinion and allowances for maximum feasible participation in decision making are characterized by a slow process of bargaining, negotiations, and compromises. Senators particularly like to call this process *deliberation*. Others might see it as an attempt to stalemate the opposition by responding so slowly that the opponent in the policy-making process may simply give way because of exhaustion.

Congressional government by committees is also parochial government. In the Congress, committees are organized largely based on constituency interests: Education and Labor, Agriculture, Interior, Public Works and Transportation, Energy and Commerce, Judiciary, and Small Business are typical House committees. Public Works is a much sought-after body, especially for junior members who want to engage in pork-barrel politics for their districts; it is the committee that constructs dams and produces hydroelectric energy. Judiciary, of course, handles civil rights legislation but also the more politically salient questions of resolving claims against the government and expediting immigration and naturalization procedures. Interior is the guardian of the national parks, as well as the protector of the environment. Energy and Commerce handles much, although not all, energy legislation, but also virtually everything that can be sold, bartered, or regulated—from the nation's airwaves to health care to railroads. These committees attract members from districts most directly affected by their principal subjects. While jurisdictions are not always clearly defined, membership on a committee that seems most relevant to one's district concerns can be of great benefit in reelection drives. Precisely because jurisdictions are not always clear-cut, the potential for slowing the progress of a major bill—or even stopping it completely—is very real in the Congress. A bill selected at random for all of those introduced in any given Congress (almost 20,000 now in the House alone) may not have as good a chance of passage as a camel trying to find an oasis in the desert. The long and tortuous path that a bill must take, involving at least one committee and one subcommittee in both the House and the Senate, makes its enactment into a public law a major event.

The "big three" committees in the House are Appropriations, Ways and Means, and Rules. Members assigned to any of these committees are generally not given any additional committee assignments. They are considered "power committees," bodies where members who want to gather institutional power jockey for positions. These committees are important because they handle the key aspects of legislative decision making: money and procedure. All bills that provide for the direct spending of money must go to the House and Senate Appropriations committees. The money, in turn, must come from taxes, which are handled by Ways and Means in the House and Finance in the Senate. In the House, but not the Senate, most important bills *must* be sent to the Rules Committee, which determines which amendments (if any) can be offered on the floor and what the ground rules (including time limitations) for debate will be. The Rules Committee also serves as the arbiter when there are conflicting claims among committees over alternative bills—or simply which body ought to have jurisdiction over a specific piece of legislation. Some bills are "privileged" in that they can go directly to the House floor without getting a rule. These include appropriations bills, but the power of the Rules Committee to restrict the amendments that might be offered provides strong incentives for virtually all committees to seek rules for debate for their bills. The situation is different in the Senate. Time limits can only be established by unanimous consent (the norm) or by a motion of cloture to break a filibuster, a prolonged period of "debate" designed to kill a bill. During a filibuster, members may argue the merits of a piece of legislation for days, weeks, or even months; in earlier days, the quality of Senate debates during filibusters varied widely as some members cited the arguments on their side of the bill and others read from telephone books merely to consume time. Senate procedures restricting amendments are so weak that a powerful committee such as the House Rules Committee could never develop. There is a Rules Committee in the Senate, but it deals with internal housekeeping (like the House Administration Committee), not the resolution of critical procedural issues.

The slow pace of congressional decision making is perhaps best illustrated by a change in House procedures in 1974 to permit greater participation in its decision making by junior members. In previous years, committees had been dominated by strong chairs. The seniority system—and indeed the entire committee system—was systematically weakened through a series of reforms (which we shall discuss later). But the change in referral procedures in the House in 1974 to make this chamber's procedures similar to those in the Senate dramatically demonstrates how the drive for power by a large number of actors can lead to a legislative stalemate. The situation is made even more cumbersome by the constituency politics that marks the fight over which committees and subcommittees get control over a piece of legislation.

The change in referral procedure permitted more actors to get involved in the processing of each bill. Previously, a bill was filed by a member; then the clerk of the House, acting through the speaker, would assign it to a committee. In several key instances, this referral procedure permitted the leadership to avoid recalcitrant chairs. The reform of 1974 in the House, following similar action in the Senate, permitted several different types of bill referral, including joint, sequential, and split referrals. The first permitted several committees to consider a bill simultaneously; the second allowed several committees to handle a bill in sequence; while the last let the speaker break a bill into several components and assign them to different committees.

While the rationale behind this proposal was to increase participation by all House members on legislation in which they were particularly interested, the reform had one major drawback: politically, the speaker could hardly reject the demand of any committee (or of a subcommittee through the full committee) as long as jurisdiction, determined by House rules, gave the committee a legitimate claim to the subject matter of the bill. The new participatory environment gave virtually every member the opportunity to have some say on a policy decision of concern to him or her. What ensued over the next several years was a series of jurisdictional conflicts that Representative Toby Moffett (D-Conn.) called "jungle warfare."[46] Thus virtually every committee could claim jurisdiction over energy policy (Chapter 9). The situation is even worse on health policy, where national health insurance is the concern of the Health Subcommittee of Energy and Commerce and a similar subcommittee on Ways and Means (which has primary jurisdiction over Medicare, a Social Security program financed through taxes); in addition every special interest committee (Veterans' Affairs, Small Business, Merchant Marine and Fisheries, Education and Labor, Interior, and so forth) controls decision making on health care within its general jurisdictions. The situation is no better on foreign policy, where questions of restrictions on foreign trade were matters of concern to Ways and Means (primary jurisdiction over trade policy), Foreign Affairs, Government Operations (oversight of both commerce and national security), Agriculture (food exports), Small Business, and Energy and Commerce—at a minimum. Should any of these committees, or the relevant subcommittees, refuse to report the bill to the Rules Committee, the legislation would die unless extraordinary measures were taken to rescue it.

The increasing use of multiple referral procedures in both the House and the Senate and the greater emphasis on the reelection goal have both served to weaken congressional initiatives in policy making. Approximately 10 percent of all bills filed in the House of Representatives are referred to more than one committee. However, these tend to be among the most controversial pieces of legislation. Multiply referred legislation is about half as likely to be enacted as bills that are sent only to one committee. Neither the Foreign Affairs nor the Armed Services Committee are among the panels with the largest number of multiple referrals. However, both fall right in the middle of the list of committees. Their legislation is thus controversial enough to cause other panels to want to get a piece of the action. Their Senate counterparts also rank toward the middle of all Senate panels.[47]

The Foreign Affairs Committee shares the Food for Peace program with the Department of Agriculture; foreign intelligence activities with Armed Services and the Select Committee on Intelligence; international banking with Banking, Finance, and Urban Affairs; the ACTION program (including the Peace Corps) and other educational programs, as well as the United Nation's International Labor Organization, with Education and Labor; immigration, claims, and passports with Judiciary; international fishing rights and environmental legislation (as well as the Panama Canal) with Merchant Marine and Fisheries; and trade with Ways and Means, among other committees (see Chapter 9). The committees that have the most multiple referrals are those dealing with intermestic issues such as energy (Science and Technology, Energy and Commerce, and Interior) and agriculture.

The referral system clearly adds many delays to the congressional process and may be particularly problematic in foreign policy, where quick responses to changes in the international system may often be required. Additionally, the Congress often uses temporary select committees to investigate the executive branch, as the Senate did to examine Watergate and as both chambers did in the Iran–Contra affair. These temporary committees are only permitted to conduct investigations and to suggest possible legislation. They may not refer bills to the floor. Only permanent committees may do so, so these temporary investigative bodies may add to legislative fragmentation. The more actors who become involved in foreign policy, the less expeditiously the nation can act.

Too Many Cooks?

Congressional decision making is also slowed down by the lack of any committee similar to the House Rules Committee in the Senate, where debate may continue at great length on virtually any subject. The lack of a strong procedure limiting amendments in the Senate means that a foreign policy question can be attached as a "rider" (an amendment not directly connected to the bill under consideration) to any other piece of legislation. There are rules in both houses prohibiting new legislation in an appropriations bill, so that it should not be possible to constrain, say, foreign trade on a foreign aid appropriation. However, virtually every subject imaginable involves the expenditure of money. All programs require someone to manage them at the least, and these managers must be paid salaries, so the jurisdictional lines become even more blurred and the process can be delayed at virtually any time for almost any reason.

Multiple referral of bills complicates the policy process; so does a 1971 reform that greatly eased the requirements for roll-call votes. Before that action, there were approximately 150 to 200 recorded votes a year; now there are about 800 such votes. Each voter takes between fifteen minutes and half an hour (often longer in Senate, where computerized voting has been resisted), adding yet further delays to the slow process. It is small wonder, then, that members often do not know the details of the bills on which they are voting. Much of the time, they do not even know what the basic substance of the bill is and rush to the floor from their offices or committee meetings, ask a trusted colleague who has followed the proceedings what the bill is and how he or she is voting, and vote accordingly.[48]

The concern for maximum possible participation, then, clearly slows down the legislative process and gives many more outside interests, as well as members themselves, the opportunity to block legislation before it can be adopted. But the commitment to a greater role for individual members, which led to the change in House referral procedures, is a hallmark of the open politics of the Congress of the 1970s and 1980s. Until 1980 the president, as cited earlier, had to report covert CIA activities to eight committees of the Congress, four each in the House and the Senate. No member trusted the others in making policy decisions for the country. Speed and coherence became clearly secondary goals to those of openness and participation. Critics charged that such a philosophy of policy making might prevent an "imperial presidency," but would also militate against a chief executive who could command enough authority and respect within his administration, as well as his own congressional party, to demand the attention and loyalty of our allies in international politics. The bill referral reform is but one of the factors that makes legislative decision making on foreign policy so much less expeditious than executive policy formation. The congressional reforms of the 1970s led to an increased policy activism in both the House and the Senate. We shall discuss these reforms shortly. But here we stress that this very activism and the longer deliberations that precede any final action on behalf of the nation have led foreign leaders, both in friendly and adversary countries, to wonder who exactly is in charge of our foreign policy—if anyone. A former British foreign minister reportedly once suggested, and not completely in jest, that foreign embassies ought to be built across from the Congress. More recently, and certainly not in jest, Representative Lee Hamilton (D-Ind.)—now chair of the Foreign Affairs Committee, formerly chair of the Select Intelligence Committee, and chair of the House Select Committee on the Iran–Contra affair—stated: "When I first came to Washington a head of government would visit the president, the secretary of state, the World Bank, and go home. Today, it's rare for a head of state to come to Washington without meeting members of Congress."[49] In 1987, as the Congress grew critical of American policy in the Persian Gulf following the Iraqi attack on the U.S.S. *Stark*, the Congress dispatched Senator James Sasser (D-Tenn.) to prepare its own report on the situation even as the administration sent an investigative team to the same site. Later that year, the administration clashed with House Speaker Jim Wright (D-Tex.) when the Democratic leader met with Nicaraguan officials to try to arrange for peace talks with the Contras. Administration officials, including the president himself, charged the Speaker with violating the separation of powers.

In 1979, both the House and the Senate voted to restore diplomatic relations with Taiwan after the administration broke such relations to recognize the People's Republic of China; the fight over congressional prerogatives in this area was finally settled in the administration's favor, but not until the Supreme Court refused to overturn a decision by the U.S. Court of Appeals that supported the contention that while initial recognition of Taiwan was accomplished by legislative action, the president could reverse that decision without congressional assent. Had the Court ruled otherwise, the newly established relations with China might well have been broken; they surely would have been very strained. During 1978 and 1979, the Congress wrestled with an amendment proposed by Senator

Jesse Helms (R-N.C.) that would have repealed American participation in the United Nations trade embargo on the white minority government of Rhodesia, a policy endorsed by every other nation except South Africa. Rhodesia, now the black majority-controlled nation of Zimbabwe, had been involved in a civil war for over a decade since the small white minority had unilaterally declared independence from Britain. The Carter administration, working with the British government under a United Nations mandate, was attempting to resolve the impasse in that African nation. Repeal of the embargo would certainly have set back such efforts, but in the eyes of the Senate supporters it would also have freed the United States from virtually complete dependence upon the Soviet Union for chrome imports. The Helms amendment cleared the Senate by a wide margin, but administration and party leadership pressure finally prevailed as the House refused to go along with the upper chamber.

In 1986, the Congress approved, over President Reagan's veto, a package of sanctions against the apartheid regime in South Africa. Reagan had strongly opposed such actions, arguing that the United States would be better off pursuing the policy of "constructive engagement." This policy was aimed at using moral persuasion rather than economic boycotts to convince South African authorities to change their policies. However, a bipartisan majority in Congress believed that Reagan's policy had failed to make any meaningful changes in South African policies to date and overrode the president's veto to impose the sanctions on South African imports. In 1987 Congress wrestled with a proposal to reduce or eliminate foreign aid to Pakistan, which had reportedly constructed an atomic bomb that some members of Congress believed might be shared with Libya. Successive administrations have perceived Pakistan as a strong American ally in southern Asia and as a particularly critical base for insurgents fighting the Soviet-backed regime in Afghanistan. In a funding bill for the Department of State in 1987, the Senate sought to initiate a wide spectrum of foreign policy objectives, ranging from condemnation of China for its policies in Tibet to closing the office of the Palestine Liberation Organization in the United States to demanding reimbursement from Persian Gulf nations for American protection of shipping in the waterway. The House concurred in the movement to close the PLO offices, but a federal court ruled that the legislature could not take such action. For good measure, the Senate also expressed its disapproval of the long honking motorcades and heavily armed guards established by the State Department for foreign officials visiting its chamber.

Congress has been more reactive than innovative toward Bush. It tried to ease immigration requirements for Chinese dissidents in 1989, but failed to override a presidential veto. The only other major initiative also involved China—denying most favored nation status. Attempts to deny China favored trading status also failed. After Congress again failed to upset the president on authorizing the use of force in the Persian Gulf and a swift military victory followed, the legislative branch retreated from activism. So did Bush in 1992 when polls indicated an increasingly isolationist public. There were simply fewer opportunities for confrontation.

Most of these issues took many months of congressional time. The legislative process is designed to be deliberative rather than expeditious. There is a far greater premium placed on hearing diverse points of view and reflecting constituency opinion than on quick coordinated action. The Senate, even though it has fewer members and a smaller number of committees (eighteen), is even slower than the House. First, Senate procedures are designed to be more reflective. Second, House members generally serve on only one or two committees; senators, on the other hand, serve on three to five committees and often have eight to ten subcommittee positions. A Senator running from one meeting to another, having to ask what the subject of today's hearing is, is commonplace. The heavy work load necessarily slows down the pace of action. The 535 members of the Congress rarely speak with a single voice and that makes decisive action on "crisis" issues much more difficult. Congress, on the other hand, excels at reflecting constituency opinion—and performs reasonably well at deliberative decision making. Whether it does as well as the executive is not readily resolved. Many of our views of process are colored by the decisions actually reached. Those who favored establishing relations with China would regret congressional "interference" with the foreign policy process, while supporters of sanctions against South Africa might hail the actions of the legislature against a recalcitrant chief executive. It is not implausible for people to hold both views—to be thankful for a Congress when one believes the president is wrong and to argue that the legislature is being obstructionist when one agrees with executive decisions. The democratic dilemmas stress these difficulties, but do not have ready answers to them.

One area in which the executive does have considerable advantages over the Congress is information about international politics. While both representatives and senators have large staffs, and the Congress has provided itself with three research organizations, the General Accounting Office, the Office of Technology Assessment, and the Congressional Research Service of the Library of Congress (as well as the Congressional Budget Office), even these facilities are dwarfed by the administrative bureaucracies of the Executive Office of the President, the Office of Management and Budget, and the State Department. Also each congressional research unit serves all 535 members of the House and Senate and examines not only foreign policy questions, but domestic ones as well. Furthermore, the congressional research service does many studies of internal congressional organization and fulfills specific research requests from members' offices which may have been forwarded from constituents needing information.

Could the Congress establish a research and investigative arm for foreign (and domestic) policy that would rival that of the executive branch? Probably not, given the vast resources of the entire federal bureaucracy available to the White

House. Even with its recent increases of staff and the strengthening of its research organizations, jurisdictional conflicts have arisen to weaken the potential for real coordination. The subcommittee system, a set of governments numbering over 300 in the House and Senate, which has replaced committees as the center of congressional power, further fragments authority. The growth of subcommittee autonomy, together with other reforms of the 1970s, has meant that policy specialists are now not only competing with the executive branch but also with each other. We turn now to an examination of these reforms and their impact.

The New Congress: The Impact of Reforms

In the 1970s, committee government gave way to subcommittee domination. A series of reforms in the 1971–1975 period radically changed the way in which the House of Representatives conducted its business. Committee chairs were no longer automatically selected by seniority. Democratic party members were no longer to be assigned to positions by the Ways and Means Committee; instead, a party organization, the Steering and Policy Committee, a third of whose members are appointed by the Speaker, controlled appointments to committees and the naming of chairs. The Democratic caucus, composed of all party members in the House, then voted on the recommendations of Steering and Policy, and agreement was not automatic. Furthermore, in an attempt to control the agenda, the Rules Committee was brought under party control. The Speaker was given the authority to appoint all Democratic members of Rules directly. In 1974, Appropriations also fell prey to the party leadership when its subcommittee chairs were to be appointed by Steering and Policy, subject to caucus approval.

Other reforms of even greater import include the "subcommittee bill of rights" and the creation, in both the House and the Senate, of budget committees which were designed to rationalize the relationship between spending and revenue raising. The first has had the greatest impact and is the most widely discussed.[50] In 1971, the Democratic caucus began the process that liberated junior members from the tyrannical chairs. The initial reforms restricted Democratic members from chairing more than one legislative subcommittee (although a member could retain a second chair of an investigative body that did not report original legislation) and guaranteed subcommittees the power to hire their own professional staff members. The biggest block of reforms occurred two years later when the selection of subcommittee members was made the responsibility of the full committee caucus and could not be dominated by the committee chairs; subcommittees were also guaranteed fixed jurisdictions, so that full committee chairs could not create new subcommittees at will to reward friends and punish enemies; committee members were guaranteed their choice, based on seniority, of subcommittee assignments; and subcommittees were forced to have ratios of party members which reflected the full committee party balances, so that conservative chairs could not stack certain subcommittees, for instance, with Republicans and overbalance less powerful ones with liberal Democrats.

In December 1974, in addition to the change in Appropriations subcommittee chairmanship appointments, the caucus mandated the following reforms: committees with more than twenty members (Ways and Means) but with no subcommittees would have to establish at least four such bodies; numbered subcommittees, such as those on Armed Services, were abolished so that the conservative chair could no longer prevent some of the new liberal members of the committee from serving on subcommittees that were examining racial and sexual discrimination in the armed forces through the assigning of bills to subcommittees without specific subject jurisdictions; committees were required to establish an oversight subcommittee; and members would be restricted to membership on two subcommittees in each full committee on which they serve (four years later, they would be restricted to five subcommittees in total—at least in principle).

These reforms encompassing the "subcommittee bill of rights" were not intended to "punish" all chairs of full committees, and, in fact, many were very highly regarded by the other members. The major objective of this reform, which was enormously successful, was to disperse power within the House. The focal point of activity shifted from the twenty-two standing committees to the approximately 120 subcommittees. The prestige of the title "Mr. (or Madame) Chairman" was reduced since almost two thirds of the Democrats in the House now hold it. The days of the strong chairs were over. The younger members who had been entering the House since the late 1960s found their cause bolstered by the Democratic landslide of 1974, which brought into the Congress a large bloc of post-Vietnam politicians distrustful of highly structured decision making.

The demise of the strong committees opened up two possibilities for future congressional decision making: an increased role for the two parties or an extreme decentralization so that each member would, in essence, become a sovereign. In the mid-1970s a resurgence of party government seemed possible. The Democratic caucus had gone on record three times (1971, 1973, and 1975) calling for a withdrawal of American troops from Vietnam and many in the party saw the prospect of using the caucus as a forum for coordinating policy making in Congress. But the old-line conservatives, including many chairs of full committees who had seen their power eroded, feared that the caucus would impose a liberal orthodoxy on the congressional party. The newer, more progressive members, on the other hand, were distrustful of any hierarchical decision-making structure, and they, too, opposed an increased role for the caucus. Thus, in early 1975, the caucus forbade itself from binding members to specific voting stands on the House floor and then voted to open future meetings to the public to stem any possibility that party leaders might try to resurrect the caucus as an internal forum for policy decision.

One measure designed to centralize decision making in the Congress was the Budget and Impoundment Control Act of 1974, which created Budget committees in the House and the Senate and also a Congressional Budget Office to formulate an alternative budget to that of the president and to coordinate spending and revenue raising in the Congress. The idea of a legislative budget was initiated as one of the anti-Nixon reforms of the Democratic Congress, but it drew support from liberals and conservatives alike. Each saw the potential for the Congress to put its budgetary process in some sort of order, for the new law required the budget committees to propose and enact a legislative budget. The limits established for expenditures in the final act passed each year could not be exceeded by the Appropriations committee of either House for any of the approximately twenty categories of federal spending.

The existing expenditure process was a classic example of group politics designed to produce many "winners" and few real "losers." Before any money could be expended, it must first be *authorized*, that is, made legal. Authorizations are determined by the substantive policy committees of the House and the Senate, so that Armed Services in each chamber would determine a maximum (and also possibly a minimum) amount to be spent on the military, while Education and Labor (House) and Labor and Human Resources (Senate) would set spending limits for federal aid to education, and so forth. Should the two houses disagree, as they usually do, a *conference committee* would be appointed by the Speaker of the House and the Senate party leadership (generally the majority and minority leaders working together) to work out a compromise within the limits of the original House and Senate bills. The conferees are, virtually without exception, members of the (sub-) committee(s) that handled the original legislation. House and Senate conferees each had to vote as a bloc and no bill would be enacted unless both groups reached agreement. Once agreement was reached, the House and Senate could only vote to accept or reject the conference report; no amendments are allowed. Failure to pass the report by either House would require the convening of another conference.

Even assuming that the conference report is accepted by the two houses, the spending process is far from over. Authorizations do not provide for the expenditure of any money; all they do is to make it legal for the appropriations committees in the House and Senate to propose actual expenditures, as restricted by the authorizations bills' maximum (or minimum) amounts. But at this point tension arises: The appropriations committees are faced with authorizations that, when added up, would break any conceivable budget. Thus they work to cut back the authorized amounts from the special interest committees to produce a more coherent relationship between taxing and spending. The House Appropriations Committee, therefore, has historically served as the budget cutter in the expenditure process, with the Senate body as a "court of last resort" for the authorizing committees and their supporting constituency groups.[51] The armed services committees have been notably active in pursuing their claims for more money and, in an extremely unusual move in 1980, Carter's chairman of the Joint Chiefs of Staff of the armed services, David Jones, opposed his own president's budget recommendations and supported the authorizing committees' recommendations for further increases in military spending. While the appropriations committees did, then, serve to restrain spending somewhat, the entire budget was never discussed in overall priorities. The new budget committees were designed to remedy this flaw in fiscal planning. To date, however, the success of these committees has been greatly limited. Budget resolutions often did not pass the Congress and the norm became a system in which spending limits on particular programs were simply waived by legislative acts. The early resolutions of the budget resolutions supported by President Reagan in 1981 suggest that the process can indeed work when disciplined majorities exist in the House and Senate. But it was the very lack of such discipline that led to the formation of the budget committees in 1974.

While the reforms of the 1970s could have produced either a more centralized or a more decentralized Congress, the weakness of the party system and the reluctance of the members to subordinate their newly liberated subcommittees to party leadership tilted the balance strongly in favor of fractionalized allegiances. Individual members, motivated by power, sought the overthrow of the committee barons who replaced the strong Speaker of the late nineteenth and early twentieth centuries. The upshot of this move toward greater participation in decision making within the Congress has led to a situation in which the only real power is the ability to block consideration of proposed legislation. If domestic authorizations and appropriations are not passed, highly salient political programs (such as agriculture, housing, and transportation subsidies) will come to a sudden halt and federal paychecks will bounce. In contrast, failure to act on key foreign policy issues will leave the executive unchecked; diplomacy will not cease. Enormous costs may, therefore, result from congressional failure to act, but these will not be directly borne by angry constituents in most instances. Foreign policy has a much smaller and less organized constituency than do most domestic programs. However, when Congress does not act on foreign policy, the president might gain so much leverage that the policy does not reflect popular opinion. What Congress does best is to represent the views of organized groups within the electorate. We can debate the wisdom of making policy, either domestic or foreign, through such group demands, but the American system has been based on this concept of politics.[52] We shall turn to an examination of how well Congress might perform this representation function after discussing the structure of foreign policy decision making in Congress.

The Foreign Policy Committees

Table 4–1 presents the full range of dispersion of foreign policy decision making in the Congress. Jurisdictional lines are often not as clear-cut as the table indicates, but the very large number of bodies with significant foreign policy authority is staggering. It is small wonder that Congress rarely takes the lead in initiating foreign policy. The key foreign policy committees are Foreign Relations (Senate), Foreign Affairs (House), Armed Services and Appropriations in each chamber, Governmental Affairs (Senate), and Government Operations (House). In addition to these standing committees, there are *select* intelligence committees in both the House and the Senate. Select committees usually are established within each house for a specified time period and are restricted to either general oversight of the administration or the reporting of very few pieces of legislation. The intelligence committees, however, have been established (as of 1977 for both houses) as permanent select committees.

The key committees are Foreign Relations in the Senate and Foreign Affairs in the House. Examination of each highlights the different ways in which senators and representatives perceive foreign policy. Foreign Relations has been a highly desired committee slot; members have waited years to obtain a seat on it. Some analysts consider it the most prestigious committee in the Senate. The body has attracted the "best and the brightest" of the Senate and, historically, both chairs and ranking minority members have achieved great stature. Prominent Foreign Relations members have included Arthur Vandenburg (R-Mich.), J. William Fulbright, Frank Church, and Jacob Javits. The current chair is Claiborne Pell (D-R.I.), who has served on the committee since 1961 and spent seven years in the Foreign Service before that. He is a thoughtful senator, of a patrician background but nevertheless among the most liberal members of the committee. Like his predecessor, Richard Lugar (R-Ind.), he strives for a bipartisan consensus to the extent possible, especially on such contentious issues as arms sales to Arab countries and sanctions against South Africa.[53] Pell, although a consensus builder, has not been a strong leader. Foreign Relations has been unable to produce a foreign aid bill since Pell assumed the chair in 1987. In 1991 he agreed to let subcommittee leaders take on greater visibility and have larger staffs. He did not take a particularly active role in the Senate debate on authorizing the Gulf War. Pell's passivity can be explained in part by his other legislative interests, especially aid to education. Grants for needy college students bear his name. The senator has also been called "one of Congress's genuine eccentrics," focusing his attention on paranormal events and writing Defense Secretary Dick Cheney that he found a code word by playing officials' speeches backward.[54] Foreign Relations no longer occupies its formerly privileged place among Senate committees, and party leaders have found it difficult to recruit new members.[55]

TABLE 4.1   Committees of Congress Dealing with Foreign Policy Issues

Committee	Subjects
Foreign Relations (Senate)	General conduct of foreign policy; declarations of war; executive agreements; treaties
Foreign Affairs (House)	Same as Senate Foreign Relations except for treaties
Armed Services (Senate and House)	Military affairs; defense budget; national security; arms exports
Energy and Commerce (House)	Energy; international economic policy; telecommunications; transportation; shipping
Commerce, Science, and Transportation (Senate)	International economic policy; telecommunications; transportation; shipping; ocean and fishing rights; nonmilitary space programs; merchant marine
Merchant Marine and Fisheries (House)	Merchant marine; ocean and fishing rights; offshore oil; law of the sea; Panama Canal
Appropriations (Senate and House)	All programs requiring funding; defense budget; budget for running bureaucracies
Budget (Senate and House)	Overall spending levels and spending within specific categories
Banking, Housing, and Urban Affairs (Senate)/Banking, Finance, and Urban Affairs (House)	International monetary policy; international commerce; authorizations for Export-Import Bank, and World Bank
Intelligence (Senate and House)	Oversight of intelligence agencies (Select committees)
Science and Technology (House)	Space program; energy research and development
Energy and Natural Resources (Senate)	Energy policy; energy research and development
Environment and Public Works (Senate)	Environmental policy; water resources; nuclear energy regulation
Interior and Insular Affairs (House)	Environmental policy; nuclear energy regulation; coal mining
Public Works and Transportation (House)	Aviation; water resources; hydroelectric energy; transportation
Finance (Senate)/Ways and Means (House)	Reciprocal trade agreements; tariffs; import quotas; customs
Agriculture, Nutrition, and Forestry (Senate)/Agriculture (House)	Price supports; international food policy; food exports; Food for Peace
Government Affairs (Senate)	General oversight; nuclear energy and export; executive branch organization
Government Operations (House)	General oversight, energy policy; trade oversight (including embargos)
Rules (House)	Setting of legislative agenda for House bills
Education and Labor (House)/Labor and Human Resources (Senate)	ACTION (including Peace Corps); International Labor Organization; migration and immigration
Judiciary (Senate and House)	Immigration policy
Joint Economic Committee (Senate and House)	International economic policy (no legislative authority; research function only)

The spotlight on Foreign Affairs now goes to its ranking minority member, Jesse Helms (R-N.C.), the self-proclaimed leader of the New Christian Right in the Senate. Helms bumped Lugar as ranking Republican on the committee when the Democrats took back the Senate in the 1986 elections. Helms has been a thorn in the side of Republican presidents from Nixon to Bush, launching one-man attacks on diplomatic nominees whose anti-Communist credentials he found insufficient. He has backed dictatorships in Chile, South Africa, and the Philippines and stridently opposed the 1976 Panama Canal treaties. His Middle Eastern policy was stridently pro-Arab until 1984, when pro-Israel groups contributed heavily to his opponent and almost defeated him; he then switched to strong defense of Israeli settlements in the West Bank and Gaza. A former television commentator, Helms can readily find an audience and has overshadowed the tongue-tied Pell. The move by Senate subcommittee leaders for greater authority in 1991 has been traced to Democrats' fears that Helms was dominating the panel.[56]

The leadership of the House committee has, until 1993, reflected the lower prestige of that body within the chamber. More senior members generally choose to chair other committees. Foreign Affairs developed a reputation for dealing with only one piece of legislation a year—the unpopular foreign aid bill. The committee has eight subcommittees, four dealing with general issue areas and four arranged by geography.

For many years the dominant premise was to resist conflict with the administration, even to the point of inaction. One member told Fenno in the 1960s:

> I've been on the Europe subcommittee for five months and I haven't even heard NATO mentioned, haven't even heard the word. I read my hometown newspaper to find out what's happening to NATO. . . . The subcommittees have displayed absolute irrelevancy in foreign affairs, amazing irrelevancy.[57]

The chair from 1958 to 1977 was Thomas "Doc" Morgan (D-Pa.), who was succeeded by Clement Zablocki. Morgan believed that the proper role of the committee was to pass the president's foreign aid request and little more.[58] He rarely interfered with subcommittee chairmen and gave them considerable leeway in the 1970s when several members, including Zablocki, became more activist. Zablocki in 1972 cosponsored (with Senator Clifford Case) a successful move to require prompt reporting to the Congress of executive agreements. But the greatest degree of activism in the 1970s came from other members, mostly representatives from relatively safe seats. These younger members, mostly Democrats, were quite ambitious. Stephen J. Solarz (D-N.Y.) now chairs the committee's Subcommittee on Asian and Pacific Affairs. In 1986, he was the leading congressional actor in moving the Reagan administration to press for the resignation of Marcos in the Philippines. Paul Sarbanes (D-Md.) moved on to the Senate; John Brademas (D-Ind.) became the House Democratic Whip before his defeat in the 1980 Republican tide; Pierre duPont (R-Del.) became governor of his state and in 1988 sought the Republican nomination for president; Hamilton rose to second in seniority among Democrats on the panel and chaired both the Select Committee on Intelligence and the Iran–Contra Select Committee; and Benjamin Rosenthal (D-N.Y.) mounted an unsuccessful challenge to Zablocki in 1977, arguing that he was not dynamic enough.

When Zablocki died in 1983, Dante Fascell (D-Fla.) became chair. He faced a daunting task, given the ideological splits on the panel. Nevertheless, he fashioned a bipartisan approach, working with ranking Republican William Bloomfield (Mich.) to get foreign aid bills through the House, supporting strong measures against Cuba, forging compromises with Republicans on aid to Central America, and leading the floor fight to support President Bush's authorization of military action against Iraq. He was called "the committee's strongest chairman in many decades,"[59] yet many Democrats feared that he was too cozy with Republican presidents and the party leadership in Congress.

Fascell and Bloomfield both joined the large list of retirees in 1992. Their replacements will dramatically reshape Foreign Affairs. The new chair, Lee Hamilton (D-Ind.), will present the Democrats' "best foot forward . . . since J. W. Fulbright (D-Ark.) and Mike Mansfield (D-Mont.) left the Senate in 1970s." Hamilton, first elected to Congress in 1964, "has been a thorn in the side of Republican presidents who have served since then."[60] He formerly chaired the House Intelligence Committee and the select committee that investigated the Iran–Contra scandal in 1987, where he was an unceasing critic of the Reagan administration. He led the House opposition to the Gulf War resolution—and has pressed for a compromise on aid to Jewish refugees to Israel from the former Soviet republics. Hamilton has often been mentioned as a possible Democratic vice presidential nominee because of his expertise on foreign policy and his strong standing with his peers. The ranking Republican is Benjamin Gilman (N.Y.), who has been a frequent critic of his own party. In 1991 Gilman voted less often with key issues on the Bush administration's agenda than all but two other House Republicans.[61] With Hamilton and Gilman in the two key leadership positions, the House Foreign Affairs Committee is likely to become both more activist and more liberal.

The challenges to the war in Vietnam, especially the War Powers Act, originated in the Senate committee. During the late 1960s and early 1970s, several attempts were made by Foreign Relations members to cut off funds for the war in Vietnam, notably by Senators Church, McGovern, Case, and John Sherman Cooper (R-Ky.). This bipartisan effort, in various forms, passed the Senate many times but always failed in the House, where members were reluctant to challenge presidential authority. Whereas Fulbright was a leading spokesman on behalf of these efforts, Morgan quietly led the opposition in the House. An amendment to forbid funding for military operations in Cambodia did pass both houses in 1975, but by that time the troops had already been withdrawn. The only real success of a congressional amendment to terminate the American involvement in Vietnam occurred *after* the Paris peace agreement of 1973, when all U.S.

combat forces had been withdrawn from Vietnam and all prisoners of war returned to America. Only then did *both* houses cut off funds for the administration's continued bombing in Cambodia, where no cease-fire had yet occurred. Yet, the legislative success was qualified, because Nixon vetoed the appropriations bill to which the cutoff on funds was attached. The president's need for funds for several executive agencies led to a compromise delaying the end of the bombing for several weeks. This gave Washington and Hanoi another chance to negotiate a Cambodian cease-fire and await the onset of the monsoon season, which would make further fighting very difficult.

The Senate, through the Foreign Relations Committee, consistently took the lead in the efforts to restrain the executive in Vietnam in the 1960s and 1970s. But the most prominent House committee initiative on foreign policy occurred on an issue that in many ways resembles the classic constituency politics of domestic policy more than the global issues of foreign policy: aid to Turkey. In July 1975, Turkey intervened militarily in Cyprus, a Mediterranean island populated by people of Turkish and Greek descent, after the Greek military government had attempted to unite Greece and Cyprus. The two countries were historical rivals, but both were NATO members. The situation was further complicated by the fact that Turkish troops used American-supplied arms in their attack. The dilemma posed to American interests was readily resolved when two factors were taken into account: (1) Turkey had not been cooperative with the United States in restricting the growth of poppy seeds, the source of heroin, despite repeated American overtures and assistance on this issue; and (2) there are many more Greek-Americans than Turkish-Americans, and these Greek-Americans tend to live in the larger cities and vote Democratic. Greek-Americans established the American Hellenic Educational Progressive Association (AHEPA) and the American Hellenic Institute Public Affairs Committee (AHIPAC) to lobby for a boycott of military aid to Turkey.

The initial move on the boycott came in the Senate but the Appropriations Committee of that body weakened the language introduced in the House to permit the president to restore aid when Turkey showed good faith in attempting to reach an agreement with Greece. The House clearly took the lead in responding to this foreign policy initiative with strong constituency politics elements. From a position of strength, the House insisted on its position and won in the conference with the Senate, although it agreed to delay the embargo until February 1976, when arms shipments were finally cut off. The success of the House in foreign policy making was, however, short-lived. By the fall of 1976, the good-faith effort language of the Senate was adopted by both houses. The ban was finally lifted in 1978, when Carter was basking in the glory of the Camp David accord between Israel and Egypt. The president's foreign policy leadership had been clearly established, and the Congress was in no mood to reject such a foreign policy initiative, particularly one with such clear-cut implications for NATO.

Throughout the 1970s, then, the House Foreign Affairs Committee was no match for either the president or the Senate Foreign Relations Committee. The 1980 election changed that dramatically. The Republicans not only captured the White House, but also the Senate—for the first time since 1953. The House Foreign Affairs Committee in 1981 became the focal point of Democratic opposition to many of the president's initiatives—especially aid to the Contras, the imposition of sanctions on South Africa, movements toward democracy in the Philippines and South Korea, the blocking of arms sales to Arab countries, and human rights issues. It was not so much that the committee itself had changed; it had not. Instead, it became the only governmental forum in which the Democratic party could air its views. When the committee could force the administration to change policy—as in the South African, Philippine, and South Korean instances—it instantly became a major actor in foreign policy.

While the Foreign Affairs/Foreign Relations committees have generally pushed the president to the left, the Armed Services Committees have tilted to the right. Following the 1986 elections, Sam Nunn (D-Ga.) assumed the chair of the Senate committee. Widely considered the expert in Congress on military matters, he has been a strong supporter of increased defense spending, as have virtually all of his predecessors. Yet Nunn emerged in 1986 as a persistent critic of the Reagan administration's position on the SALT II treaty (see Chapter 9). He argued that the treaty prohibited testing of a "Star Wars" defense system. The ranking minority member, Senator John Warner (R-Va.), served as under secretary and then secretary of the navy from 1969 to 1974. A consistent supporter of increased military power, Warner is nevertheless a low-key legislator without the clout of either Nunn or the four senators who chaired the committee before the Georgia senator took the reins: Republicans Barry Goldwater (Ariz.) and John Tower (Tex.) and Democrats John Stennis (Miss.) and Henry Jackson (Wash.). All have been vocal supporters of defense spending; Jackson was sometimes called the "senator from Boeing" since the defense contractor was a major employer in his state.

The House committee traditionally has been an equally strong defender of the military. Additionally, its members have sought to ensure that their districts receive their fair share (or more) of defense contracts. The most venerable chair of the committee, Mendel Rivers (D-S.C.), who headed the body in the 1950s and 1960s, came from Charleston, which is a veritable armed fortress with every conceivable type of military base. Rivers reputedly once said that "I didn't come to Congress to preside over the demise of the first congressional district." In the 1970s, however, a new group of legislators joined the committee. They were less committed to high levels of defense spending and were often highly critical of the military, especially on the recruitment of women and minorities.

One, Patricia Schroeder (D-Colo.), contemplated running for president in 1988; another, Les Aspin (D-Wis.), shocked the House when he toppled Melvin Price (D-Ill.) as chair in 1985 despite ranking only seventh in seniority. Aspin was just the opposite type of what one would expect as chair of the House Armed Services Committee. He did not spend years working in local politics before his election to the House; instead, he was an economics professor in Wisconsin. He did not practice the inside strategy of bargaining with his colleagues on the committee; instead, he wrote lengthy, scholarly, yet often quite partisan articles in national newspapers and magazines criticizing the committee's policies. He did not concentrate on doling out military contracts to his colleagues; instead, he called for Pentagon reorganization.[62]

Aspin achieved power because a growing majority of the full Democratic caucus—if not the Armed Services Committee itself—wanted a more dynamic leader than the aging and moderate Price to challenge the president's proposed defense buildup. The Wisconsin Democrat pledged to fellow Democrats to do just that—as he had done as a member of the panel—and to oppose military assistance to the Contras and the MX missile. However, he voted for *both* programs favored by the president and in late 1986 the Democratic caucus stripped him of his position for violating his pledge to it. Aspin immediately set out to win back his position and in early 1987 eked out a narrow victory in a four-member race. He won his seat back because he publicly apologized for his errant votes and because his principal rival was a Texas legislator who also had voted for Contra aid.[63] Neither party in the House or the Senate routinely punishes legislators for voting against the majority of their fellow partisans. What made the Aspin case so different is that the legislators sought to send the Armed Services Committee a message in selecting a more activist chair and wound up with a spokesman who sounded like more of the same. If there was to be a leadership on Armed Services, it would have to come from the Democrats' former ranking minority member William Dickinson (R-Ala.), who was low key and hard-line on defense.

Aspin gained considerable respect during the Gulf War, when he authored a series of thought-provoking position papers supporting the president. His renewed reputation loomed large in his selection as Clinton's secretary of defense in 1993. Aspin was succeeded as chair of Armed Services by Ronald Dellums (D-Cal.), the first black to head this committee. Dellums came to Congress in 1970 from "self-consciously radical Berkeley politics" as a self-declared socialist. On Armed Services, he focused on cutbacks in military expenditures, opposition to American intervention abroad, and racial problems in the military. Yet, he also developed a "passion for democratic fair play in public policy making" and was "scrupulously fair" in running his subcommittees. He worked on issues of common concern with conservative Republicans and Democrats as well as his liberal colleagues.[64] Dellums is likely to be the guiding force on the committee. Floyd Spence (R-S.C.), who succeeded Dickinson in 1993, is not likely to become more of an activist. His primary focus on Armed Services has been protection of the military base in his district, Fort Jackson, not policy issues.[65]

The Armed Services committees have faced difficult times in the 1980s and

1990s. Huge budget deficits, conflicts between Republican presidents and Democratic Congresses, the changing ideological composition of the House panel, and the demise of the Soviet threat have limited the constituency benefits that members could expect from these committees. Representatives and senators still seek appointment to the Armed Services panels to secure military contracts for their constituencies or to protect bases in their districts or states.[66] Yet, a declining military budget has made this task more difficult. In 1988 and 1990 Congress established independent commissions to close down unneeded military bases. Armed Services members in both Houses have been able to shield their highest priority programs—the Seawolf submarine for Representative Herbert Bateman (R-Va.) and Senators Joseph Lieberman and Christopher Dodd (both D-Conn.), and the Trident submarine for Representative John Rowland (R-Conn.)—but protecting constituency projects has become more difficult. The House Armed Services Committee has led the fight for sharp cuts in the Pentagon budget.[67] Since the late 1960s, ideology has become more important than constituency benefits in legislators' voting decisions on strategic weapons systems.[68] In the 1980s and 1990s there simply are not enough benefits to go around in the full House and Senate. Committee leaders can shelter some military contracts, but they can no longer defend key military installations.

Armed Services power now rests in their leaders' policy roles. Senate chair Nunn and House chair Aspin became their party's leading spokesmen on defense issues. Nunn had achieved prominence as his party's leading hawk. However, in 1987 he challenged the Reagan administration with a dovish interpretation of the Soviet Union's adherence to the antiballistic missile treaty. In 1989 his opposition to John Tower's nomination as secretary of defense helped to ensure the former senator's defeat. In 1991 he led the opposition to the resolution endorsing military action against Iraq. Nunn has been mentioned as a possible presidential candidate, though his stand on the Gulf War weakened his position in the party.[69] After his public chastisement by the Democratic caucus, Aspin established himself as a major leader in the House. He balanced the demands of his committee and the full House, usually siding with the liberal floor majority. He backed the Bush administration on the Gulf War when Nunn did not, establishing himself as "possibly the strongest figure on military issues in Congress."[70] As the Foreign Relations and Foreign Affairs Committees lost prestige, the Armed Services panels became the focus of Democratic opposition to the foreign policies of the Reagan and Bush administrations.

The remaining foreign policy committees have substantially less clout than do Foreign Relations/Foreign Affairs and Armed Services. The subcommittees on Defense on the House and Senate Appropriations Committees have considerable power over the defense budget. But the balance of power has shifted away from these panels. The House Appropriations committee, as already noted, is expected to play a different role than as booster for the armed forces or for constituency benefits. Before 1981, when the Republicans took control of the Senate, John Stennis chaired both the Armed Services Committee and the Appropriations Defense Subcommittee—something not permitted under House rules restricting any member to one major committee.

The Budget committees in each chamber have major influence on overall levels of spending, but (1) since their scope is so general, these panels can devote limited attention to foreign policy–related expenditures; and (2) more often than not, Congress fails to enact binding budget resolutions, thus circumscribing the committees' influence. Periodically, issues such as energy, trade, and agriculture play a prominent role in the legislative debate over foreign policy. But such instances are intermittent and do not dominate the arena of international politics within the American system. Each of the committees that handles these issues is primarily concerned with domestic affairs.

Finally, the Select Committees on Intelligence have largely faded from the public view. They arose from the abuses of CIA and FBI power in the 1970s, but failed to write a charter for the CIA in 1979–80. They did prevent outright repeal of many of the Hughes-Ryan provisions, as urged by members who thought that the restrictions might have contributed to the failure of the government to respond to the revolutions in Iran and Nicaragua. These committees briefly returned to public view in 1986 when they conducted hearings on the Iran–Contra affair. But they were quickly upstaged by special panels that took over the investigative function. Both the House and the Senate panels have rotating memberships—and shifting chairs—so that legislators have few incentives to develop expertise on intelligence operations. The House and Senate Intelligence Committees both had new activist chairs in 1993. Dennis DeConcini (D-Ariz.) took over the Senate panel, while Dan Glickman (D-Kans.) became the new chair of the House committee. Both DeConcini and Glickman favored cutting the intelligence budget and shifting the focus of the intelligence agencies away from military issues and toward economic and political concerns.

The many different committees that have jurisdiction over aspects of foreign policy weaken the ability of Congress as an institution to propose and carry out an alternative foreign policy. But they also provide opportunities for the administration to seek support from different constituencies within the Congress for its foreign policy as well as pitfalls for the implementation of some policies. In many instances, the administration only needs to block a restive committee effort to undermine the president's program, and, as stressed before, it is much easier to defeat something in Congress than to pass a bill. But when congressional *support* is required, the battle may become more difficult to win, as the examples of SALT II, the Panama Canal treaties, and even the Turkish arms embargo indicate. Trade-offs on other questions of foreign policy or on domestic issues may have to be employed, and in this sense foreign policy formation by—or with—Congress comes to resemble the constituency politics of domestic policy.

Congressional Fragmentation: Congressional Caucuses

In the beginning there was the floor of the Congress. Then things got a little complicated, so the legislature established a system of standing committees to help divide the work load among many people, each of whom would specialize in particular areas. Then, as the subjects of legislation became more complex, the number of committees proliferated so that by 1946 the Congress had to take some action to curtail their growth. In turn, subcommittees bloomed—to as many as 140 in each chamber at one time in the late 1970s and early 1980s. Then members realized that the subcommittee system so compartmentalized decision making that there was no way to get an overall perspective on a particular problem. The multiple referral process further complicated the situation. Rather than coordinating action on a particular problem, this procedure merely divided the work load further. Trade, for example, is such a broad-ranging issue that nine committees in the Senate alone must consider any legislation proposing changes in federal law; energy is even worse (see Chapter 9).

The congressional response, beginning in the 1960s but becoming very important in the 1970s and 1980s, has been the establishment of caucuses dealing with particular policies. (These are not to be confused with party caucuses in the House and Senate, which include all members of each party.)[71] These caucuses focus on particular topics—some broad (energy, trade, black issues, regional concerns), some narrow (footwear, travel, ports). They bring together members from many committees and often both houses. Some are partisan, but most include both Democrats and Republicans. Legislators contribute part of their allowances to support these caucuses. These bodies do not write legislation as committees do; they have no official legislative status, but they often hold their own informational hearings and their members can propose legislation that arises from caucus interactions.

In 1985 there were ninety-three caucuses in the Congress; sixty-three of them (or more than two thirds) had some foreign policy concerns.[72] Some of the caucuses dealing primarily with foreign policy are concerned with the great issues of war and peace; the Arms Control and Foreign Policy Caucus; the Members of Congress for Peace Through Law, founded during the Vietnam War to seek a legal (rather than confrontational) resolution of that conflict; the Members of Congress for Peace Through Strength, established to support the prosecution of the war; and the Senate Human Rights Caucus. Others are concerned with ethnic or regional politics: the Congressional Coalition for Soviet Jews; the Ad Hoc Committee on Irish Affairs, which advocates support for the Catholics in the religious conflict in Northern Ireland; the Friends of Ireland, which proposes a more moderate approach; and the Ad Hoc Congressional Committee on the Baltic States and Ukraine, among others. The Congressional Black Caucus concerned itself primarily with domestic issues until 1985–86, when it led the fight for sanctions on South Africa. Some are quite narrow—the House Task Force on Coal Exports and the Task Force on the Devaluation of the Peso.

Other caucuses are not primarily concerned with foreign policy issues, but do address them. Eight deal with energy at least in part; eighteen deal with trade. The Grace Commission Caucus investigates waste in federal spending, including that of the military. While the caucuses do provide members with the possibility of taking detailed looks at questions that might not interest committees (or subcommittees) and let legislators from different panels join together to discuss issues of common interest,[73] they also further fragment congressional policy making. Even nine Senate committees pale by comparison to eighteen caucuses dealing with trade that fall into our list of informal groups only partially dealing with foreign policy. At least eight, and possibly more, of the first group of caucuses fall into the trade category. While these bodies do not consider legislation, they can reinforce the parochial interests of their members. They certainly do not make it any easier for Congress to speak with one voice—so as to convey a straightforward message either to the president or to foreign countries.

The committee system has not only been losing power to subcommittees (see above) and caucuses, but also it has been self-destructing. Bills come to the floor of the House and Senate from committees and are no longer "safe" from attack by legislators not on the committee. As late as 1977 the House Armed Services Committee proposed a military spending bill that passed the House after three days of debate with no amendments added to it. Ten years later a military funding bill came to the floor with over 200 amendments proposed.[74] This bill may be somewhat unusual, but it is not atypical. Members of Congress no longer respect committee lines in proposing amendments. Truly, today everyone is an expert on everything.

Members are increasingly ready to challenge committee expertise in both the House and the Senate. The number of amendments to bills from the Senate Armed Services Committee increased from 3 per Congress during the 1950s to 71 in the 1970s and 1980s. For Foreign Relations, the jump was less dramatic: from 55 to 82.[75] The Foreign Relations Committee ranked below the mean in amending activity for the Senate in the 1950s and 1960s; in the 1970s and 1980s it ranked well above the mean. The same pattern holds for House Foreign Affairs. House Armed Services became more contentious in the late 1970s; its Senate counterpart followed in the mid-1980s. Defense authorization bills, which originate in the Armed Services panels, became particularly controversial as interest groups such as the Union of Concerned Scientists repeatedly challenged Pentagon assumptions. The number of amendments to defense authorization bills rose from fewer than 20 in 1961–62 to over 250 in 1981–82. Overall, the foreign policy committees in both the House and Senate experienced far greater increases in controversy from the 1950s through the 1980s than most other panels.[76]

Can Congress Make an Effective Foreign Policy?

For all of the increased activism of Congress in recent years, it would be a mistake to conclude that the legislative branch has assumed a role in foreign policy on the magnitude of its concern for domestic policy. The stakes are too different for that to happen, and the data would not support such a conclusion. We present in Table 4–2 a comparison of the number of treaties and executive agreements between 1930 and 1986. While the number of treaties has not increased dramatically, executive agreements have become much more frequent.[77] A study of executive agreements formulated between 1946 and 1972 found that the overwhelming majority of them (87 percent) had been authorized by congressional statute.[78] But this analysis indicates only a greater procedural role for Congress in enacting legislation which permits the agreements to be signed. An agreement signed in 1988 may have been authorized by statute twenty years earlier.

TABLE 4.2   Treaties and Executive Agreements, 1930–1982

Year	Treaties	Executive Agreements	Year	Treaties	Executive Agreements
1930	25	11	1976	13	402
1935	25	10	1977	17	424
1940	12	20	1978	15	417
1944	1	74	1979	28	378
1945	6	54	1980	26	321
1946	19	139	1981	12	322
1950	11	157	1982	17	343
1955	7	297	1983	23	282
1960	5	266	1984	15	336
1965	14	204	1985	8	336
1970	20	183	1986	17	400
1971	17	214	1987	12	434
1972	20	287	1988	21	387
1973	17	241	1989	15	363
1974	13	230	1990	20	398
1975	13	264	1991	11	280
Totals, 1946–1991				694	12,403

Furthermore, the study produced no evidence—and, indeed considerable skepticism—that such statutory grants were based on a knowledge of what types of agreements were to follow. Indeed, Carter threatened to implement the Panama Canal legislation as an executive agreement had the Senate defeated the treaties. This suggestion led to heavy criticism of the president and was promptly withdrawn—although Carter's threat may have alleviated some momentum building at the time among treaty opponents. In any event, the idea was unrealistic since the treaties required implementing legislation which appropriated funds to pay Panama for the operation of the canal in the years before the land reverts to Panamanian sovereignty. The critical House roll call on this funding in 1979 passed by only a single vote. The administration had assumed that the battle had been won after the Senate consented to the treaties. It could not have been more mistaken. On the other hand, the Congress in 1979 refused to approve the SALT II treaty negotiated with the Soviet Union by the Carter administration despite the president's strong push for ratification. Carter announced that the United States would abide by it anyway and Reagan, despite his strong criticism of the treaty in the 1980 presidential campaign, also agreed to follow its dictates. By 1986, when Reagan argued that SALT II stood in the way of the testing of his "Star Wars" missile defense program, it was the Congress that pressed for continued adherence to the treaty's terms (see Chapter 9). The assertiveness of the Congress on foreign policy questions may not occur often, but at least often enough *on important issues* that the legislative branch can no longer be consigned to a third circle of decision making.

Can Congress make foreign policy? Not by itself, to be sure. Should Congress make foreign policy? The members themselves have answered the question in the affirmative. The president is still the leading spokesman on foreign policy questions, but there is little doubt that his power will not be unchecked in the future. Congress had become more assertive in challenging the president through the use of the legislative veto, especially on foreign policy through the War Powers Act and through stipulations on military sales permitting either or both houses of Congress to block arms transfers after the president had proposed them. However, the 1983 Supreme Court decision invalidating the legislative veto has limited this form of congressional intervention in the foreign policy process.

While the Court has not ruled on the War Powers Act itself, President Reagan interpreted the 1983 decision as implying that the act *is* unconstitutional. At times he complied with it anyway—as when marines were sent to Lebanon—but he also resisted congressional dictates on other occasions (when American ships were sent to the Persian Gulf to protect Kuwaiti oil tankers). The Congress is reluctant to give up the War Powers Act. It is even more concerned that it will be restricted to using joint resolutions, which the president can veto, to assert itself on foreign policy. When the administration refused to invoke the act in September 1987 after an American helicopter fired on an Iranian ship in the Persian Gulf, many in Congress were irate. But they had no clear idea what to do, so the

Congress responded by establishing a commission to study how to make the act work.

Yet, even if the War Powers Act is overturned, Congress will continue to assert itself on international affairs. On arms sales, for example, it might—as it has in the past—put forward such strong objections that the administration is compelled to withdraw these proposals. On other areas of international politics, the Congress can be more confrontational by putting limits on what types of aid or military action the administration might pursue *before* any presidential decisions are made.

How desirable is such a trend? Crisis decision making is unlikely to be affected, since the Congress, as well as the mass public, tends to rally around the president during such moments. However, for noncrisis decision making, the question comes down to a very difficult choice which lies at the heart of the problem of foreign policy decision making in a democracy: How can we reconcile the need for swift and united national action and the demand for a set of policy goals that are responsive to public opinion and also meet the requirements of constitutional government? There are inherent tensions here, and every increase in speed and flexibility leads to a decrease in public participation. On the other hand, the greater the degree of public and legislative initiatives in foreign policy, the more difficult it might be for the administration to negotiate (particularly when secret talks are required) with foreign governments and conduct its foreign policy.

The issue of expeditious action versus reflection of public preferences is, however, more complex. The Congress certainly does reflect what its members believe to be public opinion in their districts (or states for senators). Some legislators go so far as to make such opinions the deciding factor in their policy decisions, as Senator Edward Zorinsky (D-Nebr.) did on the Panama Canal treaties in 1978. Zorinsky pledged that he would be bound by poll results he obtained and even went so far in support of the treaties as to convince Carter to invite 250 Nebraska residents to the White House to increase support among influential citizens in the state.[79] The polls consistently showed a majority against the treaties, and Zorinsky reluctantly followed public sentiment. This localism in congressional foreign policy making is clearly aided by the large staffs and tremendous expenditures for offices, supplies, and trips back home. The resources available to members have changed dramatically. Contrast this with the concern of Robert A. Dahl more than thirty years ago over how to make foreign policy making in Congress more consistent with public opinion:

> Representative Jacob Javits employed the Roper agency to poll opinion in the Twenty-first congressional district of New York prior to the 1948 elections. But this is not a readily available technique; the expense rules it out as more than a rare device. One polling agency estimates that it would cost $2,000 to $2,500 to poll a "typical" Congressional district—pretty clearly an expense not many Congressmen or local party organizations can often afford.[80]

In contemporary politics, virtually every candidate for Congress conducts polls which are a regular part of the campaign. Even at inflated prices, polls are now regarded as necessities and well within campaign budgets, which averaged almost $300,000 for the House of Representatives ($400,000 for incumbents) and over $2.5 million for the Senate (over $3.5 million for incumbents) in 1990.[81] This increased use of polling certainly induces more localism into decision making, including that on foreign policy.

However, it would be all too facile to assume that presidents are immune from public pressure in the conduct of foreign policy. Indeed, in his first major speech after resigning in protest as secretary of state in the Carter administration, Cyrus Vance charged in June 1980 that the administration's policies regarding SALT II, Afghanistan, the Middle East, and human rights were based more on election year political considerations—public opinion—than on global political considerations.[82] Carter spent the better part of his early campaign in the White House during the 1980 Democratic party primaries, in which Kennedy challenged him, stressing his role as president. To be sure, the president argued that he was preoccupied with the crisis in Iran, but when he felt that political pressures forced him to resume active campaigning, the hostages were still not free. During the campaign, Reagan roundly criticized Carter for refusing to take decisive action and preferring to negotiate with Iran for the hostages' release. This made for good press and studies of the 1980 election indicate that Reagan benefited from the public's perception of Carter as a weak leader, especially on issues of national defense (see Chapter 6). Yet, six years later the revelations that Reagan had in fact approved negotiating with the Iranians for the release of American hostages showed that even the most strident of candidates was actually seeking more leeway than popular sentiments might permit. The Iran–Contra affair tested the limits of public opinion and severely constrained the Reagan administration's initiatives in foreign policy thereafter. In 1992 George Bush's refusal to sign binding accords at the Earth Summit in Rio de Janeiro was attributed to electoral pressures: Bush advisers felt that he had already lost the environmentalist vote and needed to concentrate on winning support from supporters of economic growth in the West (see Chapter 9).[83]

The 1992 election brought presidential candidates ever closer to public opinion. Independent H. Ross Perot promised that he would resolve pressing issues through televised national town meetings. Citizens would call toll-free numbers to register their opinions. Public policy would be set by these referenda, which do not provide for the possibility of deliberation or compromise and permit—even encourage—the most militant on each side to make multiple calls. One can image rabid partisans with speed dialers trading in their obsessions with radio giveaway contests for decisions on using military force against Iraq or on letting abortion be legal. Less extreme—but equally telling—is the increased reliance of presidential candidates in 1992 on television talk shows. Such appearances do give candidates more exposure than the typical sound bite of less than ten seconds. They also suggest new forums—such as shock radio and shock television—that might not be so hospitable to informed debate.

The 1992 elections posed a challenge for Congress. The president and Congress were at loggerheads on both domestic and foreign policy during the Reagan and Bush administrations. Congressional leaders became independent policy entrepreneurs on foreign policy, often going so far as meeting with foreign chief executives. House and Senate Democrats wished to impress upon all who would listen that the president's foreign policy was not necessarily the position of the entire government. Now, faced with a president of their own party, legislators had to reconcile their own activism on foreign policy with the need to present a united front for their party. Is unified party control consistent with an activist Congress? Ought the legislature to follow the party leader?

Congressional Democrats were immediately put in a bind. During the campaign and in the Democratic platform (see Chapter 6), the Democrats called for a stricter policy on human rights in China. Candidate Clinton echoed these sentiments. Shortly after the election President-elect Clinton stressed the need to keep up good relations with China. Congressional Democrats were highly critical of the North American Free Trade Agreement with Canada and Mexico (see Chapter 9). Clinton expressed reservations during the campaign, but pledged to implement the accord.

In 1972, before the Republican convention, Nixon made his historic trip to China and traveled to Moscow to sign SALT I. Presidents, no less than members of Congress, are political animals and have a keen sense of how to use the advantage of incumbency to increase their standing in public opinion polls. Foreign policy initiatives—or even crises—are particularly useful in this regard because they focus directly on the president in a "we–they" perspective. The chief executive is seen dealing with other heads of state, thus avoiding a direct confrontation with political rivals. To a certain extent, a president serving his second term is shielded from such political pressures, but we should not overestimate the impact of the two-term limitation mandated by the Twenty-second Amendment to the Constitution. For no president wants to leave office unpopular—and perhaps charged with contributing to the election of a successor of the opposite party because his policies were out of step with public opinion.

The question, in the final analysis, is which institution better represents public opinion? In turn, we must ask: Is there a single national opinion to be represented, as defenders of the strong presidency maintain, or is the nation composed largely of groups of citizens with different interests? The answer we give largely determines which institution should dominate foreign policy decision making, assuming that one wants to argue that foreign policy, like domestic policy, should be subject to such public concern and influences. Perhaps the major questions each of us must ask ourselves are whether the two types of policy making require basically similar or different approaches and whether the benefits of participation by the legislative branch in foreign policy making, thus checking a potential "imperial president," are greater, equal to, or less than the costs imposed by the concern of Congress with issues of interest to the constituencies and by the delays (deliberations) involved in participatory decision making.

Notes

1. Alfred deGrazia, ed., *Congress: The First Branch of Government* (Washington, D.C.: American Enterprise Institute, 1966).
2. Arthur M. Schlesinger, Jr., *The Imperial Presidency* (Boston: Houghton Mifflin, 1973).
3. Hanna Fenichel Pitkin, *The Concept of Representation* (Berkeley: University of California Press, 1967), chap. 4.
4. Roger Hilsman, *The Politics of Policy-Making in Defense and Foreign Affairs* (New York: Harper & Row, 1971), pp. 118–20.
5. J. Lieper Freeman, *The Political Process*, rev. ed. (New York: Random House, 1965).
6. Roger H. Davidson, "Breaking up Those 'Cozy Triangles': An Impossible Dream?" in *Legislative Reform and Public Policy*, eds. S. Welch and J. G. Peters, (New York: Praeger Publishers, 1977), pp. 30–53.
7. David R. Mayhew, *Party Loyalty among Congressmen* (Cambridge: Harvard University Press, 1966).
8. Robert A. Dahl, *Polyarchy* (New Haven: Yale University Press, 1971), esp. p. 120.
9. Thomas M. Franck and Edward Weisband, *Foreign Policy by Congress* (New York: Oxford University Press, 1979), pp. 283–84.
10. John Felton, "Reagan Again Finds El Salvador 'Making Progress' on Rights; Critics in Congress Skeptical," *Congressional Quarterly Weekly Report*, January 29, 1983, p. 218.
11. John Felton, "Democrats Falter on Nicaragua Covert Aid Ban," *Congressional Quarterly Weekly Report*, May 21, 1983, p. 1009.
12. Steven R. Weisman, "Nicaragua Vote: How White House Ran Aground," *New York Times*, August 1, 1983, p. A3.
13. David S. Broder, "New Potential for Dividing Democrats," *Washington Post*, May 8, 1983, pp. A1, A9.
14. For a detailed explication of this thesis, see Eric M. Uslaner, *The Decline of Comity in Congress* (Ann Arbor: University of Michigan Press, 1993).
15. Joanne Omang, "Reagan to Bypass Congress to Fund El Salvador Fight," *Washington Post*, April 14, 1984, pp. A1, A14.
16. John M. Goshko, "Appointing Loyalists as Envoys" and "Clout and Moral Decline: Reaganites' Raid on the Latin Bureau," *Washington Post*, April 28, 1987, pp. A1, A16, and April 26, 1987, pp. A1, A12.
17. David B. Ottaway and Patrick E. Tyler, "New Era of Mistrust Marks Congress' Role," *Washington Post*, May 19, 1986, pp. A1, A10.
18. Quoted in Steven V. Roberts, "Foreign Policy: Lot of Table Thumping Going On," *New York Times*, May 29, 1985, p. A16.
19. Steven V. Roberts, "The Mood in Congress Is Bold and Bitter," *New York Times*, June 2, 1987, p. B6.

20. Gary C. Jacobson, *The Electoral Origins of Divided Government* (Boulder, Colo.: Westview, 1991) chap. 6.

21. David S. Cloud, "China MFN Vote Falls Short of Veto-Proof Margin," *Congressional Quarterly Weekly Report*, July 27, 1991, pp. 2053–56.

22. Carroll J. Doherty, "Consultation on the Gulf Crisis Is Hit-or-Miss for Congress," *Congressional Quarterly Weekly Report*, October 13, 1990, p. 3441.

23. Richard F. Fenno, Jr., *Congressmen in Committees* (Boston: Little, Brown, 1973), p. 103.

24. Frank Smith, *Congressman from Mississippi* (New York: Pantheon, 1964), p. 127. Cf. David R. Mayhew, *Congress: The Electoral Connection* (New Haven: Yale University Press, 1974), esp. chap. 1.

25. Warren Weaver, Jr., "Books of the Times: Review of *Man of the House: The Life and Political Memoirs of Speaker Tip O'Neill*," *New York Times*, September 3, 1987, p. C24.

26. Walter Dean Burnham, *Critical Elections and the Mainsprings of American Politics* (New York: W. W. Norton, 1970).

27. Gary C. Jacobson, *The Politics of Congressional Elections*, 3d ed. (New York: HarperCollins, 1992), p. 38.

28. The figures are drawn from Norman J. Ornstein, Thomas E. Mann, and Michael J. Malbin, comps., *Vital Statistics on Congress 1991–1992* (Washington: CQ Press, 1992).

29. Eric M. Uslaner, "The Case of the Vanishing Liberal Senators," *British Journal of Political Science* 11 (January 1981), pp. 105–13.

30. Data from the House Commission on Administrative Review, 1977, survey of members of the House of Representatives.

31. Samuel P. Huntington, "Congressional Responses to be Twentieth Century," in *The Congress and America's Future*, 2d ed., ed. D. B. Truman (Englewood Cliffs, N.J.: Prentice-Hall, 1973), pp. 6–38.

32. Fenno, *Congressmen in Committees*, chap. 1.

33. Richard F. Fenno, Jr., *Home Style* (Boston: Little, Brown, 1978), p. 160.

34. Fenno, *Congressmen in Committees*, p. 110.

35. Eileen Burgin, "Representatives' Decisions on Participation in Foreign Policy Decisions," *Legislative Studies Quarterly* 16 (November 1991), pp. 521–46.

36. Fenno, *Congressmen in Committees*, p. 141.

37. Mark Shields, "One Man's Dynasty," *Washington Post*, September 10, 1986, p. A19.

38. Jacobson, *The Politics of Congressional Elections*, chap. 5.

39. Ibid. Also see Richard F. Fenno, Jr., *The United States Senate: A Bicameral Perspective* (Washington: American Enterprise Institute, 1982).

40. Uslaner, "The Case of the Vanishing Liberal Senators."

41. Quoted in Norman J. Ornstein and David W. Rohde, "Shifting Forces, Changing Rules and Political Outcomes," in *New Perspectives on the House of Representatives*, 3d ed., Robert L. Peabody and Nelson W. Polsby, eds., (Chicago: Rand McNally, 1977), p. 222.

42. See the remarks of the Honorable Bob Carr (D., Mich.), *Congressional Record*, Daily Edition, Ninety-sixth Congress, First Session (March 5, 1978), p. E838; and Bruce A. Ray. "Committee Attractiveness in the U.S. House, 1963–1981," *American Journal of Political Science* 18 (August 1982), pp. 609–13.

43. Rhodes Cook, "Many House Members Survive, but Many Margins Narrow," *Congressional Quarterly Weekly Report*, November 10, 1991, pp. 3798–3800.

44. Fenno, *Home Style*, pp. 151–57.

45. Steven S. Smith and Christopher J. Deering, *Committees in Congress*, 2d ed. (Washington: CQ Press, 1990), pp. 87, 101.

46. Quoted in Eric M. Uslaner, *Shale Barrel Politics: Energy and Legislative Leadership* (Stanford: Stanford University Press, 1989), p. 12.

47. Roger H. Davidson, Walter J. Oleszek, and Thomas Kephart, "One Bill, Many Committees: Multiple Referrals in the House of Representatives," *Legislative Studies Quarterly* 13 (February 1988), pp. 3–28; and Davidson, "Multiple Referral of Legislation in the U.S. Senate, "*Legislative Studies Quarterly* 14 (August 1989), pp. 375–92.

48. See Donald R. Matthews and James A. Stimson, *Yeas and Nays* (New York: John Wiley, 1975).

49. Roberts, "Foreign Policy."

50. For a general discussion of these reforms, see Leroy N. Rieselbach, *Congressional Reform in the Seventies* (New York: General Learning Press, 1977).

51. Fenno, *The Power of the Purse* (Boston: Little, Brown, 1966), esp. chap. 11.

52. Theodore J. Lowi, *The End of Liberalism*, 2d ed. (New York: W. W. Norton, 1979).

53. John M. Goshko, "For Pell, Tests Await on a Resurgent Panel," *Washington Post*, November 11, 1986, p. A19.

54. Michael Barone and Grant Ujifusa, *The Almanac of American Politics 1992* (Washington: National Journal, 1992), pp. 1101–1103.

55. Leslie H. Gelb, "For Senate Foreign Relations Panel, More Partisanship and Less Influence," *New York Times*, November 27, 1984, p. A27; and Jonathan Fuerbringer, "Senate Foreign Relations Committee: Some Political Chasms That Await the Arms Treaty," *New York Times*, December 7, 1987, p. B6.

56. Barone and Ujifusa, *The Almanac of American Politics 1992*, p. 913.

57. Fenno, *Congressmen in Committees*, p. 108.

58. Ibid., pp. 71–72 and 134; see also Ornstein and Rohde, "Shifting Forces" p. 223.

59. Barone and Ujifusa, *The Almanac of American Politics 1992*, p. 291.

60. David E. Rosenbaum, "Turnovers: The Talk of the House," *New York Times*, June 2, 1992, p. A12.

61. "Leading Scorers: Presidential Support," *Congressional Quarterly Weekly Report*, December 28, 1991, p. 3752.

62. Michael Barone and Grant Ujifusa, *The Almanac of American Politics 1986* (Washington: National Journal, 1985), pp. 1458–1460.

63. Jacqueline Calmes, "Aspin Makes Comeback at Armed Services," *Congressional Quarterly Weekly Report*, January 24, 1987, pp. 139–42.

64. Michael Barone and Grant Ujifusa, *The Almanac of American Politics 1992* (Washington: National Journal, 1992), pp. 103–104; and Pat Towell, "Dellums Will Bring Savvy, Not Just Anger, to Chair," *Congressional Quarterly Weekly Report* (January 2, 1993), p. 33.

65. Alan Ehrenhalt, ed., *Politics in America 1986* (Washington: CQ Press, 1985), pp. 1403–1404.

66. Steven S. Smith and Christopher J. Deering, *Committees in Congress*, 2d ed. (Washington: CQ Press, 1991), pp. 87, 101.

67. Dan Morgan, "House Bill Blends Policy, Patronage," *Washington Post*, August 8, 1990, p. A19.

68. James M. Lindsay, "Parochialism, Policy, and Constituency Constraints: Congressional Voting on Strategic Weapons Systems," *American Journal of Political Science* 34 (November 1990), pp. 936–60.

69. Barone and Ujifusa, *The Almanac of American Politics 1992*, pp. 297–98.

70. Ibid., p. 1342.

71. Only Democrats have caucuses. The Republicans call their organizations *conferences*.

72. Samuel Kernell, *Going Public* (Washington: CQ Press, 1986), pp. 28–32.

73. Arthur G. Stevens, Jr., Daniel P. Mulhollan, and Paul S. Rundquist, "U.S. Congressional Structure and Representation: The Role of Informal Groups," *Legislative Studies Quarterly* 6 (August 1981), pp. 415–37.

74. John H. Cushman, Jr., "Amending Military Spending," *New York Times*, May 5, 1987, p. A32.

75. Barbara Sinclair, *The Transformation of the U.S. Senate* (Baltimore: Johns Hopkins University Press, 1989), p. 119.

76. Steven S. Smith, *Call to Order* (Washington: Brookings Institution, 1989), pp. 178–80, 216.

77. This table is taken from Marjorie Ann Browne, "Executive Agreements and the Congress" (Washington: Congressional Research Service, Library of Congress, 1980), p. 2. Updated and revised figures were provided by Ms. Browne and by the Department of State.

78. Loch Johnson and James M. McCormick, "The Making of International Agreements: A Reappraisal of Congressional Involvement," *Journal of Politics* 40 (May 1978), pp. 468–78.

79. Thomas M. Franck and Edward Weisband, *Foreign Policy by Congress* (New York: Oxford University Press, 1979), pp. 277.

80. Robert A. Dahl, *Congress and Foreign Policy* (New York: W. W. Norton, 1950), p. 37.

81. Ornstein, Mann, and Malbin, *Vital Statistics on Congress 1991–1992*, pp. 74, 78.

82. *New York Times*, June 6, 1980, p. A12.

83. Michael Wines, "Bush and Rio," *New York Times*, June 11, 1992, pp. A1, A12.

CHAPTER 5

The Fourth Circle I: Public Opinion

One of the key differences between foreign and domestic policy making lies in the power of the president. Domestic policy formation is always a matter of give-and-take between the legislative and executive branches. In foreign policy crises, however, the smallest, inner circle (see Figure 1–1) makes the decisions and the other actors simply "react." Prior to the 1960s, the executive dominated other aspects of foreign policy decision making as well. Now, however, other actors such as the Congress, public opinion, the political parties, the media, local political leaders, and interest groups play a much larger role in foreign policy decision making than in the past. This is particularly the case on "intermestic" policies that are a mixture of foreign and domestic issues such as energy, trade, and agriculture (see Chapter 9).

The actors in the outermost circle highlight the democratic dilemmas. On the one hand, foreign policy has become much more participatory and thus more like domestic politics. On the other hand, the stakes of foreign policy in a nuclear age have remained much higher than those of domestic issues. The distrust of presidential authority that began during the Vietnam War lasted through the Carter administration. Faith in government—and in a strong presidency—was restored early in the Reagan administration, only to plunge again during the Iran–Contra affair. It rebounded after the Gulf War, but fell precipitously thereafter.

World leaders looking to the United States for action on foreign policy found no central authority and conflicting policy initiatives. During the televised hearings on the Iran–Contra crisis, some key witnesses testified that Congress and the actors in the two outer circles were confounding effective policy making by opposing aid to the Contras. Outraged senators and representatives responded that the United States is, after all, founded on a respect for law, even if one disagrees with specific statutes. Regard for law in democratic societies implies accepting disagreeable statutes as expressions of the popular will.

Ought foreign policy to be guided by the public will? Few will dispute the superiority of democratic government over tyranny. Virtually everyone in Western nations hailed the demise of communism. The movement for more democracy spread throughout the world, and some optimists even proclaimed the emergence of a new world order with representative government triumphant.[1] Should our enthusiasm be tempered by the high stakes in foreign policy and most citizens' inattention to international politics? Since the Vietnam War, the old politics of consensus crossing the two major parties has given way to one of multiple factions. Some will see a danger in this trend, as James Madison, in *Federalist Papers* 10 and 51 on domestic political issues, over 200 years ago warned of the "mischiefs of faction." The founders of the American republic feared that the people could be easily swayed by the passions of the moment. Without sufficient checks and balances, the wrath of public opinion could produce a "tyranny of the majority."[2] The stakes are high on foreign policy, and policy decisions are not readily reversible. Could popular whims endanger our dealings with foreign countries? In the twentieth century the noted journalist Walter Lippmann warned that voters do not possess the knowledge or interest to set policy for the nation: "If the voter cannot grasp the details of the problems of the day because he has not the time, the interest or the knowledge, he will not have a better public opinion because he is asked to express it more often."[3]

The founders and Lippmann worried that the public might force leaders into unwise decisions on foreign—and domestic—policy. Gabriel A. Almond elaborated, but with a different emphasis:

> There are inherent limitations in modern society on the capacity of the public to understand the significance of most important problems of public policy. This is particularly the case with foreign policy where the issues are especially complex and remote.... The superficiality and instability of public opinion places enormous power in the hands of the policy and opinion elites. There is no corrective available in matters calling for immediate action if serious miscalculations are made at the elite level.[4]

Almond worried that the instability of public opinion gives too much power to decision makers. Public opinion changes quickly—the public does not have opinions as much as "moods"—and leaders may choose to ignore such rapid changes in popular sentiments and instead focus on what they think is best.

If the founders and Walter Lippmann are correct, elites are bound by ill-informed foreign policy beliefs of the public. If Almond is right, elites may have too much leeway. Either way, the relationship between public opinion and foreign policy making is problematic. The need to act quickly and for the nation to speak with one voice appears to put democratic governance at odds with foreign policy decision making. Leaders might be too constrained by popular passion or free enough to subvert democratic principles. Defenders of representative government will argue that democratic decision making requires a give-and-take and that it is more important that a policy be arrived at democratically than be correct. In international crises the executive still retains the flexibility to act expeditiously. And should not the people have a say in forming the very policies that will decide whether they live or die?

Can foreign policy be governed democratically? How much does the public know about foreign policy? Do they know substantially more about domestic policy? Do they know enough about either domain—and does it matter? What does the public need to know? Is public opinion fickle? If it is merely a "mood," then it may not provide a basis for setting national policy. If it is more stable and if it moves in response to events in the world, then there may be less conflict between the requirements of a sound foreign policy and democratic governance.

We examine the role of public opinion on foreign policy making by considering how much people know about international relations and how stable these opinions are. We compare attitudes on foreign policy to those on domestic issues. What do people need to know? How stable are Americans' attitudes on each type of policy? Do rapid shifts in presidential popularity during international crises indicate a fickle public that is readily manipulated? Or is there some underlying stability in public opinion? Do political leaders respond to changes in public opinion when they make foreign policy? How much might popular attitudes constrain leaders? Do the public and its leaders generally agree on key issues of foreign policy? The public's responses to the Iran–Contra scandal and the crisis in the Persian Gulf suggest that the American people can respond rationally to international events and can even shape leadership positions. Candidates for office increasingly offer voters distinctive worldviews on foreign policy and, when international events are salient to the public, the people can respond. Nevertheless, public opinion can conflict with the demands of foreign policy decision making that we identified in Chapter 1. Before we consider the evidence, we first examine some alternative perspectives on public opinion and policy making.

Popular Control of Foreign Policy

At the heart of any discussion of democratic government is popular control of decision making by the citizenry. Parties, interest groups, and the media serve to shape public opinion, which is the fountain of legitimacy in democratic politics.[5] Without popular control of decision making, democratic government becomes little more than a myth. Yet, the question remains of how competent the public is to make the difficult decisions on complex issues such as nuclear deterrence. It is also unclear that the public is sufficiently interested in these issues to take an active role in ensuring that government leaders adopt the positions that a majority of the public wants. If the public does not give the actors in the first three circles clear cues as to what it wants, then the leadership will have few incentives to follow what is called "public opinion." In turn, however, the public may complain that its leaders, be they in government or the "opinion leaders" of political parties, interest groups, or the media, do not present these complex issues in terms the ordinary citizen can understand.

These issues in popular control of government were less salient twenty years ago because there were few lines of cleavage on most foreign policy questions. Political parties did not take divergent stands on foreign policy questions. Foreign affairs intruded less frequently on the domestic scene in the era before the world economy became so interconnected. Thus, the press did not focus on the international arena except during crises. And there were very few interest groups active on these issues.

The Vietnam War changed all of this in two important ways. First, television coverage of the war brought home a new dimension of international conflict. New technology made it possible, for the first time, for viewers to see the war fought as it happened. Second, and more critical, as the war dragged on, so did public cynicism. In the late 1960s there were sharp increases in the percentages of citizens who felt that the government was unresponsive and could not be trusted. Furthermore, the high levels of faith in the political system in the early 1960s have not been restored.[6] The conflict over the war translated not only into public cynicism, but also into the breakdown of the prewar consensus on the proper role of the United States in world affairs.

Many Americans have always agreed with President George Washington's warning in his farewell address about "entangling alliances." Yet this isolationist segment of public opinion has been a distinct minority; it did not succeed in preventing American entrance into either World War. But in the post-Vietnam period, a new attitude of "noninternationalism" has arisen and now accounts for almost half of the electorate. It is skeptical of international involvements of any kind. Some say that this picture is too simplistic and that there are two overlapping worldviews. Militant internationalists are willing to use American military might to gain security; cooperative internationalists favor détente and multilateral initiatives to secure world peace. Yet, however one defines internationalism, about half the public has been isolationist and half internationalist since the mid-1970s.[7] Elites, who had always been more united than the mass public, were now split along even more complex lines than prior to the war in Vietnam. Some of these opinion leaders remained ready to use American military power wherever needed (the Cold War internationalists). Yet others, especially those who opposed the war in Vietnam from the beginning, were either outrightly skeptical of the use of force (the semiisolationists) or at least much more wary of where military action would do any good (the post-Cold War internationalists).[8]

The Vietnam War brought an end to the era of bipartisanship on foreign policy. No longer was it clear that the United States was united on the goals of "making the world safe for democracy," the expressed purpose for entering World War I. The breakdown of consensus led to increasing partisanship and the formation of a large number of interest groups taking part on international issues. Foreign policy had, in short, become democratized. Yet, for all of the din, it was not at all clear that the public was so concerned with international issues.

Does the public respond rationally to international affairs or is it readily manipulated by executive leadership?[9] In contrast to domestic issues—which are often very salient to the everyday lives of citizens—foreign affairs often seem remote. People respond to external events, but they tend to rally behind the president in an international crisis *even when it is clear that the president's policy has failed.* Only when policy failure clearly extends over a long period of time does the public turn fickle. Then it does so with a vengeance, demanding that the government refrain from any similar initiatives, no matter how well intentioned. Public opinion thus offers little guidance to elected leaders as to what they should do. Rather, it serves to set limits as to what is prohibited.[10] In either case, however, "the reaction has no depth and no structure."[11]

There is another perspective that is more optimistic. It acknowledges that there are different patterns of public responses to domestic and foreign policy—public opinion shifts more abruptly and by larger amounts on foreign policy—but the public is rarely misled by its leaders. Instead, it responds in predictable, and thus rational, ways to external events.[12] These differing perspectives are based upon alternative views of what popular control of foreign policy means. The former requires that the public understand events, formulate opinions about them, and hold consistent "belief systems" across a range of foreign policies. Furthermore, for public opinion to be really effective, citizens should translate their policy preferences into voting decisions. As we shall see below, there is little evidence that any of these conditions hold. The alternative view, however, requires only that people can react *retrospectively* to foreign policy decisions. It stems from a conception of democracy that places less emphasis on detailed knowledge than on the ability to form judgments about what the government has done. As the leading proponent of this view, E. E. Schattschneider, argued almost three decades ago, one doesn't have to be an obstetrician to have a baby, just as one doesn't have to be a policy expert to form a rational opinion about government decisions.[13]

What Does the Public Know and How Much Does It Need to Know?

Skeptics argue that Americans simply don't know much about world affairs. Events across the world are simply too remote to excite most people. How much does the public know? What does it need to know? Is public opinion consistent over time? How does it change? If we are looking for "rational" public opinion, shouldn't we at least insist that people know what they are talking about? Shouldn't they give the same responses to identical questions asked at different times, assuming that nothing in the real world has intervened that might stimulate opinion change?

A 1986 poll found that only 38 percent of Americans knew that the United States was supporting the Contras as opposed to the government in Nicaragua. An equal number of respondents in 1986 thought that the Nicaraguan government was right-wing as those who responded that it was Communist. Similarly, only 34 percent of a national sample knew that "Star Wars" referred to Reagan's space missile defense; 28 percent could remember only the movie. And two-thirds of the public admitted knowing "nothing at all" about the SALT II treaty in 1986.[14] Just 20 percent of a sample reported that they had followed the news about Central America "very closely." Four of the five most important foreign goals cited by the public were intermestic issues, and two of the top three concerned protecting American jobs and exports.[15]

Americans are not very knowledgeable about foreign affairs, but they don't do very well on domestic concerns either. Table 5–1 presents a sampling of Americans' political knowledge between April 1989 and December 1991. Three-quarters of Americans could identify July 4, 1776, as the date on which the Declaration of Independence was signed, but an almost equal share said that they had "heard of" the North Atlantic Treaty Organization, the Western military alliance. Just under three-quarters knew that the Bill of Rights is part of the Constitution.

For specific knowledge, Americans fare poorly on both domestic and foreign policy concerns. About half know which party controls the Senate and the House. Few could identify Canada as America's largest trading partner or Brian Mulroney as Canada's prime minister. Virtually no one in December 1991 knew the name of Japan's prime minister. Yet, more Americans could identify Nelson Mandela, who had just been released from a South African jail and was visiting the United States, in February 1990, than could recognize either Supreme Court nominee David Souter, House Speaker Tom Foley (D-Wash.), or Senate Majority Leader George Mitchell (D-Me.) that fall. The same share of people could identify Robert Gates, President Bush's nominee to head the Central Intelligence Agency, in August 1991, as admitted hearing of the highly controversial civil rights bill pending before Congress three months earlier. An almost identical percentage could name the former Communist country that had a prolonged civil war—even though the battles in what was Yugoslavia were vividly portrayed on network television night after night. Yet almost half got the name of the country with a new Disney theme park (France) correct, and over 40 percent knew that South Africa had voted to end its apartheid system.

If the public doesn't know much at any given time, it fares even worse when we consider the stability of people's attitudes. If the public is to help shape policy decisions, it should know what it wants. At a minimum, citizens should express

TABLE 5.1   Americans' Political Knowledge

Question	Percent Correct
Heard of North Atlantic Treaty Organization	79
Know what happened July 4, 1776	77
Know that Bill of Rights is part of Constitution	72
Know U.S. troops did not help Romanians topple government	68
Identify Nelson Mandela (head of African National Congress, South Africa)	68
Know which party controls Senate	52
Identify David Souter, Supreme Court nominee	51
Identify George Mitchell, Senate Majority Leader	50
Identify Tom Foley, Speaker of the House	47
Identify country (France) where new Disney park is located	47
Know which party controls House of Representatives	44
Know that South Africans voted to scrap apartheid system	43
Heard of civil rights bill pending before Congress	23
Identify Robert Gates, nominee to head CIA	23
Identify Yugoslavia as former Communist nation with prolonged civil war	21
Know that Canada is U.S.'s largest trading partner	12
Identify prime minister of Canada (Brian Mulroney)	11
Identify Japanese prime minister (Kiichi Miyazawa)	1

SOURCES: News stories and press releases from CBS News/*New York Times; Los Angeles Times;* NBC News/*Wall Street Journal;* Times-Mirror surveys; and *Maclean's,* April 1989 through July 1992.

the same preferences on core issues over time. Philip E. Converse shocked students of public opinion when he found in panel surveys in 1956–1958–1960 that Americans' attitudes on issues were loosely structured and inconsistent over time. On both foreign and domestic policies, people had no coherent "belief systems." One could not predict someone's position on foreign aid from that same person's attitude on whether the United States should take an active role in world affairs. Even worse, attitudes on the same questions over time were unstable. So many people gave different answers to the same questions that attitudes appeared to be random. Positions on foreign policy were less stable than those on domestic issues.[16] From 1972 to 1976 foreign policy issues again ranked below domestic issues with respect to stability over time. Moreover, attitudes were more stable in the 1950s than in the 1970s.[17]

The public is not very knowledgeable on either domestic or foreign affairs. It is fickle on both, but more so on international questions. In their comprehensive survey of repeated survey questions from 1935 to 1990, Benjamin I. Page and Robert Y. Shapiro found that attitudes on foreign policy were more likely to have sharp changes over time (49 percent) than positions on domestic policy (37 percent). Changes that are particularly sharp are far more likely to occur on foreign policy (58 percent) than on domestic policy (27 percent)—and the magnitude of the shifts was far greater (31 percent compared with 12 percent).[18]

Public opinion on the president's handling of his job provides fertile evidence of fickleness. During international crises the public rallies behind presidential leadership even when the chief executive's policy is widely viewed as a failure. The Japanese attack on Pearl Harbor boosted Franklin D. Roosevelt's popularity from an already-high 72 percent to 84 percent. The Communist invasion of South Korea led to a nine-point gain for Harry S Truman (from 37 to 46 percent). Kennedy's popularity jumped sharply after the abortive Bay of Pigs invasion by Cuban émigrés, while Ford's surged by eleven points immediately after the *Mayaguez* incident. The seizure of the American embassy in Teheran resulted in a nineteen-point gain for Carter. Public approval of President Reagan increased after the hijacking of TWA flight 847 to Beirut.[19]

Why do presidents seem to benefit from setbacks in foreign policy? In such crises, the public tends to "rally around the flag" because it sees international conflicts in "we–they" terms.[20] People place the blame for international crises on the opposition—and this is quite understandable since the "they" is almost always a hostile power such as the Soviet Union. Presidents benefit from setbacks; they also gain when things seem to go their way. Even as the Grenada intervention and the bombing of Libya in early 1986 were widely condemned internationally and by many members of Congress, both events were viewed as shows of American strength by the American public and led to sharp increases in the president's popularity. The bombing of Libya resulted in Reagan's second highest level of public support during his presidency. Bush's approval climbed 18 percent with the onset of the air war in the Persian Gulf.[21] Even staged events such as summits—and even summits that fail to reach accords—can lead to significant increases in presidential popularity.[22] Overall, when public approval of the president's handling of foreign policy increases by 3 percent, overall favorability ratings jump by 1 percent. While this is just half the effect for the chief executive's handling of the economy, it is powerful.[23]

Yet, presidents are hardly unconstrained by public opinion. The quick jumps in presidential popularity are usually short-lived. Presidents can gain some support from international events, but since the public's attention span on foreign policy is limited, other factors will soon intervene to shape its view of presidential performance. Foreign policy is different from domestic policy in its impact on popularity. Domestic issues rarely have measurable impacts on the approval of the incumbent chief executive. Yet, international events can be two-edged swords. As crises drag on and the expectation of victory disappears, public support for the president declines. Five months after the American intervention in Korea, public support for Truman dropped sharply. The drop took longer with Vietnam: Public support for the president did not reach a low point until more than two years after the initial troop commitment; the Communist Tet offensive in early 1968 led to a temporary rebound for Johnson. As the number of casualties increased in each contest, public support for the policy and for the president decreased dramatically; the impact of the casualty rate was sharper for Vietnam than for Korea.[24]

Following the seizure of hostages by Iran, Carter's approval more than doubled from its nadir of 30 percent. Approval of the president's handling of the hostage crisis stood at almost 80 percent in December 1979. But as the situation wore on without resolution, public confidence in Carter declined. By April 1980 support for the way he was handling the crisis dropped to 39 percent, his overall job performance to 40 percent, and foreign policy performance to just over 30 percent from 50 percent approval five months earlier.[25] Carter's descent was much more precipitous than Truman's or Johnson's. As in the Vietnam era, however, the constant media attention served to highlight the president's inability to resolve the issue.

Presidents lose popularity slowly, except when some major event intervenes. Nixon lost considerable popularity in 1973 over the Watergate scandal, and Ford's popularity declined sharply in just six weeks following his pardon of Nixon the next year. Truman, battling a hostile Congress controlled by the opposite party, gradually lost popular support in 1947. Reagan's drop of twenty-one approval points in one month following the revelations of illegal arms sales to Iran set a contemporary record. Some argued that the quick fall occurred because news travels faster than it did twenty years ago.[26] Yet, Reagan had done much to restore public confidence in the presidency, so it is hardly surprising that the public would react against the rescuer of the mantle of the White House with severity. Bush's popularity stood at 89 percent in a Gallup survey in early March 1991; by the end of the year it had fallen to 50 percent, yet only two surveys showed drops of 6 percent or more and most declines were in the range of 1 to 2 percent.[27] Reagan's drop in popularity was sharp and sudden; Bush's was more like Chinese water torture. Even in the media age, presidential approval does not always tumble quickly.

The "rally" effect provides insight into the rational basis of public opinion.

People do respond to real world events. Public opinion on policy issues moves most strongly on questions of war, other armed conflict, or the threat of hostilities.[28] In 1980, with the Iran hostage crisis looming large and following the Soviet invasion of Afghanistan, public support for increased military spending jumped 30 percent in just two years.[29] When there is a security threat to the United States, Americans tend to back their president strongly as well. Yet, once the danger has passed, the public turns its attention to other issues—mostly economic—as its key to judging presidential performance. Typically, the "rally" effect is no more than 5 percent additional support for the president. It fades after a month or two. If a crisis lingers, the president risks heavy losses in popularity. Thus, presidents cannot readily manipulate public opinion by creating "crises." Such tactics are likely to backfire.[30]

If the public is changeable, so are events in the world. Presidential popularity represents reasoned responses to real conditions. But how reasoned? Can we expect sophisticated responses from an uninformed citizenry? Perhaps we have judged the American people too harshly. Page and Shapiro argue that many of the questions in surveys "amount to little more than trivia quizzes." People don't need to know the name of the Speaker of the House or the name of the prime minister of Japan to make informed judgments about what the direction of foreign policy should be.

The amount of knowledge people have depends upon what information is currently salient—in the news. In a three-year period the percentage of Americans who knew which side the United States supported in Nicaragua doubled—from 29 to 59 percent from 1983 to 1986, when the Contras were much in the news. Americans don't know much about candidates for president early in the campaigns, but become quite well informed by the time of the election.[31] Similarly, the high level of knowledge about NATO presented in Table 5–1 stands in sharp contrast to a 1964 survey in which 42 percent of Americans did not know that the United States was a member of that organization.[32] In 1964 the nation was focused on domestic policy; in June 1991 the dissolution of the Eastern bloc's military alliance and the future role for NATO were much in the news.

The public also makes "rational" judgments on the state of the economy, even relatively sophisticated ones that punish the president's party more for inflation than for unemployment.[33] People are confronted with the same economic problems again and again and thus can make reasoned judgments easily. On the other hand, many (if not most) foreign policy issues are new (Grenada, Libya, the Iran hostage crisis) and catch the nation unaware. It is far more difficult for citizens to make sophisticated evaluations on international issues. The public will make the linkage when foreign policy events are well publicized. Responses to events are not the same things as fickleness. People become informed when they see some rationale for devoting their precious time and energy to issues, when they see some link between their own lives and policy concerns.[34]

Is Public Opinion on Foreign Policy Rational?

The public responds coherently to presidential performance on foreign policy. It becomes informed when events in the world demand attention. People can make judgments on past performance. These retrospective evaluations run the gamut from the state of the economy to presidential performance in international crises. Such verdicts are relatively undemanding. Citizens judge overall achievements without having to choose among alternative policy options. How well do people do when they have to decide where they stand on issues? Americans don't have firm belief systems. They change their minds on core questions of foreign policy—as well as domestic policy—too frequently for comfort. Is the role of public opinion limited to expressing likes and dislikes?

Bruce Russett, Page, and Shapiro all think not. They argue that individuals may not have coherent beliefs, but aggregate public opinion—the total numbers of pro and con responses in surveys—are very stable over time. Shifts in attitudes correspond to changes in the policy environment. Individuals have stable "long-term" preferences, resembling ideologies, on policies. They may give different answers to specific questions over time, but their fundamental positions change slowly.[35]

Foreign policy preferences do shift—and do so more quickly than domestic positions. First, the external world is far more subject to disruption than domestic politics or issues. Second, international events often define the world in us-versus-them terms, not in partisan or ideological conflicts within the nation.[36] Third, foreign policy conflicts often revolve around unfamiliar places such as Grenada or Libya, while domestic issues recur. People are more likely to develop more deep-seated preferences on issues they know a lot about, and these are largely domestic concerns.

Opinion change is most likely when the public is most attuned to foreign affairs. People focus on international politics when there is an actual or potential military threat that demands attention. In the early years of the Cold War and during the Korean War, many Americans named foreign affairs or security policy as the nation's "most important problem" in surveys. Concern tapered off during the 1950s, only to rise again during the Cuban missile crisis in 1963. It fell thereafter, only to rise during the Vietnam War. The share of mentions dropped in the mid-1970s until the Iran hostage crisis and the Soviet invasion of Afghanistan. It fell once more, only to rise again in 1983 and thereafter, when United States troops were dispatched to Lebanon and Grenada, Korean Air flight 007 was shot down by the Soviets, and the United States bombed Libya.[37]

Major international events not only grab people's attention. They also have the potential to change public opinion. The pro-Communist coup in Czechoslovakia in February 1948 led to a 17 percent jump in the share of Americans who said that the United States was too soft on the Soviet Union and a 10 percent jump in support for universal military training. In both Korea and Vietnam, public backing fell with the number of casualties. The fall in support was interrupted by "rally points" such as the Tet offensive. American attitudes toward the Israeli-Arab dispute track events in the Middle East. Public opinion became more pro-Israel following the 1967 and 1973 wars and after Israel suffered missile attacks from Iraq during the Gulf War; spurts in support for the Arabs occurred following Israel's invasion of Lebanon, the Palestinian uprising (*intifada*), and the controversy over loan guarantees (see Chapter 7). As military spending fell in the 1970s and the American strategic position weakened, public support for increased defense appropriations rose sharply. So did the share of Americans ready to use the nation's military might.[38]

Just prior to Nixon's decision to send American troops into Cambodia, only 7 percent of the respondents to a national survey approved of such a move. Afterward, support had increased to 50 percent. The initial reaction to the invasion of Grenada was mixed at best, with just a bare plurality supporting the president's initiative. After the president made a televised speech defending his policy there and in Lebanon, support for the Grenada invasion increased by nine points in one poll and thirteen points in another. In Lebanon, where 225 marines had been killed in a terrorist attack, the public registered an eleven-point increase in approval of the president's handling of the crisis even though there was no change at all in the public's disapproval of maintaining troops in that beleaguered country.[39]

Just 39 percent of Americans favored an invasion of Panama before President Bush gave a speech warning of such a possibility in May 1989; afterward, there was a 14 percent increase in support. Following the invasion early the next year, approval jumped to 74 percent. Yet the public was not expressing simple jingoism: By 57 percent to 37 percent, it held that Panama was a special case and that the United States would not send troops elsewhere. By 41 to 28 percent, the public argued that the United States should not generally participate in overthrowing foreign leaders.[40]

The Panama case highlights several aspects of rational public opinion, according to the formulation by Page and Shapiro. Attitudes change in response to events in the world and to new information that citizens receive. Bush's speech informed the public of the stakes in Panama. However, people do not necessarily receive a full education. The president has a decided advantage, if not a monopoly, in presenting his side to the American people. Leaders have strong incentives to slant the information they present to the people. Especially on foreign policy, where citizens may have less information than on longer-standing domestic issues, they may even distort the truth. Bush at least exaggerated how readily Panama would make the transition to democracy. Yet, the overall stability of public opinion over time limits the effects of executive manipulation of public opinion; recall the short duration of "rally effects" on presidential approval. Finally, in the Panama case and more generally, public opinion shifts are usually very broad. There are some variations within groups on key foreign policy questions—women are less supportive of military action than men, and Jews back Israel more strongly than Catholics or Protestants. However, when presidents "inform" the public, they have similar impacts on virtually all of the people.[41]

Even though the public may not generally be well informed on foreign policy and may not have coherent belief systems, it fulfills some key conditions for rationality. Knowledge increases when foreign policy concerns become salient. Public opinion shifts in response to events in the world—and in quite predictable and reasonable ways. Attitudes are subject to some short-term manipulation, as demonstrated by shifts in presidential approval. Yet, over a rather brief time (one to two months), the halo effects wear off. These patterns in presidential popularity suggest that the public at least is capable of making retrospective judgments on performance. It makes reasoned evaluations of how well the executive has done.

Shifting patterns of support for specific policies also demonstrate that the public can react with reasonable sophistication to events in the world. Can it do more? Might voters fulfill the ideal model of rational citizens who take clear positions on issues, identify where candidates stand, and cast their ballots on the basis of those positions? We shall see below that sometimes they can. Perhaps we should not demand so much. Often the public fares better at reacting than at issuing directions for future policies. The people do not always speak with one voice. Sixty-four percent of a November 1965 sample of Americans did *not* think that American involvement in Vietnam was a mistake, as compared with 21 percent who believed that it was. By October 1967, the balance had shifted to the position that the war was a mistake (44 percent in favor, 46 percent opposed). By the summer of 1968 a sizable majority took the latter position.[42] Yet the pattern of support for proposals to end the war—including both a stepped-up military posture and total withdrawal—had not changed accordingly from 1965 to 1968. John Mueller has argued that, at any given time, "support should be considered a chord rather than a note."[43] This was no less true of the Iranian hostage crisis, when citizens critical of the president nevertheless did not offer a mandate as to what should have been done.[44]

When is the public most likely to react to the president and when might it do more, even shape leaders' positions? We consider two cases of rational public opinion: the Iran–Contra affair and the Gulf War. In Iran–Contra, the situation was complex and it was unclear what policy prescriptions would be acceptable to a large number of people. In the Gulf crisis, the decision was more straightforward: Should the United States go to war? The public was split, and some leaders recognized this. How people respond generally depends upon the clarity of the options presented to them.

Rational Public Opinion
and the Iran–Contra Affair

Not only does the public no longer simply follow presidential initiatives, but also citizens more readily criticize the president than in the pre-Vietnam era. Vietnam, Watergate, the Iran hostage crisis, and the Iran–Contra affair have all left deep scars on presidential popularity and reputations. Unlike Vietnam and the hostage crisis, the Iran–Contra affair resulted in an immediate loss of popularity for Reagan. The clear reason for this is that there was no external enemy to blame. Iran did nothing to the United States in this example; the administration, rather, shot itself in the foot. A substantial percentage of the American public, up to a third, was uninterested in the affair as late as February 1987, and even the chairman of the House committee investigating the incident found his constituents wishing that the Congress would move on to weightier matters.[45]

Yet, the considerable majority that did follow the affair was able to make reasonably sophisticated judgments. In Figure 5–1 we present graphs of trends in presidential popularity and the percentage of respondents who believed that the president was telling the truth about the matter. Reagan's popularity was near its peak prior to the revelation of the problem in early November, and after that it quickly plummeted. When the president made a televised speech in which he agreed to name an independent counsel to investigate the affair in early December, his popularity continued to decline, as people evidently felt that where there is smoke there is fire. Following the testimony of former NSC chairman Robert McFarlane in early December, Reagan's popularity did not fall further, but the share of people saying that the president was telling the truth increased by 5 percent. McFarlane did not specifically exonerate the president, but accepted much responsibility himself.

Following the January release of the Tower Commission report indicating that the president didn't know of the diversion of funds to the Contras, Reagan's popularity slightly increased. It fell sharply in mid-February, following McFarlane's attempted suicide. Other events such as the replacement of Chief of Staff Donald Regan by Howard Baker in late February and Reagan's television speech in early March admitting that "mistakes were made" had little impact on either the president's popularity or the percentage of people who believed he was telling the truth. The former was of little interest "outside the Washington beltway." Presumably Reagan's television speech made so little impact because most people already realized that mistakes *had* been made. However, the beginning of televised hearings on May 5 led to a sharp drop (seven percentage points) in the share of the public believing that the president was telling the truth, even as Reagan's personal popularity marginally increased. By early June, however, no new major revelations had damaged the president, and Rea-

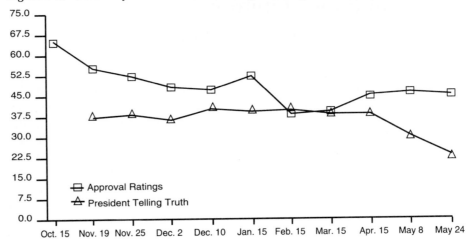

Figure 5–1. Public Opinion on President Reagan During Iran–Contra Affair.

gan's popularity and truthfulness ratings each increased by approximately 5 percent.

While the testimony of Lt. Col. Oliver North dramatically changed the tenor of the hearings, as North became something of a national hero, Reagan did not appear to benefit personally from the boomlet of public support for the colonel. There was little change in early July in the percentage of Americans who thought the president was not telling the truth. Some surveys indicated that the public believed that North was simply "taking a fall" for the president. Yet, when Admiral John Poindexter testified that he engineered the diversion of funds to the Contras and there appeared to be no "smoking gun" linked to the White House, the public turned a deaf ear. Most believed that Poindexter was not telling the truth. While there was a sharp increase in the percentage of Americans who believed that Reagan was telling the truth in just one week, the conversion came primarily from the ranks of citizens who previously had no opinion. There was but a modest drop in the share of the public (still a majority) who believed the president to be lying. More generally, the president appeared no more popular than two months earlier. Ironically, the major shift in public opinion as a result of the hearings—in particular, of North's testimony—was a dramatic increase in public support for aid to the Contras, as reported in most (but not all) polls. Supporters of the president's policy argued that the hearings made the American people more aware of the stakes involved in Central America, so Nicaragua no longer seemed like just a remote place where American soldiers might be sent to be killed. Opponents charged that these results would prove fleeting, representing little more than patriotic zeal and "Olliemania."

Reagan's popularity never fully recovered from the Iran–Contra affair. The percentage of people who approved his performance was generally about the same as that who disapproved for the remainder of 1987, with just a few exceptions. Two raids on Iran in September and October (each of which was supported by over 75 percent of Americans) led to surges in presidential popularity, but each time Reagan fell back to the break-even point shortly thereafter. Reagan did finish the year on a high note, with approval rising from 50 to 58 percent following the summit with Soviet leader Mikhail Gorbachev. Even worse for the president, support for his Central American policies quickly evaporated. Within one month, all polls indicated that the public's opposition to aid for the Contras was once again in the 50 to 60 percent range, the same level as before North's testimony. Public resistance to assistance to the Contras stabilized at this level through 1989.[46]

Well after the dispute faded from public attention, Americans continued to believe that they had not been told the truth. In early 1990 a plurality of 45 to 39 percent believed that President Bush was hiding something about the Iran–Contra affair; over a year later, 57 percent favored a congressional investigation (initiated in 1992) that Reagan–Bush campaign operatives conspired to delay release of American hostages until after the 1980 elections.[47]

The Iran–Contra affair, the hostage crisis, and the wars in Vietnam and Korea had profound effects on presidential popularity. Yet, other presidential failures such as the Reykjavik summit with Gorbachev in 1986 did not. Richard A. Brody and Catherine R. Shapiro noted that Reagan's popularity actually increased by 4 percent following the failed summit. They argued that the difference between the two situations is found in the president's ability to control the flow of information. When events are moving quickly, as in the summit, the administration effectively controls the news. Leaders of the opposition hesitate to criticize the president for fear of appearing unpatriotic. The press behaves similarly. When a crisis begins to drag out, however, the president becomes a target for all sorts of opposition.[48]

Public opinion in the Iran–Contra affair responded to revelations about the roles of key actors. The greatest impact was on Reagan's popularity and perceptions that the president was telling the truth. Both are clearly retrospective judgments. The issues involved were complex. The trail of money from selling arms to Iran and funding the Contras did not capture the public's imagination as the Watergate saga did over a decade earlier. The inability of congressional investigators to implicate the president dampened public interest in the scandal and permitted Reagan's popularity to rise again. In Watergate there were clear public policy remedies: Remove the incumbent president and tighten laws on campaign financing. There were few such solutions in Iran–Contra. Critics of the president pointed out that the administration had violated strong laws already enacted against such covert operations. The issues involved—the proper role of the president in covert operations—were not so salient to the public to shift attitudes on a key policy question. Nevertheless, the scandal did polarize the electorate. Support for the Contras rose, albeit temporarily, especially among

Republicans who saw the affair as a political rather than a constitutional dispute. Iran–Contra invoked evaluations of presidential performance—and, as such, the public gave rational retrospective evaluations.

Public Opinion and the Gulf War[49]

Nothing rallies a country like a popular war. The Gulf War against Iraq was the most popular conflict since World War II. The military action was stunning, victory was quick, casualties few. Confidence in government rebounded. Presidential popularity soared to record heights. The Democrats in Congress who voted against military action feared the electoral retribution promised by the head of the Republican National Committee.[50] The war ended in February 1991. Just a few weeks later the public mood began to sour. Americans were no longer so optimistic about the future. Saddam Hussein was still in power in Iraq; he stepped up repression of the Kurdish minority, and details of his continuing program of nuclear and chemical weapons emerged. The Kuwaiti government was restored but refused to make democratic reforms. The implicit promises by the moderate Arab states to initiate peace moves toward Israel were stalled. The public no longer saw the war as such a great success. Throughout the rest of the year—and much of the next—President Bush's popularity tumbled as the domestic economy weakened.

Attitudes toward the Gulf War conform to rational retrospection, but they also provide policy direction. The people quickly supported the president's decision to send troops to the Persian Gulf after Iraq invaded Kuwait in August 1990. Yet they remained skeptical of military intervention—and of the reasons for taking such action. As Bush's January 15 deadline for Iraqi withdrawal from Kuwait approached, Americans became more supportive of military action. After the hostilities ended, they indicated that the conflict ended too soon. Not only did the public provide policy prescriptions, but it even led decision makers. Democratic congressional leaders initially wavered in their positions on the conflict. Many House Democrats were taken aback when Speaker Thomas Foley (D-Wash.) joined the ranks of opponents of military action.[51] The hesitant Democratic leadership ultimately responded not to President Bush's call for national unity, but to the positions of rank-and-file Democrats throughout the country.

Shortly after troops were dispatched to Saudi Arabia, three-quarters of Americans backed the president's decision. As the threat of war loomed larger, people hesitated. The share saying that the United States did the right thing dropped by 10 percent in October and did not increase until hostilities began on January 16. Then it shot up to 80 percent, rising to almost 90 percent in the immediate afterglow of the military victory in late February/early March before falling to the high 70s in late spring/early summer.

While the public was supportive of sending troops abroad, it was hesitant about sending them into battle. Between one-fifth and one-third of Americans were ready to go to war (as opposed to giving sanctions more time) from mid-October to mid-January. Just before the air war began, between 55 and 68 percent favored military intervention. After the conflict began, between 75 and 81 percent felt that it was justified over the next month. Yet, by April, over half the public believed that the war had ended too soon. Two-thirds held that belief in the summer.[52]

Americans believed that it was worth going to war to show other nations that they could not get away with aggression, to protect hostages, to remove Saddam Hussein from power, and to destroy Iraq's nuclear and chemical warfare capabilities. By a substantial margin, they objected to military action to protect oil supplies. By the fall, many more Americans believed that war was inevitable. Yet, they worried about the costs. In November as many people believed that the war would be long and have many casualties as thought that it would end quickly with few deaths. Yet they rejected the analogy with Vietnam.[53]

John Mueller argues that opinion during the prewar period did not change much. The most notable shift was a drop in public support for sending troops to Saudi Arabia in October. The public did not egg the president on toward war. "The public was being led to it," even as it searched for a "properly packaged compromise."[54] Democratic legislative leaders initially strongly backed the president, but began to waffle as they read the polls. Table 5–2 shows patterns of support among Republicans, Democrats, and Independents in four surveys that broke down results by partisanship. Democrats were consistently less supportive of the Gulf policy than were either Republicans or Independents. Right up to the start of hostilities, they were reluctant to employ the military option. Moreover, Democratic support for the initial decision to send troops to Saudi Arabia fell sharply—from 70 percent in September to 56 percent in November to 50 percent in January. Republican and Independent support fell as well.

The critical result was the polarization of the American public on the war option. It is unusual for foreign policy issues to affect congressional electorates. In November 1990, however, the impending Gulf War did so. Supporters of sending troops to Saudi Arabia divided their ballots almost equally between the two parties (50 percent Republican), but opponents voted Democratic by a two-to-one margin. Thirty-seven percent of the House Democratic electorate was opposed even to stationing troops in the Gulf.[55] In January Democrats preferred by 56 to 36 percent to wait for sanctions. Republicans by 55 to 39 percent were ready to go to war, while Independents were equally divided. Democrats in Congress got a clear message that translated into overwhelming majorities from their party in Congress in January against the use of force. However, the moral was received selectively. Only 16 percent of Democratic legislators whose districts were carried by Dukakis in 1988 voted to endorse the use of force in the Gulf, compared with 46 percent whose districts were carried by Bush and 56 percent in whose districts Bush received more than 60 percent of the vote.[56]

TABLE 5.2   Partisanship and Attitudes Toward the Gulf War

Month	Question	Republicans	Democrats	Independents
September	United States right in sending troops to Saudi Arabia	89	70	70
	United States should invade Kuwait	63	47*	46*
November	United States right in sending troops to Saudi Arabia	79	56	64
	United States should take military action now	48*	39	38
December	Bush moving too quickly toward war	24	46	36
January	United States right in sending troops to Saudi Arabia	72	50	61
	Bush too quick to get military involved	29	51	47*
	Wait longer for sanctions to work	39	56	45

* Figure represents plurality in favor of option.

SOURCES: CBS News press releases, September 11, 1990; November 3, 1990; January 8, 1991; and Yankelovick, Clancy, Schulman press release (for *Time* and CNN), December 5, 1991.

Once the war began, there was a surge in public support for specific policy options, the direction the country was taking, and for Bush's conduct of the presidency (see Table 5–3). Overall there was a 13 percent decline in the number of Americans who said the initial decision to send troops to Saudi Arabia was a mistake. Among Democrats, there was a 23 percent increase in the belief that the U.S. decision was correct in less than two weeks.[57] Bush's popularity surged at the beginning of the crisis (August), but fell sharply in October when he and the Congress battled over the budget. There was a very modest recovery thereafter. The initiation of hostilities led to an eighteen-point rise in support; the brief ground war in late February added nine points to Bush's approval ratings—setting a record at 89 percent. In April, with Saddam Hussein entrenched in power and more than half of the citizenry convinced that the war should not have ended, presidential popularity began a slow but steady descent for the rest of the war.

The war renewed American optimism. Americans had worried that their nation was no longer a world power. Just 44 percent said that it *was* in 1989, but 73 percent agreed following the ground war. A majority of Americans said that the country was on the right track, and there was an 8 percent rise in the share believing that the next generation would have a better life than the current one. Nevertheless, hopefulness was restrained. Just 36 percent had great hopes for the next generation, and a plurality still believed that Japan would replace the United States as the world's leading economic power in the twenty-first cen-

TABLE 5.3 Changes in the Public's Evaluations of the Situation in the Gulf Before and After Hostilities Began

Question	Percent Change
Policy options	
Favor going to war	+24
Mistake to send troops to Saudi Arabia	−13
Situation in Middle East worth going to war	+25
War might resemble Vietnam	−21
Expect short war	+13
U.S. actions in Middle East morally justified	+10
Retrospective Evaluations	
Approve Bush's performance as president	+18
Approve Bush's handling of Persian Gulf crisis	+19
Approve Bush's handling of Iraq	+28
Satisfied with the way things are going in the country	+30

SOURCE: Computed from John Mueller, "American Public Opinion and the Gulf War: Trends and Comparisons." Paper presented at the 1992 Annual Meeting of the Midwest Political Science Association, Chicago, April, 1992, p. 19.

tury.[58] By May a plurality (40 percent) believed that the war was only partially successful, yet the United States was correct (68 percent) to keep out of the conflict between the Kurds and the Iraqi government.

As the economy weakened throughout the rest of the year, Bush's popularity fell. So did the share of Americans believing the country was on the right track. By December only 50 percent approved of Bush's performance; consumer confidence had fallen by 30 percent since January. Just 19 percent believed that the country was on the right track. Americans were less likely to express confidence in the future after the Gulf War than they had been during the Iran hostage crisis.[59] Even in the immediate aftermath of the war there were fears that we were spending too much money abroad and not enough at home and that the Vietnam experience was not behind us (by 58 to 41 percent).

The Gulf War did not become a potent electoral issue. When the vote took place, half of the electorate didn't know their legislator's position; only 16 percent said that the issue would be the most important factor in their congressional balloting, and this group split evenly in favor of and opposed to the war. Party identification figures were not altered by the war or presidential popularity.[60]

Legislators defended their votes in their districts as votes of conscience. Representative Nita Lowey (D-N.Y.), a Jewish member from a district in which 20 percent of the voters are Jewish, found that her constituents were more concerned with her overall record of support for Israel than for the vote on the Gulf War. First-term Representative Larry LaRocco (D-Id.), narrowly elected from a traditionally Republican seat, came under Republican attack early, but he assessed the situation strategically: "I'm a former stockbroker and I know when a stock [Bush's popularity] is at its high. I will fight back if my patriotism is challenged." Southern senators who voted against Bush reported by April that criticism of their votes had largely faded.[61]

Americans were turning inward, but selectively. They resisted suggestions for the further use of force and turned sharply against foreign aid. There were large declines in the percentages of people seeing the Philippines, France, Israel, Egypt, and China as vital to American security—reflecting tensions with most of those countries. There were increases in support for Gulf ally Saudi Arabia and newly democratic Poland.[62] Richard A. Brody and Richard Morin suggest that this reluctance to get involved in foreign affairs, particularly in crises, typifies "normal" politics. Americans were reluctant to fight not only in Vietnam, but also in World War II and other conflicts. The Gulf War was atypical and the American public was able to separate the stakes in the conflict against Iraq from those in other trouble spots.[63]

The public was wary of initial involvement in the Gulf War. Yet, it was hardly uninvolved. The opposition of rank-and-file Democrats seems to have pushed congressional Democrats into firm opposition. It is hardly implausible to argue that the military strategy was affected by public pressure for a short war with few casualties. Public opinion set the parameters for getting involved; recall the sharp jump in support for military action in early January. It provided the retrospective support for the president during and immediately after the conflict. And it set the parameters for what could be accomplished thereafter. As with Vietnam and the Iran hostage crisis, it sent a mixed message. A disappointed public thought that the war should not have ended. Seventy-six percent favored action to remove Saddam Hussein from power in July, yet a few months earlier a plurality opposed using American ground troops to do the job. Such ambiguity gives politicians room to pick and choose. Bush, sensing the mood of greater concern for domestic problems, chose not to reintroduce troops. Had he selected otherwise, he would have risked a protracted war and a charge that he took military action solely to boost his lagging approval.

Public Opinion and the Democratic Dilemmas

The patterns of public opinion on the Iran–Contra affair and the Gulf War indicate that the public, when it is sufficiently interested in a foreign policy issue, can respond quite rationally to events—even events that are not dramatic. And the public certainly found the Iran–Contra affair disturbing: as many people believed that it was at least as serious as Watergate as who thought that the Nixon affair was worse.[64] Events such as the Iran–Contra affair, the hostage crisis, and wars such as Korea, Vietnam, and the Gulf occur over months and years. The public's attention is focused on such issues, and thus citizens can respond ''rationally'' to even relatively ''minor'' incidents. Issues such as ''peace'' and ''strength'' also appear on the nation's agenda continuously. On the other hand, short-lived international crises such as the Bay of Pigs, the Tet offensive, the *Mayaguez*, Grenada, Libya, Panama, and hostage takings vanish from public attention quickly. People are unfamiliar with these international scenarios. Indeed, sometimes so are the State Department and even the CIA, both of which were caught unaware on the fall of the Shah and the hostage crisis that ensued. In those circumstances people follow the only cue that is available—presidential leadership. Indeed, so does the Congress. The ''we–they'' conflict inherent in such crises provides the president with a key advantage: More than at any other time, there is a need to focus on a single actor to reinforce the ''we'' in domestic politics.

Issues that linger in the background—especially the American role in world affairs—form a middle ground. Mostly, they are not terribly salient to the average citizen. The public is skeptical of getting deeply involved in world affairs, fearing another protracted conflict such as Vietnam, and worries more about protecting the United States—both militarily and economically. Here the debate on foreign policy and the democratic dilemmas shift. Even those who argue that the public does not closely follow all of the issues in world politics do not argue that the public is ''irrational.'' Noninternationalism is based upon clearly articulated fears of becoming too entangled in international conflicts. Thus, the debate shifts from the desirability of broad participation (the third dilemma) to the need for the president to maintain flexibility in dealing with other nations (the first dilemma) and to process versus output (the second dilemma). In dealing with other countries, the president needs to be able to respond quickly to international crises, on the one hand, and to pursue policies that are acceptable to our allies, on the other hand. Public opinion can act as a strong constraint on both. There is no guarantee, as we stated in Chapter 1, that foreign policy guided by public opinion will lead to policies that are ''right'' in either sense.

The ''correct'' policies, as seen by presidents, are sometimes held to be those of elites who, unlike the public, confront international issues on a regular basis. These elites are more likely to be ''internationalists,'' to favor a more active role in world affairs, and to be willing to place short-term domestic gains for the United States aside in favor of what they believe to be wise policy in the long run. Periodically, the Chicago Council on Foreign Relations surveys both the mass public and elites, including representatives and senators, State Department officials, business leaders, representatives of the media, educational institutions, labor unions, ethnic and religious groups, and the like. The results of the most recent survey, conducted in 1990, are presented in Table 5-4.[65]

The public is less interventionist than the elites. On most issues the public is

TABLE 5.4   Differences in Public and Elite Attitudes on Foreign Policy, 1990*

Question	Public	Leaders	Gap
Best for U.S. to take an active role in world	69	98	+29
Containing communism very important	58	10	−48
Favor economic aid to Soviets to modernize economy	40	71	+31
Cut defense spending	33	77	+44
Decrease commitment to NATO	31	62	+31
Use military force if Iraq invades Saudi Arabia	58	90	+32
Use military force if Arabs invade Israel	43	70	+27
Use military force if North Korea invades South Korea	44	57	+13
Use military force if Mexico threatened by revolution	54	20	−34
Use military force if El Salvador government threatened	28	13	−15
Use military force if Philippines threatened by revolution	22	7	−15
Favor foreign economic aid	50	91	+41
Cut back foreign economic aid	64	21	−43
Increase economic aid to Eastern Europe	27	75	+48
Protecting U.S. interests abroad very important	65	27	−38
Favor 25 cents a gallon gasoline tax	11	62	+51
European Community practices unfair trade with U.S.	40	56	+16
Japan practices unfair trade with U.S.	71	78	+7
Tariffs are necessary to protect U.S. industries	54	33	−19
U.S. has declined as world power	66	71	+5

* Entries are percentages agreeing with each statement; figures exclude respondents with no opinion. Gap is the percentage difference between leaders and the public.

more favorable to a less active role in international affairs, especially on the question of the use of American forces abroad, and to economic retaliation. Virtually all leaders favor the United States taking an active role in world affairs, compared with just under 70 percent of the public. Overall, the elite are more willing to use military force than the mass public when one country is threatened by another. They were also more sanguine that communism was no longer a peril to the United States and more favorable to foreign aid to the Soviets, Eastern Europeans, and other countries. Elites are thus willing to cut defense spending, but as internationalists are far less willing to cut ties to the NATO alliance. On the other hand, they are consistently less willing to support the use of American troops to quell rebellions from within (in Mexico, El Salvador, or the Philippines)—even though only a small share of the public is ready to do so.

The leaders were more interventionist in 1986 than they were in 1990. In the earlier survey the elite were more willing to use American military power to intervene in world conflicts.[66] However, they have consistently been more supportive of foreign aid and less sympathetic to tariffs even though they are more likely to see foreign trade practices as unfair than the public.

On many key issues the gap between an internationalist elite and an increasingly noninternationalist public is growing. Presidents may look on public opinion with disdain, or may ignore it completely, when confronted with an international crisis. They do so with the expectation that following decisive action, they can count on public support. Chief executives hope to retain the flexibility to act decisively because they are convinced that ultimately the "process versus output" dilemma will be submerged as the public rallies behind the president.

Members of Congress, who must run for reelection every two years, are more likely to respond to citizen attitudes on international affairs. This sets up a direct confrontation between the executive and legislative branches. Congress has been decidedly more protectionist on trade (see Chapter 9) and, at least since Vietnam, less interventionist on security issues. In the post-World War II/pre-Vietnam era consensus, a decision such as Reagan's to place Kuwaiti oil tankers in the Persian Gulf under American protection in 1987 would have met with bipartisan support. Instead, it met with bipartisan opposition, including that of Senate Minority Leader Robert Dole (R-Kans.). Congress, as noted in Chapter 4, took the lead in restricting aid to right-wing insurgent movements in Latin America and in imposing sanctions on South Africa. In its battle with the executive for control over foreign policy, Congress can use public opinion to force changes in administration decisions.

Congress and the president engage in a delicate minuet over the conduct of foreign policy. Presidents use what Theodore Roosevelt call the "bully pulpit" to shape mass opinion. When the public is not paying close attention, they have greater freedom of action. Even so, they are constrained by the electoral calendar and the need to maintain popular support. Early in a first term, presidents typically focus on domestic policy, since this is what new chief executives know best and because it is important to reward domestic constituencies during the "honeymoon" between presidents and the public at the beginning of an administration. When the midterm election approaches, foreign policy becomes a distraction that presidents cannot always afford. The beginning of a second term offers experienced leaders a window of opportunity for foreign policy initiatives, but only a brief one. The president quickly turns attention again to midterm congressional elections and then becomes a lame duck unable to seek reelection. Other people's attention focuses on the next election. The president thus has few opportunities to concentrate on foreign affairs; achieving a second term at all has eluded many contemporary chief executives.[67]

While public opinion may hem in presidents, it can also give them leverage. When the public favors the president's position, the chief executive will generally prevail. The defense build-up in the Reagan years is a case in point. Levels of defense spending generally correspond closely to public attitudes. In the early Reagan administration, constituency opinions favoring a defense build-up resulted in a $16 billion increase in defense spending, even though the Democratic-controlled House of Representatives was not predisposed toward higher expenditures.[68] Reagan also gained support for aid to the Contras by "educating the public" through televised addresses in 1986. The Iran–Contra hearings at least temporarily boosted public backing for assistance, and Democrats in Congress could not prevail over the president even as they were lambasting his administration for illegal support for the rebels.[69]

The battle for public opinion can give a powerful weapon to the Congress. After the initial military build-up achieved by the Reagan administration, public attitudes turned away from increased defense spending and toward the nuclear freeze. One member of the House of Representatives said that the drive for a freeze was "the most powerful, spontaneous grass-roots movement I have seen since I was elected to Congress."[70] Congress enacted freeze resolutions, which the president ignored; yet, the movement, supported by a shifting public opinion on levels of defense spending, led to cuts in defense expenditures. Polls do not show as clear-cut evidence on sanctions against the apartheid regime in South Africa, but it appears that support for such measures—which were strongly opposed by the Reagan administration yet supported by bipartisan majorities in the Congress—was increasing during the period leading to the congressional action in 1986.[71] When public support for the Contras fell once more, Presidents Reagan and Bush were forced to accede to only "humanitarian" assistance. Congress does not need majority opinion to *challenge* the president. The unsuccessful congressional attempts to place sanctions on China were bolstered by an almost even division of public opinion on whether to criticize the Beijing regime or to maintain good relations.[72] The mixed signals of public opinion on the Gulf War energized congressional Democrats to oppose the president's resolution on the use of force.

While the Congress can challenge the president when public opinion is divided, the chief executive retains the upper hand. The president has the veto, which has been used increasingly on foreign policy issues in recent years. To sustain his position, all he needs is just more than one-third support in *either* the House or the Senate. Despite overwhelming support for sanctions against China in the House, President Bush was able to sustain his position in the Senate. Presidents may also circumvent Congress by resorting to executive agreements when treaties cannot receive sufficient support.

Most critically, the president has a decided advantage in swaying the public. The chief executive can command public attention in a way that the 535 members of Congress, most of whom are invisible to the public, cannot. When public opinion is strongly tilted against the president—as with more recent defense spending cutbacks—or clearly moving against the executive—as with aid to the Contras or support for sanctions on South Africa—Congress may become energized. The president, no less than legislators, is ultimately a creature of public opinion. Without popular support, a president cannot hope for either his own reelection or the continuation of his program by a successor from the same party. Yet, opinion alone, no matter how "rational," cannot suffice to guide policy making. Elections provide the critical mechanism for translating public opinion into policy. Parties shape the options that citizens choose from and the media send out the messages, perhaps shaping them along the way. In the next chapter, we consider the electoral linkage, as well as the impacts of political parties and the media.

Notes

1. Francis Fukuyama, *The End of History and the Last Man* (New York: Macmillan, 1992). But see Alan Ryan, "Professor Hegel Goes to Washington," *New York Review of Books,* March 26, 1992, pp. 7–13.
2. Alexander Hamilton, James Madison, and John Jay, *The Federalist Papers* (New York: New American Library, 1961).
3. Walter Lippmann, *The Phantom Public* (New York: Macmillan, 1925), pp. 36–37.
4. Gabriel A. Almond, *The American People and Foreign Policy* (New York: Frederick A. Praeger, 1965), pp. 5, 85.
5. See Giovanni Sartori, *The Theory of Democracy Revisited*, Part One (Chatham, N.J.: Chatham House, 1987), chap. 5.
6. See Seymour Martin Lipset and William Schneider, *The Confidence Gap*, rev. ed. (Baltimore: Johns Hopkins University Press, 1987).
7. William Schneider, "Conservatism, Not Interventionism: Trends in Foreign Policy Public Opinion, 1974–1982," pp. 33–64, in Kenneth A. Oye, Robert J. Lieber, and Donald Rothchild, eds., *Eagle Defiant: United States Foreign Policy in the 1980s* (Boston: Little Brown, 1983), esp. p. 41; Eugene R. Wittkopf, *Faces of Internationalism* (Durham, N.C.: Duke University Press, 1990), p. 24.
8. Ole R. Holsti and James N. Rosenau, *American Leadership in World Affairs* (Boston: George Allen and Unwin, 1984), esp. pp. 117–23, 141.
9. See, on the one hand, Angus Campbell, Philip E. Converse, Warren E. Miller, and

Donald E. Stokes, *The American Voter* (New York: John Wiley, 1956); and, on the other hand, V. O. Key, Jr., *The Responsible Electorate* (New York: Random House, 1966).

10. Schneider, *Conservatism, Not Interventionism,* p. 53.

11. Almond, *The American People and Foreign Policy,* p. 232.

12. See Benjamin I. Page and Robert Y. Shapiro, "Changes in Americans' Policy Preferences," *Public Opinion Quarterly* 46 (Spring 1982), pp. 24–42.

13. E. E. Schattschneider, *The Semisovereign People* (New York: Holt, Rinehart and Winston, 1960), p. 137.

14. David Shipler, "Poll Shows Confusion on Aid to Contras," *New York Times,* April 15, 1986, p. A6; "Star Wars Status," *Public Opinion,* August/September, 1985, pp. 33–35; Barry Sussman, "Public Would Preserve SALT II Treaty, Not Help Nicaragua Contras," *Washington Post,* June 6, 1986, p. A16.

15. John E. Rielly, ed., *American Public Opinion and U.S. Foreign Policy 1987* (Chicago: Chicago Council on Foreign Relations, 1987), pp. 8, 13.

16. Philip E. Converse, "The Nature of Belief Systems in Mass Publics," in David E. Apter, ed., *Ideology and Discontent* (New York: Free Press, 1965), pp. 206–61, esp. pp. 229 and 240.

17. Philip E. Converse and Gregory B. Markus, "Plus ca change...: The New CPS Election Study Panel," *American Political Science Review* 73 (March 1979), pp. 32–49.

18. Benjamin I. Page and Robert Y. Shapiro, *The Rational Public: Fifty Years of Trends in Americans' Public Opinion* (Chicago: University of Chicago Press, 1991), pp. 45, 54.

19. See, among other citations, Adam Clymer, "Analyzing the Drop in Reagan's Ratings," *New York Times,* December 7, 1986, p. E5; and Lou Cannon, "What Happened to Reagan the Gunslinger?" *Washington Post,* July 7, 1985, pp. B1, B4.

20. See John E. Mueller, *War, Presidents, and Public Opinion* (New York: John Wiley, 1973).

21. R. W. Apple, Jr., "And Now the Political Plowshares: Boost for Bush Campaign, but Will It Last?" *New York Times,* June 17, 1992, pp. A1, A11.

22. Barry Sussman, "Grenada Move Earns Reagan Broad Political Gains"; and "76% of Americans Polled Back Bombing of Libya," *Washington Post,* April 30, 1986, p. A4; NBC News Press Release, May 12, 1986.

23. Miroslav Nincic and Barbara Hinckley, "Foreign Policy and the Evaluation of Presidential Candidates," *Journal of Conflict Resolution* 35 (June 1991), pp. 333–55; see esp. p. 341.

24. The Vietnam War cost Johnson seventeen points in popularity in 1968 alone, far more than it hurt Nixon later on, or that Korea cost Truman. See Charles W. Ostrom, Jr., and Dennis M. Simon, "Promise and Performance: A Dynamic Model of Presidential Popularity," *American Political Science Review* 79 (June 1985), p. 351.

25. Adam Clymer, "Poll Finds Reagan-Carter Choice Unsatisfactory," *New York Times,* April 18, 1980, pp. A1, B5.

26. Clymer, "Analyzing the Drop in Reagan's Ratings."

27. John Mueller, "American Public Opinion and the Gulf War: Trends and Comparisons." Paper presented at the 1992 Annual Meeting of the Midwest Political Science Association, Chicago, April, 1992. We are grateful to Professor Mueller for providing us with the very detailed tables he prepared for that paper, which we use extensively in this chapter.

28. Page and Shapiro, *The Rational Public,* pp. 332–36.

29. Ibid., p. 270.

30. Bruce Russett, *Controlling the Sword: The Democratic Governance of Foreign Policy* (Cambridge: Harvard University Press, 1990), p. 94.

31. Page and Shapiro, *The Rational Public*, pp. 12–13.

32. Russett, *Controlling the Sword*, p. 89.

33. Voters react more strongly to inflation than to unemployment because the former affects all citizens, whereas unemployment only a small percentage of people. Furthermore, many unemployed people do not vote and, most critically, the average length of unemployment is a few months. See Kay Lehman Schlozman and Sidney Verba, *Injury to Insult* (Cambridge: Harvard University Press, 1979).

34. Russett, *Controlling the Sword*, p. 90.

35. Page and Shapiro, *The Rational Public*, pp. 15–16.

36. Ibid., p. 283.

37. Russett, *Controlling the Sword*, p. 90.

38. Page and Shapiro, *The Rational Public*, chaps. 5 and 6.

39. David Shribman, "Poll Shows Support for Presence of U.S. Troops in Lebanon and Grenada," *New York Times*, October 29, 1983, p. 9; Barry Sussman, "Reagan's Talk Gains Support for Policies," *Washington Post*, October 30, 1983, pp. A1, A18; and Barry Sussman, "Grenada Move Earns Reagan Broad Political Gains," *Washington Post*, November 9, 1983, p. A3.

40. CBS News press releases, May 12, 1989 and January 18, 1990; NBC News press release, February 14, 1990.

41. Page and Shapiro, *The Rational Public*, chaps. 7, 9, and 10.

42. Mueller, *War, Presidents, and Public Opinion*, pp. 54–55.

43. Ibid., p. 50.

44. Louis Harris, "Carter Rated as 'Failure' in Handling of Hostage Crisis," *Washington Post*, March 17, 1980, p. A18.

45. *Los Angeles Times* Poll press release, February 20–23, 1987; Kenneth B. Noble, "Iran Wave Is a Ripple Back Home," *New York Times*, May 26, 1987, p. A10.

46. In December 1989, 35 percent favored some form of aid to the Contras, while 50 percent opposed it (NBC News press release, December 29, 1989).

47. CBS News press release, January 18, 1990; *Los Angeles Times* press release, June 30, 1991.

48. Richard A. Brody and Catherine R. Shapiro, "Policy Failure and Public Support: Reykjavik, Iran, and Public Assessments." Paper presented at the 1987 Annual Meeting of the American Political Science Association, Chicago, August-September. The sources for the public opinion data cited above were the *New York Times*, the *Washington Post*, and *Newsweek*. All three used essentially the same question wording, so problems of comparability are minimized. When more than one poll was available for a particular week, the results were averaged.

49. This section depends heavily upon Mueller, "American Public Opinion and the Gulf War." We cite the results of many surveys, some of which are summarized in Mueller's paper. Others derive from press releases from CBS News; NBC News; Yankelovich, Clancy, Schulman for *Time* and the Cable News Network; the *Los Angeles Times;* the Times-Mirror Center for People and the Press; and Americans Talk Issues; and from stories in the *Washington Post*.

50. Thomas B. Edsall, "Political Warfare Erupts over Gulf," *Washington Post*, January 25, 1991, p. A4.

51. Walter Pincus and Thomas B. Edsall, "Debate in Congress Reshuffles Disparate Democrats," *Washington Post,* January 11, 1991, p. A25.
52. The precise figures depend upon the wording of questions. The general question was not asked prior to October.
53. Mueller, "American Public Opinion and the Gulf War," pp. 11, 14, 15.
54. Ibid., pp. 13, 10.
55. "How Issues Influenced Votes in the Election for U.S. House of Representatives," *New York Times,* November 11, 1990, p. E5. The latter figure was calculated from the table in the *Times.*
56. Rhodes Cook and Ronald D. Elving, "Even Votes of Conscience Follow Party Lines," *Congressional Quarterly Weekly Report,* January 19, 1991, pp. 190–95.
57. CBS News press releases, January 8 and 18, 1991.
58. Robin Toner, "Poll Finds Postwar Glow Dimmed by the Economy," *New York Times,* March 8, 1991, p. A14.
59. Mueller, "American Public Opinion and the Gulf War," p. 28. The figures were 59 and 64 percent respectively.
60. Ibid., p. 29.
61. John E. Yang, "Words and Images Intended to Reassure Skeptical New Yorkers," *Washington Post,* February 19, 1991, p. A14; Tom Kenworthy, "Answering the Critics: Hard-Learned Lesson in Conservative Idaho," *Washington Post,* February 19, 1991, p. A14; Helen Dewar, "Absence of Malice on War Vote," *Washington Post,* April 9, 1991, p. A4.
62. John E. Rielly, *American Public Opinion and U.S. Foreign Policy 1991* (Chicago: Chicago Council on Foreign Relations, 1991), pp. 18–19.
63. Richard A. Brody and Richard Morin, "From Vietnam to Iraq: The Great American Syndrome Myth," *Washington Post,* March 31, 1991, pp. B1, B2.
64. *Los Angeles Times* Poll press release (February 20–23, 1987).
65. The data in Table 5–4 are compiled from Rielly, ed., *American Public Opinion and U.S. Foreign Policy 1991.*
66. See Rielly, *American Public Opinion and U.S. Foreign Policy 1987.*
67. Russett, *Controlling the Sword,* pp. 12–14.
68. Ibid., p. 99; and Larry M. Bartels, "Constituency Opinion and Congressional Policy Making: The Reagan Buildup," *American Political Science Review* 85 (June 1991), pp. 457–74.
69. Richard Sobel, "Public Opinion About United States Intervention in El Salvador and Nicaragua," *Public Opinion Quarterly* 53 (Spring 1989), p. 117.
70. Schneider, "Conservatism, Not Interventionism," pp. 43–48, 35.
71. "Americans Evaluate the Situation in South Africa," *Public Opinion* (August/September, 1985), pp. 26–28; Rielly, *American Public Opinion and U.S. Foreign Policy 1987,* p. 27.
72. A January 1990 survey found a 42 to 46 split on punishing China. Four months later the figures were 42 to 44. Yet, most respondents (by 52 to 37 percent) favored maintaining China's most favored nation status. See CBS News press releases, January 18, 1990, and May 25, 1990.

CHAPTER 6

The Fourth Circle II: Elections, Political Parties, and the Media

People can make reasoned decisions on foreign policy questions. Changes in public opinion reflect events in the world. Presidents are constrained by mass attitudes. However, the ultimate check on leaders is not public opinion, but electoral sanctions. If people don't translate their views to voting decisions, the impact of public opinion will be limited. Do Americans vote on foreign policy issues? Voters' choices become clearer if the parties take distinctive stands on foreign policy. During and after World War II there was a strong emphasis on bipartisanship on foreign policy (see Chapters 1 and 2). As the consensus on American goals broke down after Vietnam, so did bipartisanship. In the Reagan and Bush years party conflict reemerged on foreign policy. The United States is now less able to speak with one voice. Stronger partisanship enhances the role of public opinion: Voters clearly see differences between the two parties and can cast their ballots on the basis of foreign policy issues. Since the 1970s, the media have played an increasingly prominent role in discussions of foreign policy. Does this "unelected elite" shape foreign policy—and, if so, how? Are the media the tools of corporate America, reflecting a nationalistic bias that glorifies American power and the president, as some have argued? Or does the press constantly carp at the White House, as others have suggested? More critically, how much power does the press have? Does it transform public opinion—or mostly reflect it?

The Electoral Connection

The battle for control of foreign policy between the legislative and executive branches implies a struggle for the hearts and minds of the American people. But popular control of government is hardly a one-way street. Public opinion can affect policies in two ways. The first occurs when politicians simply decide to do what the people want. This is a less powerful means of control because public attitudes do not sanction errant behavior on the part of the president or Congress. The second is through elections. If citizens do not like the policy decisions of their officials, they can vote them out of office. In order for the message to be clear, however, it is imperative that there be some connection between electoral outcomes and policy preferences—or at least between retrospective evaluations of leaders' performance on foreign policy and vote choice.

There are two views of electoral accountability. The stronger argues that public opinion should be "converted" into public policy by the representative system of government. These theorists expect leaders to "re-present" the views of the public. How well the public's viewpoints are translated into public policy gives us an idea of how well the democratic system is working. This "conversion" function assumes that it is the task of officeholders to represent faithfully the majority position (for Congress in their constituencies, for the president of the nation) between elections as well.[1] The weaker theory of retrospective voting maintains that voters can replace an officeholder whose views or simply whose performance they do not like at the next election.[2]

Conversion makes strong demands. Voters must have positions on issues, identify the stances of both major party candidates, find differences (where they exist) in candidate stands, and be able to identify which nominee is more liberal than the other.[3] For retrospective voting, voters need only evaluate performance. People might turn away from Jimmy Carter because of his performance on the Iran hostage crisis and Ronald Reagan because of Iran–Contra, yet support John F. Kennedy for his success on the Cuban missile crisis and George Bush for his victory in the Gulf War. Such voters would reward outcomes, not ideological similarity.

Presidential elections have historically revolved around domestic concerns, especially the state of the economy, rather than foreign policy issues. In 1948 Harry S Truman and Thomas E. Dewey, the Republican nominee, did not take divergent positions on the general thrust of foreign policy, thus limiting the impact of international concerns on voting decisions.[4] In 1956 and 1960 the net contribution of the parties' foreign policy stands on voting behavior changes from one election to the next was, at a maximum, one-half of 1 percent.[5] On the other hand, retrospective evaluations of presidential performance had powerful effects on vote choice.[6] In 1952 the public tired of American involvement in Korea.[7] In 1968 concern over Vietnam mounted.[8] In 1980 there was a sharp negative reaction to the Iranian hostage crisis. Each election marked a change in the governing party. Voters may have also expressed their disappointment with the foreign policy record of the second Eisenhower administration. The Soviet Union launched the first space satellite, Sputnik, in 1957, challenging American technological preeminence; in 1960, an embarrassed president had to admit that the Soviets had shot down the U-2 spy satellite, and a summit meeting in Paris with Soviet leader Nikita Khrushchev ended in disaster.

Voters are more likely to rely upon retrospective evaluations, which are easy to form, than positions on issues. In presidential elections from 1952 to 1980, performance was more important than policy for almost all candidates. Only three challengers, all of whom stressed ideology (Barry Goldwater in 1964, George McGovern in 1972, and Ronald Reagan in 1980), were evaluated more on policy than on estimates of their likely performance.[9]

Foreign policy issues are not always electoral stepchildren. Voters sometimes care mightily about international issues and *can* make distinctions between candidates. There are three reasons that the impact of foreign policy on elections may be increasing. First, cues are more readily available. Parties are increasingly differentiated on foreign policy positions, making it easier for voters to see clear differences between candidates and to cast ballots on that basis (see below). Second, people have greater exposure to foreign policy news and higher levels of education that might predispose them to follow such events more closely. In 1990, 36 percent of Americans paid attention to news about other countries, up from 28 percent as recently as 1982. Fifty-three percent were concerned about news of American relations with other nations, compared with 45 percent in 1982. Attention to state and local governments declined over this period, while interest in national news remained essentially stable.[10] Finally, the world has become more interdependent, and major events in the news increasingly focus on international events. Ironically, however, since the 1970s people have been *less* likely to see foreign affairs as the nation's most important problem than in the 1940s, 1950s, or 1960s.[11] This is understandable, since the 1940s were a decade of war and the 1950s and 1960s were marked by the Cold War. Détente ushered in a concern for domestic problems. During the hot and cold wars, foreign policy was more bipartisan, so there was less to choose from. Other issues predominate in the current era, but there is greater debate between the parties on foreign policy. We suggest that: *When foreign policy salience is highest, its impact on vote choice should be greatest, provided that voters are offered distinct alternatives by the presidential candidates. Even if candidates do not take divergent positions on foreign policy, voters may cast their ballots retrospectively on these issues if public concern is sufficiently high.*

This is generally what we find. Consider two polar cases. In 1948, almost 70 percent of Americans considered foreign policy to be the nation's most important problem. Yet, there were few clear differences between Truman and Dewey. Nor were there compelling reasons to throw Truman out based upon performance, so foreign policy had little impact on the election. In 1964, Johnson and

Barry Goldwater took widely divergent positions on both domestic and foreign policy. Yet, foreign policy was less salient than in any election since 1940. That contest was also decided largely on domestic issues.

In 1952 concern for foreign policy was high—and rising. While both Eisenhower and Democrat Adlai Stevenson were internationalists, there were real differences between them. Stevenson was substantially less interventionist. Eisenhower's competitor for the Republican nomination, Senator Robert Taft (Ohio), was a strong isolationist. Their contest reopened old sore wounds in the party. Democrats were on the defensive because of the Korean conflict. Americans voted retrospectively—to punish poor Democratic performance—and on the basis of issues. By one estimate, foreign policy concerns were equal to domestic ones in 1952.[12]

Foreign policy did not seem to loom large in the 1956 rematch between Eisenhower and Stevenson. While people were energized over international issues in 1956, differences between the candidates were muted.[13] Voters did cast retrospective ballots on foreign policy concerns, but there was little evidence of policy voting. As we noted, 1964 was largely a referendum on domestic politics. There were new cleavages between the major party nominees in 1968, Republican Richard M. Nixon and Democrat Hubert H. Humphrey. Humphrey backed away from Johnson's Vietnam policy and adopted a more dovish position. Nixon refused to be specific about his "secret plan" to end the war. The third-party challenge of Alabama Governor George Wallace was very hawkish. Wallace's running mate, former General Curtis LeMay, suggested "bombing North Vietnam back to the Stone Age." Moreover, the Democratic primaries were dominated not by Humphrey, but by Senators Eugene McCarthy (Minn.) and Robert F. Kennedy (N.Y.), both of whom based their challenges on opposition to the war. While there were ultimately few opportunities for policy voting, there were ample ones for retrospective evaluations.

The Nixon–McGovern contest of 1972 was marked by moderately high salience for foreign policy concerns and deep divisions between the candidates. McGovern, following McCarthy and Kennedy four years later, made the Vietnam War the principal focus of his campaign. Voters responded on the basis of both performance and policy. Yet four years later foreign policy concerns fell to a post-World War II low. Just 4 percent of Americans said that foreign or defense issues were the nation's most important problem. The two candidates, Republican incumbent Gerald Ford and Democrat Carter, came from the moderate wings of their parties. Voters were overwhelmingly concerned with the state of the economy.

In 1980 Carter faced a hostile electorate, concerned about the Iranian hostage crisis, the Soviet invasion of Afghanistan, a defense budget most Americans considered too low, and the twin economic problems of inflation and unemployment. The election was a referendum on both the economy and foreign policy, while one analyst found that the election was largely a referendum on Carter rather than on his policies.[14] However, most other studies found that issues, especially foreign policy concerns, mattered mightily.[15] Foreign and defense issues were as salient to the electorate in 1980 as in 1972. Carter and Ronald Reagan disagreed on most issues. Overall approval ratings of Carter were strongly related to his handling of the hostage crisis and the Soviet invasion of Afghanistan.

Retrospective evaluations heavily focused on foreign policy. The principal reason voters gave for supporting Carter or opposing Reagan was the outlook for peace. The dominant reason for opposing Carter was his handling of the hostage crisis. The percentage of respondents who "strongly disapproved" of Carter's performance on the hostage crisis jumped from 30 to 49 during 1980, compared with increases from 37 to 47 and 23 to 36 on inflation and unemployment, respectively.[16] The desire for a change in policy on defense contributed almost 9 percent to Reagan's vote, more than any other pro-Republican factor; party identification had a slightly greater impact, but it favored the Democrats. Voters were significantly closer to Reagan on defense spending and getting along with the Soviet Union. These issues polarized the electorate more than most domestic concerns. The policy reasons people gave for their vote choices also centered on foreign policy.

The conditions for policy voting were fulfilled in 1980. Forty percent of voters said that foreign policy and defense issues were important to the nation, themselves, or both. Over 80 percent of survey respondents took positions on foreign policy issues. More than half met all of the criteria: taking positions, attributing stands to candidates, seeing differences between them, and identifying the Democrat as more liberal. Eight percent more voters fulfilled these conditions on foreign policy than on domestic issues. And the overall impact of international issues on the vote was slightly weaker than domestic concerns.[17]

The 1984 race pitting Reagan against former Vice President Walter F. Mondale was not quite a rerun of 1980. Foreign policy issues were important, but they were not decisive. Mondale made the nuclear freeze one of the major issues in his ill-fated campaign, while Reagan repeatedly chastised the Democratic-controlled House of Representatives for cutting defense expenditures. A *Los Angeles Times* poll found that foreign relations generally and nuclear arms control were, at 19 and 18 percent respectively, of concern to the electorate. Reagan's 2 to 1 advantage on foreign affairs was exactly balanced out by an edge for Mondale on the nuclear arms issue.[18] Yet, other analyses indicated that by the eve of the election in October, Reagan had surged ahead, even if barely, on *all* salient foreign policy issues except for keeping the United States out of war. Reagan's performance evaluations were largely, though not exclusively, based on the state of the economy. Pro-Reagan policy reasons were focused on defense spending.[19]

These poll results, however, do not consider the *relative* importance of foreign policy compared with other factors in the voting decision. Voters once again were able to fulfill the conditions for issue voting. There is no consensus on the impact of foreign policy issues in 1984. One study found international concerns somewhat more important than domestic positions in 1984.[20] Another found that a diverse set of foreign policy concerns—defense spending, détente, and Central American policy—motivated voters, but none contributed much to Reagan's margin of victory.[21] Each of these concerns benefited not Reagan, but Mondale, in 1984. The 4 to 1 majority favoring more defense spending in 1980 had become a 3 to 1 majority supporting cuts in expenditures. Yet, most voters preferred to maintain the status quo on *general* policy direction.[22] Foreign policy clearly mattered in 1984, even if it did not swing the outcome of the election.

Public concern for international affairs plummeted in 1988: Only 10 percent cited foreign or defense issues as the most important problem, down from 34 percent four years earlier and the lowest share since 1976. Economic and social issues predominated: 41 percent of voters most liked their candidates' stands on economic issues, compared with 25 percent on social policies and 22 percent on defense and foreign policy. Democratic nominee Michael Dukakis had a twelve-point lead on social issues. Bush had just a two-point advantage on economic concerns, but a seventeen-point edge on foreign and defense problems. Bush's supporters were twice as likely to cite foreign policy considerations as were Dukakis's, but still just 12 percent cited such reasons. By one estimate, people who were most concerned with national defense voted for Bush by a margin of 84 to 15, adding almost 12 percent to Bush's vote. Yet, considerably more people cited the state of the economy than cited foreign issues as the reason for their vote choice. There was some evidence of issue voting on defense issues in 1988, but it was far less than in either 1980 or 1984. People's evaluations of Reagan were still largely based on foreign policy accomplishments, but these did not readily translate into backing for Bush.[23]

Bush became a foreign policy hero with the Gulf War, but the halo of that conflict did not last. He lost the 1992 elections to Bill Clinton, whom he derided as "the failed governor of a small state" whose only foreign policy experience was "eating breakfast at the International House of Pancakes." Yet, the election of 1992 was almost exclusively a referendum on the economy, not on international affairs. In the summer of 1992, Americans were simply not worried about foreign policy: No international issue was cited as the most important national problem by even two percent of the public. The nine most widely cited issues were all domestic concerns.[24]

Things did not improve for the president in November. People who thought that foreign policy was one of the two most important issues in their vote choice cast 87 percent of their ballots for Bush, but they constituted just eight percent of the electorate. Bush got two-thirds of the vote of people who said the Persian Gulf War was "very important" in making up their minds, but only one in four voters cited this issue.

In the weekend preceding the election, Iran–Contra Special Prosecutor Lawrence Walsh announced another indictment of former Secretary of Defense Caspar Weinberger. Weinberger was accused of lying about personal notes that allegedly revealed that Vice President Bush knew more than he had admitted.

This issue was as salient to the electorate as the Gulf War. Only a quarter of voters said that Bush was telling the truth about Iran–Contra; two-thirds of the voters who said that Iran–Contra was important backed Clinton; another quarter backed independent H. Ross Perot.

On the surface, specific foreign policy issues cancelled each other out. The most important story about 1992 is how unimportant foreign policy concerns were. By far, the most important issues were about the economy. On the three major economic concerns, the economy (42 percent of voters), the deficit (21 percent), and health care (20 percent), Bush received between 20 and 27 percent of the vote. Clinton won considerable majorities on the economy and health care and split the deficit vote with Perot. Bush got 82 percent support among people who thought that the national economy was doing well, but only 12 percent who thought that it was doing poorly. Just 8 percent were optimists, while 32 percent were pessimists.[25] Overall, foreign policy played a very modest role in the 1992 elections, largely because voters were primarily concerned with domestic issues and because Clinton stressed his agreement with Bush on such key issues as the Gulf War and the extent of cutbacks in defense spending. Bush and Clinton appeared closer to each other on foreign policy issues than either did to Perot, a Texas businessman who campaigned on a platform that advocated tariffs and a shrinking American role in the world.

There is an overall pattern that emerges from this discussion of the elections of 1948 onward. Table 6.1 summarizes the results. Retrospective voting is common. There is evidence for it in each contest except 1956 and 1976. Substantial policy voting occurs far less frequently, only in 1952, 1972, 1980, and 1984. Retrospective evaluations on foreign policy will occur when *either* international affairs are highly salient (with 50 percent or more saying that such issues are the nation's most important problem) *or* there are substantial differences between the candidates on international questions. Since 1972 the public has been less concerned with foreign policy, but there has been more interparty conflict. The conditions for retrospective voting have "balanced out." Substantial policy voting will occur only when at least one of the two dimensions—salience and cleavage—is high and the other at least moderate. In 1952 the public was very concerned about foreign policy, and the candidates took somewhat different stands, making foreign policy issue voting possible. In 1972, 1980, and 1984, public concern was moderate (above 20 percent naming foreign and defense issues as the most important problem) but cleavages were strong. Issue voting occurs less frequently than retrospective evaluations because it makes fewer demands on the voter. Whenever one finds policy balloting, there are also retrospective concerns.

Presidential elections often turn on foreign policy issues, but congressional contests rarely do. International questions have been less salient in years without presidential elections. Without the national debate on foreign policy issues that presidential contests bring, domestic policy, especially the state of the economy, becomes central. In 1978, for example, fewer than 1 percent of the voters cited

TABLE 6.1   Conditions for Retrospective and Policy Voting on Foreign Policy

Year	Salience of Foreign Policy*	Extent of Cleavage	Evidence of Retrospective Voting	Evidence of Policy Voting
1948	High	Low	No	No
1952	High	Moderate	Yes	Yes
1956	Moderate	Moderate	No	No
1960	High	Low	Yes	No
1964	Low	High	Yes	No
1968	High	Moderate	Yes	Slight
1972	Moderate	High	Yes	Yes
1976	Low	Low	No	No
1980	Moderate	High	Yes	Yes
1984	Moderate	High	Yes	Yes
1988	Low	High	No	Slight
1992	Low	Low	No	No

* Based on share of people citing foreign policy as most important problem.

foreign policy issues as the most important questions facing the country.[26] When international issues are highly salient and the lines of polarization are clear, they can spill over into congressional elections. As noted above, the Gulf War played a role in 1990. So did positions on defense spending: 56 percent of voters who did not want to cut back on military expenditures voted Republican, while 61 percent endorsing such reductions cast Democratic ballots for Congress.[27]

Nevertheless, congressional elections are becoming increasingly local events, tied less to national trends than in the past, even in presidential election years.[28] In 1984, Reagan's forty-nine-state landslide brought only fourteen new Republicans into the House of Representatives. Bush won the same percentage of the vote in 1988 as Eisenhower did in 1952. The earlier election gave control of the Congress to the Republicans; in 1988 the victorious party actually lost seats in the House. National trends do still affect congressional elections, but when they do they are more likely to be referenda on the state of the economy and political scandals than on specific issues such as foreign policy.[29] Member of the House and Senate initially seemed threatened by their 1991 votes on the Gulf War, but even this prominent issue faded.

The 1992 elections saw an unusually large number of House incumbents defeated in the general election; twenty-four members went down to defeat. Yet, 93 percent still prevailed and almost all of those who lost either were charged with improprieties or were adversely affected by changes in their constituencies attributable to redistricting. No member of the House or Senate seemed to lose because of a vote on the Gulf War.[30]

Foreign policy has played a more prominent role in Senate elections than in

House contests. The Senate has a greater constitutional role in foreign policy decision making. Issues are more important in Senate contests. Yet, in both the Senate and the House, legislators seem to be most affected by foreign policy when they pay *too much* attention to it. Voters in congressional elections have looked more for personal attention and responsiveness to local problems. Responsibility for foreign policy still rests with the White House.

International events are more important in people's voting decisions for president than for Congress. The growing interdependence of the world impinges on an electorate that has become less preoccupied with foreign policy than in the past. The growing divergence of party stands on foreign policy has brought these issues to the forefront of political debate. Presidents cannot give low priority to the international arena. When candidates differ on the issues, such conflicts readily spill over into the election campaign.

Political Parties: Do They Provide the Basis for Linkage?

Voters do not make up their minds in a vacuum. They cast ballots for candidates who almost always are Democrats or Republicans. Partisanship structures issue positions of both the mass public and the political elites. What, then, is the impact of political parties on foreign policy?

There have long been clear lines of partisan cleavage on many domestic issues, both among the electorate and within the Congress. Domestic policies that are primarily distributive—general appropriations measures, agriculture price supports, public works bills, and legislation relating to the size of the bureaucracy and the overall level of spending—are highly partisan. These issues involve the spending of money by the government. Democrats have traditionally supported domestic spending programs, while Republicans have emphasized fiscal restraint. The differences between the parties on these issues are quite real and long-standing. As the North-South split within the Democratic party dissipated in the 1970s, issues concerning civil liberties and social welfare also became very partisan, while differences on the new intermestic issues such as energy and agriculture became more regional. After a period during which the ideological distance between the parties on domestic policy was declining, the Reagan and Bush years were marked by dramatic rises in partisanship.[31]

A system of strong political parties would resolve much of the tension in foreign policy making and the democratic dilemmas. If the president were the leader of a party, he could count on the support of fellow partisans in pursuing his foreign policy objectives. If the president's partisans controlled both houses of Congress, this backing would provide solid majorities for the initiatives of the chief executive. The electorate could then decide between competing visions of what the nation's foreign policy should be. Such a system would provide for democratic accountability for the decisions of government and for executive leadership. It is the hallmark of parliamentary government.

However, the United States has not been marked by strong political parties as most parliamentary systems are. American parties traditionally have been neither distinctive ideologically nor internally cohesive. Most roll-call votes in the House of Commons in Great Britain are strictly along party lines. A member who deviates from the party position on a major vote can be denied renomination for another term in Parliament. In the United States, however, the only votes that can be safely predicted to come out along strictly partisan lines are those that choose the leaders of each house of Congress. Parties do not demonstrate the cohesiveness that we find in parliamentary systems because the American public has never been enamored with the idea of majority rule that goes hand in hand with strong parties. Majority-rule politics means that whichever party gains control of the government can implement any policies it chooses. Instead, Americans place a higher value on individual rights and set limits on what the government can do, as set forth in the Bill of Rights. The division of powers between separately elected legislative and executive branches reflects the American aversion to majoritarian institutions. Parties have always been regarded with guarded skepticism by Americans.[32]

On no issue has this apprehension about the role of political parties been so evident as on foreign policy. There has been a search for a consensus that crosses party lines. As we noted in Chapter 3, bipartisanship ensures continuity in policy making across administrations.[33] Bipartisan support for foreign policy was very strong in the Eisenhower administration. Modest cleavages arose during the Kennedy and Johnson presidencies. It was under Nixon that foreign policy became the focal point of partisan conflict, as most Democratic hawks reassessed their prior support for the Vietnam War. They sought to blame the Republican president for dramatically escalating the conflict beyond the confines of Vietnam and into Laos and Cambodia. The Congress enacted the War Powers Act over Nixon's veto, even as the president threatened not to comply with it. A new, more partisan era in foreign policy formation had begun.[34]

During the Carter, Reagan, and Bush administrations, partisan cleavages on foreign policy issues became more pronounced, although regional differences continued to persist within each party.[35] During the Reagan administration, when all issues facing the Congress were marked by high partisanship, foreign policy was marked by almost as much party-line voting as economic issues. Party cohesion on foreign policy was similar to unity on social welfare votes.[36] This continued into the Bush administration, as the growing budget deficit produced conflict over spending cuts in defense and social programs.

Party conflict on foreign policy began to increase in 1964 when conservatives took control of the Republican party. Four years later anti-Vietnam War activists almost captured the Democratic party. They succeeded in 1972, this time with a neoisolationist message that changed the general direction of the party's foreign policy.[37] Democrats, beginning with Woodrow Wilson through Franklin D. Roosevelt through John F. Kennedy, had stressed the centrality of America's role in the world, even when such views were not popular. George McGovern instead called for an end to interventionism and pleaded, "Come home, America." Senate Majority Leader George Mitchell (D-Me.) expressed similar sentiments in 1992:

> The president came to us and said, "There's an emergency in Turkey, let's help them, don't worry about the budget [deficit]." He said the same thing with respect to aid to Bangladesh, with respect to aid to people in Iraq, in Israel, and other places. But when it comes to Americans, the president has said, "No, no, no." . . . Why is the president so willing and eager to help people overseas, so unwilling, so reluctant to help Americans in need?[38]

Republican conservatives had traditionally been isolationist. Now, following Barry Goldwater and Ronald Reagan, they highlighted the need for a military ready to police the world. The spread of primaries as methods for nominating candidates made it easier for activists to challenge the old order in each party. Democratic internationalism and Republican isolationism were on the wane anyway. The South, long a bastion of internationalism, began moving toward the Republicans and away from the Democrats in 1964. Residents of the two coasts had long provided the Republican base of "liberal internationalism" associated with Eisenhower. In the late 1960s and early 1970s they became increasingly neoisolationist and Democratic, leaving the Republican party more open to capture by the more militant internationalists of the Goldwater and Reagan wings.

There was a foreign policy consensus in the Congress after World War II. Bipartisan voting in Congress was high in the Truman and Eisenhower years. The peak of bipartisan foreign policy voting in the post-World War II era came at the end of the Eisenhower administration for the House, and in the middle of the Truman administration in the Senate. There is some indication of a post-Vietnam drop in bipartisanship for the House, though not for the Senate. Foreign aid and a more general category of "foreign relations" votes became more partisan in the 1970s and 1980s.[39]

Bipartisanship has traditionally helped chief executives maintain control of foreign policy, giving rise to the idea of "two presidencies." Recent presidents have had less success on both foreign and domestic issues. Democratic chief executives do as well on each type of policy. Republican presidents have an advantage on international issues, but only because they fare much more poorly on domestic issues than Democratic executives.[40] Nixon, Reagan, and Bush have all battled mightily with Congress over foreign policy, but these conflicts pale by comparison with those on domestic issues. The overall decline in presidential success clearly reflects increasing party struggles.

Partisanship has historically been most intense on foreign policies that most closely resemble domestic issues. The parties have traditionally divided over the size of the defense budget, with the Democrats supporting increases in military spending and the Republicans calling for cutbacks prior to the 1970s. These positions reflected Republican opposition to government spending and Democratic beliefs that defense expenditures would stimulate local economies. Recent years have witnessed a reversal of this pattern, as defense spending has become increasingly a security concern and less a reward for politically important constituencies. Another area that has traditionally divided the parties is reciprocal trade legislation. The Democrats historically supported lower tariffs, with Republicans backing protection for domestic industries. Since the 1970s party positions have shifted. Democrats now largely favor protectionist policies, while the Republicans have shifted toward free trade. Democrats have been pressured by labor, which argues that American jobs will flock to countries with lower wage rates. Republicans respond to business firms that depend heavily upon exports.[41]

The parties are becoming more distinctive on foreign policy issues. There is more partisanship in congressional voting on foreign affairs, and delegates to each party's conventions diverge on these issues. These delegates nominate presidential candidates and write the platforms for each party. Hence, they are an important elite that generally differs substantially from the rank-and-file voters. Overall, Republican delegates have moved further away from the mass public from 1972 to 1980, while Democrats did not move significantly. In 1984 foreign policy issues greatly polarized delegates. Democratic delegates became far more dovish, Republican delegates considerably more hawkish, than either was just four years earlier. There were also considerable differences on détente with the Soviet Union, though much of the change had occurred earlier. A somewhat distant third, just behind attitudes toward the women's movement, was détente. The shift over time in defense attitudes—indicating increasing partisan divisions—was far greater than for any other issue.[42] The polarization continued into the Bush presidency. In 1988 Republican delegates were substantially more likely than the public to favor high levels of defense spending. Democrats overwhelmingly favored expenditure cuts. Just 37 percent of the electorate was more worried about a Communist takeover in Central America than involvement in a war there, compared with 12 percent of Democrats but 80 percent of Republicans. In 1992, 60 percent of Republican delegates agreed that "there is nothing wrong" in undermining hostile foreign governments, while 64 percent of Democrats disagreed.[43]

Party platforms reflect these tensions, but to a more limited degree. From 1944 through 1964, 47 percent of all party platform pledges on foreign policy were bipartisan, a higher percentage than for any other issue. One-third of defense promises were also bipartisan, close to the overall mean. In 1968 through 1976, the percentage of bipartisan pledges fell by almost half on foreign policy (to 25 percent) and to just 10 percent on defense. Parties fulfilled 79 percent of their foreign policy pledges in the less partisan era, but only 61 percent thereafter. The parties did *not* make conflicting promises, as much as focus their attention on different aspects of foreign policy. Just 6 percent of commitments on foreign policy were conflicting in each period, while the share of divergent promises on defense rose from 2 to just 7 percent.[44]

While Reagan and Mondale certainly had very different views about how foreign policy should be conducted and Democrats and Republicans in both Houses of Congress sharply differed with each other on these issues, the 1984 platforms offered little guidance on what each party would do differently from the other if elected. This is not to say that each party's platform was vague. When one party was specific, the other was not. The Republican platform pledged continued economic and military aid to the Contras; the Democrats called for an increased reliance on a negotiated resolution to the problems of Central America, but did not specifically propose a cutoff of Contra aid. Democrats endorsed the reimposition of tough sanctions on South Africa in a detailed policy statement; Republicans simply condemned apartheid and urged support for "well-conceived efforts to foster peace, prosperity, and stability." Both parties endorsed a strong defense, human rights, support for anti-Soviet Afghan forces, arms control, American peace efforts in the Middle East (including an undivided Jerusalem), and even efforts to restore free trade. The Democratic platform overall was far more specific, the Republican quite general. This is what one would expect from an out-party, trying to garner new votes, and an in-party, attempting to alienate as few previous supporters as possible. On domestic issues, the differences between the parties were far more dramatic.[45]

Strung by three successive electoral defeats, the Democrats decided to downplay ideology in their 1988 platform. The statement of principles became drastically shorter and more ambiguous. On foreign policy, it endorsed broad principles such as military strength, human rights, and cooperation with other nations. It was specific only in opposing military operations in Lebanon and Honduras and calling for stronger action against South Africa. The Republicans issued a detailed platform. Despite its length and the extensive number of sections dealing with different parts of the world, the document pledged few specific actions and even fewer that might have differentiated the parties. Most of the platform revolved around what the party believed its accomplishments in foreign policy were and how the Democrats had taken the wrong track. The Republicans opposed a Palestinian state and a role for the Palestine Liberation Organization in peace talks between Israel and the Arabs; they pledged to take strong actions to oust Cuban leader Fidel Castro, to defend Taiwan, to continue the isolation of Cambodia and Vietnam, and to back the Contras.[46] Only the question of the Contras was both highly salient and strongly partisan. The Democrats endorsed the peace plan of Costa Rican President Oscar Arias, but did not even mention the Contras. The documents clearly showed different emphases— the Democrats stressed human rights, the Republicans military strength—but there were no conflicting pledges that promised specific actions.

The 1992 Democratic platform represented a shift to the center, endorsing the use of military force when needed and becoming more ambiguous on trade. It was also more specific than the 1988 document, albeit on just a few issues. The Democrats endorsed trade restrictions on China, maintenance of sanctions on South Africa, and the biodiversity treaty the Bush administration rejected at the 1992 environmental summit in Brazil.[47]

The Republican platform was much longer. Yet, it did not emphasize details as much as highlight the accomplishments of the Bush administration and pledge further gains in world peace and the spread of democracy. The party pledged not to force Israel to negotiate with the Palestine Liberation Organization, re-iterated support for the Strategic Defense Initiative, promised to retain television and radio broadcasts to Cuba, and backed the North American Free Trade Agreement. The Republicans backed "constructive engagement" in South Africa without mentioning sanctions and encouraged "maintain[ing] the relationship with China." It would take a careful reader to pinpoint how the parties differ on these two areas. Only on the environmental summit did the Republicans take a readily identifiable position in opposition to the Democrats.[48]

If foreign policy issues divided the parties more than they did in the past, why do the platforms not reflect such partisanship? Platforms proclaim the party positions to the electorate; parties must reassure voters that they stand for popular ideals such as a strong defense, human rights, and democratic governance throughout the world. Platforms must be vague and bipartisan to a certain extent, especially on "we–they" issues. Yet, they also reflect the interests of the most strongly committed. Increasingly, the parties are responding to distinct constituencies on foreign policy. Democrats cared about the nuclear freeze in 1984, Republicans did not. Blacks and other liberals pressed for a strong statement on sanctions against South Africa in the Democratic platform. There were few blacks or liberals to make the case for the Republicans. Conservative Republican activists placed high priority on aid to the Contras. Few Democrats cared enough in 1984 to press the issue, although this changed four years later.

Platforms tell only part of the story of foreign policy partisanship. Party leaders increasingly take divergent stands on international affairs both inside and outside Congress. Voters in presidential elections have responded to candidates' foreign policy themes when the issues are presented clearly and when international issues are highly salient. Yet, we have not entered an era of responsible parties. Politicians still recognize that foreign policy issues may unite the country. After the Gulf War resolution passed the Congress, most opponents rallied behind the president—and, ultimately, the troops. When the war began, it became difficult to tell the supporters from the opponents of the original resolutions from their public statements. Representative Nita Lowey (D-N.Y.), who did not back the president initially (see Chapter 5), wore a yellow ribbon in solidarity with the troops when the hostilities started.[49] While foreign policy issues have become more partisan, leaders are often reluctant to politicize popular causes. To tie the hands of the commander in chief might be politically suicidal.

Party Dealignment and Accountability

There is not always a ready audience for international affairs. Foreign policy was salient in 1972, 1980, and 1984, but not in 1976, 1988, or 1992. These contests were *not* marked by significant issue voting on foreign policy—or, for that matter, on domestic policy. Each was largely a referendum on the party in power, a retrospective context with relatively low issue content. Many recent elections have been issueless because the electorate is less loyal to parties than it once was. Election analysts call this the *dealignment* of the American party system, rather than a realignment in which the two parties and their supporters in the electorate are clearly identifiable by their party stands.[50]

The weaker partisan ties explain the dwindling coattails effect in presidential election years. Yet, dealignment means more than just fewer national tides. Since the late 1960s, it has usually meant divided government—Republican control of the White House and Democratic control of Congress, or at least the House of Representatives. From 1969 to 1993, the Republicans held the White House for all but four years. They controlled the Senate for just six years and the House of Representatives not at all. Gary C. Jacobson has explained voters' penchant for divided government by examining their attitudes on policy and performance. Americans have expressed greater confidence in the Republicans to manage the economy; they also believe that economic management is the principal responsibility of the president. Democrats are more trusted to provide constituency benefits on domestic programs such as education, social welfare, and the environment. Congress is best equipped to handle such programs, voters say. Thus, voters make rational decisions to give Democrats control of the Congress and Republicans dominance of the White House—even if their overall preferences (lower taxes, higher services) may seem illogical.[51]

We can see a similar dynamic on foreign policy. The public has been closer to Democrats on several key issues of foreign policy in recent years: aid to the Contras, sanctions on South Africa, reducing defense spending, and restraining executive power. Yet, people still perceive the president as the major actor on foreign policy and prefer Republican performance by a wide margin. In September 1990, Americans thought that Republicans would perform better on a wide range of international issues (see Table 6.2). The Republican edge on defense increased to 48 to 10 after the Gulf War. By 61 to 14 percent, Americans said that the Republicans were more likely to keep military defenses strong, but by 45 to 23 percent believed that the Democrats were better able to keep the United States out of another war. Americans were ambivalent enough about foreign policy to give *both* parties credit for the Gulf War. While 65 percent said that they had gained confidence in the Republicans after the war (only 16 percent lost faith), a plurality (41 to 34 percent) also became more favorable to the Democrats.[52]

TABLE 6.2   Voter Preferences for Party Best Able to Handle Foreign Policy Issues, 1990

Party Better at Handling	Republicans (%)	Democrats (%)
Dealing with Soviet Union	55*	17
Making United States more respected in world	41	26
Defense	39	28
Relations with Central and Eastern Europe	39	20
Making United States competitive	41	25

* Percentages do not add to 100 because of respondents who said "both," "neither," or "don't know."

SOURCE: Times-Mirror Center for the People and the Press, *The People, the Press, and Politics 1990.* Washington, 1990.

Even when issues favored the Democrats (as in 1984), performance evaluations helped the Republicans. Most people don't pay a great deal of attention to foreign policy until some international event makes them pay heed. Presidents often exhort the Congress to provide bipartisan support for the nation's foreign policy. Chief executives ask voters for continued support on the basis of their overall record in foreign policy, not specific decisions. Members of Congress who find interested electorates—and they are not numerous—can and must be more specific simply because the Congress *does not manage foreign policy.*

We thus confront a paradox. Voters seem to be casting ballots more often on the basis of foreign policy. Yet such votes don't decide elections nearly as much as do retrospective evaluations of performance. The elites—members of Congress and delegates to party conventions—are increasingly polarized on foreign policy, but voters aren't so sharply split. This is not new. What is distinctive is how rapidly rational public opinion shifts. Issue voting on foreign policy helped the Republicans in 1980, the Democrats in 1984, and the Republicans again in 1988. Retrospective evaluations favored the Republicans in each year. When party ties were stronger, voters were less likely to desert their partisanship on the basis of issues or performance evaluations. Now they are more fickle and more willing to split their tickets.

The 1992 elections marked a shift in voters' preferences. For the first time since 1976 more Americans preferred single-party control of the legislative and executive branches than divided government.[53] Americans believed that George Bush would handle foreign policy better than Clinton—by a margin of 57 percent to 36 percent. Yet, they thought that the two candidates would perform equally well on keeping the United States out of war and that Clinton was substantially more likely to protect American jobs from foreign competition.[54] The Republicans, and especially President Bush, had lost their advantage on foreign policy for two reasons. First, while voters most concerned with foreign policy backed the president by substantial margins, they were a small share of the electorate. The issues that mattered most, the economy and health care, favored the Democrats at both the presidential and congressional levels. Second, when foreign policy issues were phrased in economic terms, as in protecting American jobs, the Republican edge had evaporated.

The increased emphasis on foreign policy has opportunities and pitfalls for presidents. There are now voters who can be wooed by a strong presidential performance in the international arena. The "Reagan Democrats" who favor a strong defense have been an important source of strength for recent Republican presidential candidates. People who disagreed with the policy directions of Republican candidates may nevertheless have approved of their overall performance. Presidents have considerable freedom to set their own foreign policy, since what matters most is the general record. Yet, retrospective evaluations change much more quickly than attitudes on policy. Today's hero may become tomorrow's scapegoat—as Bush's popularity during and after the Gulf War demonstrated. Moreover, initial success on foreign policy may raise the stakes for a president. The electorate expects continued good performance. Small failings after initial achievements may bring down the wrath of a disappointed public (see Chapter 10). Without the fear of communism or an Iraqi takeover of Kuwait, the Reagan Democrats of 1984 voted 2–1 for Bill Clinton over George Bush in 1992.[55]

An electorate that consistently elects a Congress of one party and a president from another rejects the notion of responsible party government. Responsible government must rely upon policy agreement between the governors and their electoral base. When the voters send mixed messages to decision makers, the power of parties is weakened. Thus, while parties have become more distinctive on foreign policy issues, they cannot impose their positions on unwilling members. The positive aspect of this constraint is that presidents can still appeal for bipartisan support on "we–they" issues. The negative side of the ledger is that leaders rarely receive an unambiguous mandate from the public to take foreign policy in a particular direction. If the United States had sharper partisan divisions on foreign policy, we might have two major actors (the Democratic and Republican parties) rather than 536 (the president, the 435 members of the House, and the 100 Senators).

The Media Factor: You Are What You Watch?

If the parties' role in foreign policy is limited, what about the media's? The media have played a critical role in shattering the post-Vietnam consensus. Public support declined more precipitously for the war in Vietnam and Cambodia than for the Korean conflict in no small part because the fighting was brought home to Americans' living rooms every night. The violence, including massacres such as that in My Lai, turned many viewers against the war. So did the public opposition to the war from America's great folk hero, CBS anchor Walter Cronkite. In earlier wars, including Korea and World War II, people learned about fighting through newspapers and radio, neither of which could provide the explicit graphics of television. Visual portraits were available only through highly edited newsreels shown at movie theaters.

As in Vietnam, the constant media exposure served to highlight the president's difficulties. To be sure, Carter focused attention on himself by holding many press conferences and insisting that he could not leave the White House to campaign or even to meet with other public officials outside Washington. But the media also paid a great deal of attention to Iran, with ABC television news scheduling a nightly program on the events (or nonevents) of the day. (The program, hosted by Ted Koppel, later became "Nightline.") Americans became very familiar with the militants holding the hostages at the embassy; their spokeswoman, called Mary, generally had higher late-night ratings than Johnny Carson did on NBC. Meanwhile, on the top-rated "CBS Evening News," Cronkite ended each broadcast counting the number of days that Americans had been held hostage in Iran. The evaporation of public support permitted other sources of information to gain a public following.

The two principal alternative sources are congressional hearings and the media. Lacking the power to change the president's Vietnam policies, Senator Fulbright used the mechanism of his Foreign Relations Committee hearings to dramatize opposition to the war. At times, the major television networks would carry live coverage of these hearings. At a minimum, the hearings would be covered on the evening network news programs and in the major newspapers across the country. The influence of such hearings—which are often long and tedious and may not bring out any new information—may be slight, but it is often almost all that opponents of a policy have in their attempt to affect public opinion. With the growth of the medium of television, the roles of the congressional committee hearings and the media have become ever more closely intertwined.

Television gives opponents of a policy a more direct line to the public than do newspapers or radio. Its pictures make vivid points. However, the gains that opponents of a policy have made through this newest medium have also accrued to the president. The chief executive can almost always obtain free network time for an address to the nation, and he can use such speeches to rally public opinion behind his policies. The round-the-clock coverage of the Gulf War helped the country rally behind Bush's leadership. On balance, the advent of television probably has meant more to opponents of a president's policy than to the chief executive himself. Since public opinion is generally permissive and supportive of presidential initiatives, any gain in exposure of the opposition's point of view may well enhance the opponents' strength. A president needs less exposure to rally support for his position than does the opposition.

When the issues can readily be presented in "we–they" terms, extensive media attention may help the president. When Reagan and Soviet leader Mikhail Gorbachev held a summit in Reykjavik, Iceland, in 1986, television coverage focused heavily on the agreements the two men reached. There was virtually no criticism of the president. When conflicts cross over into domestic politics, as the Iran–Contra case did one month later, the executive's message meets strong competition. A quarter of television coverage of Iran–Contra, and slightly less in the *New York Times,* dealt with elite criticism. Reagan's popularity declined as the amount of television coverage of the scandal increased. The linkage between attitudes on aid to the Contras and overall approval of Reagan increased sharply, especially among people who did not normally pay close attention to politics.[56]

The media are more than just vehicles for presenting alternative views of public officials to the public or, in turn, representing the public to the foreign policy establishment. The media also have their own impact on public opinion. Although most voters are usually not terribly concerned with foreign policy issues, the nightly television coverage of events in Vietnam brought an overseas war into millions of American homes each night, as did the reports on Iran a half decade after American involvement in Vietnam ended. Furthermore, the media have not always presented presidential decisions in a favorable light. Virtually every president of the United States in recent years has believed that the press was hostile. Indeed, the Nixon administration brought its hostilities toward the media—the television networks and national newsmagazines, as well as the newspapers—out into the open. Johnson was less hostile to the press but did criticize several reporters and nationally syndicated columnists for their opposition to his Vietnam policies. And both Carter and Reagan, at various times, lamented the treatment they received from the press. Bush established greater rapport with the press, but his vice president, Dan Quayle, launched a verbal assault on the "cultural elite" (including the press) that was reminiscent of Vice President Spiro Agnew's attacks during the Nixon administration.

Presidents respond in different ways to criticism from the press. At one extreme, Nixon was so angered by the *Washington Post's* coverage of the Watergate affair that he threatened to have the Federal Communications Commission deny the applications for license renewals of two television stations the *Post* owned in Florida. At the other extreme was the reaction of Kennedy, who canceled his subscription to the *New York Herald Tribune* following a series of uncomplimentary articles the paper ran about him. The subscription was quietly renewed after the incident proved embarrassing to the president. Carter, withdrawing from criticism of his handling of foreign and domestic policy before the hostage crisis, refused to hold press conferences in Washington for several months, traveling to distant locales where the local press might be somewhat more sympathetic to his situation. After the hostages were seized, Carter actively sought out the press, even as his popularity was declining.

Reagan, a former actor quite at home with cameras, established a reputation as the "Great Communicator." He used press conferences and televised addresses to build support for his programs and to disarm the opposition with his quick wit. Reagan is the master practitioner of a presidential strategy born of the television age: "going public," circumventing negotiations with the Congress and directly appealing to the public to pressure their elected representatives to support the president's program. Such tactics bring about a more confrontational relationship between the president and the Congress, as each attempts to appeal to the public. Nixon and especially Carter used the same strategy, but since neither was a master of the media—indeed, Carter generally performed poorly on television—they were not as successful at it as Reagan.

Direct appeals to the people played a critical role in convincing many members of Congress to vote for Reagan's program of tax and budget cuts in 1981. As the president's popularity sagged in 1982 and again in 1986–87 during the Iran–Contra affair, his use of the media declined—as did positive public responses to his infrequent appearances. Television has also become the medium of choice for foreigners, from the leaders of the Soviet Union, China, and Iran to terrorists. They seek to affect public opinion—and thus to "go public" over the heads of the president, the Congress, and the State Department.[57] Bush was a noticeable exception to this pattern. He did not perform well on television and avoided prime-time press conferences and public addresses. Apparently, he believed that television was unnecessary when he was popular and could not rescue him when his approval ratings sank.

The media focus people's attention on foreign policy issues beyond those such as hearings on the Vietnam War, the Iranian hostage crisis, or the Iran–Contra affair. Many members of Congress argued that the United States government was ultimately compelled to take action forcing Philippine President Ferdinand Marcos to resign because of television. The extensive coverage of the Philippine election of 1986 and the widespread allegations of vote fraud against Corazon Aquino were in sharp contrast to television's usual one-shot two-minute stories about international politics. Furthermore, the Filipinos interviewed were usually middle-class English speakers with whom Americans could identify. Almost 60 percent of respondents to a poll said that they followed the contest very or fairly closely, and by a 5 to 1 margin they believed that Aquino, not Marcos, was the legitimate victor.[58]

Television has had a major impact on electoral politics as well. Media expenditures constitute the largest share of candidates' disbursements.[59] Negative advertising has come to play a prominent role in campaigns. Candidates for both the presidency and Congress emphasize "looking good" over substance.[60] In the 1984 presidential primaries, Senator Gary Hart (D-Colo.) traversed the country, stopping only at airports where he met with television reporters for interviews that would be taped for the local evening news. The stories would make it appear that the candidate actually spent time in each city, although following the interviews he would reboard his campaign plane to fly to the next set of waiting reporters. Three years later, while running once more for the presidency, Hart found the press to be more of an adversary. Allegations of sexual impropriety by the *Miami Herald* and the *Washington Post* led Hart to withdraw from the race for the Democratic nomination for the presidency.

Television has replaced newspapers as the primary source of news: 64 percent of Americans rely on television for news, as compared with just 44 percent for newspapers.[61] Television news differs radically from print news. First, viewers are likely to skip stories in which they are not vitally interested, such as foreign affairs. Flipping the page in a newspaper is easy; turning off the television or changing the channel generally requires people to get out of their chairs. Second, as previously noted, televised news is more dramatic than print stories. Third, television news covers stories quickly and without repetition. Reading a newspaper permits one to return to a story at leisure. Fourth, newspapers must be purchased—and in fact have never been purchased by a majority of citizens. Television news come into people's homes for free, and virtually every American home owns a television set. Fifth, televised coverage of news, including but not limited to congressional hearings, gives the viewer a keener sense of the adversarial nature of contemporary politics. The public thus becomes less patient with and more cynical about its leaders, whom they perceive as divided.[62]

In another sense, however, television and newspapers are very similar. Both tend to give short shrift to issues of substance in presidential elections, particularly during the primaries. Even "prestige" newspapers and newsmagazines give the same disproportionate coverage to the "horse race" aspect of the campaign as do local papers and mass-circulation dailies that emphasize "lifestyle" stories. During the conventions and the general election campaign, quality newspapers and newsmagazines do put greater emphasis on issues than the network newscasts and other press outlets, but on balance even then the elite press focuses more on the "game."[63]

How responsible is television for the breakdown of the post-Vietnam consensus? Some observers have attributed the growth of television to the loss of trust among the American public as well as to the waning of partisan attachments.[64] More to our point, is television biased? If so, how? Conservative critics charge the press with a left-wing bias. Stanley Rothman and S. Robert Lichter argue that contemporary journalists are part of a "new-class' intellectual elite stemming from the radical politics of the 1960s and 1970s. These reporters became politicized by the antiwar protests against Vietnam and racial discrimination. Their stories about both domestic and foreign policy are slanted toward the views of contemporary protest groups.[65] Alternatively, Benjamin I. Page and Robert Y. Shapiro maintain that the media tilts toward the status quo, especially to the conservative side. Television and the press rally to the pro-American position, trumpeting our military accomplishments and downplaying the claims of ethnic groups who are not powerful in the United States (blacks, Latinos, Arabs, etc.).

The media play to their audience: an ethnocentric American population. They are also commercial enterprises, not the surrogates for public interest groups that Rothman and Lichter see.[66]

Which view is correct? Both are! Reporters are liberal. Newspapers owners are conservative. Some news sources will slant stories, but there is little evidence that most do. There is not even consensus on the impact of the media on public opinion. Page and Shapiro find that the most important determinant of opinion change on a wide range of policy areas is commentary on news programs. A single comment by a network personality or an expert can change opinion by as much as 4 percent; such figures had particularly strong effects on SALT II and on the 1981 sale of AWACS to Saudi Arabia (see Chapter 7). Each broadcast has a bigger impact on public opinion than presidential remarks. The more frequent appearances by chief executives tilted the balance toward presidential power, especially for popular leaders.[67]

On the other hand, Richard A. Brody shows that there is a close connection between presidential popularity and the flow of good and bad news in the media. Yet, he attributed the impact to events in the world, not to the press. The media report what they see—sometimes bad news (in the Johnson, Nixon, and Carter administrations) and sometimes good news (in the Kennedy and Reagan years). A press that accurately reflects the state of the world must be reasonably unbiased.[68] It is also less powerful than critics would have us believe. We wonder how many Americans pay attention to the comments of experts who appear on television. The two foreign policy issues cited by Page and Shapiro as shaped by media commentary—SALT II and the AWACS sale—became subjects of intense public controversy. Did the media or the messengers lead to change in public opinion?

We do not deny that television has become a major factor in how we perceive international politics. Yet, it seems dubious to maintain that television is the *cause* of many of our contemporary problems. Rather, it is more reasonable to argue that it is a *symptom* of the state of public attitudes in the nation. For one thing, television coverage of major American political figures does *not* emphasize the "blow-dried" politicians seeking thirty seconds of notoriety on the major networks. Instead, congressional leaders rather than "show horses" receive the bulk of coverage.[69] For another, if television coverage worked to undermine faith in the political system, we would expect that further media expansion would lead to less confidence in leadership. Yet just the opposite occurred. As cable television grew dramatically in the 1980s, a master of the media (Reagan) presided over a nation in which trust in government was *increasing*.[70] Rather, media politics, including going public, reflects the breakdown of party coalitions in American politics rather than causes it. Without a dependable bloc of support in the Congress, presidents feel compelled to seek support outside the legislative branch.[71]

All of this is not to say that the media are impotent. They play a critical role in transmitting information to the public, and the way the news is presented can make a difference in peoples' interpretations of it. Both news commentary on television and stories depicting alternative policies in a positive light can change public opinion by three percentage points or more—considerably more than presidents. Indeed, the impact of commentary is especially strong when presidents are unpopular. Television can have a particularly strong effect in enhancing negative images of presidents. When Nixon took to the airwaves during Watergate to state, "I am not a crook," the very fact that a president of the United States had to plead his innocence added to beliefs that something really must be wrong. Carter's poor performance on television certainly led to the sharp decline in his popularity. His vice president, Walter Mondale, attributed his poor showing in the 1984 elections to his failure to master the medium of television. Even Reagan as the "Great Communicator" found that television was a double-edged sword. During the Iran–Contra affair, Reagan often appeared ill at ease on television. Many Americans put aside his geniality and began to concentrate more on the president's misstatements and inconsistencies. Bush, as we have noted, also seemed ill at ease on television. The 1992 presidential contest was marked by round after round of candidates appearing on talk shows for up to two hours at a time. Such exposure gave the candidates more control over public discourse than they had in earlier campaigns when voters had to rely on sound bites lasting under ten seconds.

Yet even these effects may reflect elite or public consensus rather than the unique influence of the media.[72] Most of the time television coverage *intensifies* views already held and makes them more volatile.[73] Yet negative advertising and stories about candidates' sex lives would not play such a prominent place in the media if viewers did not respond so favorably to them. If the electorate really preferred more debates on international affairs to more lurid stories, the networks would oblige and "Roseanne" would be replaced by live debates from the Oxford Union. It would be truly remarkable, and regrettable, if citizens in a democracy abdicated the accountability of their political leaders to the press. It is reassuring that they do not.

There is a strong irony about the changing role of the media. On the one hand, there has been a veritable news explosion on the airwaves. All-news television and radio have become a staple of American life in recent years. Additionally, there are the public affairs programming on the two C-SPAN cable networks, the growth of public radio news programming, and more news programming on the major networks. More and more local television stations and newspapers have opened Washington bureaus, and the foreign bureaus of both television/radio and newspapers have expanded greatly. There are also many more specialized magazines on politics and foreign affairs than there were just a decade ago. On the other hand, many newspapers have closed, ceding the news dissemination function to radio and television. And, for all the greater concern with public affairs on television, the growth of cable has created alternatives to informational programming. The rise of independent television stations and especially cable networks means that the American public is no longer a captive audience for the network news or even the State of the Union address. Many people tune instead to music videos, reruns of 1950s programs, or "Wheel of Fortune."

The number of actors in the fourth circle is quite large—too much so to do justice to them in a single chapter. We therefore continue our consideration of these actors in Chapter 7, where we focus on the growing role of local political actors in foreign policy making and the impact of interest groups, long associated with domestic policies, in the international arena. We shall also delay our consideration until Chapter 7 of what this all means for the democratic dilemma. We do so because it is important to examine all of the actors in the fourth circle together. There are different aspects of public participation in decision making, and these need to be compared systematically.

Notes

1. See Hannah Fenichel Pitkin, *The Concept of Representation* (Berkeley: University of California Press, 1967), chap. 4.
2. See V. O. Key, Jr., *The Responsible Electorate* (New York: Random House, 1966); and Austin Ranney and Willmoore Kendall, *Democracy and the American Party System* (New York: Harcourt Brace Jovanovich, 1956), chap. 4.
3. John H. Aldrich, John L. Sullivan, and Eugene Borgida, "Foreign Affairs and Issue Voting: Do Presidential Candidates 'Waltz Before a Blind Audience'?" *American Political Science Review* 83 (January 1989), p. 128.
4. Richard W. Boyd and Adam Berinsky, "The Influence of Foreign Policy Issues in the American Elections of 1948 and 1952." Paper presented at the 1992 Annual Meeting of the Midwest Political Science Association, Chicago, April 1992, p. 32.
5. Warren E. Miller, "Voting and Foreign Policy," in James N. Rosenau, ed., *Domestic Sources of Foreign Policy* (New York: Free Press, 1967), p. 229.
6. Morris P. Fiorina, *Retrospective Voting in American National Elections* (New Haven: Yale University Press, 1981), chap. 8.
7. Miller, "Voting and Foreign Policy," pp. 215–216.
8. John E. Mueller, *War, Presidents, and Public Opinion* (New York: John Wiley, 1973), p. 227.
9. Arthur H. Miller and Martin P. Wattenberg, "Throwing the Rascals Out: Policy and Performance Evaluations of Presidential Candidates, 1952-1980," *American Political Science Review* 79 (June 1985), pp. 359–372, esp. p. 365.
10. John E. Rielly, ed., *American Public Opinion and U.S. Foreign Policy* (Chicago: Chicago Council on Foreign Relations, 1991), p. 9.
11. Bruce Russett, *Controlling the Sword: The Democratic Governance of Foreign Policy* (Cambridge: Harvard University Press, 1990), p. 90. The figures below on the salience of foreign affairs are taken from Figure 4.1 on this page and from Paul R. Abramson, John H. Aldrich, and David W. Rohde, *Change and Continuity in the 1988 Elections*, rev. ed. (Washington: CQ Press, 1991), p. 157.
12. Boyd and Berinsky, "The Influence of Foreign Policy Issues in the American Elections of 1948 and 1952," pp. 32–33.

13. The summaries of presidential elections from 1960 to 1976 derives from Aldrich, Sullivan, and Borgida, "Foreign Affairs and Issue Voting," p. 135; Fiorina, *Retrospective Voting in American National Elections*, ch. 8; Abramson, Aldrich, and Rohde, *Change and Continuity in the 1988 Elections*, p. 157; and Miller and Wattenberg, "Throwing the Rascals Out."

14. Gregory Markus, "Political Attitudes in an Election Year: A Report on the 1980 NES Panel Survey," *American Political Science Review* 76 (September 1982), pp. 558–559.

15. Aldrich, Sullivan, and Borgida, "Foreign Affairs and Issue Voting"; Warren E. Miller and J. Merrill Shanks, "Policy Directions and Presidential Leadership," *British Journal of Political Science* 12 (October 1982), p. 318; Warren E. Miller and J. Merrill Shanks, "Policy Direction and Performance Evaluation: Complementary Explanations of the Reagan Elections," *British Journal of Political Science* 20 (1990), pp. 143–235; Martin P. Wattenberg, *The Rise of Candidate-Centered Politics* (Cambridge: Harvard University Press, 1991); and Miroslav Nincic and Barbara Hinckley, "Foreign Policy and the Evaluation of Presidential Candidates," *Journal of Conflict Resolution* 35 (June 1991).

16. Markus, "Political Attitudes During an Election Year," pp. 550, 558–559.

17. Aldrich, Sullivan, and Borgida, "Foreign Affairs and Issue Voting."

18. Scott Keeter, "Public Opinion in 1984," in Gerald Pomper et al., *The Election of 1984* (Chatham, N.J.: Chatham House, 1985), p. 96. The percentages for each issue are based upon respondents' mentions of up to *two* concerns that were most important to them in the election.

19. William Schneider, "The November 6 Vote for President: What Did It Mean?" in Austin Ranney, ed., *The American Elections of 1984* (Durham: Duke University Press, 1985), pp. 216–217, 226; and Wattenberg, *The Rise of Candidate-Centered Politics*, pp. 119, 138.

20. Aldrich, Sullivan, and Borgida, "Foreign Affairs and Issue Voting," p. 133.

21. Miller and Shanks, "Policy Direction and Performance Evaluation."

22. Wattenberg, *The Rise of Candidate-Centered Politics*, p. 112; and Miller and Shanks, "Policy Direction and Performance Evaluation."

23. The discussion of the 1988 elections is based upon Wattenberg, *The Rise of Candidate-Centered Politics*, pp. 140, 147; Gerald M. Pomper, "The Presidential Election," in Gerald M. Pomper, ed., *The Election of 1988: Reports and Interpretations* (Chatham, N.J.: Chatham House, 1989), p. 143; J. Merrill Shanks and Warren E. Miller, "Alternative Interpretations of the 1988 Election," paper presented at the 1989 Annual Meeting of the American Political Science Association, Atlanta, August-September, p. 51; and exit poll data from ABC News graciously provided by John Brennan. Candidate advantages reflect the relative percentages supporting each candidate multiplied by the share of the electorate concerned with the issue.

24. CBS News press release, July 12, 1992.

25. The results in this paragraph and the one above come from exit polls of the electorate by Voter Research and Survey. They are repeated in: "Portrait of the Electorate," *New York Times*, November 5, 1992, p. B9; and "Exit Poll," *Washington Post*, November 4, 1992, p. A24, and November 5, 1992, p. A30.

26. Computed from the National Election Study of the Center for Political Studies, University of Michigan.

27. *New York Times*, "How Issues Influenced Votes in the Election for U.S. House of Representatives," November 11, 1990, p. E5.

28. Randall L. Calvert and John A. Ferejohn, "Coattail Voting in Recent Presidential Elections," *American Political Science Review* 77 (June 1983), pp. 407–419.

29. Ibid., p. 417; and Eric M. Uslaner and M. Margaret Conway, "The Responsible Congressional Electorate: Watergate, the Economy, and Vote Choice in 1974," *American Political Science Review* 79 (September 1985), pp. 788–803.

30. Dave Kaplan and Charles Mahtesian, "Election's Wave of Diversity Spares Many Incumbents," *Congressional Quarterly Weekly Report,* November 7, 1992, pp. 3570–3576.

31. Barbara Sinclair, *Congressional Realignment 1925–1978* (Austin: University of Texas Press, 1982), pp. 77-78; Steve Blakely, "Partisanship in Congress Up Sharply in 1985," *Congressional Quarterly Weekly Report,* January 11, 1986, pp. 86–91.

32. Austin Ranney, *The Doctrine of Responsible Party Government* (Urbana, Ill.: University of Illinois Press, 1962).

33. Ernest A. Gross, "What Is a Bipartisan Foreign Policy?" *Department of State Bulletin,* October 3, 1949, pp. 504–505.

34. Sinclair, *Congressional Realignment 1925–1978.*

35. Barbara Sinclair, "Agenda, Policy, and Alignment Change from Coolidge to Reagan," in Lawrence C. Dodd and Bruce I. Oppenheimer, eds., *Congress Reconsidered,* 3d ed. (Washington: Congressional Quarterly Press, 1985), pp. 291–314.

36. William Schneider, "A Year of Continuity," *National Journal,* May 17, 1986, pp. 1162–1191.

37. I. M. Destler, Leslie H. Gelb, and Anthony Lake, "Breakdown: The Impact of Domestic Policies on American Foreign Policy," in Charles W. Kegley and Eugene R. Wittkopf, eds., *The Domestic Sources of American Foreign Policy* (New York: St. Martin's, 1988), p. 23.

38. Quoted in Carroll J. Doherty, "Democrats Aim to Strike Chord Playing 'America First' Tune," *Congressional Quarterly Weekly Report,* November 6, 1991, p. 3394.

39. James M. McCormick and Eugene R. Wittkopf, "Bipartisanship, Partisanship, and Ideology in Congressional-Executive Foreign Policy Relations," *Journal of Politics* 52 (November 1990), pp. 1077–1100; and James M. McCormick and Eugene R. Wittkopf, "At the Water's Edge: The Effects of Party, Ideology, and Issues on Congressional Foreign Policy Voting," *American Politics Quarterly* 20 (January 1992), p. 39.

40. Jon R. Bond and Richard Fleisher, *The President in the Legislative Arena* (Chicago: University of Chicago Press, 1990), pp. 158, 165.

41. See Eric M. Uslaner, "Political Parties, Ideas, Interests, and Free Trade in the United States," in Charles F. Doran, ed., *Trade and Party: Foreign Trade Relations and Party Politics in North America* (forthcoming, 1993).

42. Warren E. Miller and M. Kent Jennings, *Parties in Transition* (New York: Russell Sage Foundation, 1986), p. 207; and Miller, *Without Consent* (Lexington, Ky.: University Press of Kentucky, 1988), pp. 17, 19.

43. *New York Times,* "Convention Delegates and the Public on the Issues," August 14, 1988, p. A32; and *Washington Post,* ABC News Survey #479, provided by Richard Morin of the *Washington Post.*

44. See Gerald M. Pomper, *Elections in America* (New York: Dodd, Mead, 1965), p. 194; and Gerald M. Pomper and Susan Lederman, *Elections in America,* 2d ed. (New York: Longman, 1980), pp. 164, 169. The results on bipartisan and conflicting pledges were computed from tables in the two editions.

45. For the texts of the Democratic and Republican platforms, see *Congressional Quarterly*

Weekly Report, July 21, 1984, pp. 1747–1780, and August 25, 1984, pp. 2096–2117. The quote from the Republican platform on South Africa is on p. 2113. Foreign policy issues occupied nine of thirty-four pages in the Democratic platform and seven of twenty-two in the Republican plank.

46. Ronald D. Elving, "Comity on Platform Collapses As Angry Jackson Forces Dig In," *Congressional Quarterly Weekly Report,* July 16, 1988, pp. 1967–1970; and "Republican Party Issues Detailed, Long Platform," *Congressional Quarterly Weekly Report,* August 20, 1988, pp. 2369–2399.

47. "Party's Statement of Policies Mirrors Clinton's Goals," *Congressional Quarterly Weekly Report,* July 4, 1992, (Supplement), pp. 59–67.

48. "The Platform: Party Stresses Family Values, Decentralized Authority," *Congressional Quarterly Weekly Report,* August 22, 1992, pp. 2560–2581.

49. John E. Yang, "Words and Images Intended to Reassure Skeptical New Yorkers," *Washington Post,* February 19, 1991, p. A14.

50. See especially Walter Dean Burnham, *Critical Elections and the Mainsprings of American Politics* (New York: W. W. Norton, 1970).

51. Gary C. Jacobson, *The Electoral Origins of Divided Government* (Boulder, Colo.: Westview, 1991).

52. NBC News press release, March 29, 1991; CBS News press release, March 17, 1991; and Yankelovich, Clancy, Schulman press release (for *Time* and CNN), March 15, 1991.

53. Forty-seven percent preferred that the president and Congress be controlled by the same party, while only 31 percent opted for divided government. CBS News press release, September 15, 1992. By the time of the election, 63 percent wanted single-party control and just 27 preferred divided government, according to the Voter Research and Survey exit poll.

54. Times-Mirror Center for the People and the Press, *The People, the Press, and Politics Campaign '92: 1993–Priorities for the President,* October 28, 1992, pp. 19–20. Americans thought that H. Ross Perot would be better at protecting American jobs than either Bush or Clinton.

55. Voter Research and Survey exit poll, November 4, 1992.

56. Richard A. Brody and Catherine Shapiro, "Policy Failure and Public Support: Reykjavik, Iran, and Public Assessments of President Reagan." Paper presented at the 1987 Annual Meeting of the American Political Science Association, Chicago, September, pp. 8, 18, 21. See also Jon A. Krosnick and Donald R. Kinder, "Altering the Foundations of Support for the President Through Priming," *American Political Science Review* 84 (June 1990), pp. 497–512.

57. Samuel Kernell, *Going Public* (Washington: Congressional Quarterly Press, 1986), pp. 3–35; and John Corry, "Even Revolutionaries Smile for the Camera," *New York Times,* October 4, 1987, p. H31.

58. Steven V. Roberts, "The Global Village: A Case in Point," *New York Times,* February 20, 1986, p. B8; and John M. Goshko, "Most in Poll Say Marcos Won by Fraud," *Washington Post,* February 25, 1986, p. A11.

59. Robert E. DiClerico and Eric M. Uslaner, *Few Are Chosen: Problems in Presidential Selection* (New York: McGraw-Hill, 1984), p. 59; and Edie N. Goldenberg and Michael W. Traugott, *Campaigning for Congress* (Washington: Congressional Quarterly Press, 1984), p. 85.

60. Nelson W. Polsby, "The Washington Community, 1960–1980," in Thomas E. Mann

and Norman J. Ornstein, eds., *The New Congress* (Washington: American Enterprise Institute, 1981), pp. 7–31.

61. William Schneider, "Conservatism, Not Interventionism: Trends in Foreign Policy Public Opinion, 1974–1982," p. 61, in Kenneth A. Oye, Robert J. Lieber, and Donald Rothchild, eds., *Eagle Defiant: United States Foreign Policy in the 1980s* (Boston: Little, Brown, 1983).

62. Ibid., pp. 61–62; Theodore J. Lowi, *The Personal President* (Ithaca, N.Y.: Cornell University Press, 1985), pp. 63–70; and *The World Almanac and Book of Facts 1984* (New, York: Newspaper Enterprise Association, Inc., 1984), p. 429.

63. Thomas Patterson, *The Mass Media Election* (New York: Praeger, 1980), p. 29.

64. Austin Ranney, *Channels of Power* (New York: Basic Books, 1983), p. 144.

65. Stanley Rothman and S. Robert Lichter, "Elite Ideology and Risk Perception in Nuclear Energy Policy," *American Political Science Review*, 81 (June 1987), pp. 383–404.

66. Benjamin I. Page and Robert Y. Shapiro, *The Rational Public: Fifty Years of Trends in Americans' Public Opinion* (Chicago: University of Chicago Press, 1991), p. 376.

67. Ibid., p. 344.

68. Richard A. Brody, *Assessing the President: The Media, Elite Opinion, and Public Support* (Stanford: Stanford University Press, 1991), esp. pp. 140, 153.

69. Stephen Hess, *The Ultimate Insiders* (Washington: Brookings Institution, 1986); and Timothy E. Cook, "House Members as Newsmakers," *Legislative Studies Quarterly* 11 (May 1986), pp. 203–226.

70. E. J. Dionne, Jr., "Government Trust: Less in Western Europe Than in U.S.," *New York Times*, February 16, 1985, p. 20.

71. Kernell, *Going Public*, p. 9.

72. Benjamin I. Page, Robert Y. Shapiro, and Glenn R. Dempsey, "What Moves Public Opinion?" *American Political Science Review* 81 (March 1987), pp. 23–43.

73. See Schneider, "Conservatism, Not Interventionism," p. 62.

CHAPTER 7

The Fourth Circle III:
Local Activists and
Interest Groups

The role of public opinion in foreign policy formation has been a subject of concern since the very first days of democratic government. Debates over what the proper role for the public should be has formed the core of the debate on not only electoral sanctions, but also on bipartisanship and media coverage of international events. Yet, there has been little attention paid to local activists and interest groups. Until recently, what we have called "local diplomacy" simply did not exist. Governors and mayors, not to mention city councils, were much more concerned with sewers than with Sandinistas. Interest groups—apart from a few on the fringes of both left and right—were considered the stuff of which domestic, not foreign, policy was made. The shattering of the bipartisan consensus in the post-Vietnam era has changed all of this. Today, the fourth circle is bursting with participants. It may be the farthest removed from the centers of power in international politics, but it is becoming one of the most important, especially as issues that formerly were purely domestic are now increasingly matters of concern in the international arena. As Secretary of State George Shultz stated in the Iran–Contra hearings, quoting the late entertainer Jimmy Durante, "Everybody wants to get into the act!"

The Newest Actors: All Politics
Are Local

In the pre-Vietnam period the focus of national policy making on international affairs was just that: *national* policy formation. However, in the post-Vietnam era, new actors have emerged on the foreign policy scene: state and local governments. In one sense this is not surprising. As former Speaker of the House

Thomas P. O'Neill was fond of saying, "All politics are local." Yet, it is difficult for the nation to speak with one voice if presidents must contend with governors, mayors, unelected officials, presidential candidates, and even private citizens (as in the Iran–Contra affair) attempting to make foreign policy.

Concern with international relations is not new for local governments. However, as the consensus on what foreign policy should be has broken down, many local officials, such as Larry Agran, former mayor of Irvine, California, argue that they have an *obligation* to speak out against administration policies they oppose so that citizens will have an alternative set of leaders. For years localities have established "sister cities" with localities in other countries; there are now more than 1,200 such arrangements. These relationships have traditionally been little more than signs of neighborliness, a sort of "hands across the ocean."

More recently, the emergence of an interdependent world economy—as well as the large budgetary surpluses run by exporting countries such as oil producers and Japan—added greatly to local politicians' interest in the international arena. Concern with other foreign policy questions followed naturally. Indeed, in 1987 the annual meeting of the National Governors' Association declared that state leaders must take an active role in foreign policy making, especially on issues such as trade, in order to prevent economic wars among the states.

In 1988, 3.5 million Americans worked for foreign-owned companies, and 6 million more had jobs dependent on exports. Forty-one states established 110 offices in 24 countries promoting trade, investment, and tourism. More states had offices in Tokyo (39) than in Washington (38). Approximately 1,000 local governments have established international programs. Twenty-three states have established offices to provide financial assistance to firms in the export business, and more than 200 cities have sent trade envoys abroad. Yet, at the same time, 46 states have established "buy American" or "buy state" provisions for their own governments—possibly thwarting their own international programs.

States have begun to adopt the "industrial policies" that have eluded the federal government. These arrangements bring government, business, and labor together to enhance competitiveness. The public role involves subsidies and tax breaks to assist firms that wish to modernize and expand. Twenty-four states have taken active roles in venture capital; 21 provide financing for exports. The imminent liberalization of European economies has both excited and terrified American firms. Military exporters in California, Maryland, New York, and Texas and aircraft manufacturers in Kansas, Missouri, and Washington face stiffer competition. Eastern states, closest in geographical proximity to Europe, and some Midwestern ones, such as Illinois, see opportunities for greatly expanded markets.[1]

State and local politics have crossed the boundary of economic relationships and good neighborliness. Now they are actively involved in shaping foreign policy. Thirty-seven cities established such relations with Managua, the capital of Nicaragua, in protest against the United States policy of providing aid to the Contras; 33 other Nicaraguan cities have similar arrangements with American communities. Seattle, sometimes described as a "city with its own foreign policy," has 11 such sister cities and a Mayor's Commission on Central America.[2] San Francisco has declared itself a sanctuary for refugees from El Salvador and Guatemala, one of more than 20 cities to do so. It has instructed its police department not to cooperate with the Immigration and Naturalization Service, which seeks to deport many of the illegal aliens. Together with over 70 other cities and more than 20 states, it has begun selling its stocks in companies still doing business with South Africa. In 1988 it held a referendum on whether the United States should support the establishment of a Palestinian homeland.

Massachusetts, with a large Irish Catholic population, has prohibited state pension funds from investing in companies that sell arms to Great Britain for use in the religious conflict in Northern Ireland. Michigan had limited university investments in companies trading with the Soviet Union. Over 160 cities, including Chicago, have declared themselves "nuclear-free zones." They ban the manufacture, transport, or disposal of nuclear weapons within city limits. Almost as many refused to participate in the federal government's program for test relocations in the event of a nuclear war. Oakland took the federal government to court to block the installation of nuclear weapons within city limits. In 1982, 28 out of 30 communities and 8 of 9 states conducting nonbinding referenda supporting the nuclear freeze adopted such proposals.[3]

One issue has pitted states against each other. The federal government has argued that the National Guard is part of the country's defense system and has assigned guard units to build roads (among other projects) in Honduras, which is battling left-wing guerrillas and which also served as a launching base for raids by the American-backed Contras in neighboring Nicaragua. Ten states followed the lead of Minnesota in a challenge to a statute enacted in 1986 that prohibited governors from withholding their approval of the use of guards outside the country in the absence of an emergency within the states. These governors argued that the guard units are state organizations. Eight other states entered the legal fray as "friends of the court" *supporting* the guard's right to dispatch troops abroad.[4] Eight of the eleven states challenging the law have Democratic governors, while seven of the eight supporting the statute have Republican chief executives. One state in which the governorship changed parties in 1986— Arizona—has seen a reversal in policy on this issue: The new governor, Evan Mecham, reversed his Democratic predecessor's ban on sending guard members other than military police to Honduras.[5] A federal court ruled in late 1987 against the Minnesota challenge, maintaining that the National Guard fell under the jurisdiction of the Congress. One Illinois state legislator, upset at his state's policies, filed a bill to prohibit the guard from being sent abroad, visited the troops in Honduras, and reported on the trip in a newsletter to his constituents (see Figure 7–1). The Montana legislature, the Missoula (Montana) County Commission, and the Missoula City Council passed resolutions requesting that Bush give sanctions more time before beginning hostilities against Iraq.[6]

The new activism of subnational governments reflects the breakdown of the pre-Vietnam consensus on foreign policy. Yet it symbolizes something more. The good economic times of the 1950s and especially the 1960s and the great in-

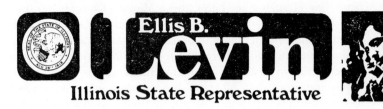

Illinois State Representative

SPRING, 1987

REP. LEVIN INTRODUCES LEGISLATION TO GET THE ILLINOIS NATIONAL GUARD OUT OF CENTRAL AMERICA, FOLLOWING, TRIP TO HONDURAS AND NICARAGUA

REP. LEVIN WITH MEMBERS OF THE ILLINOIS NATIONAL GUARD IN NORTHERN HONDURAS

Dear Friend:

In late February and early March I traveled to Honduras and Nicaragua on a fact finding trip in connection with the deployment of the Illinois National Guard to Honduras. What we saw and heard demonstrated beyond any possible doubt that the Illinois National Guard does not belong in Honduras

This newsletter gives me a chance to report to my constituents and others in Illinois on what we saw and the conclusions we reached. While there, we had the opportunity to meet with all sides in both countries, including being helicoptered by the U.S. military to the base where the Illinois National Guard is deployed in Honduras, meeting with Contra leaders, members of the majority and opposition Honduran parties, as well as members of the Sandinistan Government in Nicaragua. Everyone we met with was extremely cooperative. This gave us an extraordinary opportunity to reach some hard conclusions as to what is really going on down there.

The Illinois National Guard does not belong there and it is our role as citizens to make this conclusion known to the legislators in the State. One wonders if it would have been possible to undertake a similar type of trip before the Vietnam War.

Sincerely,

Ellis B. Levin
State Representative

crease in the role of government in the nation's economy led to a new participatory environment throughout American politics—on domestic as well as foreign policy issues. The number of lobbyists in Washington increased from 4,000 in 1976 to 14,500 in 1991; as far back as 1975, however, there were reported to be 15,000 individuals, including unregistered lobbyists, working on some form of foreign lobbying activity in Washington.[7] As noted in Chapter 4, the number of special interest caucuses in the Congress has also skyrocketed.

The arguments of radicals protesting the Vietnam War and the lack of progress in civil rights in the 1960s—"Power to the People"—was taken quite literally by Americans. The range of issues that excited people increased dramatically. Concern over the environment, civil rights, women's rights, and other social issues (abortion, prayer in schools, etc.)—as well as foreign policy—changed the atmosphere in Washington. When the boom of the 1960s gave way to very high rates of inflation in the 1970s and the recession of 1982, local politicians—both mayors and governors—traversed the world to seek new outlets for investment in their communities and states. The distrust of governmental authorities in Washington led people to become more active in all sorts of issues; Americans have traditionally believed that the most representative governments are the ones closest to home. The activism, both through local politics and interest groups, reflects the reemergence of this motif in the 1970s, 1980s, and 1990s.

Interest Groups

Nothing has so directly challenged the idea of presidential dominance over foreign policy in the past two decades as the increase in the role of interest groups in foreign policy. In the pre-Vietnam period there was a scattering of groups on the ideological fringes as well as some ethnic groups pressing for congressional statements of support for their causes, but little more. To be sure, some interest groups were active on issues such as trade but they were far fewer in number than they are today. Groups pressuring for free trade generally canceled out those demanding protection, so that presidents retained the upper hand in negotiating tariff agreements with other countries. As Bauer, Pool, and Dexter argued:

> The stereotype notion of omnipotent pressure groups becomes completely obsolete once there are groups on both sides. The result of opposing omnipotent forces is stalemate. But, even taken by themselves, the groups did not appear to have the raw material of greater power. We noted shortages of money, men, information, and time.[8]

Interest groups on trade also tended to concentrate their efforts on legislators who agreed with their own stands, and there was hardly unanimity even within the corporate and union sectors. Much lobbying took the form of speaking to the already converted.

On domestic policies, where the stakes more clearly involve "winners" and "nonwinners" rather than "winners" and "loosers," interest groups have been much stronger actors. Weak political parties, moreover, generally indicate that interest groups are powerful.[9] Farmers' lobbies have an important say on agriculture, veterans' organizations are forceful proponents of their demands for more government services, and business lobbies fight against government regulation and for tax deductions for investments. On foreign policy there have been far fewer interest groups active. When there is a clearly perceived "national interest" at stake, it appears unseemly for groups to seek some private interest.

Yet there are some important areas of foreign policy in which interest groups have traditionally been active. In addition to trade, one prominent issue has been the defense budget. Since defense expenditures are in the range of $300 billion, it is reasonable to presume that military contractors would attempt to play a major role in the defense budgetary process. Military contractors have supported specific services in their competition for funds and weapons. However, the military services are not themselves united over which weapons should be built: The navy wants more ships, the army more tanks, the air force more jets. Not all can be purchased, and rivalries between the services are fierce.

Members of Congress fight for military projects for their districts, but even in this realm there is no strong evidence to support a linkage between serving on the armed services committees and getting more than a "fair share" of military expenditures in one's district or state.[10] Legislators do a better job of protecting military installations already in their districts than in obtaining new bases. Cost-effectiveness is one criterion. As the military budget now is mainly spent on personnel, there is simply less flexibility in locating installations for political purposes. In 1988 and 1990 Congress enacted legislation establishing a bipartisan commission to recommend the closing of unneeded military bases. There are some other constraints that we tend to gloss over: You cannot locate a naval base in Kansas. Finally, as we noted in Chapter 4, the choice of weapons systems and the size of the defense budget reflects legislators' own ideologies and public pressures on members for higher or lower expenditures.

The intermestic policies of food and energy also involve group conflict, just as trade and the defense budget do. However, the policy-making process on these issues is considerably more complex. In addition to the range of domestic interest groups involved, there are foreign actors who can restrict the range of alternative policies from which a decision can be made. There are also multinational corporations, for example, the oil companies and telecommunications giants such as AT&T, ITT, and IBM, which operate both in the consuming nations (particularly the United States) and in the producing nations (such as the OPEC countries). These corporations are, of course, among the domestic interests involved in the policy-making process. But multinational corporations are not easily controlled by the American government. They can act in concert with the producing nations (as the oil companies cooperate with the OPEC nations) and are not subject to U.S. regulations outside American borders. Pharmaceutical firms can market products abroad that have not been approved by American authorities. The leverage that the United States has over such companies is limited, since the multinationals can threaten to move their bases of operation abroad. The policy-making process on these issues becomes much more complex, and often the result is no coordinated policy at all.

The sharp rise in energy prices (up to $36 per barrel) and their rapid descent (to a low of $8 per barrel) within the course of a decade led to increased economic turmoil in the developing nations of the Third World. The nations that had relied on cheap energy to industrialize had to resort to borrowing instead during the 1970s, often at levels far beyond their capacity to pay back the loans. Energy-rich countries such as Mexico and Nigeria profited mightily from the boom in oil prices and rushed to diversify their economies with massive building projects, again financed by loans. When prices plummeted in 1985–86, these countries were unable to pay back even the interest on loans. Together with other developing nations, they threatened not to repay the loans at all. Since popular support for foreign aid among the mass public has plummeted in the post-Vietnam era and direct grants are more difficult to obtain, banks took the place of governments in financing Third World loans. Many of the banks are themselves multinational corporations. In one's travels abroad, it is no longer a surprise to see offices of Citicorp, the Bank of America, or the First National Bank of Chicago, among many others. These financial institutions have become the principal financiers of development and, in turn, have large deposits from Japan and of "petrodollars" from oil-producing nations. Banks have loaned money not only to American friends in the Third World such as Mexico, Argentina, Brazil, Turkey, and Zaire (among many others), but also to the Communist nations of Eastern Europe and even to the Soviet Union itself. By making these loans, the banks not only make calculated business decisions but foreign policy as well.

Such private loans often serve the same function as government loans or direct aid. Just as critical, many of these loans are made to facilitate purchases of American goods by foreign nations. The banks, then, control the flow of international commerce, and international banking regulations are few in number and difficult to enforce. When Carter froze Iranian assets in American banks in 1980 (including overseas branches) following the seizure of hostages, observers in the financial community wondered whether the banks would go along; many even doubted that foreign branches would comply. The banks did not challenge the president, however, and America's allies were quite supportive in permitting American branches in their nations to follow presidential orders. An international, financial, and political crisis might have developed otherwise.

The issue was resolved without substantial difficulty, because most banks involved also were holding unpaid notes from the shah's government, and it was far from clear that the new Islamic regime would honor past debts. The possibility that the government might have to bail out some banks that lost large amounts of money through loans to American allies was fortunately avoided in the Iranian case, but is a question that worries both policy makers and bankers. It is far from clear what the government would do should a major nation such as Argentina, Brazil, or Mexico default or refuse to pay its debts. Nor is it immediately evident whether the government of the United States or the banks, which control much of the domestic money supply, would ultimately emerge from such a struggle as the dominant actor.[11]

The government won the first round of what promised to be a protracted legal battle when the Supreme Court ruled unanimously in July 1981 that President Carter had authority under the Constitution to conclude the agreement which finally won the hostages' release. In May 1987 the banks had to confront a far more serious problem. Several of the nation's largest banks, led by Citicorp, increased their reserve deposits to cover possible defaults on Third World loans. Citicorp put aside $3 billion, but its total outstanding loans to developing countries amounted to $14.7 billion. The five largest American banks alone had losses in 1987 estimated at $7 billion.[12] These figures, of course, do not include obligations owed to financial institutions in Western Europe, Japan, and Canada. Should many Third World countries default, the major banks in North America, Western Europe, and Japan could be thrown into turmoil—and with them the economies of each nation. The federal government already has had to rescue one bank—Continental Illinois—from imprudent lending practices to the domestic energy sector. Some leading politicians, especially Senator Bill Bradley (D-N.J.), have recommended forgiving part of the loans if the debtor nations agree to restructure their economies. With increased environmental concern throughout the world (see Chapter 9), industrialized nations, including the United States, have begun to reduce the debt of developing nations in exchange for stricter environmental regulations. Brazilian debt has been slashed in an effort to preserve its rain forests. While such decisions are made by governments, the financial institutions involved must absorb much of the loss.

The government argues that banks recognized the risks in loaning money to poor nations. Getting back even some of the money would be better than default. The 1980s and 1990s have been a rough time for financial institutions. A large number of savings and loans failed in the United States, resulting in a taxpayer bailout that could cost up to $500 billion. There were fears that a similar fate would befall the banks, including some of the larger ones with considerable foreign debt. One of the world's largest banking conglomerates, the Pakistan-based Bank of Credit and Commerce International (BCCI), collapsed amidst international scandal. BCCI had several subsidiary banks in the United States.

The increased interdependence of the world economy has brought a whole new range of actors into the foreign policy process: foreign companies that have invested in the United States. Foreigners now own more than 10 percent of all United States government securities and often obtain special tax advantages for opening plants in the United States. Many states have engaged in bidding wars against each other to attract Japanese car manufacturers, for example. In 1986 Sony, Nestle (the Swiss chocolate conglomerate), the Alcan Aluminum Company of Canada, and ICI American (a British-owned chemical firm) formed the Organization for the Fair Treatment of International Investment to lobby on federal and state tax issues; it now has thirty-three member firms. The Association for International Investment, with sixty members, lobbies on nontax issues; it was founded by Elliot L. Richardson, who served in a variety of cabinet posts under Nixon and Gerald R. Ford.[13]

Altogether the 850 foreign lobbyists who did register in 1985 spent $150 million in their activities. The political action committees of American companies owned by foreign nationals donated more than $1 million to congressional campaigns in 1984, twice as much as two years earlier; two years later, the figure had more than doubled again to $2.3 million. The rate of increase leveled off in 1988, when spending by 118 committees amounted to $2.8 million.[14] While foreign nationals are prohibited from making contributions to American political campaigns, the Federal Election Commission has ruled that foreign-owned companies operating within the United States are the political arms of their employees rather than their stockholders. The Federal Election Commission, which regulates campaign financing, has held hearings on whether foreign-owned companies should be banned from establishing political action committees. The commission voted to outlaw political action committees with majority foreign ownership in June 1990, but it took no further action. It is unclear whether such restrictions would be constitutional.

Japanese firms have also donated large sums of money to California state legislative candidates who pledged to overturn a law that imposed taxes on the worldwide earnings of corporations operating in California. As Japan came under increasing criticism for its large trade surplus with the United States, it mounted a political offensive in Washington in an attempt to forestall stringent trade legislation in the Congress. Japanese government agencies, corporations, and foundations spent an estimated $250 million on lobbying in 1989, far more than any other country. They hired as many as 300 lobbying firms to assist them, as well as eighty-nine Washington lawyers and public relations experts at a cost of $100 million. When a Japanese firm, Toshiba, was charged with selling advanced American technology to the Soviet Union in violation of American laws, the firm was able to mobilize not only the resources of the government of Japan but also leaders of many American corporations doing business in the Far East to lobby against a ban on the import of Toshiba products. This effort cost $9 million and saved Toshiba $10 billion in lost sales. Japan has also spent $5 million in a lobbying effort to dispute charges that it sold superconductors for computers at prices below cost to American suppliers. Yet, the Japanese have been very discrete in electoral politics. Only 12 of the 118 political action committees with foreign ties are connected to Japanese interests.[15]

The Korean-based Unification Church has established daily newspapers in Washington and New York to compete with the *Washington Post* and the *New York Times,* as well as a newsmagazine to compete with *Time* and *Newsweek.* Former presidential aide Michael Deaver was accused in 1986 of using his influence with President Reagan on behalf of his employer, the government of Canada, to affect acid rain legislation. Deaver, who also worked for Saudi Arabia and South Korea, is just one example of prominent federal officials who went to work for foreign countries. From 1980 to 1985, at least seventy-six former high-ranking government officers worked for over fifty foreign governments, including former Vice President Spiro T. Agnew, two former secretaries of state (Dean Acheson and William P. Rogers), a former secretary of defense (Clark Clifford), the ex-director of the CIA (William Colby), an erstwhile national security adviser (Richard Allen), and many former representatives and senators, including one who chaired the Foreign Relations Committee (J. William Fulbright). Howard Baker, formerly Senate majority leader and Ronald Reagan's White House chief of staff, has lobbied for the Japanese government.[16] More recently, South Africa has hired eleven lobbying firms at $2 million a year, while China employed the prominent Hill and Knowlton public relations firm to press for continuation of its most favored nation status.[17] Taiwan, which has not had diplomatic relations with the United States since the establishment of American ties with China in 1979, has mounted a lobbying effort that rivals Japan's to expand its exports to the United States.[18]

Ideological and Religious Lobbies

Ideological interest groups, such as the Committee of One Million and the Women's Strike for Peace, played a prominent role in the foreign policy of the 1950s and 1960s. The first group consistently battled to prevent the recognition of the Peking government of China, whereas the latter organization pressed for nuclear disarmament. Neither of these groups was successful in its goal, and both have disappeared from public view. During the 1970s and 1980s new and temporarily influential groups did arise. One such organization, the Committee on the Present Danger, arose in the 1970s to combat what it considered to be public apathy in the wake of Vietnam about the growing military threat of the Soviet Union. One of its major efforts was to prevent ratification of the SALT II treaty. Its principal impact, however, came during the Reagan administration, when many of the committee's most prominent members—including Reagan himself and Secretary of State George P. Shultz—found themselves in positions in government.[19]

Among the "ideological" interest groups that have emerged since the Vietnam War are religious organizations, especially churches. Churches have traditionally been active politically in the United States, fighting for the abolition of slavery prior to the Civil War, for Prohibition in the early twentieth century, for civil rights in the 1950s and 1960s, and on both sides of the new social issues of the 1970s and 1980s (abortion, prayer in schools, etc.). Church activism on foreign policy dramatically increased during the Vietnam War and has continued apace since then. In 1986, the National Conference of Catholic Bishops approved almost unanimously a pastoral letter calling for significant increases in foreign aid and a ban on sales of military hardware abroad. The next year it announced that it would divest $5.3 million of investments in American firms doing business in South Africa.

The Catholic Church went on record opposing aid to the Contras, while the Presbyterian General Assembly has actively lobbied members of Congress on the same issue. Together with the United Church of Christ, the United Methodists, the American Baptists, the United Council of Churches, and pacifist churches such as the Mennonites and the Society of Friends, they have formed the Inter-Religious Task Force on El Salvador and Central America. A few secular groups also lobby on the left. Conservative organizations include the Heritage Foundation, the American Security Council, the Council for Inter-American Security, and the Institute on Religion and Democracy. Most of these organizations have little or no staffs, and only the religious groups have had much of an impact on Capitol Hill. Even the Bahai faith, whose members accept the principles of most of the world's major religions and who are prohibited from participating in partisan politics, have formed a lobbying organization to call attention to the persecution of their co-religionists in Iran.[20]

Religious and ideological interest groups were very active on the issues of the Gulf War. The National Conference of Catholic Bishops opposed the conflict as morally wrong. The National Council of Churches not only condemned potential military action, but charged the Bush administration with maintaining a double standard of pressuring Iraq to withdraw from Kuwait but not insisting that Israel withdraw from the West Bank and Gaza strip. The council called on its member churches to engage in both conventional and unconventional protest strategies—both lobbying Congress and demonstrating at recruitment centers and military bases. The Church of the Brethren called for an "oil-free Sunday" to demonstrate that Americans could withstand a petroleum cutoff by Iraq without going to war. The United Methodists warned of growing intolerance of Arabs and Muslims in the United States. The church groups were joined by the Coalition to Stop U.S. Intervention in the Middle East, organized by former Attorney General Ramsey Clark, who has long been a strong opponent of most American foreign policy, especially concerning the Arab world. More mainstream opposition came from nine union leaders who signed an "open letter" to President Bush in the *Washington Post* opposing hostilities. Some women's groups opposed joining a coalition with Arab nations that limited women's rights. Many civil rights leaders charged that blacks and other minorities were overrepresented in the military and thus might suffer more casualties than their share of the population would warrant.

As the protests against Central American policy indicate, churches have taken an increasingly active role in the peace movement. Yet, there was not unified religious opposition in previous wars. Many churches rallied behind the anti-Communist cause in World War II. Others, including the mainline Protestant denominations, focused their attention on internal church issues. The religious opposition to the war in Vietnam was not unified. There was at least one prominent holdout. The Council of Jewish Federations was split on military action, but urged "the maintenance of a firm position of opposition to Saddam Hussein."[21]

Not all action takes place within the confines of the mile-long road that both joins and separates the Capitol and the White House. One organization, loosely affiliated with some Protestant and Catholic church groups and deriving its inspiration from a Jesuit concept of the harmony that binds people together, pursues its goals through a more adversarial venue—the legal system. The Christic Institute filed suit in 1986 to force the Reagan administration to abandon its support for the Contras, charging that some of the antigovernment military operations in Nicaragua had been financed by illegal narcotics sales assisted by American officials.[22] Churches and synagogues have been at the forefront of the sanctuary movement. Evangelical churches have mobilized their members in support of aid to the Contras. Jews have, in addition to their strong support for Israel (see below), lobbied heavily for penalizing the Soviet Union until it no longer restricted Jewish emigration. In 1974, they pressured Congress to enact the Jackson–Vanik amendment restricting trade with the Soviet Union. This statute was finally repealed in 1991 when the Soviets permitted emigration to Israel and reestablished diplomatic relations with the Jewish state. Ironically, the opening of the Tel Aviv embassy was the last major international venture of the Soviet Union before it dissolved on New Year's Eve, 1992.

Some of the most effective groups are ethnic lobbies. The preeminent organizations are those supporting Israel, especially the American Israel Public Affairs Committee (AIPAC). The Jewish organizations (AIPAC, the American Jewish Committee, and the B'nai B'rith Anti-Defamation League) are concerned almost exclusively with American policy toward Israel, although emigration of Soviet Jews has also been a major focus of their efforts. While these organizations have been unusually successful, they are not always victorious. The failure to block the sale of military aircraft to Egypt and Saudi Arabia in 1978 and to prevent the transfer of AWACS planes to the Saudis are two examples. On those issues where AIPAC has been least successful, it faced strong opposition from the administration.

While AIPAC could not prevent an additional arms deal with Saudi Arabia in 1986, it reasserted its strength later that year and in 1987, when Congress forced Reagan to withdraw proposed arms sales to Jordan and the Saudis. Legislators feared that the arms might be used against Israel and believed that neither Jordan nor Saudi Arabia had been sufficiently forthcoming in furthering the Middle East peace process.[23] Many Americans were up in arms in 1987 against Saudi Arabia's refusal to shoot down the Iraqi plane that fired at the USS *Stark* in the Persian Gulf. Israel receives by far the largest amount of foreign aid from the United States—$3 billion a year—and has received other unique forms of aid. The United States and Israel signed a free-trade pact in 1985 that eliminates tariffs between the two countries. The United States has also permitted Israel to use some of the military credits its receives to develop its own technology; additionally, contributions by Americans, largely from the Jewish community, to Israel are tax-exempt.

How powerful are ethnic lobbies? We shall examine the range of such groups in small detail, but focus primarily on the most powerful, the pro-Israel lobby and especially AIPAC. This force has become the model for most other ethnic actors—the Greeks, the Cuban-Americans, and even the Arab-Americans. The story of the ups and downs of the pro-Israel lobby is best told by considering two case studies, the AWACS sale and the issue of loan guarantees for housing immigrants from the former Soviet Union.

The AWACS Sale and the Housing Loan Guarantees

The transfer of five AWACS planes to Saudi Arabia sorely tested relations between the Israeli lobby and both White House and congressional supporters. Neither AIPAC nor the president was accustomed to losing battles on Capitol Hill; moreover, the administration seemed an unlikely adversary for the Israeli lobby, since Reagan had actively campaigned in 1980 as a strong supporter of Israel. However, the security of Saudi Arabia, one of America's leading suppliers of oil, was also of prime concern to the president, who wished to create a security zone in the Middle East composed of all of America's friends. However, regional animosities were too strong for such a unified stance to come about, and the stage was set for a confrontation between the administration, which wanted to sell the planes to the Saudis, and the Israeli lobby, which feared that they would be used to spy on Israel's military moves. The constellation of forces involved in the fight was quite wide, and as such the AWACS sale provides a fascinating case study on the interaction of interest groups, the president, and Congress in foreign policy decision making.

Under the 1976 law which permitted Congress to veto major arms sales (since June 1983 of dubious constitutionality), a majority in both the House and the Senate had the power to kill the sale of the AWACS planes to Saudi Arabia. No president had ever lost an arms sales agreement before, even to nations for which the American public had little affinity. Americans, however, generally agreed that Saudi Arabia was vital to their interests; a 1982 poll indicated that 77 percent of the public felt so, compared with 75 percent for Israel (Israel had a slightly higher overall favorable rating than did Saudi Arabia). Yet a wide variety of polls also indicated varying degrees of opposition to arms sales to the Saudis, with none showing majority support for such deals (including AWACS) or demonstrating that the sales would have even the level of support that supplying Israel did.[24]

Thus, the stage was set for a dramatic confrontation between the White House and the Congress. Many also interpreted it as a test between presidential power and the lobbying power of the friends of Israel. Israel contended that the sale would pose a threat to its existence, since the AWACS would alter the military balance of strength in the Middle East. The administration countered that the planes were to be used exclusively for defensive purposes against threats to the Saudi regime, although it was unable to persuade Saudi Arabia to agree to have both its own and American pilots operate the planes. Instead, the president sent a letter to key Republican senators promising to cancel the deal if the planes were not used exclusively for defensive purposes. This hardly mollified the opponents of the sale, since they believed that the deal could not be canceled retrospectively.

The pro-Israeli lobby strongly mobilized against the sale. AIPAC has an annual budget of $15 million, 50,000 dues-paying members, a staff of more than 100 operating only a block away from Capitol Hill, and eight regional offices. It regarded stopping the AWACS sale as its top legislative priority in 1981. AIPAC operates mostly on Capitol Hill and carefully attempts to distance itself from the Israeli embassy uptown.[25] Also involved were the Conference of Presidents of Major American Jewish Organizations, an umbrella organization of forty groups; and the larger members of the conference, including the American Jewish Committee, the American Jewish Congress, B'nai B'rith, and the Union of American Hebrew Congregations, all of which have their own Washington offices. Most of these organizations focus on domestic issues or on raising funds for Israel rather than on lobbying for foreign policy issues. But the AWACS sale was viewed as too important an issue to ignore.

The effort appeared to be paying off in the summer of 1981. In June AIPAC secured a letter opposing the AWACS deal signed by 224 members of the House and 54 senators, enough to defeat the sale in both houses. The timing of the letter was fortuitous; it was circulated after the Israeli bombing of an Iraqi nuclear reactor and, hence, gave the impression that the signatures constituted the minimum basis of support for the Israeli lobby's position.[26] The power of the lobby has been attributed to its success in fund-raising. Nonetheless, electoral reprisal from Jewish voters was feared even though it rarely, if ever, materialized. Many key members of Congress, including AWACS opponent Senator Bob Packwood (R-Ore.), had raised substantial portions of their campaign funds from Jewish contributors.[27] Senator Charles McC. Mathias, Jr. (R-Md.), reflecting the congressional obsession with the disposition of the "Jewish vote," wrote in *Foreign Affairs* that

> as a result of the activities of the lobby, congressional conviction [that Israel must remain strong] has been measurably reinforced by the knowledge that political sanctions will be applied to any who fail to deliver.[28]

AIPAC was clearly a formidable foe. Its reputation in Washington is comparable not to other foreign policy lobbies, but to domestic actors such as organized labor. Presidential candidates seek its advice, even though AIPAC itself does not endorse candidates for office, and administrations have often sought AIPAC's assistance in gaining congressional support among friends of Israel for other foreign policy issues. The organization has also mobilized local networks of supporters of Israel who meet with members of Congress back in their districts, as well as with those candidates who seek to defeat incumbents. More recently, it organized 1,500 "citizen lobbyists," armed with individualized computer printouts of their legislators' backgrounds, to press for additional aid to Israel because of the damage it incurred in the Gulf War.[29]

The "Arab lobby" consists primarily of the National Association of Arab Americans (NAAA). While openly modeled on AIPAC, it has far fewer resources, including a mailing list of only 80,000 names, most of whom are inactive, and a budget reported to be $500,000 annually to fund a staff of twenty-five.[30] While AIPAC has been able to maintain a separate identity from the Israeli government, much of the funding of NAAA (through advertisements in the organization's publication) comes directly from Arab governments and the Palestine Liberation Organization. NAAA leaders complain that many Arab Americans are apolitical, but a rival organization, the American Lebanese League, is harshly critical of the NAAA and views it as essentially anti-American.[31] There have been some efforts to get American businesses with interests in the Middle East, especially oil companies, to do more lobbying and fund-raising for the Arab cause, but they have not yielded much success to date. One analysis concludes: "Most Arab embassies throw impressive parties, but have little day-to-day contact with Congress, according to lawmakers and aides. Israel, by comparison, has a staff of congressional relations counselors who keep in touch with Capitol Hill."[32]

With all of these advantages, it would appear that victory was almost guaranteed for the Israel lobby on the AWACS votes. The vote in the House was a ringing endorsement for its position; on October 1, 1981, it vetoed the sale by a margin of 301 to 111. But on October 25, the Senate upheld the president by the narrow vote of 48 to 52. The president had convinced eight senators—seven Republicans and one Democrat—to vote with the administration. What happened to turn what seemed to be a sure victory for the Israeli lobby into a humiliating defeat?

First was the hard lobbying done by the president himself. Reagan had won rave reviews as a legislative persuader earlier in the year when he successfully maneuvered a very controversial domestic budget through a Congress which was initially skeptical. On the AWACS issue, he asserted the need for the Republican-controlled Senate to back a Republican president on a key foreign policy issue. The fact that a president had never before lost an up-or-down arms sales vote worked to his advantage, as did arguments that the United States would be embarrassed in the Arab world should the sale be vetoed. The specter of another oil embargo, although not specifically raised, was on many people's minds. Second, five days after the House vote, Egyptian President Anwar Sadat was assassinated by Muslim radicals in Cairo. Many senators were worried about further instability in the Middle East and decided that they must rally around the president. Third, simple party loyalty played an important role. Many of the senators whom Reagan converted were elected in 1980 and identified with the "New Right." Most leaders of the religious right, particularly the Moral Majority's Jerry Falwell, have a strong affinity for Israel as the Holy Land and actively opposed the AWACS sale. But pressure to support their fellow conservative, the president, proved too strong to resist. Senator Roger Jepsen (R-Iowa), one of the earliest and strongest opponents of the sale, ended up voting with the president "after prayerful and careful deliberation."[33] Fourth, the letter that the president sent to wavering senators promising to cancel the sale if the planes were not used for defensive purposes permitted some senators to argue that the White House had made concessions. Finally, there were also charges that the president engaged in logrolling on the AWACS vote, promising a political appointment to an Iowa senator, a hospital for a Washington Republican, a power plant for a Montana Democrat, and even a pledge not to campaign in 1982 against an Arizona Democrat.[34]

Whatever the relative impacts of each factor, the senators assuaged their consciences and bolstered the Israeli lobby five weeks later when the Senate Appropriations Committee voted to increase foreign aid to Israel by $475 million more than the administration requested. Ultimately, the administration prevailed on its original lower request for aid, but in 1983, following the accord between Lebanon and Israel on the withdrawal of foreign forces from Lebanon, the administration agreed to congressional action increasing assistance to Israel. Congress dealt the administration a further setback when a House Foreign Affairs subcommittee voted to ban arms sales to Jordan until King Hussein publicly recognized Israel and agreed to negotiate with it under the terms of the 1979 Camp David accords.

A further test of AIPAC's effectiveness might have come had Reagan pushed his 1982 peace plan, under which the Israelis would withdraw from most of the West Bank and Gaza (captured from Jordan and Egypt in 1967) and permit a self-governing Palestinian entity to be formed in association with Jordan. The plan was proposed after the Israeli invasion of Lebanon in late spring of 1982. To many, the invasion appeared not only as an effort to destroy the Palestine Liberation Organization (PLO), but as an attempt to destroy Palestinian nationalism and tighten Israeli control of the West Bank. While Israeli forces were in control of Lebanon's capital of Beirut, Christian Lebanese forces massacred Palestinians in two camps. As a result of the invasion and the massacre, Israel's position in America—in the eyes of both the public and the Congress—was seriously undermined.

American pressure on Israel to withdraw from Lebanon was initially resisted, as the Israelis insisted on a long list of preconditions. In response, the United States postponed the transfer to Israel of U.S.-made fighter planes. Finally, Secretary of State Shultz journeyed to the Middle East and worked out a Lebanese–Israeli agreement under which the Israelis would withdraw if the Syrian and remaining PLO forces did so simultaneously. The Reagan administration's relationship with American Jews improved as a result of these mediation efforts. Responsibility for an Israeli failure to pull its forces out of Lebanon now lay clearly with the Syrians and the PLO. A test of the strength of the Israeli lobby was also avoided because the PLO and Jordan's King Hussein refused to negotiate a settlement of the Palestinian problem based on the Reagan plan, after an initially cautious but favorable reaction. Had Jordan and the PLO accepted the plan, the administration would have had to pressure the Israeli government, and the administration's relationship with the Jewish community, already badly strained by the AWACS deal, would have been severely tested.

The United States "brokered" an agreement for the withdrawal of Israeli troops from Lebanon between Israel and the government then dominated by Maronite Christians in Beirut. This further strengthened American–Israeli ties, as most people in the United States viewed the American role as another step toward fostering peace treaties (which the Israel–Lebanon agreement was not!) between Israel and her neighbors. When Syria successfully pressed the Beirut government to abandon the agreement, Israel's stock in the United States rose even further; it was viewed as proposing a peace to unwilling or incapacitated neighbors.

The AWACS defeat and the Israeli invasion of Lebanon changed the environment for AIPAC. Congressional support was no longer automatic. It thus shifted its strategy in several ways. First, it recognized that it had to pay more attention to the Republican-controlled Senate, rather than restricting its focus on the House. Second, it began working with Republicans as well as Democrats. Third, and most critical, it expanded its membership base beyond the states with large Jewish populations. It opened a regional office in Austin, Texas. These tactics paid off. Not only did Southern and Southwestern support for Israel increase dramatically, but AIPAC regained the offensive more generally. It blocked proposed arms sales to Jordan and Saudi Arabia in the late 1980s. In 1986, Secretary of State Shultz reportedly asked AIPAC what kind of arms and aid package the Reagan administration could get passed.[35]

The lobby's preeminence was not to last. The Iraqi invasion of Kuwait led to further strains in relations between Israel and the United States. The Palestinian uprising (*intifada*) in the West Bank and Gaza Strip was two years old. It drew public support from the Arab world. The United States was forming a broad coalition against Iraq that included virtually all of the other Arab states, including its long-time enemy, Syria. To secure Arab support, the United States voted twice within two weeks in October 1990 to condemn Israel's treatment of the Palestinians. President Bush reportedly viewed Israel as an "unruly partner and a nuisance."[36]

Israel sought $10 billion in loan guarantees to build housing for immigrants from the Soviet Union and Ethiopia the next fall. Bush was lukewarm to the idea. Many in Congress supported the plan. The president insisted that for the loan guarantees to go through, Israel must agree to stop building Jewish settlements in the West Bank and Gaza Strip. Israel refused, counting on the support of its friends in Congress. Yet, Bush would not agree and persuaded Congress to accept a 120-day delay until an accord could be reached. There was a sour public mood toward Israel in the United States. Legislators in Congress normally sympathetic to the Jewish state agreed with the president's plan. American Jewish groups, including AIPAC, mounted a frenzied lobbying effort. Thousands of volunteers came to Washington to demand action; others wrote letters or faxed their comments to the legislative and executive branches. Bush not only refused to budge, but he also became the first president to attack the pro-Israel lobby: "I am up against some powerful forces, but I owe it to the American people to tell them how strongly I feel."

Israel's restrained role in the Gulf War bolstered its public support (see below). Yet, the issue of settlements refused to go away, and the president rejected congressional compromises that would have granted Israel the $10 billion minus what it spent on settlements. When the 120-day period ended in March 1992, the president remained strongly opposed to any compromise. AIPAC and other pro-Israeli forces, chastened by Bush's attack on the lobby, lay low. Some Jewish organizations even preferred not to fight the president because their members favored the freeze on settlements.[37] When Congress did not challenge the president, the pro-Israel lobby suffered a major defeat and a blow to its prestige. When a coalition devoted to stronger moves toward peace defeated Israel's rightist government in June 1992, the president agreed to restore the loan guarantees. The presidential election appeared close. Bush hoped the move would win back Jewish support. It did not work: Jews gave Clinton 78 percent of their vote, the highest share of the Jewish vote any candidate had received in several decades and virtually tied with blacks as the most loyal Democratic constituency in 1992.[38]

Nevertheless, AIPAC's reputation was not readily restored. The new Israeli prime minister, Yitzhak Rabin, lambasted AIPAC in a private meeting before the Israeli election. He charged that the lobbying effort on the loan guarantees had damaged Israel's public image in the United States and had shifted AIPAC's role from a neutral broker on behalf of Israel to a partisan supporter of the right-wing government. AIPAC's stature in the American Jewish community was tarnished by charges that the organization was attempting to infiltrate and undermine dovish Jewish groups.[39] In November of 1992, the president of AIPAC resigned after boasting, without any evidence, that he could dictate to newly elected President Bill Clinton who the major foreign policy figures in the new administration would be. Even so, AIPAC remains more powerful than other ethnic lobbies. Before we consider the basis for AIPAC's strength, let us examine some other ethnic actors on foreign policy.

Ethnic Lobbies[40]

The strength of ethnic groups is not a new phenomenon in American politics; they have played a major role in foreign policy debates throughout the twentieth century. Irish groups, opposed to Britain, argued against American participation in World War I and later opposed U.S. entry into the League of Nations. Italian and German groups were active opponents of American entry into both world wars. German groups were extremely powerful in the Midwest throughout the century, helping elect several senators and members of the House. While often quite liberal on domestic policies, the midwestern members of Congress elected from districts with heavy concentrations of Germans were decidedly isolationist in their foreign policy. Their rationale for not fighting a war against Germany was that the United States should not attempt to resolve what essentially were conflicts between other nations.

Isolationist strength reached its peak between the two wars, when Robert LaFollette, Sr., ran for president on a third-party ticket in 1924. Although LaFollette carried only his home state of Wisconsin, he ran a close second in several midwestern states and compiled what was then the second largest number of votes a third-party candidate for president had ever received. The strength of the LaFollette movement raised serious questions about American entry into World War II before Pearl Harbor. The Irish, Italian, and German groups failed because they each opposed the government's established policies, whereas the Jewish groups have been more successful at least partially because of the government's official position of support for Israel.

The Greek lobby was "for years . . . widely rumored to have influence second only to the supporters of Israel" on foreign policy issues facing the Congress.[41] The American Hellenic Institute Public Affairs Committee and the American Hellenic Educational Progressive Association were successful in gaining substantial foreign assistance as well as in enacting a partial arms embargo on Turkey following that nation's invasion of Cyprus in 1974. Historically, the Greek and Israeli lobbies worked together in providing support for each other's causes, thus making each more effective than either would have been alone.[42] But the alliance broke down in 1978 when Israel feared that the embargo on sales to Turkey might lead to a loss of U.S. bases in that country, so many key supporters of Israel in the Congress, led by Representative Steven Solarz (D-N.Y.), supported President Carter's proposal to repeal the embargo. The election of a Socialist government in Greece and Greek threats to leave NATO further weakened both the Greek–Israeli lobbying alliance in Washington (especially since Greek Prime Minister Andreas Papandreou is outspokenly pro-Arab) and the efforts of the Greek lobby itself. In 1983, Turkey insisted that the traditional 7 to 10 ratio of American aid to Greece and Turkey be revised further in Turkey's favor. Greece in turn demanded far greater aid if the United States were to maintain bases there. The House insisted that the traditional ratio be maintained, a defeat for the administration and a victory for the Greek lobby, its first notable win in more than five years.

Despite the belligerence of the Greek government, which periodically threatens to demand that the United States military base outside Athens be shut, Greek-Americans continue to be more successful in lobbying Congress than Turkish-Americans. One reason is the greater sophistication of the Greek lobby, which traditionally worked closely with the Jewish lobby and, indeed, was consciously modeled after AIPAC. Moreover, there are far more Greek-Americans— estimated to be between 600,000 and three million—than Turkish-Americans, who number only 200,000 and have no lobbying group of their own.[43] In 1987 the Congress not only reduced military aid to Turkey, but also stipulated that none of the arms could be used in Cyprus, which Turkey had invaded in 1974; the Congress also enacted a resolution condemning the massacre of hundreds of thousands of Armenians in Turkey in 1915—an event strongly disputed by the Turks themselves. Greek-Americans took a particularly active role in the 1988 presidential campaign as one of their own, Massachusetts Governor Michael Dukakis, sought the presidency. The community raised over 15 percent of the Massachusetts governor's early war chest.[44]

The Greeks maintain a much larger Washington presence than the Turks. The Turkish government plays an active role in pressing its cause, but until recently it primarily relied upon support from the American Legion and the Veterans of Foreign Wars, who are concerned about the Turkish link to NATO. More recently the Turkish government has employed a Washington public relations firm at a cost of $600,000 a year. The Turks, aside from constituting a small portion of the American population, are not clearly perceived in the national consciousness as a significant force in either the United States or in NATO. As one member of Congress said, "I don't have any Turkish restaurants in my district."[45]

Hispanic Americans now constitute 9 percent of all Americans, up from 6.4 percent in the 1980 census. Yet, there is little unity among them. Mexican-Americans constitute 60 percent of all Hispanics, but many are not American citizens and even those who are have ambivalent feelings toward Mexico. The next largest group of Hispanics are Puerto Ricans. Yet they too are divided over the status of Puerto Rico, some favoring statehood, others continuation of the commonwealth status, and some independence. Mexican-Americans and Puerto Ricans are generally less well off than many other Americans. They overwhelmingly identify with the Democratic party.[46] On the other hand, the third largest group of Hispanics, Cuban-Americans, are much better off financially and vote heavily for Republican candidates. They are strongly motivated by anticommunism and have contributed heavily to the Florida Republican party and to anti-Castro groups throughout the nation. Cuban-Americans account for up to 10 percent of the Republican vote in Florida and have elected a Cuban-American mayor of Miami. They have helped to fund Lt. Col. Oliver L. North's legal expenses during the Iran–Contra affair and a lobbying effort to force Cuban troops from the African nation of Angola.[47]

The Cuban-American National Foundation's leader, Jorge Mas Canosa, "may be the most significant individual lobbyist in the country."[48] The CANF is consciously modeled on AIPAC. It lobbied successfully in 1990 for TV Marti, a direct broadcast station aimed at Cuba from the United States that has been effectively jammed by the Cuban government. State Department officials privately state that CANF has been responsible for maintaining the American hard line against Fidel Castro's regime. The lobbying firm has 100 directors, each of whom contributes $10,000. It claims 50,000 donors. CANF contributed to fifty-six congressional campaigns in 1988 and to forty-eight in 1990, focusing largely on members of the House Foreign Affairs Committee.[49]

Black lobbying groups have been active in urging increased aid to African nations, but in recent years have shifted their attention to the struggle to defeat apartheid in South Africa. The Congressional Black Caucus and Trans-Africa, an ethnic lobbying organization with a budget of $325,000 in 1982 and a membership of 10,000, played key roles in arranging demonstrations outside the South African embassy and in pushing Congress to impose sanctions on the apartheid regime.[50]

Irish activity focuses not on Ireland, but on Northern Ireland. There are two Irish caucuses in the Congress and two lobbying groups. The Irish National Aid Committee is strongly pro-IRA. It was required in 1971 to register as a foreign agent. The Irish National Caucus, with a budget estimated at $500,000 raised from 100 local chapters, has contacts with the National Aid Committee, and is more moderate. The Northern Ireland issue is both too complex and too hot for most decision makers, thus limiting the impact of Irish lobbying. Representative Brian Donnelly, an Irish Democrat from Massachusetts, admitted, "Irish-American politicians have never been marked as a finely oiled, high-stepping cohesive unit."[51]

Given the impressive lobbying efforts of Japan and Taiwan and the size of the Asian population (7.3 million), one might expect considerable power from this group. Yet Asian-Americans have not been active in politics. New immigrants focus on economic issues and eschew politics. Older Japanese and other Asians who faced discrimination in earlier periods (especially during World War II) shy away from politics, in contrast to blacks who have used politics to gain civil rights. The Asian-American community, like the Hispanics, is very diverse and there are few common bonds between Koreans, Japanese, Chinese, Vietnamese, and Cambodians. Japanese-Americans have been in the United States longer than most and have become more active in politics than other Asian groups. They tend to be Democrats, while Vietnamese and Cambodians, who fled Communist regimes, favor Republicans.

The Japanese-American community was particularly active in obtaining reparations for the internment of their parents and grandparents during World War II. It has shied away from direct involvement in American-Japanese relations, which have often been strained because of the trade issue (see Chapter 9). Koreans, in contrast, have become more vocal recently. The speaker of the Korean parliament even sent a letter to House Speaker Thomas Foley asking Congress to consider compensation for Korean-Americans whose property was damaged in the 1992 Los Angeles riots.[52]

Some ethnic lobbies have lost influence. The stereotypical "ethnic lobby" of the 1950s and 1960s was the Eastern European immigrant organization (representing Ukrainians, Latvians, Lithuanians, and Estonians) seeking demonstrations of congressional support for freedom for their countrymen who resided in formerly independent states or regions that became part of the Soviet Union. These groups still exist, but they no longer occupy the privileged position on Capitol Hill that they did during the Cold War days. These lobbies reasserted themselves in 1988 when nationalist movements in the Soviet republics demanded autonomy as part of Mikhail Gorbachev's policy of *perestroika* (restructuring).

When Lithuania asserted its independence in 1990, the Lithuanian-American community of 120,000 sent almost 4,000 telegrams to Congress pressing for a cutoff of American aid to the Soviet Union and formal diplomatic recognition. Yet, it could not convince the Senate to adopt a resolution urging President Bush to extend recognition "immediately." Bush finally established diplomatic ties seventeen months later, but only after the Soviet Union agreed to let the Baltic republics go. The president argued that it was more important to help save Gorbachev's rule in the Soviet Union—an ultimately unsuccessful goal—than to expedite the liberation of the Baltic republics. While Baltic-Americans were highly critical of Bush, the president retained the support of the American people for his go-slow approach: Just 31 percent favored immediate recognition in March 1990, compared with 41 percent who favored bolstering Gorbachev. After Lithuania, Latvia, and Estonia gained independence in 1991, the longtime alliances in the Baltic-American community threatened to come apart as each ethnic group fought for a share of the decreasing American foreign-aid pie.[53]

The potential power of economic and ethnic interests raises important issues related to the democratic dilemma on foreign policy decision making. What price might our foreign policy pay for its openness? Does the opportunity for groups to participate mean that they might come to dominate foreign policy making? An argument for the thesis that economics may on occasion determine policy choices can be made through examples.[54] The attempt by the International Telephone and Telegraph Company to rig the 1970 election for president of Chile against the Marxist Salvador Allende to protect its financial interests there is a case in point. Although Nixon and Kissinger specifically rejected a plan that would have entailed the cooperation of the White House in what proved to be an unsuccessful attempt to prevent Allende from becoming president, in 1973 the CIA "destabilized" the Allende government. While there is no direct evidence that multinational corporations were also involved in the 1973 incident, Nixon did know about the CIA involvement. Thus, even if there was no firm conspiracy between business and the government, in this instance at least, American foreign and economic policies certainly coincided. Such occurrences are, apparently, relatively rare. But we must always be concerned about the potential for a private interest to determine public policy. On the other hand, grass-roots organizations such as the Emergency Coalition to Save the Panama Canal do attempt to mobilize support in the Congress to persuade members to espouse certain policy positions based on public opinion. In such efforts, as in the ethnic lobbies, foreign policy making resembles domestic policy formation.

Are Interest Groups Dangerous?

In *The Federalist* (no. 10) James Madison warned of the "mischiefs of faction."[55] The ambivalence early felt toward parties is analogous to current attitudes toward interest groups. On the one hand, everyone has interests, so certain interest groups are seen as legitimate. The ones we tend to think of most positively are those with whose goals we agree. Certainly those groups that do not stand to benefit directly by their actions, such as the environmental lobby and the various ideological groups on both the left and the right, are often accorded the right to represent their members without suspicion. On the other hand, when groups do benefit directly, the public may regard them with suspicion. Particularly on foreign policy, when the stakes are so high, we may wonder whether these groups or the president is running the country. We have argued that various lobbying groups active on foreign policy questions generally have not succeeded in changing the policies of a government. But in instances where they have, was their influence in the interest of the nation as a whole?

The argument against foreign policy lobbies has been framed by former Maryland Senator Charles Mathias in terms of ethnic lobbies. We must also consider the relationship between foreign policy lobbies and public opinion. A key theme in many critiques is that public opinion is a more appropriate determinant of foreign policy than lobbying pressure. But do they generally conflict with one another? Mathias argues:

> Factions among us lead the nation toward excessive foreign attachments or animosities. Even if the groups were balanced—if Turkish-Americans equaled Greek-Americans or Arab-Americans equaled Jewish-Americans—the result would not necessarily be a sound, cohesive foreign policy because the national interest is not simply the sum of our special interest and attachments . . . ethnic politics, carried as they often have been to excess, have proven harmful to the national interest. . . . Public debate becomes charged with accusations of "betrayal" and "sellout," which is to say, of moral turpitude, when in truth the issues that divide us are, with few exceptions, questions of judgment and opinion as to what is best for the nation. . . . There is a clear and pressing need for the reintroduction of civility into our public discussions of these matters.[56]

We cannot resolve the question of whether lobbies are beneficial or harmful in the formulation of foreign policy, but only determine to what extent the activities of these organizations conform to the broad outline of public opinion on a few issues. We examine here public attitudes toward the Middle East and El Salvador. Periodically, polling organizations survey the American public about its sympathies toward Israelis and Arabs. Should the poll reveal a generally pro-Arab sentiment among Americans, or indeed even a reasonable split, then the reputed power of the Israeli lobby would be pernicious indeed, notwithstanding its loss on the AWACS vote.

The American public has consistently been more pro-Israel than pro-Arab, as Table 7.1 reveals. The greatest Israeli advantage occurred, not surprisingly, following the Six-Day War in June 1967, when the ratio in favor of Israel was 14 to 1. It has now fallen to slightly more than 3 to 1 and, indeed, once fell to an almost even level (following the siege of Beirut during the 1982 Israeli invasion of Lebanon). Even with the increase in the overall level of support for the Arab nations, Israeli support within the United States remained very high indeed, especially considering the controversy surrounding many of Israel's actions and the level of the American commitment and involvement in events not of its making. In late 1987 young Palestinians on the Israeli-occupied West Bank and Gaza Strip began a prolonged "uprising." They attacked Israeli military and civilian personnel on the West Bank and threw stones at the police. Israel retaliated with tactics that many in the West, including the United States, believed were stronger than necessary. As a result, public support for Israel dropped sharply in 1988. Table 7.1 shows that in three polls there were pronounced drops in the level of popular backing for Israel. Two surveys show declines of 15 to 18 points, another a drop of 25 points.

TABLE 7.1   Public Sympathies in the Middle East Conflict

Date of Poll	More with Israel	More with Arab Nations	Neither/ Both	Don't Know
June 1967 (following Six-Day War)	56	4	25	15
December 1973 (following Yom Kippur War)	50	7	25	18
January 1975	44	8	22	26
March 1978	38	11	33	18
January 1979	40	14	31	15
July 1981	49	10	20	11
June 1982	52	10	29	9
September 1982 (following Lebanon invasion)	32	28	21	19
January 1983	49	12	22	17
Feburary–March 1983	52	16	13	19
July 1985 (following TWA hostage crisis)	49	11	18	22
October 1985 (following *Achille Lauro* incident)	64	14	13	9
June 1986	62	13	13	12
January 1988 (during Palestinian uprising)	37	11	37	16
May 1988 (during Palestinian uprising)	44	13	21	22
April 1989 (after Pan Am 103 bombing)	69	16	10	4
June 1990 (during Palestinian uprising)	40	19	18	23
March (early) 1991 (following Gulf War)	49	20	18	13
March 1991 (following Gulf War)	51	16	22	11
October 1991 (during loan guarantee debate)	48	19	11	5

All polls up to January 1983 were conducted by the Gallup organization and are reported in Alvin Richman, "American Attitudes Toward the Middle East Since Israel's Invasion of Lebanon," Table 4B (paper presented at the Annual Meeting of the American Association of Public Opinion Researchers, May 1983). The remaining polls through 1986, except for the October 1985 survey, were conducted by the *Washington Post* and ABC News; the October 1985 poll was conducted by the Harris organization. They are reported in Eytan Gilboa, "Terrorism and Trust; How We See the Middle East," *Public Opinion*, November/December 1986, pp. 52–55. The January and May 1988, surveys were prepared by Penn and Schoen Associates for the B'nai B'rith Anti-Defamation League and were reported in Penn and Schoen Associates, "Summary of National Survey for Anti-Defamation League," Penn and Schoen Associates, May 13, 1988. The April 1988 survey was prepared for the American Jewish Committee by the Roper Organization and was reported in David Singer and Renae Cohen, "In the Wake of the Palestinian Uprising: Findings of the April 1988 Roper Poll" (Washington, D.C.: American Jewish Committee, April 1988). Both 1988 polls included the option that respondents support both Israel and the Arabs. Respondents selecting this option (eight and six percent respectively in the Penn and Schoen polls and eleven percent in the Roper survey) are included in the "neither" category in the table.

The April 1989 survey was conducted by the *Washington Post* and ABC News and reported in a *Washington Post* memorandum provided by Richard Morin, director of surveys for the paper. The June 1990, early March 1991, and October 1991 surveys were conducted by CBS News and the *New York Times* and reported in CBS News press releases dated July 8, 1990, March 7, 1991, and October 10, 1991. The late March survey was conducted by NBC News and the *Wall Street Journal* and reported in an NBC News press release dated March 29, 1991. The NBC/*Wall Street Journal* surveys included "both" and "neither" responses. The CBS/*New York Times* surveys included "both," "neither," and "it depends."

Yet the American public still supports Israel over the Arabs by a substantial margin, even as it disapproves of specific Israeli policies in handling the uprising. Popular backing for Israel is found for virtually every group among the American citizenry (data not shown). Americans were no more sympathetic to the Arab cause in 1988 than they were during the more peaceful times of the late 1970s. There has been some increase in support for the Arab position (up to 20 percent in one 1991 survey), but Israel's favor has rebounded to a level not seen since the Yom Kippur War in 1973.

Public opinion reacts rationally toward Israel and the Arabs. American support for Israel has been highest following the 1967 and 1973 wars against her Arab neighbors, after the *Achille Lauro* incident in which Arab terrorists destroyed a cruise ship with American and Israeli tourists on board, in the aftermath of the terrorist attack on Pam Am 103 in December 1988, and following the Gulf War. By a 3 to 1 margin (31 percent to 9 percent, with 57 percent unchanged), Americans became more sympathetic to Israel, and by 2 to 1 (20 percent to 9 percent, with 65 percent unchanged) less favorable to the Palestinians, whose leaders supported Saddam Hussein. There were sharp declines in public backing for Israel after the Lebanon invasion and the massacre of Palestinian refugees in Israeli-controlled territory, when American Jonathan Pollard admitted spying for Israel, and during the *intifada*.[57] The spurt in public support following the Gulf War has lasted longer than most. Even the flap with President Bush over loan guarantees for new immigrants in October 1991 had little effect on public sympathies.

Israel's supporters do have a very effective lobby and one that many in Congress fear can threaten electoral sanctions, although the data do not support this assertion. But even Mathias admits that the tactics of AIPAC consist largely of providing information as well as informational letters and visits from lobbyists and influential constituents. These are the tactics of any lobbying organization. The threats of electoral sanctions, however, would appear to be far more disturbing if the lobbying organization were out of step with public opinion. Exactly the contrary seems to be the case with AIPAC. As in the AWACS sale, AIPAC "lost" the battle to block the beginning of an American dialogue with the PLO in 1988 after Yasir Arafat recognized Israel's right to exist and renounced terrorism. Even though public opinion polls showed a plurality in opposition to this move, many American Jewish leaders differed with AIPAC and supported the Reagan administration's initiative.

The power of the Israeli lobby does not depend on threatening tactics. Instead, it relies on public support for Israel, especially when contrasted with that for the Arabs.[58] Americans have never expressed more sympathy with the Arabs than with Israel. This has translated into strong congressional backing for Israel, even as some presidents have been neutral to hostile to the Jewish state.[59] Traditionally, pro-Israel groups have formed alliances with unions, churches, and civil rights groups. The weakness of pro-Arab groups made the task even easier.

Much of this has changed, which has complicated U.S.–Israel relations. Unions concern themselves with other battles. Many churches have shifted to a more pro-Palestinian position. The Episcopal Church and the Evangelical Lutheran Church in America opposed the loan guarantees unless settlements were halted.[60] Some of the religious opposition to the Gulf War reflected the view that American Middle East policy was biased against the Arabs and toward Israel (see above).

In 1979 several major black civil rights leaders, including the Reverend Jesse Jackson, visited the Middle East and made statements in support of the PLO. The civil rights leaders were upset when United Nations Ambassador Andrew Young, the first black to hold a major foreign policy position in the American government, was forced to resign following an unauthorized meeting with a PLO representative at the United Nations. Jackson and others met with key Arab leaders, including Yasir Arafat of the PLO, but did not meet with Israeli Prime Minister Menachem Begin. On returning home, the black leaders made strong statements in support of Palestinian rights and on the need for a cease-fire in the areas under military threat.

Black-Jewish tensions were exacerbated by some poll data showing a weakening in the traditional black support for Israel and by revelations that Arab groups had made donations to black civil rights organizations. The traditional black-Jewish alliance was in danger, and there were serious questions of what the impact on foreign policy in both the Middle East and Africa might be. Other black leaders reasserted traditional support for Israel and rejected the argument that blacks must be concerned with Palestinian rights because in any conflict involving American armed intervention in the Middle East, an interruption of oil supplies would most adversely affect the most disadvantaged economic groups, notably blacks.

Several factors worked to defuse the conflict, at least temporarily. One was the strong defense of Israel and the need for a continuation of the black-Jewish alliance established by Urban League President Vernon Jordan. A second was the revelation of financial inducements made by Arab groups and allegedly demanded by some black leaders in return for political support. Finally, the takeover of the American embassy in Iran by Islamic militants united black and white Americans in support of the president's policies, at least temporarily. These issues between blacks and Jews have not been resolved. A major conflict between these two important constituent groups, both strongly associated with the Democratic party, might affect policy through the ballot box: Should the party lose the support of either group, it could not hope to gain a majority in presidential elections for years to come. The loss of both groups would virtually guarantee it perpetual minority status.

In 1984 such a split did threaten the Democrats, as the simmering conflict for the first time spilled over into the electoral arena. Jackson, who ran for the Democratic nomination for the presidency, not only vociferously supported the creation of a Palestinian state and welcomed the backing of Arab-Americans, but also admitted calling Jews *Hymies* and New York City *Hymietown* in private conversations with black reporters. Furthermore, Jackson refused to denounce one of his most vocal supporters, Minister Louis Farrakhan of the Nation of Islam, who had reportedly threatened the life of the *Washington Post* reporter who broke the "Hymie" story and who had called Hitler a "great man." Many key Jewish leaders denounced Jackson as a racist, while black leaders rallied to his support. Jews threatened to boycott the Democratic party if Jackson's views on the Middle East were reflected in the party's platform, while many in the Jackson camp said that they would do likewise if their perspective were *not* included. While most blacks were not as hostile to the Jewish perspective on the Middle East, the importance of Jackson's role in mobilizing black voters was not to be taken lightly by Democratic party leaders, who had to confront a great dilemma about how to handle two of the party's most loyal voting blocs. The same conflict reasserted itself in 1988 when Jackson unsuccessfully proposed a Democratic party platform plank calling for an independent Palestinian state.

In 1992, just before the Democratic convention, Jackson addressed the World Jewish Congress and made amends by calling Zionism a "liberation movement." He linked racism and anti-Semitism and demanded that blacks' anti-Semitism come to a halt. Yet, he did not condemn Farrakhan, much to the dismay of Jewish leaders. The black-Jewish rift may have cooled, but the old union of the civil rights days has passed. Blacks are among the least supportive groups toward Israel in public opinion surveys; black members of Congress have become increasingly less likely to support foreign assistance for Israel. Jackson's speech served to highlight differences between the two groups rather than their past unions.

The Arab cause has also received more publicity. Former Senator James Abourezk (D-S.D.) heads the Arab American Institute, while James Zogby, co-chair of Jackson's 1988 campaign, directs the Arab-American Anti-Discrimination Committee. Zogby's organization, modeled after the B'nai B'rith Anti-Defamation League, has 25,000 members. It fights negative stereotypes of Arab-Americans. Zogby himself is quite visible in promoting the Arab position and attacking Israeli policies, even as these organizations (as well as the NAAA) now acknowledge Israel's right to exist. In 1992 the chairs of both the Democratic and Republican national committees addressed an Arab-American gathering. Arab-Americans raised $750,000 for Jackson in 1988 and have formed grass-roots organizations in several large states. Moreover, as we noted, there are strains within the pro-Israel lobby and the Jewish community more generally. While Arab influence is growing, its power still pales compared with that of the pro-Israel forces. Zogby admits, "We don't make policy," while Abourezk states, "We are not powerful."[61]

The pro-Arab lobbies do not have the organizational clout that AIPAC and other pro-Israeli forces do. The Arab American Institute and the Anti-Discrimination Committee do not lobby. NAAA does, but its resources are meager. Arab countries hire public relations firms from time to time, but have no long-term lobbying effort. The Arab cause is often carried by American economic interests that are themselves unpopular. The American Petroleum Institute (API), which represents 350 corporations, has been lobbying for a shift in American Middle Eastern policy for over a decade. The API is primarily concerned with oil politics, of course, but it has acted in the not unreasonable belief that American relations with the oil-producing nations are related to the willingness of the country to consider alternative political solutions in the Middle East. The oil companies have not been able to dictate foreign policy to the president or the Congress.

The pro-Israel lobby has been more successful because it has largely had public opinion on its side. When it has run into trouble, American attitudes have not been favorable to Israel (especially at the time of the AWACS sale). In 1986 AIPAC could set the terms for the administration's Middle East policy; its popularity was at almost its record high since 1967. Yet, there is much in its strength that is constant. Some is organizational, but there is more as well. Jews have the highest rate of voting of any ethnic group, and almost 90 percent live in twelve states with a sufficient number of electoral votes to choose a president. They also have a long tradition of working together as a community; while only 100,000 (or 5 percent) of the two million Arab-Americans belong to any ethnic organization, two million of the 5.9 million American Jews (or one-third) belong to a Jewish group.[62] Theirs is a community that is strongly energized toward pro-Israel causes and has been able to spread the word to other Americans. Even though fewer than 4 percent of Americans are either Jews or Arab-Americans, 18 percent said in 1988 that the Middle East conflict was of high personal importance to them and 5 percent said it was *the* most important issue in the campaign.[63]

The continued success of the pro-Israel lobby depends on the breadth, not just the depth, of public support. Here the pro-Israel forces have two worries. First, public opinion on the Middle East has become more volatile in recent years. AIPAC could depend on a strong base in Congress for years; this solidarity weakened as public support has wavered. Second, at least some observers worry that the broad basis of *activist* support for Israel may be waning and that the pro-Israel lobby may be left to the American Jewish community.[64] Bolstering the pro-Israel lobby is the reservoir of good will among Americans, despite the more recent public opinion roller coaster, and the emergence of a more flexible government in Jerusalem. In 1989 more Americans thought that Israel had too much influence than too little (31 to 11 percent) on American policy, yet the majority (54 percent) said that it had "the right amount." Yet, there are limits. When President Bush publicly attacked the pro-Israel lobby in the fall of 1991, he found a responsive public. Even though overall support for Israel remained high, a plurality (40 percent) now thought that Israel had too much power.[65]

American support for Israel, as opposed to the Arabs, remains bipartisan. Although Democrats are more sympathetic to the Arabs than are Republicans or Independents, they are also more friendly to Israel. Democrats back Israel by 2 to 1, Republicans by almost 3 to 1.[66] The Labor government of Prime Minister Vitzhak Rabin will provoke fewer confrontations with the United States than its Likud predecessors (Menachem Begin and Yitzhak Shamir). Rabin campaigned on restoring better ties with Washington. He not only served a previous term as prime minister, but was also Israel's ambassador to the United States. It will be easier for him to reassert the common bonds between Israel and the United States than it was for any recent Israeli leader—and this will only complicate the problems for Arab-Americans and the Arab nations.

The Power of Interest Groups?

The American Petroleum Institute's poor record of influencing policies suggests that any view of foreign policy based on economic determinism is a vast oversimplification. Economic interest groups have been active on foreign policy issues, but, as we noted, they obtain what they want only if these demands do not conflict with preestablished policies of the government. An economic interest group may benefit from a foreign policy decision, but this does not imply anything about the role that the group actually played in the formulation of the decision. A good example of this is the economic boom that some farmers and grain speculators enjoyed because of the decision of the United States to make major wheat sales to the Soviet Union in 1973, without their having initiated or lobbied for the deal.

Opponents of American policy in El Salvador argued that the ideological and church-related interest groups opposing administration policy might have a salutary effect on the congressional attempts to limit American involvement there. In turn, the restricted U.S. role induced the right-wing government to reach an accord with the left-wing opposition. Opposition on the part of interest groups to the war in Vietnam played a major role in turning public opinion against the conflict, a key ingredient in the final American defeat in Southeast Asia. A decade and a half later, various polls indicated that Americans feared that the United States would become entangled in Latin America much as it did in Vietnam. A Gallup poll in June 1983 found that 71 percent of Americans were concerned that the United States would become more deeply involved in El Salvador, compared with only 24 percent who thought otherwise. Three years later, even though no American troops had been committed to Latin America, 62 percent of Americans believed that Nicaragua would become the next Vietnam. The minority who knew which side the United States was backing was 17 percent more strongly opposed to aid to the Contras than were the citizens with less knowledge of the situation.[67]

Interest groups have led public opinion away from the president's program. But the widespread public opposition to a troop commitment in Central America has also been reflected in congressional skepticism about the appropriate role for the United States. Groups opposed to U.S. involvement in Latin America have not only challenged the administration, but also strengthened the hands of the congressional majority opposed to the president's policy. It is precisely because the churches do not stand to benefit directly from any specific policy in Latin America that there have been relatively few charges that their role is illegitimate.

Yet, the impact of interest groups is limited. In the Gulf War, a range of interests led by churches opposed the initiation of hostilities. Th ey could not prevent military actions. Once the conflict began, public opinion sh.fted toward strong support for Operation Desert Storm. The moral appeals of religious leaders fell upon deaf ears. Religious opposition to U.S. involvement in Central America, found a more supportive public from the beginning. As with economic interest groups, the impact of interest groups on foreign policy seems greatest when they press for positions that public officials are ready to adopt anyway.

When Is Lobbying Worrisome?

Lobbying on foreign policy becomes worrisome for the same reasons that lobbying on domestic policy does: There is concern that policy formation is subjected to undue pressure or when there is a potential loss of accountability in policy formation. Let us consider one instance of each.

Ethnic lobbying on foreign policy generally succeeds when the group pursues policies that are in accord with public opinion and with existing governmental decisions. The efforts of the pro-Israel lobby certainly meet both criteria. In recent years, pro-Israel groups have relied increasingly on electoral competition: they have tried to single out for defeat candidates who challenge the lobby or who make pro-Arab statements.[68] In 1980 and 1982 they focused on Representative Paul Findley (R-Ill.), who had called for recognition of the Palestine Liberation Organization (PLO). Findley was defeated in the latter contest and argued that he was the target of the lobby. His view was not entirely unjustified: over 90 percent of his opponent's campaign expenditures reportedly came from Jewish sources. Two years later a Jewish donor from California contributed $1 million of his own money in independent expenditures that helped defeat Senate Foreign Relations Chair Charles Percy (R-Ill.), also a critic of Israel. Yet, the largest recipient of pro-Israel money was North Carolina Governor James Hunt, who barely failed to unseat Senator Jesse Helms. After the election, Helms, previously a strong critic of Israel, became one of its most determined supporters in the Senate.

In 1984, fifty-four pro-Israel political action committees contributed more than $4.25 million to House and Senate candidates—considerably more than was spent by the largest domestic political action committee, that of the real estate industry. Almost 80 percent of the contributions went to Democrats; more than a third of all money given to Republicans went to Senator Rudy Boschwitz (R-Minn.), who is Jewish and who chaired the Senate Foreign Relations Committee's Subcommittee on the Middle East. In the 1986 contests, eighty pro-Israel political action committees spent $6.9 million, of which $3.9 million was contributed to candidates. In 1990, House and Senate candidates received $8.7 million, of which 70 percent went to Democrats. National PAC, the largest of the pro-Israel groups, has given relatively more to Republicans than others have given, though it still favors Democrats. Pro-Israel PACs also favor incumbents. In contrast, Arab-Americans have not been at all active in contributing to political candidates. One of their two political action committees neither raised nor spent any money in 1982; the other, which supports moderate candidates, gave only $5,500 to six campaigns in 1982. In 1986, the National Association of Arab Americans contributed just about $70,000 to congressional aspirants.[69]

Making foreign policy hostage to campaign contributions is at least as dangerous as buying votes on domestic legislation. For, if domestic groups can purchase influence, so can foreign companies. When confronted with demands by foreign companies to withdraw taxes on their worldwide earnings, Florida complied and California did not. Japanese companies responded, as noted above, with large donations to legislative campaigns in the latter state.[70] In time this might provoke not only legal action, but, more important, hostile public attitudes toward the companies that pursue such strategies. Similarly, the tactics of the pro-Israel lobby may result in a backlash against what has been relatively consensual support for Israel. Indeed, even as the post-Vietnam consensus on foreign policy has broken down, the one issue that draws support across the ideological spectrum of elites is the moral obligation to prevent the destruction of Israel.[71]

Policy making through threats of electoral retribution can only serve to disrupt such a consensus. Pro-Israeli groups seemed to recognize this in 1985 and 1986 when they contributed heavily to Republicans, especially to those New Right senators who have backed Israel. Making contributions bipartisan does not depoliticize the issue. Focusing on an electoral strategy may make it appear that American Jews have no other concerns than the support of Israel—and can raise the issue that American Jews fear most: that of dual loyalty, that is, loyalty not only to the United States but also to Israel. Furthermore, electoral support through campaign contributions, with the sanctions that are implicit in that strategy, will ultimately raise questions of private interests competing with national interests. When then-Representative (now Senator) John Breaux (D-La.) was asked if his vote could be bought, he responded, "No, but it can be rented."[72] Perhaps more than anything else, such a charge would destroy a policy consensus.

The other concern about interest group activity on foreign policy is accountability. To be sure, electoral activity such as pro-Israeli groups have pursued *does* enhance accountability, even if it results in divisions within a policy community. This strategy works to limit presidential—congressional—flexibility in foreign policy formation. Yet the privatization of foreign policy, as in the Iran-Contra affair, makes us worry about whether foreign policy can be conducted democratically. In a very different way, so does the Third World debt crisis. Because of public opposition to foreign aid, the funding of Third World loans has been left to banks, which are clearly private institutions. What happens if some countries default on their loans, as now appears increasingly likely? Will the government bail out the banks? Many argue that it should *not* do so. If government maintains a hands-off policy, it is effectively delegating foreign policy formation to the banks. Even if the banks were not to act against any conception of the public interest, even if they were to make what we might consider the "correct decisions," ought private institutions to be placed in the position of making foreign policy? Does the government, then, have the right to delegate foreign policy formation?

Similarly, foreign lobbying raises the question of accountability as well. While it is always difficult to hold interest groups "responsible" for governmental decisions, the problem is compounded for international lobbyists. Former Senator Lloyd Bentsen (D-Tex.) has proposed legislation that would outlaw any campaign contributions by foreign nationals. Independent presidential candidate H. Ross Perot sought to ban foreign lobbying in his 1992 campaign. There are already laws that prohibit many former high-level government officials from working as foreign lobbyists. President Clinton required that all administration appointees refrain from lobbying for foreign countries for five years after their service ends. Yet some opponents of this legislation argue that such statutes might lead highly qualified individuals to forgo government service altogether. There is also the problem of balancing the interests of American firms and international corporations. Should foreign companies be put at a disadvantage in influencing governmental policy when, other than in their ownership, they are quite similar to domestic firms? Also, should other governments restrict the activities of American companies' political activities? Ought American firms refrain from such "mild" politicking as trying to change South Africa's apartheid laws through extensive minority recruitment?

The Public and Foreign Policy

The actors in the fourth circle of decision making are strongest on foreign policy when they respond to the same pressures as found in domestic and even intermestic policies. A bipartisan foreign policy aids the executive branch in its battle with the Congress since the president can build a new coalition of his own on each foreign policy roll call. The leaders of both parties can generally be counted on to seek out support for the president's positions. As the traditional bipartisanship is threatened, so is the president's strategic advantage. Particularly when such consensus may be replaced by conflicts between traditional allies—the members of the Democratic coalition—and when American foreign policy may become more dependent on international economic conditions (as have the policies of Western Europe and Japan on Middle Eastern issues), the executive branch faces severe challenges ahead. The Congress is not in a position to fill any such leadership vacuum, because it has not resolved, and hardly seems willing to try to resolve, the difficult question of which interests are ultimately to be represented.

The democratic dilemmas of foreign policy making apply more to the fourth circle than to any other. This is no accident, because the dilemmas focus on whether a coherent foreign policy can result from democratic policy. Public opinion, elections, the media, and interest groups are the heart of popular control of democratic institutions. We have seen that public opinion does affect foreign policy and that the post-Vietnam electorate can exercise some control over decision making on foreign affairs. Politics is increasingly a story of public opinion polls. Presidents are thus more constrained by public opinion than they ever have been. The people may not provide detailed instructions to decision makers on what they ought to do. At the least, they indicate what actions they do not like. This overall balance gives political leaders some flexibility to respond to the actions of other nations. Yet the electorate's tether is often very short. With political parties increasingly taking divergent positions on key issues, leaders in both the legislative and executive branches are more and more tied down to positions espoused by their parties. Parties and public opinion can mightily constrain executive leadership.

The role of the media has changed considerably. Gone are the days when press barons can play a major, if not dominant, role, as William Randolph Hearst did, in pushing the nation into intervening in the Mexican revolution of 1913–14.[73] Nowadays the media are more likely to terminate a war than to start one. Yet media impacts can be—and often have been—overemphasized. There is little evidence that the media have actually changed the balance of power in any policy area, foreign or domestic. Some say that the media want to have it both ways: On the one hand, television is said to be too superficial; on the other hand, it is charged with having too much power over public opinion. More likely, the media have some effects—it would be truly remarkable if they had none—but hardly such to constitute a threat either to a democratic order or to presidential government. Similarly, the activities of local political leaders may make it difficult for presidents to claim that American speaks with one voice, but then so does Congress.

More than anything else, the rise of interest groups in foreign policy marks a sharp break with the past. Are interest groups dangerous? To the extent that they promote fragmentation of decision making, they challenge presidential authority. But again, so does the wide swath of congressional decision making on foreign policy. Like the Congress, interest groups cannot formulate their own foreign policy for the nation—unless, as in the case of the Third World debt crisis, the government abdicates responsibility to them. To the extent that foreign policy more and more resembles domestic policy, however, there is a threat to coherent decision making and to the flexibility that chief executives require. The stakes are far higher in foreign policy than in domestic issues. International issues affect elections only when passions are high and there is widespread dissatisfaction with administration policy. Groups that actively seek to make foreign policy issues the main focal points of political campaigns must contemplate the likely consequences of their acts.

The fourth circle has become increasingly important in recent years. Presidents are more constrained than they have ever been on foreign policy because public opinion plays a larger role in all of politics. There are more interest groups than ever, and the media are increasingly paying attention to foreign policy. The decline of bipartisanship on foreign policy makes each of these actors more important. Presidents must now respond to a wide range of forces—and so must leaders of most other nations. Foreign policy throughout the world is increasingly a reflection of domestic politics. To the extent that democratic politics conflicts with the needs of a strong foreign policy—responding quickly with a single voice— international relations become more complex and hazardous.

Notes

1. William K. Stevens, "Governors Assert Key to Prosperity Is in Global View," *New York Times*, July 26, 1987, pp. A1, A22; Kathleen Sylvester, "Exporting Made Easy (Or How States and Cities Are Selling Products Overseas)," *Governing*, January 1988, p. 38; Larry Agran, "Local Officials Should Speak Out on Foreign Policy," *Governing*, December 1987, p. 74; Earl H. Fry, "U.S. States and International Economic Relations." Paper presented at the Conference on Comparative Federalism, Dartmouth College, June 1989, pp. 2, 5, 11, 15; and Penelope Lemov, "Europe and the States: Free Trade, But No Free Lunch," *Governing*, January 1991, pp. 49–52.

2. Agran, "Local Officials," p. 74; and Denis Farney, "In Seattle, Rep. Miller Is Drawing Fire for Support of Contra Aid," *Wall Street Journal*, October 13, 1986, p. 34.

3. David Brock, "Municipal Hue and Cry Makes Foreign Policy Waves," *Insight*, April 4, 1986, pp. 18–20; Katherine Bishop, "Oakland Battles U.S. to Be Nuclear-Free," *New York Times*, December 22, 1989, p. B6; and William Schneider, "Conservatism, Not Interventionism: Trends in Foreign Policy Opinion. 1974–1982," in Kenneth A. Oye, Robert J. Lieber, and Donald Roth, eds., *Eagle Defiant: United States Foreign Policy in the 1980s* (Boston: Little, Brown, 1983), p. 58.

4. Reuters, "11 States Seek to Bar Foreign Training of Guard," *New York Times*, June 17, 1986, p. A10. The ten states joining Minnesota are Arkansas, Colorado, Delaware, Hawaii, Iowa, Maine, Massachusetts, Ohio, Rhode Island, and Vermont. The eight states supporting sending the guard abroad are Florida, Illinois, Louisana, Nevada, New Mexico, Oklahoma, South Carolina, and Wisconsin. Iowa, Maine, and Rhode Island have Republican governors, while Louisiana has a Democratic chief executive (see the text below).

5. *Washington Post*, "Arizona Troops Deploy," May 31, 1987, p. A8.

6. Michael deCourcy Hinds, "Drawing on Vietnam Legacy, Antiwar Effort Buds Quickly," *New York Times,* January 11, 1991, p. A1.

7. Mark P. Petracca, "The Rediscovery of Interest Group Politics," in *The Politics of Interests* (Boulder, Colo.: Westview, 1992), p. 14; and Deborah M. Levy, "Advice for Sale," *Foreign Policy,* Summer 1987, p. 67.

8. Raymond A. Bauer, Ithiel de Sola Pool, and Lewis Anthony Dexter, *American Business and Public Policy,* 2d ed. (Chicago: Aldine-Atherton, 1982), pp. 300–301.

9. E. E. Schattschneider, *The Semisovereign People* (New York: Holt, Reinhart, and Winston), esp. ch. 2.

10. Bruce Ray, "Congressional Losers in the U.S. Federal Spending Process," *Legislative Studies Quarterly* 5 (August 1980), pp. 359–372.

11. Jack Zwick and Richard K. Goeltz, "U.S. Banks Are Making Foreign Policy," *New York Times,* March 18, 1979, p. F14.

12. Leonard Silk, "Citicorp's Step: Mixed Effects," *New York Times,* May 22, 1987, p. D2; and Anne Swardson, "Losses Mount as Banks Cope with Bad Third-World Loans," *Washington Post,* July 14, 1987, pp. A1, A12.

13. Carol Matlack, "Sizing the Shackles," *National Journal,* August 11, 1990, p. 1937.

14. John Burgess, "FEC and Role of Foreign Money in U.S. Politics," *Washington Post,* July 7, 1990, p. A7.

15. John B. Judis, "The Japanese Megaphone," *The New Republic,* January 22, 1990, pp. 20–25; and Matlack, "Sizing the Shackles," p. 1938.

16. "As Investments by Foreigners Surge, Their Influence in U.S. Politics Grows," *New York Times,* December 30, 1985; Martin Tolchin, "U.S. Elections Got More Foreign Cash," *New York Times,* May 24, 1987; Bill Whalen, "Japan Builds a Lobbying Leviathan," *Insight,* September 21, 1987, pp. 22–23; Susan F. Rasky, "Top U.S. Corporations Lobbying Against Curb on Toshiba Imports," *New York Times,* September 14, 1987, pp. A1, D12; Levy, "Advice for Sale," pp. 68–71; and Gary Lee, "Japan Article: A Question of Partiality," *Washington Post,* May 13, 1992, p. A21.

17. Gary Lee, "S. Africa's Low-Profile Lobbyists," *Washington Post,* July 15, 1991, p. A9; and Gary Lee, "With Vote Approaching, China Hires Hill and Knowlton to Lobby for MFN," *Washington Post,* July 10, 1991, p. A19.

18. James McGregor, "Taiwan Cultivates America's Support with Lobbying Force the Size of Israel's," *Wall Street Journal,* November 7, 1989, p. A26.

19. *New York Times,* November 23, 1981.

20. Robin Toner, "Those Who Beg to Differ on Aid to Nicaragua," *New York Times,* March 14, 1986, p. A14; Bill Keller, "Interest Groups Focus on El Salvador Policy," *Congressional Quarterly Weekly Report,* April 24, 1982, pp. 895–897; and Lena Williams, "Bahais Open a Lobbying Operation," *New York Times,* October 22, 1987, p. A32.

21. Hinds, "Drawing on Vietnam Legacy, Antiwar Effort Buds Quickly"; Ari L. Goldman, "Council of Churches Condemns U.S. Policy in Gulf," *New York Times,* November 16, 1990, p. A13; Religious News Service, "Religious Leaders Turn Up Heat on Bush over Gulf Crisis," *Washington Post,* September 29, 1990, p. B6; Holly Idelson, "Lobbyists Off to Slow Start," *Congressional Quarterly Weekly Report,* January 5, 1991, p. 17; and Laura Sessions Stepp and E. J. Dionne, Jr., "Churches' Anti-War Effort Marks Departure," *Washington Post,* January 26, 1991, pp. A13, A18.

22. Keith Schneider, "A Liberal Group Makes Waves with Its Contra Lawsuit," *New York Times,* July 20, 1987, p. A16.

23. The Israeli government itself did not object to the arms sale proposal to Jordan.
24. John E. Rielly, *American Public Opinion and U.S. Foreign Policy 1983* (Chicago: Chicago Council on Foreign Relations, 1983), pp. 16, 19; and Connie deBoer, "The Polls: Attitudes Toward the Arab-Israeli Conflict," *Public Opinion Quarterly* 47 (Spring 1983), pp. 128–129.
25. Ben Bradlee, Jr., "Israel's Lobby," *Boston Globe Magazine,* April 24, 1984, p. 64; Lloyd Grove, "On the March for Israel," *Washington Post,* June 13, 1991, p. D10; and Robert I. Friedman, "The Wobbly Israel Lobby," *Washington Post,* November 1, 1992, pp. C1, C4.
26. Bill Keller, "Supporters of Israel, Arabs Vie for Friends in Congress, at White House," *Congressional Quarterly Weekly Report,* August 25, 1981, p. 1524.
27. Ibid., p. 1527.
28. Charles McC. Mathias, Jr., "Ethnic Groups and Foreign Policy," *Foreign Affairs* 59 (Summer 1981), p. 993. Mathias's home state has a large Jewish population; not surprisingly, he did not seek reelection after publishing the article.
29. David K. Shipler, "On Middle East Policy, a Major Influence," *New York Times,* July 6, 1987, pp. A1, A4; Robert Pear with Richard L. Berke, "Pro-Israel Group Exerts Quiet Might As It Rallies Supporters in Congress," *New York Times,* July 7, 1987, p. A8; and Grove, "On the March for Israel," p. D1.
30. Keller, "Supporters of Israel," pp. 1527–1528; David A. Dickson, "Pressure Politics and the Congressional Foreign Policy Process." Paper presented at the 1990 Annual Meeting of the American Political Science Association, San Francisco, August–September.
31. Keller, "Supporters of Israel," p. 1528.
32. Ibid.
33. Richard Whittle, "Senate Supports Reagan on AWACS Sale," *Congressional Quarterly Weekly Report,* October 31, 1981, p. 2098.
34. Ibid., p. 2099.
35. Hedrick Smith, *The Power Game: How Washington Works* (New York: Random House, 1988), pp. 222–228.
36. John M. Goshko, "Persian Gulf Crisis Drives U.S.-Israeli Relations to Historic Ebb," *Washington Post,* October 27, 1990, p. A20.
37. Thomas L. Friedman, "Bush Aid to Israel Subject to Conditions," *New York Times,* October 6, 1991, p. E3; Friedman, "Israeli Loan Deal Is Linked by Baker to a Building Halt," *New York Times,* February 25, 1992; and Friedman, "Uneasy Debate for Jews in U.S. on Loan Guarantee," *New York Times,* March 2, 1992, pp. A1, A6.
38. Editorial, "Portrait of the Electorate," *New York Times,* November 5, 1992, p. B9.
39. Friedman, "The Wobbly Israel Lobby," p. C4.
40. Much of the discussion below follows Eric M. Uslaner, "A Tower of Babel on Foreign Policy?" in Alan J. Cigler and Burdett Loomis, eds., *Interest Group Politics,* 3d ed. (Washington: CQ Press, 1990), pp. 299–313.
41. John Felton, "Military Aid Requests Presented to Congress," *Congressional Quarterly Weekly Report,* February 12, 1983, p. 345.
42. Thomas M. Franck and Edward Weisband, *Foreign Policy by Congress* (New York: Oxford University Press, 1979), pp. 195–196.
43. Ibid., pp. 191–193.
44. Alan Cowell, "Turkish Leader Puts Off U.S. Visit over Anger at Congress," *New York Times,* May 9, 1987, p. 3; and Richard Berke, "Heeding Plato, Greek-Americans

Aid in Effort to Raise Money for Dukakis," *New York Times,* December 27, 1987, p. A30.

45. Barbara Gamarekian, "Turkey Focuses on Its Image," *New York Times,* January 20, 1987, p. A18; Franck and Weisband, *Foreign Policy by Congress,* pp. 191–193; and Neil A. Lewis, "Greece and Turkey: The Local War," *New York Times,* March 26, 1987, p. B8.

46. Barbara Vobejda, "Asians, Hispanics Giving Nation More Diversity," *Washington Post,* June 12, 1992, p. A3; and Bernard Weinraub, "Wooing Cuban-Americans in G.O.P.," *New York Times,* May 22, 1987, p. A14.

47. Robert S. Greenberger, "Right-Wing Groups Join in Capitol Hill Crusade to Help Savimbi's Anti-Communists in Angola," *Wall Street Journal,* November 25, 1985, p. 58.

48. John Newhouse, "Socialism or Death," *The New Yorker,* April 27, 1992, p. 77.

49. Ibid., pp. 76–81; and Lee Hockstadter and William Booth, "Cuban Exiles Split on Life After Castro," *Washington Post,* March 10, 1992, pp. A1, A14.

50. Michael Beaubien, "Making Waves in Foreign Policy," *Black Enterprise,* April 1982, pp. 37–42.

51. William Glaberson, "Threads of Irish Politics Woven into Mayoral Race," *New York Times,* November 3, 1989, p. B5; Robert J. Thompson and Joseph R. Rudolph, "Irish Americans in the American Foreign-Policy-Making Process," in Mohammed E. Ahrari, ed., *Ethnic Groups and U.S. Foreign Policy* (Westport, Conn.: Greenwood Press, 1987), pp. 135–154; and Tom Kenworthy, "Unity Eludes Hill's Irish-Americans on Thorny Ulster Issue," *Washington Post,* April 10, 1990, p. A4.

52. Rob Gurwitt, "Have Asian-Americans Arrived Politically? Not Quite," *Governing,* November 1990, pp. 32–38; and *Washington Post,* "Korea Urges Recompense as World Protest Mounts," May 3, 1992, p. A27.

53. *New York Times,* "Lithuanian-Americans Urge Bush to Take a Firmer Stand," January 14, 1991, p. A8; John Felton, "Lithuanian Events Highlight U.S. Stake in Gorbachev," *Congressional Quarterly Weekly Report,* April 7, 1990, pp. 1084–1085; CBS News press release, April 5, 1990; and Isabel Wilkerson, "A Battle Is Over for Baltic-Americans," *New York Times,* September 3, 1991, p. A9.

54. Detailed analyses of American imperialism may be found in, among other books, Carl Ogelsby and Richard Shaull, *Containment and Change* (New York: Macmillan, 1967), and in any of the several volumes by Gabriel Kolko on U.S. foreign policy during World War II and since; a briefer statement of Kolko's view is presented in *The Roots of American Foreign Policy* (Boston: Beacon Press, 1969).

55. Alexander Hamilton, John Jay, and James Madison, *The Federalist Papers,* with an introduction by Clinton Rossiter (New York: Mentor, 1961), pp. 77–84.

56. Mathias, "Ethnic Groups and Foreign Policy," pp. 981, 997.

57. Yankelovich, Clancy, Shulman press release for *Time* and CNN, February 12, 1991; see also Benjamin I. Page and Robert Y. Shapiro, *The Rational Public* (Chicago: University of Chicago Press, 1992), chap. 6.

58. The April 1989 *Washington Post*/ABC News survey of American attitudes toward the Middle East (see Table 7.1 above) found that 32 percent of Americans believed that Arab leaders want peace, compared with 50 percent for Israeli leaders. While 69 percent said that their sympathies were more with Israel and just 16 percent with the Arabs, only a small majority (51 to 46 percent) held that Israel was a reliable ally.

59. Steven Spiegel, *The Other Arab-Israeli Conflict* (Chicago: University of Chicago Press, 1985).

60. Associated Press, "Lutherans Decry Israeli Settlements," *Washington Post,* September 4, 1991, p. A7.

61. Nora Boustany, "Arab-American Lobby Is Struggling," *Washington Post,* April 6, 1990, p. A10; and Maralee Schwartz, "Parties Are Paying Greater Attention to Arab Americans," *Washington Post,* January 20, 1992, p. A10.

62. Mitchell Bard, "The Influence of Ethnic Groups on American Middle East Policy," in Charles W. Kegley and Eugene R. Wittkopf, eds., *The Domestic Sources of Foreign Policy* (New York: St. Martin's Press, 1988), pp. 57–69, esp. p. 58; David A. Dickson, "Pressure Politics and the Congressional Foreign Policy Process," paper presented at the 1990 Annual Meeting of the American Political Science Association, August, San Francisco, p. 9; and Boustany, "Arab-American Lobby Is Struggling."

63. Jon A. Krosnik, "Public Attitudes and American Policy Toward Israel," Ohio State University. Mimeo, n.d.

64. Thomas L. Friedman, "U.S. and Israel at Sea," *New York Times,* September 22, 1991, pp. A1, A14.

65. *Washington Post*/ABC survey of April 3, 1989; and CBS News press release, October 10, 1991. In the latter survey, only 17 percent favored the loan guarantees and 67 percent were opposed.

66. CBS News press release, July 8, 1990; the figures are 52–26–6 (don't know) for Democrats, 49–16–16 for Republicans, and 27–18–38 for Independents.

67. Lindsey Gruson, "Poll Reveals Fear of a New Vietnam," *New York Times,* July 24, 1983, pp. A1, A6.

68. See Uslaner, "A Tower of Babel on Foreign Policy?" pp. 312–315 for more details on this strategy.

69. See Ed Zuckerman, "Pro-Israel PACs: What Role Do They Play?" *PACs & Lobbies,* September 2, 1987, pp. 1, 7; Ed Zuckerman, comp., *The Almanac of Federal PACs: 1990* (Washington: Anward Publications, 1990); Charles R. Babcock, "Israel's Backers Maximize Political Clout," *Washington Post,* September 26, 1991, p. A21; and Barbara Levick-Segnatelli, "The Washington Political Action Committee: One Man Can Make a Difference," in Paul Herrnson and Clyde Wilcox, eds., *Risky Business* (forthcoming).

70. *New York Times,* "As Investments by Foreigners Surge, Their Influence in U.S. Politics Grows," December 30, 1985.

71. Ole R. Holsti and James N. Rosenaul, *American Leadership in World Affairs* (Boston: Allen & Unwin, 1984), p. 206.

72. Thomas B. Edsall, "Democrats' Lesson: To the Loyal Belong the Spoils," *Washington Post,* January 14, 1983, p. A7.

73. Thomas A. Bailey, *The American Pageant* (Boston: D.C. Heath and Company, 1961), p. 701.

CHAPTER 8

The Rational Actor Model and Crisis Decisions

Two Models of Policy Making

How do the various actors who participate in foreign policy making interact? To examine this question, we will analyze two models of the policy-making process. The first model is the rational actor; the second is the bureaucratic/governmental politics model. These models are devices by which we, as outside observers and analysts, organize our perceptions about how decisions are made. We do not assume that the various actors necessarily "choose" one model or the other and then make their decisions based on that model. Rather, we describe possible methods of decision making when we posit the models. We will then examine several specific foreign policy decisions in light of these models.

The Rational Actor

The rational actor model is based on the assumption that the government is a unitary actor and that there is some agreed-on goal to be attained; the problem, then, is to find the most effective way to reach that goal. This model is most useful in studying crisis decision making, as we shall indicate later in the chapter. In contrast, the bureaucratic/governmental politics model assumes that there are a multiplicity of actors, each with different goals, who see the stakes involved in a situation in different terms. The outcome reached will be one that is most politically feasible, the result of a bargaining agreement among the parties involved. This model best fits noncrisis decisions involving security policies and particularly those policies that are intermestic—partly international, partly domestic. The characteristics of the policy-making process on each of these types of policies are detailed in Table 8–1.

Crisis decision making involves a response to a perceived threat, a rational calculation of what to do given the actions of an opponent. Such situations involve relatively few actors, with the president preeminent, and require the capacity for both swift and careful planning. The group is normally small enough to arrive at quick decision while allowing vigorous debate on how the crisis ought to be managed. In that respect, crisis decision making approximates rational decision making. There is little or no time for bureaucratic infighting or the executive-legislative conflicts that characterize routine policy making.

There is also little time for prolonged discussion within the legislature or among the public about what the response to the crisis should be. All actors perceive—or are expected to perceive—a common stake in responding to the external threat and forming a united front. The focus of the decision-making process is on arriving at the most effective solution to the question of how to respond. Otherwise, the crisis may escalate into military confrontation and war. The rational actor approach and crisis decision making thus stress a strong executive, the ability to act swiftly, and domestic unity. This concentration of decision making in a small circle of executive officials, generally unrestrained by congressional or public opinion during a critical and relatively short period, means that the normal shortcomings of decision making said to characterize the American separation of powers are downplayed or disappear altogether. The policy makers can focus on the means-end problem.

The bureaucratic/governmental politics model, on the other hand, emphasizes other values: checks and balances, fair opportunities for bargaining among diverse actors, and the need for widespread participation by as many interested parties as possible. The emphasis here is on the representation of diverse interests, each of whom may see the stakes involved in a decision-making situation differently. There is no "best" outcome. The decision is evaluated based on the opportunities that various actors have to influence the bargaining that produces some outcome—which may very well end up supporting the status quo, because each of the various participants may check and balance each other effectively and prevent anyone from emerging as dominant and thus changing the status quo. This model applies to noncrisis policies—security issues such as arms control policies within the United States—and even better, to intermestic policies (for instance, energy) since the origin of this model lies in the domestic policy process.

Let us return to the rational actor model. The term rational has a very specific meaning. It refers to a decision-making process and involves four steps: (1) selecting the objectives and values that a given policy is supposed to achieve and maximize; (2) considering the various alternative means to achieve these purposes; (3) calculating the likely consequences of each alternative course; and (4) choosing the course that is most likely to attain the objectives originally selected. Furthermore, as noted, the government is viewed as a unitary actor when the

TABLE 8.1 Policy Characteristics

Type of Policy	Chief Characteristic	Primary Actors	Principal Decision Maker	Role of Congress	Role of Interest Groups	Role of Public Opinion	Relationship among Actors
Crisis	Short run; bureaucracy and Congress short-circuited. Common stake: all win or lose together.	President, responsible officials, and ad hoc individuals from in and out of government	Executive (presidential preeminence)	Postcrisis legitimization	None	Supportive; legitimization	Cooperation
Noncrisis (security)	Long run; bureaucratic–legislative participation; winners and losers	President; ex-executive agencies; Congress; interest groups; public opinion	Executive bureaucracy	Congressional participation	Low to moderate	Low to moderate	Competition and bargaining
Intermestic (welfare)	Long run; bureaucratic–legislative participation; winners, nonwinners, and losers	President; ex-executive agencies; Congress; interest groups; public opinion	Executive-congressional sharing	High	High	High	Competition and bargaining

SOURCE: This table is adapted from Randall B. Ripley and Grace A. Franklin, *Congress, the Bureaucracy, and Public Policy* (Chicago, Ill.: Dorsey Press 1976), p. 17.

rational actor model is used. This is implicit in the phrases we use or read: "The United States has decided . . . ," "It is believed that Moscow seeks . . . ," and "China has announced. . . ."

Decision makers have goals and attempt to maximize them in the policy-making arena. Deterrence of nuclear war, for example, assumes that a potential aggressor will not attack if the price of destroying the adversary is far higher than any conceivable gains taken. Nuclear devastation is clearly a price totally dispro-portionate to any possible profit. Deterrence thus rests on the assumption that the party to be deterred is rational and will reject alternative courses of action—that is, not attack and commit suicide or choose a third course such as refusing to defend national interests and withdrawing into isolationism. Or, consider the rationale for limited war. In 1957, at the height of the Cold War, Henry A. Kissinger published a book, *Nuclear Weapons and Foreign Policy*, in which he ar-gued that since the U.S. strategy of massive retaliation gave the president only two options—deterrence or, if challenged, fighting a total war—America's ad-versary (then still perceived as a united Sino-Soviet bloc) would be able to confront it with limited challenges in areas of vital interest to the United States.[1] This would then put Washington up against a dilemma: either respond com-pletely and risk nuclear immolation, or don't respond and appease or yield. The rational alternative in these circumstances was to have a limited war capability to respond to challenges in a measured way.

The rational actor model has been dominant in explaining international pol-itics to a far greater degree than in domestic politics.[2] Because most decisions studied in international politics have involved relations among nations, students of international politics have tended to view nations as unitary actors. It is our view that for crisis decision making, this assumption is a reasonable one. In a crisis, the scope of the decision-making arena is rather small. The inner circle makes the decisions and is almost invariably supported by Congress, the bureau-cracies, and public opinion. This is less true for noncrisis security decisions, and we shall see in the next chapter that these present a different model for explain-ing and understanding the decision-making process in more normal or everyday type of security policies.

Bureaucratic/Governmental Politics

In contrast to the rational actor model, the bureaucratic/governmental politics model does not assume that the government is a unitary actor.[3] It does not use phrases such as "the U.S.," or "the Soviet Union"; or refer to Paris or London as shorthand terms for their governments. Government is the sum of many parts. The executive branch of the U.S. government consists of more than the office of the presidency—it is also, as we know, composed of the senior foreign policy departments, such as the State Department; junior foreign policy departments, such as the International Communication Agency and the Arms Control and

Disarmament Agency; and such essentially domestic departments as the Departments of Commerce, Labor, Agriculture, and Treasury, all of whom have some interest in foreign policy, because they wish to enhance exports, protect U.S. labor, or seek a favorable balance of trade. Similarly, as we saw earlier, the Congress is composed of two houses, each of which is further decentralized into committees that in turn, fragment into a multitude of subcommittees. And in this context, a whole host of interest groups representing every conceivable group from business and labor to environmental and other self-styled public interest groups are additional actors.

Second, each of these actors—the presidency, executive departments, committees, subcommittees, and interest groups—approaches a problem or issue from a different perspective. This should not be surprising. They have different responsibilities; often they have received training to fulfill these responsibilities; they view the world from different perspectives and their stakes are different as well. It is surely understandable that all actors should believe that what they are doing is important (otherwise, why bother?) and that they should actively seek to gain the adoption of their solutions for the problem being confronted. There is a phrase for this: where you stand depends on where you sit. State Department Foreign Service officers not unnaturally believe that given patience, and the kinds of skills they possess, almost any problem can be resolved by diplomacy. By contrast, military officers are more prone to dismiss the possibilities of a compromise settlement and feel that the use of force or threat is more likely to yield fruitful results. Similarly, a congressional committee concerned with foreign affairs may well see a specific issue quite differently than one concerned with military affairs.

Actually, government can be broken down even further. Thus the State Department, as noted earlier, is hardly a single actor, even if the secretary of state officially presents his viewpoint. For the department in turn is composed of desks representing each major area of the world. Thus, as often happened in the past, the European desk and the African desk would be at odds. If a colony were seeking its independence, as often happened after World War II, the African desk would urge U.S. support of the independence movement, even if it annoyed one of our European allies, while the European desk would recommend caution. Preserving the cohesiveness of NATO against the Soviet threat was from its point of view more critical. Similarly, the Defense Department is composed of the air force, army, and navy, each of which quite naturally feels that its contribution to the defense and security of the United States is the most important and, therefore, seeks the larger share of the budget to best equip itself for any tasks it might be called on to do. Therefore, not only are the three services rivals, but each is subject to further conflict, for example, between the Strategic Air Command, Tactical Air Command, and Military Air Transport (air force); armor, artillery, and infantry (army); and aircraft carriers, regular surface navy, and nuclear submarines (navy). The United States thus has three navies. The aircraft carrier navy, which has been dominant since World War II, believes that should war occur with the Soviet Union, it can best project U.S. naval power; and in limited war and crisis situations it can bring U.S. air power to bear even if land bases are absent. The surface navy is preoccupied with control of the sea lanes in case of war, so that American troops and munitions can be shipped to Western Europe and American industry can continue to have access to the raw materials it needs from all regions of the world. The nuclear submarine navy, of course, feels it is the most important of these three navies since its task is the deterrence of war and, should that fail, retaliation against the Soviet Union. To repeat: where you stand depends on where you sit.

Third, the inevitable result of so many executive and legislative actors, each with a different stake and viewpoint on an issue, is conflict. Making a decision is thus not a matter of selecting a particular value or goal, calculating the various means by which it can be attained, and then selecting the one means that will most fully realize it at the least possible cost. Rather than reflecting a calm, considered, dignified, and reasoned process, decision making resembles a brawl, usually an unseemly one at that. For the issue is not whose policy position and recommendation is correct. There is no single correct policy that, but for every actor's narrow and self-interested perspective, would clearly emerge. Let us be clear about this. There is no objective ''national interest'' that would be clearly visible to all policy makers if they would but give priority to a broader, unselfish, patriotic view and subordinate their own parochial and selfish perception of a problem and do ''what's right for the country.'' The issue is not who is right but how to reconcile—if that is possible—many conflicting interpretations of what the correct policy should be.

The reason the term *bureaucratic politics* is used more frequently than *governmental* politics should be obvious from our earlier analysis: the executive branch has the primary responsibility in the formulation and implementation of foreign policy. Thus the focus of the policy struggle is among the many executive actors; the conflict is between the various bureaucracies. But, as is also clear from our earlier discussion, the Congress can never be neglected in noncrisis decisions. Since Vietnam, indeed, interested legislative actors have participated more consistently and assertively than before. Hence, our emphasis on governmental politics, encompassing all the decision-making circles. In nondemocratic societies such as the Soviet Union, of course, one focuses only on the executive.

Fourth, as noted, this pluralism of actors, interests, and views means that the policy process is one of attempting to reconcile these conflicting perspectives and building a consensus or majority coalition so that a decision can be made. This is not done by considering only whose policy recommendation has the most merit; it is also a question of which actor is the more powerful. Indeed, the degree of an actor's influence, skill in negotiating, ability to attract some actors and accommodate others are probably more important than the wisdom of his or her position. Indeed, the reason for the use of the word *politics* in the terms *governmental politics* or *bureaucratic politics* reflects the fact that a policy emerges from a process of simultaneous conflict and accommodation among a multitude of actors with competing viewpoints and possessing different amounts of power. Policy making means bargaining; negotiations are required and compromises must be struck. Those *for* a policy and those *opposing* the policy negotiate with other actors, seeking to organize a coalition of a majority of the actors to advance their collective policy interests or oppose a change of policy. Negotiations thus occur throughout the executive branch as officials, bureaus, and agencies in one department seek support in another; attracting the president and/or some of his advisers is especially important and is, therefore, a cause of fierce struggle. Policy making is thus a matter of widening the base of support within the executive while also seeking allies within Congress. This occurs through the constant modification of the proposed policy as concessions are made to potential allies to satisfy their needs and overcome their objections in the hope of building a majority coalition. Coalition building, in short, crosses institutional lines.

Fifth, the characteristics of the conflict and the coalition-building process affect the policy output. One of the most important results of this continuous bargaining within the "policy machine" is that policy moves forward one step at a time and tends to focus on momentary concerns and short-range aims. This is usually called *incrementalism*. Another word is *satisficing*. This word suggests that policy makers do not, each time they have to make a decision, sit down and go through the rational procedure of decision making. Policy makers have neither the time nor the resources to go through this process. Instead, they pick the policy that is likely to be the most satisfactory; and they judge this by whether a policy has been successful in the past. If a policy has been satisfactory up to that point, why not take another step forward on the same path? The presumption is that what worked in the past will work now, as well as in the future. In addition, once a majority coalition has been forged after hard struggle, a winning coalition will normally prefer modification of existing policy decisions. This is not necessarily true. The negotiating process among different groups with conflicting perspectives and vested interests can produce a stalemate and paralysis of policy—that is, no policy at all.

Sixth, a further characteristic of the policy process, and implicit in our analysis so far, is its time-consuming nature. Incrementalism suggests a policy machine in low gear, moving along a well-defined road rather slowly in response to specific short-run stimuli. A proposed policy is normally discussed first within the executive branch. It then passes through official channels, where it receives clearances and modifications as it gathers a broader base of support on its way up the executive hierarchy to the president. The constant conferences and negotiations among departments clearly slow the pace. The process takes even longer when a policy needs congressional and public approval. Potential opponents can occupy many veto points to block legislation within Congress; such veto points are in the House Rules Committee, the House and Senate committees and a multitude of subcommittees, and on the floor during debates and votes in both chambers. The advantage normally lies with those who oppose a specific policy, because it is difficult to jump all the hurdles along its route of legislative enactment. An additional result, given this slow policy process, the formidable obstacles and great effort needed to pass major policy, is that old policies and the old assumptions on which they are based, tend to survive longer than the conditions that produced these policies initially.

Seventh, one further characteristic of American foreign policy decision making is that it is usually public in nature. In a democracy, this is inevitable. While policy may be made primarily by the executive, the confines of this policy are established by public opinion. No American government before the fall of France could have intervened in Europe to preserve the balance of power. During World War II and most of the Cold War, however, Congress and public opinion tended to be permissive and supportive as far as the presidential conduct of foreign policy was concerned. Aware of their lack of knowledge, information, and competence in an area remote from their everyday involvement—in the more familiar area of domestic policies, public opinion is much more structured and knowledgeable—the legislature and public looked to the president for leadership. Only when setbacks or painful experiences arose would Congress and public opinion react, broadly clarify the limits of its tolerance, and perhaps punish the party in power. But even if most of the time public opinion did not act as a restraining factor, policy makers were always aware of its existence. Because mass opinion does not tend to take shape until after some foreign event has occurred, it can hardly act as a guide for those who must make the policy. Nonetheless, the last will take into account what they think "the traffic will bear," because they know that if a decision is significant enough, there is likely to be some crystallization of opinion and, possibly, retribution at the polls. Since Vietnam, this has changed considerably. There is more widespread skepticism of presidential wisdom, greater congressional capability, more extensive public concern about dangerous involvements; and the emergence of intermestic policies with their pocketbook effects on voters arouses legislators and interest groups. Congress and public opinion tend to be both less permissive and supportive of presidents now; presidential capacity for leadership has become more constrained.

We shall examine the bureaucratic politics model as it relates to the antiballistic missile system (ABM), strategic arms limitation talks, and energy politics in the next chapter. But we shall first focus on the rational actor model and its application to crisis decision making on Cuba and Iraq in this chapter.

Crisis Decision Making: Cuba and Iraq

A Definition of Crisis

The rational actor model is probably the most relevant to explaining and understanding crisis decisions. A crisis is characterized by a number of features: decision makers are taken by surprise; they feel that they must make decisions rapidly; and they perceive that vital interests are at stake.[4] In these circumstances, decisions cannot be made in the routine manner characteristic of bureaucracies. The element of surprise is likely to forestall use of standard operating procedures in management of the crisis. The need for quick decisions will limit the number of officials involved. Above all, the perception that vital interests are at stake will quickly centralize the decision making and take it to the top: to the president and the chief presidential advisers in the United States, and equivalent officials in other governments.

When vital interests are threatened by another *major* actor, the reason a crisis erupts is, of course, that one party threatens the status quo and the other is determined to defend it. A crisis is so called in the first place primarily because of the *heightened expectation of violence* that it raises. A crisis exists at the crossover point between peace and war. The chance for escalation to war becomes ever greater as the crisis goes on. It is the fear of this that drives policy makers to act quickly and try to resolve the issues involved before the crisis gets out of hand. Time is therefore of the essence. During the Cold War, crises were particularly dangerous because an escalation could result in a nuclear war that would obliterate both of the superpowers. A crisis, then, involved the likelihood that the United States itself would be attacked and destroyed beyond any hope of quick recovery.

In that sense, the Iraqi crisis of 1990 was not a crisis. To be sure, there was a rapid deployment of U.S. forces after Saddam Hussein invaded Kuwait on August 2, 1990, and there was great fear in both Washington and the Saudi Arabian capital that he would try to seize the oil kingdom. U.S. forces were therefore dispatched to the area. Thus the "crisis" dragged on for five and a half months and, after Iraq's refusal to withdraw from Kuwait, hostilities erupted. Clearly, the American–Iraqi confrontation was not comparable to an American–Soviet crisis, such as the 1962 Cuban missile crisis which, by its very nature, confronted both states with the possibility of extinction. That *was* a crisis in every sense of that word; and the longer such a face-off lasted, the greater the likelihood that a misstep by one or the other party would lead to a dangerous escalation. That kind of danger was only a potential in the Iraqi instance. It was precisely because Iraq might someday acquire nuclear arms that some observers—and probably some policy makers—felt that war to destroy Saddam Hussein was better now rather than later. If left in power and able to develop nuclear and perhaps biological weapons in addition to his chemical warfare arsenal, he would be far more dangerous to face down, let alone defeat, at a "reasonable" cost at some future point. Thus a real crisis might yet occur. But, in current terms, the Iraqi leader was perceived as threatening vital interests of the United States and other Western countries. Not only had he increased the share of oil he controlled by adding Kuwaiti oil to Iraq's, but if the militarily vulnerable Saudi Arabia and other Gulf oil kingdoms knuckled under to his threats, Saddam Hussein would be left virtually in control of OPEC's decision on the supply and price of oil, upon which all Western industrial economies depended. So his invasion of Kuwait did represent a real crisis, even though Iraq was hardly a superpower.

Decision Making Flows Upward

In terms of the decision-making process, the various characteristics of a crisis listed above tend to be highly functional. The usual drawn-out haggling over differences in policies between different bureaucracies, the separation of powers between the executive and Congress, and all the efforts of interest groups to influence policy, if not to undermine it, are, in these circumstances, short-circuited. The different way in which a crisis is managed by the government means that the policy process works speedily and efficiently, free of the traditional domestic pressures, for the short duration of the crisis. And the fact that crisis decisions flow upward to the top officials has another important consequence: the careful and cautious management of superpower crises.

In the case of Cuba, Kennedy's advisors considered all the various options of how to get the Soviets to take their missiles out of Cuba without having to go to war after the president had made their withdrawal the American objective. The president's advisors had the rare luxury of time, thanks to photos taken by a U-2 spy plane, and took the better part of a week to debate alternative courses, from taking the issue to the United Nations to launching a "surgical strike" on the missiles.[5] They chose a blockade to prevent further shipments of missiles; this action was also to underline the seriousness of the U.S. demand that the missiles must be removed, although the blockade could not remove those already in Cuba. Any further escalation of pressure to achieve this objective was left for later. Whether the United States would increase the pressure thus depended on what the Soviets did. In the meantime, the blockade was not too risky a course and placed the responsibility for the next step—whether to escalate or de-escalate—on Moscow. Bush's handling of the Iraqi crisis was also the result of decisions made by a few individuals: the president, the secretaries of state and defense, the national security adviser and, in this case, the chairman of the Joint Chiefs of Staff;[6] the secretary of state was equally restrictive in whom he talked to in his department. These four individuals and the president appeared to agree on all fundamentals, thus reinforcing their thinking on policy rather than examining its bases. In turn, this inner war cabinet was part of what was dubbed as the Big Eight, the inner circle which, like Kennedy's executive committee during the Cuban crisis,[7] took over from the more formal National Security Council.[8] Presidents during crises tend to favor being surrounded by an informal network of advisers and friends and to cut out policy makers mandated by law.

It is indeed not uncommon for policy makers, coming to power with strong convictions, to ignore or downgrade the best advice available within the government, that of bureaucrats in the various foreign, defense, and intelligence agencies. These are the experts who have the knowledge and experience; those who win power or who are appointed to high office by the president are "generalists." They may be the "best and brightest," but they usually lack the expertise of bureaucrats. This does not mean that the latter are always right and the former usually wrong. The experts often cannot see the forest for the trees; and bureaucracies, wedded to their policies, tend to resist policy changes, even when the president seeks such changes. The point is that the generalists ought to consult the available experts in the government—and sometimes former officials and academics outside the government—before making critical decisions.[9] The reason they often do not is that when a president and his people come to office they have great confidence in their own political judgment; they do not therefore feel that they need defer to the political analysis of the bureaucracies, whose policy preferences are, after all, also reflections of their political judgments.

Presidential Perceptions and Policy Choices

A second characteristic of crisis decision making is the central role of the president, who interprets events and evaluates the stakes in the crisis. Kennedy's reading of the situation he confronted during the Cuban missile crisis, the consequences it might have for American security, and his political future and ability to lead the nation, were responsible for his actions. (The latter two factors can hardly be separated, for the external challenges, as the president sees them, do not really leave a choice of accepting a loss of personal prestige without a loss of national prestige. For the president of the United States, personal and national cost calculations tend to be identical.)

Kennedy saw the installation of Soviet missiles in Cuba as a personal challenge, with potentially damaging national effects. In response to earlier congressional and public clamor about possible Soviet offensive missiles in Cuba—as distinct from ground-to-air or ground-to-ship defensive missiles—Kennedy had publicly declared that the United States would not tolerate offensive missiles on an island ninety miles off the Florida coast. Intended primarily as a declaration to cool domestic criticism that had come largely from Republicans, Kennedy's statement had also led Soviet leaders to respond that they had no intention of placing missiles in Cuba. Kennedy thus was pledged to act if the Soviets had lied—as it turned out they had—unless he wished to be publicly humiliated. If he did not act, the Soviet leaders would not believe other pledges and commitments the president had made or inherited from his predecessors. At least, that is how Kennedy perceived the situation.

He saw the consequences as very dangerous, because he feared that Soviet premier Nikita Khrushchev had interpreted previous acts—the abortive 1961 Bay of Pigs invasion of Cuba and the inaction of U.S. troops when the Berlin Wall went up the same year—as signaling a lack of will, an absence of sufficient determination to defend vital American interests. Khrushchev spoke openly of an American failure of nerve. It was not so much the effect of the Soviet missiles on the military equation between the two powers that mattered, although that was important; it was the political consequences of the *appearance* of a change in the balance of power that were deemed critical by Kennedy. The Soviet Union was supposed to be on the short end of the missile gap, but Kennedy feared that American inaction would convince the world that Soviet claims of missile superiority were accurate. This would lead allied governments to fear that in the new situation in which the United States would be vulnerable to nuclear devastation, they could no longer count on this country to defend them. Above all, it might tempt the Soviets to exploit the situation and seek to disrupt American alliances—especially the North Atlantic Treaty Organization. Khrushchev had already restated his determination to eject the Western allies from West Berlin. If Khrushchev succeeded in Cuba, why should he take Kennedy's pledge to defend West Berlin seriously? And if he did not, would not Soviet and American troops soon be clashing in an area where they would be hard to separate?

The real irony of the Cuban missile crisis is that Kennedy was also determined to seek a more stable and restrained basis for coexistence with the Soviet Union during his years in office. This long-range goal, which hardly had the massive support it would have later, could not be realized if Khrushchev did not take Kennedy seriously and tried to push him around. Then earnest negotiations, in which each party would recognize the other's legitimate interests, would be impossible. A major change in the Cold War atmosphere was at stake, in addition to the United States' reputation for power and willingness to keep commitments. Domestically, of course, another "defeat" in Cuba, discrediting Kennedy's foreign policy, was bound to affect his personal standing with his party, Congress, and the public. It also would lead to strong right-wing Republican pressures to be more forcible in foreign policy and would give less priority to the president's liberal domestic reform program. Thus, the foreign policy and domestic pressures for Kennedy to act were overwhelming.

The dominant role of the president in crises was reaffirmed by President Bush during the Iraqi confrontation from August 1990 to March 1991. We already know how from the beginning he interpreted the Iraqi invasion of Kuwait: as an attempt by Saddam Hussein to make Iraq the dominant power in the Gulf, controlling OPEC oil production and pricing policies; as an effort to establish Iraq as the hegemonic power in the Middle East, eliminating pro-Western moderate Arab leaders; and to place itself as leader of an anti-Israeli and anti-American campaign. These goals had to be opposed. Furthermore, if Saddam Hussein could conquer and rape Kuwait with impunity, it would set a bad precedent for other potential aggressors in the newly emerging post-Cold War period. In making his decision to oppose the Iraqi strongman, to apply sanctions and use force, if necessary, to evict him from Kuwait, President Bush was guided by two powerful convictions. The first, derived from World War II in which he served as the navy's youngest fighter pilot, was that aggressors had to be stopped in their tracks; appeasement was folly. The president viewed Saddam Hussein's threat as one similar to Hitler's in the 1930s. The horror stories of the brutal behavior and atrocities committed by the Iraqis in Kuwait only reinforced his belief that the Iraqi leader, like the Nazi one, was an evil and immoral man who had to be stopped. The second conviction was Bush's continuing belief in the worth and purposes of American power. Unlike many of his countrymen who had lost much of their confidence in both after Vietnam, the president remained steadfast; he told an interviewer that "because of the role of the United States in the world, we have a disproportionate responsibility."[10]

Having decided at the outset that the occupation of Kuwait "will not stand," Bush kept his eye on the central strategic issue, which in fact was the neutralizing of Saddam Hussein as a threat to the entire Middle East. He then proceeded to organize a coalition of the Soviet Union, key Western allies such as Britain and France, and important Arab states, including Egypt, Syria, and Morocco, besides the threatened Gulf states. Had anyone on August 1, 1990, the day before the Iraqi invasion of Kuwait, predicted that the president of the United States would not only take a firm stand on an issue that might involve the use of force, but that he could organize a coalition of such disparate nations, he would have been laughed at and dismissed as crazy. In addition, Bush proceeded to mobilize the United Nations in support of his aim of getting Iraq out of Kuwait; this certainly made it easier for Moscow and several of the Arab states to justify cooperation with the United States, former Cold War rival and friend of Israel. It also gave legitimacy to the U.S. aim of ejecting Iraq from Kuwait and the application, initially, of economic sanctions to achieve that aim; and when these were not successful, of setting a deadline for an Iraqi withdrawal which, if not met, would lead to the use of force.

Bush's domestic handling of the crisis was equally skillful. He mobilized public opinion in support, despite cries of "Vietnam!" The initial deployment of more than 100,000 troops, and then a build-up to about 250,000 troops, met little opposition. The Democratic party, which, as noted earlier had since Vietnam become an essentially pacifist party, first supported the president's use of economic sanctions. Only later, when the president virtually doubled the military force in an effort to convince Saddam Hussein that if he did not get out voluntarily he would be forced out, did the Democrats oppose Bush, arguing that while they were committed to the same goal as Bush they preferred to avoid war and the large numbers of casualties that a conflict with a million-man Iraqi army might involve. If economic sanctions were given a year, eighteen months, perhaps two years, to work, Iraq would have to comply because its loss of oil revenues would bring it to economic collapse. The Democrats demanded that the United States not go to war except as constitutionally mandated, that is, with congressional support. Bush eventually did go to the Congress for support. The United Nations, the United States' allies, had already given support for military action. Would the Congress be the one exception? It was a gamble, but despite the almost wholesale opposition of the Democrats, the president squeaked by in the Senate, where the issue had been in doubt.

Once the deadline passed on January 15, 1991, Bush did not hesitate, but ordered the war to start. It lasted forty-three days. The initial weeks were fought only in the air. Air power basically won the war, destroying Iraq's capability to become a great regional power by building up its weapons of mass destruction; it also pounded the Iraqi army in Kuwait and southern Iraq mercilessly. Nevertheless, the critics, again, many of them in Congress, urged the president to continue the fight in the air; they pleaded that he avoid a ground war. But when his generals told him that they were ready for action on land, he gave them the permission they needed. In less than 100 hours it was all over; the total number of American casualties in the war (some caused by U.S. fire) was an astonishingly low 263. The vaunted Iraqi army was only too glad not to fight but to surrender or retreat.

However, it was Bush's diplomatic performance that dominated the fighting. First, he prevented a split-up of the coalition that Saddam Hussein thought he could achieve by attacking Israel with missiles. He expected Israel to retaliate, thus forcing the Arab states out of the war. Not only did the Israelis show remarkable restraint by not retaliating (allied planes, including those of the Saudis, were diverted to finding and destroying Iraqi missile launchers), but all Arab members of the coalition stuck and their peoples did not rise up in anger against their governments for joining in an attack on a fellow Arab state—despite widespread predictions, by many experts on the Middle East, besides Saddam Hussein, that this would happen.

Second, and more important, Bush prevented an outcome that would have allowed Saddam Hussein to save face and to preserve much of his conventional fighting capability. As the likelihood of a ground war was becoming obvious, Soviet leader Gorbachev tried to end the war by getting the Iraqi leader to withdraw from Kuwait and save Iraq, as well as position himself as a major postwar player at the bargaining table. Saddam Hussein agreed to pull out, seeking to lure Gorbachev from the coalition, but on terms unacceptable to Bush: Economic sanctions would have to be ended before the Iraqi withdrawal was complete; no economic reparations would be imposed on Iraq for its pillaging and mistreatment of tiny Kuwait (most of whose oil wells the Iraqis set on fire at the last moment and which took months to extinguish); and Saddam Hussein would not be required to formally disavow Iraq's annexation of Kuwait. In addition, without a ground war the United States could not ensure the destruction of the Iraqi army, especially Saddam Hussein's elite and loyal Republican Guard forces. Bush thanked Gorbachev but told him that the terms did not go far enough; instead, he cut short a potentially troubling diplomatic situation which could have delayed the ground war and been troublesome for the alliance's cohesion by giving Saddam Hussein a twenty-four-hour ultimatum to get out of Kuwait or face a ground war. Once the ground war started, again after the Iraqi leader had ignored another deadline, Saddam Hussein accepted Soviet terms more favorable to U.S. demands; he even announced Iraq's withdrawal without any conditions.

But Bush, with a rout of Iraqi forces in sight, would have none of these maneuvers. The added ground sweep around all of the Iraqi forces in Kuwait, especially the Republican Guard, whose strength had to be destroyed before the fighting ceased, remained his top priority. Saddam Hussein's threat to the area had to be ended; that had been the central and strategic aim from the beginning of the crisis. Restoring Kuwait was the subsidiary goal. All in all, it was a flawless performance by the commander in chief in what turned out to be a widely popular victory, watched by Americans in their living rooms via extensive television coverage. American pride in their armed forces and in their country was at an all-time high. Bush's job approval rating was the highest of any president in nearly a half century and the second highest since public opinion polls had begun.

Bureaucracy and the Execution of Policy

The third characteristic of crises is the subordination of bureaucratic interests to the need to make a decision to safeguard the "national interest." A crisis is accompanied by a sense of urgency, as well as by policy makers' perception that the nation's security is at stake and that war looms. Thus, although decision making has risen to the top levels of the government, and the men and women in those positions reflect their departmental points of view, they do not necessarily feel themselves limited to representing those points of view. Organizational affiliation is not a good predictor of such points of view. Senior participants in crises behave more as "players" than as "organizational participants." Secretary of Defense Robert McNamara did not reflect the Joint Chiefs' readiness to bomb and invade during the Cuban missile crisis (just as late in the Vietnam War he was to disagree increasingly with their views and recommendations); he became the leading proponent of the blockade. Other players in that crisis did not even represent foreign policy bureaucracies—the two men closest to the president, the attorney general and the president's special counsel, along with the secretary of the Treasury and a former secretary of state, for example, represented only themselves. The bureaucratic axiom that "you stand where you sit" is thus not necessarily correct, at least during a crisis.

The bureaucracy's principal role in a crisis is carrying out policy. This applies especially to the military because use of the threat of force, if not some limited application of force, becomes quickly visible in such a confrontation. Military organizations, like all organizations, operate according to certain standard operating procedures. While these serve the purpose of the organization, they may not serve the policy makers' goals of preventing a dangerous escalation and preserving the peace. Thus, the air force, when asked about the possibility of a "surgical strike" on the missiles, dusted off old plans drawn up for an invasion of Cuba and simply added the missiles to hundreds of other targets—that is, the air force produced a disproportionate response, which might have led Moscow to respond differently if it suspected the U.S. goal was not only the withdrawal of Soviet missiles but—despite the president's words—the elimination of Castro as well. And the navy wanted the blockade to be imposed outside the range of Cuban-piloted Soviet MIG fighters, while Kennedy wanted the blockade pulled in to give Khrushchev extra time to think about his next move. Both goals were legitimate, but obviously incompatible. The risks of war by inadvertence, then, are real. No one wants war, but a loss of control in the implementation phase of a crisis may well provoke an unintentional escalation. It is, therefore, imperative that the president ensure that his political goals remain primary, and that military operations do not jeopardize them.

For military operations may, indeed, tend to drive policy. They can set deadlines for political action, foreclosing diplomacy and determining the nation's course. In Vietnam, the U.S. military had become disillusioned by the gradual escalation of pressure and the restraints imposed upon the conduct of the war. The officers in charge of the campaign against Iraq, led by General Colin Powell, Chairman of the Joint Chiefs of Staff and Vietnam veteran, believed in gathering sizable forces so that if hostilities erupted, the United States could act with overwhelming force and, unhampered by political constraints, try to win quickly and with the least cost of lives. Thus the initial commitment to defend Saudi Arabia was more than 200,000 U.S. troops, in addition to Saudi and other countries' forces. Such a large commitment, it was hoped, would also convey to Saddam Hussein the seriousness of the American determination to defend the oil kingdom and deter a possible Iraqi attack. But as the Iraqi build-up continued, the U.S. military sought to reach greater strength in order to deal an offensive punch if war came. A political objective was admittedly also present, that is, communicating to Iraq's leader that if he did not withdraw from Kuwait he would be forcefully ejected. But the military's purpose in virtually doubling U.S. forces, including tank divisions from Germany where they had long faced the Soviets, was to have the capability to seize the initiative at the outset of the war, to destroy all key military targets in Iraq immediately, and to contain Iraqi forces in Kuwait while cutting their supply lines. While no one could promise a quick victory and few casualties, the military planned on as quick a victory as possible, holding casualties down by attacking with large forces and exploiting U.S. technology to the full.

But once Operation Desert Shield, as it was called, reached full strength, the critics feared that the military option might become unstoppable. Once the forces were in place, war would become hard to avoid; they could not be kept in place month after month, much of the time in the desert heat. A long stay of Western "infidels" in Saudi Arabia might also jeopardize the monarchy, especially if the troops were still there when the faithful visited Mecca in the late spring. Thus committing military forces, particularly such large forces, might limit, if not undermine, any possible diplomatic efforts to resolve differences peacefully. Admittedly, the possibility of war might just give Saddam Hussein the incentive to withdraw from Kuwait. The hope for that solution, however, was never high. The annexation of Kuwait as a province of Iraq did not suggest that Saddam Hussein would withdraw even if in return he were to be granted certain objectives, such as access to the Gulf; and his firm belief that America would not fight meant that President Bush's warnings and sending of troops to Saudi Arabia tended to be dismissed as a bluff. Thus, while the military build-up probably did place a time limit on diplomatic efforts, the likelihood of a peaceful settlement of the issue of Kuwait was never strong.

Once hostilities started, the main emphasis was on the air war. Eventually, it would take ground forces to eject the Iraqi army from Kuwait. Air power has never won a war by itself, but the air force argued that carpet bombing and cutting supply lines could perhaps destroy up to half of the well-dug-in land forces, as well as demoralize and starve them. Air force officers claimed that no war had ever been more winnable, because the desert, unlike the jungles of Vietnam, would allow no concealment unless the troops stayed on the defensive in entrenched positions. In general, then, the air force could soften up the land forces in advance of a ground engagement. The principal issue was one of time. The air force had to be given sufficient time. And this position was supported by those in the Congress and by outside experts who wished to minimize U.S. and allied ground casualties. The problem, some critics believed, was that the war was planned by army officers: the Chairman of the Joint Chiefs of Staff, Colin Powell, and the commanding officer in Saudi Arabia, Norman Schwartzkopf. Quite naturally, army officers believe that only ground forces can capture territory and dislodge enemy forces—that is, that wars are won on land. They were quite correct in this estimation, but despite their belief, they in fact waged an essential air-war strategy, consisting of more than 100,000 sorties, to destroy and demoralize the Iraqi forces in Kuwait. By the time the army rolled in, the ground war had become a quick mopping-up operation. Thus in this superbly planned combined arms operation, the army planners did not act parochially, as might have been expected. In large part, this was due to a fact that the critics had overlooked, namely, the reorganization of the Joint Chiefs of Staff, which eliminated much of the previous interservice rivalry. The Chairman of the Joint Chiefs was now its most powerful member, placing him in direct touch with the local theater commander or commander in chief—General Norman Schwartzkopf in this case—and depriving the other chiefs of much of their authority.[11]

Role of Congress

Finally, decision making in a crisis is characterized by congressional noninvolvement. Congressional leaders are usually called in and informed of the president's decision just before he announces it publicly. This form is followed as a matter of courtesy, and their advice is not requested. Presidents consider themselves more representative of the country than any senator or House member and as representative as Congress as a whole. Interestingly, Kennedy, after informing a congressional delegation of his decision to blockade Cuba, did ask for its members' opinions. When the response was to question the utility of the blockade and to propose an air strike instead, Kennedy reacted angrily. After the members left, he consoled himself by saying that had they had more time to think it over, they also would have decided on the blockade. If presidents assure themselves like this, why indeed consult members of the legislative branch? In any event, in American–Soviet crises, the members of Congress have generally supported the president.

A characteristic of a crisis is its brevity. There is not sufficient time to develop criticism and opposition; even if there is disagreement, there is great reluctance to voice it in the early stages of a confrontation. The country "rallies around the flag." Time is the critical factor. If a crisis does not end quickly, however, congressional opposition does grow. During the confrontation with Iraq, Congress initially supported the president's goals and actions fully. But after the substantial increase of forces in November, three months after the first deployment, questions about the future course of events multiplied. Did the military build-up make war inevitable? Had economic sanctions been given enough time to work? What about diplomatic efforts to resolve the Kuwaiti issue without resorting to force? If war came, how would the war be conducted? Would the emphasis be on a long air war, relying mainly on air power to win the war, or would the focus, after a short air campaign, be on the ground engagement? Would the result be heavy U.S. casualties? Even if war were unavoidable, and it ended quickly and without many U.S. deaths, would the aftermath of a war in which Westerners again killed Arabs further destabilize the Middle East, making America's Arab friends more vulnerable and poisoning relations with the Arab world for generations to come? Even if Iraq were defeated, would this not result in Iran's once more seeking to become the hegemon in the Gulf while Syria resumes its drive for Arab leadership?

As war threatened, the Congress, having been witness to presidential uses of force time and time again during the Cold War, began to insist on its authority to declare war. Given the institutional rivalry between the executive and legislative branches (if not also between the House and the Senate), and partisan and ideological differences on national security issues, with one party much of the time occupying the presidency and the other the Congress, it was not easy for the United States to confront its adversary with unity at home. Since Vietnam, it has become increasingly clear that short of an attack on the United States or on American forces overseas, Congress is unlikely to support overwhelmingly any use of force. Bush declared repeatedly in public that he would like congressional support if he felt it necessary to use force against Saddam Hussein, but unless Congress could give him overwhelming support he would rather do without it. A close vote would send the wrong signal to Iraq, only confirming its dictator's belief that the United States was too divided to go to war against him. With the U.N. vote sanctioning the use of force if Iraq did not pull out from Kuwait by January 15, 1991, Bush believed that as commander in chief, he already possessed the authority to go to war. But at the last minute, given the size of the U.S. commitment and assuming that Congress would not dare undermine the pres-

ident before the entire world, he did seek a congressional equivalent of a declaration of war. Despite the opposition of the entire Democratic leadership, he
gained just enough Democratic votes to slide past in the Senate and win com-
fortably in the House.

One reason for the post-Vietnam involvement in only relatively short wars has
been to hold congressional involvements to a minimum. It is notable that even
against Iraq Bush called off the war as soon as the Iraqis had been driven out of
Kuwait with minimal U.S./U.N. casualties. He rejected driving to Baghdad, because he believed not only that Iraq's nuclear facilities had been destroyed, but
that assuming responsibility for governing Iraq and becoming drawn into its civil
war would prolong U.S. involvement and raise the number of casualties. As it is,
later revelations that Iraq's nuclear facilities had not been destroyed, as had been
believed before a defector informed the United Nations of secret nuclear sites,
have led to criticisms of the quick ending of the war before Saddam Hussein had
been deposed in Baghdad. But Bush was probably right. Had the hostilities
lasted six months or possibly a year, and, above all, had casualties ranged upward
from 5,000 to 20,000, with perhaps 7,000 dead, he would have faced a growing
peace movement and growing criticism from Congress.

Crisis Decision Making and the Democratic Dilemmas

Crisis decision making is predominantly characterized by a "rational" mode of
operation. The fact that vital interests are considered to be at stake, that the
decision makers are usually surprised by the occurrence of the crisis and feel
under great pressure to make quick decisions ensures that crisis decisions will
not be handled routinely. Decision making rises to the top and is narrowed to a
few participants who may be organized for the duration of the crisis as a special
task force. The president plays the key role; he has a greater opportunity in these
circumstances to determine policy than he does in more normal security policies, let alone intermestic policies. He and his specially selected advisers are not
hampered by an aroused Congress, irate interest groups, or an inquisitive public.
The crisis itself tends to unite everyone. There is not enough time to stimulate
sufficient opposition. The cabinet officers participating in the decision making
process are usually not fundamentally motivated by the organizational and bureaucratic interests of their departments, as when "normal" policy is being
made. In any case, there is normally little time for bargaining among actors with
different perspectives.

Thus, in a way, there are no dilemmas. As Lowi said many years ago, "only
command positions were involved; the public and its institutions were far removed. . . . In sum, there was hardly any politics at all." The men in these
"command positions" are "institutional leaders . . . *without their institutions*."[12]
Thus the U.S. political system ironically may work more efficiently when it acts

in an authoritarian manner, when the normal democratic participation of the bureaucracy, Congress, interest groups, and public opinion is at a minimum. Some refer to this presidential dominance and freedom from political constraint as *democratic Caesarism.*

Yet while the consequences of surprise, high threat, and short time can be very functional by considerably reducing, if not eliminating, the "traditionally acclaimed disabilities and deficiencies of United States democracy in foreign affairs,"[13] one final point deserves to be discussed briefly: the possibility that when decision making is limited to a few individuals—as noted earlier regarding the Iran–Contra affair—they will not make rational decisions but will fall victim to *groupthink.*[14] This term refers to the tendency of a small group of decision makers to become a cohesive group and the possibility that individual members may silence their doubts and qualifications about the policy views the majority holds; those who disagree tend to be rejected. Thus the consensus reached may be superficial because it does not reflect the sound judgment of the group reached after critical examination; without the give-and-take of debate in which all options are carefully analyzed, this consensus may represent a collective misjudgment—or just plain bad judgment. Groupthink, claims Irving Janis, is a deterioration of the mental efficiency, reality testing, and moral judgment that is the product of group pressure to conform.[15]

In the Cuban missile crisis, the president avoided becoming a victim. First, he absented himself from the executive committee's discussions so that its members would be free to say what they wanted to. Had he been present and expressed his views, the tendency would have been for the committee members to take their cue from him. Who, after all, dares to challenge the president's views? Second, the committee was divided into smaller groups who debated and cross-examined one another. In this way, all members became thoroughly familiar with the pros and cons of the arguments for specific options. Robert Kennedy, the attorney general who was his brother's confidante, often played devil's advocate, probing and asking what some felt were rude questions that demanded a justification of their position.

If the Cuban missile crisis was handled so well that it has become a classic case study of crisis management, it is because the administration learned from the disaster of the Bay of Pigs operation a year earlier. This operation too has become a classic of sorts—of a "perfect failure." The operation was launched on a series of assumptions, all of which proved wrong. Among these were: no one would discover that the United States was responsible for this invasion; the Cuban Air Force could be knocked out before the invasion started; Castro's army was weak; and the invasion would touch off uprisings that would probably lead to Castro's overthrow. How could such flimsy assumptions go unchallenged by a group of men who were considered "the best and the brightest"? A number of reasons have been cited, including the fact that the CIA's own intelligence experts and the State Department's Cuban desk people, who could have predicted the failure of sending 1,400 men to Cuba to topple the regime, were excluded, and the illusion of these able people that they were invincible and that they were unanimous in their support of the CIA plan. Doubts were not loudly voiced, silence was taken for consent, and any disagreements that surfaced were suppressed by a "mindguard" who guarded the consensus from intellectual assault as a bodyguard would protect an individual from physical injury. The evidence also suggests that if widespread democratic participation in crisis decision making is not feasible, the failure to subject policy to critical evaluation has been greatest when the U.S. adversary was not a nuclear or even a major power. When the Soviet Union has been the opponent, U.S. policy makers have been cautious and careful, continuously reviewing their policies. The awesome cost of miscalculations and actions based on wrong assumptions have been the best antidotes to the pressures for groupthink.[17] One misstep could transform the superpowers' confrontation into a nuclear disaster for which the label World War III would be a misnomer. The scale of destruction would so greatly exceed those of World Wars I and II that new language and words would have to be found to describe it.

Notes

1. Henry A. Kissinger, *Nuclear Weapons and Foreign Policy* (New York: Harper & Row, 1957).
2. Graham Allison, "Conceptual Models and the Cuban Missile Crisis," *American Political Science Review,* September 1969, p. 716.
3. See Roger Hilsman, *To Move a Nation* (Garden City, N.Y.: Doubleday, 1967); Graham T. Allison, *The Essence of Decision* (Boston: Little, Brown, 1971); Morton H. Halperin, *Bureaucratic Politics and Foreign Policy* (Washington, D.C.: Brookings, 1974); Morton H. Halperin and Arnold Kanter, eds., *Readings in American Foreign Policy* (Boston: Little, Brown, 1973); and David C. Kozak and James M. Keagle, eds., *Bureaucratic Politics and National Security* (Boulder, Colo.: Lynne Rienner, 1988).
4. Oran Young, *The Politics of Force* (Princeton, N.J.: Princeton University Press, 1968), pp. 6–15; Charles F. Hermann, ed., *International Crises* (New York: Free Press, 1972); and Phil Williams, *Crisis Management* (New York: John Wiley, 1976).
5. Irving Janis, *Victims of Groupthink* (Boston: Houghton Mifflin, 1972), pp. 138–166.
6. Michael R. Gordon, "Cracking the Whip," *New York Times Magazine,* January 27, 1991, pp. 16ff; Bob Woodward, *The Commanders* (New York: Simon & Schuster, 1991), claims that the chairman of the Joint Chiefs of Staff preferred continuing economic sanctions to military action in the early phase of the confrontation with Iraq.
7. For the Cuban missile crisis, see Elie Abel, *The Missile Crisis* (New York: Bantam Books, 1966); Alexander L. George et al., eds., *The Limits of Coercive Diplomacy* (Boston: Little, Brown, 1971); and Robert F. Kennedy, *Thirteen Days* (New York: Norton, 1967); James Blight, *The Shattered Crystal Ball* (Savage, Md.: Rowman & Littlefield, 1990); James Blight and David Welch, *On the Brink* (New York: Farrar, Straus, 1989); and Michael R. Beschloss, *The Crisis Years* (New York: HarperCollins, 1991).

8. Gerald W. Seib, "How President Bush Deftly Orchestrated Swift Victory over Iraq," *Wall Street Journal*, March 1, 1991.

9. On mainly domestic issues, see Walter Williams, *Mismanaging America* (Lawrence, Kans: University of Kansas Press, 1990).

10. Fred Barnes, "The Hawk Factor," *The New Republic*, January 2, 1991, pp. 8–9, and Paul A. Gigot, "Bush's View: This Is Still America's Century," *Wall Street Journal*, January 24, 1991.

11. Kurt M. Campbell, "All Rise for Chairman Powell," *The National Interest*, Spring 1991, pp. 51–60.

12. Theodore Lowi, "Making Democracy Safe for the World," in *Domestic Sources of Foreign Policy*, ed. James Rosenau. (New York: Free Press, 1967), p. 301 (italics in original).

13. Phil Williams, *Crisis Management* (New York: John Wiley & Sons, 1976), p. 72.

14. Janis, *Victims of Groupthink*.

15. Ibid., p. 9.

16. Ibid., pp. 14–49; and Theodore C. Sorenson, *Kennedy* (New York: Bantam Books, 1966), pp. 326–346.

17. Williams, *Crisis Management*, pp. 79–80.

CHAPTER 9

The Bureaucratic Politics Model and Noncrisis Decisions

The bureaucratic/governmental politics model described in Chapter 8 stands in sharp contrast to the rational actor model. Different participants see the stakes in different ways and there is no objective solution to be sought. Conflict occurs both within and across the branches of government and the outcome is the result of intense bargaining. Congress, the bureaucracies, interest groups, and public opinion all play key roles—as does, of course, the president—and there is no single actor who is determinative in most cases. By focusing on the broader governmental context rather than only on presidential leadership or the bureaucratic players, the governmental politics perspective is a reminder of the broader American political system and how it influences the conduct of foreign policy. In this chapter, we shall outline how decisions are made according to this model.

We first discuss Lyndon Johnson's decision to deploy an antiballistic missile (ABM) system—and contrast that briefly with Nixon's later decision to go forward, based on rational actor logic, with an expanded ABM and the ultimate governmental decision to dismantle the entire system. The emphasis on the ABM case is on the bureaucracy. Besides being a very interesting case study of what has been called "making a decision without really choosing" (to govern is supposed to be to choose among alternative courses of action), the ABM decision remains of current interest because in 1983 President Reagan called for a Strategic Defense Initiative (SDI), a major scientific effort to come up with defensive weapons that could shoot down incoming missiles. And during Reagan's second term, the ABM treaty itself became the issue as the administration sought to reinterpret it to allow it to test components of this defensive system. Thus the issue of producing and deploying defensive weapons for protection against nuclear attack was not a new one. Indeed, the Reagan administration gave strategic defense an emphasis that it had not received before. "Star Wars" was the name the critics gave to this new stress on ABM defense, now renamed ballistic missile defense (BMD). While the focus of the original ABM is on conflict within the bureaucracy, there was none of this on SDI, for the president sprung it on the bureaucracy, Congress, and the nation; but SDI gave rise to an increasing confrontation with the Congress.

Finally we consider the Byzantine politics of energy, farm, trade, and environmental policy, all examples of intermestic policy, where the stakes are perceived as very high by all actors and there is widespread participation in decision making (see Chapter 4) but virtually no coordination. In energy, this lack of coordination fails to produce international or national energy policy for the developed nations of the world, especially the United States. Energy politics typifies some of the more extreme aspects of the bureaucratic model, particularly because participation is so widespread, very few actors have common interests, and the capacity for not reaching a decision is great. Indeed, energy policy remains more of a domestic issue because the leading industrial nations—either collectively or individually—have not been able to come to grips with the international politics of oil and other energy supplies. The same is true for the other policy areas.

The Politics of Strategic Defense: From ABM to SDI

The seven characteristics of noncrisis decision making discussed in the preceding chapter by no means exhaust the characteristics of the foreign policy process in the federal government, but they are the most obvious and are reflected in the following case study of the politics of strategic defense. In 1983 President Reagan proposed his Strategic Defense Initiative, or "Star Wars," as his critics dubbed SDI because it relied largely on space-based defenses. The program is still being funded. It has survived the end of the Reagan and Bush presidencies, the end of the Cold War, and the end of the Soviet missile threat, against which it was originally conceived. It was therefore ironic that despite the gutting of SDI by Congress, it received a new boost from the fear that states such as Iraq, hostile to the United States, will develop long-range missiles and that Washington must increasingly worry about the use of chemical or nuclear-armed warheads against friendly states or the United States itself. How did it survive the very threat against which it was proposed? A look back at the original antiballistic missile (ABM) decision made by President Johnson during the 1960s will place SDI in some perspective. That decision provides a keen insight into governmental decision making and is especially important because the ABM treaty, incorporated into SALT I, became part of the controversy over SDI. In the 1960s the United States' deterrent policy was based on a retaliatory capability. It was generally assumed that defense of either the missiles or the U.S. population was unnecessary. The deterrent forces were supposed to be invulnerable to a first strike, and, if they were, it was assumed that the people in the cities were also protected; no enemy would be foolish enough to attack America's cities if the United States could retaliate in kind. A first strike made sense only if U.S. retaliatory capability could be destroyed; therefore, as long as this force was invulnerable, the enemy would be deterred.

From time to time, however, the defense of either the population and/or America's land-based deterrent forces has been proposed and debated publicly. The first time was in 1967 when Secretary of Defense Robert McNamara made a speech that seemed to make no sense because it included contradictory themes. On the one hand, he denounced the ABM—designed to knock down incoming missiles or warheads before designated targets were hit—as an expensive venture that would stimulate another round of the arms race and leave the United States less secure in the end; on the other hand, he proposed building a "small" ABM system against the Chinese (who were verbally more radical and militant than the Soviets but had few ICBMs). To say the least, it was a strange speech, but it reflected the opposing views on defense within the government.[1]

Antiballistic Missiles: The Principal Actors and Arguments

On the anti-ABM side were McNamara and Secretary of State Dean Rusk, as well as the Arms Control and Disarmament Agency. All believed that the decision to deploy ABMs would mean a spiraling and costly arms race and would destroy all chances for a stabilization of the American–Soviet deterrent balance. McNamara believed that such deployment would virtually preclude any possibility of initiating arms limitations talks with the Soviets. He was also skeptical of the technical feasibility of the proposed ABM. The secretary, however, was in the minority within his own department on this question. The Pentagon's Office of Defense Research and Engineering, concerned with development of modern weapons, and its Office of Systems Analysis both supported development of ABMs. Within the Defense Department only the Office of International Security Affairs agreed with McNamara.

The principal bureaucratic supporters of the ABM were the armed services, which, in contrast to their situation on most defense issues, were united in their support. Although the army, navy, and air force each "saw a different face of ABM and reached different conclusions,"[2] the very fact of this interservice agreement is worth noting. Earlier, McNamara had exploited divisions between the services to prevail on issues of defense spending. Their united front, however, compelled him to go above the services and to appeal directly to the president. Different departments and, indeed, different bureaus within the various departments thus all saw different "faces" of the same ABM problems and had different stakes in the issue.

Congress too had interests and stakes in the ABM debate. Supporting the services were several senior members of the Senate Armed Services Committee, including Chairman Richard Russell, John Stennis, and Henry Jackson. These Democratic senators were supporters of Johnson's Vietnam policy and had been friends of the president when he served as the Democratic majority leader in the Senate during the administration of Dwight Eisenhower. Indeed, Johnson had served with them on the Armed Services Committee and trusted their judgment. He was particularly close to Russell.

In arguing their case, proponents and adversaries often emphasized different factors. Supporters stressed that the Soviets had already developed such a system, that it threatened the U.S. deterrent capacity, and that the ABM would save American lives. They argued that an ABM would provide Americans with an extra bargaining chip in any negotiations on a mutual defensive-weapons limitation. Opponents, however, were less concerned about the Soviet deployment of ABMs than about the potential for a new arms race. Another factor that concerned them was the price tag. Estimates of the cost of an ABM system ranged from $30 billion to $40 billion.

View from the Presidency

In the presence of these opposing pressures, no decision below the presidential level was possible. But a president's stake in any given issue is always greater than that of anyone else, and the White House perspective is different from that of any other player. For one thing, unity in the administration is a primary goal. Thus, Johnson sought to avoid, if at all possible, a direct break with McNamara. They were already at odds over the war in Vietnam, but the president still valued his secretary of defense too highly to reject his advice out of hand. McNamara viewed the ABM choice as a direct confrontation between himself and the Joint Chiefs of Staff, and he would have seen a decision to deploy the system as a rejection. In addition, a president also needs congressional support for foreign and domestic policies. A negative decision on the ABM would have alienated key senators who were also longtime friends and colleagues and whose opinions and convictions Johnson respected. But presidents are more than the chief officers of their administrations and chief architects of legislation to be submitted to Congress. They are also the heads of their parties and concerned with reelection and their parties' fortunes at the polls. The Republicans were already talking of an ABM gap, threatening to do to the Democrats what Kennedy and Johnson had done to Nixon in 1960—use the powerful charge of neglecting the nation's defenses. Johnson, who had not yet decided to forego a reelection bid, had to be worried about the possible impact of such an accusation.

But presidents must take other considerations and pressures into account as well. They know that in the final analysis they are responsible for the country's security and protection. Others can advise them, but only presidents can make the required decisions, and it is they who will be judged, not only by the people but also by history.[3] And that judgment is their ultimate stake. They will be compared with others: George Washington, Thomas Jefferson, Abraham Lincoln, Theodore Roosevelt, Franklin Roosevelt, Harry Truman. No one who occupies the White House (or its equivalent in other countries) can possibly ignore his or her future historical reputation. Johnson, whose involvement in Vietnam was already arousing popular and congressional criticism and casting doubt on his place in history, was keenly interested in a major arms limitation agreement with the Soviet Union to help his standing at that time and in the future; he needed a major breakthrough in the area of international reconciliation.

Minimal Decision Making

In this situation, given the "pitfalls" he saw in the ABM issue and the stakes he had in it, yet buffeted by conflicting pressures, the president would have preferred to make no decision at all and to allow the proponents and opponents of ABM to reach some kind of compromise among themselves. The problem of gaining presidential support for one side or another thus is not limited to the ability to reach presidents, but also includes persuading them to make decisions. Their tendency is to procrastinate or to make only a "minimal decision." "How to decide without actually choosing" is the way political observer Warner Schilling aptly put it, in connection with another important presidential decision:

> The President did make choices, but a comparison of the choices that he made with those that he did not make reveals clearly the minimal character of his decision. It bears all the aspects of a conscious search for the course of action which would close off the least number of future alternatives, one which would avoid the most choice. . . .

> One of the major necessities of the American political process [is] the need to avert conflict by avoiding choice. The distribution of power and responsibility among government elites is normally so dispersed that a rather widespread agreement among them is necessary if any given policy is to be adopted and later implemented. Among the quasi-sovereign bodies that make up the Executive the opportunities to compel this agreement are limited.[4]

Truman put this need to gain support to decide policy in fewer and more picturesque words: "They talk about the power of the president, how I can push a button and get things done. Why, I spent most of my time kissing somebody's ass."[5]

The critical question thus became: What will be the nature of the ABM compromise? At least part of the answer became clear in a meeting between Johnson and McNamara and Soviet premier A. N. Kosygin in Glassboro, New Jersey, in June 1967. Johnson pressed the Soviets for a date for the opening of arms limitation talks. This declaration would allow him to postpone the decision on the ABM. But Johnson did not receive an answer. Kosygin described the Soviet ABM system as defensive and therefore unobjectionable. As a weapon that would save lives, it was, in the Soviet premier's judgment, a good weapon that would not destabilize the arms balance and was not a proper subject for strategic arms limitation talks. McNamara's principal objection to the ABM had been refuted by the Soviets. Consequently, Johnson no longer saw the ABM as a possible stumbling block to beginning arms limitation talks.

Johnson then made his minimal decision: to adopt a small anti-Chinese ABM system. McNamara announced the decision in a contradictory speech. He said, on the one hand, that the most effective way to overcome a Soviet ABM was to saturate the defense with offensive missiles, suggesting that the Soviets could do that to the United States as well. On the other hand, should the Chinese be as irrational as their militant revolutionary rhetoric suggested, a "thin" or small ABM system might help to deter a strike. In one sense, McNamara had won a victory against the Joint Chiefs of Staff and ABM supporters in Congress, who favored a "thick" or nationwide anti-Soviet (and more expensive) ABM system. The very fact that he made the speech showed that he had by no means suffered a major defeat on this issue. He could view the president's decision as leaving open the possibility that the system would never be deployed at all if the Soviets would later agree to limitation of mutual defensive weapons. The administration had come out *not* in support of deployment but only in support of increased funding for the procurement of certain ABM parts that would require a long lead time. But the administration had publicly changed its position, and that represented a victory for ABM supporters in Congress and the Joint Chiefs. Proponents of the more extensive system viewed the change in the administration's position as a hopeful sign and expected that they could accomplish their goal later. There were as yet no "winners" or "losers." Compromises prevented that.

The fight over ABM continued into the Nixon administration. At the time, the large Soviet missile buildup, which overtook the United States in the number of ICBMs and to which there seemed to be no end in sight, was perceived as an increasing threat to U.S. ICBMs. The fear was that the number of missiles, plus the number of warheads the Soviets would place on them over the coming years, would give the Soviet Union a first-strike capability. President Nixon, therefore, switched the ABM from defending cities to defending ICBMs. This would counter the possibility of a successful Soviet strike and help keep the mutual deterrent balance stable.

Nixon also wanted a bargaining chip for the Strategic Arms Limitation Treaty (SALT). There had been no U.S. missile build-up, so he could not trade some U.S. missiles against the larger number of Soviet missiles. The ABM might be the only thing the United States could trade. As it turned out, the strategic arms limitation treaty placed a low limit on ABMs (the Soviets had already deployed about sixty around Moscow), so low that the United States abandoned it. At the same time, the two powers agreed to freeze all offensive systems for a five-year period, during which they would renegotiate mutually acceptable ceilings on all strategic systems.

Neither Johnson nor Nixon was strongly committed to a strategic defense. Johnson was concerned that the Republicans would make the lack of an ABM defense a key issue in the next presidential election, and he was also worried about his relations with his own secretary of defense and several senators whose friendship and support he needed for his Great Society domestic reform program. Nixon, in his turn, wanted a trade-off between defensive and offensive systems at a time when the public and Congress were in an antimilitary mood and the defense budget had reached its lowest percentage of the gross national product since 1950, *before* Korea.

Reagan and Star Wars

President Reagan, by contrast, was committed to a strategic defense and did not think of SDI as a bargaining chip.[6] Moreover, Reagan's advice on some sort of defensive system had come from outside the government, primarily from Edward Teller, the "father" of the hydrogen bomb. There was no pressure within the executive branch or Congress for SDI. Indeed, at the time of the president's speech proposing it, the Defense Department's assessment of a strategic defense was that it was not feasible. Many in the administration were surprised by the president's speech. The SDI conclusion to Reagan's speech had been added by the president at the last moment. The idea had not been submitted to the relevant departments for their examination, analysis, and recommendations. The president surprised most members of his administration.

This is not to say that SDI reflected a momentary whim. Reagan had expressed concern both before and immediately after he became president that the U.S.

population was not being defended. The strategic balance when he assumed the office of presidency was, in his judgment (although not that of most experts), shifting in the Soviet Union's favor. Whether or not it was, the president worried about the long-term consequences of a deterrent balance that depended on the threat of wiping out millions of Russians. He had little faith in deterrence. Nuclear weapons, instead of preventing war, would produce Armageddon, the biblical prophecy of the end of the world. Would it not be better to build deterrence on a defense that would shoot down incoming missiles and protect, rather than incinerate, the civilian population of *both* countries? And, if the Soviets were behind the United States technologically, he offered to share SDI technology with them.

SDI AND THE ANTINUCLEAR MOVEMENT.   The security of the United States was not Reagan's only reason for advancing SDI; domestic politics was another. The president was seen by many as a militant anti-Communist crusader. He and other members of his administration had made a number of careless comments about nuclear war. Moreover, members of the administration had talked of *nuclear war fighting,* of *limited nuclear war,* and of *prevailing* in a nuclear exchange, not of deterrence. Partly because of all this talk, partly because détente had ended and the United States was embarking on a major modernization of its strategic forces, and partly because the administration was clearly opposed to arms control, many people feared a possible nuclear war. The media, physicians, Catholic and Methodist bishops, and other groups made constant reference to a "nuclear winter" and "the day after"; the nuclear freeze movement gained a large public following. In these circumstances, the president was on the defensive, especially against the bishops who denounced the immorality of using, if not possessing, nuclear weapons—which, in effect, was tantamount to saying that nuclear deterrence was immoral. SDI placed the president back in charge and gave him the initiative in the nuclear debate. If nuclear war was bad for the nation's health and bad for Americans' souls, why not propose a nuclear shield that would protect the population? Why not seek mutual assured survival instead of mutual assured destruction? "Warmonger" Reagan thus stole his critics' antinuclear thunder. There was something profoundly ironic about the most conservative president in postwar history adopting the nuclear abolitionist stance of the most left-wing nuclear disarmers.

SDI 1–3.   In his speech the president proposed that SDI be able to render missiles "impotent and obsolete." A three-phase system, SDI would try to shoot down missiles while they were in their initial boost phase, lasting about five minutes; it would then try to destroy the multiple warheads after they had separated from the missiles in midphase flight (an infinitely more difficult task because of the far larger number of targets); and last, a terminal defense would try to destroy the warheads that had escaped. Nevertheless, SDI was controversial from the beginning. However shrewd a move in the context of American politics, it also suddenly undermined the deterrent basis on which U.S. and Western security had rested for four decades. Deterrence assumed that the threat of retaliation and extinction was sufficient to prevent an attack; SDI assumed that deterrence would fail. Moreover, it turned out that there was not one but three SDIs. SDI 1—the president's proposed nonnuclear population defense shield based in space—was quickly dismissed by most technologists and arms controllers. Such a futuristic system was deemed so complex and technically demanding that it was doubtful that it could offer the 100 percent protection the president had promised. Even if it were 80 to 90 percent effective—which was dubious— enough Soviet missiles would still be able to penetrate the "space shield" to destroy the United States. The point was that no matter how good U.S. technology might be eventually—and no one was likely to know that for a decade or two—it was questionable whether SDI would work perfectly the first time it was needed. Indeed, because no full-scale test of all the components could be carried out beforehand, the Congressional Office of Technology Assessment thought SDI would be a "catastrophic failure."[7]

Moreover, because the Soviets were hardly likely to accept the president's assurance that the United States would share this new technology with them so that both powers could substitute SDI for their offensive missiles simultaneously —as Gorbachev sarcastically remarked, the Americans would not even share their oil-drilling technology with the Russians—SDI was likely to stimulate not one but two arms races. One way the Soviets could seek to overcome SDI was by flooding it with more warheads than it could possibly handle. This meant a further Soviet offensive build-up, just as the United States had responded to the Soviet ABMs in the 1970s by MIRVing, or multiplying the warheads on its missiles, to inundate and thereby overwhelm any Soviet defenses. Simultaneously, the Soviets would accelerate their own SDI research. Thus, the critics said, SDI would result in offensive and defensive arms races, which would be enormously expensive and in the end leave both powers less secure than before.

SDI 2 did not create such intense controversy. Relying largely on then-or-soon-to-be-available technology (fundamentally ground based), SDI 2 was limited to missile protection. Given the large numbers of Soviet missiles and increasingly accurate warheads with their potential for a first strike, SDI 2 had some appeal. It would reduce the potential vulnerability of land-based missiles, thereby stabilizing the deterrent balance. Because such a defense was not based mainly on exotic space-based technologies, it also would be more affordable and feasible. And, unlike a population defense, a defensive capability of 50 percent would suffice. If a potential attacker knows that even half of the adversary's missiles will survive to retaliate against it, it will remain deterred. Not surprisingly, many military officers, including the Joint Chiefs of Staff (who hoped for an only 30 percent shoot-down rate) and members of Congress, skeptical about SDI 1, were attracted to SDI 2, and the Senate Armed Services Committee specifically went on record favoring this more attainable goal.

One critical difference distinguished SDI 1 from SDI 2. It was assumed that with the deployment of SDI 1, offensive missiles would be eliminated. They would become "impotent and obsolete" and therefore could be scrapped. With SDI 2, however, it was assumed that offensive missiles would remain; deterrence, rather than being abolished, would be made safer by sending the message to the other side that it cannot prevent a devastating second strike—even if it struck first. SDI 2 was also compatible with further arms control efforts.

SDI 3 was the *Soviet* perception of the president's proposal as an offensive, not defensive, system. If SDI 1 could not be made "leak proof" against an attack by thousands of warheads, a certain number of which would still be able to penetrate it to create enormous destruction, it could be effective against a retaliatory blow already weakened by the opponent's first-strike capability. This, the Soviets claimed, was what the Reagan administration was really seeking. Interestingly, the Soviet objection to SDI was the same as the U.S. objection to Soviet ABM deployment in the early 1970s. Washington had viewed the Soviet ABM as part of a first-strike strategy, since Soviet military doctrine had emphasized a preemptive strike if nuclear war appeared likely and destruction of as much of the U.S. retaliatory capacity as possible to limit damage to itself. The ABMs might then further weaken the retaliatory blow by the remnants of the crippled U.S. forces, reducing the damage to the Soviet Union even further. In fact, SDI's aims remained defensive, although the military sought to promote the use of lasers offensively against satellites.[8]

INCENTIVE OR OBSTACLE TO ARMS CONTROL?   The Reagan administration, worried that U.S. ICBMs were becoming more vulnerable to a Soviet attack, had from the outset sought a radical reduction of Soviet ICBMs and warheads to decrease this danger. But this proposal had little to offer the Soviets in return. SDI thus proved, no doubt to Reagan's surprise, a powerful counter. In part, this stemmed from the Soviet fear of SDI as part of an offensive strategy. It stemmed as well from the fear of Soviet leadership—beset with a stagnating economy at home and already unable to keep up with Western technological advances—that SDI research would result in a quantum leap forward in the very area in which the United States had a successful past and the Soviet Union did not: technological innovation. The consequences of such a forward leap would be even further setbacks for the Soviet Union technologically. Moreover, the expense of a Star Wars race would have profound consequences for the Soviet standard of living, already low.

Thus, the Soviet interest in preventing SDI deployment, or at least slowing it down and allowing Soviet science to catch up, was intense. The research could continue in the laboratories; that could hardly be prevented. But there was to be no testing or deployment of any SDI technology in space, as the two powers had agreed in the 1972 ABM treaty. SDI had thus given the Reagan administration the lever with which to gain a radical reduction in the Soviet first-strike capability. SDI, like the U.S. ABM, was potentially a very powerful bargaining chip. But while Nixon had been willing to use the ABM that way, Reagan was unwilling to do so. The president clung to his vision, talking of SDI as if it were already a reality instead of a research program that could only in ten to twenty years reveal whether SDI was even technologically feasible. Unwilling to accept any limitations on U.S. research and *testing*, Reagan rejected Gorbachev's "grand compromise" of a 50 percent cut in offensive weapons, even as his secretary of state and others were seeking to negotiate such an agreement and make it so attractive that neither the president nor other SDI supporters could turn it down.[9]

Thus, instead of being a bargaining chip, SDI became an obstacle to an arms control agreement on strategic weapons. The Soviets repeatedly stated that they should not be expected to greatly reduce the numbers of their strategic missiles when they did not know whether they had enough to cope with SDI. Again, they were merely echoing President Nixon's argument that he could not accept limits on U.S. offensive missiles until he knew whether the Soviets intended to deploy a nationwide ABM system. If the Soviets were going to deploy such a system, Nixon had said, the United States would need large numbers of missiles to penetrate this defense; if not, the United States was willing to accept an upper ceiling on missile deployment. Now Gorbachev presented Reagan with the same argument, but the president would not accept the linkage between the offensive and defensive arms races that had made SALT I possible in 1972.

It was hard to understand why the president was not more compromising on SDI, because he was not being asked to abandon his vision and the Soviets were willing to make him a good offer while SDI research could continue in the laboratories. But what the Soviets were unable to achieve, Congress did. SDI stimulated governmental politics in the form of an executive–legislative confrontation. The Congress, especially the Democrats, who controlled the House and, after the 1986 midterm election, the Senate as well, had never been enthusiastic about SDI, about whose purposes, feasibility, and costs even the administration appeared to be divided. The enormous cost of SDI at the time of a huge budget deficit was an added factor inciting congressional resistance and funding cuts after 1985. The Reagan administration had made support for SDI a loyalty test. SDI thus became a "Republican weapon." Michael Dukakis, the 1988 Democratic presidential candidate, had denounced the entire program and, although he backtracked on SDI research, he declared SDI largely a waste of money badly needed for many more pressing domestic programs.

A Bush Reprieve

The election of George Bush to succeed Reagan in the White House gave SDI at least a partial new lease on life. Conservative Republicans remained loyal to SDI, and they were a strong faction within the Republican Party. Bush, however, remained subject to the same constraints that his predecessor faced: the technical-scientific limits; the opposition from the still Democratic-controlled Senate, especially Senator Nunn, who favored only a limited system against accidental launches; and the huge Reagan-inherited budget deficit. Thus Bush was in a good position to achieve the "grand compromise" deal on missiles if he downgraded SDI from a vision to a long-term research program on the feasibility of the exotic technologies involved.[10]

In fact, that was the deal the Soviets offered the administration soon after it came into office: a 50 percent cut in strategic forces; a prior agreement on SDI would not be necessary as long as the United States did not violate the 1972 ABM agreement. This would allow START to be completed, permit Gorbachev to avoid a high-tech arms competition that would interfere with his transfer of military resources to his failing civilian economy, and allow Bush to claim that he had not sacrificed SDI. Gorbachev, of course, knew that Congress, already lukewarm in its support of SDI, would be even less likely to fund it after a START agreement reduced U.S. concerns about a Soviet missile threat to American forces, a concern that had largely disappeared anyway because of the changed atmosphere of Soviet–American relations in the wake of the Cold War.

Thus SDI, after a $24 billion investment, seemed largely a dead issue—until the war with Iraq erupted in January 1991. The Iraqis then used Soviet-made SCUD missiles to attack Saudi and Israeli urban targets; the missiles, a product of 1960s technology, were too inaccurate to use against military installations. In response, the American ground-to-air Patriot missile had dramatic successes— vividly relayed by satellite to millions of Americans watching the war unfold on their television screens—destroying many of the incoming SCUDs against Saudi Arabia and Israel. The Patriot, which was adapted by the army during the Reagan years from an antiaircraft system to shoot down missiles, admittedly was not perfect in its performance. But even its high success rate did not mean that a Patriot defense was equivalent to a major Star Wars defense against Soviet ICBMs; the SCUD travels at five times the speed of sound whereas an ICBM warhead flies at twenty times the speed of sound. The SCUDs came one at a time; Soviet warheads and their multistage missiles come by the thousands and at a high altitude. Nevertheless, the performance of the Patriot suggested that U.S. industry might indeed be able to solve the problem of shooting down a missile with another missile. Indeed, a January 1991 test firing of a ground-based interceptor destroyed a mock warhead 100 miles up in space.[11]

The point of all this was that the Iraqi attacks, launched mainly against urban targets to terrorize their inhabitants, raised the question of whether U.S. civilians did not deserve equal protection against the possibility of a future missile attack by states whose chemical, nuclear, and even biological warheads and long-range missiles were expected to proliferate. The Central Intelligence Agency has conservatively estimated that fifteen nations will acquire ballistic missiles by the year 2000. Will the threat of retaliation in these circumstances continue to deter an attack by such weapons of mass destruction? Will the Saddam Husseins, Qaddafis,* and Khomeinis refrain from using their arsenals of modern weapons as Soviet leaders did, or will their missionary ambitions lead them to take risks that less ambitious and more cautious and rational leaders would not? Should the nation therefore deploy or not deploy a defensive system so that the United States can do more than watch such incoming missiles land?

The issue of strategic defense, in short, remains very much alive in the changing strategic environment of the post–Cold War world. Only its focus may change: A possible mix of ground and space-based interceptors against a small attack of up to 100 enemy warheads, such as a deliberate Third World state attack.[12] In the words of President Bush's 1991 state of the union address, Star Wars should be "refocused on providing protection from limited ballistic missile strikes—whatever their source"—something that some congressmen, including the influential chairman of the Senate Armed Services Committee, Sam Nunn (D-Ga.), had long favored.[13] In 1991 the president's defense budget proposed $4.6 billion for SDI, $1.7 billion more than the administration and Congress had agreed upon for 1990. SDI had become the Global Protection Against Limited Strikes (GRALS). More specifically, a new generation of interceptor would emphasize two missions. The first would extend the range of an antimissile defense so that a larger area could be protected from missiles moving at greater heights and speeds than SCUDs. The second would create separate, mutually supporting layers of defense so that a missile that evades one could be attacked by another. Such a backup system might be particularly critical when the hostile warhead may be nuclear and even one miss spells catastrophe for the city at which it is aimed. The Senate Armed Services Committee version, however, would also concentrate 100 interceptors against 100 enemy warheads, and unlike SDI it would be based solely on land. Star Wars would thus come back to earth, as envisaged in the original ABM conception.[14] Also, as in McNamara's proposal at the time, the new SDI plans are for a thin defensive system. Will it at some point grow into a thick nationwide protective screen, and will its deployment—thin or thick—in fact require a renegotiation of the 1972 ABM treaty? President Bush proposed precisely this; but SDI's future now lies in President Clinton's hands. Given his focus on deficit reduction, SDI is bound to lose more funds.

Energy Policy: An Intermestic Issue

In examining energy policy at the international and national levels, we see the democratic dilemma in very straightforward terms. This intermestic policy clearly demonstrates bureaucratic/governmental politics to the ultimate degree, be-

---

* When in 1986 U.S. planes attacked Libya in retaliation for what was believed to be Libyan-inspired terrorism against U.S. service personnel in a West Berlin discotheque, Qaddafi was reported to have said that if he had possessed a missile with a range to hit New York City, he would have fired it. (See Malcolm Wallop, " 'Patriots' Point the Way," *New York Times,* January 31, 1991.)

cause virtually no participants see the stakes in the same way others do, and each is in some position to check the actions of most others. What we are studying, then, is nonpolicy making. There are no energy policies, but also there are too many such policies. We find ourselves in the situation of Buridan's ass, which found two bales of hay each so attractive that it starved to death trying to decide which one to devour. On energy policy, there are more actors, and few mind starving others if that means more of a scarce commodity for themselves. Alas, it does not, however, and what we see is a classic lack of coordination across and within the developed nations—and particularly in the United States. When so many actors become so intensively involved in an issue, conflict resolution becomes virtually impossible. When we have both national and international stakes involved, hopeless may be the only way to describe the situation that begs for international coordination.

In an increasingly interdependent world, the traditional distinctions between foreign and domestic policy making break down. For many years, policy making in such areas as energy and food was viewed as domestic in scope. There were some international implications of these policies—such as the Food for Peace program, trade quotas on specific food commodities particularly when American markets were weak, and the problem of taxing multinational oil companies. But most of the supplies of both energy and food were both produced and consumed in the United States. The energy imported from abroad was extremely cheap—and plentiful.Thus, there was little concern with the foreign policy implications of resource policy.

The price explosion for oil that followed the outbreak of the Yom Kippur War in the Middle East in 1973, when Arab member nations of the Organization of Petroleum Exporting Countries (OPEC) imposed an embargo on nations supporting the political position of Israel, setting the stage for international concern for energy prices and availability. The realization in that year that supplies of oil could be shut off and that once supplies were resumed the cost would more than quadruple transformed energy into an international issue. One direct effect was to change the positions of Japan and most Western European nations to favor the Arabs in the Middle East conflict. These countries are far more dependent on Arab oil than is the United States. Six years later, following the fall of the shah, Iran cut off oil supplies to the West and the price spiral resumed.

However, the worldwide recession of the 1980s and increased conservation led to an abundance of petroleum and the price of oil fell to as low as $8 a barrel in 1986 from the high of $36 in the early 1980s. Some producing countries that had benefited so much from the boom of the 1970s found themselves saddled with enormous debts to Western (mostly American) banks. Many could not pay even the interest, producing a different type of international crisis (see Chapter 7). Domestic producers also suffered and the economies of Alaska, Texas, Louisiana, and Oklahoma that had also boomed during the 1970s plunged into deep recessions. Prices rebounded somewhat in 1987 to about $20 per barrel.

Some analysts warned of another oil crisis by the end of the twentieth century.

By 1992 United States oil production had dropped to a post–World War II low, and the country was importing over half of the oil it consumed. Energy experts considered this level dangerously low, making the country vulnerable to an oil shutoff. The nation had not learned a critical lesson from the Gulf War—that Middle East oil was not a secure supply.[15] It is almost beyond question that oil resources will be exhausted much sooner than anyone had forecast before the 1970s. Unlike food, oil is not a renewable resource—there is not a "new crop" every year. Furthermore, while new areas of arable land can be created by irrigation or other technological breakthroughs, one cannot so easily will another oil field.[16] Energy resources are clearly now an issue of intermestic policies. The scarcity of energy resources had led Western nations to establish the International Energy Agency to pursue a joint strategy for reducing energy consumption and sharing burdens in the event of future shortages. However, domestic political considerations within each of the member nations have precluded effective action. No government can risk facing an electorate after it has agreed to give up some of its scarce energy resources. When Iran expanded its war with Iraq in 1987 and attacked neutral ships in the Persian Gulf, threatening much of the world's oil supply, the Reagan administration put eleven Kuwaiti tankers under American protection in the Gulf. However, America's Western European allies, who get far more of their oil from the Gulf than the United States does, refused to join the patrols.

The most disturbing element in facing an uncertain energy future is the set of political problems in domestic politics that dwarfs the problems in reaching agreement in international politics. One cannot expect an international energy program to be developed in the absence of agreement on a national energy strategy. But, within the United States, the political problems in confronting this issue are overwhelming. The problem is largely one of stakes. The stakes are large indeed, because energy affects everything we do—from driving to school or work to producing the energy itself and the food that sustains us all—as well as shipping that food to where we live. The amount of gasoline wasted simply when Americans throughout the country waited in gasoline lines in 1973–74 and 1979 is staggering. There also are virtually no winners in energy shortages—only different levels of losing. To be sure, the oil companies may be profiting immensely as might some other speculators or inventors. But there are few who benefit from shortages; even the oil companies might prefer greater supplies and somewhat lower prices, if for no other reason than to improve their public image. Even such diverse "capitalist" nations as Canada, Mexico, and the countries of Western Europe have either nationalized oil companies or established government controlled corporations to oversee imports because they view the issue of energy shortages as one of overwhelming importance.

But such coordination has eluded the Americans. There have been no major movements to nationalize the oil companies, but Presidents Nixon, Ford, and Carter each proposed at least one comprehensive national energy policy. None met with much success in the Congress. The reason for this lack of action is straightforward: if all politics are local, as former House Speaker Thomas P. O'Neill has maintained, then energy politics are the most local of them all. The producing areas of the South, especially Texas and Louisiana, have little in common with the consumers of the North and the West. In the first states, temperatures are mild and oil consumption is not nearly so great in the winter as it is in New England. One can drive on the wide Texas freeways and see many cars with bumper stickers reading, "Drive faster, freeze a Yankee!" In 1986–87, when oil prices fell, the bumper stickers' message was different: "Please Lord, Give Us One More Oil Boom. We Promise Not to Abuse It This Time." In the meantime, consumers in the producing states, which benefited strongly from the drop in energy prices, proclaimed that the North had risen again.

Congressional Committees and Energy Policy

Not surprisingly, the Congress has reflected these divergent local concerns. Furthermore, the jurisdictional battles in the Congress make a coordinated attack on energy virtually impossible. Congressional committees are based on jurisdictions that affect major interests in the country: Agriculture, Armed Services, Education and Labor, Banking, Veterans' Affairs, and so forth. These interests are largely, but not exclusively, unaffected directly by each other. Few farming lobbies are concerned with the fate of a housing project for New York or Cleveland. But energy is different. As stated above, it affects everyone. A gallon of gas allocated to New Hampshire means a longer wait on a line in California. So almost every committee in the Congress has some jurisdiction over energy policy. In the Ninety-fifth Congress (1977–78), eighty-three committees and subcommittees actually held hearings on some aspect of energy policy in the House of Representatives, encompassing every member of the House who serves on a committee.[17] Five committees share jurisdiction over the Department of Energy authorization—Energy and Commerce, Science and Technology, Interior and Insular Affairs, Public Works and Transportation, and Foreign Affairs. The last body has not exercised its jurisdiction, but executive spokesmen still must repeat the same testimony to four different authorizing committees in the House and then appear before the Appropriations and Budget Committees in that chamber and the Appropriations, Budget, and Energy and Environment Committees in the Senate.

An attempt to restructure and rationalize energy jurisdictions in the House failed in 1980 because key legislators did not want to yield their power over various aspects of energy legislation and convinced others that power, that goal of all politicians, was not something they should be forced to yield.

The House of Representatives generally has had a more proconsumer tilt because it better represents the more populous consuming states of the East, the Midwest, and the West Coast. The Senate provides the producers a more congenial forum since Louisiana, Oklahoma, and Alaska are entitled to the same two senators per state as are New York and California. These regional splits were reflected in many legislative battles. In 1977–78 Carter, newly inaugurated, sent to Capitol Hill the most ambitious energy program ever proposed. The new president recognized that he faced severe political problems. When he proposed the program in a televised address to the nation in April 1977, he warned: "I am sure each of you will find something you don't like about the specifics of our proposal. . . . We can be sure that all the special interest groups in the country will attack the part of the plan that affects them directly."[18] He was correct. Business leaders and conservatives generally opposed the program's emphasis on conservation rather than on production. Environmentalists found the level of support for solar energy pitifully low and objected to plans for the development of nuclear technology. Labor thought the program would cut back the number of jobs in energy related fields and feared that the proposed gasoline tax of 50 cents a gallon would affect only the middle and lower classes; it also argued that further taxation of gas-guzzling cars would take jobs away from the automobile industry—not yet fully recovered from the recession following the oil embargo and certainly not yet anticipating the even worse slump of 1980. Rural members thought the taxes would discriminate against their constituents, while urban legislators believed that the administration's plan to rebate some of the proposed energy taxes signaled an abandonment of the president's commitment to mass transit. The oil companies viewed the program as a consumer plot to keep petroleum prices regulated, but consumer groups felt that the modest energy savings that would be accomplished at great costs to everyone but industry constituted a giant ripoff by the oil companies and OPEC. The House of Representatives quickly passed the president's bill but the Senate tore the legislation to shreds. Ultimately the two chambers reached an accord much closer to the Senate's bill—a far cry from the comprehensive legislation that Carter sought.

Little changed in the next couple of years. Many pressures on Carter and the Congress to produce some national energy program continued, but no one could produce a program that was acceptable to 435 members of the House and 100 senators. Senate Majority Leader Robert Byrd (D-W.Va.) summed up the dilemma: "Energy is so divisive, because here all of the parochial—all of the parochial and regional interests surface."[19] Following the long summer of 1979 when residents of California and major cities throughout the country spent thankless hours on gasoline lines, the president proposed a *standby* gasoline rationing plan that could be implemented in the event of a national emergency—not a plan to implement rationing itself, which he opposed (and Kennedy espoused in his bid to deny Carter renomination the following year)— but again parochial, local interests prevailed on the first Carter proposal despite a most unusual plea by the speaker to members to put aside parochial interests and vote for the plan. In contrast, Representative Tom Hagedorn (R-Minn.) stated:

> I care less about supplies in the Washington area and more about the citizens of the Second District of Minnesota who would be forced to wait for their ration checks in the mail. . . . I care about the citizens of the Second District who would be forced to pay the white market value for extra coupons that could be sold in downtown Manhattan and brought out to the Midwest and sold for three to four times as much.[20]

The Energy Policy Roller Coaster

The Reagan administration came into office with a commitment to letting the open market resolve the problem of energy supply. In 1981 the memories of gasoline lines of the summer of 1979 faded as an oil glut developed throughout the world. Reagan announced in his inaugural address that the price of gasoline, subject to regulation since the cutoff of supplies following the Yom Kippur War in 1973, would now be free to find its market level. Congress in 1978 had authorized the president to take this step, but Carter felt it would be both bad policy and politically too risky in any event. As the oil companies cheered "Free at last!" they proclaimed that the days of shortages were over, since the additional revenue would allow them to tap previously undiscovered or unprofitable sources of oil. For a short time exploration efforts skyrocketed, but these were washed away by the oil glut. There were now abundant supplies and the price of gasoline actually went down considerably.

The decline in oil supplies was not the result of decontrol, but rather of the worldwide recession brought about by the fiscal policies of the Reagan administration and some Western European governments. As the oil glut grew the incentives to develop other sources of fuel vanished. Synthetic fuel experimental projects were canceled in the United States and cut back in Canada, even though they were backed by governmental loan guarantees. The Reagan budgets dramatically cut back funding for research and development of solar energy. Yet, despite the glut in both oil and natural gas, gas prices actually were increasing in many parts of the country. The Natural Gas Policy Act of 1978, part of the compromise legislation reached in that year, had produced a strange result. Even as gas was in surplus in 1981–82, gas pipelines were permitted to sell their highest cost supplies to consumers, so prices were increasing at levels almost as great as those of the years of shortages. Reagan proposed deregulating the price of natural gas, but with prices rising it is no surprise that the attempt to do so failed.

In 1986–87 when prices for all energy products plummeted, the very same producer-state representatives who had clamored for decontrol of pricing now were back in Washington begging the government to save the oil industry.

Before the price shocks of the 1970s, these producers would respond to the laws of supply and demand. If prices were lifted, more supplies would become available since producers would have incentives to seek higher profits. Yet by the late 1980s producers were arguing that energy was a distinctive commodity. The wells that had been "shut in" because they were no longer profitable could not simply be reopened. Oil wells were not like shoe stores; you could not simply reopen them when the public wanted more shoes. To shut in a well, one had to block it with cement and it was terribly expensive to blast out the cement and start pumping again. Energy was vital to national security. Producers demanded taxes on imported oil so that those supplies would become more expensive. In turn, people would use more domestic energy. This brought cries of foul play from northerners, who use more foreign than domestic oil. Northerners felt that the producing states had gouged them during the shortage years and they were not about to become suckers again. They now argued vigorously in favor of letting the market take its course. The issues had not changed—only which participants were on each side.

Congress and the Bush administration finally agreed on a "comprehensive energy act" in 1992. The situation was ripe for some action. Many legislators worried that an oil cutoff, as might have occurred had Iraq taken over Saudi Arabia before the Gulf War, would paralyze the American economy. The current oil glut produced prices per barrel that were less than half of those during the 1979–80 crisis. Steady prices meant that few people were paying attention to the energy issue. If this meant that the public was not demanding action, it also implied that legislators did not hear from irate constituents demanding that *nothing* be done that might injure them.

The legislation relaxed licensing requirements for natural gas pipelines and nuclear power plants, reformed the regulation of electric utilities, gave special emphasis to the development of vehicles that run on alternative fuels, and prohibited offshore oil drilling. The legislation was truly "comprehensive" because of its scope. Yet, critics charged that it would not do much to resolve the nation's long-term energy problems. Producers charged that the prohibition of offshore drilling would ensure continued U.S. dependence on foreign oil. Consumer groups argued that the bill did little to fill the Strategic Petroleum Reserve and added no new taxes. The reserve is the nation's emergency energy source; higher taxes, many claim, are the only way that people will conserve enough energy to make a difference. The legislation tackled all of the questions in the wide range of energy issues—except the most important ones: oil and taxes. Eli Bergman, director of Americans for Energy Independence, an interest group, commented: "The most potentially valuable provisions were the most controversial and there wasn't the will to tackle them. Senators and Congressmen will whisper that the thing that would do the most would be a $1 hike in the gasoline tax. They'll whisper it, but they won't do anything about it." The legislation did not tackle the question of long-term energy security.[21]

The crux of the domestic problem lies in the constituency politics of energy policy. International energy politics is a captive of the localism of energy policies in the nation and the states. We refuse to acknowledge that sacrifices might have to be made in the face of shortages. Half of all Americans believe that the country does not face a serious energy shortage, and just slightly more than a third believe that another energy crisis will be very likely to occur in the 1990s. Fewer than half believe that the growing use of imported oil threatens national security. In the 1992 campaign, independent H. Ross Perot proposed a 50-cent-a-gallon tax on gasoline to reduce the budget deficit and restrain consumption. Only 28 percent of Americans favored this proposal.[22]

These responses are perhaps understandable in the midst of an energy glut, but they do not augur well for a more reasoned response to the next crisis compared to the previous ones. The United States is the world's largest importer of oil and the biggest exporter of food. We could perhaps reach agreement on some national energy policy if there was any evidence that we could use the food weapon as OPEC has employed the oil weapon, but this is highly questionable because such a small portion of our food exports go to OPEC nations. If such a strategy existed, we could find some way of reaching agreement on a national policy to determine how to allocate the new gains from our agricultural surplus, and we could reconcile such a strategy with the international political environment, since we export so much of our food to our allies and to Third and Fourth World nations, which would then face very high prices for both fuel *and* food. Could such a strategy bankrupt the national economy on which all nations, but particularly the dominant economic powers such as the United States, Europe, and Saudi Arabia, depend for their prosperity or simple survival? The international energy problem is not likely to be resolved in the immediate future despite the compelling need to do so. But the interconnections between domestic and international considerations makes the political problem seem even less tractable than the technological one.

Agriculture: A Domestic Issue Gone International

There were hard times on American farms in the 1980s. Movies starring Jane Fonda, Jessica Lange, and Sissy Spacek have described the new traumas of farming families much as *The Grapes of Wrath* did for the Great Depression of the 1930s. The farm economy has not been as depressed at any time since the 1930s as it was in the 1980s. Twenty years ago we heard threats of imminent famine throughout much of the developing world. Yet today the problem is not one of shortages, but one of *surpluses*. Saudi Arabia is giving away wheat it cannot store, China is exporting corn, and the small African state of Malawi is trading maize.[23]

The world has experienced a "green revolution" over the past two decades.

New technologies have led to dramatic increases in production of many food commodities. When countries grow their own foodstuffs, they have less need to import them. As recently as the 1970s, agriculture was the largest single contributor to America's trade surplus.[24] Since 1981 agriculture exports have declined from their high of $44 billion to about $26 billion in 1986. In that year the United States imported more food than it exported for the first time this century. The American share of the market for all agricultural commodities has fallen by more than 20 percent. Wheat, feed grains, and soybeans have been hit particularly hard.[25] Increased production is only one reason for the decline in American food exports. A second cause is the Third World debt. Countries that have severe financial constraints simply have to cut back on their export purchases. Often they lack the Western currency to make the purchases. These developing countries had been the fastest growing market for American agricultural exports.

A third cause is more aggressive pricing policies by other nations. Japan, Canada, Argentina, Australia, and the European Economic Community all subsidize their agricultural products to make them more competitive in the international market. In 1985 the United States began using farm export subsidies as well, although the government had been indirectly subsidizing agriculture for many years.[26] Fourth, during the 1970s the high inflation induced by spiraling energy costs actually worked to the benefit of farmers. Their prices also dramatically increased, aided in part by poor Soviet grain harvests. The United States Department of Agriculture urged farmers to augment their own production. To do so, many farmers bought more land and expensive equipment to aid in planting and harvesting. When world supplies surged and demand remained steady—or declined in the developing countries—farmers were faced with massive debts. By 1986, 20 percent of farm loans had been declared "nonperforming" (or essentially uncollectible), as opposed to just 5 percent three years earlier. Farm income had plummeted and the average value of farmland dropped by almost 30 percent.[27] Movies about farmers once again focused on bankruptcy foreclosures.

There were calls for the government to step in to save the family farm. There was nothing new about this proposal. Government has been involved in the agricultural economy for three quarters of a century. The philosophy of government assistance for the farmers was to stabilize prices, the same logic that led originally to government controls on natural gas prices a half century ago.[28] By paying farmers to withhold excess supplies from the market, the government ensured that prices did not fluctuate wildly from one year to the next. This strategy not only provided farmers with a secure income, but also protected consumers from large swings in their grocery bills. By 1986, however, the disarray in world markets had resulted in a government bill of $26 billion compared to just $4 billion in 1980. Yet the depression in the agricultural sector continued. There were signs of improvement in 1987, but the prognosis for a long-term recovery was poor.[29]

Agriculture stands in contrast to energy, then. Most experts predict a sharp rise in energy prices in the 1990s, but farm exports are expected to remain depressed. The difference is one of shortage versus surplus. Yet, despite these distinctions, the politics of the two intermestic issue areas are rather similar.

Both energy and agriculture traditionally have been regarded as domestic issues. Throughout American history, most of our energy has been produced domestically. Yet domestic oil sources account for just half of our consumption. We have historically produced most of our own food. Indeed, even though we now import slightly more than we export, the United States still sells about 30 percent of its farm products abroad. Both commodities have now been internationalized. While the United States has long imported energy from abroad, the price was so cheap that nobody paid any attention to the issues of international politics that might be raised. Indeed, there were few such questions to be answered, as price fixing for energy is a phenomenon of the 1970s. Similarly, before the 1980s the major question that Americans confronted in the agricultural arena was how to maintain the country's position as the world's dominant exporter. For both sets of commodities, all of this changed dramatically.

Like energy, agriculture has produced a politics in which traditional coalitions have broken down. Historically, agricultural politics in the Congress have been marked by cooperation. Legislators from agricultural districts, particularly those in the South, have supported urban aid programs for northern Democrats in return for the lasts' votes on government price supports for commodities. It was particularly critical for the farm bloc to maintain a united front. In recent years, however, northern Democratic support for farm programs has slipped and the farm coalition itself has fallen apart.[30] Consider the following remarks by two Democratic members of Congress, the first from the urban Northeast and the second from the farmbelt in the Midwest.[31]

> In my part of the country, if an industry can't cut the mustard they close down. Do we have too many farmers? Do we have $25 billion a year thrown at a problem that has no solution?

> We should reduce the exposure to the taxpayer. And the way you do that is to increase the exposure to the consumer. God forbid that the consumer should have to pay 1 percent more of his disposable income for food.

Not only has the urban-rural coalition for farm support split, but so has the farm bloc itself.

Different commodities face disparate problems—and a host of alternative farm programs has been proposed ranging from massive new subsidies to the Reagan administration's suggestion that all federal farm aid be phased out. These alternative policies have split the commodities that had been essential for the enactment of previous farm bills. Cotton, rice, dairy, tobacco, peanuts, and sugar interests, for example, opposed legislation that would limit how much farmers would be permitted to grow, while wheat farmers strongly backed the idea. The dairy interests themselves lost many of their subsidies in a 1981 bill; corn growers (who produce sweeteners that compete with sugar) joined the chorus of interests who argued for sharp cutbacks in sugar subsidies that were set at three times the world price.[32]

The economic troubles for agriculture in the 1980s renewed, at least temporarily, the coherence of the farm coalition. The U.S. government spent $133.5 billion in farm subsidies in the 1980s as exports fell. In 1986 government subsidies for rice exceeded the value of the crop.[33] The Department of Agriculture spent $566 million that year to export food at a loss and $3.3 billion to induce farmers to leave their land idle.

Agriculture in the Mind of America

Why did the American public go along with such high levels of farm supports at all? How did the $26 billion get approved in the first place when on energy the Congress seemed tied up in knots? The answer is simple: while Americans have little love for oil companies, they idealize farmers. They cling to the myth of the "yeoman farmer" who played such a prominent role in the development of the American frontier.[34] The same Americans who refused to believe that the energy shortages of the 1970s were real expressed concern that farm failures might lead to inadequate levels of food; they were willing to assist farmers if it meant increasing taxes; they said that farmers were more honest than other Americans; and half of the public even expressed the desire to live on a farm. Furthermore, people from the city were even more likely to support aid to farmers than were rural residents.[35] However, as the problem got worse with no end in sight, the coalition began to fall apart. Despite the sympathy for the farmer, people and their representatives in Congress quickly began to worry about the costs of this policy, particularly at a time when the federal deficit was such a problem.

The farm problems, however, were not restricted to the United States. World agriculture was in crisis and other countries that compete for markets with the United States were sending similar amounts to protect their own farmers: $23 billion by the twelve-nation European Economic Community and $15 billion by Japan alone.[36] In 1986, with the Republicans facing difficult Senate races in the farm states, the president overrode his own philosophical objections and agreed to sell the Soviet Union 3.85 million tons of subsidized American wheat. Reagan certainly recalled how unpopular the wheat embargo imposed by Carter in 1979 following the Soviet invasion of Afghanistan had been. Indeed, repeal of the embargo was one of the new president's first acts on taking office in 1981. But such actions only reinforce the same problem of collective action as in world energy supplies.

Each national leader looks after his or her own constituents. Thus, although every leader recognizes that all would do better by eliminating subsidies, each worries that his/her country might be the only one to do so. This would lead to a loss of market share for the country following "wise" policy and an increase in sales for the other countries. Only if everyone agreed to cooperate to eliminate subsidies would *anyone* agree to do so. But the political costs of doing so, especially if others fail to comply, would be very high indeed. Since world leaders have no way to ensure that even their allies would stand by any agreement reached, no accord is likely. This is precisely what didn't happen at the Venice economic summit in 1987. All seven of the leaders of the major Western economies—the United States, Great Britain, France, Canada, West Germany, Japan, and Italy—went into the meeting promising an agricultural agreement. With little fanfare, they emerged without one.

Trade disputes on agriculture have strained relations among the industrialized nations since the 1950s.[37] The United States and the European Economic Community fought over the importing of American poultry in the 1960s. There have been continuing battles with Japan over access to the Japanese market for American beef, citrus, tobacco, and especially rice. American farmers have charged that Canada and Australia subsidize their wheat growers to permit them to undercut U.S. prices on the world market. Agriculture policy has been among the most contentious of all trade issues: Between 1974 and 1989, almost 40 percent of all "unfair trade practice" petitions filed with the U.S. trade representative dealt with agriculture, even though farm exports constitute less than 10 percent of all American exports. While overall tariff levels have fallen from over 40 percent in 1947 to less than 5 percent today, agricultural levies have not declined significantly.

Each national leader looks after his or her own constituents. Thus, although every leader recognizes that all would do better by eliminating subsidies, each worries that his or her country would be the only one to do so. This would lead to a loss of market share for the country following "wise" policy and an increase in sales for the other countries. Only if everyone agreed to cooperate to eliminate subsidies would *anyone* agree to do so. But the political costs, if others fail to comply, would be very high. U.S. Trade Representative Carla Hills commented, "I am absolutely against trade-distorting subsidies, but will not unilaterally disarm."[38]

Farmers account for a small share of the economy and the work force in the major industrial nations. Yet, they have extracted large shares of government assistance (see Table 9.1). The United States heavily subsidizes its few farmers, but pays out relatively less than the European Community and substantially less than Japan. The Japanese government subsidizes a network of small farmers who are substantially less efficient than their competitors in the United States or Western Europe. It protects the farmers by restricting the imports of a wide range of goods, but conflicts with the United States have been particularly harsh over beef and rice. Two-thirds of the Japanese farmers' income stems from government subsidies.

TABLE 9.1   Agriculture in the Industrial Nations

	United States	European Economic Community	Japan
Farming as share of Gross National Product	2.0%	3.9%	3.0%
Farmers as percentage of work force	3.3%	7.5%	8.9%
Share of farm income attributable to government intervention, 1982–86	26%	33%	66%
Cost to farm sector of hypothetical trade agreement (in billions)	$16.2	$22.7	$21.8
Reduction in output from hypothetical trade agreement	1%	7%	32%

SOURCE: Robert L. Paarlberg, "Agricultural Policy," in Robert Art and Seyom Brown, eds., *U.S. Foreign Policy: The Search for a New Role* (New York: Macmillan, 1993), pp. 195–196.

The hypothetical trade accord proposed at the Venice summit would drastically cut farmers' welfare and lead to reduced agricultural production. While output would shrink by just 1 percent in the United States and by 7 percent in the European Economic Community, it would fall by almost one-third in Japan. No wonder it has been so difficult to reach an accord on farm subsidies! Any nation can block an international accord by refusing to sign. Japan's farmers are politically powerful; they support the governing Liberal Democratic party, which has been increasingly challenged by both the Socialists and various "clean government" slates. Alienating the farmers would be most precarious in Japan. European governments are not quite so dependent upon farmers' support as Japan's. Yet, they have often held office by slender margins and could not afford to alienate farmers.

Farmers in the United States are no longer quite so pivotal in most political contests. Only 46 congressional districts (of 435) were "farm oriented" in 1988: In such districts at least one-third of counties derived 20 percent or more of their total income from agriculture.[39] However, farmers can be critical in Senate elections, which are often quite competitive. In 1986 the Democrats regained control of the Senate by winning nine Republican seats while losing just one of their own. Six of the new Democrats came from states hit particularly hard by the farm crisis of the 1980s (Alabama, Florida, Georgia, North Carolina, North Dakota, and South Dakota). Farmers clearly blamed the Bush administration and the Republican party more generally for their economic woes. Farmers thus have clout beyond their numbers—and the Congress has responded with generous price supports. By 1989, 82 percent of growers of crops such as wheat, corn, and rice received government subsidies, accounting for about one-third of their total income, up from 8.1 percent in 1980. Payments to these farmers grew from 7 percent of the crops' values in 1980 to 57 percent in 1986.[40]

An unusual coalition of liberals and conservatives tried to slash farm subsidies in 1990, but could not prevail in the Congress. Nevertheless, a five-year, $13.6 billion cut in farm subsidies was enacted that year. What happened? The budget deficit had grown out of control. The president and Congress both lost public confidence when they could not reach an accord to reduce spending and raise taxes. After the embarrassment that came from temporarily shutting the entire federal government down, they reached a budget agreement that slashed agriculture subsidies. Why focus on the farmers? The liberal–conservative axis that tried to cut price supports split the agriculture coalition. The economic crisis in agriculture eased. And public support for farmers fell by 8 percent from 1987 to 1990, making agricultural assistance one of the least favored public expenditures.[41] The place of farmers in American public opinion was no longer quite so special.

After the United States cut subsidies, it pressured its allies to follow suit. Japan refused to budge, but the European Community agreed to do so in 1992. Facing high employment rates and soaring budget deficits, governments felt that they had to respond to broader constituencies than the farmers. The economic unification accord slated to take effect in 1993 dictated more uniform policies. The accord was strongly challenged by French farmers, who dumped produce in market towns, stranded almost 300 pigs aboard a truck before they were set free to devour watermelons that had been left behind, and engaged in violence. Together with truckers protesting new safety regulations, the farmers strangled French daily life for over a month.[42] The longer-term prospects for an agricultural accord remained bleak. Leaders of the seven major industrial powers failed to achieve a breakthrough in reducing subsidies and easing import restrictions at their annual economic summit in July 1992. Even in the United States, which positioned itself as the leader in cutting subsidies, price supports remained considerably higher than they were two decades earlier. Shortly after he lost the election, President Bush threatened French farmers with 200 percent tariffs on white wine unless the European Community agreed to reduce subsidies on oilseeds. The EEC soon capitulated, but French President Francois Mitterand, whose own popularity had fallen dramatically, blocked the accord. French farmers once more took to the offensive to protest American demands: They blockaded entrances to Coca-Cola bottling plants and McDonald's restaurants and tore down a street sign for Woodrow Wilson Avenue in Paris. With increased competition throughout the world, each country will naturally seek to protect its own farmers first.

Trade: The Ties That Bind Everyone Up

Few issues have been as divisive in the 1980s and 1990s as trade. The energy crisis of the 1970s led to billions of dollars sent abroad to pay the increasing petroleum bills of American consumers. The problems of agriculture in the 1980s led to decreased American exports of foodstuffs. There were depressions in sectors of the economy such as timber, lead, aluminum, and zinc. American raw materials and manufactured goods were no longer competitive either in world markets or even in the United States. Wages in the United States are among the highest in the world and the costs of extracting raw materials and producing manufactured goods are correspondingly great. In contrast, in developing nations both sets of costs are much lower. In other developed nations, especially Japan, government subsidizes much of the research and development costs of manufacturing.

In both cases, the producing countries have what economists call a *comparative advantage* over the United States. Because their costs are lower, so are their prices. As Third World nations have been developing their industrial bases, they have become more important players in the international political economy. Their emergence has hurt the United States in two important ways. First, the simple fact of cost advantage makes American raw materials and manufactured goods less competitive. Few have failed to notice the flood of imported electronics consumer goods, clothing, and shoes—among other products—in American stores. Second, increasing production by developing countries means that more goods are entering the marketplace. In several important arenas, there already was more than sufficient production to meet world demand. The entry of new producers glutted the market. The high inflation and the booming economy of oil producers in the 1970s spurred tremendous growth in the manufacturing sectors.[43] This alone would be sufficient to depress prices. Automobiles, steel, semiconductors, and petrochemicals are among the industries that have been particularly hard hit, with excess production in the range of 15 to 30 percent in the mid 1980s.[44] However, because American costs of production are higher than those of most other nations, the overcapacity hurts the United States more than most.

In 1950 the United States produced 40 percent of the world's goods and services. Three decades later the percentage had dropped almost in half—to 22 percent. Germany had replaced the United States by 1986 as the world's leading exporter, with Japan close behind.[45] The United States had lost as many as two million jobs related to exports from 1980 to 1986, even as total employment in the nation increased by 10 percent. What had been trade surpluses turned into trade deficits.

Why the Trade Deficit?

The causes of the trade deficit are hotly debated. Some argue that the very large budget deficits are the most important factor in the imbalance of trade. The budget deficits mean that the United States government has to borrow money to pay the interest on the debt. This increases interest rates by the financial institutions that lend the money. In turn, inflation rises, making foreign goods relatively cheaper than goods produced in the inflated American economy. A related explanation is the high value of the American dollar relative to other currencies. When the American dollar is overvalued, it is cheaper for consumers to purchase goods produced abroad. Third, a frequently heard argument is that American workers are not as productive as their counterparts in other countries. There are cries that both workers and corporations care more about maximizing their salaries and profits than they do about the quality of their products. Consumers who want excellent quality, then, will seek out goods made abroad. Fourth, the decline of manufacturing in the United States is held to be part of a more general shift in the world economy. Developing countries will continue indefinitely to have cost advantages in manufacturing. The economies of the developed nations, and especially that of the United States, have been moving for at least two decades toward service industries. This service sector includes technology (computers, computer programming, and other high-tech areas), information/entertainment (publishing, television, movies), and recreation (restaurants, hotels, resorts, etc.), among others.

Fifth, many countries have been accused of unfair trade practices. The United States has charged that Japan was "dumping" semiconductors on the American market—subsidizing these computer chips so that Japanese companies could sell them to American wholesalers and retailers below the cost of production. In addition, Japan and other countries have not opened their markets to exports in the same way that the United States has done. Some domestic industries in these countries are directly subsidized by the government. Other practices include either outright bans on importing commodities or manufactured goods and very high tariffs on these goods that would make imports noncompetitive with domestic products. Both Japan and West Germany, for example, restrict the import of telephone equipment. Japan also places barriers on rice, while Norway, Sweden, and Finland, worried over plant parasites, ban American softwood.[46]

In the mid-1980s the strong economy led to rising demand for consumer products, most of which are now manufactured abroad. The trade deficit reached a record $159.5 billion in 1987. Since then it has fallen consistently, reaching $73.6 billion in the 1991 recession—the first time it had dropped below $100 billion since 1983. Yet the deficit with Japan is increasing at the same time. In 1981 the United States became a debtor nation for the first time this century. As the budget deficit ballooned to over $400 billion, foreign debt grew even as the trade imbalance shrank.

Each of these explanations has its supporters and detractors. We shall not consider them here. But just as there is little agreement on why the trade deficit has grown, there is also no consensus on what to do about it. There are noncontroversial proposals to establish commissions that would study how to make America more competitive by producing superior products. No one is against better quality. Yet few would agree that making American products better would resolve the trade deficit. There is less consensus on what to do about the other possible "causes." Noting that there has been a long-term shift in the nature of the American economy away from manufacturing jobs does not tell us what we can do to redress the balance of trade. Should we attempt to preserve our manufacturing base, as some have argued,[47] or ought the United States to "recognize reality" and find a new way to compete?

Politicians find it far easier to place the blame on other nations than on themselves. Almost all elected officials agree that it is important to reduce the nation's budget deficit, but few want to curtail programs that would hurt their constituents. Thus members of Congress seek ways to reduce the trade deficit without cutting the budget deficit. Similarly, bringing down the value of the dollar in relation to other currencies would certainly bring about inflation. Americans would have to pay more for imported goods simply because the dollar buys fewer yen than it previously did. So a video cassette recorder made in Japan with salaries and production costs paid in yen will cost more in dollars when the dollar's value fails. Consumers thus would react *against* the sort of policies designed to reduce the value of the dollar. Yet the expectation is that a dollar that is no longer overvalued would entice other countries to increase their purchases of American products. This would stimulate the economy and reduce unemployment. A drop in the value of the dollar might not be sufficient to have a measurable impact on the balance of trade.[48] Could the United States wind up with inflation without more trade?

The idea of other countries' subsidizing their industries and restricting imports is also controversial. Many in the Congress argue that without import barriers, other nations would import much more from the United States than they already do. On the other hand, the Japanese maintain that their consumers do not purchase American products because the United States does not produce the type of goods that Japanese consumers want. Should the United States impose tariffs on other nations to redress the trade balance or might this make the situation only worse? Representative Dan Rostenkowski (D-Ill.) stated:

> Trade is becoming very, very parochial. It's employment, it's our jobs. Legislators, whether they want to be international or national, when there's nobody working at home, become very local.[49]

It is far easier for politicians to place the blame for the trade imbalance on other nations than on America's own problems. Television advertisements featuring prominent entertainers exhort Americans to look for labels stating that the product was made in the United States. Even President Reagan, a strong opponent of trade barriers, imposed restrictions on the number of Japanese cars imported into the United States and placed tariffs of up to 100 percent on electronics components in 1987. He responded to political pressures in 1986 and agreed to subsidize American wheat sales to the Soviet Union. President Bush, who has called protectionism "a smokescreen for a country that is running scared,"[50] nevertheless has supported key restrictions on Japanese trade. He backed Super 301 and the Structural Impediments Initiative in 1989 (see below). He also traveled to Japan in 1991 and threatened to close markets if the Japanese were not more forthcoming on trade.

Americans are ambivalent on trade. A variety of surveys from 1970 to the present indicate that between 60 and 70 percent of Americans favor restricting imports and increasing tariffs. They believe that other countries compete unfairly with the United States. Americans are even willing to pay higher taxes if that is the cost of trade barriers. They are particularly incensed by foreign purchases of major American firms (such as Sony's buying Columbia records, and the acquisition of Rockefeller Center by Mitsubishi, the purchase of the Seattle Mariners by the American subsidiary of Nintendo).[51] President Clinton promised during the 1992 campaign to block a merger of USAir with British Air. Perot railed against foreign ownership of American companies in 1992 and promised to end foreign lobbying.

We tend to see the trade world as an almost exclusively Japanese–American battle. Canada is the United States' largest trading partner, but almost 70 percent of Americans believe that Japan is number one. Almost two-thirds of Americans hold that Japanese trading practices are unfair, more than double the share holding that view about the European Economic Community and nine times the number who say that about Canada. Almost 60 percent of Americans say that Japanese real estate purchases are a threat to the United States, and nearly 40 percent claim that Japan is trying to dominate the world. Yet, in 1989, Japan's direct investment in the American economy was just 17.4 percent of all foreign stakes, whereas Europe's was 65.4 percent.

Americans single out Japan because they see her as the principal threat to their economic leadership. More Americans believe that Japan is now the world's leading economic power and that her advantage will grow in the next century. Yet they overwhelmingly say that they hold Japan in high esteem and that Japan's success is attributable to a strong work ethic and better technology. The Japanese have stronger family values, work harder, have a better education system, are more productive, and have higher standards for quality. Americans buy imported cars, mostly from Japan, because of quality, not because of special advantages from their country of manufacture. Americans thus seek retribution, while simultaneously accepting most of the blame for their fall from economic predominance.[52]

While placing the blame abroad *appears* to be a politically astute move, the consequences are not beneficial for all. Senator Robert Packwood (R-Ore.) noted that 10,000 people in his state work in the automobile import business in such jobs as unloading Japanese cars from ships: "When anyone talks about restricting imports, they are talking about losing jobs in Oregon."[53] States and localities are actively seeking foreign markets, as we noted in Chapter 7. Much that is familiar is now foreign: Shell Oil is owned by a Dutch–British consortium, Hardee's by Canadians, and even the American National Can Company is French. So while lawmakers have proposed restrictions on foreign investments, they have rarely succeeded. A 1988 law gave the president the power to restrict foreign takeovers, but only on national security grounds; the law received a critical test in 1992 when the Thomson firm, partly owned by the French government, was refused permission to buy LTV's aerospace division. Greater restrictions proved elusive. Foreign investments remained inviolate, but other pressures for protection found a more receptive audience.

Those who worry about the impact of sanctions fear a spiraling trade war. Sanctions imposed by the United States on Japan would lead to similar actions by Japan on the United States; this would lead to further restrictions by the United States on Japanese products and the process would continue indefinitely. In 1986 the United States and the European Economic Community narrowly averted such a trade war over agricultural goods, including Italian pasta. Sanctions make goods more expensive for consumers so that continued rounds of such reactions would raise inflation for all consumers. We have another problem of collective action, much as we found on energy and agriculture. Everybody would be better off if there were no trade barriers at all, that is, if there were what economists call *open markets*. However, once one nation imposes some restrictions—be they government subsidies on computer chips or agricultural products or tariffs or even outright prohibitions on imports (as Japan bans American baseball bats to protect its own domestic industry)—then every other nation will see its best interest in doing likewise. Thus, we are likely to wind up with all countries imposing barriers on each other—making everyone worse off than if all markets were open.

The president and Congress implemented two strong actions against Japan that were seen as departures from the traditional norms of enhancing trade. "Super 301" required the executive branch to single out discriminatory trading partners and to threaten retaliation if they did not remove commercial barriers. The Structural Impediments Initiative (SII) looked at deeper, or "structural," causes of trade imbalances, such as the purchasing practices of Japanese firms, the work and leisure habits of the Japanese people, and public expenditures by the government. Japan reacted sharply to both initiatives and invoked its own "SII," challenging the high budget deficits in the United States, the lesser quality of education and labor training, and the lack of an American long-term strategic plan for the economy.[54] As in other intermestic politics, there is a clear-cut strategy for actors in international politics to pursue: open markets. Yet, pressures from domestic constituents lead politicians to deviate from that course.

Open or Closed Markets?

American trade policy has wavered between promoting open markets and seeking protectionism through trade restrictions and high tariffs. The last major protectionist legislation was the Smoot-Hawley tariff of 1930, which many said caused the Great Depression. Since then, Congress has followed the presidential lead in pushing for more open markets in the world economy. American trade policy has taken as its principal objective the lowering of existing tariff barriers. After World War II, the industrialized nations formed the General Agreement on Tariffs and Trade in 1947 to coordinate trading practices and to work toward open markets. The support for these policies from 1930 through the 1970s was often overwhelming.[55] Congressional decisions reflected the prevailing consensus among economists that open markets promoted economic growth.[56] The nation's business executives, strongly influenced by the prevailing economic theories, also provided consistent support for free trade. As the U.S. position in the world economy shifted, so did the views of many business executives. While only 15 percent favored some type of import restrictions in 1980, this figure jumped to 38 percent in 1982 and to 44 percent three years later.[57] Obviously, elite opinion reflects the regional split in public opinion. Those people living in states such as the industrial Midwest where manufacturing has been particularly hard hit by imports were much more likely to support restrictions on trade than those in states that have been the pioneers in the service industries (the Southwest and some southern states).[58]

The post-1930 consensus on free trade has broken down and legislators are struggling to find a way out of the trade dilemma. The import deficit may be the greatest threat of all to maintaining the standard of living of Americans. With no apparent resolution to the American budget problem, legislators have turned their attention to restricting imports. Democrats have taken the lead in pushing for retaliation, arguing that workers in industries in America's heartland—the Northeast, the industrialized Midwest, and manufacturing communities in some areas of the South (especially the Carolinas and Tennessee)—have been hurt by foreign competition. Labor, a traditional ally of the Democratic party, has been at the forefront of the movement to impose tariffs and other sanctions on countries with low-paid work forces and nations that block American imports. This is a reversal of the party's historical role in the post-1930 era. Under Kennedy, some of the sharpest cuts in tariff rates in American history took place. The Republicans have been split, largely along regional lines. Reagan, as noted, has strongly opposed any restrictions on free trade. Yet Republican members from states or districts that have been adversely affected by imports have joined the Democratic chorus for strong legislation. When a subsidiary of the Japanese electronic firm Toshiba sold sensitive military equipment to the Soviet Union, Republican members of Congress took the lead in pursuing retaliatory measures against the parent company. Senator Jake Garn (R-Utah) proposed banning all imports of Toshiba products into the United States, while three Republican House members staged a demonstration outside the Capitol in which they smashed several Toshiba electronics products. The restrictive trade bill that passed the Senate in July 1987 garnered unanimous Democratic support, but also 40 percent of the votes of Republican legislators.

The Congress enacted a protectionist trade bill in 1986 with support from both the Democratic-controlled House of Representatives and the Republican-controlled Senate. The president vetoed it and the issue came up again in 1987 after the Democrats had won control of the upper house. While some Democrats interpreted this victory as a mandate to enact a strong trade bill—and polls showed the public as more supportive of restrictions than even two years ago— they nevertheless feared that the situation could get out of hand. First, they worried about retaliation from exporters. Should there be an all-out trade war and the worldwide economy go into a deep recession, Democrats feared that they might be blamed for this downturn. Second, they worried about specific industries attempting to write the bill to their own specifications. Steel, oil, textiles, and footwear firms, for example, were seeking special protection. Were they to succeed, they might set off a massive scramble for a similar action by many other industries and thus lead to a bill more protectionist than anyone wanted.[59] The conflict became exquisitely complex as sectors that a protectionist bill was designed to protect found themselves worrying about possible adverse affects. Wheat growers, for example, complained about subsidized exports from Canada and Argentina, yet feared that tariffs on other items might provoke European retaliation against American wheat. So did the Computer and Business Equipment Manufacturers Association, which also found itself straining under competition from Japan and Korea.[60]

Trade affects everything. The intermestic issues that are particularly contentious share this trait. So everyone has a position and every congressional player wants to get a piece of the action. In the Senate in 1987, nine committees considered the legislation. The Finance Committee has primary responsibility for trade legislation. The Judiciary panel prepared a section protecting American patent rights overseas; the Governmental Affairs Committee was concerned with reorganizing the executive branch to place a greater emphasis on competitiveness; the Department of Agriculture sought to expand farm subsidies; Labor and Human Welfare proposed to assist workers who lost their jobs through layoffs; the Foreign Affairs Committee examined proposals to enhance Third World investment through international agencies; the Banking, Housing, and Urban Affairs Committees restricted the right of foreign (almost exclusively Japanese) brokers to act as the primary agents in buying and selling government securities unless American agents receive reciprocal rights; the Department of Commerce wrestled with blocking foreign takeovers of American corporations; and the Small Business Committee added segments directing itself to place more emphasis on exports. The large number of actors indicates just how complex the politics of trade are—and how difficult it is to enact legislation that would command a majority of both houses of Congress. The bill that passed the Senate in 1987 was filled with special interest provisions such as (1) $300 million in rebates to sugar refiners for tariffs paid between 1977 and 1982; (2) $39 million for tobacco export promotion; (3) restrictions on imports of lamb, pork, strawberries, and steel fence panels; and (4) an amendment requiring that all imported food products be labeled as such.[61]

The stock market crash of October 19, 1987, temporarily derailed protectionist pressures. Many economists were concerned that a trade war with nations that had fewer economic worries might send the market into a free-fall that would invoke a recession or even a depression. (The protectionist Smoot–Hawley tariff of 1929 was blamed by many for the Depression.) The next year Congress enacted a trade bill that was considerably less protectionist than the 1987 proposal. Reagan vetoed it, but ultimately let it become law. The pressures were renewed the following year, when President Bush agreed to the congressional proposals on Super 301 and the Structural Impediments Initiative (see above).

Yet, trade policy was not all protection. In 1988 and 1991 Congress took steps toward more open markets. First the Congress approved, with just a handful of negative votes, a major free-trade accord with Canada. In 1991 there was strong bipartisan support for an expanded North American Free Trade Agreement that would also include Mexico. Even Representative Richard Gephardt (D-Mo.), who sought the 1988 Democratic presidential nomination on a protectionist platform, joined the vast majority of representatives and senators in giving the president "fast-track" authority to negotiate an accord with Mexico and Canada. Under the "fast-track," the executive can conclude an accord without intervention by Congress. The legislature reserves the right to reject the agreement or to insist upon modifications, but only after the negotiations have concluded. Congress and the president were willing to eliminate tariffs on Canada (and presumably also Mexico) because Americans do not see it as an unfair trading partner: Just 7 percent of Americans argue that Canada's practices are inequitable to the United States.[62]

The issue became politicized in 1992 when Gephardt reversed his stance and called for tariffs to underwrite retraining of American workers who lost their jobs under the accord and to pay for the cleanup of Mexican plants that pollute. Labor and environmental groups strongly opposed the deal. Together with congressional Democrats, they pressed presidential nominee Clinton to oppose the agreement. Clinton nevertheless endorsed the accord, but promised to amend it to provide for retraining and environmental assistance to Mexico.

Presidents have historically championed free trade, while support for protection has been greatest in Congress.[63] Executive behavior does not always match rhetoric. Even the most ardent supporters of free trade—such as Nixon, Reagan, and Bush—have backed strongly protectionist measures.[64] Trade has historically been a partisan issue, with Democrats supporting tariff reduction and Republicans favoring protection—until the 1970s. Then the parties shifted positions, even though significant portions of each party still held their historical stands. This switch partly reflected the changing views of the party's constituents. Organized labor, which had long backed tariff reduction, switched to protection in the 1970s when foreign competition endangered American jobs. Big business shifted the other way. It used to worry about foreign competition, but now it is more concerned with opening export markets. Yet the parties changed positions *before* their major constituents did. The Republicans became associated with the message of free trade, even if they did not always follow it, as part of their overall strategy of becoming the party of prosperity. The Democrats forsook the message of economic growth that had been the hallmark of their success in favor of protecting the status of groups that were hurt by increasing international competition (labor union members, minorities, the poor). Free trade leads to economic growth, and the party seen strongest on maintaining prosperity is the one that promises open markets.[65] The 1992 campaign marked a shift toward less protectionism among the Democrats; the challenge in the Republican primaries by columnist Pat Buchanan saw the reemergence of protectionism in that party. The antifree trade banner was carried in 1992 by H. Ross Perot.

The Environment: A New World Order?

Few issues have risen so quickly on national agendas, or created as much controversy, as the environment. What started as a domestic issue, initially in the United States, quickly became a worldwide movement. Even though political movements vary dramatically from one country to another, ecological problems cannot be contained within geographical boundaries. Pollution knows no borders. The environment now has a prominent place on the international stage. Representatives from 178 countries attended the Earth Summit (the United Nations Conference on Environment and Development) in June 1992. They heard warnings that further economic development might bring about an ecological catastrophe, that the deterioration of the earth's ozone layer would lead to widespread skin cancer and climatic change, and that cutting down tropical rain forests would unleash noxious carbon dioxide into the common air space of all humanity.

The conference produced few concrete results, largely because of domestic political considerations in developed and developing nations. Most industrialized nations (the "North") favored strong action to limit pollution, especially in the rapidly growing industrializing nations in the Southern hemisphere. The South responded that it could not afford the enormous costs of the cleanup. It demanded that the North bear the expense for maintaining biological diversity and reducing pollutants. Alone among the industrialized nations, the United States refused to go along, even though public support for environmental regulation was at least as strong as in any other country.

The modern environmental movement began in the United States with the celebration of Earth Day in 1969, launched largely by the counterculture. Ecology became a mainstream concern in the next decade, as politicians of all stripes jumped aboard. The Clean Air Act of 1970 was enacted by a Democratic Congress and a Republican president, with few dissenting voices. In the 1980s and 1990s environment had become a contentious issue. Public support for strong environmental policies was as high as ever. The two-party consensus evaporated, as Republicans under Reagan and Bush saw ecological regulations inhibiting economic growth.

Environmental politics in the United States, unlike that in most other countries, has been contained within the two-party system. Throughout Europe, the issue has become the preserve of Green parties. The Greens reject compromise and espouse a wide range of countercultural values. They have been most successful electorally in Germany, where they have held the balance of power in several state legislatures. They won 2500 seats in the 1989 French local elections, up from 300. Greens more than doubled their share of the vote in Great Britain in 1992 after winning 15 percent of the British vote in elections to the European parliament. They have pressed for the elimination of fossil fuels. Half of all voters in the European Economic Community say that they might vote for a Green party.[66]

Environmental politics in the United States has historically been a consensus issue. While the contemporary ecological movement began in the 1960s very much along the lines of protest politics, the issue has a much longer and rather different history. Environmental protection was salient to upper income moderate Republicans in the late nineteenth and early twentieth centuries. The wealthy owned vast tracts of land and wanted to preserve them from environmental damage. One of the earliest public exponents of environmentalism was Theodore Roosevelt. "Conservation," as it was called then, comes from the same root as "conservative." Preservation of ecological quality was hardly a radical idea. The early environmentalists wanted to protect not only land, but also birds and furry animals. The most prominent traditional conservation organizations were the Sierra Club and the National Audubon Society, both of which maintained—and still do—conservancies. The ecology movement throughout the world was devoted to conservation. The largest movement in England was the Royal Society for the Preservation of Birds. Almost all international treaties prior to 1954 dealt with restrictions on the killing or selling of migratory birds. One of the few exceptions was the 1911 accord on the preservation of fur seals, which has not been strongly enforced.[67]

The rise in environmental consciousness in the 1960s led to sharp increases in the memberships of traditional organizations. From 1968 to 1972 the Sierra Club doubled its membership, while the increase was threefold for the Audubon Society. Newer, more confrontational associations came into being: Environmental Action, the Environmental Defense Fund, Greenpeace, and Friends of the Earth. They focused more on air and water pollution, the protection of endangered species, nuclear energy, energy-environmental trade-offs, toxic wastes, and similar issues. The older societies were reserved, the new ones were media conscious.

Environmental Action started a trend in American politics in 1970 when it rated members of Congress on their ecological voting record and selected a "Dirty Dozen" of incumbents to be targeted for defeat. Pressure from public opinion and these new interest groups led to a spate of new institutions—the

Council on Environmental Quality and the Environmental Protection Agency—and legislation. Congress enacted the National Environmental Policy Act in 1969, the Clean Air Act Amendments in 1970, and the Federal Water Pollution Control Act of 1972. Sometimes there was a rush to action in the drive to make policy catch up with public opinion: The Clean Air Act Amendments of 1970 set standards that scientists did not know how to implement and that bureaucrats could not readily regulate.[68]

According to David Vogel, "the United States has made measurable progress in reducing emissions and ground concentration levels of both particulates and sulfur oxides" so that "by 1980 almost all air pollution control regions had met the [Environmental Protection Agency's] primary standards for these two hazardous pollutants." Automobile emissions have significantly fallen since 1970. Between 1977 and 1980 ambient lead concentrations fell 64 percent in a ninety-two-city survey. The number of days with unhealthy air pollution levels dropped by more than 50 percent (and even more for "hazardous" days) between 1974 and 1981. While two-thirds of the states reported "generally improving" water quality to EPA in 1982, ameliorations in rivers and streams have been offset by deteriorating lakes and reservoirs.[69]

By margins as large as 74 to 21 percent Americans say that "protecting the environment is so important that cost is irrelevant."[70] Over 80 percent hold that pollution is a serious problem. Despite considerable evidence of progress, most Americans remain unconvinced that much has been done. Two-thirds believe that the environment is worse than in 1970; only 16 percent say that it has improved. Three-quarters believe air pollution has deteriorated, only 6 percent that it has gotten better. The figures for water quality are similar: 80 versus 8 percent. There is a need for concerted action: Over 90 percent say that the United States should use its position to get other nations to join in taking action on world environmental problems.

Growing concern and pessimism led to increased, and more strident, demands for action on environmental problems. The early environmental legislation did not provoke much conflict, perhaps because few foresaw how complex and strict the regulations stemming from the 1970 Clean Air Act Amendments would be. Environmental politics in the United States became increasingly confrontational.[71] Business interests sought the effective dismantling of the Environmental Protection Agency and were almost successful under Reagan. Secretary of the Interior James Watt and Environmental Protection Agency head Anne Gorsuch Burford tried to dismantle the regulatory regime until public pressure forced them to resign.

Environmental organizations similarly "believe that they thrive on conflict and cannot successfully raise funds from their constituent groups without portraying the other side as an implacable foe."[72] Radical environmental organizations forsake the political process: Earth First employs violent tactics to protect older trees against loggers. Even the more traditional interests such as the Sierra Club have resorted to confrontation.

Charges beget countercharges. Have we resolved most of our fundamental environmental issues, or is ecological doomsday around the corner? Must we trade in our automobiles for bicycles, or is the real challenge to give more people in the developing world the blessings of modern technology? Most people have little idea, in part because the issues are so technologically complex but also because neither side in the debate really talks to the other. Eighty percent of Americans agreed in 1990 that "there are so many contradictory things said about the environment that it is sometimes confusing to know what to do."[73]

Confrontation increases public attention to problems, but it also makes them more difficult to resolve. The environment remains a consensual issue among the public, but elected officials are now split along partisan lines. Democrats favor strict environmental regulations. Republicans worry that stringent require- ments will stunt economic growth. President Bush and the Congress finally reached an accord on extending the Clean Air Act Amendments in 1990, but could not agree on a strategy for the Earth Summit in Rio de Janeiro. The parties also split over a 1990 California referendum, "Big Green," that would have banned all pesticides found to cause cancer in laboratory animals, protected redwoods, prohibited offshore drilling, and taxed oil companies to pay for fu- ture oil spills. The electorate, tired of competing scientists charging each other with creating "hysteria," rejected the proposal.[74]

The contemporary environmental movement may have begun in the United States, but neither public concern nor contention is unique to America. The early conservation movement was more prominent in Great Britain.[75] Other Europeans, especially the young, have become more environmentally conscious since the 1970s. More so than Americans, Europeans accept the notion that there are limits to growth and that economic development must be restricted to control pollution. Some of the most dramatic conflicts have occurred on the issue of nuclear energy, as activists throughout Europe (including England) have tried to close power stations. Environmentalist pressures have led to re- strictions on coal mining and burning and on automobile emissions throughout Europe.[76] The onset of the unified market in 1993 will make regulations both stronger and more uniform.

Environment in the International Arena

Environmental regulation has largely been the preserve of national governments in the industrialized world. International coordination has not been quite so prominent. A biosphere conference was held in Paris in 1968. An international convention on trade in endangered species was signed in 1973; signatory coun- tries have contributed voluntarily to a trust fund to protect flora and fauna since 1980. The convention also banned dumping of toxic materials in the ocean, established a moratorium on the hunting of whales (which several Scandinavian countries abrogated in 1992), and established a United Nations program on the environment. Half of all U.N. specialized agencies now deal with ecological problems.[77] Recent years have seen greater progress on international coordination on the environment, but not without domestic politics playing a major role. The failure of the Earth Summit in Rio to enact binding accords is directly traceable to domestic concerns in the United States.

A major breakthrough on world environment problems occurred in 1987, when 28 nations signed an accord in Montreal calling for a 50 percent reduction in ozone depletion by the year 2000. A 1989 conference called by British Prime Minister Margaret Thatcher drew 123 nations and agreed to phase out ozone-depleting chlorofluorocarbons (CFCs) and halons entirely by the end of the century. (CFCs and halons are the chemicals used in refrigerators.) The ozone layer is a protective shield that prevents the sun's rays from wreaking havoc. The United States Environmental Protection Agency estimated that continued dissipation of the earth's ozone layer would lead to 150 million cases of skin cancer and more than 3 million deaths by 2075; there would also be 18 million additional cases of cataracts, many of which would lead to blindness. Substantial crop losses have already occurred, especially for soybeans. The weakened ozone layer also has led to increased urban smog.[78]

Domestic politics almost scuttled the accord.[79] The United States, Canada, and Norway took the lead in pressing for expanded action, while Britain and France, major manufacturers of halon, initially resisted. American support was never assured. Backing strong action was an unlikely coalition of environmentalists and chemical companies, joined by the State Department. Opposing the ban were conservative forces within the Reagan administration and Representative John Dingell (D-Mich.), chair of the Energy and Commerce Committee. In 1974 the largest American manufacturer of CFCs, duPont, pledged that it would press for a ban if evidence showed that these chemicals damaged the ozone layer. Three major producers—duPont, Allied Chemical, and Pennwalt—felt that American regulations had put them at a competitive disadvantage against their European counterparts. By 1987 duPont led the business interests in pressing for a ban, citing studies that confirmed the harm done by CFCs and halons. Activists had succeeded in getting legislation adopted or introduced in New York, California, Michigan, Minnesota, and Oregon. The chemical firms preferred a uniform international policy, even if that meant the substitution of new chemicals for CFCs and halons.

Dingell, one of the most powerful members of Congress, objected to the accord because he represented a Detroit district in which automobile companies were major employers. Car and truck manufacturers feared that substitute chemicals would not be readily available for vehicle air conditioners. The Office of Management and Budget, White House science advisor William Graham, and the Departments of Commerce and Interior also opposed the Montreal protocol. Interior Secretary Donald Hodel was not worried about the ozone layer: "People who don't stand out in the sun—it doesn't affect them." He suggested that others wear broad-brimmed hats and sunglasses. Hodel's comments backfired. They brought about an outcry from environmentalists and gave the upper hand to Secretary of State George Shultz, who favored a strong accord. The unified support of environmentalists, the chemical industry, and the State Department was too powerful for the isolated band of strong conservatives. Faced with American backing, the British and French capitulated and the accord was signed.

Protecting the ozone layer was relatively easy compared with the rest of the international agenda. Not only was there an unusual coalition of environmentalists and business within the United States, but the problem was manageable. CFCs and halons were manufactured largely in the developed nations, which also were responsible for almost 90 percent of consumption. Other issues, which would be addressed at the 1992 Earth Summit, were far more difficult. There were diverse national agendas and pressures.

The Rio meeting was billed as the first international meeting to discuss the full gamut of international environmental issues. The most salient topics included (1) the spread of carbon dioxide in the atmosphere and the consequences for climatic change; (2) conservation of tropical rain forests; (3) the preservation of biological diversity, especially in the developing world, and who would benefit from the benign exploitation of biodiversity; (4) shifting energy consumption away from fossil fuels; and (5) who would pay the enormous bill for all of these good works. Some observers believed that the most critical issue was one that the Rio conference largely overlooked: the population explosion in the developing world. The South needs to create a billion new jobs by the end of the decade just to keep up with population growth. At some stage the planet would simply run out of room for all of these people: By 2100 there could be 13 billion people on the earth, compared with 5 billion now. A more immediate problem was that we would all choke to death from the pollution caused by so many people. Most of the South rejected even discussing population. So did the Vatican, the Islamic states, and feminists who charged that male-dominated governments should not determine women's priorities.[80]

None of the issues that the conference tackled had anything like a consensus, so it was remarkable that the summit came as close as it did to an agreement. American domestic politics derailed action on climatic change, biological diversity, and protection of the rain forests. Even though the United States seemed to stand outside an international consensus, that accord was considerably more fragile than public posturing indicated. Many countries left Rio griping to the press, but relieved of facing powerful constituencies back home.

The most contentious issue could never be resolved: Who would pay the costs. The meeting's official document, Agenda 21, called for a worldwide effort amounting to $125 billion a year, more than double the $55 billion in all aid to developing nations. The South could not possibly afford even a token contribution; as of 1989, developing nations' debt constituted 44 percent of their total Gross National Product. To pay back their Northern creditors, they are exporting their natural resources. Twenty-three of thirty-three timber-exporting countries will exhaust their supplies by 2000. They will be left with a reduced economic base and few trees to enrich the soil and soak up greenhouse gases (see below). Developing nations argue that it is their turn to enjoy the fruits of economic growth. If the wealthy North wants to save the environment that it is largely responsible for polluting, it should pay the bill. India and China delayed phasing out CFCs and halon until industrialized countries picked up the cost. Edward Kufuor of Ghana, former chair of the Group of 77 developing nations, justified this strategy: "Those who make $200 a year should not pay so that those who make $10,000 a year can breathe clean air."[81]

Why the expense of $125 billion a year? Environmentalists argue that the world is facing an ecological crisis. While world food production has been rising, population has been climbing faster so that between 1985 and 1989 per capita harvests fell in ninety-four countries. The world fish catch fell by 4 million tons in 1990—for the first time in two decades. Thailand banned commercial logging in 1989 after a landslide from denuded hills destroyed the homes of 40,000 people. Canada predicts that the older, taller trees in its logging province, British Columbia, will vanish in the first decade of the twenty-first century.[82]

Burning fossil fuels—oil and coal, in particular—leads to increased carbon dioxide emissions. Carbon dioxide in turn leads to rising world temperatures (global warming) and to acid rain. Higher temperatures—of up to 9 degrees—could lead to the melting of polar ice caps, causing sea levels to rise and flooding cities such as New York, London, Shanghai, and Tokyo. The tiny island nation of Tuvalu in the South Pacific is only five feet above sea level; its leaders feel that the entire country could, like the fictional Atlantis, sink below the sea. When temperatures change, so do rainfall patterns. Deserts may bloom, but fertile fields may become fallow. Carbon dioxide levels in the atmosphere have risen 20 percent over the past century. Additionally, sulfur dioxide exhausts from cars, trucks, and coal-fired power plants mix with water vapor in the atmosphere, yielding "acid" rain and snow far from their sources. Acid rain can kill lakes, destroying fish and other parts of the ecosystem, and trees.[83]

Acid rain is not the only danger to trees. Tropical rain forests soak up these "greenhouse" gases and are being destroyed at the rate of 42.5 million acres a year, a rate more than 50 percent greater than a decade and a half ago. These forests also are the habitat of more than half of the world's species. Tropical nations such as Malaysia, India, and especially Brazil (the Earth Summit's host) have been cutting down the rain forests to build cities and provide grazing land for cattle. The trees and the insects, plants, and microorganisms they host offer great promise for medicine. Bark, wasp glands, snake venom, spider webs, and ant hill matter may provide cures for cancer, diabetes, and AIDS. Some scientists worry that up to one-fourth of the planet's species may become extinct over the next half century. The effects on the total ecosystem are unknown. Each species occupies a niche in the overall system, and we don't know what the consequences of losing any might be.[84]

The Rio meeting set out to tackle these diverse issues. How could the world cut back on the use of fossil fuels to reduce carbon dioxide emissions and limit global warming and acid rain? How could it protect rain forests? Who would pay, and who would own the rights to new pharmaceuticals developed from the rain forests' species? The most divisive issue was the division of costs. Japan took the lead in offering support from an industrialized nation. It backed a German proposal to stabilize all carbon dioxide emissions at 1990 rates by the year 2000 and pledged $1.45 billion a year for the next half decade, an almost 50 percent increase in its foreign aid. Stung by charges that it did not pull its weight in the Gulf War, Japan sought to assert a leadership role on the environment.[85]

European nations backed the German proposal to limit carbon dioxide emissions. The European Economic Community proposed a stiff tax on oil, starting at $3 a barrel and reaching $10 a barrel by 2000 (oil currently sells for under $20 a barrel). The Germans, the Dutch, and the Danes took the lead on oil taxes, dragging the reluctant poorer nations of the Community—Spain, Portugal, and Greece—along. The same North–South split that emerged over the larger question of costs divided the Community; the poorer nations were more concerned with economic growth. The Saudis, who long have urged the industrialized world to conserve energy, successfully fought the tariff, which they called ''yet another form of excise tax to raise government receipts.'' The revenues of the oil exporters, especially the Saudis, would plummet if consumers used less energy as the price went up.[86]

The poorer nations were unenthusiastic about taxes that would ultimately raise the price of oil by 50 percent. They perceived these levies, together with pressures to reduce greenhouse gases to protect the environment and preserve biodiversity, as demands by the North that the South forsake development in favor of ecological purity. People in the richer countries already had refrigerators and automobiles. Why should Chinese and Indians forsake the benefits of modern technology? The North used more energy than the South even though its share of world population was much smaller (see Table 9.2). The United States was the world's greatest energy hog and its biggest polluter. Poorer countries contributed far less to the world's carbon dioxide levels. The industrialized countries admitted this, but they were worried about what might happen when the South became wealthier. People in large cities in China already wear surgical masks on the street to protect themselves from urban smog. If China and India were to industrialize along the Northern model, the worldwide plan to reduce pollution would be sabotaged.[87]

The South also demanded that the industrialized world pay to protect the tropical rain forests and share in whatever bounty came from exploiting biodiversity. Merck, the world's largest pharmaceutical company, paid Costa Rica $1.3 million in 1991 for a two-year experiment to see whether insects, plants, and microorganisms from the country's forests could yield materials for medical research. The American firm would maintain intellectual property rights and most profits, but Costa Rica would share in the royalties. The draft biodiversity

TABLE 9.2 Energy Consumption and Pollution: North and South

Nation	Percent World Population	Percent Carbon Dioxide Emissions	Energy Use (Metric Tons)
United States	4.7	22.3	5.4
Japan	2.3	4.8	2.3
Germany	1.5	2.9	2.9*
China	21.0	10.9	.6
India	16.0	3.0	**
Indonesia	3.6	.6	**

* Figure for West Germany only.
** Not reported.
SOURCES: William K. Stevens, "Rio: A Start on Managing What's Left of This Place," *New York Times*, May 31, 1992, p. E6; and Michael Weisskopf, "Rust-Belt Emissions Cloud Earth Summit," *Washington Post*, June 2, 1992, p. A8.

treaty would give the host country control over property rights and require an equitable sharing of profits.[88]

The North–South conflict ultimately became a battle between the United States and the rest of the world. The Bush administration fought all of the major proposals, motivated by both ideology and domestic political concerns. Many conservatives, including the president, were not convinced that an ecological disaster was at hand. Some scientists argued that it was unclear whether world-wide temperatures have been rising faster now than they have for billions of years, before modern technology spewed out carbon dioxide throughout the world. Even if temperatures are rising, the net impact may be benign: Warming and increased precipitation may make some lands fertile that heretofore were barren.[89]

Bush saw the Rio summit as an effort by the developing nations to force the North, especially the United States, to pay for the Third World's problems and to extort Western technology. He offered more American aid, proposing to double assistance for forest conservation to $150 million, but far less than other industrialized nations wanted to give. The president also objected to the biodiversity treaty, charging that it did not protect the intellectual property rights of U.S. pharmaceutical firms. The firms that develop the new medicines should retain the patents, regardless of where the discoveries occur.

The president perceived his Western allies, and Japan in particular, as being hypocritical in pushing for an activist agenda:

> Japan's out there killing whales and running driftnets, for God's sake, while we've got the world's toughest environmental laws and we're twisting ourselves into knots over how many jobs to abolish [in the logging industry] to save a subspecies of an owl. And these guys presume to lecture us about environmental responsibility?

The president's critics charged that Japan and Europe had done much on environmental regulation and that Germany outpaced even the United States in some areas. They also found his concern for the spotted owl suspect since the administration had tried to override the Endangered Species Act that protected the bird against loggers.[90]

Conservatives also see a trade-off between regulations and economic growth. Directives that mandate environmental cleanups cost firms money and in turn inhibit job creation. The president said: "I will not sign a treaty that in my view throws too many Americans out of work," especially in the midst of a recession. Do environmental regulations cost jobs? Some suggest not: The directives have led to the establishment of 70,000 cleanup firms, employing two million Americans, with $130 billion in sales. After firms' initial investments in new technology have been absorbed, reducing greenhouse gases will produce more efficient use of energy and higher profits.[91]

Critics of the president charged that ideology played a smaller role in his decision to reject most of Agenda 21 than domestic political concerns. Bush's concern for the economy stemmed less from ideology—after all, he promised in his 1988 campaign that he would be the "environmental president"—than from poor economic performance in the United States and his own political problems. Economic growth in the first three and a half years of Bush's presidency was slower than in any administration since the end of World War II. Fifty-five percent of Americans disapproved of Bush's handling of the environment, while just 31 percent approved; 19 percent said that the president had made progress on the environment, and 70 percent said that he just talked about the problem without taking action. Only 9 percent expected the Rio summit to produce substantial results. Facing a three-way race for the White House, Bush was ready to concede the environmental vote to Democrat Bill Clinton to secure Republican loyalists in the South and the West and "Reagan Democrats" throughout the country. The former are ideological conservatives and the latter care more about jobs than the environment.[92]

The Democrats actively courted the environmental vote. Vice presidential candidate Albert Gore had written a scholarly book about a pending ecological disaster. Bush called him "Mr. Ozone" and charged that the Democrats were more interested in the spotted owl (an endangered species) than in jobs. The president turned out to be half right and half wrong. Voters who said that the environment was one of the two major issues that decided their choice cast almost three quarters of their vote for Clinton and Gore and just 12 percent for Bush. Yet the Democrats also beat Bush by more than 2–1 among voters most concerned with jobs.

The conferees ultimately agreed to a variety of documents, including the controversial biodiversity treaty that Bush refused to sign, but President Clinton accepted. The United States agreed to a global warming treaty curbing greenhouse gases, but insisted that carbon dioxide targets be voluntary rather than mandatory. All other documents were nonbinding statements of principles.

Great Britain and Germany joined with the United States in opposing firm monetary commitments. Developing countries lamented the North's lack of generosity. Friends of the Earth called the summit "a failure."[93]

Of all intermestic issues, ecological ones are perhaps most critical to international politics. Pollution knows no national boundaries. Greenhouse emissions from one country may travel throughout the world. Environmental concerns increasingly impinge on foreign relations. Canada and the United States have battled for more than two decades over acid rain issues. The North American Free Trade Agreement has become embroiled in questions of air and water pollution emanating from Mexico's low-wage manufacturing plants along the United States border. Yet ecological concerns are central to domestic politics in many countries. As with agriculture, environmental groups hold the balance of political power in many countries. Progress on international accords has thus been very difficult and subject to the same problems encountered in achieving collective action on agriculture. Because the stakes are even higher in the environment than in agriculture and public concern for the ecology is more widespread, progress is even less likely even with a president and vice president committed to an environmental program.

Bureaucratic/Governmental Politics and the Democratic Dilemmas

Crisis politics is marked by executive-led politics. It also provides the strongest public support for presidential leadership. Most of the citizenry perceives one policy as the "correct one." In crises, then, the democratic dilemmas are often resolved by default. Yet it is the strong presidency of crisis politics that gives rise to the "imperial presidency" of noncrisis periods. The weak Congress of crises becomes the bulwark of public opinion against the president who has gone too far. In bureaucratic politics, however, things are rarely that straightforward. Few people see the stakes in the same light. On issues that are primarily international, presidents must confront a fragmented bureaucracy. On intermestic issues, they must deal with a Congress divided along the lines of constituency interests. It is difficult to determine what the "correct" policy is—and even if one can do that, achieving it might not be so easy.

Even on strategic issues such as the ABM, SALT II, and the Strategic Defense Initiative, there is no consensus on what ought to be done. Different actors see the stakes in alternative ways—and these cannot be divorced from the domestic political issues involved in the decisions. Not only do the various services and branches of the foreign policy bureaucracy (the State Department versus the Defense Department, for example) have alternative perspectives, but so do members of the Congress and candidates for the presidency. In 1980, Carter responded to the Soviet invasion of Afghanistan with a ban on wheat sales to the U.S.S.R. Reagan, usually the hawk, reacted sharply in a bid for the farm vote and promised to repeat the embargo if he were elected. He did so on inauguration day in 1981, pleasing midwestern farmers whose markets had otherwise been shrinking.

In 1986, Nunn—also generally regarded as a hawk—led the opposition to the administration's interpretation of SALT II that would permit SDI deployment. Many observers argued that what motivated Nunn was not simply a concern for an arms control agreement, but also domestic political factors. On the one hand, the Democrats had regained control of the Senate in the 1986 elections and as chair of the Armed Services Committee, Nunn would be acting as a party spokesman. On the other hand, Nunn was considering running for the presidency in 1988 and his overall conservative voting record would not sit well with many Democratic activists. By taking a strong stand on the SALT II limitations, he could take a major step in establishing better relations with the mainstream of his party.

While crisis policy making points to the benefits—and potential dangers—of a strong executive leading the way on foreign policy, bureaucratic/governmental politics emphasizes checks and balances. The more bureaucratic policy making resembles domestic bargaining, as on intermestic issues such as energy and agriculture, the less powerful a president is to dictate the outcome. The chief executive is stronger on those issues—including the intermestic policy of trade—that more directly involve other nations. Yet even on these the chief executive must confront an often unruly bureaucracy or a divided Congress. The president becomes less a dictator and more a referee.

Even when presidents seem to get their way, as Bush did on the Rio de Janeiro Earth Summit, they may be still quite constrained. Bush did prevail at Rio, but largely because Congress had no direct role in setting U.S. policy. The domestic response to the environment bears more a congressional imprint than an executive one. The 1990 Clean Air Act Amendments extension was largely shaped in Congress. A reluctant White House, prodded by public opinion, signed on to the legislation.

When we cannot readily agree on what the "right" policy is, the question of process versus output may be reduced to which actor we wish to have more power. Do we favor open markets because we believe the president should have the flexibility to negotiate tariff rates? Or do we favor presidential power on trade because we believe in open markets? Would Democrats be so concerned with the conditions under which a president followed—or did not follow—a treaty that a Democratic-controlled Senate refused to ratify (SALT II)? Had the public been more willing to go to war against Iraq, would the Democratic Congress have pushed so hard for a vote authorizing the conflict?

Crisis decision making is of necessity policy formation by a small elite. Bureaucratic decisions involve a wider range of actors. Intermestic issues on which the public might become energized involve an even larger number of actors than policy decisions that focus on more than bureaucracies. Ecological politics may be the most inclusive intermestic issue: Forty-six percent of Americans claim to contribute money to environmental groups regularly or occasionally.[94] There is a potential for stalemate on bureaucratic and intermestic issues. Does that mean that crisis decision making is preferable? The failure to reach agreement on contentious intermestic issues should not lead us to believe that crisis decision making would work better on these questions. During the 1970s we called the policy problems on energy *crises*, much as many call environmental problems today. But this didn't do much to affect the way we make—or don't make—energy or environmental policy. Nor did the labels *agricultural crisis* or *trade crisis* result in fewer groups demanding to have a say. As the environmental struggle suggests, the more intense the conflict and the greater the public concern on an intermestic issue, the *more* actors we can expect to find.[95] Bureaucratic/governmental politics are more democratic, but is more democracy always desirable in foreign policy? If you say no, recall how the expansion of presidential authority beyond the "crisis arena" in the Watergate scandal led to a long ordeal in which the fundamental aspects of presidential accountability underwent severe challenge.

Notes

1. This section relies heavily on the account by Morton H. Halperin, "The Decision to Deploy the ABM: Bureaucratic and Domestic Politics in the Johnson Administration," *World Politics*, October 1972, pp. 62ff. For the development of the ICBM, see Edmund Beard, *Developing the ICBM* (New York: Columbia University Press, 1976).
2. Halperin, "Decision to Deploy the ABM," pp. 67–69.
3. Morton H. Halperin, *Bureaucratic Politics and Foreign Policy* (Washington, D.C.: Brookings, 1974), pp. 81–82.
4. Warner R. Schilling, "The H-Bomb: How to Decide Without Actually Choosing," in Morton H. Halperin and Arnold Kanter, eds. *Readings in American Foreign Policy* (Boston: Little, Brown), pp. 253, 255.
5. Quoted in *Time*, January 25, 1968.
6. For the background of SDI, see Ashton B. Carter and David N. Schwartz, eds., *Ballistic Missible Defense* (Washington, D.C.: Brookings, 1984); and Philip M. Boffey et al., *Claiming the Heavens*, subtitled "The *New York Times* Complete Guide to the Star Wars Debate" (New York: Times Books, 1988). Two anti-SDI books are Sidney Drell, Phillip Farley, and David Holloway, *The Reagan Strategic Defense Initiative* (Cambridge, Mass.: Ballinger, 1985); and Robert McNamara, *Blundering into Disaster* (New York: Pantheon, 1986). Two pro-SDI books are Zbigniew Brzezinski et al., *Promise or Peril* (Lanham, Md.: University Press of America, 1986); and Keith B. Payne, *Strategic Defense* (Lanham, Md.: Hamilton Press, 1986). Also see Harry Waldman, *The Dictionary of SDI* (Wilmington, Del.: Scholarly Resources, 1988) for the terminology of SDI. For historical and Soviet perspectives, among other issues, see Samuel F. Wells, Jr. and

Robert S. Litwak, *Strategic Defenses and Soviet-American Relations* (Cambridge, Mass.: Ballinger, 1987). The Congressional Office of Technology Assessment reports, the second one of which is very critical, may be found in *Strategic Defense Initiative* (Princeton, N.J.: Princeton University Press, 1988). The economic aspects are examined in Rosy Nimroody (for the Council on Economic Priorities), *Star Wars* (Cambridge, Mass.: Ballinger, 1987).

7. Warren E. Leary, "Report Depicts 'Star Wars' as an Unworkable System," *New York Times,* April 25, 1988.

8. William J. Broad, "U.S. Promoting Offensive Role for 'Star Wars' " and "Military to Ready Laser for Testing as Space Weapon," *New York Times,* November 27, 1988 and January 1, 1989, respectively.

9. See Strobe Talbott's *The Master of the Game* (New York: Knopf, 1988) for details of the "grand compromise" negotiations and the progress made during the Reagan administration. Also see Lou Cannon, *President Reagan* (New York: Simon & Schuster, 1991), pp. 163–171, 287–292, 219–333 for Reagan's early obsession with strategic defense.

10. Talbott, *Master of the Game.*

11. William J. Broad, "In Test, 'Star Wars' Hits Warhead in Space," *New York Times,* January 30, 1991.

12. William J. Broad, "A New Course for 'Star Wars' from Full to Limited Defense" and Eric Schmitt, "Republicans Split Over 'Star Wars,' " *New York Times,* January 31 and June 15, 1991, respectively.

13. "President Bush's State of the Union Message to the Nation," *New York Times,* January 30, 1991. Yet questions about the success of the Patriot missiles began to surface after the war. See, for instance, Bob Davis, "Patriot Missile, High Tech Hero in Gulf, Comes Under Attack as Less Than Scud's Worst Enemy," *Wall Street Journal,* April 15, 1991.

14. William J. Broad, "As Anti-Missile Era Dawns, Planners Eye Panoply of Weapons," and "Anti-Missile Plan Exploits Controversial Technology," *New York Times,* February 5 and July 30, 1991.

   The Senate plan would require renegotiation of the 1972 ABM treaty to allow for five or six sites, instead of two, for added protection. For Senator Nunn's defense of the Armed Services Committee plan, "Needed: An ABM Defense," ibid., July 31, 1991. For a critical evaluation, raising some of McNamara's original criticisms of a thick defensive shield, see Tom Wicker, "Shades of Sentinel," ibid., August 4, 1991.

15. National Petroleum Council, *Factors Affecting U.S. Oil and Gas Outlook* (Washington: National Petroleum Council, Department of Energy, 1987); Joint Economic Committee, *The 1987 Joint Economic Report,* 100th Congress, First Session, March 5, 1987; and Thomas Lippmann, "U.S. Oil Output at Lowest Level in 30 Years," *Washington Post,* June 17, 1992, p. A11.

16. There are some new developments in the field of superconductivity that promise great energy savings and hence may revolutionize the field of energy.

17. These data were compiled by the United States House of Representatives Select Committee on Committees, 1979–80, and are reported in Eric M. Uslaner, *Shale Barrel Politics: Energy and Legislative Leadership* (Stanford: Stanford University Press, 1989), chap. 1.

18. Quoted in *Congressional Quarterly Almanac* 1977 (Washington, D.C.: Congressional Quarterly, 1977, p. 710.

19. Remarks made on the National Broadcasting Company's "Meet the Press" February 10, 1980 (Washington, D.C.: Kelly Press, 1980), p. 8.

20. *Congressional Record,* Daily edition, Ninety-sixth Congress, First session, May 10, 1979, p. H2997.

21. Holly Idelson, "House Gives Energy Bill Big Win; Lengthy Conference Expected," *Congressional Quarterly Weekly Report,* May 30, 1992, pp. 1530–1532; and Matthew L. Wald, "The Energy Strategy," *New York Times,* May 29, 1992, pp. A1, D13.

22. NBC News press release, April 23, 1986; data from a national survey on energy attitudes in 1991 by the Congressional Institute for the Future's Public Interest Polling Project; and *Business Week,* "Who Will Raise Taxes? Try Clinton, Bush, and Perot," October 19, 1992, p. 32.

23. Wendy Wall, "World's Grain Output Surges as Nations Seek Food Self-Sufficiency," *The Wall Street Journal,* April 6, 1987, pp. 1, 10.

24. Art Pine, "Agricultural Subsidies Would Be Jointly Cut under U.S. Trade Plan," *The Wall Street Journal,* April 7, 1987, pp. 1, 26.

25. M. Ann Tutwiler and George E. Rossmiller, "External Events and the Recovery of U.S. Agricultural Exports," *Resources,* Winter 1987, p. 20.

26. Ibid.

27. Joint Economic Committee, *The 1987 Joint Economic Report,* p. 127.

28. See M. Elizabeth Sanders, *The Regulation of Natural Gas* (Philadelphia: Temple Univ. Press, 1981).

29. William Robbins, "Farmers Are Reaping Optimism by the Bushel," *New York Times,* May 5, 1987, p. A16.

30. On the coalitional strategy, see David R. Mayhew, *Party Loyalty Among Congressmen* (Cambridge, Mass.: Harvard Univ. Press, 1966); for more recent results, see Barbara Deckard Sinclair, "Agenda, Policy, and Alignment Change from Coolidge to Reagan," in *Congress Reconsidered,* 3d ed., eds. Lawrence C. Dodd and Bruce I. Oppenheimer (Washington, D.C.: CQ Press, 1985), pp. 291–314; and David Rapp, "For the Farmer, It's a Question of Necessity," *Congressional Quarterly Weekly Report,* February 21, 1987, pp. 303–8.

31. The first is Representative Frank Guarini (D-N.J.), the second the late Senator Edward Zorinsky (D-Nebr.). Cited in Rapp, "For the Farmer, It's a Question of Necessity," p. 303.

32. David Rapp, "Hill Fervor for Farm Bill Changes Died Slowly," *Congressional Quarterly Weekly Report,* November 1, 1986, pp. 2725–2726; Martha Derthick and Paul J. Quirk, *The Politics of Deregulation* (Washington, D.C.: Brookings Institution, 1985), p. 231; and Ward Sinclair, "USDA Targets Domestic Sugar Productions," *Washington Post,* March 8, 1987, p. A4.

33. Rapp, "For the Farmer, It's a Question of Necessity," pp. 303–8.

34. Richard Hofstadter, *The Age of Reform* (New York: Vintage, 1955), pp. 23–59.

35. William Robbins, "Surge in Sympathy for Farmer Found," *New York Times,* February 25, 1986, pp. A1, A22; and Adam Clymer, "Poll Finds Most Americans Cling to Ideals of Farm Life," *New York Times,* February 25, 1986, p. A22.

36. Peter T. Kilborn, "U.S. Will Stress Farm-Aid Issues in Global Talks," *New York Times,* March 23, 1987, pp. A1, D4.

37. Robert L. Paarlberg, "Agricultural Policy," in Robert Art and Seyond Brown, eds., *U.S. Foreign Policy: The Search for a New Role* (New York: Macmillan, 1993).

38. Ibid.

39. Steven E. Nelson, "Distributive Politics and Representation: Support for Agriculture in the U.S. Senate, 1965 to the Present." Paper presented at the 1990 Annual Meeting of the Southern Political Science Association, Atlanta, November, p. 3.

40. David Cloud, "Logic Doesn't Always Apply to Multiyear Farm Bills," *Congressional Quarterly Weekly Report*, February 4, 1990, pp. 576–582; and Rapp, "For the Farmer, It's a Question of Necessity," p. 304.

41. Times-Mirror Center for the People and the Press, *The People, the Press, and Economics* (Washington: Times-Mirror Corporation, 1989), p. 109.

42. William Drozdiak, "Now Truckers Peeve La France," *Washington Post*, July 4, 1992, p. A14.

43. While much of the new demand occurred in energy-producing nations, the energy crisis of the 1970s led to the development of a new market for smaller cars in the United States. See Bruce Stokes, "Coping With Glut," *National Journal*, November 1, 1986, p. 2608.

44. Ibid.

45. Stuart Aberbach, "America, the 'Diminished Giant,' " *Washington Post*, April 15, 1987, pp. A1, A18.

46. John Cranford, "Trade Bill: Partial Remedy for Complex Problem," *Congressional Quarterly Weekly Report*, April 25, 1987, p. 771.

47. Stephen S. Cohen and John Zysman, *Manufacturing Matters* (New York: Basic Books, 1987).

48. Peter Behr, "Is America Running Out of Steam?" *Washington Post*, April 17, 1987, pp. A1, A18.

49. "The Evolution of a Trade Bill," *Washington Post*, March 27, 1987, p. H3.

50. Andrew Rosenthal, "Bush Announces Candidacy, Claiming Reagan Mantle," *New York Times*, February 13, 1992, p. A24.

51. Susan Chira, "Poll Blames U.S. on Japan Trade," *New York Times*, August 13, 1985, pp. A1, D6; Clyde Farnsworth, "U.S. and Japan: Fraying Ties," *New York Times*, June 5, 1987, pp. D1, D5; CBS News press releases, February 22, 1988, May 12, 1989, and July 9, 1990; NBC News press release, October 28, 1988; Roper Survey for "Wall Street Week" (PBS television series), January 1990, provided by Maryland Public Television; Times-Mirror Center for the People and the Press, *The People, the Press, and Economics*, p. 15; "A North-South Dialogue?" *Maclean's*, July 3, 1989, p. 50.

52. NBC News press releases, February 14, 1990, and September 28, 1990; CBS News press releases, July 9, 1990, and December 16, 1991.

53. Anne Swardson, "Senate Panel Takes Up Trade Bill," *Washington Post*, January 14, 1987, p. F4.

54. David Spiro, "Trade Policy," in Art and Brown, eds., *U.S. Foreign Policy: The Search for a New Role*.

55. Robert A. Pastor, *Congress and the Politics of U.S. Foreign Economic Policy* (Berkeley: University of California Press, 1980), pp. 196–199.

56. I. M. Destler, *American Trade Politics: System Under Stress* (Washington: Institute for International Economics, 1986), p. 4.

57. See William Schneider, " 'Rambo' and Reality: Having It Both Ways," in *Eagle Resurgent: The Reagan Era in American Foreign Policy*, eds. Kenneth A. Oye, Robert J. Lieber, and Donald Rothchild (Boston: Little, Brown, 1987), p. 6. Note that the last survey

cited asked a somewhat different question than the two earlier ones, so comparisons must be made with caution.

58. Clyde Farnsworth, "Most in Poll Found to Favor Import Limits to Protect Jobs," *New York Times,* June 9, 1985, pp. A1, A40.

59. Jonathan Fuerbringer, "Congress Seeking Harmony on Trade," *New York Times,* February 6, 1987, pp. D1, D4.

60. Clyde Farnsworth, "One Day as a Trade Lobbyist," *New York Times,* June 16, 1987, p. A32.

61. "The Senate Trashes Trade," *New York Times,* July 24, 1987, p. A34.

62. Times-Mirror Center for the People and the Press, *The People, The Press, and Economics,* p. 15.

63. Judith Goldstein, "Ideas, Institutions, and American Trade Policy," in G. John Ikenberry, David A. Lake, and Michael Mastanduno, eds., *The State and American Foreign Economic Policy* (Ithaca, N.Y.: Cornell University Press, 1988), p. 215.

64. Eric M. Uslaner, "Political Parties, Ideas, Interests, and Free Trade in the United States," in Charles F. Doran, ed., *Party and Trade* (forthcoming).

65. Ibid.

66. Jessica Tuchman Mathews, "Environmental Policy," in Art and Brown, eds., *U.S. Foreign Policy: The Search for a New Role;* William K. Stevens, "Rio: A Start on Managing What's Left of This Place," *New York Times,* May 31, 1992, p. A1; and Ronald Inglehart, *Culture Shift in Advanced Industrial Society* (Princeton: Princeton University Press, 1990), p. 267.

67. The next three paragraphs are based on David Vogel, *National Styles of Regulation* (Ithaca, N.Y.: Cornell University Press, 1986), pp. 20, 175. See also Lynton Keith Caldwell, *International Environmental Policy,* 2d ed. (Durham, N.C.: Duke University Press, 1990), pp. 31–35.

68. Charles O. Jones, *Clean Air* (Pittsburgh: University of Pittsburgh Press, 1975), chaps. 7 and 8.

69. Vogel, *National Styles of Regulation,* pp. 156–159.

70. The next five paragraphs follow Eric M. Uslaner, *The Decline of Comity in Congress* (Ann Arbor, Mich.: University of Michigan Press, 1993), chap. 6. See also CBS News press release, April 16, 1991; and Americans Talk Issues, *The New World Order—What the Peace Should Be,* Washington, March, 1991.

71. Vogel, *National Styles of Regulation,* chaps. 4 and 5.

72. Rochelle Stanfield, "Resolving Disputes," *National Journal,* November 15, 1986, p. 2765.

73. Yankelovich, Clancy, Shulman press release, December 17, 1990.

74. Jay Mathews, "Tide Is Turning Against Big Green," *Washington Post,* October 30, 1990, p. A5.

75. Vogel, *National Styles of Regulation,* p. 20.

76. Inglehart, *Culture Shift in Advanced Industrial Society,* pp. 91, 92, 267–271.

77. Caldwell, *International Environmental Policy,* pp. 105, 217, and 263; and William K. Stevens, "Earth Summit Finds the Years of Optimism Are a Fading Memory," *New York Times,* June 9, 1992, p. C4.

78. Caldwell, *International Environmental Policy,* p. 263; Mathews, "Environmental Policy"; and Richard Elliot Benedick, *Ozone Diplomacy* (Cambridge: Harvard University Press, 1991), pp. 1, 21.

79. This account follows Benedick, *Ozone Diplomacy*.

80. William K. Stevens, "Lessons of Rio: A New Prominence and an Effective Blandness," *New York Times*, June 14, 1992, p. A10; and Emily T. Smith, "Growth vs. Environment," *Business Week*, May 11, 1992, p. 69.

81. Smith, "Growth vs. Environment," p. 69; Paul Lewis, "Poor vs. Rich in Rio," *Washington Post*, June 3, 1992, p. A1, A12; and Sharon Begley, "Is It Apocalypse Now?", *Newsweek*, June 1, 1992, p. 42.

82. Begley, "Is It Apocalypse Now?", p. 37.

83. Caldwell, *International Environmental Policy*, pp. 263–265; Julia Preston, "National Interests Preside at Rio," *Washington Post*, June 7, 1992, p. A28; and Smith, "Growth vs. Environment," p. 70.

84. Smith, "Growth vs. Environment," p. 70; Eugene Robinson, "At Earth Summit, South Aims to Send Bill North," *Washington Post*, June 1, 1992, p. A14; Julia Preston, "A Biodiversity Pact with a Premium," *Washington Post*, June 9, 1992, p. A16; and Steven Greenhouse, "Ecology, the Economy, and Bush," *New York Times*, June 14, 1992, p. E6.

85. John Newhouse, "The Diplomatic Round: The Earth Summit," *The New Yorker*, June 1, 1992, pp. 64–78.

86. Marlise Simons, "Europe Sees Oil Tax as a Way to Dampen Demand," *New York Times*, June 1, 1992, p. A6.

87. Lewis, "Poor vs. Rich in Rio," p. A12.

88. Preston, "A Biodiversity Pact with a Premium," p. A16.

89. Boyce Rensenberger, "As Earth Summit Nears, Consensus Still Lacking on Global Warming's Cause," *Washington Post*, May 31, 1992, pp. A1, A22.

90. Michael Wines, "Bush and Rio," *New York Times*, June 11, 1992, pp. A1, A12; Greenhouse, "Ecology, the Economy, and Bush," p. E6; and Ann Devroy, "Bush: $150 Million Hike in U.S. Aid for Forests," *Washington Post*, June 2, 1992, p. A9.

91. Keith Schneider, "Environmental Policy: It's a Jungle in There," *New York Times*, June 7, 1992, pp. E1, E4; and Greenhouse, "Ecology, the Economy, and Bush," p. E1.

92. Greenhouse, "Ecology, the Economy, and Bush," p. E6; John Holusha, "Poll Finds Skepticism About U.S. Earth Summit," *New York Times*, June 11, 1992, p. A13; Wines, "Bush and Rio," pp. A1, A12; and Voter Research and Survey exit poll, November 4, 1992.

93. Lewis, "Storm in Rio."

94. CBS News press release, April 19, 1989.

95. See E. E. Schattschneider, *The Semisovereign People* (New York: Holt, Rinehart and Winston, 1960).

CHAPTER 10

Balancing the Scales?

Where Does the Balance Lie?

The Great Depression, followed by the New Deal and the Nazi and Japanese threats, followed after Japan's and Germany's defeat by the Cold War, all contributed to the steady growth of presidential power. But for the Vietnam War, this unchallenged growth might have continued. This trend toward increasing presidential power had gone unchallenged because crisis after crisis, domestic and foreign, required strong action and often speedy reaction. The need for a powerful presidency seemed obvious. More than that, the growth of presidential power was identified with the use of this power domestically for progressive social legislation (the New Deal, Fair Deal, New Frontier, and Great Society programs) and externally for the defense of what used to be called the *free world*, although it included nondemocratic societies. The confrontation of Stalin's Soviet Union—which, not surprisingly so soon after World War II, looked a lot like Hitler's Germany to Western eyes—with the United States, Britain, and France, made the Cold War appear to be fundamentally a continuing struggle of totalitarianism against democracy. Thus the expansion of presidential power was identified with liberal causes, with domestic changes to help the underprivileged and to correct social injustices and a foreign policy to protect liberal values that had first been assaulted by Hitler and then by Stalin. In fact, it had simply come to be assumed that the president is a liberal and that, therefore, he can, like the kings of old, do no wrong.

During those days it was conservatives who opposed the trend toward increasing presidential power. As exponents of small government and congressional supremacy, they opposed New Deal and other domestic reforms as well as the conduct of a vigorous foreign policy, all of which required big government, especially "big executive government." Liberals championed the last. But Vietnam reversed the liberal attitudes toward presidential power. Liberals, who had always expected "their" presidents to back good causes whether eliminating poverty, doing away with racial injustice, or stopping totalitarian aggression, became schizophrenic as the war escalated. Johnson's domestic record surpassed that of John F. Kennedy, whose style and charm attracted liberals but who by the time of his death had not managed to get Congress to pass any major social legislation; Johnson, unlike Kennedy, was able to achieve the passage of a vast amount of social legislation. But Vietnam disillusioned many liberals. A war in defense of an undemocratic government, often fought by methods that repelled people of humane sentiments and springing from commitments made by Presidents Eisenhower and Kennedy and transformed into major war by Johnson, not only seemed incompatible with the very values America proclaimed to the world but was carried on in a way that seemed unconstitutional.

The Gulf of Tonkin Resolution, the blank check Congress gave Johnson but did not expect him to use to initiate a large land war in Asia, only made the war an even more bitter experience. Vietnam, a "presidential war," was perceived to be the culmination of the trend toward increasingly powerful presidents who were not subject to the legislative restraint envisaged by the Founding Fathers. Had they not with good reason, in the Constitution, specifically provided against the danger of locating absolute power in the hands of one man by assigning to Congress the authority to "declare war" and the president the authority to "make war"? In the future asked critic and *New York Times* journalist Tom Wicker, "could a president, for example, bomb Lima in order to forestall or retaliate for some act of expropriation by Peru? If Fidel Castro refuses to help put an end to airline hijackings to Cuba, can Mr. Nixon constitutionally bomb Havana to make him negotiate seriously?"[1]

If the Vietnam War traumatized many liberals, the Iran–Contra affair had the same effect on many conservatives. It was those to the right of center who had so strongly stressed that the United States was founded on a respect, indeed a reverence, for law. Yet there were former representatives from what was arguably the most conservative administration of this century arguing before national television audiences that it was acceptable to disobey some bad laws. Some even testified that there were so many different Boland amendments that National Security Council officials did not know which one to follow at any given time—a view that *New Yorker* columnist Elizabeth Drew regarded as somewhat disingenuous since the administration did not tell people to file their income taxes under the old rules if they found the new reformed law too complicated to understand.[2] The Iran–Contra affair, perhaps more than anything else in recent American diplomatic history, is a classic example of putting outcomes ahead of process and thereby losing respect for law. It leads one to an interpretation that the Constitution, amended by years of presidential practice and congressional acquiescence, reads in effect: "The president may conduct a war unless Congress halts him." Hence, to redress the balance between the executive and legislative, to prevent another Vietnam and avoid a second costly disaster and strain of the American social fabric, a flood of proposals has been put forward, almost all of which aim at a greater role in the making of foreign policy, and especially the use of force for Congress—and, through it, presumably, "the people."

The belief that the presidency—when occupied by bellicose presidents—needs to be restrained by a pacific Congress, acting as the representative of the people, assumes that Congress, especially the Senate, would demonstrate wisdom, moderation, and virtue, qualities that have frequently been lacking in the postwar period.

> This spring the land is filled ... with a resounding chorus demanding that the United States Senate reassert its "right" over foreign policy. . . .
>
> But hold on a moment. Which Senate are we speaking of? Are we talking of the Senate which has over and over again balked at constructive foreign initiative, crippled foreign efforts, ignored foreign opportunities? Are we talking of the Senate which blocked American entry into the League of Nations, held back full support for the World Court, is presently cutting back further and further on foreign aid, which has no hesitation over passing resolutions mixing in the affairs of other countries for political rather than diplomatic reasons?
>
> Of course, this is not the Senate which today's "strengthen-the Senate" advocates have in mind. They visualize an upper chamber full of wisdom and goodwill, a bulwark of reason and foresight in a reckless world. In short, they dream of a Senate which will hew to their own concept of where foreign policy should go and how it should be conducted.[3]

However, these expectations are of a Congress whose foreign policy stance for most of the postwar period has been intensely anti-Communist and nationalistic. Presidents have therefore moved with great caution, if and when they have moved at all, in their relations with Communist countries lest they be tainted as "soft on communism."

But the fall of pro-American governments in Nicaragua and Iran, as well as the weakness of other friends and allies such as Guatemala, El Salvador, Zaire, Turkey, and Morocco, led to increased demands that the country take a more activist role in international politics. Many of these arguments were heard most loudly in the Congress. The nomination of Ronald Reagan by the Republicans intensified the political debate on foreign policy, especially the growing concern with defense policy. The congressional activism, in contrast to that of the late 1960s and early 1970s, was now once more directed toward an interventionist foreign policy that conflicted with the policies of the president. The Congress of the 1970s was concerned with too much presidential power *and* prowess, while that of the early 1980s, especially the Republican-controlled Senate, was determined to reassert American power. Few members of the Congress during the Vietnam War period could have imagined that a president would not win universal acclaim for pronouncing that no American soldiers had died in overseas combat during his term of office, as Carter often reminded the country. The Iran–Contra affair led to another change of direction. The public feared that support for antigovernment rebels in Nicaragua would lead to another American embroglio in Latin America. Memories of the hostage crisis, Iranian-backed terrorism throughout the world, the killing of American marines in Lebanon, and the attack on the USS *Stark* in the Persian Gulf led many Americans to argue that the United States need not make itself a sitting target for anyone who would dare to attack. The Congress quickly picked up on this theme. It joined the chorus for restraint in government policy.

This reluctance to get involved in the international arena contributed to the ambivalent American attitudes toward initiating hostilities in the Gulf War. The public was anxious to reassert American power in the world, but reluctant to risk soldiers' lives in what might be a protracted war. As we saw in Chapter 5, public support for military action did not become widespread until after hostilities had begun.

There is an irony to the post-Vietnam appointment of Congress as the watch-dog of presidential temptations to go to war. For it overlooks the fact that Congress approved U.S. participation in both limited wars. Had President Tru-man requested a declaration of war after North Korea's invasion of South Korea, he would have received it; support for Truman's decision to intervene militarily with U.S. forces received virtually unanimous congressional and popular sup-port. Only after the war became domestically unpopular did a few conservative senators raise the question of its constitutionality. Similarly, President Johnson had the support of large majorities in Congress and the country not only at the time of the Gulf of Tonkin incident during the summer of 1964, but also when the sustained bombing of North Vietnam began in the spring of 1965. If a War Powers Act had existed at the time, it would not have prevented either of the two limited wars in which the United States has become engaged since 1945. It is also plausible to presume that Congress would have dictated that troops be with-drawn in sixty days in either case. For this would have been too short a period for any congressional investigation to turn up facts beyond those—as in the North Korean invasion—already evident or explained by the president. Congress' Tonkin Gulf investigation did turn up additional information—three years after the events. Similarly, even in the Iran–Contra affair, where foreign policy ap-peared to have been privatized, many legislators argued that Congress had to shoulder some of the blame. The legislative branch had not been diligent enough in its oversight to prevent the affair.[4] Indeed, James Sundquist has argued that the power of the contemporary presidency can be traced to the actions of the Congress. The legislature has, until the 1970s, delegated much responsibility to the chief executive, generally to achieve more coordination and coherence in policy formation.[5]

If there is one rule that has become clear in the post-World War II period, it is that during real or alleged crises, Congress and the public turn to the presi-dent for information and interpretation. For example, it was Kennedy's inter-pretation of the impact of Soviet missiles in Cuba that precipitated the Cuban missile crisis. Put in different words, the president has a superior ability to manipulate the picture of reality in the short run; this advantageous presidential position if reinforced by an emotional fact of life—namely, that if the president sends troops into action, be it in the name of freedom or security or both, the patriotic feelings that are aroused will make it extremely difficult to oppose him and refuse him the troops and money he requests. In fact, it will take a great deal more willingness on the part of Congress to accept responsibility for its decisions in case history should vindicate the president.

Why Things Always Appear to Go Wrong

Our concern in this chapter is with reconciling the democratic dilemmas of foreign policy making with the argument, advanced by many, that we seem to be trapped in a cycle of strong and weak presidents and congresses that leads to frustration and a sense that things seem to go wrong more often than they go right. The ideal balance seems to elude us. If Vietnam taught us that foreign policy making needed to be made more accountable to both Congress and the public, the Iran–Contra affair reminded us that we have not learned that lesson well enough.

What is the source of our difficulties? Are our presidents too strong or is the Congress too weak? Do we have too much partisanship on foreign policy or too little? Or is there a mismatch between our expectations of the president and the occupants of the Oval Office? All of these possibilities have been raised by serious observers. We shall consider each of them.

Deadlocked Democracy

In 1987, the bicentennial anniversary of the Constitution of the United States, a bipartisan group of distinguished citizens issued a report warning that the distinguished document might be in need of revision. The Committee on the Constitutional System was cochaired by Senator Nancy Landon Kassebaum (R-Kans.), former Secretary of the Treasury C. Douglas Dillon (a Republican who served in the Kennedy and Johnson administrations), and Lloyd Cutler, former counsel to President Carter. The committee's membership included sitting and former members of Congress from both parties, current and past governors and mayors, others who had served in the cabinet, as well as representatives from business, labor, and universities. It argued that the increasing responsibilities placed on modern governments were putting severe burdens on the contemporary political order. The committee argued:

> Consistency in our foreign and national security policies is . . . frustrated by an institutional contest of wills between presidents and shifting, cross-party coalitions within the Congress. Over forty treaties submitted to the Senate for ratification

since World War II have either been rejected or have never come to a vote. ... Meanwhile presidential concern over "leaks" and frustration with congressionally imposed restrictions have led presidents and their staffs to launch important diplomatic, military and covert activities in secret and without consulting Congress.[6]

The report rejected the notion that the problem lay with the quality of national leaders: "Our public officials are no less competent, either individually or as a group, than they used to be."[7]

The committee viewed the period before World War II as one in which the legislative and executive branches got along reasonably well. The "dealignment" of the party system since the 1930s has served to weaken the ability of legislative leaders to deal with the president. When party ties were strong, voters typically chose a legislature and a chief executive of the same party. Before World War II, the voters selected a president of one party and a Congress with at least one house controlled by the opposition less than 25 percent of the time. Since 1956, this has happened 66 percent of the time and since 1968 it has occurred over 80 percent of the time.

The Committee on the Constitutional System saw the need to try to put the genie back in the bottle, to achieve some greater coordination between the legislative and executive branches. Yet the past that it wanted to replicate was not one of bipartisan cooperation between the parties, but rather a time of renewed vigor for the parties. Strong parties, in its view, advance accountability. On the one hand, the people would know which party they could hold responsible for the decisions of the government. On the other hand, if the legislature and the executive were in the same hands, there would be added incentives for each branch to cooperate with the other. There would be no repetition of the long and arduous impeachment hearings of the Nixon administration or of the Iran–Contra hearings, though less momentous, of the Reagan era.

Reformers such as those in the Committee on the Constitutional System take the parliamentary form of government as their model for legislative–executive cooperation. In such systems, which are found in Great Britain, Canada, and many Western European nations, strong party government is possible. The prime minister is not elected by the people at large, but by the party (or coalition of parties) that wins the most seats in the legislature. Divided control of the legislative and executive branches is thus impossible. Furthermore, the prime minister must tailor policies to the wishes of the parliamentary party. A major defeat on a policy question can lead to the formation of a new government. Anthony Eden was replaced as prime minister of Great Britain in 1957 by Harold Macmillan after a major foreign policy blunder in the Middle East. Eden had committed British troops during the Egyptian–Israeli war to a joint effort with the French to recapture control of the Suez Canal from the Egyptians, who had seized the waterway. The British–French attempt failed and Eden resigned. In the United States, on the other hand, Woodrow Wilson argued that:

> Our system is essentially astronomical. A president's usefulness is measured not by efficiency, but by calendar months. It is reckoned that if he be good at all, he will be good for four years. A prime minister must keep himself in favor with the majority; a president need only keep alive.[8]

American presidents can afford to take actions that risk failure early in their administrations. Because they have as long as three and a half years to recover from their "mistakes," they are virtually unchecked. When presidents ignore congressional criticism, as did Johnson in Vietnam, Nixon in Cambodia and on Watergate, and Reagan on the Iran–Contra affair, they lose popularity but retain their offices. What we have is a weakened presidency but a leader who cannot be dislodged from office.

How did the Committee on the Constitutional System propose to restore a sense of partisanship to the American political system? The reforms it suggested included four-year terms for House members and eight-year terms for senators, so that legislators would always be elected at the same time as presidents. In midterm elections the party of the president almost always loses seats in the Congress, often in substantial numbers. This situation provides incentives for legislators to divorce themselves from the president's policy initiatives and hinders legislative–executive cooperation. The committee also proposed permitting cabinet members to serve in the Congress to foster a less confrontational attitude between the bureaucracy and the Congress. Recognizing that the president's party would rarely achieve the two thirds of the Senate needed to ensure treaty ratification, it proposed that this requirement be lowered to 60 percent. The committee also noted a series of proposals on which its membership could not reach a consensus, but nevertheless deserved further consideration. These included encouraging the president to appear before the Congress to answer legislators' questions about administration policies, as prime ministers do at question time in parliamentary systems; permitting the states to make straight-ticket voting—at least for the president and Congress—compulsory rather than optional as it currently is; and permitting either the president or Congress to call a new election in the event of prolonged deadlock, as prime ministers in most parliamentary systems can do.[9]

A Constitutional Dilemma?

To what extent are the sources of America's difficulties in forming a coherent foreign policy (not to mention a domestic policy) found in our Constitution? To be sure, the document does provide for a division of powers between the legislative, executive, and judicial branches. The separate elections for the president and Congress do permit the members of Congress to vote to establish their own political bases as opposed to contests in parliamentary systems where all candidates for office run based on party appeals and where the prime minister is selected from the ranks of legislators. Mid-term contests also provide voters with ready opportunities to select a Congress in which the dominant party is different from that of the president.

It is facile to blame all of the problems of deadlock on the constitutional system. First, the Constitution *permits* but hardly *requires* voters to choose divided government. In the presidential elections of 1968, 1972, 1980, 1984, and 1988, the electorate cast ballots for a president of one party and a Congress in which at least one house was controlled by the opposite party. Two of these contests, those of 1972 and 1984, were landslides of historic proportion in American electoral history, yet the Republicans did not gain control of both houses of Congress in either one. In 1988, when Republican George Bush carried 40 states to win the presidency, the Democrats gained strength in both houses of Congress. In the 1930s and 1940s only about 10 to 15 percent of congressional districts produced a plurality with one party for president and the other for Congress. In the 1970s and 1980s this figure had increased to a range of 30 to 40 percent.[10]

Further, the behavior of voters gives members of Congress ample reason to assert their independence from the White House. Not only do a third or more districts divide their vote between the parties for the legislative and executive branch, but even in districts carried by the president, the chief executive more often than not does not fare as well as the district's representative. When presidents do not score overwhelming victories (as in 1960 and 1976), members of the House run ahead of the president in more than 90 percent of congressional districts.[11] The Constitution does not dictate such behavior. There is deadlock between the parties because the people seem to prefer it that way. In several polls citizens have expressed the belief that split control of the legislative and executive branches is good for the country.[12]

The other devices suggested by the committee similarly might not achieve their objectives. Placing the secretary of state or defense in the Congress would not necessarily improve relations with the members of the legislature. First, there are already many opportunities for consultation between the secretaries and key congressional leaders.[13] Second, the lack of party discipline among legislators is not likely to increase simply because key White House officials sit among them. Even the idea that the president go before Congress to answer legislators' questions, as worthy as it is, might not lead to greater support for the chief executive among his own party. Question time in parliaments is useful mostly when prime ministers want to make some type of policy statement or might be trapped into explaining controversial programs. In the United States the press conference accomplishes the same goal with as much adversarial tenor as we would find in any parliamentary system.

The party system has been weakened without any change in the constitutional order. Indeed American presidents have had difficulties even when their parties controlled the Congress, as Carter's tenure demonstrated clearly. We should also recall that Johnson's Vietnam policy appeared to draw more unified support among Republicans than among his fellow Democrats in the Congress. In such cases it is highly unlikely that either the president or Congress would seek to resolve deadlock by calling a new election, if this proposal were to be adopted. When the president is unpopular, so too will be his party. Its members will be very reluctant to call for an election that would likely benefit the opposition party. When deadlock is between the parties, it is unclear who would be responsible for calling a new election, and the wrangling over who could do so might exacerbate the conflicts between the parties rather than resolve them. The United States does not have strong parties because Americans have always had ambivalent feelings toward these organizations. As Sundquist argues:

> The revitalization of political parties cannot be willed. If it could be, it already would have been; party leaders have not lacked the desire to preside over stronger organizations.[14]

Instead, the tendency toward deadlock in the American political system is "normal" and "irresistible."[15]

It is unclear that restoring the comity between the legislative and executive branches involves strengthening political parties. One can make a good argument that it might be desirable to have the two parties taking divergent stands on many policy issues, both domestic and foreign. It might have been preferable to have one party take a hard line on dealing with the Soviet Union and the other a position more favorable to détente, so that the electorate might be able to choose which course it prefers. But this is not the same argument as restoring legislative–executive cooperation. The "good old days," if they were that, were marked by *bipartisanship*, not by ideologically distinctive parties. With the pre-Vietnam consensus broken down, it is very difficult to restore it. Constitutional reform seems an unlikely method for altering public opinion.

Government by strong political parties might not be possible within the American context for another reason. Americans often express foreign policy attitudes that do not form the consistent basis for party appeals. For example, strong majorities of both parties opposed aid to the Contras in Nicaragua, yet they overwhelmingly supported the invasion of Grenada and expressly back Israel over the Arab states in the Middle East conflict. Other policy proposals, such as the level of defense spending, have shifting majorities. At times a plurality of Americans support more money for the military and at other times it favors reduced expenditures. These data suggest that there may be no single set of policies that voters prefer. Would the country be better off if one party endorsed lower defense spending, criticized the Grenada episode, opposed aid to the Contras, and supported the Arab cause in the Middle East while the other party took the opposite positions? It is far from clear that this would be desirable. In the era of the post-Vietnam dissensus, it is equally unlikely that both parties would adopt the same positions on all foreign policy issues.

We have seen in Chapters 5 and 6 that Americans increasingly divide along partisan lines on many questions of foreign policy and often cast ballots on foreign policy issues. When the candidates are clearly divided on foreign policy, the electorate follows suit. Whether this is a good or bad thing is debatable. Yet, the polarization on foreign policy took place without any institutional reforms. Would a changed constitutional system have produced even more partisanship? It seems doubtful. Americans are proud of their Constitution—and believe that it has worked better in providing for the national defense than in any other area.[16]

Is the President the Problem?

If the constitutional order is not the problem perhaps it is the presidency itself. We consider two arguments that focus on the White House. Both criticize the current selection process for presidential nominations, but they come to very different conclusions. The second thesis posits that the system of primary elections produces candidates who are better qualified to run for office than to serve once elected. The thesis we shall consider first presents a more damning conclusion: many of the people who have been elected president do not have the proper temperament to serve in the job. Furthermore, through appropriate analysis, it is possible to isolate such potential misfits and call their unsuitability for public office to the public's attention. Presumably the electorate would then reject such candidates for the nation's highest office.

Personality and the Search for a President: Why Not the Best?

Increasing presidential power has spawned a heightened interest and concern about the type of individuals who have occupied—and will occupy—the highest office in the land and perhaps the world. Most schoolchildren can recite a list of "great" presidents such as Washington, Jefferson, Lincoln, Wilson, and the two Roosevelts. We hear substantially less about other presidents—from those who were simply not successful to those we consider outright scoundrels—and virtually nothing at all about vice presidents. In 1972, the McGovern presidential campaign suffered a major setback when it became known that the vice presidential nominee, Senator Thomas Eagleton (D-Mo.), had undergone psychiatric treatment earlier in his life. Eagleton was ultimately forced to withdraw from the ticket although he has continued to serve quite effectively in the Senate. Vice President Quayle's qualifications to serve as chief executive were severely questioned in 1988. In an era of the strong presidency, the nominees' personal traits are being critically scrutinized by the press, the public, and scholars.

The tensions of Vietnam and Watergate have made Americans somewhat fearful of presidential power. In turn, these events have called attention to the problems of determining in advance who might be an exceptional president, or at least a very good one. Could there be a prescreening, a sort of presidential leadership test that might not guarantee us great leaders but perhaps could save us from our previous errors? At least one school of thought leads to a positive answer to this question. Called *psychohistory* or *psychobiography,* this approach to studying leadership is based on the development of personality in potential leaders and the use of psychoanalytic methods of investigation to determine what brought some leaders to success and others to failure. The 1970s did not mark the beginning of psychohistory, but rather a renewed and enlarged concern for the capacity of academic research to guide us in screening out potentially bad presidents.

Psychobiography has been applied to such diverse figures as Martin Luther and Woodrow Wilson. But in 1972, James David Barber's book, *The Presidential Character,* the first psychohistory of American presidents, was published.[17] Barber's analysis dealt with presidents comparatively, presented a framework for classifying presidents, claimed to have predictive utility, and specifically and strikingly predicted the ultimate failure of the Nixon presidency. Barber's argument is itself complex, so we shall necessarily over-simplify it here.

Barber clearly maintains that the early development of a president's personality is the key to understanding how he will perform in office. In examining this personality through the tools of psychoanalysis, we must be careful to avoid accounts that are too popular (press reports or biographies that may be overly critical or flattering) and obtain detailed information on the future leader's early development. What is one to look for in examining whether someone will be a successful leader? *Style* involves the way the president balances rhetoric, personal relationships, and detailed "homework"—ranging from the very intense patterns of Nixon, Johnson, and Wilson to the more relaxed style of Eisenhower and particularly Coolidge, who would not miss his daily nap. *World view* consists of the president's perception of what the great issues of the time are and what forces shape them, including both Franklin Roosevelt's dictum that "We have nothing to fear but fear itself" to Nixon's (and Johnson's) identification of such struggles as involving, among other things, elements of good and evil, white and black, the forces of incumbency versus the challenge from without and sometimes even from within. Finally, there is the element of *character,* the president's outlook on life and his role in the world "not for the moment, but enduringly."[18] From these considerations Barber outlines two basic dimensions of the presidential character: activity-passivity and positive-negative affect toward one's activity. On the question of activity, style is stressed. Affect toward activity reflects world view and character; more specifically, affect poses the question: Does the (potential) president enjoy the job and have a positive outlook on his capacity to handle the problems he confronts?

Putting these two dimensions together, Barber constructs four types of presidential character. The active-positive chief executive puts much effort into the job and enjoys doing it. He values productivity and sees himself as developing over time to meet new challenges within well-defined personal goals. There is an emphasis on rationality; such a president sees events in terms of diverse factors and the political battles that must be won, within the contexts of rational action, to achieve productivity.[19] Among the active-positive presidents have been Franklin Roosevelt, Harry Truman, John Kennedy, Gerald Ford, and Jimmy Carter. In contrast, the active-negatives have a conflict between a very strong effort to succeed and low emotional reward for that attempt. Activity is compulsive, the president himself ambitious and aggressive. Unlike the active-positive, who relates well to others who may oppose his policies, the active-negative retreats from opposition, often into a lonely inner struggle that produces confrontation and despair for the leader and isolates him from the nation. Such presidents include Wilson, Johnson, Herbert Hoover, and Nixon. Barber implicitly suggested that Bush might be an active-negative president when he noted the president's penchant for secrecy and his "very bizarre and dangerous" fondness for "surprises." Elsewhere he called him an active-positive president with no coherent world view.[20]

The passive-positive president is simultaneously optimistic and agreeable, friendly and compliant. Such a leader has a positive outlook on the job of being president but does not believe that much is demanded of him personally in commitment to new programs or national leadership. The emphasis is on personality, as Barber argues regarding the ever-smiling William Howard Taft and later about Warren Harding during the "return to normalcy" after World War I, a period of relative calm in the country. A passive-positive is popular because of what he does not do and because of what he is—either a hero to the nation or a likable sort of person (Harding). A passive-negative, in contrast, would rather be almost anything but president. He is in politics because he believes he ought to be. The job is unrewarding and this type of leader has little patience for it. The classic case is Coolidge, who cultivated the image of someone sleeping through his administration; another, less clear-cut example is Dwight Eisenhower.[21] Neither appeared to want the position. Coolidge simply walked away from renomination when he said, "I do not choose to run." Eisenhower turned down the Democratic nomination in 1948, while the battle on his behalf for the Republican nomination was largely waged without his seeming involvement.

In the era of strong presidents, however, passive chief executives are increasingly unlikely to be selected. Rather, Barber sees the major struggle in American politics as one between active-positives and active-negatives. The former are, of course, almost ideal types. The great presidents were all active-positives and others who fit into this category are viewed at least as reasonably successful. All were well adjusted and did not allow the office of the presidency to insulate them from the nation, whatever their other failings may have been. Active-negatives, on the other hand, are self-destructive and thus potentially fatal to the nation. Their world vision is limited by their concern for their respective places in history and their insistence that each of them has the answers to the nation's problems. Their opponents are simply wrong. Barber predicted in 1972 that Nixon's presidency would come to an unhappy end, and the utility of his framework was established for many.[22] In 1980, he predicted that if elected, Reagan would be a "jelly bean"—a softie—rather than the danger that President Carter was trying to portray him as. Reagan, according to Barber, would be a nine-to-five president. His passivity had been shown by his lifetime practice of taking it easy; his positive side is evident in his generally cheerful optimistic attitude. Reagan hates to fight and seeks to please and may cave in to pressure; the greatest danger will be that the president may be done in by his friends, as were many of his passive-positive predecessors. Who presidential friends are is thus critical and a considerably more important issue to consider than it would be for a president possessing a different character.

The strengths of the approach of psychohistory are its comparative evaluation of president and its recognition of the role of childhood development on a leader's personality. The active-positives are well adjusted and the active-negatives poorly adjusted. But historical records, even psychoanalytic ones, are subject to multiple interpretations. The same evidence can by used to adduce either a positive or a negative evaluation of even childhood experiences.[23] Often value judgments are a function of hindsight. Truman seems to be a much better president now than he did when he was in office. Revisionist psychohistory has, in fact, leapfrogged Eisenhower from a borderline passive-negative to a passive-positive.[24] Reagan's high profile and very effective bargaining style during his first several months in office seemed to dispute predictions of his passivity. Psychohistory is certainly a useful way of generalizing about leadership that has previously been beyond the political scientists' scope. But what happens when not just the journalists but the specialists, the psychohistorians, disagree on what the evidence means? Furthermore, Barber's linkage of the presidential character to early childhood experiences and teenage development seems to belie the traditional notion of a president "growing into the job." How much more likely is someone with earlier emotional problems to develop into an active-negative president? Has the country actually been better served by ensuring that an Eagleton will never be elected to either the presidency or the vice presidency? How do we determine the most appropriate methods of evaluating the evidence? Psychoanalysis is hardly an exact science.

What kind of foreign policy president will a particular personality type make?

It is in this area that there is the greatest potential for further development, because handling foreign affairs from the White House necessarily involves on-the-job training. Two classic active-negatives, Wilson and Johnson, failed on key foreign policy issues important to them. Wilson lost a pitched battle with the Senate over American entry into the League of Nations while Johnson was overcome by events in Vietnam. Both presidents had been primarily interested in domestic politics—and, despite Barber's analysis, Wilson is often listed in both public and academic surveys as one of the nation's great presidents.[25] The disparity lies in Wilson's remarkable achievements in social welfare legislation, his New Freedom, mostly accomplished during his first administration (1913–1917). Johnson was also a leader in domestic politics, where he sought "to heal and to build" and was a compassionate champion of civil rights and war against poverty. Probably more social legislation was passed during 1965–1966 than in the rest of this century (including the New Freedom and Franklin Roosevelt's New Deal). Could Johnson have been an active-positive president on domestic policy but not on foreign policy? On the other hand, Nixon's foreign policy accomplishments kept his personal popularity at levels that let him retain the presidency for at least several months longer than would otherwise be the case. As much as Wilson and Johnson were bedeviled by foreign policy and sought refuge in social welfare legislation, Nixon and Bush believed that their worlds centered on international events. Reagan was even more complex. His management style was not so neatly broken up into foreign and domestic realms. Rather, he seemed to be an active-positive when he was popular—in the first years of each of his terms and in the last year of his first term. When public opinion was less supportive, Reagan seemed to fall into a much more passive phase. His presidency, as much as any other since Johnson, demonstrated the difficulties of attempting to sum up a president's style so simply. It is indeed difficult to understand the makeup of a president who took charge with such vigor and success in 1981 and 1985 but who seemed content to delegate so much of his authority in most other years.

These questions are not meant to disparage the contributions of psychohistory, but only to recognize the limitations of any approach that seeks to determine who might be a "great" president or even an "acceptable" one. A president successful in foreign policy is not necessarily the same as a strong leader in domestic policy. Perhaps the personality types involved in each are sufficiently different so that we expect the impossible. Traditional foreign policy leadership requires a command style, the establishment of a hierarchy so that there is a single leader for the nation. Domestic policy success, on the other hand, requires strong bargaining skills, an ability to deal with legislators on their own terms, and, most critically, an understanding of the complex political relationships among members of Congress and the president. One style emphasizes almost complete control over a situation; the other tremendous flexibility. It is a rare president, particularly in these days of an increasingly interdependent world, who possesses both traits. Perhaps only Franklin Roosevelt achieved such success.

How could we adopt presidential screening even if we had so few reservations about putting candidates on the couch? Would candidates submit themselves to a board of psychiatrists? How much about the personal background of candidates do we really need to know? And how much are we likely to learn even if we don't hanker to find out about it? The 1988 presidential contest has answered some of these questions for us. The revelations about former Senator Gary Hart's alliances with model Donna Rice and other women forced him out of the race. Following those divulgences by the *Miami Herald* and the *Washington Post,* the *New York Times* asked all active presidential candidates to supply written answers to a detailed questionnaire about their personal backgrounds. The *Times'* questions covered the gamut—from tax returns to health to personal relationships. Almost all of the candidates refused to answer at least some of the questions and the *Times* apologized for its poor taste. Yet the very fact that a major American newspaper felt that it could even broach the subject indicates that every aspect of the private lives of candidates is a matter for public examination.

In 1992 the supermarket tabloids reported charges by model Gennifer Flowers that she had had an affair with Bill Clinton. The mainstream press downplayed the story, but it quickly spread and led to a sharp decrease in the Arkansas governor's popularity. The leading news media were responsible for stories about H. Ross Perot's investigations of people in and out of government. These accounts may have been responsible for Perot's temporary withdrawal from the race in the summer of 1992. If the electorate preferred stories about arms control positions, as Hart suggested, the media—though perhaps not the tabloids—would have filled their pages and air time with debates rather than stories about sex in high places.

It seems that we are destined to know virtually everything that can be learned about presidential candidates. It is no surprise that even candidates who might have nothing to hide might decide to forego the trauma of having every aspect of their personal lives dragged before the network audiences of the nightly news. It is far from clear that only the least qualified candidates are the ones who withdraw from the fray. Yet the information garnered by the press is not likely to permit the detailed type of psychiatric investigation that Barber recommends. At most it will provide a pseudoscientific analysis that many citizens might be willing to accept as a substitute for more sophisticated studies. The very politicians who feel hounded by the press are unlikely to subject themselves to detailed analysis by a panel of psychiatrists so that the public might be better informed. Even if psychohistory were more reliable, they could rightly argue that leaving the decision to a panel of experts is undemocratic. The people have every right to select whomever they wish. The specter of experts quarreling among themselves in a field that has not reached anything like consensus would hardly dignify the presidential selection process.

The Troubled Presidency: The Selection Process Is the Problem

It was Jimmy Carter who asked "Why not the best"? He also promised to give the United States "a government as good as its people." When he did so, governing as an outsider not born of the "Washington establishment," the people roundly rejected his administration in the 1980 elections. Yet they chose as his successor another outsider, Ronald Reagan. There are some who argue that the difficulty lies not so much with the psychological makeup of the candidates, but with their lack of experience in dealing with national and international affairs. This is especially problematic in a country that has come to look to the White House for the solution to all of its problems.

This perspective agrees with the constitutional reformers that the president no longer serves as party leader. It offers little hope that the party system can be restored and sees the real root of the problem with the people who occupy the office and the public's expectations of the president. On the one hand, the system of primary elections that has dominated the presidential nominating system since 1972 has put a premium on candidates who make good impressions on television, who simplify issues, and who run against the establishment in Washington. A wheelchair-bound Franklin Roosevelt, a short and stocky Harry Truman, or a tall and sometimes vulgar Lyndon Johnson would not fare well in the media age where everyone seeks to be the next John F. Kennedy. On the other hand, the electorate now has a very high set of expectations of what the president should do, so that even superhumans might not be able to fulfill them, much less the "outsiders" who fare so well on television.

The problem is not simply the abuses of power in an "imperial presidency," but rather a combination of poor presidents and overly optimistic views by the public about what the president can accomplish. In the nineteenth century, when the federal government had few responsibilities compared to the present and when the conduct of foreign affairs consisted largely of appointing ambassadors, the Congress rather than the president was the center of the federal government. The legislature was a part-time job whose members served but a few terms in Washington.[26] The popular view was that governing was anything but an art.

> We are too apt to think both the work of legislation and the work of administration easy enough to be done readily, with or without preparation by any man of discretion and character. No one imagines that the drygoods or hardware trade, or even the cobbler's craft, can be successfully conducted except by those who have worked through a laborious and unremunerative apprenticeship, and who have devoted their lives to perfecting themselves as tradesmen or as mendors of shoes. But . . . administration is regarded as something which an old soldier, an ex-diplomatist, or

a popular politician may be trusted to take by instinct. No man of tolerable talents need despair of having been born a presidential candidate.[27]

Another keen observer, Lord James Bryce, argued that intelligence and eloquence were useful, but perhaps superfluous traits for a president. Instead, the nineteenth-century president's job was such that the skills needed to perform the job were similar to those of "the chairman of a commercial company or the manager of a railway": firmness, common sense, and, most critical, honesty.[28] In the twentieth century, however, the role of the central government grew tremendously. The New Deal brought Washington into the lives of most American citizens. The two world wars, the conflicts in Korea, Vietnam, and the Persian Gulf, and, most important, the growing internationalization of the world economy made the central government the focal point of people's attention. So did the rise of national media, especially television networks, that led to a more homogenous culture throughout the nation's regions.

Do We Expect Too Much of Our Presidents?

The new focus on Washington, the growth of national media to spread the word about what was happening in the Capitol, and the declining power of political parties meant that people looked more and more to the president as the single source of authority in the country. The presidency thus became an almost mythical institution. The people viewed the occupant of the White House as the single person who could coordinate the activities of the government and who thus could solve the nation's problems. Presidents in turn encouraged this lavish attention by constantly appealing for popular support through the act of " going public." The people and their chief executive built up a rapport that excluded the Congress or other actors in the government. The parties were not left out. It was their weakness that led presidents to seek out a direct relationship with the public.[29]

This "special relationship" between the people and their leader is not a simple love story. One suitor, the public, is often quite fickle in its feelings toward the other, the president. Given the great expectations that people initially have of their leaders, it is only natural that disappointment sets in at some time during the president's administration. Even partial successes can become failures if the people expect too much; thus presidents appear doomed to failure. Contemporary presidents have succeeded for the most part in making their successors look better than they did while in office.[30] During the Iran–Contra hearings, many Americans came to upgrade their evaluation of Carter who, after all, took full responsibility for the hostage crisis. During the Carter administration Ford's hapless tenure in office, marked primarily by overridden vetoes, seemed a happy memory. Witness not only the rehabilitation, but the revival of Nixon's fortunes, including a 1986 cover story in *Time* magazine showing the former president making the "V for Victory" sign of happier days. Bush rode a virtually unprecedented wave of popularity during and immediately after the Gulf War, only to lose popularity consistently through the summer of 1992: He withstood a nearly 60-point drop in favorability.

What factors contribute to the roller-coaster contour of presidential popularity in the post-Vietnam era? Clearly our expectations of presidential performance are critical, but suggestions that we lower our sights are unrealistic.[31] The presidency occupies too important a role in our political system. If we cannot convince the public that they are demanding the impossible, perhaps we can find presidents who are up to the task. When we look to recent history, we find that those presidents who have failed sought the office as "outsiders." They ran against the Washington establishment, promising a whole new way of doing business. More than any other recent presidents, they went public. Carter established a reputation as the "people's president" by carrying his luggage into the White House himself. Reagan continually pressed viewers to write their representatives and senators to demand support for his policies. Both gave short shrift to their party leaders in Congress. As Meg Greenfield argued:

> We have developed something new in our politics: the professional amateur. It is by now a trend, a habit, a cult. You succeed in this line of activity by declaring your aversion to and unfitness for it. That will bring you the cheers of the multitude. It will also bring in time . . . the kind of troubles the Carter presidency has sustained and seemed, almost perversely, to compound.[32]

Both Carter and Reagan, as well as "amateur" candidates who failed to win the presidency (George McGovern in 1972, John Anderson in 1980) ignored the traditional party organizations through which presidents used to be selected.

Presidential candidates focus on the media instead of the parties. They spend their time going public and confer with a handpicked set of personal advisers, many of whom have had no contact with politicians in Washington. At the 1980 Democratic convention, only 14 percent of the Democratic members of the House and Senate attended as delegates.[33] The party recognized the error of its ways when it provided for additional "superdelegates" who would comprise 14 percent of the 1984 convention delegates. This group would consist of party members and elected officials, two thirds of whom might be members of the House and Senate. However, the party's ties to its Washington base had long been weakened. Between 1968 and 1980 the number of primaries doubled from seventeen to thirty-five and the percentage of delegates selected through this route increased from forty to seventy-five. The focal point of Washington politics had shifted back to the heartland of the country.

The backgrounds of Carter, Reagan, Dukakis, and Clinton are also no accident.

Presidential candidates no longer come primarily from the Senate. Both Carter and Reagan were *former* governors who became full-time presidential candidates. In 1984 Walter F. Mondale's background in the Senate and as vice president were considered by many to be handicaps, and a legislative outsider with few accomplishments in the Senate (Hart) captured the imagination of many Democrats and almost the nomination as well. In 1988, only three of the candidates had won statewide races for national office on their own more than once: Robert Dole, Paul Laxalt, and Joseph Biden. Just three had risen to positions of leadership in their parties: Dole as majority (and later minority) leader of the Senate and Gephardt as chair of the Democratic Caucus in the House. Three prominent candidates (Jesse Jackson, Alexander Haig, and Pat Robertson) had never been elected to any position. Two senators ran in their first terms (Albert Gore and Paul Simon).

Two factors conspired to deter established Washington figures from seeking the Democratic nomination in 1992. Bush's popularity was so high in early 1991, when potential candidates had to establish organizations for the primaries, that leading figures decided to pass up the race. At least of equal importance was the anti-Washington mood in the country. The three leading candidates—Clinton, former Senator Paul Tsongas (Mass.), and former California Governor Jerry Brown—jousted with each other for the mantle of the outsider most hostile to the Washington establishment. What is even more remarkable is the large number of trial balloons sent up by rather ordinary political figures who had virtually no name recognition beyond their own states. The presidency had become democratized, so that the refrain one learned in elementary school—that any little boy or girl could grow up to become president—seemed quite true indeed.

Presidents get into trouble, this thesis goes, because they come to Washington as enemies of the government and bring their own staffs—be they from California or Georgia—with them. This is the "cult of the amateur" that the public seems to reward. Yet chief executives must confront congressional leaders still chosen largely in accord with the seniority system, and heads of other countries who rise through the ranks of their political parties and legislatures. How do we get such presidents—those who disdain the type of bargaining that past leaders recognized as necessary to accomplish the successful enactment of their legislative programs, and their dealings with foreign heads of state?

According to many, the villain is the nomination system. The proliferation of primaries and caucuses places a premium on candidates' willingness to spend two to three years traversing such states as Iowa and New Hampshire, shaking hands with potential supporters rather than developing ties with party leaders who in previous years could deliver delegate support at the nominating conventions. The British magazine, *The Economist*, expressed this view succinctly.

> America gets bad presidents because it gets bad candidates, and it gets bad candidates because they are now chosen chiefly in a series of primary elections in which voters put a premium on superficial qualities televisually conveyed, with little consideration of the attributes needed to run the most powerful country in world.[34]

Since many of the delegates themselves are attending conventions for the first time, there are few ties that bind the presidential candidates to the party, or the party to its eventual nominee.[35] The delegates are nowhere to be found when the winner takes office.

The new president must deal with the "entrenched Washington establishment," in the Congress and in the bureaucracy. After having run against these same people—and having run behind most congressional candidates even in districts carried by the victorious party—the president cannot rely on them for support. Thus, the only alternative is to go over their heads and demand that the public put pressure on these officials to support the administration's policies. This leads presidents not only to chastise the Congress, but ultimately to ignore it. In turn this produces either an isolated chief executive such as Carter or an irate one such as Reagan, whose hand-chosen advisers feel free to take policy initiatives into their own hands when Congress seems obstructionistic. The Iran–Contra affair thus can be seen not as a unique event, but as the culmination of a political crisis between the two major branches of government. In turn, it produces a downward spiral in public confidence in the presidency that can only be reversed by the same type of anti-Washington appeals that led to the difficulties in the first place. Thus, the cure for the ills of amateurism—to paraphrase the late Robert LaFollette, the Progressive party candidate for president in 1924—is more amateurism.[36]

Is there a way out of this seemingly vicious cycle? Some have suggested that if the primary system is the cause of the problems, taking the nomination out of the hands of the public might resolve the predicament of "the cult of the amateur." One proposal would make all of the party nominees for the House and Senate in addition to senators not due for reelection automatic delegates to the party conventions. This proposal is designed to increase the ties that bind the presidential candidate to the party's congressional delegation.[37] A more radical suggestion would abolish primaries altogether and rest the nominations with the party's membership in Congress, as was the case before 1824. Not only might this bring more harmony to legislative–executive affairs, but it would also make the nomination of an outsider extremely unlikely.[38] Legislators would hardly be apt to select as their party's standard-bearer someone who refused to acknowledge any ties to the caucus. Both of these reforms, it should be noted, do not require any legislation. The national parties could adopt them.

The difficulty with the first suggestion is that it has already been substantially adopted without much effect on the nominating process. In 1984, the Democrats provided that up to two thirds of the sitting members of the House and Senate would be delegates to their convention. Even with the same system in place for 1988 and 1992, a whole raft of unknown and untested candidates sought their party's nomination. Merely adding a handful of additional members, plus party nominees for the Congress who have not yet served in Washington and may never be elected, is unlikely to have a measurable impact. This "reform" would not do away with the long arduous nominating system that places a premium on outsider strategies. The second, more radical proposal *would* do away with primaries and caucuses. However, for that very reason, it is not likely to be adopted. It is especially unlikely that the very amateurs who gather at conventions would vote to eliminate their base of power and give it back to party leaders.

In any event, there is reason to doubt that the primary system itself is the cause, rather than the effect, of the decline of parties. Many of the trends of the new long campaign, with its numerous candidates, actually predated the 1972 reforms that made the nominating system for the Democratic party so wide open.[39] As noted in Chapter 5, the decline of party strength dates back to the 1930s. A more proximate cause of the success of the outsider strategy than the primary system is the decline in political trust in America that began in the 1970s. This makes perfect sense. Candidates for the White House succeed with the outsider strategy because people see the Washington establishment as not trustworthy. Each new crisis of the presidency further erodes trust in government—and makes it more difficult for an "insider" to gain a nomination.

If this argument is correct, there is little we can do to stop the cult of amateurism. To get better presidents, we need a successful presidency. Yet presidencies seem doomed to failure, if for no other reason than because the public expects more of the office than any human being can deliver. The nominating system puts a premium on successful politicians rather than on men and women who can govern well, so our leaders are sure to fall very short of public expectations. We do indeed have a vicious cycle. Perhaps we can gain some solace from recognizing that this is not a novel problem of the television age. Writing of the "mediocre" candidates of the nineteenth century, Bryce argued that "the merits of a president are one thing and those of a candidate another thing."[40] The stakes, especially in international politics, have increased enormously and thus it is more crucial than ever that we find some way to balance executive and legislative power and responsibilities.

What Kind of Foreign Policy Does the Public Want?

If the search for better presidents is not likely to be fruitful, perhaps one way to avoid the cycles of presidential popularity is for the legislative branch to become stronger. A more active role for the Congress might restrain the president from engaging in the sort of policies that ultimately and it seems inevitably lead to failed presidencies. A stronger Congress might also make legislators less parochial and more willing to view foreign policy from a global perspective.

Whom does the public believe makes foreign policy in the United States and whom does it trust the most to formulate the great issues of international affairs? Surveys by the Chicago Council on Foreign Relations in 1982 provide some insight into these questions.[41] Interviewing both a national sample of the public and 341 elite opinion leaders, the council asked each who had the most power on foreign policy decision making and who *ought* to be the most important. The results of the surveys are presented in Table 10.1.

The president is seen by both samples as the most important actor, although 70 percent of the general public has this perception compared to almost the entire elite sample. Almost equally powerful from the public's perspective—and still a strong second in the eyes of the elite—is the secretary of state. Slightly less than half of the public sample and just about a third of the elite sees an important role for Congress. This represents a considerable shift from a 1974 set of surveys when only 20 percent of the elite sampled and 40 percent of the public perceived Congress as playing an important role on foreign policy. However, it also represents somewhat of a decline, at least among the elite, from the 45 percent who saw Congress as very important as recently as 1978–1979, the most recent survey taken after the legislature began to challenge the executive during the Nixon years on domestic and foreign issues. Most of the actors, ranging from the bureaucrats at the State Department to the United Nations to labor and business as well as the military and the CIA, are perceived as less important by the elite than they are by the public at large. The elite tends to view the foreign policy-making process in dominance by the president and the secretary of state, with some power for the Congress and more limited influence by the bureaucracy, the military, and public opinion. The elite perceives the president's na-

TABLE 10.1   The Importance of Various Actors in Foreign Policy Making: The Chicago Council on Foreign Relations Mass and Elite Surveys, 1982*

Actor	Actor Perceived as Very Important		Actor Should Be Important	
	Public	Elite	Public	Elite
President	70	91	39	17
Secretary of state	64	83	33	22
State Department	47	38	34	34
Congress	46	34	44	34
Military	40	36	26	3
Public opinion	23	15	54	36
United Nations	29	2	37	33
American business	35	22	23	22
Labor unions	17	3	17	14
Private organizations	9	3	10	21
Central Intelligence Agency	28	20	16	9
National security adviser	35	46	31	13

*In percentages

tional security adviser as more powerful than does the general public. Ordinary citizens may be less likely to understand the unique role of this adviser, much less to know who he is, than the more attentive elite. But the public does acknowledge executive dominance on foreign policy while perceiving substantial roles for most other actors. Most of the public, however, does not view public opinion as a particularly powerful voice on foreign policy when compared to Congress, the military, the State Department, business, or even the United Nations.

While the public does not see its own opinions as having a major impact, it does believe (by a margin of 54 percent) that it should be the most important determinant of foreign policy making. Congress is second, ahead of the president, who barely edges the United Nations and is not far ahead of the State Department, the secretary of state, or the national security adviser. Indeed, the public seems to have lost confidence in all actors—including public opinion itself—since 1978–1979. Thirteen percent more of the public (67 percent in all) felt that its attitudes should be very important in 1978–1979, while 46 percent believed that the president should be important. Of the other actors, there were drops of between 3 and 7 percent except for the Congress and labor unions, which stayed at almost similar levels to four years earlier. The elites became somewhat less trustworthy as well of most actors. Public opinion fell 8 points. On the other hand, there were small increases in elite opinions about the roles that Congress, the State Department, and labor ought to play.

The opinion leaders remain distrustful of presidential dominance, perhaps because of the lack of foreign policy experience that the men who have recently become president had before assuming office. The Iran–Contra affair demonstrates that perceptions of poor performance lead to crises of trust in *all* institutions. Although more people lost confidence in the executive branch (24 percent) than in any other institution, 20 percent reported losing faith in the Congress and about 16 percent each in the press, business, and labor.[42] When the news was better, during and in the immediate aftermath of the Gulf War, confidence in most institutions rose. The anti-Washington mood in the nation meant that the increases in support for Congress were relatively modest compared with those for other institutions.[43] The elite seems to prefer a more dispersed pattern of authority on foreign policy than does the public, although the difference is not nearly as sharp as it was in earlier surveys. The public is more willing to entrust policy making to business than to labor or other private organizations, but it already sees business as having more power than is desirable. The elites recognize that business is powerful, but do not seem to think that it is quite as strong as the public believes it to be. Indeed, its influence is seen as "just about right," while both labor and private organizations ought to be more powerful.

The deflation of public confidence in political institutions has hit Congress harder than other bodies. Americans have not turned against Congress in its struggle for control over foreign policy, but have become more evenly divided in the legislative–executive conflict. Pluralities of both the public and elites believe that the balance between the president and the Congress on foreign policy is "about right." There have been increases in the number of people claiming that Congress is too strong and that the executive is too weak. Most Americans believe that we have two presidencies. Almost twice as many people say that Congress takes the lead on domestic policy as argue that the president does. On foreign policy, the balance is 3.5 to 1.0 in favor of the executive. Most Americans favor coequal branches; of those who do not, a slim plurality (28 to 20 percent) believe that Congress should be more powerful. Americans are *not* willing to cede foreign policy making to the White House: 71 percent said that the president needed congressional approval to begin military action in the Persian Gulf. Sixty percent—including majorities of Democrats, Republicans, and Independents—believed that Congress should be required to declare war.[44]

The elite prefers a foreign policy conducted by the unusual coalition of Congress, the State Department, public opinion, and the United Nations. On the other hand, the public prefers more of a partnership among its own opinions, the Congress, and the executive. In essence, it calls for a more evenly distributed balance of power between the legislative and executive branches than we now have, with somewhat more power given to the legislature.

How might the Congress take on a more assertive role in foreign policy? The institutional barriers we discussed in Chapters 3 and 4 remain. It is simply unrealistic to expect the 435 members of the House of Representatives and the 100 members of the Senate to coalesce in support of a single foreign policy. It might even be too much to demand that the major foreign policy committees in each house reach agreement. Even if they could, who would negotiate with international leaders, the president, or the Congress? When the two branches agree on key issues, this question is of little consequence. However, the entire question of which branch should predominate is predicated on the idea that the legislative and executive will generally *not* agree. This, of course, is the heart of the democratic dilemmas. If whatever process we used had the same outcomes, the problem of making foreign policy in a democracy would not exist.

The President Proposes, the Congress Reacts?

Perhaps we should admit that the Congress is not well suited to formulate an independent foreign policy and that it is unlikely to impose its own views on the president in many instances. Is there an alternative role for Congress? The answer is "yes." Like the role of public opinion in a democracy, the Congress can—and often does—evaluate foreign policy retrospectively. That is, it responds to administration proposals and actions by examining them, holding hearings, and proposing alternative policies. The Legislative Reorganization Act of 1970 indeed mandated increased oversight for all committees in the Congress.

The prospects for oversight can perhaps best be summed up by the traditional refrain. The word *oversight* has two meanings: critical evaluation of executive performance and a passing thought. In the Congress, where many committee hearings are routine and not very investigative, there has been an overemphasis on the meaning not intended by those who want more of a balance of power in the national government. The difficulty is that in too many cases, the regulators (congressional investigators) become the accomplices of the groups or organizations they are supposed to investigate and control.[45] Furthermore, as Morris Ogul argues, the oversight function is not terribly salient to most members of Congress.[46] Even when members do become concerned with their oversight duties, the close working relationships that develop among the legislators, bureaucrats, and interest groups ("those cozy triangles"[47]) are not conducive to critical examinations of the behavior of each other.

Yet there has been an increase in critical oversight in recent years. In particular, both the House and the Senate established oversight committees to investigate the abuses of power of the Central Intelligence Agency and the Federal Bureau of Investigation in the Ninety-fourth Congress (1975–1976). Yet, the very fact that such committees were established points to one of the weaknesses in the congressional oversight procedure. Institutional loyalties prevailed, so that no thought was given to a joint committee—which would have saved duplication of effort. In each House, a select committee (as opposed to one of the more traditional standing committees) was formed for the investigations. Yet there existed committees on foreign relations, armed services, government operations, and judiciary (in the case of the FBI) in each House that could just as effectively have conducted the oversight. Why were select committees employed? Again, the question of institutional loyalties arose within congressional committees, and there was also a problem of where the ultimate jurisdiction was to be placed.

Once established, the intelligence committees did not function smoothly. In the Senate, many critics claimed that Chairman Frank Church was headline hunting and was trying to conclude the hearings as quickly as possible to enter the Democratic presidential primaries. The committee in the House, known as the Pike Committee, drew better "press notices," but the lower house produced a spectacle of its own. The original House Intelligence Committee was chaired by Representative Lucien Nedzi (D-Mich.). A conflict within the committee developed when maverick Representative Michael Harrington (D-Mass.) leaked to the press classified material on the CIA's role in destabilizing the Allende government in Chile in 1973. Nedzi demanded that Harrington be removed from the committee, and there was a movement within the House to censure Harrington. The Harrington case was overshadowed by further leaks to the press and the entire matter was finally closed on a rather obscure technicality that saved Harrington from possible action by his fellow House members. Speaker

Carl Albert finally resolved the dispute between supporters of Nedzi and those of Harrington by reconstituting the committee without either member. Like its Senate counterpart, the House Intelligence Committee was established as a permanent committee in 1977.

What did the intelligence committees accomplish? They did bring to public attention a large number of abuses of power by the FBI and particularly by the CIA. Yet much of this publicity arose through leaks and much of what we learned about the intelligence agencies came from newspapers and magazine follow-up stories rather than from congressional testimony. Indeed, Pike and Ford were at loggerheads on what the committee could or could not release. The full House ultimately sided with the president against a moderate Democrat. Much of the impetus for reform was slowed when Richard Welch, a CIA operative in Greece, was assassinated. Many people thought that the congressional hearings were divulging too much information about the agency, thereby making the intelligence operations of the United States vulnerable throughout the world. Ultimately, the Congress did take some action: It forbade the CIA from engaging in domestic intelligence operations, and it also passed a law that made the assassination of foreign leaders illegal—an action that undoubtedly would make a few foreign chiefs of state sleep more soundly at night. Attempts to make the CIA budget available to at least the relevant congressional personnel failed. No wide-ranging reorientation of foreign intelligence was mandated by Congress. The decision in 1977 to place all intelligence operations dealing with foreign policy under a single agency, headed by CIA Director Stansfield Turner, was made in the White House, not on Capitol Hill.

In 1980 the Congress voted to restrict the number of committees to which the president must report any covert action to two, the intelligence chambers in the House and the Senate. A congressional move, backed by the Carter administration, to formulate a charter for the CIA failed to win approval, but so did a conservative bid in the Congress to repeal the provisions of the Hughes-Ryan amendment and "unleash" the intelligence community. The actions of 1980 were taken by many as a sign that the CIA and other agencies had learned to live with the new requirements, indeed that the reporting procedures were not particularly onerous. There had been considerable concern that if the president reported to eight committees, leaks of national security information from the Congress would occur, which was the case with the single committee in the House in 1973. Thus, the administration had simply not informed all relevant committees and subcommittees of foreign intelligence operations.

There were few congressional complaints until the attempt to rescue the hostages from Iran in 1980 failed, and some members of Congress claimed that they had not been given advance notice. However, this did not prevent them from restricting the Hughes-Ryan amendment shortly thereafter. Oversight of the CIA, particularly in a period of international tensions when the American will was being severely tried, was not a politically beneficial issue in 1980, so few members pressed for it. Oversight on foreign policy has thus tended to become regularized since the early 1970s but is not nearly as rewarding as many members thought it might be. Thus, it has taken a lesser role in congressional politics than domestic policy or even other foreign policy issues; and the permanent select committees have not been made standing committees, a move that would indicate greater importance for these bodies within the Congress.

Congressional oversight on foreign policy has not been totally ineffective. Congress did interrogate Kissinger to a greater extent than during any other recent period on the details of the 1975 Sinai accord. As discussed earlier, Congress passed, over Nixon's veto, a War Powers Act; and, against the wishes of the Nixon administration, the legislature required the secretary of state to submit the final text of any executive agreement on foreign policy to Congress within sixty days. In 1983, the House attempted to rein in the CIA once again by voting to prohibit covert aid to insurgents trying to overthrow the Nicaraguan government.

This was clearly one of the most conspicuous failures of the oversight process. Three years later the Iran–Contra affair broke and the Congress had to admit that it did not make the sanctions strong enough to block covert assistance. The Reagan administration's policies in both the Middle East and Latin America stood in shambles as the Congress merely stood by in anger. Similarly, the War Powers Act has not given Congress the new tool it sought to control the executive. Critics of the Grenada invasion, the bombing of Libya, and the reflagging of Kuwaiti tankers in the Persian Gulf found themselves acting too late with too little authority to reverse the Reagan administration policies. They found themselves with insufficient support on Capitol Hill and lacking alternative programs with which to reverse course.

The independent Special Prosecutor Lawrence Walsh continued to investigate Iran–Contra. In mid-1992 Walsh indicted former Defense Secretary Caspar Weinberger for failing to reveal notes from cabinet meetings that the special prosecutor believed might reveal greater knowledge of the affair by President Reagan. Congress lost interest and moved on to other foreign policy questions. It probed the allegation that Reagan and Bush, while candidates in 1980, convinced the Iranian government to hold up the release of the American hostages until after the election. The legislative branch and the media (especially ABC's "Nightline") suggested that Bush and the late CIA director William Casey had met with Iranian officials in Paris in 1980. Bush emphatically denied the meetings, and Casey was deceased. Ultimately Congress admitted it had no evidence that Bush was in Paris at all in 1980. Representatives Henry Gonzalez (D-Texas), chair of the Banking Committee, and Jack Brooks (D-Texas), chair of the Judiciary Committee, probed the Bush administration's early dealings with Iraq. They charged that the president and Secretary of State James Baker illegally used the American grain export program to permit American firms to sell arms and nuclear technology to Saddam Hussein's regime in 1989. *New York Times* columnist William Safire described "a pattern of obstruction of justice and lying to Congress" that he called "Iraqgate."[48] As with Iran–Contra, the "Iraqgate" accusations formed a complex web of international financial transactions that made the issue difficult to exploit in the arena of public opinion.

However, these examples of frustration should not obscure the substantial initiatives of the Congress on foreign policy. Congress has reversed the administration course of action on South African sanctions and in providing aid to the Contras. It blocked aid to Angolan rebels in the 1970s. Since the founding of Israel, it has been the legislature rather than various presidents that has insisted on strong American support for the Jewish state.[49] This backing has included not only economic and military aid, but also several successful attempts to block arms sales to Arab countries. Presidents virtually always win on these arms sales, so the magnitude of the victories of pro-Israeli groups should not be underestimated. These are but a few of the examples of congressional initiatives that have succeeded. The legislature is more active on domestic policy. These issues permit greater legislative initiatives and, indeed, the Congress has often taken the lead on domestic questions.[50] On foreign policy, however, the legislature is consigned to act in response to executive initiatives. This is not because of inherent weaknesses of Congress, for the same institutional structure that takes the lead on domestic policy must take a back seat on foreign policy. Rather, the distinction lies in the nature of the issue areas. The foreign policy agenda is set not by legislators' constituents exclusively, but by other nations as well. Country-to-country negotiations necessarily take place at the level of executives. When domestic legislatures do react to executive initiatives on foreign policy issues, especially intermestic ones, they protect the interests of their own citizens (see Chapter 9). This is the case even in strong party systems in parliamentary regimes.

Those who want to strengthen the role of Congress in determining what the foreign policy of the United States *will be,* as opposed to what it should have been, may seek a more active role for the legislature than oversight. However, they must answer the question, do legislators want to do more policy initiation? One study has found that rational members of Congress would not devote all of their time to examining the minute details of any policy area. In this "police-patrol" model of oversight, legislators examine a sample of executive activities in a search for violations of legislative dictates. Alternatively, the Congress might pursue a "fire-alarm" model, in which the legislature delegates much of the oversight responsibility to interest groups and citizens who ring "fire-alarm boxes" to indicate to Congress that the executive has breached its congressional mandate. Sometimes the legislature responds directly to its own indications of transgressions. The analogy is to community protection agencies. Police patrols drive around neighborhoods more or less at random and keep their eyes open for unusual occurrences. Fire departments, on the other hand, respond only to calls from citizens, unless they notice fire themselves.

The fire-alarm strategy of responding primarily to crises—and often through the assistance of interest groups or citizens—is a rational use of legislators' time and resources.[51] Police-patrol oversight cannot examine every issue area; it must sample and in doing so it is likely to miss some important violations of congressional intent in administrative practices. Fire-alarm oversight, in contrast, is less likely to miss any important transgressions because it delegates responsibility to interested groups in the public. While this strategy dictates a more limited role for the legislature than do police patrols, it may actually provide Congress with more leverage over executive decisions by highlighting questions that the legislators believe are critically important. Ironically, then, the Congress can have a greater say in foreign policy formation by acting selectively than by trying to compete with the administration on every front.

One explanation for this conclusion is that legislators are not as accountable for their actions, especially on foreign policy, as the president.[52] Legislators will thus focus their activities on policy questions on which they can make electoral gains. These do not generally include foreign policy. Devoting too much time to international issues can, as was argued in Chapter 4, lead to electoral problems. Instead, the fire-alarm approach permits legislators to delegate foreign policy concerns to interested constituents. By the time these issues trickle up to the Congress, legislators already know that there is at least some group who might reward them for taking an active role on such questions. How large the group is will determine the amount of effort legislators will expend on foreign policy oversight.

Once an issue catches the public's imagination many legislators will become involved in it. As noted in Chapter 5, however, there are a few issues on which the public is so aroused—or even where there are sufficiently powerful interest groups to entice members of Congress to devote considerable attention to international problems. Yet those issues that do arouse the public's attention for more than fleeting moments—in contrast to short-lived events such as the Grenada invasion and the bombing of Libya—are those on which the president's position proves unpopular. Here the Congress can have the greatest effect. It can reverse administration policy on South African sanctions and aid to the Contras and put pressure on Marcos to leave the Philippines. It can reinforce American support for Israel in the Middle East even as successive administrations have sought to reverse course.

Even when public opinion is not mobilized, interest groups may well be. When groups are well organized *and* have no powerful opposition, they can prevail on foreign policy just as they do on domestic issues—even in the face of presidential opposition to their points of view. The blocking of arms sales to Arab countries, as sought by the pro-Israel lobby, is perhaps the most striking example of this effect. However, very few of the examples of the "effects" of foreign policy rest entirely on the reactions of the unorganized citizenry. The most vocal exponents of any point of view are the interest groups. Groups, however, would not get their way, especially on foreign policy, if they did not begin with at least potential support among the mass public and a predisposition by most members of Congress to agree with their positions. In effect, what Congress can do is bring public concerns to bear on American foreign policy. When congressional initiatives fail, it is either because public opinion supports the administration more than the legislature or simply because there is no clear mandate from the electorate. This was the case in Vietnam. As unpopular as that war was, critics could not convince the public that withdrawal was preferable to a stepped-up military presence. Those who demand that Congress play a greater role in the initiation of foreign policy must confront the incentives facing legislators. That brings us back to a reconsideration of the democratic dilemmas.

The Democratic Dilemmas Reconsidered

We have seen that one way of resolving the problem of how much power each branch of the government should have on foreign policy is by strengthening the power of Congress, which can at least in part be accomplished by reforms such as the War Powers Act or increased oversight. But this will not necessarily lead to further congressional *control* over foreign policy decisions. On the other hand, a change that would give Congress more power on foreign policy, strengthening political parties to the point of sharing responsibility with the executive, might not be possible to initiate.

Is there an answer to the problem of foreign policy decision making in a democracy? Probably not, if one insists on a panacea for failures in foreign policy and a guarantee that successful policies will continue to be chosen. The decision-making process on foreign policy questions appears to work best in crisis situations, when immediate and decisive action is required. Perhaps leaders function best in crises—or perhaps the "followers" are simply more likely to support the leaders. On security and intermestic policies, the system appears to work less well. These issue areas may have high stakes, but they are not perceived as external threats. Furthermore, there is not always agreement about what the stakes are for all actors or what the most desirable outcome is. A democratic political system appears to handle foreign policy decisions best when the fewest actors—the inner circle—are involved in the process of decision making. As more and more actors in all four circles become involved, the conflict between presidential formation of foreign policy and the desires of other actors to have a say in foreign policy becomes intense. In crisis decision making, the administration chooses a course of action designed to maximize a given goal. The decision that is reached is directly related to that goal. Students of the foreign policy-making process have praised the decisions made in crises and concluded that democratic governments can indeed rival monolithic dictatorships in response to external threats, citing the pattern of rational decision making in such situations as the reason why the American political system has fared as well in crises. Lowi has stated:

> *Crisis decisions in foreign policy are made by an elite of formal, official officeholders.* Rarely is there time to go further . . . the people who make decisions in times of crisis are

largely those who were elected and appointed to make such decisions. That is to say, *in foreign affairs crises our government has operated pretty much as it was supposed to operate.* There is a normative corollary as well: Since our record of response to crisis is good, then the men in official positions have been acting and are able to act rationally. . . . Indeed, a fundamental feature of crisis decisions is that they involve institution leaders (holders of the top posts) *without their institutions.* Only when time allows does the entire apparatus of the foreign policy establishment come in play.[53]

On security and intermestic policies, however, the decisions reached through bureaucratic/governmental politics are often "minimal" ones; they do not resolve issues one way or the other and often cannot be justified on the basis that they maximize any particular foreign policy goal. Indeed, it is possible that, as in energy policy, bureaucratic/governmental politics may lead to no decisions at all—if the contending forces are each strong and obstinate enough to prevent a compromise acceptable to all (or even most) parties.

In addition, in security policies—including limited wars—the objectives of the policy as well as the proposed ways of handling them often lack the clarity of crisis decision making.* In Vietnam, for example, the objectives of American policy were never clearly delineated. On the one hand, a policy of total war was never seriously considered by the Johnson or Nixon administration. However, neither was the policy of withdrawal of all American troops. Both administrations flatly rejected what might appear to have been a "rational" compromise first suggested by other nations and then advocated by North Vietnam: a coalition government in South Vietnam. The result was a sequence of minimal decisions: to increase American troop strength during the Johnson administration, but to continue to press for a negotiated settlement to the conflict. By contrast, Nixon reduced American troop strength but increased the bombing of North Vietnam, again continuing to search for a negotiated settlement. Yet the strategies of both administrations involved contradictory policies, producing what Burns has called an *immoderate moderation.* The United States finally extricated itself from the war without ever having resolved the question of what goals were accomplished by the many years of costly fighting.

If it is then concluded that decision making works best—produces the best results or garners the most public support—in crisis situations, we must, in conclusion, address ourselves again to the democratic dilemma posed at the beginning of the study. To ensure its security in the essentially anarchical international system, a state must have a concentration of executive authority so that it can respond quickly and with unity of purpose to events in the international political system. A democratic state, on the other hand, requires a restraint on executive power to preserve the constitutional system. This tension between the

---

*Limited wars are much like program policies in that both types of foreign policy decisions (1) involve multiple actors; (2) take a considerable amount of time to reach a conclusion; (3) involve conflicting goals on what a policy is supposed to accomplish; (4) involve bargaining—generally among the combatants rather than domestically—and are ultimately resolved by a negotiated settlement; and (5) are often marked by minimal decisions.

needs of international and domestic systems spills over into the distinction between crisis decision making on the one hand and security and intermestic policies on the other. Decision making in crisis situations very much resembles authoritarian decision making: policies are determined by a relatively small number of actors who must act with dispatch and unity. Democratic politics, on the other hand, is often marked by the necessity to compromise, to consider issues at great length in the attempt to reconcile conflicting interests, and to highlight the different goals of the actors involved rather than to assume that the decision makers all agree on the goals to be maximized.

What Role for Democratic Institutions?

The three aspects of the democratic dilemmas pervade all aspects of policy making, but are particularly difficult to resolve on foreign policy issues, where the stakes are so high and the actors all share at least one common goal: the survival and defense of the nation. The need to act quickly on foreign policy issues means that the president, as chief diplomat and commander in chief of the armed forces, must be able to respond to events in the international environment. But presidents may claim many things in the name of national security. (Nixon went as far as to include conversation with his aides on the Watergate scandal) and the question remains of how democratic the nation will be so that the president must protect these claims. What should the proper role of Congress be in foreign policy decision making—particularly when the Founding Fathers expected the legislature to dominate domestic politics and domestic policies to dominate the nation's agenda? If the Congress should have some role in foreign policy making, how great should that role be? Should other actors, such as interest groups, public opinion, and the media, also have their interests represented, as is the case with domestic policy? Does the Congress, with its more limited resources compared to the vast foreign policy bureaucracy of the executive branch, have the capacity to reach the "correct" foreign policy? In this same regard, how do we determine what the "correct" decision is—and how might we reconcile what we believe to be the proper course of action on an international issue with what popular sentiment might be? When the public is supportive of administration policies, this issue does not arise. But the public and the administration may both be right or may both be wrong. Hindsight is a great teacher, but it gives us little guidance about how widespread the scope of participation should be for present decisions.

The irony of foreign policy decision making is thus that the American political system appears to function best when decisions are made in the very way authoritarian states formulate policies.[54] When foreign policy decisions become more "democratic" by encompassing more actors, the policies selected may not have as clear a relationship to the strategic problem at hand. The democratic dilemmas do not admit of a ready answer. The framers of the Constitution did indeed produce a document with "missing powers," allowing for the growth of presidential power to meet changing needs. And by consciously creating a form of government that was inimical to responsible party government,[55] the framers of the Constitution ensured that the legislative branch could not take the foreign policy initiative away from the executive—an initiative they had given him. Believing that the nation would engage in no "entangling alliances," against which George Washington was to admonish the country in his farewell address, the Founding Fathers expected the war-making powers given to Congress in the Constitution would provide an adequate check on presidential dominance of the foreign policy process.

The president will, however, remain the dominant actor in foreign policy decision making. The conduct of an activist foreign policy—as distinct from a neoisolationist one—will continue to require a strong foreign policy president. Thus, the basic dilemma remains. What is a virtue internationally may be a vice domestically, and what is virtue domestically—a restraint on executive power—may become a vice internationally. The basic question is whether the United States can grant its government sufficient authority to safeguard the nation while preserving its democratic system. In the final analysis, the purpose of America's foreign policy is to protect the country's democratic way of life. Yet, will the policy subvert the very purposes it was intended to serve?

After Vietnam, it appeared that presidents would be less willing to seek out the sort of confrontations with Congress that led to Nixon's surprising defeat on the Cambodian and War Powers issues in 1973 and the refusal of Congress to authorize funds for Ford's request on Vietnam and Angola. Yet the Iran–Contra affair indicates that administrations continue to challenge congressional dictates on foreign policy—indeed, even to defy them. The Congress has found itself always having to play catch-up with the executive. By the time the Congress took action prohibiting further aid to Vietnam in 1975, the South Vietnamese government had fallen and public support for continued American aid had virtually evaporated. Not until the Iran–Contra affair broke—and even then not expeditiously—did the Congress follow public opinion and stop aid to the Contras. Taking the lead can be risky. Congressional Democrats responded to a divided public opinion by urging the president to go slow on initiating military action. They could not block the passage of the resolution authorizing the use of force, even though they came close in the Senate. Once the president was free to take military action, public backing for Operation Desert Storm soared. Republican leaders sharply criticized the Congress—and some even suggested that legislators who opposed the war were less than patriotic.

The American people and their Congress have learned the lesson of restraint from the Vietnam experience more than have presidents. Yet the public's very high expectations of American presidents may lead chief executives to be *more* adventurous than in the past. Since the people demand so much of their presidents, and because it is becoming increasingly difficult for leaders (especially outsiders) to live up to these expectations, presidents may well be tempted to do something dramatic to shore up lagging popularity. There is nothing new in such presidential initiatives to build up popular support. However, in a period when presidential popularity can fall very far very quickly—and do so several times within an administration—the potential for adventurism by the chief executive may be much greater than even in the years before Vietnam.[56]

An irony of the post-Vietnam breakdown in the foreign policy consensus is that, even in what are called *crises,* there may be no agreed on course of action for the nation to take (see Chapters 2 and 3). What should the United States' response have been to the situations in Grenada and Libya? While the invasion of Grenada and the bombing of Tripoli both were very popular, there was also widespread criticism of each action—in a manner that we would not have seen before Vietnam. Much of the difficulty faced by foreign policy makers can be traced to the breakdown in consensus in the nation. Yet as the Iran hostage crisis demonstrated, the changing international environment also plays a critical role. Policy makers simply did not know what to do in response to a regime that practiced international terrorism. Some believed that quiet diplomacy was the best course, while others favored a military solution. Carter tried both. Reagan chided Carter in the 1980 elections for being too soft on terrorist regimes, but he himself approved arms sales to the same regime in the attempt to resolve another hostage crisis. Another reason, then, why crises do not automatically unite the nation is that it is simply unclear how to deal with the aggressor other than to get angry.

When there is no agreement on what the nation should do, questions of the best policy become intertwined with issues of who should decide what the country's policy ought to be. The Iran–Contra affair brought the issue into striking relief. As we argued in Chapter 3, members of the House and Senate committees investigating the affairs stressed the importance of following democratic procedures in enacting foreign policy. Even supporters of aid to the Contras, such as Senator Warren Rudman (R-N.H.), were highly critical of the diversion of arms sales profits. Yet many present and former administration officials—especially Lt. Col. Oliver North and Admiral John Poindexter—emphasized that support for the Contras was so vital that it justified misleading the Congress regarding what the executive branch was doing. While polls showed that the American public strongly disapproved of the entire affair, there is no clear pattern showing which offense Americans thought was worse: conducting a bad policy or violating legislatively mandated procedures. One survey found that 81 percent objected to selling arms to Iran, while 80 percent were upset that "a small group of unelected representatives [made and carried out] foreign policy without Congress or the public knowing about it."[57] In the case of the Iran–Contra affair, the public response was so overwhelmingly negative that there hardly seemed a tension between outcomes and process. Yet that crisis highlights the potential conflict that might arise and the public concern with both process and outcomes.

The Clinton administration faced this dilemma in its first 100 days. What could—or should—the United States do to stop the bloodshed in Bosnia-Hersegovina, a republic of the former Yugoslavia, where Serb nationalists are engaged in "ethnic cleansing" of Muslims in Bosnia? When Yugoslavia fell apart,

Muslims formed the largest population group in Bosnia (44 percent). By May 1993, Serbians controlled almost three-quarters of Bosnian territory. The carnage had been so devastating that Nobel Laureate Elie Wiesel used the opening ceremonies of the U.S. Holocaust Museum in Washington to call upon President Clinton to take military action against the Serbs. He likened the hatred in Bosnia to the sentiments that led to the Holocaust in Nazi Germany. Secretary of State Warren Christopher announced plans to engage the United States and its allies against the Bosnian Serbs in early May, 1993—but he faced a reluctant public. Americans were about evenly split (46 percent to 42 percent) as to whether military action would lead to a quick success as in the Gulf War or a long and costly involvement such as in the Vietnam War. By 52 percent to 36 percent they believed that the United States had already done enough to stop the bloodshed.[58] The public had no taste for a long conflict with many casualties. The president had to confront the dilemma of how to respond to moral leaders, such as Wiesel who warn of potential holocausts, while respecting the public's reluctance to get involved in other countries' conflicts.

On other policies, the roles of the presidency and Congress will depend on at least two circumstances. First, events in the developing world will have an enormous impact. Events in the Persian Gulf–Indian Ocean area—the fall of the shah in Iran and the subsequent Islamic revolution, the signs of potential internal instability in Saudi Arabia and other oil sheikdoms, and the Iran–Iraq war—have led an energy-dependent United States to commit itself to the protection of the oil kingdoms. This is one of several signs that instead of withdrawing from many of its commitments, which it is unable to do, the United States has discovered that it has become more involved than during the pre-Vietnam era. Second, because of the Vietnam War and the subsequent cries of "No More Vietnams," the question is how long the mood of the country, as expressed in this slogan, will constrain a foreign policy that is becoming activist once more and might again include the possibility of military action.

With the demise of the Soviet Union, the stakes in foreign policy may appear to be lower. However, the Gulf War suggests that the world is not yet free of crises. Instability in any of the oil-producing nations poses a greater threat to Western security than ever, as domestic production falls below the "critical" 50 percent level in the United States. A friendly Russia only highlights the dangers of the emergence of new nuclear powers such as North Korea, Libya, Pakistan, and Iraq. The burden of security will fall exclusively on the West—and, thus, the United States. The Gulf War did not liberate American policy makers from the "Vietnam syndrome." The public was relieved that the conflict ended quickly. It was not ready for further military involvement. Nationalist conflicts in the former Soviet Union and Yugoslavia came to the fore, posing security problems for the West. Who would resolve them—and how?

International politics will shift from security concerns to interdomestic issues. The critical international issues of the twenty-first century may well be trade and the environment. The collapse of communism in Eastern and Central Europe brought about democratic regimes eager to join Western economic organizations. Can the already strained industrialized economies accommodate more poor relations? Might this lead to warring trading blocs and a reversal of the liberalization of tariffs since World War II? The environment, as we saw in Chapter 9, will be one of the most contentious and expensive issues. The new democracies of Eastern and Central Europe need economic assistance to make the transition from communism to free markets, as well as substantial aid to repair decades of inattention to their environment. Their centralized planning focused on heavy industry. The new democracies—and the older autocracies (such as China)—were ecological basket cases. Americans have become increasingly polarized on international issues, but they have always been divided on domestic issues. As the two increasingly intersect, foreign policy making in the next century will likely be even more contentious.

World War I was the "war to end all wars." World War II started only twenty-one years after the earlier conflict had ended. The United States was propelled into this war against Germany and Japan despite congressional attempts to constrain presidential freedom of action to maintain America's isolationist stance. It was not to be the last time that, despite a preference for peace, the country found itself at war. This long war ended with the detonation of two atomic weapons over Japan and was supposed to underline the dangers of any future international conflict. A few years later, General Douglas MacArthur, commenting on the Korean War, stated that it was sheer folly for the United States to fight a land war in Asia; but his warnings did not prevent Vietnam. As George Santayana noted, any nation that doesn't learn from history is doomed to repeat it. The question is: Which lesson should it learn—the lesson of 1940–1941 or that of Vietnam?

Notes

1. Tom Wicker, *New York Times,* January 14, 1973.
2. Elizabeth Drew, "Letter from Washington," *The New Yorker,* June 22, 1987, p. 82.
3. "Will the Real Senate Stand Up?" *Christian Science Monitor,* May 29–June 1, 1970.
4. David Ignatius, "Contra-Funding Affair Illustrates Failure of Oversight Process," *Washington Post,* December 16, 1986, p. A16.
5. James Sundquist, *The Decline and Resurgence of Congress* (Washington, D.C.: Brookings Institution, 1981), esp. p. 155.
6. Committee on the Constitutional System, *A Bicentennial Analysis of the American Political Structure* (Washington, D.C.: 1987), p. 3. For a similar analysis that contrasts "the freebooting adventurism of a go-it-alone executive" with the "535 secretaries of state who cannot resist any opportunity to . . . micromanage foreign policy" with the result of "mutual suspicion and a state of flux," see the comments of two senators: David L. Boren [D-Okla.] and John C. Danforth [R-Mo.], "Why This Country Can't Lead," *Washington Post,* December 1, 1987, p. A21.
7. Ibid.
8. Woodrow Wilson, *Congressional Government* (Cleveland: Meridian Books, 1967), pp. 167–168. Originally published in 1885.

9. Committee on the Constitutional System, *A Bicentennial Analysis,* pp. 10–16.

10. Norman Ornstein et al., *Vital Statistics on Congress, 1984–1985 Edition* (Washington, D.C.: American Enterprise Institute), p. 56.

11. Computed from ibid., p. 57.

12. James L. Sundquist, *Constitutional Reform and Effective Government* (Washington, D.C.: Brookings Institution, 1986), p. 87. A 1991 NBC News/*Wall Street Journal* survey showed that 67 percent of Americans favored split-party control, while just 24 percent backed single-party government (NBC News press release, November 8, 1991). Even 56 percent of Republicans, who ought to be the strongest constituency for single-party control of government during an era of Republican dominance of the White House, favor divided control (NBC News press release, February 14, 1990).

13. Sundquist, *The Decline and Resurgence of Congress,* p. 470.

14. Ibid., p. 477.

15. Ibid., p. 476.

16. Douglas Martin, "Views on Constitution: Promises Kept, Miles to Go," *New York Times,* May 26, 1987, p. A20.

17. James David Barber, *The Presidential Character,* 2d ed. (Englewood Cliffs, N.J.: Prentice-Hall, 1977).

18. Ibid., p. 8.

19. Ibid., chaps. 2 and 3.

20. Ibid., chap. 5; and Andrew Rosenthal with Joel Brinkley, "Old Compass in New World: A President Sticks to Course," *New York Times,* June 25, 1992, p. A24; Barber, *The Presidential Character,* 4th ed., p. 465.

21. Barber, *The Presidential Character,* 4th ed., chap. 5.

22. Ibid., pp. 345–442.

23. Alexander George, "Assessing Presidential Character," *World Politics* 26 (January 1974), pp. 234–282; and Robert C. Tucker, "The Georges' Wilson Reexamined," *American Political Science Review* 71 (June 1977), pp. 606–618.

24. Fred I. Greenstein, *The Hidden-Hand Presidency* (New York: Basic Books, 1982).

25. Robert E. DiClerico, *The American President* (Englewood Cliffs, N.J.: Prentice-Hall, 1979), p. 332.

26. Theodore J. Lowi, *The Personal President* (Ithaca, N.Y.: Cornell Univ. Press, 1985), p. 25; and Nelson W. Polsby, "The Institutionalization of the U.S. House of Representatives," *American Political Science Review* 62 (March 1968), pp. 144–68.

27. Wilson, *Congressional Government,* p. 170.

28. James Bryce, *The American Commonwealth,* vol. 1, rev. ed. (New York: Macmillan, 1915), p. 80.

29. This is the thesis, very briefly stated, of Lowi, *The Personal President.*

30. Ibid., p. 11.

31. Richard Neustadt, *Presidential Power* (New York: John Wiley & Sons, 1980), pp. 204–5. For a set of proposals, including the adoption of a multiparty system in the United States, that are based on lower expectations, see Lowi, *The Personal President,* pp. 191–210.

32. Meg Greenfield, "The Cult of the Amateur," *Washington Post,* June 11, 1980, p. A19.

33. William Crotty, "Two Cheers for the Presidential Primaries," in *Rethinking the Presidency,* ed. Thomas Cronin (Boston: Little, Brown, 1982), p. 68.

34. "Only Freaks," *The Economist,* May 9, 1987, p. 12. See also David S. Broder, "Would You Prefer a Mondale-Baker Race?" *Washington Post,* June 4, 1980, p. A19.

35. Lowi, *The Personal President,* pp. 107–8.

36. LaFollette's statement was that the cure for the ills of democracy is more democracy.

37. Committee on the Constitutional System, *A Bicentennial Analysis of the American Political Structure*, p. 8.

38. Robert E. DiClerico and Eric M. Uslaner, *Few Are Chosen: Problems in Presidential Selection* (New York: McGraw-Hill, 1983), chap. 6.

39. See Howard L. Reiter, *Selecting the President* (Philadelphia: Univ. of Pennsylvania Press, 1985).

40. Bryce, *The American Commonwealth*, vol. 1, p. 79.

41. The data in Table 10–1 are reported in John E. Rielly, ed., *American Public Opinion and U.S. Foreign Policy 1983* (Chicago: Chicago Council on Foreign Relations, 1983). No similar questions were posed in the 1986 surveys cited in Chapter 4. The 1990 results were not reported in detail.

42. *Los Angeles Times* press release, February 20–23, 1987.

43. Times-Mirror Center for the People and the Press, *The People, the Press, and the Gulf War, II*. Washington, March 25, 1991.

44. John Rielly, *American Public Opinion and U.S. Foreign Policy 1991* (Chicago: Chicago Council on Foreign Relations, 1991), p. 8; *Los Angeles Times* news release, January 12, 1991; Martin, "Views on Constitution," p. A20; and NBC News press release, December 27, 1990.

45. Seymour Scher, "Conditions for Legislative Control," *Journal of Politics* 25 (August 1963), pp. 526–551.

46. Morris S. Ogul, *Congress Oversees the Bureaucracy* (Pittsburgh: University of Pittsburgh Press, 1976), esp. chaps. 1, 6, and 7.

47. Roger H. Davidson, "Breaking Up Those 'Cozy Triangles': An Impossible Dream?" in *Legislative Reform and Public Policy*, eds. Susan Welch and John G. Peters (New York: Praeger, 1977), pp. 30–52.

48. William Safire, "Obstructing Justice," *New York Times*, July 9, 1992, p. A21.

49. Steven L. Spiegel, *The Other Arab–Israeli Conflict* (Chicago: Univ. of Chicago Press, 1985).

50. See David E. Price, *Who Makes the Laws?* (New York: Schenkman, 1969).

51. Mathew D. McCubbins and Thomas Schwartz, "Congressional Oversight Overlooked: Police Patrols versus Fire Alarms," *American Journal of Political Science* 28 (February 1984), pp. 165–279.

52. Sundquist, *The Decline and Resurgence of Congress*, p. 454.

53. Theodore J. Lowi, "Making Democracy Safe for the World," in *Domestic Sources of Foreign Policy*, ed. James N. Rosenau (New York: Free Press, 1967), p. 301.

54. Contrast this argument with the one made by Kenneth N. Waltz that democratic institutions in the United States *do not* hinder foreign policy decision making. See Waltz, *Foreign Policy and Democratic Politics* (Boston: Little, Brown, 1967), esp. chap. 11.

55. See Richard Hofstadter, *The Idea of a Party System* (Berkeley: Univ. of California Press, 1970), p. 68.

56. We owe this insightful argument to a June 1987 graduate seminar paper by Walter Schaefer at the University of Maryland.

57. "A Distinct Sense of Unease," *U.S. News & World Report*, July 13, 1987, pp. 22–23.

58. We are grateful to T. Keating Holland of Yankelovich Partners, Inc., for providing us with these figures from their survey for *Time* and CNN.

Further Readings

Chapter 1

Art, Robert. "Bureaucratic Politics and American Foreign Policy: A Critique." *Policy Sciences,* December 1973.

Henkin, Louis. *Foreign Affairs and the Constitution.* Mineola, N.Y.: Foundation Press, 1973.

———. "Foreign Affairs and the Constitution."*Foreign Affairs,* Winter 1987/88, pp. 284–310.

Hilsman, Roger. *The Politics of Policy Making in Defense and Foreign Affairs.* New York: Harper & Row, 1971.

Hughes, Barry. *The Domestic Context of American Foreign Policy.* San Francisco: W. H. Freeman, 1978.

Lowi, Theodore, J. "American Business, Public Policy, Case Studies, and Political Theory." *World Politics,* July 1964.

Manning, Bayless. "The Congress, the Executive and Intermestic Affairs: Three Proposals." *Foreign Affairs,* January 1977.

Neustadt, Richard. *Presidential Power.* New York: John Wiley & Sons, 1980.

Peppers, Donald. "The Two Presidencies: Eight Years Later." In *Perspectives on the Presidency,* ed. Aaron Wildavsky. Boston: Little, Brown, 1975.

Wildavsky, Aaron. "The Two Presidencies." *Transaction,* December 1966.

Chapter 2

Brzezinski, Zbigniew. *Power and Principles.* New York: Farrar, Straus, Giroux, 1983.

Campbell, John. *The Foreign Affairs Fudge Factory.* New York: Basic Books, 1972.

Cannon, Lou. *President Reagan.* New York: Simon & Schuster, 1991.

Clarke, Duncan L. "Why State Can't Lead." *Foreign Policy,* Spring 1987, pp. 108–142.

Fulbright, J. W. *The Crippled Giant.* New York: Random House, 1972.

George, Alexander. *Presidential Decision Making in Foreign Policy.* Boulder, Colo.: Westview Press, 1980.

Haig, Alexander. *Caveat.* New York: Macmillan, 1984.

Inderfurth, Karl F., and Loch K. Johnson, eds. *Decisions of the Highest Order.* Pacifica Grove, Calif.: Brooks/Cole, 1988.

Kissinger, Henry A. *White House Years.* Boston: Little, Brown, 1979.

Rubin, Barry. *Affairs of State: The State Department and the Struggle over U.S. Foreign Policy.* New York: Oxford University Press, 1985.

Shultz, George. *Turmoil and Triumph.* New York: Charles Scribner's Sons. 1993.

Sick, Gary. *All Fall Down.* New York: Random House, 1985.

Spanier, John. *American Foreign Policy since World War II.* 11th ed. Washington, D.C.: CQ Press, 1988.

Vance, Cyrus. *Hard Choices.* New York: Simon & Schuster, 1983.

Chapter 3

Cheever, Daniel S., and Field H. Haviland. *American Foreign Policy and the Separation of Powers.* Cambridge, Mass.: Harvard Univ. Press, 1952.

Crabb, Cecil V. *Bipartisan Foreign Policy.* New York: Row, Peterson, and Co., 1957.

Destler, I. M., Leslie Gelb, and Anthony Lake. *Our Own Worst Enemy.* New York: Simon & Schuster, 1984.

Hodgson, Godfrey. "The Establishment." *Foreign Policy,* Spring 1973, pp. 3–40.

Holsti, Ole R., and James N. Rosenau. *American Leadership in World Affairs.* Boston: Allen & Unwin, 1984. (Also see the update in the December 1986 issue of *International Studies Quarterly.*)

Isaacson, Walter, and Gran Thomas. *The Wise Men.* New York: Simon & Schuster, 1986.

Quandt, William B. *Camp David: Peacemaking and Politics.* Washington, D.C.: The Brookings Institution, 1986.

Spiegel, Steven L. *The Other Arab-Israeli Conflict.* Chicago: The Univ. of Chicago Press, 1985.

The Iran-Contra Affair. Washington, D.C.: U.S. Government Printing Office, 1987.

Woodward, Robert. *Veil.* New York: Simon & Schuster, 1987.

Chapter 4

Bond, Jon R., and Richard Fleisher. *The President in the Legislative Arena.* Chicago: University of Chicago Press, 1990.

Fenno, Richard F., Jr. *Home Style: U.S. House Members in Their Districts.* Boston: Little, Brown, 1978.

———. *Congressmen in Committees.* Boston: Little, Brown, 1973.

Jacobson, Gary C. *The Politics of Congressional Elections.* 3d ed. New York: HarperCollins, 1992.

———. *The Electoral Origins of Divided Government.* Boulder, Colo.: Westview, 1991.

King, Anthony, ed. *Both Ends of the Avenue.* Washington: American Enterprise Institute, 1983.

Mayhew, David R. *Congress: The Electoral Connection.* New Haven: Yale University Press, 1974.

Ornstein, Norman J., Thomas E. Mann, and Michael J. Malbin, comps. *Vital Statistics on Congress 1991–1992.* Washington: CQ Press, 1992.

Sinclair, Barbara. *The Transformation of the U.S. Senate.* Baltimore: Johns Hopkins University Press, 1989.

Smith, Steven S., and Christopher J. Deering. *Committees in Congress.* 2d ed. Washington: CQ Press, 1990.

Wilcox, Francis O. *Congress, the Executive, and Foreign Policy.* New York: Harper & Row, 1971.

Chapter 5

Holsti, Ole N., and James N. Rosenau. *American Leadership in World Affairs.* Boston: George Allen and Unwin, 1983.

Kernell, Samuel. *Going Public.* Washington: CQ Press, 1986.

Mueller, John E. *War, Presidents, and Public Opinion.* New York: John Wiley, 1967.

Page, Benjamin I., and Robert Y. Shapiro. "Changes in Americans' Policy Preferences," *Public Opinion Quarterly* 46 (Spring 1982), pp. 24–42.

———. *The Rational Public.* Chicago: University of Chicago Press, 1992.

Reilly, John E., ed. *American Public Opinion and U.S. Foreign Policy 1991.* Chicago: Chicago Council on Foreign Relations, 1991.

Russett, Bruce. *Controlling the Sword.* Cambridge: Harvard University Press, 1990.

Schneider, William. "Conservatism, Not Interventionism: Trends in Foreign Policy Public Opinion, 1974–1982." In *Eagle Defiant: United States Foreign Policy in the 1980s,* ed. Kenneth A. Oye et al. Boston: Little Brown, 1983.

Wittkopf, Eugene R. *Faces of Internationalism.* Durham, N.C.: Duke University Press, 1991.

Chapter 6

Abramson, Paul R., John H. Aldrich, and David W. Rohde. *Change and Continuity in the 1988 Elections.* Rev. ed. Washington: CQ Press, 1991.

Aldrich, John H., John L. Sullivan, and Eugene Borgida, "Foreign Affairs and Issue Voting: Do Presidential Candidates 'Waltz Before a Blind Audience'?" *American Political Science Review* 83 (January 1989), pp. 123–142.

Cook, Timothy J. *Making Laws and Making News.* Washington: Brookings Institution, 1989.

Fiorina, Morris P. *Retrospective Voting in American National Elections.* New Haven: Yale University Press, 1981.

Hess, Stephen. *The Ultimate Insiders.* Washington: Brookings Institution, 1986.

McCormick, James M., and Eugene R. Wittkopf. "Bipartisanship, Partisanship, and Ideology in Congressional–Executive Foreign Policy Relations." *Journal of Politics* 52 (November 1990), pp. 1077–1100.

Miller, Warren E., and J. Merrill Shanks, "Policy Direction and Performance Evaluations: Complementary Explanations of the Reagan Elections." *British Journal of Political Science* 20 (1990), pp. 143–235.

Patterson, Thomas E. *The Mass Media Election.* New York: Praeger, 1980.

Pomper, Gerald M., ed. *The Election of 1988.* Chatham, N.J.: Chatham House, 1989.

Wattenberg, Martin P. *The Rise of Candidate-Centered Politics.* Cambridge: Harvard University Press, 1992.

Chapter 7

Ahrari, Mohammed E., ed. *Ethnic Groups and Foreign Policy.* Westport, Conn.: Greenwood Press, 1987.

Bauer, Raymond A., et al. *American Business and Public Policy.* 2d ed. Chicago: Aldine-Atherton, 1972.

Cigler, Alan J., and Burdett A. Loomis, eds. *Interest Group Politics.* 3d ed. Washington: CQ Press, 1990.

Gilboa, Eytan. *American Public Opinion Toward Israel and the Arab–Israeli Conflict.* Lexington, Mass.: Lexington Books, 1987.

Mathias, Charles McC., Jr. "Ethnic Groups and Foreign Policy." *Foreign Affairs* 59 (Summer 1981), pp. 975–998.

Schattschneider, E. E. *The Semisovereign People.* New York: Holt, Rinehart, and Winston, 1960.

Schlozman, Kay Lehman, and John T. Tierney. *Organized Interests and American Democracy.* New York: Harper & Row, 1986.

Smith, Hedrick. *The Power Game: How Washington Works.* New York: Random House, 1988.

Spiegel, Steven L. *The Other Arab–Israeli Conflict.* Chicago: University of Chicago Press, 1985.

Uslaner, Eric M. "A Tower of Babel on Foreign Policy?" in Cigler and Loomis, eds., *Interest Group Politics.* 3d ed. pp. 299–313.

Chapter 8

Brown, Harold. *The Strategic Defense Initiative* (Boulder, Colo.: Westview Press, 1987).

Doran, Charles F. *Myth, Oil, and Politics.* New York: Free Press, 1977.

Flanagan, Stephen J. "Congress, the White House and SALT." *The Bulletin of Atomic Scientists* (November 1978), pp. 34–40; and "The Domestic Politics of SALT II: Implications for the Foreign Policy Process," in Spanier and Nogee, *Congress, the Presidency and Foreign Policy,* pp. 44–76.

Halperin, Morton. "The Decision to Deploy the ABM: Bureaucratic and Domestic Politics in the Johnson Administration." *World Politics,* October 1972.

———. *Bureaucratic Politics and Foreign Policy.* Washington, D.C.: Brookings Institution, 1974.

Herkin, Gregg. *Counsels of War.* New York: Oxford University Press, 1987, especially pp. 331–357.

Payne, Keith. *Strategic Defense.* Lanham, N.Y.: Hamilton Press, 1986.

Smoke, Richard. *National Security and the Nuclear Dilemma.* 2d ed. New York: Random House, 1987, especially pp. 247–282.

Talbott, Strobe. *The Master of the Game.* New York: Alfred A. Knopf, 1988

Chapter 9

Art, Robert, and Seyom Brown, eds. *U.S. Foreign Policy: The Search for a New Role.* New York: Macmillan, 1993.

Benedick, Richard. *Ozone Diplomacy.* Cambridge: Harvard University Press, 1991.

Caldwell, Lynton Keith. *International Environmental Policy.* 2d ed. Durham, N.C.: Duke University Press, 1990.

Cohen, Stephen S., and John Zysman. *Manufacturing Matters.* New York: Basic Books, 1987.

Destler, I. M. *American Trade Politics.* Washington: Institute for International Economics, 1986.

Drell, Sidney D., Philip J. Farley, and David Holloway. *The Reagan Strategic Defense Initiative.* Cambridge, Mass.: Ballinger, 1985.

Flanagan, Stephen J. "Congress, the White House, and SALT." *Bulletin of Atomic Scientists,* November 1978, pp. 34–40.

Halperin, Morton. "The Decision to Deploy the ABM: Bureaucratic and Domestic Politics in the Johnson Administration." *World Politics,* October 1972.

———. *Bureaucratic Politics and Foreign Policy.* Washington: Brookings Institution, 1974.

Nivola, Pietro. *The Politics of Energy Conservation.* Washington: Brookings Institution, 1986.

Pastor, Robert A. *Congress and the Politics of U.S. Foreign Economic Policy.* Berkeley: University of California Press, 1980.

Stein, Arthur A. "Strategy as Politics, Politics as Strategy." In *The Logic of Nuclear Terror,* ed. Roman Kolkowicz. Boston: Allen and Unwin, 1987.

Tugwell, Franklin. *The Energy Crisis and the American Political Economy.* Stanford: Stanford University Press, 1988.

Uslaner, Eric M. "Political Parties, Ideas, Interests, and Free Trade in the United States." In *Trade and Party: Foreign Trade Relations and Party Politics in North America,* ed. Charles F. Doran (forthcoming).

Chapter 10

Crabb, Cecil V., Jr. *Bipartisan Foreign Policy: Myth or Reality?* White Plains, N.Y.: Row, Peterson and Co., 1957.

DiClerico, Robert E., and Eric M. Uslaner. *Few Are Chosen: Problems in Presidential Selection.* New York: McGraw-Hill, 1984.

Lowi, Theodore J. *The Personal President.* Ithaca, N.Y.: Cornell University Press, 1985.

McCubbins, Mathew D., and Thomas Schwartz. "Congressional Oversight Overlooked: Police Patrols Versus Fire Alarms." *American Journal of Political Science* 28 (February 1984), pp. 165–179.

Polsby, Nelson W. *Consequences of Party Reform.* New York: Oxford University Press, 1983.

Reiter, Howard L. *Selecting the President.* Philadelphia: University of Pennsylvania Press, 1985.

Robinson, Donald L., ed. *Reforming American Government: The Bicentennial Papers of the Committee on the Constitutional System.* Boulder, Colo.: Westview, 1985.

Rockman, Bert A. *The Leadership Question.* New York: Praeger, 1984.

Sundquist, James L. *The Decline and Resurgence of Congress.* Washington: Brookings Institution, 1981.

———. *Constitutional Reform and Effective Government.* Washington: Brookings Institution, 1986.

Wilson, James Q. "Does the Separation of Powers Still Work?" *The Public Interest,* Winter 1987, pp. 36–52.

Index